A MANUAL

OF

ANCIENT HISTORY,

FROM THE EARLIEST TIMES

TO THE FALL OF THE WESTERN EMPIRE.

COMPRISING THE HISTORY OF

Chaldæa, Assyria, Media, Babylonia,
Lydia, Phœnicia, Syria, Judæa, Egypt, Carthage, Persia,
Greece, Macedonia, Parthia, and Rome.

BY

GEORGE RAWLINSON, M.A.,

CAMDEN PROFESSOR OF ANCIENT HISTORY IN THE UNIVERSITY OF OXFORD.

NEW YORK:
HARPER & BROTHERS, PUBLISHERS,
FRANKLIN SQUARE.
1871.

PREFACE

THE work here given to the public has been contemplated by the Author for several years. The "Handbuch" of Professor Heeren, originally published in 1799, and corrected by its writer up to the year 1828, is, so far as he knows, the only modern work of reputation treating in a compendious form the subject of Ancient History generally. Partial works, i. e., works embracing portions of the field, have been put forth more recently, as, particularly, the important "Manuel" of M. Lenormant (*Manuel d'histoire ancienne de l'Orient jusqu'aux guerres Médiques.* Paris, 1868–9; 3 vols. 12mo). But no work with the scope and on the scale of Professor Heeren's has, so far as the present writer is aware, made its appearance since 1828. That work itself, in its English dress, is, he believes, out of print; and it is one, so great a portion of which has become antiquated by the progress of historical criticism and discovery, that it can not now be recommended to the student, unless with large reserves and numerous cautions. Under these circumstances, it seemed to the present writer desirable to replace the "Handbuch" of Heeren by a Manual conceived on the same scale, extending over the same period, and treating (in the main) of the same nations.

Heeren's Hand-book always appeared to him admirable in design, and, considering the period at which it was written, excellent in execution. He has been content to adopt, generally, its scheme and divisions; merely seeking in every case to bring the history up to the level of our present advanced knowledge, and to embody in his work all the really ascertained results of modern research and discovery. He has not suffered himself to be tempted by the example of M. Lenormant to include in the Manual an account of the Arabians or the Indians; since he has not been able to convince himself that either the native traditions of the former, as reported by Abulfeda, Ibn-Khaldoun, and others, or the Epic poems of the latter (the *Maha-Bharata* and *Ramayana*), are trustworthy sources of history. With more hesitation he has decided on not including in his present work the history of the Sassanidæ, which is sufficiently authentic, and which in part runs parallel with a period that the Manual embraces. But, on the whole, it appeared to him that the Sassanidæ belonged as much to Modern as to Ancient History—to the Byzantine as to the Roman period. And, in a doubtful case, the demands of brevity, which he felt to be imperative in such a work as a Manual, seemed entitled to turn the scale.

OXFORD, *Nov.* 23, 1869.

CONTENTS.

INTRODUCTION.

BOOK I.

PART I.—Asiatic Nations.

PART II.—African Nations.

BOOK II.

BOOK III.

FIRST PERIOD.

SECOND PERIOD.

THIRD PERIOD.

BOOK IV.

BOOK V.

PART I.—History of Rome.

PART II.—History of Parthia.

SECOND PERIOD.

THIRD PERIOD.

APPENDIX.

GENEALOGICAL TABLES.

MANUAL OF ANCIENT HISTORY.

---

1. THE word "HISTORY," which etymologically means "inquiry" or "research," and which has many slightly differing uses, is attached in modern parlance pre-eminently and especially to accounts of the rise, progress, and affairs of NATIONS. The consideration of man, prior to the formation of political communities and apart from them, belongs to Natural History—and especially to that branch of it which is called Anthropology—but not to History Proper. History Proper is the history of States or Nations, both in respect of their internal affairs, and in regard to their dealings one with another. Under the former head, one of the most important branches is Constitutional History, or the history of Governments; under the latter are included not only accounts of the wars, but likewise of the friendly relations of the different States, and of their commercial or other intercourse.

Anthropology, though not History Proper, is akin to it, and is a science of which the historical student should not be ignorant. It treats of man prior to the time when "History" takes him up, and thus forms, in some sort, the basis on which History rests. The original condition of man, his primary *habitat* or place of abode, the mode and time of his dispersion; the questions of the formation of races, of their differences, and of their affinities: these, and similar subjects, which belong properly to Anthropology, are of interest to the historian, and underlie his proper field. The most important works bearing on these matters are:

The Book of Genesis—the only extant work which claims to give an authoritative account of the creation and dispersion of mankind, and which is universally admitted to contain most interesting notices of the primitive condition of the human race, and of important facts belonging to very remote times. KALISCH's *Historical and Critical Commentary*, London, Longman, 1855, contains a mass of valuable, though not always quite sober, illustration from the best modern sources.

The Physical History of Mankind, by Dr. PRICHARD, London, 3d edition, 1836—a work of great grasp and power, elaborately illustrated, and in many respects of enduring value; but in some points behind the existing state of our knowledge. Not, however, at present superseded by any general work.

Prehistoric Man, by Sir JOHN LUBBOCK. London, 1866. This book is based mainly on recent researches into the earliest vestiges of man upon the earth, as those believed to have been found underneath the floors of caves, in ancient gravel deposits, in the soil at the bottom of lakes, in the so-called "kitchen-middings," and the like. It is well illustrated.

2. HISTORY PROPER is usually divided either into two, or into three, portions. If the triple division is adopted, the portions are called respectively, "Ancient History," the "History of the Middle Ages," and "Modern History." If the twofold division is preferred, *the middle portion is suppressed*, and History is regarded as falling under the two heads of "Ancient" and "Modern."

3. "ANCIENT" HISTORY is improperly separated from "Modern" by the arbitrary assumption of a particular date. A truer, better, and more convenient division may be made by regarding as ancient all that belongs to a state of things which has completely passed away, and as modern, all that connects itself inseparably with the present. In Western Europe the irruption of the Northern Barbarians, in Eastern Europe, in Asia, and in Africa the Mohammedan conquests, form the line of demarkation between the two portions of the historic field; since these events brought to a close the old condition of things, and introduced the condition which continues to the present day.

4. The SOURCES of History fall under the two heads of *written records*, and *antiquities*, or the actual extant remains of ancient times, whether buildings, excavations, sculptures, pictures, vases, or other productions of art. These *antiquities* exist either in the countries anciently inhabited by the several nations, where they may be seen *in situ*; or in museums, to which they have been removed by the moderns, partly for their better preservation, partly for purposes of general study and comparison; or, finally, in private collections, where they are for the most part inaccessible, and subserve the vanity of the collectors.

No general attempt has ever been made to collect into one work a description or representation of all these various remains; and, indeed, their multiplicity is so great that such a collection is barely conceivable. Works, however, on limited portions of the great field of "Antiquities" are numerous; and frequent mention will have to be made of them in speaking of the sources for the history of different states and periods. Here those only will be noticed which have something of a general character.

OBERLIN, *Orbis antiqui monumentis suis illustrati primæ lineæ.* Argentorati, 1790. Extremely defective, but remarkable, considering the time at which it was written.

CAYLUS, *Recueil d'Antiquités Egyptiennes, Etrusques, Grecques et Romaines.* Paris, 1752–67. Full of interest, but with engravings of a very rude and primitive character.

MONTFAUCON, *L'Antiquité expliquée et representée en figures.* Paris, 1719–24; 15 vols. folio.

SMITH, Dr. W., *Dictionary of Greek and Roman Antiquities.* London, 2d edition, 1853.

FERGUSSON, JAMES, *History of Architecture in all Countries, from the Earliest Times to the Present Day.* London, 1865–7.

BIRCH, SAMUEL, *Ancient Pottery.* London, 1858.

5. The second source of Ancient History, *written records*, is at once more copious and more important than the other. It consists of two main classes of documents—1st, Inscriptions on public monuments, generally contemporary with the events recorded in them; and 2dly, Books, the works of ancient or modern writers on the subject.

6. Whether INSCRIPTIONS were, or were not, the most ancient kind of written memorial is a point that can never be determined. What is certain is, that the nations of antiquity made use to a very large extent of this mode of commemorating events. In Egypt, in Assyria, in Babylonia, in Armenia, in Persia, in Phœnicia, in Lycia, in Greece, in Italy, historical events of importance were from time to time recorded in this way—sometimes on the natural rock, which was commonly smoothed for the purpose; sometimes on obelisks or pillars; frequently upon the walls of temples, palaces, and tombs; occasionally upon metal plates, or upon tablets and cylinders of fine clay—hard and durable materials all of them, capable of lasting hundreds or even thousands of years, and in many cases continuing to the present day. The practice prevailed, as it seems, most widely in Assyria and in Egypt; it was also in considerable favor in Persia and among the Greeks and Romans. The other nations used it more sparingly. It was said about half a century ago that "of the great mass of inscriptions still extant, but few comparatively are of any importance as regards his-

tory." But this statement, if true when it was made, which may be doubted, at any rate requires modification now. The histories of Egypt and Assyria have been in a great measure reconstructed from the inscriptions of the two countries. The great inscription of Behistun has thrown much light upon the early history of Persia. That on the Delphic tripod has illustrated the most glorious period of Greece. It is now generally felt that inscriptions are among the most important of ancient records, and that their intrinsic value makes up to a great extent for their comparative scantiness.

General collections of ancient inscriptions do not as yet exist. But the following, which have more or less of a general character, may be here mentioned:

MURATORI, LUD. ANT., *Novus Thesaurus Veterum Inscriptionum.* Mediolani, 1739, etc. Together with DONATI, *Supplementa.* Luccæ, 1764.

GRUTER, *Inscriptiones antiquæ totius orbis Romani*, cura J. G. GRÆVII. Amstel. 1707; 4 vols. folio.

POCOCKE, R., *Inscriptionum antiquarum Græcarum et Latinarum liber.* Londini, 1752; folio.

CHANDLER, R., *Inscriptiones antiquæ pleræque nondum editæ.* Oxonii, 1774; folio.

OSANN, FR., *Sylloge Inscriptionum antiquarum Græcarum et Latinarum.* Lipsiæ, 1834; folio.

A large number of cuneiform inscriptions, Assyrian, Babylonian, and Persian, will be found in the *Expédition Scientifique en Mésopotamie* of M. JULES OPPERT. Paris, 1858. The Persian, Babylonian, and Scythian or Turanian transcripts of the great Behistun Inscription are contained in the *Journal of the Asiatic Society*, vols. x., xiv., and xv., to which they were contributed by Sir H. RAWLINSON and Mr. NORRIS. A small but valuable collection of inscriptions, chiefly cuneiform, is appended to Mr. RICH's *Narrative of a Journey from Bussora to Persepolis.* London, 1839.

7. Under the head of Inscribed Monuments must be included COINS, which have in most instances a legend, or legends, and which often throw considerable light upon obscure points of history. The importance of coins is no doubt the greatest in those portions of ancient history where the information derivable from authors — especially from contemporary authors—is the scantiest; their use, however, is not limited to such portions, but extends over as much of the historical field as admits of numismatic illustration.

Collections of ancient coins exist in most museums and in many libraries. The collection of the British Museum is among the best in the world. The Bodleian Library has a good collection; and there is one in the library of

Christ Church, Oxford, possessing many points of interest. In default of access to a good collection, or in further prosecution of numismatic study, the learner may consult the following comprehensive works:

SPANHEIM, *Dissertatio de usu et præstantia Numismatum.* London and Amsterdam, 1706–17; 2 vols. folio.

ECKHEL, *De Doctrina Nummorum Veterum.* Vindebonæ, 1792–8; 8 vols. 4to.

MIONNET, *Description des Médailles.* Paris, 1806–37; 16 vols. 8vo., copiously illustrated.

HUMPHREYS, *Ancient Coins and Medals.* London, 1850. In this work, by means of embossed plates, fac-similes of the obverse and reverse of many coins are produced.

LEAKE, *Numismata Hellenica.* London, 1854.

Works upon coins, embracing comparatively narrow fields, are numerous, and often specially valuable. Many such works will be noticed among the sources for the history of particular times and nations.

8. The "Books" from which ancient history may be learnt are of two kinds—(1) Ancient; and (2) Modern. Ancient works which treat the subject in a general way are neither numerous, nor (with one exception) very valuable. The chief of those now extant are:

DIODORUS SICULUS, *Bibliotheca Historica*, in forty books, of which only books i.–v. incl. and xi.–xx. incl. have come down to us entire. The best editions are those of WESSELING (Bipont. 1793–1800; 10 vols. 8vo) and DINDORF (Parisiis, 1843–4; 2 vols. 8vo). This work was a universal history from the earliest times down to B.C. 60.

POLYBIUS, *Historiæ*, likewise in forty books, of which the first five only are complete. Originally, a universal history of the period commencing B.C. 220 and terminating B.C. 146. Bad in style, but excellent in criticism and accuracy. The best edition is SCHWEIGHÆUSER's (Lips. 1789 et seqq.; 8 vols. 8vo. Reprinted at Oxford, 1823, together with the same scholar's *Lexicon Polybianum*, in 5 vols. 8vo). A good edition of the mere text has been published by Didot, Paris, 1859.

JUSTINUS, *Historiæ Philippicæ*, in forty-four books, extracted, or rather abbreviated, from Trogus Pompeius, a writer of the Augustan age. This is a universal history from the earliest times to Augustus Cæsar. It is a short work, and consequently very slight and sketchy. Of recent editions, the best is that of DUEBNER (Lips. 1831). The best of the old editions is that of Strasburg, 1802, 8vo.

ZONARAS, *Chronicon* sive *Annales*, in twelve books. A universal history, extending from the Creation to the death of the Emperor Maximin, A.D. 238. Greatly wanting in criticism. The best edition is that in the *Corpus Scriptorum Historiæ Byzantinæ.* Bonnæ, 1841–4.

Besides these, there remain fragments from the universal history of NICOLAUS DAMASCENUS (*Fragm. Hist. Græc.* vol. iii. ed. C. MÜLLER, Parisiis, 1849), which are of very considerable value.

Modern works embracing the whole range of ancient history are numerous and important. They may be divided into two classes: (*a*) Works on Universal History, of which Ancient History forms only a part; (*b*) Works exclusively devoted to Ancient History.

(*a*) To the first class belong:

The Universal History, Ancient and Modern, with maps and additions. London, 1736–44; 7 vols. folio. Reprinted in 8vo in 64 vols. London, 1747–66; again, in 60 vols., with omissions and additions.

RALEIGH, SIR W., *History of the World*, in his *Works.* Oxford, Clarendon Press, 1829; 8 vols. 8vo.

BOSSUET, *Discours sur l'Histoire Universelle.* Paris, 1681; 4to. (Translated into English by RICH. SPENCER. London, 1730; 8vo.)

MILLOT, *Elémens de l'Histoire Générale.* Paris, 1772 et seqq. Reprinted at Edinburgh, 1823; 6 vols. 8vo. (Translated into English, 1778; 2 vols. 8vo.)

EICHHORN, *Weltgeschichte.* Leipsic, 1799–1820; 5 vols. 8vo.

KEIGHTLEY, TH., *Outlines of History*, 8vo, being vol. ix. of LARDNER'S *Cabinet Cyclopædia.* London, 1835 et seqq. A convenient abridgment.

TYTLER and NARES, *Elements of General History.* London, 1825. "Owes its reputation and success to the want of a better work on the subject."

(*b*) Under the second head may be mentioned:

NIEBUHR, B. G., *Vorträge über alte Geschichte.* Berlin, 1847; 3 vols. 8vo. Edited after his death by his son, MARCUS NIEBUHR. (Translated into English by Dr. LEONHARD SCHMITZ, with additions and corrections. London, 1852; 3 vols. 8vo.) A work of the highest value, embodying all the results of modern discovery up to about the year 1830.

SCHLOSSER, *Universal-historische Uebersicht der Geschichte der alten Welt.* Frankfort, 1826; 3 vols. 8vo.

BREDOW, *Handbuch der alte Geschichte.* Altona, 1799; 8vo. (Translated into English. London, 1827; 8vo.)

SMITH, PHILIP, *An Ancient History from the Earliest Records to the Fall of the Western Empire.* London, 1865; 3 vols. 8vo. Embodies the latest results of modern discovery.

HEEREN, *Ideen über die Politik, den Verkehr, und den Handel der vornehmsten Völker der alten Welt;* 4th edition. Göttingen, 1824. (Translated into English. Oxford, 1833 et seqq.; 5 vols. 8vo.) A work which, so far as the commerce of the ancients is concerned, has not been superseded.

A few modern works of a less comprehensive character than those hitherto described, but still belonging rather to *general* than to particular history, seems also to deserve mention here. Such are—

ROLLIN, *Histoire Ancienne des Egyptiens, des Carthaginiens, des Assyriens, des Mèdes et des Perses, des Macédoniens, et des Grecs.* Paris, 1824; 12 vols. 8vo, revue par LETRONNE. "The last and best edition." (Translated into

English. London, 1768; 7 vols. 8vo.) The earlier portion of this work is now antiquated, and must be replaced by writers who have had the advantage of recent discoveries.

RAWLINSON, G., *The Five Great Monarchies of the Ancient Eastern World, or the History, Geography, and Antiquities of Chaldæa, Assyria, Babylonia, Media, and Persia.* London, 1862–7; 4 vols. 8vo. With numerous illustrations.

9. The fact that all historical events must occur at a certain time and in a certain place, attaches to History two branches of knowledge as indispensable auxiliaries; viz., CHRONOLOGY and GEOGRAPHY. By the universal historian these sciences should be known completely: and a fair knowledge of them ought to be acquired by every historical student. A fixed mode of computing time, and an exact or approximate reckoning of the period occupied by the events narrated, is essential to every methodized history; nor can any history be regarded as complete without a more or less elaborate description of the countries which were the theatres of the events recorded in it.

10. Exact CHRONOLOGY is difficult, and a synchronistic view of history generally is impossible, without the adoption of an era. Nations accordingly, as the desire of exactness or the wish to synchronize arose, invented eras for themselves, which generally remained in use for many hundreds of years. The earliest known instance of the formal assumption of a fixed point in time from which to date events belongs to the history of Babylon, where the era of Nabonassar, B.C. 747, appears to have been practically in use from that year. The era of the foundation of Rome, B.C. 752 (according to the best authorities), was certainly not adopted by the Romans till after the expulsion of the kings; nor did that of the Olympiads, B.C. 776, become current in Greece until the time of Timæus (about B.C. 300). The Asiatic Greeks, soon after the death of Alexander, adopted the era of the Seleucidæ, B.C. 312. The era of Antioch, B.C. 49, was also commonly used in the East from that date till A.D. 600. The Armenian era, A.D. 553, and the Mohammedan, A.D. 622 (the Hegira), are likewise worthy of notice.

The most important chronological *monuments* are the following:

The ASSYRIAN CANON (discovered by Sir HENRY RAWLINSON among the antiquities in the British Museum, and published by him in the *Athenæum*, Nos. 1812 and 2064), an account of Assyrian Chronology from about B.C. 909 to B.C. 680, impressed on a number of clay tablets in the reign of Sardanapalus, the son of Esarhaddon, all now more or less broken, but supplying each other's deficiencies, and yielding by careful comparison a complete chronological scheme, covering a space of 230 years. The chronology of the whole period is verified by a recorded solar eclipse, which is evidently that of June 15, B.C. 763.

The APIS STELÆ (discovered by M. MARIETTE, close to the Pyramid of Abooseer, near Cairo), published in the *Zeitschrift für die Kunde des Morgenlandes* for 1864, and also by M. DE ROUGÉ in his *Recherches sur les monuments qu'on peut attribuer aux six premières Dynasties de Manethon.* Paris, 1866. Most important for Egyptian Chronology.

The PARIAN MARBLE (brought to England from Smyrna in the year 1627 by an agent of the Earl of Arundel, and presented to the University of Oxford by his son; preserved among the "Arundel Marbles" in the *Schola Philosophiæ Moralis*, but in a very decayed condition), a chronological arrangement of important events in Greek history from the accession of Cecrops to the archonship of Callistratus, B.C. 355. Best editions: *Marmora Arundeliana*, ed. J. SELDEN. Londini, 1628. *Marmora Oxoniensia*, ed. R. CHANDLER. Oxoniis, 1763; folio. *Marmor Parium*, ed. C. MÜLLER, in vol. i. of the *Fragmenta Historicorum Græcorum.* Parisiis, 1846. The inscription is also given in BOECKH'S *Corpus Inscriptionum Græcarum*, vol. ii. No. 2374.

The FASTI CAPITOLINI (discovered at Rome on the site of the ancient Forum, partly in the year 1547, partly in 1817 and 1818, and still preserved in the Museum of the Capitol), a list of the Roman magistrates and triumphs from the commencement of the Republic to the end of the reign of Augustus. Best edition of the fragments discovered in 1547, the second of SIGONIUS, Venet. 1556. Best edition of the fragments of 1817-8, that of BORGHESI, Milan, 1818. These Fasti are reproduced in appendices to the first and second volumes of Dr. ARNOLD'S *History of Rome*, down to the close of the first Punic War. An excellent reprint and arrangement of the fragments will be found in MOMMSEN'S *Inscriptiones Latinæ Antiquissimæ.* Berlin, 1863.

Ancient works on Chronology were numerous; but not many have come down to our times. The subject first began to be treated as a science by the Alexandrians in the third century before Christ. Eratosthenes, Apollodorus, Sosicrates, and others, undertook the task of arranging the events of past history according to exact chronological schemes, which were no doubt sufficiently arbitrary. These writers were succeeded by Castor (about B.C. 100–50), Cephalion, Julius Africanus (A.D. 200), and Hippolytus, of whom the last two were Christians. The earliest work of a purely chronological character which has come down to us is the following:

Eusebius Pamphili, *Chronicorum Canonum libri duo.* The Greek text is lost; but the latter book has been preserved to us in the Latin translation of Jerome; and the greater part of both books exists in an Armenian version, which has been rendered into Latin by the Armenian monk, Zohrab, assisted by Cardinal Mai. (Mediolani, 1818; folio.)

Other chronological works of importance are—

Georgius Syncellus, *Chronographia*, in the *Corpus Hist. Byzant.*, ed. Dindorf. Bonnæ, 1829; 2 vols. 8vo.

Johannes Malalas, *Chronographia*, in the same collection, ed. Dindorf. Bonnæ, 1831; 8vo.

Chronicon Paschale, in the same collection. Bonnæ, 1832; 2 vols. 8vo.

Scaliger, Jos., *De Emendatione Temporum.* Genevæ, 1629.

Ideler, *Handbuch der Chronologie.* Berlin, 1825–6; 2 vols. 8vo.

L'Art de Verifier les Dates. Paris, 1819–44; 36 vols. 8vo.

Hales, W., *New Analysis of Chronology, explaining the History and Antiquities of the Primitive Nations of the World.* London, 1809–12; 3 vols. 4to. New edition, corrected and improved, 1830; 4 vols. 8vo.

Clinton, H. F., *Fasti Hellenici*, or *The Civil and Literary Chronology of Greece from the Fifty-fifth Olympiad to the Death of Augustus.* Oxford, Clarendon Press, 1827–30; 3 vols. 4to. A valuable work, not confined to the chronology of Greece, but embracing that of all the Asiatic kingdoms and empires from the earliest times to Alexander's conquest of Persia.

11. Geography, the other ancillary science to History, was recognized from a very early date as closely connected with it. The History of Herodotus is almost as much geographical as historical: and the geographical element occupies a considerable space in the histories of many other ancient writers, as notably Polybius and Diodorus. At the same time the separability of geography, and its claims to be regarded as a distinct branch of knowledge, were perceived almost from the first; and works upon it, whereof only fragments remain, were written by Hecatæus of Miletus, Scylax of Caryanda, Charon of Lampsacus, Damastes, Eratosthenes, Agatharchides, Scymnus of Chios, and others. The most important of the extant classical works on the subject are—

The *Periplus Maris Mediterranei*, ascribed to Scylax of Caryanda, but really the work of an unknown writer belonging to the time of Philip of Macedon. Ed. D. Hoeschel, August. Vind., 1608. Printed also in Hudson's *Geographi Minores*, Oxoniis, 1703; and in C. Müller's *Geographi Græci Minores.* Paris, 1855.

Strabo, *Geographica*, in seventeen books, the most important ancient work on the subject. Best editions: that of Is. Casaubon, Parisiis, 1620, fol.; that of Th. Falconer, Oxoniis, 1807, 2 vols. folio; that of Sieben-

KEES, Lipsiæ, 1796–1811, 6 vols. 8vo; and that of KRAMER, Berolini, 1847–52, 3 vols. 8vo.

DIONYSIUS, *Periegesis*, written in hexameter verse. Published, with the commentary of Eustathius, by H. Stephanus. Parisiis, 1577. It will be found also in the *Geographi Græci Minores* of BERNHARDY (Leipsic, 1828) and of C. MÜLLER.

PLINIUS, *Historia Naturalis*, in thirty-seven books. Best edition, that of SILLIG. Gothæ; 8 vols. 8vo.

PTOLEMÆUS, *Geographia*, in eight books. Ed. BERTIUS, Amstel., 1618; folio.

POMPONIUS MELA, *Cosmographia*, sive *De Situ Orbis*, in three books. Edited by H. STEPHANUS, together with the *Periegesis* of DIONYSIUS. Parisiis, 1577. Best edition, that of TZSCHUCKE. Lipsiæ, 1807; 7 vols. 8vo.

And for the geography of Greece—

PAUSANIAS, *Periegesis Helladis*, in ten books. Best editions: that of SIEBELIS, Lipsiæ, 1822–8, 5 vols. 8vo; and that of BEKKER, Berlin, 1826–7, 2 vols. 8vo.

Modern works on the subject of Ancient Geography are numerous, but only a few are of a general character. Among these may be noticed—

CELLARIUS, *Notitia Orbis Antiqui*. Lipsiæ, 1701–6; 2 vols. 4to. *Cum observationibus* J. C. SCHWARTZII. Lipsiæ, 1771 and 1773.

MANNERT, *Geographie der Griechen und Römer*. Nürnberg, 1801–31; 10 vols. 8vo.

GOSSELIN, *Recherches sur la Géographie systématique et positive des Anciens*. Paris, 1798–1813; 4 vols. 4to.

RENNELL, J., *Geography of Herodotus*. London, 1800; 4to. And the same writer's *Treatise on the Comparative Geography of Asia Minor*, with an Atlas. London, 1831; 2 vols. 8vo.

RITTER, *Erdkunde*. Berlin, 1832 et seqq. A most copious and learned work, embracing all the results of modern discovery up to the date of the publication of each volume.

SMITH, Dr. W., *Dictionary of Greek and Roman Geography*. London, 1854; 2 vols. 8vo.

Among useful compendiums are—

LAURENT, P. E., *Introduction to Ancient Geography*. Oxford, 1813; 8vo.

ARROWSMITH, A., *Compendium of Ancient and Modern Geography, for the use of Eton School*. London, 1830; 8vo.

The best Atlases illustrative of Ancient Geography are the following:

KIEPERT, *Atlas von Hellas*, with supplementary maps. Berlin, 1846–51. Also the same geographer's *Atlas Antiquus*. Berlin, 1861.

MÜLLER, C., Maps accompanying the *Geographi Græci Minores*. Paris, 1855.

JOHNSTON, A. KEITH, *Atlas of Classical Geography*. Edinburgh, 1866; 4to.

SMITH, Dr. W., *Biblical and Classical Atlas*. London, 1868; small folio.

12. The field of Ancient History may be mapped out either synchronistically, according to certain periods and epochs, or ethnographically, according to states and nations. Neither of these two methods is absolutely superior to the other, each having merits in which the other is deficient. It would be embarrassing to have to choose between them; but, fortunately, this difficulty is obviated by the possibility of combining the two into one system. This combined method, which has been already preferred as most convenient by other writers of Manuals, will be adopted in the ensuing pages, where the general division of the subject will be as follows:

BOOK I.—History of the Ancient Asiatic and African States and Kingdoms from the Earliest Times to the Foundation of the Persian Monarchy by Cyrus the Great, B.C. 558.

BOOK II.—History of the Persian Monarchy from the Accession of Cyrus to the Death of Darius Codomannus, B.C. 558–330.

BOOK III.—History of the Grecian States, both in Greece Proper and elsewhere, from the Earliest Times to the Accession of Alexander, B.C. 336.

BOOK IV.—History of the Macedonian Monarchy, and the Kingdoms into which it broke up, until their absorption into the Roman Empire.

BOOK V.—History of Rome from the Earliest Times to the Fall of the Western Empire, A.D. 476, and Parallel History of Parthia.

BOOK I.

HISTORY OF THE ANCIENT ASIATIC AND AFRICAN STATES AND KINGDOMS FROM THE EARLIEST TIMES TO THE FOUNDATION OF THE PERSIAN MONARCHY BY CYRUS THE GREAT.

PART I.—ASIATIC NATIONS.

A. *Preliminary Remarks on the Geography of Asia.*

Asia—size and situation.

1. ASIA is the largest of the three great divisions of the Eastern Hemisphere. Regarding it as separated from Africa by the Red Sea and Isthmus of Suez, and from Europe by the Ural Mountains, the Ural river, the Caspian Sea, and the main chain of the Caucasus, its superficial contents will amount to 17,500,000 square miles, whereas those of Africa are less than 12,000,000, and those of Europe do not exceed 3,800,000. In climate it unites greater varieties than either of the two other divisions, extending as it does from the 78th degree of north latitude to within a hundred miles of the equator. It thus lies mainly within the northern temperate zone, but projects northward a distance of eleven degrees beyond the Arctic circle, while southward it throws into the region of the Tropics three long and broad peninsulas.

The advantages of Asia over Africa are great. Note especially the indentation of the shores, the numerous littoral islands, the great number of large rivers, and the comparatively small amount of sandy desert. Its advantages over Europe are less, consisting chiefly in its far larger size, and the greater variety of its products.

Physical features.

2. Asia consists mainly of a great central table-land, running east and west from the neighborhood of the Ægean to the north-western frontier of China, with low plains surrounding it, which are for the most part fertile and well watered. The high table-land is generally bounded by MOUNTAIN-CHAINS, which mostly run parallel to it in *latitudinal* lines. In places these primary latitudinal chains

give way to others, which run in an opposite or *longitudinal* direction.

Among the *latitudinal* chains the most important are—in the west, Taurus, Olympus, and Niphates; in the central region, Paropamisus (Elburz), and the four parallel chains of the Kuen-lün, the Himalaya (Imæus), the Thian-chan, and the Altai; while in the extreme east are the Chinese ranges of the In-chan, the Nan-chân, and the Kilian-chan. In the reverse or *longitudinal* direction run the Ural, separating Europe from Asia; the Zagros range, bounding the Mesopotamian plain on the east; the Suliman and Hala ranges, shutting in the Indus valley on the west; the Bolor chain, connecting the Himalaya with the Thian-chan; the eastern and western Ghauts in the peninsula of Hindustan; the Dzangbo-tchu of Burmah; the Yun-ling, Ala-chan, and Khingan of China; and the Jablonnoi of Siberia, in the region between Kamtchatka and Manchuria.

Rivers.

3. The RIVERS of Asia may be divided into two classes—those of the central tract, and those of the circumjacent regions. The rivers of the central tract are *continental* or *mediterranean;* i. e., they begin and end without reaching the sea. Either they form after a while salt lakes in which their waters are evaporated, or they gradually waste away and lose themselves in the sands of deserts. The rivers of the circumjacent plains are, on the contrary, *oceanic;* i. e., they mingle themselves with the waters of the great deep.

To the class of *continental* rivers belong the Ural and the Aras (Araxes), which flow into the Caspian; the Sir-Daria or Syhun (Jaxartes), and the Amoo or Jyhun (Oxus), which fall into the Sea of Aral; the Heri-rud (Arius), or river of Herat; the Zende-rud, or river of Isfahan; the Bendamir, or river of Persepolis; the Helmend (Etymandrus), the chief stream of Affghanistan; the Dehas, or river of Balkh; the Ak-Su, or river of Bokhara; the Kashgar river; the Jordan, and others. The most important of the Oceanic streams are the Obi or Irtish, the Yenisei, and the Lena, which drain the northern or Siberian plain, and flow into the Arctic Ocean; the Amoor, the Hoang-Ho, and the Yang-tse-kiang, which drain the eastern plain, and fall into the North Pacific; the May-kiang or Cambodia, the Meinam, and the Irrawaddy, the rivers of Siam and Burmah; the Brahmaputra, Ganges, and Indus, the great rivers of India; and the Tigris and Euphrates, the rivers of Mesopotamia; which all flow southward into the Indian Ocean. Of these streams only the following were known to the ancients—the Tigris, the Euphrates, the Indus, the Etymandrus, the Arius, the Oxus, the Jaxartes, the Araxes (Aras), and the Jordan. Minor streams important in Ancient History are—the Halys (Kizil-Irmak), Hermus (Ghiediz Chai), and Mæander (Mendere), in Asia Minor; the Orontes (Nahr-el-Asy) in Syria; the Phasis (Rion) in Imeritia and Mingrelia; and the Pasitigris (Kuran), the Hedypnus (Jerrahi), and the Oroatis (Tab or Hindyan), in Susiana and Persia Proper.

2

Natural divisions.

4. Asia may conveniently be divided into NORTHERN, CENTRAL, and SOUTHERN, the Southern region being again subdivided into a Western and an Eastern portion. It is with South-western Asia that Ancient History is almost exclusively concerned.

Northern Asia.

5. NORTHERN ASIA, or the tract lying north of the Caspian Sea, the Jaxartes, and the Altai mountain-chain, is for the most part a great grassy plain, of low elevation, destitute of trees, and unproductive, the layer of vegetable soil being thin. Towards the north this plain merges into vast frozen wilds capable of nourishing only a few hunters. In the west the Ural and Altai, in the east the Jablonnoi, and their offshoot the Tukulan, are the only mountains. The rivers are numerous, and abound in fish. The Ural and Altai chains are rich in valuable minerals, as gold, silver, platina, copper, and iron. This region was almost unknown to the ancients, who included it under the vague name of Scythia. Some scanty notices of it occur, however, in Herodotus.

Central Asia.

6. CENTRAL ASIA, or the region bounded on the north by the Altai, on the west by the Caspian, on the south by the Elburz, the Hindu Kush, and the Himalaya, on the east by the Yun-ling and other Chinese ranges, consists, excepting in its more western portion, of an elevated plateau or table-land, which towards the south is not less than 10,000 feet, and towards the north is from 4000 to 2600 feet above the level of the sea. This plateau is intersected by the two great chains of the Thian-chan and the Kuen-lün, and otherwise diversified by important ridges. Towards the north the soil admits of pasturage, and in the west and south are some rich plains and valleys; but the greater part of the region consists of sandy deserts. Outside the western boundary of the plateau, which is formed by the Bolor and other "longitudinal" chains, a low plain succeeds, a continuation of the Siberian steppe, which consists also, in the main, of sandy desert, excepting along the courses of the streams.

The low deserts between the Caspian and the Bolor are known under the names of Kharesm and Kizil Koum. The great sandy desert of the elevated central region is called Cobi or Gobi in its western, and Shamoo in its more eastern portions. It has a general direction from S.W. by W. to N.E. by E., and is estimated to contain 600,000 square miles, or about three times the area of France. It comprises, however, some oases where there is good pasturage.

A small portion only of Central Asia—lying towards the west and the south-west—was known to the ancients. In the low region between the Elburz range and the Siberian steppe, upon the courses of the two great streams which flow down from the plateau, were three countries of some importance. These were—

i. *Chorasmia*, to the extreme west, between the Caspian and the lower Oxus—a desolate region, excepting close along the river-bank, known still as Kharesm, and forming part of the Khanat of Khiva.

ii. *Sogdiana*, between the lower Oxus and the lower Jaxartes, resembling Chorasmia in its western portion, but towards the east traversed by spurs of the Bolor and the Thian-chan, and watered by numerous streams descending from them. The chief of these was the Polytimetus of the Greeks, on which was Maracanda (Samarkand), the capital.

iii. *Bactria*, on the upper Oxus, between Sogdiana and the Paropamisus (Hindu Kush). Mountainous, fertile, and well watered towards the east, but towards the west descending into the desert. Chief cities, Bactra (Balkh), the capital, a little south of the Oxus, and Margus (Merv), on a stream of its own, in the western desert.

Tradition makes Bactria a country of great importance at a remote date, and there is some reason to believe that Bactra, its capital, was the first great city of the Arian race. Some moderns have reported that the bricks of Balkh bear cuneiform inscriptions; but as yet the site is very partially explored.

7. Southern Asia, according to the division of the continent which has been here preferred, comprises all the countries lying north of the Black Sea, the Caucasus, the Caspian, and the Elburz, Hindu Kush, and Himalaya ranges, together with those lying east of the Yun-ling, the Ala-chan, and the Khingan, which form the eastern boundary of the central table-land. A line drawn along the ninety-second meridian (E. from Greenwich) will separate this tract, at the point where it is narrowest, into an Eastern and Western region, the former containing Manchuria, China, and the Siamo-Burmese peninsula, the latter Hindustan, Affghanistan, Beluchistan, Persia, the Russian Transcaucasian provinces, Turkey in Asia, and Arabia. With the Eastern

Southern Asia.

region Ancient History has no concern at all, since it was unknown to the great nations of antiquity, and whatever history it has belongs to the Modern rather than to the Ancient period. (See Introduction, § 3.) With the Western region Ancient History is, on the contrary, concerned vitally and essentially, since this region formed in the early times, if not the sole, yet at any rate the chief, stage on which the historical drama was exhibited.

Revelation, tradition, and the indications derivable from ethnology and comparative philology, agree in pointing to this South-western region as the cradle of the human race. The soil, climate, and natural productions are such as would have suited man in his infancy. Here, and in the adjoining part of Africa, large communities were first formed, cities built, and governments established. Here was the birthplace of agriculture and the arts; and here trade and commerce first acquired any considerable development. Numerous streams, a rich soil, abundant and most valuable natural products, among which the first place must be assigned to the wheat plant, here alone indigenous, rendered this portion of the earth's surface better fitted than perhaps any other for encouraging and promoting civilization. Here, accordingly, civil history commenced, the earliest Kingdoms and States being, all of them, in this quarter.

Regions of South-western Asia.

8. SOUTH-WESTERN ASIA is naturally divisible into four main regions—viz. (*a*) Asia Minor, or the peninsula of Anatolia; (*b*) the adjoining table-land, or the tract which lies between Asia Minor and the Valley of the Indus; (*c*) the lowland south of this table-land, which stretches from the base of the mountains to the shores of the Indian Ocean; and (*d*) the Indian Peninsula.

Asia Minor.

(*a*) ASIA MINOR consists of a central table-land, of moderate elevation, lying between the two parallel chains of Taurus and Olympus, together with three coast-tracts, situated respectively north, west, and south of the plateau. Its chief rivers are the Iris (Yechil Irmak), the Halys (Kizil Irmak), and the Sangarius (Sakkariyeh), which all fall into the Euxine. Its loftiest mountain is Argæus, near Cæsaræa (Kaisariyeh), which attains an altitude of 13,000 feet. On the highest part of the plateau, which is towards the south, adjoining Taurus, are a number of salt lakes, into which the rivers of this region empty themselves. The largest is the Palus Tattæus (Touz Ghieul), which extends about forty-five miles in its greatest length. Asia

Minor contained in the times anterior to Cyrus the following countries:—On the plateau, two: Phrygia and Cappadocia; boundary between them, the Halys. In the northern coast-tract, two: Paphlagonia and Bithynia; boundary, the Billæus (Filiyas). In the western coast-tract, three: Mysia, Lydia, and Caria, with the Æolian, Ionian, and Dorian Greeks occupying most of the sea-board. In the southern coast-tract, three: Lycia, Pamphylia, and Cilicia. The chief cities were Sardis, the capital of Lydia; Dascyleium, of Bithynia; Gordium, of Phrygia; Xanthus, of Lycia; Tarsus, of Cilicia; and Mazaca (afterwards Cæsaræa), of Cappadocia; together with the Grecian settlements of Miletus, Phocæa, Ephesus, Smyrna, Halicarnassus, and Cnidus on the west, and Cyzicus, Heraclea, Sinope, Amisus, Cerasus, and Trapezus upon the north.

ISLANDS. The littoral islands belonging to Asia Minor were important and numerous. The principal were Proconnesus in the Propontis; Tenedos, Lesbos (capital Mytilene), Chios, Samos, and Rhodes, in the Ægean; and Cyprus in the Levant or Eastern Mediterranean. The chief towns of Cyprus were Salamis, Citium, and Paphos, on the coast; and, in the interior, Idalium.

(b) The GREAT HIGHLAND extending from Asia Minor in the west to the mountains which border the Indus Valley in the east, comprised seventeen countries — viz., Armenia, Iberia or Sapeiria, Colchis, Matiênê, Media, Persia, Mycia, Sagartia, Cadusia, Hyrcania, Parthia, Aria, Arachosia, Sattagydia, Gandaria, Sarangia, and Gedrosia or the Eastern Ethiopia. As these countries were mostly of considerable size and importance, a short description will be given of each.

The central highland.

i. *Armenia* lay east of Cappadocia. It was a lofty region, consisting almost entirely of mountains, and has been well called "the Switzerland of Western Asia." The mountain system culminates in Ararat, which has an elevation of 17,000 feet. Hence all the great rivers of this part of Asia take their rise, viz., the Tigris, the Euphrates, the Halys, the Araxes, and the Cyrus. In the highest part of the region occur two elevated lake-basins, those of Urumiyeh and Van, each having a distinct and separate water-system of its own. The only town anciently of much importance was one which occupied the position of the modern Van, on the east coast of the lake of the same name.

ii. *Iberia*, or Sapeiria, adjoined Armenia to the north-east. It comprised the whole of the modern Georgia, together with some parts of Russian and Turkish Armenia, as especially the region about Kars, Ispir, and Akhaltsik. Its rivers were the Cyrus (Kur) and Araxes (Aras), which flow together into the Caspian. It had one lake, Lake Goutcha or Sivan, in the mountain region north-east of Ararat.

iii. *Colchis*, or the valley of the Phasis, between the Caucasus and Western Iberia, corresponded to the modern districts of Imeritia, Mingrelia, and Guriel. Its chief importance lay in its commanding one of the main routes of early commerce, which passed by way of the Oxus, Caspian, Aras, and Phasis to the Euxine. (Connect with this the Argonautic expedition.) Chief town, Phasis, at the mouth of the Rion river, a Greek settlement. Natives of Colchis, black: believed to be Egyptians.

iv. *Matiênê* was a strip of mountain land, running southward from Sapeiria, and separating between Assyria and Media Magna. It early lost its name, and was reckoned to one or other of the adjoining countries.

v. *Media*, one of the largest and most important of the regions belonging to this group, extended from the Araxes on the north to the desert beyond Isfahan on the south. Eastward it reached to the Caspian Gates; westward it was bounded by Matiênê, or (when Matiênê disappeared) by Armenia and Assyria. Its chief rivers were the Araxes (Aras) and the Mardus (Kizil Uzen or Sefid-rud). It consisted of two regions, Northern Media, or Media Atropatênê (Azerbijan), and Southern Media, or Media Magna. The whole territory was mountainous, except towards the south-east, where it abutted on the Sagartian desert. The soil was mostly sterile, but some tracts were fairly, and a few richly, productive. The chief cities were Ecbatana and Rhages.

vi. *Persia* lay south and south-east of Media, extending from the Median frontier across the Zagros mountain-chain, to the shores of the gulf whereto it gave name. It was barren and unfruitful towards the north and east, where it ran into the Sagartian desert; mountainous and fairly fertile in the central region; and a tract of arid sand along the coast.

Its rivers were few and of small size. Two, the Oroatis (Tab) and Granis (Khisht river), flowed southward into the Persian Gulf; one, the Araxes (Bendamir), with its tributary the Cyrus (Pulwar), ran eastward, and terminated in a salt lake (Neyriz or Bakhtigan). The principal cities were Persepolis, Pasargadæ, and Carmana, which last was the capital of a district of Persia, called Carmania.

vii. *Mycia* was a small tract south-east of Persia, on the shores of the Persian Gulf, opposite the island of Kishm and the promontory of Ras Mussendum. It was ultimately absorbed into Persia Proper.

viii. *Sagartia* was at once the largest and the most thinly peopled of the plateau countries. It comprised the whole of the great desert of Iran, which reaches from Kashan and Koum on the west to Sarawan and Quettah towards the east, a distance of above 900 miles. It was bounded on the north by Media, Parthia, and Aria; on the east by Sarangia and Sattagydia; on the south by Mycia and the Eastern Ethiopia; on the west by Media and Persia. It contained in ancient times no city of importance, the inhabitants being nomads, whose flocks found a scanty pasturage on the less barren portions of the great upland.

ix. *Cadusia*, or the country of the Cadusians, was a thin strip of territory along the south-eastern and southern shores of the Caspian, corresponding to the modern Ghilan and Mazanderan. Strictly speaking, it scarcely belonged to the plateau, since it lay outside the Elburz range, on the northern slopes of the chain, and between them and the Caspian Sea. It contained no city of importance, but was fertile, well wooded, and well watered; and sustained a numerous population.

x. *Hyrcania* lay east of Cadusia, at the south-eastern corner of the Caspian, where the name still exists in the modern river Gurgan. The chain of the Elburz here broadens out to a width of 200 miles, and a fertile region is formed containing many rich valleys and high mountain pastures, together with some considerable plains. The chief city of Hyrcania was Zadracarta.

xi. *Parthia* lay south and south-east of Hyrcania, including the sunny flank of the Elburz chain, and the flat country at its base as far as the northern edge of the desert, where it bordered on Sagartia. It was a narrow but fertile territory, watered by the numerous streams which here descend from the mountains.

xii. *Aria*, the modern territory of Herat, adjoined Parthia on the east. It was a small but fertile tract on the river Arius (the Heri-rud), with a capital city, called Aria or Artacoana (Herat).

xiii. *Arachosia*, east of Aria, comprised most of Western and Central Affghanistan. Its rivers were the Etymandrus (Helmend) and the Arachotus (Arghand-ab). The capital was Arachotus (Kandahar ?). It was an extensive country, mountainous and generally barren, but containing a good deal of fair pasturage, and a few fertile vales.

xiv. *Sattagydia* adjoined Arachosia on the east, corresponding to South-eastern Affghanistan, or the tract between Kandahar and the Indus valley. In character it closely resembled Arachosia, but was on the whole wilder and more rugged.

xv. *Gandaria* lay above Sattagydia, comprising the modern Kabul and Kaferistan. It consisted of a mass of tangled mountain-chains, with fertile valleys between them, often, however, narrowing to gorges difficult to penetrate. Its principal stream was the Cophen (or river of Kabul), a tributary of the Indus, and its chief town Caspatyrus (Kabul ?).

xvi. *Sarangia*, or Zarangia, was the tract lying about the salt lake (Hamoon) into which the Etymandrus (Helmend) empties itself. This tract is flat, and generally desert, except along the courses of the many streams which flow into the Hamoon from the north and east.

xvii. *Gedrosia* corresponded to the modern Beluchistan. It lay south of Sarangia, Arachosia, and Sattagydia, and east of Sagartia and Mycia. On the east its boundary was the Indus valley; on the south it was washed by the Indian Ocean. It was a region of alternate rock and sand, very scantily watered, and almost entirely destitute of wood. The chief town was Pura (perhaps Bunpoor).

The southern lowland.

(*c*) The LOWLAND to the south, or rather the south-west, of the great West-Asian plateau, comprised five countries only: viz., Syria, Arabia, Assyria, Susis or Susiana, and Babylonia. Each of these requires a short notice.

i. *Syria*, bounded by Cilicia on the north, the Euphrates on the north-east, the Arabian desert on the south-east and south, and by the Levant upon the west, comprised the following regions: 1st. *Syria Proper*, or the tract reaching from Amanus to Hermon and Palmyra. Chief cities in the ante-Cyrus period: Carchemish, Hamath, Damascus, Baalbek, and Tadmor or Palmyra. Chief river, the Orontes. Mountains: Casius, Bargylus, Libanus, and anti-Libanus. 2d. *Phœnicia*, the coast-tract from the thirty-fifth to the thirty-third parallel, separated from Syria Proper by the ridge of Libanus. Chief towns: Tyre, Sidon, Berytus, Byblus, Tripolis, Aradus. 3d. *Palestine*, comprising Galilee, Samaria, Judæa, and Philistia, or Palestine Proper. Chief cities: Jerusalem, Samaria, Azotus or Ashdod, Ascalon, and Gaza or Cadytis. Mountains: Hermon, Carmel. River, Jordan. Northern and Western Syria are mountainous, and generally fertile. Eastern Syria is an arid desert, broken only by a few oases, of which the Palmyrene is the principal.

ii. *Arabia*, lay south and south-east of Syria. It was a country of enormous size, being estimated to contain a million of square miles, or more than one-fourth the area of Europe. Consisting, however, as it does, mainly of sandy or rocky deserts, its population must always have been scanty, and its productions few. In the ancient world it was never of much account, the inhabitants being mainly nomads, and only the outlying tribes coming into contact with the neighboring nations. The only important towns were, in the east, Gerrha, a great trading settlement; in the west, Petra and Elath.

iii. *Assyria* intervened between Syria and Media. It was bounded on the north by the snowy chain of Niphates, which separated it from Armenia, and on the east by the outer ranges of Zagros. Westward its limit was the Euphrates, while southward it adjoined on Babylonia and Susiana. Towards the north and east it included some mountain tracts; but in the main it was a great rolling plain, at a low level, scantily watered towards the west, where the Euphrates has few affluents, but well supplied towards the east, where Mount Zagros sends down many large streams to join the Tigris. Its chief cities were Ninus, or Nineveh, Calah, and Asshur upon the Tigris; Arbela in the region between the Tigris and Mount Zagros; Nisibis, Amida, Harran or Carrhæ, and Circesium in the district between the great rivers. Its streams, besides the Tigris and Euphrates, were the Bilichus (Belik) and the Chaboras (Western Khabour), affluents of the Euphrates; the Centrites (Bitlis Chai), the Eastern Khabour, the Zabatus (or Zab Ala), the Caprus (or Zab Asfal), and the Gyndes or Physcus (Diyaleh), tributaries of the Tigris. It contained on the north the mountain range of Masius (Jebel Tur and Karajah Dagh). Its chief districts were Aturia, or Assyria Proper, the tract about Nineveh; Adiabênê, the country between the Upper Zab and the Lower; Chalonitis, the region south of the Lower Zab; and Gozan (or Mygdonia) on the Western Khabour at the foot of the Mons Masius. The Greeks called the whole tract between the two great rivers Mesopotamia.

iv. *Susis*, Susiana or Cissia, lay south-east of Assyria, and consisted chiefly of the low plain between the Zagros range and the Tigris, but comprised also a portion of the mounttain region. Its rivers were the Choaspes (Kerkheh), the Pasitigris (Kuran), the Eulæus (a branch stream formerly running from the Choaspes into the Pasitigris), and the Hedypnus (Jerrahi). Capital city, Susa, between the Choaspes and Eulæus rivers.

v. *Babylonia* lay due south of Assyria, in which it was sometimes included. The line of demarkation between them was the limit of the alluvium. On the east Babylonia was bounded by Susiana, on the west by Arabia, and on the south by the Persian Gulf. It was a single alluvial plain of vast extent and extraordinary fertility. The chief cities, besides Babylon on the Euphrates, were Ur (now Mugheir), Erech (Warka), Calneh (Niffer), Cutha (Ibrahim), Sippara or Sepharvaim (Mosaib), and Borsippa (Birs-Nimrud). The more southern part of Babylonia, bordering on Arabia and the Persian Gulf, was known as Chaldæa.

The Indian Peninsula.

(*d*) The PENINSULA OF HINDUSTAN, the last of the four great divisions of South-western Asia, contains nearly a million and a quarter of square miles. Nature has divided it into three very distinct tracts, one towards the north-west, consisting of the basin drained by the Indus; one towards the east, or the basin drained by the

Ganges; and one towards the south, or the peninsula proper. Of these the north-western only was connected with the history of the ancient world.

This tract, called *India* from the river on which it lay, was separated off from the rest of Hindustan by a broad belt of desert. It comprised two regions—1st, that known in modern times as the Punjab, abutting immediately on the Himalaya chain, and containing about 50,000 square miles; a vast triangular plain, intersected by the courses of five great rivers (whence Punj-ab=Five Rivers)—the Indus, the Hydaspes (Jelum), the Acesines (Chenab), the Hydraotes (Ravee), and the Hyphasis (Sutlej),—fertile along their course, but otherwise barren. 2dly, the region known as Scinde, or the Indus valley below the Punjab, a tract of about the same size, including the rich plain of Cutchi Gandava on the west bank of the river, and the broad delta of the Indus towards the south. Chief town of the upper region, Taxila (Attok); of the southern, Pattala (Tatta?).

B. *Preliminary Observations on the General Character of the Early Asiatic Kingdoms.*

1. The physical conformation of Western Asia is favorable to the growth of large empires. In the vast plain which extends from the foot of Niphates and Zagros to the Persian Gulf, the Red Sea, and the Mediterranean, there are no natural fastnesses; and the race which is numerically or physically superior to the other races inhabiting it readily acquires dominion over the entire region. Similarly, only not quite to the same extent, in the upland region which succeeds to this plain upon the east, there is a deficiency of natural barriers, and the nation which once begins to excel its neighbors, rapidly extends its influence over a wide stretch of territory. The upland and lowland powers are generally pretty evenly balanced, and maintain a struggle in which neither side gives way; but occasionally the equality becomes deranged. Circumstances give to the one or to the other additional strength; and the result is that its rival is overpowered. Then an empire of still greater extent is formed, both upland and lowland falling under the sway of the same people.

Large size of the kingdoms.

2. Still more remarkable than this uniformity of size is the

uniformity of governmental type observable throughout all these empires. The form of government is in every case a monarchy; the monarchy is always hereditary; and the hereditary monarch is a despot. A few feeble checks are in some instances devised for the purpose of restraining within certain limits the caprice or the cruelty of the holder of power; but these barriers, where they exist, are easily overleaped; and in most cases there is not even any such semblance of interference with the will of the ruler, who is the absolute master of the lives, liberties, and property of his subjects. Despotism is the simplest, coarsest, and rudest of all the forms of civil government. It was thus naturally the first which men, pressed by a sudden need, extemporized. And in Asia the wish has never arisen to improve upon this primitive and imperfect essay.

Despotism the sole form of government.

Note *as exceptional* the power which their independent religious position gave to the Jewish high-priests—a power which, however, would have been trampled upon if it had not been upheld by miracle. (See 2 Chron. xxvi. 16–21.)

3. Some variety is observable in the internal organization of the empires. In the remoter times it was regarded as sufficient to receive the personal submission of the monarch whose land was conquered, to assess his tribute at a certain amount, and then to leave him in the unmolested enjoyment of his former dignity. The head of an empire was thus a "king of kings," and the empire itself was an aggregation of kingdoms. After a while an improvement was made on the simplicity of this early system. Satraps, or provincial governors, court officials belonging to the conquering nation, and holding their office only during the good pleasure of the Great King, were substituted for the native monarchs; and arrangements more or less complicated were devised for checking and controlling them in the exercise of their authority. The power of the head of the empire was thus considerably increased; and the empire acquired a stability unknown under the previous system. Uniformity of administration was to a certain extent secured. At the same time, a very great diversity underlay this external uniformity, since the conquered nations were generally suffered to retain their own language, religion, and

Differences in the internal organization.

usages. No effort was made even to interfere with their laws; and thus the provinces continued, after the lapse of centuries, as separate and distinct in tone, feeling, ideas, and aspirations, as at the time when they were conquered. The sense of separateness was never lost; the desire of recovering national independence, at best, slumbered; nothing was wanted but opportunity to stir up the dormant feeling, and to shatter the seeming unity of the empire into a thousand fragments.

Prevalence of polygamy: its evil influence.

4. A characteristic of the Oriental monarchies, which very markedly distinguishes them from the kingdoms of the West, is the prevalence of polygamy. The polygamy of the monarch swells to excessive numbers the hangers-on of the court, necessitates the building of a vast palace, encourages effeminacy and luxury, causes the annual outlay of enormous sums on the maintenance of the royal household, introduces a degraded and unnatural class of human beings into positions of trust and dignity; in a word, at once saps the vital force of the empire in its central citadel, and imposes heavy burdens on the mass of the population, which tend to produce exhaustion and paralysis of the whole body politic. The practice of polygamy among the upper classes, destroying the domestic affections by diluting them, degrades and injures the moral character of those who give its tone to the nation, lowers their physical energy, and renders them self-indulgent and indolent. Nor do the lower classes, though their poverty saves them from participating directly in the evil, escape unscathed. Yielding, as they commonly do, to the temptation of taking money for their daughters from the proprietors of harems, they lose by degrees all feeling of self-respect; the family bond, corrupted in its holiest element, ceases to have an elevating influence; and the traffickers in their own flesh and blood become the ready tools of tyrants, the ready applauders of crime, and the submissive victims of every kind of injustice and oppression.

Other causes of decline and ruin.

5. The Asiatic Empires were always founded upon conquest; and conquest implies the possession of military qualities in the victors superior at any rate to those of the vanquished nations. Usually the conquering people were at first simple in their habits,

brave, hardy, and, comparatively speaking, poor. The immediate consequence of their victory was the exchange of poverty for riches; and riches usually brought in their train the evils of luxurious living and idleness. The conquerors rapidly deteriorated under such influences; and, if it had not been for the common practice of confining the use of arms, either wholly or mainly, to their own class, they might, in a very few generations, have had to change places with their subjects. Even in spite of this practice they continually decreased in courage and warlike spirit. The monarchs usually became *fainéants*, and confined themselves to the precincts of the palace. The nobles left off altogether the habit of athletic exercise. Military expeditions grew to be infrequent. When they became a necessity in consequence of revolt or of border ravages, the deficiencies of the native troops had to be supplied by the employment of foreign mercenaries, who cared nothing for the cause in which their swords were drawn. Meanwhile, the conquerors were apt to quarrel among themselves. Great satraps would revolt and change their governments into independent sovereignties. Pretenders to the crown would start up among the monarch's nearest relatives, and the strength and resources of the state would be wasted in civil conflicts. The extortion of provincial governors exhausted the provinces, while the corruption of the court weakened the empire at its centre. Still, the tottering edifice would stand for years, or even for centuries, if there was no attack from abroad, by a mere *vis inertiæ;* but, sooner or later, such an attack was sure to come, and then the unsubstantial fabric gave way at once and crumbled to dust under a few blows vigorously dealt by a more warlike nation.

C. *History of the Ancient Asiatic Kingdoms previous to Cyrus.*

SOURCES. 1. Native: including (*a*) the cuneiform inscriptions of Chaldæa, Assyria, and Armenia; and (*b*) the fragments of Berosus. 2. Jewish: including the historical books from Genesis to Chronicles, and the works of the Prophets anterior to Cyrus. 3. Classical writers: as Herodotus, Ctesias, Diodorus Siculus, and Justin; with the later chronologers, Eusebius and Syncellus. Specimens of the inscriptions themselves have been published in the *British Museum Series*, edited by Sir H. RAWLINSON and Mr. E. NORRIS (London, 1860). A large number have been translated by M. OPPERT, in his *Inscriptions des Sargonides* (Paris, 1862). The fragments of Berosus have been collected by Mons. C. MÜLLER, and will be found in the *Fragmenta Historicorum Græcorum*, vol. ii. (Paris, 1848). The fragments of Ctesias have been collected by BÄHR (Frankfurt, 1824), C. MÜLLER (Paris, 1844), and others.

The chief modern works treating of this period generally, are—

BUNSEN, *Philosophy of Universal History;* 4 vols. 8vo. London, 1854. Learned, but wild and extravagant, more especially in its chronology.

RAWLINSON, G., *Five Great Monarchies*, etc. (see p. 19), vols. i. to iii.

The subject is also discussed generally by B. G. NIEBUHR, in the first volume of his *Vorträge über alte Geschichte* (see p. 18), and by Mr. P. SMITH in the first volume of his *Ancient History* (see p. 18).

Among the works which treat of portions of the time, the following are of value:

Geschichte Assurs und Babels seit Phul, by M. NIEBUHR. Berlin, 1857.
Rerum Assyriarum Tempora Emendata, by BRANDIS. Bonnæ, 1853.
Prophecies relating to Nineveh, by G. VANCE SMITH. London, 1857.

Some other modern writers will be named under the heads of particular nations.

I. CHALDÆAN MONARCHY.

1. The earliest of the Asiatic monarchies sprang up in the alluvial plain at the head of the Persian Gulf. Here Moses places the first "kingdom" (Gen. x. 10); and here Berosus regarded a *Chaldæan* monarchy as established probably as early as B.C. 2000. The Hebrew records give Nimrod as the founder of this kingdom, and exhibit Chedorlaomer as lord-paramount in the region not very long afterwards. The names of the kings in the lists of Berosus are lost; but we are told that he mentioned by name forty-nine Chaldæan monarchs, whose reigns covered a space of 458 years from about B.C. 2000 to about B.C. 1543. The primeval monuments of the country have yielded memorials of fifteen or sixteen kings, who probably belonged to this early period. They were at any rate the builders of the most ancient edifices now existing in the country; and their date is long anterior to the time of Sennacherib and Nebuchadnezzar. The phonetic reading of these monumental names is too uncertain to justify their insertion here. It will be sufficient to give, from Berosus, an outline of the

Its antiquity.

dynasties which ruled in Chaldæa, from about B.C. 2000 to 747, the era of Nabonassar:

Chaldæan dynasty, ruling for 458 years (Kings: Nimrod, Chedorlaomer)................................	about B.C. 2001 to 1543
Arabian dynasty, ruling for 245 years....................	about B.C. 1543 to 1298
Dynasty of forty-five kings, ruling for 526 years.....	about B.C. 1298 to 772
Reign of Pul (say 25 years)............................	about B.C. 772 to 747

Changes of dynasty and condition.

2. Berosus, it will be observed, marks during this period two, if not three, changes of dynasty. After the Chaldæans have borne sway for 458 years, they are succeeded by Arabs, who hold the dominion for 245 years, when they too are superseded by a race not named, but probably Assyrian (see p. 42). This race bears rule for 526 years, and then Pul ascends the throne, and reigns for a term of years not stated. (Pul is called "king of Assyria" in Scripture; but this may be an inexactness. He is not to be found among the Assyrian monumental kings.) These changes of dynasty mark changes of condition. Under the first or Chaldæan dynasty, and under the last monarch, Pul, the country was flourishing and free. The second dynasty was probably, and the third certainly, established by conquest. Chaldæa, during the 526 years of the third dynasty, was of secondary importance to Assyria, and though from time to time engaged in wars with the dominant power of Western Asia, was in the main submissive and even subject. The names of six kings belonging to this dynasty have been recovered from the Assyrian monuments. Among them is a Nebuchadnezzar, while the majority commence with the name of the god Merodach.

Character of the monarchy.

3. The Chaldæan monarchy had from the first an *architectural* character. Babylon, Erech or Orchoë, Accad, and Calneh, were founded by Nimrod. Ur was from an early date a city of importance. The attempt to build a tower "which should reach to heaven," made here (Gen. xi. 4), was in accordance with the general spirit of the Chaldæan people. Out of such simple and rude materials as brick and bitumen vast edifices were constructed, pyramidical in design, but built in steps or stages of considerable altitude. Other *arts* also flourished. Letters were in use; and the baked bricks employed by the royal builders had commonly a legend in their centre. Gems were cut,

polished, and engraved with representations of human forms, portrayed with spirit. Metals of many kinds were worked, and fashioned into arms, ornaments, and implements. Textile fabrics of a delicate tissue were manufactured. *Commerce* was carried on with the neighboring nations both by land and sea: the "ships of Ur" visiting the shores of the Persian Gulf, and perhaps those of the ocean beyond it. The study of *Astronomy* commenced, and observations of the heavenly bodies were made, and carefully recorded.

According to Simplicius, these observations reached back a period of 1903 years when Alexander entered Babylon. This would make them commence B.C. 2234.

II. ASSYRIAN MONARCHY.

PERIODS.	B.C.
I. Previous to the Conquest of Babylon, which occurred about........	1250
II. From the conquest of Babylon to the accession of Tiglath-pileser II.	745
III. From the accession of Tiglath-pileser to the fall of Nineveh.........	625

First Period, prior to B.C. 1250.

1. The traces which we possess of the First Period are chiefly monumental. The Assyrian inscriptions furnish two lists—one of three, and the other of four consecutive kings—which belong probably to this early time. The seat of empire is at first Asshur (now Kileh Sherghat), on the right bank of the Tigris, about sixty miles below Nineveh. Some of the kings are connected by intermarriage with the Chaldæan monarchs of the period, and take part in the struggles of pretenders to the Chaldæan crown. One of them, Shalmaneser I., wars in the mountain-chain of Niphates, and plants cities in that region (about B.C. 1270). This monarch also builds Calah (Nimrud), forty miles north of Asshur, on the left or east bank of the river.

Art of this period, rude. Letters, scanty. Cities quadrangular, and surrounded by walls. Palaces are placed on a lofty mound. Temple-towers pyramidical.

Second Period, B.C. 1250-745.

2. The Second Period is evidently that of which Herodotus spoke as lasting for 520 years, from about B.C. 1260 to 740. It commenced with the conquest of Babylon by Tiglathi-nin (probably the original of the Greek "Ninus"), and it terminated with the new dynasty established by Tiglath-pileser II. The monuments furnish for the earlier portion of this period some nine or ten discontinuous royal names, while for the later portion they supply

a complete consecutive list, and an exact chronology. The exact chronology begins with the year B.C. 909.

Note, that the lists of Ctesias, which should belong to this period, differ completely from those of the monuments; that they are internally improbable, as they consist in part of Medo-Persian, in part of Greek, in part of geographic names; and that consequently they must be set aside as wholly unhistorical.

Subdivision of the period, B.C. 1250–909.

3. The great king of the earlier portion of the Second Period is a certain Tiglath-pileser, who has left a long historical inscription, which shows that he carried his arms deep into Mount Zagros on the one hand, and as far as Northern Syria on the other. He likewise made an expedition into Babylonia. Date, about B.C. 1130. His son was also a warlike prince; but from about B.C. 1100 to 900 Assyrian history is still almost a blank; and it is probable that we have here a period of depression.

B.C. 909–745.

4. For the later portion of the Second Period—from B.C. 909 to 745—the chronology is exact, and the materials for history are abundant. In this period Calah became the capital, and several of the palaces and temples were erected which have been disinterred at Nimrud. The Assyrian monarchs carried their arms beyond Zagros, and came into contact with Medes and Persians; they deeply penetrated Armenia; and they pressed from Northern into Southern Syria, and imposed their yoke upon the Phœnicians, the kingdom of Damascus, and the kingdom of Israel. The names of Ben-hadad, Hazael, Ahab, and Jehu are common to the Assyrian and Hebrew records. Towards the close of the period, the kings became slothful and unwarlike, military expeditions ceased, or were conducted only to short distances and against insignificant enemies.

LINE OF KINGS:—Asshur-danin-il I. Reign ended, B.C. 909. Successor, his son, Hu-likh-khus III. (Iva-lush). Reigned from B.C. 909 to 889. Successor, his son Tiglathi-nin II. Reigned from B.C. 889 to 886. Warred in Niphates. Asshur-idanni-pal I. (Sardanapalus), his son, succeeded. A great conqueror. Warred in Zagros, Armenia, Western Mesopotamia, Syria, and Babylonia. Received the submission of the chief Phœnician towns. Built a great palace at Calah. Reigned from B.C. 886 to 858. Followed on the throne by his son, Shalmaneser II., who reigned from B.C. 858 to 823, and was contemporary with Ben-hadad and Hazael of Damascus, and with Ahab and Jehu in Israel. Built a palace and set up an obelisk at Calah. Warred in the same countries as his father, and likewise in the highland beyond

Zagros, where he contended with the Medes and Persians; also in Lower Syria, where he was engaged against Ben-hadad, Hazael, and Ahab, and received tribute from Jehu. Succeeded on the throne by his son, Shamas-iva or Samsi-hu, who reigned from B.C. 823 to 810. This king had wars with the Medes, Persians, Armenians, and Babylonians. His successor was his son, Hu-likh-khus IV. (Iva-lush), who mounted the throne B.C. 810 and reigned till B.C. 781. He too was a warlike monarch. He took Damascus, and received tribute from Samaria, Philistia, and Edom. Babylonia acknowledged his sovereignty. His wife bore the name of Sammuramit (Semiramis). The next king was Shalmaneser III., who reigned from B.C. 781 to 771. His wars were with Eastern Armenia and the Syrians of Damascus and Hadrach. He was succeeded by Asshur-danin-il II., a comparatively unwarlike prince, under whom military expeditions became infrequent. In the ninth year of this king's reign an eclipse of the sun is recorded as having taken place in the month Sivan (June)—undoubtedly the eclipse of June 15 of that year, which was visible over the whole of Western Asia. Asshur-danin-il reigned from B.C. 771 to 753. He was succeeded by the last monarch of this series, Asshur-likh-khus, or Asshur-lush, who reigned ingloriously for eight years—from B.C. 753 to 745.

Art, etc., of this period.

5. The Assyrian art of the Second shows a great advance upon that of the First Period. Magnificent palaces were built, richly embellished with bas-reliefs. Sculpture was rigid, but bold and grand. Literature was more cultivated. The history of each reign was written by contemporary annalists, and cut on stone, or impressed on cylinders of baked clay. Engraved *stelæ* were erected in all the countries under Assyrian rule. Considerable communication took place with foreign countries; and Bactrian camels, baboons, curious antelopes, elephants, and rhinoceroses were imported into Assyria from the East.

The art of this period is largely illustrated in the *Monuments of Nineveh*, First Series. By A. H. LAYARD; folio. London, 1849.

Third Period, B.C. 745–625.

6. In the Third Period the Assyrian Empire reached the height of its greatness under the dynasty of the Sargonidæ, after which it fell suddenly, owing to blows received from two powerful foes. The period commenced with a revival of the military spirit and vigor of the nation under Tiglath-pileser II., the king of that name mentioned in Scripture. Distant expeditions were resumed, and the arms of Assyria carried into new regions. Egypt was attacked and reduced; Susiana was subjugated; and in Asia Minor Taurus was crossed, Cappadocia invaded, and relations established with the Lydian monarch, Gyges. Naval expe-

ditions were undertaken both in the Mediterranean and the Persian Gulf. Cyprus submitted, and the Assyrian monarchs numbered Greeks among their subjects. Almost all the kings of the period came into contact with the Jews, and the names of most of them appear in the Hebrew records. Towards the close of the period the empire sustained a severe shock from the sudden invasion of vast hordes of Scythians from the North. Before it could recover from the prostration caused by this attack, its old enemy, Media, fell upon it, and, assisted by Babylon, effected its destruction.

LINE OF KINGS OF THE THIRD PERIOD: — 1. Tiglath-pileser II., an usurper, ascends the throne B.C. 745, two years after Nabonassar in Babylon. Wars in Babylonia, Media, Armenia, Southern Syria, and Palestine. Receives tribute from Menahem, about B.C. 743. Takes Damascus, attacks Pekah of Israel, and accepts the submission of Ahaz of Judah, about B.C. 734 to 732. 2. Shalmaneser IV.; his first year B.C. 727. Leads several expeditions into Palestine. Conquers Phœnicia, except the island Tyre, which he attacks by sea: his fleet suffers a defeat. In B.C. 723 commences the siege of Samaria. Loses his crown by a revolution after reigning six years. 3. Sargon, an usurper; ascends the throne B.C. 721. Takes Samaria and settles the Israelites in Gauzanitis and Media. Successful war with Shebek I. (Sabaco) of Egypt for the possession of Philistia. Defeat and capture of Merodach-baladan in Babylonia, B.C. 709. Submission of Cyprus, B.C. 708 to 707. Invasion of Susiana. Conquest of Media. Wars in Niphates and Taurus. 4. Sennacherib, son of Sargon, succeeds, B.C. 705. Expedition against Babylon, B.C. 702. Deposes Merodach-baladan and sets up Belibus. First expedition into Palestine, B.C. 700. Submission of Elulæus of Sidon, and Hezekiah of Judah. Second expedition into Babylonia, B.C. 699. Belibus deposed, and Assaranadius, or Asordanes, son of Sennacherib, made king. Second expedition into Palestine, about B.C. 698. Great destruction of the Assyrian army near Pelusium, on the borders of Egypt. War with Susiana; a fleet launched on Persian Gulf, about B.C. 692 to 690. Conquest of Cilicia and founding of Tarsus, about B.C. 685. Murder of Sennacherib by two of his sons, B.C. 680. 5. Esarhaddon, son of Sennacherib, obtains the crown after a short struggle. Reigns alternately at Babylon and Nineveh. Puts down revolts in Syria and Cilicia, about B.C. 680 to 677. Conquers Edom, about B.C. 674. Invades Central Arabia, B.C. 673. Reduces Northern Media, B.C. 671. Great expedition into Egypt, about B.C. 670. Defeat of Tirhakah (Taracus). Egypt broken up into a number of petty kingdoms. Revolt and reduction of Manasseh, king of Judah. Colonization of Samaria with Babylonians, Susianians, and Persians. 6. Asshur-bani-pal (Sardanapalus), son of Esarhaddon, succeeds, about B.C. 667, or a little later. Under him Assyria reaches the culminating point of her greatness. He reconquered Egypt, which had been recovered by Tirhakah; invaded Asia Minor, and received tribute from Gyges, king of Lydia; subjugated most of Armenia; completely conquered Susiana and attached it as a province to

Babylonia; and reduced many outlying tribes of Arabs. He built the most magnificent of all the Assyrian palaces; loved music and the arts; and established a sort of royal library at Nineveh. His last year is uncertain; but was probably *about* B.C. 647. 7. Asshur-emid-ilin (the Saracus of Abydenus), son of Asshur-bani-pal, succeeded. But little is known of his reign; its two great events were the inroad of a vast Scythic horde from the tract north of the Caucasus, and the Median war which brought about the destruction of the empire. First attack of the Medes, B.C. 634, repulsed. Scythian inroad, B.C. 632. Second Median attack, B.C. 627. Defection of the Babylonians under Nabopolassar. Siege of Nineveh. Capture, B.C. 625.

Art, etc., of the Third Period.

7. Assyrian art attained to its greatest perfection during this last period. Palaces were built by Tiglath-pileser II. at Calah, by Sargon at Dur Sargina (Khorsabad), by Sennacherib at Nineveh, by Esarhaddon at Calah and Nineveh, by Sardanapalus II. at Nineveh, and by Saracus at Calah. Glyptic art advanced, especially under Sardanapalus, when the animal forms were executed with a naturalness and a spirit worthy of the Greeks. At the same time carving in ivory, metallurgy, modelling, and other similar arts made much progress. An active commerce united Assyria with Phœnicia, Egypt, and Greece. Learning of various kinds—astronomic, geographic, linguistic, historical—was pursued; and stores were accumulated which will long exercise the ingenuity of the moderns.

The best illustrations of Assyrian art during this period will be found in the *Monument de Ninive* of Mons. BOTTA (Paris, 1849–50), 5 vols. folio; and in Mr. LAYARD's *Monuments of Nineveh*, Second Series (London, 1853). On Assyrian architecture, consult *The Palaces of Nineveh and Persepolis Restored*, by Mr. JAMES FERGUSSON (London, 1851); and the Assyrian section in his *History of Architecture*, vol. i. (London, 1866).

III. MEDIAN MONARCHY.

PERIODS.	B.C.
I. Media Independent	830–710
II. Media subject to Assyria	710–650

Early history.

1. The primitive history of the Medes is enveloped in great obscurity. The mention of them as Madai in Genesis (x. 2), and the statement of Berosus that they furnished an early dynasty to Babylon, imply their importance in very ancient times. But scarcely any thing is *known* of them till the ninth century B.C., when they were attacked in their own proper country, Media Magna, by the Assyrians (about B.C. 830). At this time they were under the govern-

ment of numerous petty chieftains, and offered but a weak resistance to the arms of the Assyrian monarchs. No part of their country, however, was reduced to subjection until the time of Sargon, who conquered some Median territory about B.C. 710, and planted it with cities in which he placed his Israelite captives. The subsequent Assyrian monarchs made further conquests; and it is evident from their records that no great Median monarchy had arisen down to the middle of the seventh century B.C.

The earlier portions of the Zendavesta indicate the existence of powerful Arian states on the great plateau of Iran and in the low districts east of the Caspian at a very remote period; but they contain no mention at all of the Medes. Bactria seems to have been the seat of Arian power in these primitive times.

History according to Herodotus and Ctesias.

2. The earliest date which, with our present knowledge, we can assign for the commencement of a great Median monarchy is B.C. 650. The monarchs assigned by Herodotus and Ctesias to a time anterior to this may conceivably have been chiefs of petty Median tribes, but were certainly not the heads of the whole nation. The probability is that they are fictitious personages. Suspicion attaches especially to the list of Ctesias, which appears to have been formed by an intentional duplication of the regnal and other periods mentioned by Herodotus.

(*a*) *Median History of Herodotus.*—The Medes revolt from Assyria, about B.C. 740. Conquer their independence and continue for a number of years without a monarch. Deioces chosen king, B.C. 708. Reigns fifty-three years. Founds Ecbatana, and introduces a rigid court ceremonial. Dies B.C. 655. Phraortes, his son, succeeds. Reigns twenty-two years. Conquers Persia. Attacks Assyria. Killed while besieging Nineveh, B.C. 633. Cyaxares, his son, reigns from B.C. 633 to 593, forty years. Reorganizes the army. Renews the attack on Assyria. War interrupted by irruption of the Scyths. Takes Nineveh. Wars with Alyattes, king of Lydia, B.C. 615 to 610. Dies B.C. 593. Astyages, his son, reigns thirty-five years, from B.C. 593 to 558, when he is dethroned by his grandson, Cyrus.

(*b*) *Median History of Ctesias.*—The Medes, having revolted from Assyria, take and destroy Nineveh, in conjunction with the Babylonians, B.C. 875. Arbaces ascends the throne. Reigns twenty-eight years, B.C. 875 to 847. Maudaces reigns fifty years, B.C. 847 to 797. Sosarmus, thirty years, B.C. 797 to 767. Astycas, fifty years, B.C. 767 to 717. Arbianes, twenty-two years, B.C. 717 to 695. Artæus, forty years, B.C. 695 to 655. Artynes, twenty-two years, B.C. 655 to 633. Astibaras, forty years, B.C. 633 to 593. Astyages, *x* years, the last king. (Note the prevalence of round numbers, the repetition of every number but one, and the fact that of the eight numbers six are evidently taken from Herodotus.)

3. There is reason to believe that about B.C. 650, or a little later, the Medes of Media Magna were largely reinforced by fresh immigrants from the East, and that shortly afterwards they were enabled to take an aggressive attitude towards Assyria, such as had previously been quite beyond their power. In B.C. 633—according to Herodotus—they attacked Nineveh, but were completely defeated, their leader, whom he calls Phraortes, being slain in the battle. Soon after this occurred the Scythian inroad, which threw the Medes upon the defensive, and hindered them from resuming their schemes of conquest for several years. But, when this danger had passed, they once more invaded the Assyrian Empire in force. Nineveh was invested and fell. Media upon this became the leading power of Western Asia, but was not the sole power, since the spoils of Assyria were divided between her and Babylon.

Real history from B.C. 650-593.

HISTORICAL KINGS:—1. Phraortes (name doubtful). Conquers Persia. Attacks Nineveh. Falls there, B.C. 633. 2. Cyaxares, his son, the great Median monarch. Attacks Nineveh, B.C. 632. Called off to resist the Scyths. Second attack on Nineveh succeeds, B.C. 625. Conquers all Asia between the Caspian and the Halys. Invades Asia Minor and wars against Alyattes, B.C. 615 to 610. Dies, B.C. 593. 3. Astyages, his son, ascends the throne. His peaceful reign. Media allied with Lydia and Babylon. Revolt of the Persians under Cyrus brings the Median Empire to an end, B.C. 558. Media long remains the first and most important of the Persian provinces.

4. Less is known of Median art and civilization than of Assyrian, Babylonian, or Persian. Their architecture appears to have possessed a barbaric magnificence, but not much of either grandeur or beauty. The great palace at Ecbatana was of wood, plated with gold and silver. After the conquest of Nineveh, luxurious habits were adopted from the Assyrians, and the court of Astyages was probably as splendid as that of Esarhaddon and Sardanapalus. The chief known peculiarity of the Median kingdom was the ascendency exercised in it by the Magi—a priestly caste claiming supernatural powers, which had, apparently, been adopted into the nation.

General character of Median civilization.

IV. BABYLONIAN MONARCHY.

PERIODS.	B.C.
I. From the era of Nabonassar to the destruction of Nineveh.......	747–625
II. From the destruction of Nineveh and establishment of Babylonian independence under Nabopolassar to the conquest of Babylon by Cyrus..	625–538

First Period, B.C. 747–625.

1. After the conquest of Babylonia by the Assyrians, about B.C. 1250, an Assyrian dynasty was established at Babylon, and the country was, in general, content to hold a secondary position in Western Asia, acknowledging the suzerainty of the Ninevite kings. From time to time efforts were made to shake off the yoke, but without much success till the accession of Nabonassar, B.C. 747. Under Nabonassar and several of his successors Babylonia appears to have been independent; and this condition of independence continued, with intervals of subjection, down to the accession of Esarhaddon, B.C. 680, when Assyrian supremacy was once more established. Babylon then continued in a subject position, till the time when Nabopolassar made alliance with Cyaxares, joined in the last siege of Nineveh, and, when Nineveh fell, became independent, B.C. 625.

Line of Kings during this Period (chief authority, the famous Canon of Ptolemy):—1. Nabonassar. Reigned fourteen years, B.C. 747 to 733. Destroyed the records of the monarchs who had preceded him. 2. Nadius, reigned two years, B.C. 733 to 731. 3. Chinzinus and Porus, reigned five years, B.C. 731 to 726. 4. Elulæus, reigned five years, B.C. 726 to 721. 5. Merodach-baladan, reigned twelve years, B.C. 721 to 709. Embassy to Hezekiah, about B.C. 713. Conquered and made prisoner by Sargon. 6. Arceanus, an Assyrian viceroy, placed on the throne by Sargon, reigned five years, B.C. 709 to 704. After an interregnum of more than a year, Merodach-baladan, who had escaped from captivity, recovered the throne, and reigned six months, when he was driven out by Sennacherib, who placed on the throne a viceroy. 7. Belibus; he reigned from B.C. 702 to 699. Suspected of treason by Sennacherib and deprived of his government. 8. Assaranadius, a son of Sennacherib, succeeds. He reigns six years, B.C. 699 to 693. Babylon twice revolts and is reduced. 9. Regibelus (probably an Assyrian viceroy) reigns a year, B.C. 693 to 692. 10. Mesesimordachus (also probably a viceroy) reigns four years, B.C. 692 to 688. A period of anarchy and disturbance follows, coinciding with the last eight years of Sennacherib. No king reigns so long as a year. 11. Esarhaddon conquers Babylon, takes the title of king, builds himself a palace there, and reigns alternately at Babylon and Nineveh. He holds the throne for thirteen years, B.C. 680 to 667. 12. Saos-duchinus, son of Esarhaddon, is made viceroy by his father or brother, and governs Babylon for twenty years, from B.C. 667 to 647. 13. Cinneladanus (either an Assyrian viceroy, or the last Assyrian monarch himself) succeeds Saos-duchinus, and holds the throne for twenty-two years, from B.C. 647 to 625.

Second Period. Babylonian empire, B.C. 625–538.

2. During the Second Period, Babylonia was not only an independent kingdom, but was at the head of an empire. Nabopolassar and Cyaxares divided the Assyrian dominions between them, the former obtaining for his share Susiana, the Euphrates valley, Syria, Phœnicia, and Palestine. A brilliant period followed. At first indeed the new empire was threatened by Egypt; and for a few years the western provinces were actually held in subjection by Pharaoh-nechoh; but Babylon now aroused herself, defeated Nechoh, recovered her territory, and carrying her arms through Palestine into Egypt, chastised the aggressor on his own soil. From this time till the invasion of Cyrus the empire continued to flourish, but became gradually less and less warlike, and offered a poor resistance to the Persians.

LINE OF KINGS:—1. Nabopolassar. Becomes independent on the fall of Nineveh, B.C. 625. Assists Cyaxares in his Lydian war, B.C. 615 to 610, and brings about the peace which ends it. Loses the western provinces to Nechoh of Egypt, B.C. 608. Sends Nebuchadnezzar to recover them, B.C. 605. Dies, B.C. 604. 2. Nebuchadnezzar, his son, returns victorious from Syria, and is acknowledged as king. Wars in Phœnicia, Palestine, and Egypt. Takes and destroys Jerusalem, B.C. 586. Takes Tyre, B.C. 585. Recognized as lord-paramount of Egypt, about B.C. 569. Period of the construction of great works, B.C. 585 to 570. Madness—recovery. Death, B.C. 561. 3. Evil-merodach, his son, succeeds. Reigns only two years. Murdered by his brother-in-law. 4. Neriglissar (or Nergal-shar-uzur), who succeeds, B.C. 559 (his wife perhaps the Nitocris of Herodotus). Builds the western palace at Babylon. Dies after a reign of four years, B.C. 555. 5. Laborosoarchod, or Labossoracus, his son, a mere boy, mounts the throne. He is murdered after a few months by 6. Nabonadius (Labynetus), the last king. Not being of royal birth, he married a daughter of Nebuchadnezzar (probably Neriglissar's widow), and as soon as his son by this marriage, Belshazzar (Bel-shar-uzur), is of sufficient age, associates him on the throne. Makes alliance with Crœsus of Lydia, B.C. 555. Constructs the river defenses at Babylon. Attacked by Cyrus and defeated—throws himself into Borsippa. Babylon, carelessly defended by Belshazzar, is taken by stratagem. Nabonadius surrenders himself a prisoner, B.C. 538.

3. The architectural works of the Babylonians, more especially under Nebuchadnezzar, were of surpassing grandeur. The "hanging gardens" of that prince, and the walls with which he surrounded Babylon, were reckoned among the Seven

Characteristics of the empire. Architecture, art, etc.

Wonders of the World. The materials used were the same as in the early Chaldæan times, sunburnt and baked brick; but the baked now preponderated. The ornamentation of buildings was by bricks of different hues, or sometimes by a plating of precious metal, or by enamelling. By means of the last-named process, war-scenes and hunting-scenes were represented on the walls of palaces, which are said to have been life-like and spirited. Temple-towers were still built in stages, which now sometimes reached the number of seven. Useful works of great magnitude were also constructed by some of the kings, especially by Nebuchadnezzar and Nabonadius; such as canals, reservoirs, embankments, sluices, and piers on the shores of the Persian Gulf. Commerce flourished, and Babylon was reckoned emphatically a "city of merchants." The study of astronomy was also pursued with zeal and industry. Observations were made and carefully recorded. The sky was mapped out into constellations, and the fixed stars were catalogued. Occultations of the planets by the sun and moon were noted. Time was accurately measured by means of sun-dials, and other astronomical instruments were probably invented. At the same time it must be confessed that the astronomical science of the Babylonians was not pure, but was largely mixed with astrology, more especially in the later times.

On the commerce of the Babylonians, see the section upon the subject in HEEREN'S *Historical Researches*, "Asiatic Nations," vol. ii. On their astronomy, see Sir G. C. LEWIS'S *Astronomy of the Ancients*, ch. v., and G. RAWLINSON, *Five Monarchies*, "Babylonia," ch. v. For illustrations of Babylonian art (mixed, however, with Assyrian and Persian), see CULLIMORE, *Oriental Cylinders*, London, 1842, 8vo; and F. LAJARD, *Culte de Mithra*, Paris, 1847, folio.

V. KINGDOMS IN ASIA MINOR.

No empire in Asia Minor in the early times.

1. The geographical formation of Asia Minor, which separates it into a number of distinct and isolated regions, was probably the main reason why it did not in early times become the seat of a great empire. The near equality of strength that existed among several of the races by which it was inhabited—as the Phrygians, the Lydians, the Carians, the Cilicians, the Paphlago-

nians, and the Cappadocians—would tend naturally in the same direction, and lead to the formation of several parallel kingdoms instead of a single and all-embracing one. Nevertheless, ultimately, such a great kingdom did grow up; but it had only just been formed when it was subverted by one more powerful.

Kingdom of Phrygia.

2. The most powerful state in the early times seems to have been Phrygia. It had an extensive and fertile territory, especially suited for pasturage, and was also rich in the possession of salt lakes, which largely furnished that necessary of life. The people were brave, but somewhat brutal. They had a lively and martial music. It is probable that they were at no time all united into a single community; but there is no reason to doubt that a considerable monarchy grew up in the north-western portion of the country, about B.C. 750 or earlier. The capital of the kingdom was Gordiæum on the Sangarius. The monarchs bore alternately the two names of Gordias and Midas. As many as four of each name have been distinguished by some critics; but the dates of the reigns are uncertain. A Midas appears to have been contemporary with Alyattes (about B.C. 600 to 570), and a Gordias with Crœsus (B.C. 570 to 560). Phrygia was conquered and became a province of Lydia about B.C. 560.

Kingdom of Cilicia.

3. Cilicia was likewise the seat of a monarchy in times anterior to Cyrus. About B.C. 711 Sargon gave the country to Ambris, king of Tubal, as a dowry with his daughter. Sennacherib, about B.C. 701, and Esarhaddon, about B.C. 677, invaded and ravaged the region. Tarsus was founded by Sennacherib, about B.C. 685. In B.C. 666 Sardanapalus took to wife a Cilician princess. Fifty years afterwards we find a Syennesis seated on the throne, and from this time all the kings appear to have borne that name or title. Cilicia maintained her independence against Crœsus, and (probably) against Cyrus, but submitted to Persia soon afterwards, probably in the reign of Cambyses.

The Lydian kingdom and empire.

4. Ultimately the most important of all the kingdoms of Asia Minor was Lydia. According to the accounts which Herodotus followed, a Lydian kingdom had existed from very ancient times, monarchs to whom he gives the name of Manes, Atys, Lydus, and

Meles, having borne sway in Lydia prior to B.C. 1229. This dynasty, which has been called Atyadæ, was followed by one of Heraclidæ, which continued in power for 505 years—from B.C. 1229 to 724. (The last six kings of this dynasty are known from Nicholas of Damascus who follows Xanthus, the native writer. They were Adyattes I., Ardys, Adyattes II., Meles Myrsus, and Sadyattes or Candaules.) On the murder of Candaules, B.C. 724, a third dynasty—that of the Mermnadæ—bore rule. This continued till B.C. 554, when the last Lydian monarch, Crœsus, was conquered by Cyrus. This monarch had previously succeeded in changing his kingdom into an empire, having extended his dominion over all Asia Minor, excepting Lycia, Cilicia, and Cappadocia.

DYNASTY of the MERMNADÆ (according to the chronology of Herodotus): 1. Gyges murders Candaules, and mounts the throne, B.C. 724. Reigns thirty-eight years. Takes Colophon. Attacks Miletus. Dies, B.C. 686. 2. Ardys, his son, succeeds. Takes Priênê. Irruption of Cimmerians. Dies, B.C. 637. 3. Sadyattes, his son, reigns twelve years, from B.C. 637 to 625. Wars with Miletus. 4. Alyattes, son of Sadyattes, mounts the throne. Expels the Cimmerians. Makes peace with Miletus, B.C. 620. Carries on defensive war against Cyaxares of Media, B.C. 615 to 610. Takes Smyrna. Attacks Clazomenæ. Dies, B.C. 568. 5. Crœsus, his son, succeeds. Reduces the Ionian, Æolian, and Dorian Greeks. Conquers all Asia Minor west of the Halys, except Lycia and Cilicia. Alarmed at the success of Cyrus, makes alliance with Sparta, Egypt, and Babylon, B.C. 555. Invades Cappadocia, and fights an indecisive battle at Pteria. Attacked in his turn, defeated, and made prisoner by Cyrus, B.C. 554.

CHRONOLOGY of this dynasty, according to Eusebius:—Gyges, thirty-six years, B.C. 698 to 662. Ardys, thirty-eight years, B.C. 662 to 624. Sadyattes, fifteen years, B.C. 624 to 609. Alyattes, forty-nine years, B.C. 609 to 560. Crœsus, fifteen years, B.C. 560 to 546.

VI. PHŒNICIA.

Importance of Phœnicia. Its history fragmentary.

1. PHŒNICIA, notwithstanding the small extent of its territory, which consisted of a mere strip of land between the crest of Lebanon and the sea, was one of the most important countries of the ancient world. In her the commercial spirit first showed itself as the dominant spirit of a nation. She was the carrier between the East and the West—the link that bound them together—in times anterior to the first appearance of the Greeks as navigators. No complete history of Phœnicia has come down to us, nor can a continuous history be constructed;

but some important fragments remain, and the general condition of the country, alternating between subjection and independence, is ascertained sufficiently.

The chief sources for Phœnician history are—1. The fragments of MENANDER and DIUS preserved to us in JOSEPHUS. (MENANDER and DIUS composed their histories from native sources.) 2. The sacred writers, Ezekiel, and the authors of Kings and Chronicles. 3. Scattered notices in HOMER, HERODOTUS, and other classical authors.

The best modern authorities on the subject are the following:

MOVERS, *Die Phönizier*, 3 vols. 8vo. Berlin, 1841–50. A work of great research and of a wide grasp, but allowing undue weight to PHILO-BYBLIUS's pretended translation of the Phœnician history of SANCHONIATHON.

KENRICK, J., *Phœnicia.* London, 1855; 8vo. The best work on the subject. Carries the history down to the conquest of Syria by the Turks, A.D. 1516.

HEEREN, *Ideen*, vol. ii., part i. Peculiarly good with respect to the commerce of the Phœnicians.

TWISTLETON, Hon. E. T. B., Articles on Phœnicia and Tyre in Dr. SMITH's *Dictionary of the Bible.* London, 1860–3.

Isolation of the cities. Early pre-eminence of Sidon.

2. At no time did Phœnicia form either a single centralized state, or even an organized confederacy. Under ordinary circumstances the states were separate and independent: only in times of danger did they occasionally unite under the leadership of the most powerful. The chief cities were Tyre, Sidon, Berytus, Byblus, Tripolis, and Aradus. Of these Sidon seems to have been the most ancient; and there is reason to believe that, prior to about B.C. 1050, she was the most flourishing of all the Phœnician communities.

Sidon superseded by Tyre about B.C. 1050.

3. The priority and precedency enjoyed by Sidon in the remoter times devolved upon Tyre (her colony, according to some) about B.C. 1050. The defeat of Sidon by the Philistines of Ascalon is said to have caused the transfer of power. Tyre, and indeed every Phœnician city, was under the rule of kings; but the priestly order had considerable influence; and an aristocracy of birth, or wealth, likewise restrained any tyrannical inclinations on the part of the monarch. The list of the Tyrian kings from about B.C. 1050 to 830 is known to us from the fragments of Menander.

LINE OF KINGS:—1. Abibaal, partly contemporary with David. 2. Hiram, his son, the friend of David and Solomon. Ascended the throne about B.C. 1025. Reigned thirty-four years. 3. Baleazar, his son, succeeded, about B.C. 991. Reigned seven years. 4. Abdastartus, his son, reigned nine years, from about B.C. 984 to 975, when he was murdered by a conspiracy. 5. One of the conspirators—name unknown—succeeded, and reigned twelve years, from about B.C. 975 to 963. The line of Abibaal seems then to have been restored. 6. Astartus, reigned also twelve years, from about B.C. 963 to 951, when he was succeeded by his brother. 7. Aserymus, who, after a reign of nine years, was murdered by another brother, Phales, about B.C. 942. 8. Phales reigned eight months only, being in his turn murdered by the high-priest of Astarte, Ithobalus or Ethbaal, who seized the throne. 9. Ithobalus reigned thirty-two years, about B.C. 941 to 909. Ahab married his daughter Jezebel. Great drought in his reign. 10. Badezor, his son, succeeded. Reigned six years only, from about B.C. 909 to 903. 11. Matgen, the son of Badezor and father of Dido, then mounted the throne. His reign lasted thirty-two years, about B.C. 903 to 871. Matgen was followed by his son. 12. Pygmalion, under whom occurred the flight of Dido and the colonization of Carthage. He reigned forty-seven years, from about B.C. 871 to 824.

Phœnician colonies.

4. The commercial spirit of Phœnicia was largely displayed during this period, which, till towards its close, was one of absolute independence. The great monarchies of Egypt and Assyria were now, comparatively speaking, weak; and the states between the Euphrates and the African border, being free from external control, were able to pursue their natural bent without interference. Her commercial leanings early induced Phœnicia to begin the practice of establishing colonies; and the advantages which the system was found to secure caused it to acquire speedily a vast development. The coasts and islands of the Mediterranean were rapidly covered with settlements; the Pillars of Hercules were passed, and cities built on the shores of the ocean. At the same time factories were established in the Persian Gulf; and, conjointly with the Jews, on the Red Sea. Phœnicia had at this time no serious commercial rival, and the trade of the world was in her hands.

Geographical sketch of the Phœnician colonies:—(*a*) In the Eastern Mediterranean: Paphos, Amathus, Tamisus, and Ammochosta in Cyprus; Ialysus and Camirus in Rhodes; Thera, and most of the Cyclades; Thasos; Thebes (?). (*b*) In the Western Mediterranean: Lilybæum and Panormus (Mahaneth) in Sicily; Gaulos, Melite; Utica, Carthage, and Hadrumetum in North Africa; Carteia, Malaca in Spain. (*c*) Beyond the straits: Tartessus on the Bætis (Guadalquiver) and Gades (now Cadiz) on an island close to the Spanish coast. (*d*) In the Persian Gulf: Tylos and Aradus (perhaps Bahrein).

5. The geographical position of the Phœnician colonies marks the chief lines of their trade, but is far from indicating its full extent; since the most distant of these settlements served as starting-points whence voyages were made to remoter regions. Phœnician merchantmen proceeding from Gades and Tartessus explored the western coast of Africa, and obtained tin from Cornwall and the Scilly Islands. The traders of Tylus and Aradus extended their voyages beyond the Persian Gulf to India and Taprobane, or Ceylon. Phœnician navigators, starting from Elath in the Red Sea, procured gold from Ophir, on the south-eastern coast of Arabia. Thasos and the neighboring islands furnished convenient stations from which the Euxine could be visited and commercial relations established with Thrace, Scythia, and Colchis. Some have supposed that the North Sea was crossed and the Baltic entered in quest of amber; but the balance of evidence is, on the whole, against this extreme hypothesis.

Sea-trade; its extent and chief lines of direction.

6. The sea-trade of the Phœnicians was probably supplemented from a very remote date by a land traffic; but this portion of their commerce scarcely obtained its full development till the time of Nebuchadnezzar. A line of communication must indeed have been established early with the Persian Gulf settlements; and in the time of Solomon there was no doubt a route open to Phœnician traders from Tyre or Joppa, through Jerusalem, to Elath. But the generally disturbed state of Western Asia during the Assyrian period would have rendered land traffic then so insecure, that, excepting where it was a necessity, it would have been avoided.

Land-trade of the early period.

7. Towards the close of the period, whereof the history has been sketched above (see par. 3), the military expeditions of the Assyrians began to reach Southern Syria, and Phœnician independence seems to have been lost. We can not be sure that the submission was continuous; but from the middle of the ninth till past the middle of the eighth century there occur in the contemporary monuments of Assyria plain indications of Phœnician subjection, while there is no evidence of resistance or revolt. Native sovereigns tributary to Assyria reign in the Phœnician towns and are reckoned by the Assyrian monarchs

Phœnicia subject to Assyria, about B.C. 850.

among their dependents. The country ceases to have a history of its own; and, with one exception, the very names of its rulers have perished.

Revolts, and recovery of independence.

8. About B.C. 743 the passive submission of Phœnicia to the Assyrian yoke began to be exchanged for an impatience of it, and frequent efforts were made, from this date till Nineveh fell, to re-establish Phœnician independence. These efforts for the most part failed; but it is not improbable that finally, amid the troubles under which the Assyrian empire succumbed, success crowned the nation's patriotic exertions, and autonomy was recovered.

Revolts of Phœnicia from Assyria:—1. Under a Hiram, from Tiglath-pileser II., about B.C. 743. 2. Under Elulæus, from Shalmaneser, B.C. 727. Long resistance of New Tyre. 3. Under the same, from Sennacherib, about B.C. 704. Expedition of Sennacherib, B.C. 700. Elulæus flies. Tubal made king. 4. Under Abdi-melkarth, from Esarhaddon, B.C. 680. Crushed immediately. 5. Under Baal of Tyre and the contemporary king of Aradus, from Sardanapalus, about B.C. 667. Likewise crushed without difficulty.

Phœnicia an Egyptian dependency, B.C. 608.

9. Scarcely, however, had Assyria fallen, when a new enemy appeared upon the scene. Necholi of Egypt, about B.C. 608, conquered the whole tract between his own borders and the Euphrates. Phœnicia submitted or was reduced, and remained for three years an Egyptian dependency.

Conquered by Nebuchadnezzar, B.C. 605.

10. Nebuchadnezzar, in B.C. 605, after his defeat of Necholi at Carchemish, added Phœnicia to Babylon; and, though Tyre revolted from him eight years later, B.C. 598, and resisted for thirteen years all his attempts to reduce her, yet at length she was compelled to submit, and the Babylonian yoke was firmly fixed on the entire Phœnician people. It is not quite certain that they did not shake it off upon the death of the great Babylonian king; but, on the whole, probability is in favor of their having remained subject till the conquest of Babylon by Cyrus, B.C. 538. As usual, the internal government of the dependency was left to the conquered people, who were ruled at this time either by native kings, or, occasionally, by judges.

LINE OF KINGS AND JUDGES AT TYRE (from Menander):—1. Ithobaal II., contemporary with Nebuchadnezzar, about B.C. 597 to 573. Tyre besieged by Nebuchadnezzar for thirteen years. 2. Baal. Reigned ten years, B.C. 573 to 563. 3. Ecnibaal, judge for three months. 4. Chelbes, judge for ten months. 5. Abbarus (Abalus), the high-priest, judge for three months. 6 and 7. Mytgon and Gerastartus, judges for five years, B.C. 562 to 557. 8. Balator, king. Reigned a year, B.C. 557 to 556. 9. Merbal, king. Reigned four years, B.C. 556 to 552. 10. Hirom, king. Reigned twenty years, B.C. 552 to 532. In this king's fourteenth year, B.C. 538, Cyrus took Babylon, and Hirom became independent.

Decline of the Phœnician sea-trade, and development of the land traffic.

11. As Greece rose to power, and as Carthage increased in importance, the sea-trade of Phœnicia was to a certain extent checked. The commerce of the Euxine and the Ægean passed almost wholly into the hands of the alien Hellenes; that of the Western Mediterranean and the Atlantic Ocean had to be shared with the daughter state. Meanwhile, however, in consequence of the more settled condition of Western Asia, first under the later Assyrian, and then under the Babylonian monarchs, the land trade received a considerable development. (*a*) A line of traffic was established with Armenia and Cappadocia, and Phœnician manufactures were exchanged for the horses, mules, slaves, and brazen or copper utensils of those regions. (*b*) Another line passed by Tadmor, or Palmyra, to Thapsacus, whence it branched on the one hand through Upper Mesopotamia to Assyria, on the other down the Euphrates valley to Babylon and the Persian Gulf. (*c*) Whether a third line traversed the Arabian peninsula from end to end for the sake of the Yemen spices may be doubted; but, at any rate, communication must have been kept up by land with the friendly Jerusalem, and with the Red Sea, which was certainly frequented by Phœnician fleets.

Character of Phœnician commerce.

12. The Phœnician commerce was chiefly a carrying trade; but there were also a few productions of their own in which their traffic was considerable. The most famous of these was the purple dye, which they obtained from two shell-fish, the *buccinum* and the *murex*, and by the use of which they gave a high value to their textile fabrics. Another was glass, whereof they claimed the discovery, and which they manufactured into various articles of use and ornament. They were also skillful in metallurgy; and their bronzes, their gold and silver vessels, and other works in metal, had a high repute. Altogether, they have a claim to be considered one of the most ingenious of the na-

tions of antiquity, though we must not ascribe to them the invention of letters or the possession of any remarkable artistic talent.

VII. SYRIA.

1. SYRIA, prior to its formation into a Persian satrapy, had at no time any political unity. During the Assyrian period it was divided into at least five principal states, some of which were mere loose confederacies. The five states were—1. The northern Hittites. Chief city, Carchemish (probably identical with the later Mabog, now Bambuch). 2. The Patena, on the lower Orontes. Chief city, Kinalua. 3. The people of Hamath, in the Cœle-Syrian valley, on the upper Orontes. Chief city, Hamath (now Hamah). 4. The southern Hittites, in the tract south of Hamath. 5. The Syrians of Damascus, in the Anti-Libanus, and the fertile country between that range and the desert. Chief city, Damascus, on the Abana (Barada).

Syria divided into several petty states.

2. Of these states the one which was, if not the most powerful, yet at any rate the most generally known, was Syria of Damascus. The city itself was as old as the time of Abraham. The state, which was powerful enough, about B.C. 1000, to escape absorption into the empire of Solomon, continued to enjoy independence down to the time of Tiglath-pileser II., and was a formidable neighbor to the Jewish and Israelite monarchs. After the capture by Tiglath-pileser, about B.C. 732, a time of great weakness and depression ensued. One or two feeble attempts at revolt were easily crushed; after which, for a while, Damascus wholly disappears from history.

Kingdom of Damascus.

LINE OF DAMASCENE KINGS:—1. Hadad, contemporary with David, about B.C. 1040. Assists Hadadezar, king of Zobah, against David; is defeated, and makes his submission. 2. Rezon, contemporary with Solomon, about B.C. 1000. Revolts, and establishes independence. 3. Tab-rimmon, contemporary with Abijah, about B.C. 960 to 950. 4. Ben-hadad I. (his son), contemporary with Baasha in Israel and Asa in Judah, about B.C. 950 to 920. Wars with Baasha and Omri. 5. Ben-hadad II. (his son), contemporary with Ahab, about B.C. 900. Wars with Ahab. Murdered by Hazael. 6. Hazael, contemporary with Jehu in Israel and Shalmaneser II. in Assyria, about B.C. 850. 7. Ben-hadad III. (his son), contemporary with Jehoahaz, about B.C. 840. Oppresses Israel. Defeated three times by Joash. Kings unknown till 8. Rezin (about B.C. 745 to 732), who attacks Ahaz of Judah, and is defeated and slain by Tiglath-pileser.

VIII. JUDÆA.

1. The history of the Jews and Israelites is known to us in completer sequence and in greater detail than that of any other people of equal antiquity, from the circumstance that there has been preserved to our day so large a portion of their literature. The Jews became familiar with writing during their sojourn in Egypt, if not even earlier; and kept records of the chief events in their national life from that time almost uninterruptedly. From the sacred character which attached to many of their historical books, peculiar care was taken of them; and the result is that they have come down to us nearly in their original form. Besides this, a large body of their ancient poesy is still extant, and thus it becomes possible to describe at length not merely the events of their civil history, but their manners, customs, and modes of thought.

SOURCES OF THE HISTORY:—(*a*) Native. 1. The historical books of Joshua, Judges, Samuel, Kings, and Chronicles, with the historical parts of Jeremiah and Daniel. 2. The prophetical books, except Haggai, Zechariah, and Malachi. 3. JOSEPHUS, *Antiquitates Judaicæ;* ed. COTTA and GFRÖRER, Philadelphia, 1864. (*b*) Foreign. 1. The Fragments of NICOLAS of Damascus, in the *Fragmenta Hist. Græc.* vol. iii.; ed. C. MÜLLER, Paris. 2. TACITUS, *Historiæ*, lib. v. Curious, but of little value. 3. Occasional notices in the cuneiform inscriptions of Assyria and the hieroglyphics of Egypt.

Modern works on the subject are numerous and important. The following will be found of especial value:

MILMAN, H. H., *History of the Jews from the Earliest Period down to Modern Times.* London, 1863; 3d edition, revised and extended; 3 vols. 8vo.

EWALD, *Geschichte des Volkes Israel.* Göttingen, 1851–8. 2d edit.; 3 vols. 8vo.

STANLEY, A. P., *Lectures on the History of the Jewish Church.* First Series; London, 1863. Second Series; London, 1865; 2 vols. 8vo.

LEWIS, *Origenes Hebrææ: the Antiquities of the Hebrew Republic.* London, 1724; 4 vols. 8vo.

RELAND, *Antiquitates Sacræ veterum Hebræorum breviter delineatæ.* Traj. Bat. 1708.

EWALD, *Die Alterthumer des Volkes Israel.* Göttingen, 1851–9; 7 vols. 8vo.

And the numerous articles on the subject in Dr. W. SMITH'S *Dictionary of the Bible.* London, 1860–3; 3 vols. 8vo.

2. The history of the Jewish state commences with the

Exodus, which is variously dated, at B.C. 1652 (Poole), B.C. 1491 (Ussher), or B.C. 1320 (Bunsen, Lepsius). The long chronology is, on the whole, to be preferred. We may conveniently divide the history into three periods.

Periods of Jewish history.

PERIODS.	B.C.
I. From the Exodus to the establishment of the monarchy.....	1650–1095
II. From the establishment of the monarchy to the separation into two kingdoms........	1095–975
III. From the separation of the kingdoms to the captivity under Nebuchadnezzar........	975–586

3. During the First Period the Jews regarded themselves as under a theocracy; or, in other words, the policy of the nation was directed in all difficult crises by a reference to the Divine will, which there was a recognized mode of consulting. The earthly ruler, or rather leader, of the nation did not aspire to the name or position of king, but was content to lead the nation in war and judge it in peace from a position but a little elevated above that of the mass of the people. He obtained his office neither by hereditary descent nor by election, but was supernaturally designated to it by revelation to himself or to another, and exercised it with the general consent, having no means of compelling obedience. When once his authority was acknowledged, he retained it during the remainder of his life; but it did not always extend over the whole nation. When he died, he was not always succeeded immediately by another similar ruler: on the contrary, there was often a considerable interval during which the nation had either no head, or acknowledged subjection to a foreign conqueror. When there was no head, the hereditary chiefs of tribes and families seem to have exercised jurisdiction and authority over the different districts.

First Period, from B.C. 1650–1095. Time of the judges.

4. The chronology of this period is exceedingly uncertain, as is evident from the different dates assigned above (par. 2) to the Exodus. The Jews had different traditions upon the subject; and the chronological notices in their sacred books were neither complete, nor, apparently, intended for *exact* statements. The numbers, therefore, in the subjoined sketch must be regarded as merely approximate.

Uncertainty of the chronology.

JUDGES, etc., from the Exodus to the establishment of the monarchy:—1. Moses, the great lawgiver of the nation. Delivers the people from their Egyptian bondage, and conducts them to the borders of Palestine, B.C. 1650 to 1610. 2. Joshua. Conquers Palestine and divides it among the tribes, B.C. 1604. Dies, about B.C. 1595. Interregnum, about thirty years. Servitude under Cushan-rishathaim, eight years, about B.C. 1565 to 1557. 3. Othniel. Delivers Israel. Reigns forty years, B.C. 1557 to 1517. Interregnum, about five years. Servitude under Eglon, king of Moab, eighteen years, B.C. 1512 to 1494. 4. Ehud. Kills Eglon, and delivers Israel. Land has rest eighty years, B.C. 1494 to 1414. 5. Shamgar. (His reign probably included in the eighty years.) Servitude under Jabin, king of Canaan, twenty years, B.C. 1414 to 1394. 6. Deborah. Delivers Israel from Jabin. Land has rest forty years, B.C. 1394 to 1354. Servitude under Midian, seven years, B.C. 1354 to 1347. 7. Gideon. Delivers Israel from the Midianites. Reigns forty years, B.C. 1347 to 1307. 8. Abimelech, king. Reigns three years, B.C. 1307 to 1304. Interregnum, about five years. 9. Tola. Reigns twenty-three years, about B.C. 1299 to 1276. 10. Jair. Reigns twenty-two years, about B.C. 1276 to 1254. Interregnum, about five years. Servitude under Ammon, eighteen years, B.C. 1249 to 1231. 11. Jephthah. Delivers Israel from the Ammonites. Reigns six years, B.C. 1231 to 1225. 12. Ibzan. Reigns seven years, B.C. 1225 to 1218. 13. Elon. Reigns ten years, B.C. 1218 to 1208. 14. Abdon. Reigns eight years, B.C. 1208 to 1200. Interregnum, about five years. Servitude under the Philistines, forty years, B.C. 1195 to 1155. 15. Samson. Reigns in South-west Palestine during twenty years of these forty, B.C. 1175 to 1155. 16. Eli, High-priest and Judge. Reigns forty years, B.C. 1155 to 1115. 17. Samuel, the last Judge. Reigns probably about twenty years B.C. 1115 to 1095.

Second Period, from B.C. 1095–975.

Rapid growth of the Israelite power.

5. The Second Period of the Jewish state comprises three reigns only—those of Saul, David, and Solomon. Each of these was regarded as having lasted exactly forty years; and thus the entire duration of the single monarchy was reckoned at 120 years. The progress of the nation during this brief space is most remarkable. When Saul ascends the throne the condition of the people is but little advanced beyond the point which was reached when the tribes under Joshua took possession of the Promised Land. Pastoral and agricultural occupations still engross the attention of the Israelites; simple habits prevail; there is no wealthy class; the monarch, like the Judges, has no court, no palace, no extraordinary retinue; he is still little more than leader in war, and chief judge in time of peace. Again, externally, the nation is as weak as ever. The Ammonites on the one side, and the Philistines on the other, ravage its territory at their pleasure; and the latter people have encroached largely upon the Israelite borders, and re-

duced the Israelites to such a point of depression that they have no arms, offensive or defensive, nor even any workers in iron. Under Solomon, on the contrary, within a century of this time of weakness, the Israelites have become the paramount race in Syria. An empire has been formed which reaches from the Euphrates at Thapsacus to the Red Sea and the borders of Egypt. Numerous monarchs are tributary to the Great King who reigns at Jerusalem; vast sums in gold and silver flow into the treasury; magnificent edifices are constructed; trade is established both with the East and with the West; the court of Jerusalem vies in splendor with those of Nineveh and Memphis; luxury has invaded the country; a seraglio on the largest scale has been formed; and the power and greatness of the prince has become oppressive to the bulk of the people. Such a rapid growth was necessarily exhaustive of the nation's strength; and the decline of the Israelites as a people dates from the division of the kingdom.

6. Saul, divinely pointed out to Samuel, is anointed by him, and afterwards accepted by the people upon the casting of lots. He is remarkable for his comeliness and lofty stature. In his first year he defeats the Ammonites, who had overrun the land of Gilead. He then makes war on the Philistines, and gains the great victory of Michmash; from which time till near the close of his reign the Philistines remain upon the defensive. He also attacks the Amalekites, the Moabites, the Edomites, and the Syrians of Zobah. In the Amalekite war he offends God by disobedience, and thereby forfeits his right to the kingdom. Samuel, by divine command, anoints David, who is thenceforth an object of jealousy and hatred to the reigning monarch, but is protected by Jonathan, his son. Towards the close of Saul's reign the Philistines once more assume the offensive, under Achish, king of Gath, and at Mount Gilboa defeat the Israelites under Saul. Saul, and all his sons but one (Ishbosheth), fall in the battle.

Reign of Saul, B.C. 1095-1055.

7. A temporary division of the kingdom follows the death of Saul. Ishbosheth, conveyed across the Jordan by Abner, is acknowledged as ruler in Gilead, and after five years, during which his authority is extended over all the tribes except Judah, is formally

Temporary division of the kingdom, B.C. 1055-1048.

crowned as King of Israel at Mahanaim. He reigns there two years, when he is murdered. Meanwhile David is made king by his own tribe, Judah, and reigns at Hebron.

Sole reign of David, B.C. 1048-1015.

8. On the death of Ishbosheth, David became king of the whole nation. His first act was the capture of Jerusalem, which up to this time had remained in the possession of the Jebusites. Having taken it, he made it the seat of government, built himself a palace there, and, by removing to it the Ark of the Covenant, constituted it the national sanctuary. At the same time a court was formed at the new capital, a moderate seraglio set up, and a royal state affected unknown hitherto in Israel.

His conquests.

9. A vast aggrandizement of the state by means of foreign conquests followed. The Philistines were chastised, Gath taken, and the Israelite dominions in this quarter pushed as far as Gaza. Moab was invaded, two-thirds of the inhabitants exterminated, and the remainder forced to pay an annual tribute to the conqueror. War followed with Ammon, and with the various Syrian states interposed between the Holy Land and the Euphrates. At least three great battles were fought, with the result that the entire tract between the Jordan and the Euphrates was added to the Israelite territory. A campaign reduced Edom, and extended the kingdom to the Red Sea. An empire was thus formed, which proved indeed short-lived, but was as real while it lasted as those of Assyria or Babylon.

Rebellions of Absalom and Adonijah.

10. The glories of David's reign were tarnished by two rebellions. The fatal taint of polygamy, introduced by David into the nation, gave occasion to these calamities, which arose from the mutual jealousies of his sons. First Absalom, and then Adonijah, assume the royal title in their father's lifetime; and pay for treason, the one immediately, the other ultimately, with their lives. After the second rebellion, David secures the succession to Solomon by associating him upon the throne.

11. The reign of Solomon is the culminating point of Jewish history. Resistance on the part of the conquered states has, with scarcely an exception, now ceased, and the new king can afford to be "a man of peace." The position of his king-

Reign of Solomon, B.C. 1015-975.

dom among the nations of the earth is acknowledged by the neighboring powers, and the reigning Pharaoh does not scruple to give him his daughter in marriage. A great commercial movement follows. By alliance with Hiram of Tyre, Solomon is admitted to a share in the profits of Phœnician traffic, and the vast influx of the precious metals into Palestine which results from this arrangement enables the Jewish monarch to indulge freely his taste for ostentation and display. The court is reconstructed on an increased scale. A new palace of enlarged dimensions and far greater architectural magnificence supersedes the palace of David. The seraglio is augmented, and reaches a point which has no known parallel. A throne of extraordinary grandeur proclaims in language intelligible to all the wealth and greatness of the empire. Above all, a sanctuary for the national worship is constructed on the rock of Moriah, on which all the mechanical and artistic resources of the time are lavished; and the Ark of the Covenant, whose wanderings have hitherto marked the unsettled and insecure condition of the nation, obtains at length a fixed and permanent resting-place.

12. But close upon the heels of success and glory follows decline. The trade of Solomon—a State monopoly—enriched himself but not his subjects. The taxes which he imposed on the provinces for the sustentation of his enormous court exhausted and impoverished them. His employment of vast masses of the people in forced labors of an unproductive character was a wrongful and uneconomical interference with industry, which crippled agriculture and aroused a strong feeling of discontent. Local jealousies were provoked by the excessive exaltation of the tribe of Judah. The enervating influence of luxury began to be felt. Finally, a subtle corruption was allowed to spread itself through all ranks by the encouragement given to false religions, religions whose licentious and cruel rites were subversive of the first principles of morality, and even of decency. The seeds of the disintegration which showed itself immediately upon the death of Solomon were sown during his lifetime; and it is only surprising that they did not come to light earlier and interfere more seriously with the prosperity of his long reign.

Decline of the state.

Signs of disintegration in the empire during Solomon's reign:—1. Revolt of Damascus under Rezon, and re-establishment of the Damascene monarchy. 2. Revolt of Hadad in Edom. 3. Attempted revolt of Jeroboam.

Third Period, B.C. 975–586.

13. On the death of Solomon, the disintegrating forces, already threatening the unity of the empire, received, through the folly of his successor, a sudden accession of strength, which precipitated the catastrophe. Rehoboam, entreated to lighten the burdens of the Israelites, declared his intention of increasing their weight, and thus drove the bulk of his native subjects into rebellion. The disunion of the conquering people gave the conquered tribes an opportunity of throwing off the yoke, whereof with few exceptions they availed themselves. In lieu of the puissant State, which under David and Solomon took rank among the foremost powers of the earth, we have henceforth to deal with two petty kingdoms of small account, the interest of whose history is religious rather than political.

Kingdom of Israel, B.C. 975–721.

14. The kingdom of Israel, established by the revolt of Jeroboam, comprises ten out of the twelve tribes, and reaches from the borders of Damascus and Hamath to within ten miles of Jerusalem. It includes the whole of the trans-Jordanic territory, and exercises lordship over the adjoining country of Moab. The proportion of its population to that of Judah in the early times may be estimated as two to one. But the advantage of superior size, fertility, and population is counterbalanced by the inferiority of every Israelite capital to Jerusalem, and by the fundamental weakness of a government which, deserting purity of religion, adopts for expediency's sake an unauthorized and semi-idolatrous worship. In vain a succession of Prophets, some of them endowed with extraordinary miraculous power, struggled against this fatal taint. Idolatry, intertwined with the nation's life, could not be rooted out. One form of the evil led on to other and worse forms. The national strength was sapped; and it scarcely required an attack from without to bring the State to dissolution. The actual fall, however, is produced B.C. 721, by the growing power of Assyria, which has even at an earlier date forced some of the monarchs to pay tribute.

Note, as remarkable features of the kingdom of Israel:—1. The frequency of the dynastic changes, and the short average of the reigns. Nineteen monarchs are found in the brief space of 250 (or, according to the numbers assigned to the reigns, 230) years, giving an average of twelve or thirteen years to a reign. The kings belong to nine different families. Eight of them meet with violent deaths. Only two dynasties, those of Omri and Jehu, retain the throne for any considerable period. 2. The changes of the capital, which is first Shechem, then Tirzah, then Samaria. 3. The constant and exhausting wars (*a*) with Judah, (*b*) with Damascus, (*c*) with Assyria; and the want of an ally on whom dependence can be placed, Egypt being too remote, and Phœnicia too weak, to be serviceable.

LINE OF KINGS:—1. Jeroboam, divinely appointed to his office. Leader of the rebellion. Establishes the national sanctuaries with idolatrous emblems at Dan and Bethel, and at the same time creates a new priesthood in opposition to the Levitical. Great efflux of the Levites and other adherents of the old religion. War with Judah. Jeroboam helped by Shishak. Reigns twenty-two years (incomplete), B.C. 975 to 954. 2. Nadab, his son, reigns two years (incomplete), B.C. 954 to 953. Murdered by Baasha. 3. Baasha, reigns twenty-four years (incomplete), B.C. 953 to 930. Makes Tirzah the capital. Wars with Asa of Judah and Ben-hadad of Damascus. Exodus of pious Israelites continues. 4. Elah, his son, reigns two years (incomplete), B.C. 930 to 929. Murdered by one of his officers. 5. Zimri, against whom the army sets up Omri, the captain of the host. Zimri, in despair, burns himself in his palace. 6. Omri has a rival for some time in Tibni, but outlives him. Reigns twelve years (incomplete), B.C. 929 to 918. Transfers the capital to Samaria. Wars with Damascus and makes a disgraceful peace. 7. Ahab, his son, succeeds. Reigns twenty-two years (incomplete), B.C. 918 to 897. Strengthens himself by contracting affinity with Eth-baal of Tyre and Jehoshaphat of Jerusalem. The Tyrian alliance leads to the introduction of Phœnician idolatry. Evil influence of the Phœnician princess Jezebel over her husband and sons. Advance of corruption and futile efforts of Elijah. Wars of Ahab with Syria and Assyria. He falls fighting against the Syrians at Ramoth-gilead. 8. Ahaziah, his son, reigns little more than a year, B.C. 897 to 896. Revolt of Moab. 9. Jehoram, brother of Ahaziah, succeeds and reigns twelve years, B.C. 896 to 884. The league with Judah continues. Wars with Moab, and with Hazael of Damascus. Jehoram, and the queen-mother Jezebel, are murdered by Jehu. 10. Jehu is acknowledged king. He destroys the whole house of Ahab, and puts down the worship of Baal, but maintains the idolatry of Jeroboam. Hazael deprives him of all his territory east of the Jordan. On one occasion at least he pays tribute to Assyria. Jehu reigns twenty-eight years, B.C. 884 to 856. He is succeeded by his son, 11. Jehoahaz, who reigns seventeen years, B.C. 856 to 839. He loses cities to Damascus, and submits to have the number of his standing army limited. 12. Jehoash, or Joash, his son, reigns sixteen years, B.C. 839 to 823. A revival of the Israelite power commences. Joash defeats Ben-hadad, son of Hazael, three times, and recovers part of his lost territory. He also defeats Amaziah, king of Judah, and takes Jerusalem, but allows Amaziah to continue king. He is succeeded by his son, 13. Jeroboam II., under whom the kingdom reaches the acme of its prosperity. In his long reign, estimated at forty-one, or by some at fifty-one, years, B.C. 823 to 772, he not only recovered all the old Israelite territory, but even conquered Hamath and Damascus. He was succeeded, either immediately or after an interregnum, by his son, Zechariah, the fifth and last king of the house of Jehu. 14. Zechariah, who reigned six months only, B.C. 772, was murdered by 15. Shallum, who was in his turn assassinated, within little more than a month, by 16. Menahem of Tirzah. This enterprising prince, bent on carrying out the policy of Jeroboam II., made an expedition to the Euphrates and took Thapsacus; but having thereby provoked the hostility of an Assyrian (or Chaldæan) monarch, Pul, was attacked in his turn, and forced to become tributary. Menahem reigned ten years, B.C. 772 to 762. He left the crown to his son, 17. Pekahiah, who was murdered by one of his officers, Pekah, after a reign of two years, B.C. 762 to 760. 18. Pekah then succeeded, and reigned either twenty or thirty years, B.C. 760 to 730. He was twice attacked by Tiglath-pileser II., king of Assyria, who on the second occasion completely desolated the trans-Jordanic territory. His league with Rezin of Damascus was ineffectual against this enemy, though it reduced Judah to the verge of destruction. After the second invasion of Tiglath-pileser, Pekah was murdered by Hoshea, who succeeded him, either directly or after an interregnum. 19. Hoshea, the last king, reigned nine years, from B.C. 730 to 721. He at first accepted the position of tributary under Assyria, but, having obtained the alliance of Egypt, he shortly afterwards revolted. Shalmaneser, the Assyrian king, came up against him and commenced the siege of Samaria, which resisted for two years. It fell, however, shortly after Sargon's accession; and with its fall the kingdom of Israel came to an end.

Kingdom of Judah, B.C. 975–586.

15. The separate kingdom of Judah, commencing at the same date with that of Israel, outlasted it by considerably more than a century. Composed of two entire tribes only, with refugees from the remainder, and confined to the lower and less fertile portion of the Holy Land, it compensated for these disadvantages by its compactness, its unity, the strong position of its capital, and the indomitable spirit of its inhabitants, who felt themselves the real "people of God," the true inheritors of the marvellous past, and the only rightful claimants of the greater marvels promised in the future. Surrounded as it was by petty enemies, Philistines, Arabians, Ammonites, Israelites, Syrians, and placed in the pathway between two mighty powers, Assyria and Egypt, its existence was continually threatened; but the valor of its people and the protection of Divine Providence preserved it intact during a space of nearly four centuries. In striking contrast with the sister kingdom of the North, it preserved during this long space, almost without a break, the hereditary succession of its kings, who followed one another in the direct line of descent, as long as there was no foreign intervention. Its elasticity in

recovering from defeat is most remarkable. Though forced repeatedly to make ignominious terms of peace, though condemned to see on three occasions its capital in the occupation of an enemy, it rises from disaster with its strength seemingly unimpaired, defies Assyria in one reign, confronts Egypt in another, and is only crushed at last by the employment against it of the full force of the Babylonian empire.

LINE OF KINGS :—The throne is held by nineteen princes of the house of David and one usurping princess of the house of Omri, whose position as queen-mother enables her to seize the supreme power. The average length of the reigns is nineteen and a half years. 1. Rehoboam, son of Solomon, reigns eighteen years (incomplete), B.C. 975 to 958. Forbidden by the prophet Shemaiah to attack Jeroboam, he fortifies his towns. Invasion of Shishak; Jerusalem occupied and plundered. Jeroboam strengthened. Constant hostilities between Israel and Judah. Partial lapse of the people into idolatry. 2. Abijam, his son, reigns three years (incomplete), B.C. 958 to 956. He attacks Jeroboam and gains a great victory. Captures Bethel and other towns. Makes a league with Ben-hadad. 3. Asa, his son. Attacked by Zerah the Ethiopian (Osorkon, king of Egypt?), he completely defeats him. Attacked by Baasha, he detaches Ben-hadad from his alliance, and gains advantages. Makes efforts to put down idolatry. Reigns forty-one years (incomplete), B.C. 956 to 916. 4. Jehoshaphat, his son. Marries his son, Jehoram, to Athaliah, the daughter of Ahab, and makes alliance with the kingdom of Israel. Assists Ahab in his Syrian wars. Attempts to reopen the Ophir trade in conjunction with Ahaziah, but fails. Wars with Moab, Ammon, and Edom. Reigns twenty-five years (incomplete), B.C. 916 to 892. Succeeded by 5. Jehoram, his son, who reigns eight years (incomplete), B.C. 892 to 885. Successful revolt of Edom. The Philistines and Arabs attack and take Jerusalem. Jehoram gives encouragement to idolatry. 6. Ahaziah, his son, reigns one year only, being murdered by Jehu, king of Israel, B.C. 884. He is succeeded by 7. Athaliah, his mother, the daughter of Ahab and Jezebel, who murders all the seed royal except the infant Joash, and makes herself queen. She reigns six years, B.C. 884 to 878, and substitutes the worship of Baal for that of Jehovah. Jehoiada, the high-priest, heads a rebellion, proclaims Joash, and puts Athaliah to death. 8. Joash, son of Ahaziah, succeeds. Reigns well as long as Jehoiada lives, then becomes idolatrous. Attacked by Hazael and forced to purchase a peace. Murdered by two of his subjects, after he had reigned forty years, B.C. 878 to 838. 9. Amaziah, his son, defeats the Edomites and takes Petra. Attacks Joash, who defeats him and captures Jerusalem. Reigns twenty-nine years, B.C. 838 to 809. Murdered at Lachish. 10. Azariah or Uzziah, his son, a great and warlike prince. Re-establishes the port of Elath. Conquers most of Philistia. Defeats the Arabs. Receives tribute from Ammon. His attempt to invade the priest's office punished by leprosy. Reigns fifty-two years, B.C. 809 to 757. 11. Jotham, his son, who had been regent during his father's illness, succeeds. Reigns sixteen years (incomplete), B.C. 757 to 742. Fortifies Jerusalem. Forces the Ammonites to pay tribute. Attacked by Rezin and Pekah in his last year. 12. Ahaz, his son, reigns sixteen years, B.C. 742 to 726. Attacked by Rezin and Pekah, who defeat him and besiege Jerusalem, Ahaz calls in the aid of Tiglath-pileser II. of Assyria, and becomes his tributary. Pekah is chastised, Rezin slain, and Judæa relieved. Ahaz introduces various foreign idolatries. 13. Hezekiah, his son. Throws off the Assyrian yoke, defeats the Philistines, and re-establishes the pure worship of Jehovah. Attacked by Sennacherib, he submits and becomes tributary; but soon afterwards he revolts and makes alliance with Egypt. Second invasion of Sennacherib, directed especially against Egypt, results in the complete destruction of his army, and in the relinquishment of his designs. Hezekiah receives an embassy from Babylon. Isaiah prophesies during his reign, which lasts twenty-nine years, from B.C. 726 to 697. Hezekiah is succeeded by his son, 14. Manasseh, who reigns fifty-five years, from B.C. 697 to 642. In this reign idolatry is firmly established, the temple shut up, and the law of Moses allowed to fall into complete disuse. The worshippers of Jehovah are also violently persecuted. Manasseh, suspected of an intention to rebel by the Assyrians, is carried captive to Babylon, but afterwards restored to his kingdom, where he effects a religious reformation. 15. His son, Amon, succeeds, but reigns only two years, during which he re-establishes the various idolatries which his father had first introduced and then abolished. He is murdered by conspirators, B.C. 640. 16. Josiah, his son, a boy of eight, mounts the throne, and reigns thirty-one years, B.C. 640 to 609. Abolition of idolatry, and restoration of the temple worship. Discovery of the Book of the Law. Scythian inroad. Palestine invaded by Nechoh, king of Egypt. Battle of Megiddo, and death of Josiah. 17. Jehoahaz, his second son, is made king by the people, but within three months is removed by Nechoh, who confers the crown on his elder brother, 18. Jehoiakim, which he holds for four years as an Egyptian tributary, B.C. 609 to 605. Great expedition of Nebuchadnezzar; defeat of Nechoh at Carchemish, and extension of the Babylonian dominion to the borders of Egypt. Jehoiakim submits, but afterwards rebels and is put to death, B.C. 605 to 598. 19. Jehoiachin, son of Jehoiakim, is made king by Nebuchadnezzar, but holds the throne for three months only, when he is carried captive to Babylon, with a great number of his subjects, B.C. 597. 20. Zedekiah, third son of Josiah, uncle of Jehoiachin, then rules as a Babylonian tributary; but he too rebels, allies himself with Apries, king of Egypt, and defies the Chaldæan power. Nebuchadnezzar lays siege to Jerusalem, B.C. 588, and takes it B.C. 586. Zedekiah and the rest of the nation are carried captive to Babylon. Jeremiah prophesies during the reigns of Josiah and his three sons.

PART II.—AFRICAN NATIONS.

Preliminary Remarks on the Geography of Ancient Africa.

1. THE continent of Africa offers a remarkable contrast to that of Asia in every important physical characteristic. Asia extends itself through all three zones, the torrid, the frigid,

Contrast between Africa and Asia.

and the temperate, and lies mainly in the last, or most favored of them. Africa belongs almost entirely to the torrid zone, extending only a little way north and south into those portions of the two temperate zones which lie nearest to the tropics. Asia has a coast deeply indented with numerous bays and gulfs; Africa has but one considerable indentation—the Gulf of Guinea on its western side. Asia, again, is traversed by frequent and lofty mountain chains, the sources from which flow numerous rivers of first-rate magnitude. Africa has but two *great* rivers, the Nile and the Niger, and is deficient in mountains of high elevation. Finally, Asia possesses numerous littoral islands of a large size; Africa has but one such island, Madagascar; and even the islets which lie off its coast are, comparatively speaking, few.

Aridity and general infertility of Africa.

2. Its equatorial position, its low elevation, and its want of important rivers, render Africa the hottest, the dryest, and the most infertile of the four continents. In the north a sea of sand, known as the Sahara, stretches from east to west across the entire continent from the Atlantic to the Red Sea, and occupies fully one-fifth of its surface. Smaller tracts of an almost equally arid character occur towards the south. Much of the interior consists of swampy jungle, impervious, and fatal to human life. The physical characteristics of the continent render it generally unapt for civilization or for the growth of great states: it is only in a few regions that Nature wears a more benignant aspect, and offers conditions favorable to human progress. These regions are chiefly in the north and the north-east, in the near vicinity of the Mediterranean and the Red Sea.

General description of North Africa.

3. It was only the more northern part of Africa that was known to the ancients, or that had any direct bearing on the history of the ancient world. Here the geographical features were very marked and striking. First, there lay close along the sea-shore a narrow strip of generally fertile territory, watered by streams which emptied themselves into the Mediterranean. South of this was a tract of rocky mountain, less fitted for human habitation, though in places producing abundance of dates. Thirdly, came the Great Desert, interspersed with

oases—islands in the sea of sand containing springs of water and a flourishing vegetation. Below the Sahara, and completely separated by it from any political contact with the countries of the north, but crossed occasionally by caravans for purposes of commerce, was a second fertile region—a land of large rivers and lakes, where there were cities and a numerous population.

Divisions: 1. Eastern portion. 2. Western portion.

4. The western portion of North Africa stood, in some respects, in marked contrast with the eastern. Towards the east the fertile coast-tract is in general exceedingly narrow, and sparingly watered by a small number of insignificant streams. The range of bare rocky hills from which they flow—the continuation of Atlas—is of low elevation; and the Great Desert often approaches within a very short distance of the coast. Towards the west the lofty range of Atlas, running at a considerable distance (200 miles) from the shore, allows a broad tract of fertile ground to intervene between its crest and the sea. The range itself is well wooded, and gives birth to many rivers of a fair size. Here states of importance may grow up, for the resources of the tract are great; the soil is good; the climate not insalubrious; but towards the east Nature has been a niggard; and, from long. 10° E. nearly to long. 30°, there is not a single position where even a second-rate state could long maintain itself.

Description of the Nile valley.

5. The description of North Africa, which has been here given, holds good as far as long. 30°; but east of this line there commences another and very different region. From the highlands of Abyssinia and the great reservoirs on the line of the equator, the Nile rolls down its vast body of waters with a course whose general direction is from south to north, and, meeting the Desert, flows across it in a mighty stream, which renders this corner of the continent the richest and most valuable of all the tracts contained in it. The Nile valley is 3000 miles long, and, in its upper portion, of unknown width. When it enters the Desert, about lat. 16°, its width contracts; and from the sixth cataract down to Cairo, the average breadth of the cultivable soil does not exceed fifteen miles. This soil, however, is of the best possible quality; and the possession of the strip on either side of the river, and of the

broader tract known as the Delta, about its mouth, naturally constitutes the power which holds it a great and important state. The proximity of this part of Africa to Western Asia and to Europe, its healthiness and comparatively temperate climate, likewise favored the development in this region of an early civilization and the formation of a monarchy which played an important part in the history of the ancient world.

Region between the Nile and the Red Sea.

6. Above the point at which the Nile enters the Desert, on the right or east bank of the stream, occurs another tract, physically very remarkable, and capable of becoming politically of high consideration. Here there is interposed between the main stream of the Nile and the Red Sea an elevated table-land, 8000 feet above the ocean-level, surrounded and intersected by mountains, which rise in places to the height of 15,000 feet. These lofty masses attract and condense the vapors that float in from the neighboring sea; and the country is thus subject to violent rains, which during the summer months fill the river-courses, and, flowing down them to the Nile, are the cause of that stream's periodical overflow, and so of the rich fertility of Egypt. The abundance of moisture renders the plateau generally productive; and the region, which may be regarded as containing from 200,000 to 250,000 square miles, is thus one well capable of nourishing and sustaining a power of the first magnitude.

Political division of Northern Africa.

The nations inhabiting Northern Africa in the times anterior to Cyrus were, according to the belief of the Greeks, five. These were the Egyptians, the Ethiopians, the Greeks, the Phœnicians, and the Libyans.

i. *Egypt.* To the Egyptians belonged the Nile valley from lat. 24° to the coast, together with the barren region between that valley and the Red Sea, and the fertile tract of the Faioom about Mœris, on the opposite side of the stream. Its most important portion was the Delta, which contained about 8000 square miles, and was studded with cities of note. The *chief* towns were, however, in the narrow valley. These were Memphis, not much above the apex of the Delta, and Thebes, about lat. 26°. Besides these, the places of importance were, in Upper Egypt, Elephantine and

Chemmis, or Panopolis; in the lower country, Heliopolis, Saïs, Sebennytus, Mendes, Tanis, Bubastis, and Pelusium. The Nile was the only Egyptian river; but at the distance of about ninety miles from the sea, the great stream divided itself into three distinct channels, known as the Canobic, the Sebennytic, and the Pelusiac branches; while, lower down, these channels further subdivided themselves, so that in the time of Herodotus the Nile waters reached the Mediterranean by seven distinct mouths. Egypt had one large and several smaller lakes. The large lake, known by the name of Mœris, lay on the west side of the Nile, in lat. 29° 50′. It was believed to be artificial, but was really a natural depression.

ii. *Ethiopia.* The Ethiopians held the valley of the Nile above Egypt, and the whole of the plateau from which descend the great Nile affluents, the modern country of Abyssinia. Their chief city was Meroë. Little was known of the tract by the ancients; but it was believed to be excessively rich in gold. A tribe called Troglodyte Ethiopians—i. e., Ethiopians who burrowed underground—is mentioned as inhabiting the Sahara where it adjoins upon Fezzan.

iii. *Greek Settlements.* The Greeks had colonized the portion of North Africa which approached most nearly to the Peloponnese, having settled at Cyrene about B.C. 630, and at Barca about seventy years afterwards. They had also a colony at Naucratis in Egypt, and perhaps a settlement at the greater Oasis.

iv. *Libyans.* The Libyans possessed the greater part of Northern Africa, extending, as they did, from the borders of Egypt to the Atlantic Ocean, and from the Mediterranean to the Great Desert. They were divided into a number of tribes, among which the following were the most remarkable: the Adyrmachidæ, who bordered on Egypt, the Nasamonians on the greater Syrtis, the Garamantes in the modern Fezzan, and the Atlantes in the range of Atlas. Most of these races were nomadic; but some of the more western cultivated the soil, and, consequently, had fixed abodes. Politically, all these tribes were excessively weak.

v. *Carthage.* The Carthaginians, or Liby-Phœnicians—immigrants into Africa, like the Greeks—had fixed themselves in the fertile region north of the Atlas chain, at the point where it approaches nearest to Sicily. Here in a cluster lay the important towns of Carthage, Utica, Hippo Zaritus, Tunis, and Zama Regia, while a little removed were Adrumetum, Leptis, and Hippo Regius. The entire tract was fertile and well watered, intersected by numerous ranges, spurs from the main chain of Atlas. Its principal river was the Bagrada (now Majerdah), which emptied itself into the sea a little to the north-west of Carthage. The entire coast was indented by numerous bays; and excellent land-locked harbors were formed by salt lakes connected with the sea by narrow channels. Such was the Hipponites Palus (L. Benzart) near Hippo Zaritus, and the great harbor of Carthage, now that of Tunis. Next to the Nile valley, this was the portion of Northern Africa most favored by Nature, and best suited for the habitation of a great power.

HISTORICAL SKETCH OF THE ANCIENT AFRICAN STATES.

A. *History of Egypt from the Earliest Times to the Persian Conquest.*

SOURCES. 1. *Native:* including (*a*) the Monuments themselves, which are either inscriptions on buildings, sarcophagi, etc., or writings on papyrus. Only a portion of these have been edited. The best collections are: LEPSIUS, *Denkmäler*, Berlin; commenced in 1849, and still in progress. A magnificent work. BRUGSCH, H., *Geographische Inschriften altägyptischer Denkmäler.* Leipzig, 1857–60; 3 vols. 4to. CHAMPOLLION LE JEUNE, *Monuments de l'Egypte et de la Nubie.* Paris, 1835–45; 4 vols. folio. ROSELLINI, *I monumenti dell Egitto e della Nubia.* Pisa, 1832–43; text, 9 vols. 8vo; plates, 3 vols. folio. Important works on single subjects are LEPSIUS, *Konigsbuch der alten Ægypten.* Berlin, 1858; 2 vols. 4to; and WILKINSON, *Turin Papyrus.* London. (*b*) The history of Manetho, written in Greek, about B.C. 260, but now existing only in fragments, and in the epitomes of Eusebius and Africanus (the latter known to us through Syncellus). The fragments have been collected and edited by C. MÜLLER in his *Fragmenta Historicorum Græcorum*, vol. ii.

2. *Jewish.* Important notices of the condition of Egypt are contained in the Pentateuch, especially in Genesis and Exodus; and likewise in Kings, Chronicles, and Jeremiah. Until the time of Rehoboam, however, the Egyptian monarchs, unfortunately, are not mentioned by name, the title, Pharaoh, being used instead. This renders it impossible to identify, except conjecturally, the earlier Egyptian monarchs of Scripture with monumental or Manethonian kings.

3. *Greek.* (*a*) The earliest, and in most respects the best Greek authority, is HERODOTUS, who reports faithfully what the Egyptian priests communicated to him as the history of their country, when he visited Egypt about B.C. 460 to 450. If he is credulous with regard to the exaggerated chronol-

ogy required by the priestly system, we must remember that he had no means of knowing how long mankind had existed upon the earth. The sketch of Egyptian history supplied to him was scanty and incomplete, but in few respects untrue. It was, in a peculiar sense, *monumental* history, i. e., it was such a history as would naturally be obtained by a traveller who inquired principally concerning the founders of the great public edifices which came under his notice. The list of monarchs obtained in this way was, of course, not consecutive; but the kings themselves were real personages, and the actual order of their reigns was only at one point seriously deranged. Herodotus adds to his account of the Egyptian history a most graphic description of their manners, customs, and religious rites—a description which, though disfigured by some rhetorical exaggerations, and not free from mistakes of the kind which a foreigner who pays a short visit to a country always makes, is yet by far the best and fullest account of these matters that has come down to us from ancient times. (*b*) The Greek writer who comes next to Herodotus in the copiousness with which he treats Egyptian affairs is DIODORUS, who, like Herodotus, visited Egypt, and who also professed to draw his narrative from information furnished him by the priests. The Egyptian history of Diodorus is, however, so manifestly based on that of Herodotus, which it merely supplements to a certain extent, that we can scarcely suppose it to have been drawn quite independently from native sources. Rather we must regard him as taking Herodotus for his basis, and as endeavoring to fill out the sketch with which that writer had furnished his countrymen. Apparently he was wholly ignorant of the history of Manetho. It is remarkable that the additions which Diodorus makes to the scheme of Herodotus are in almost every instance worthless. He deserves credit, however, for pointing out that the monarchs in Herodotus's list are often not consecutive, but separated from each other by intervals of several generations. (*c*) ERATOSTHENES of Cyrene, and APOLLODORUS the chronographer, treated Egyptian chronology from their own point of view, manipulating it at their pleasure in a way that was sufficiently arbitrary. They are of scarcely any value.

Modern works on the subject of Egyptian History are numerous and important. The best are:

CHAMPOLLION LE JEUNE, *L'Egypte sous les Pharaons, ou Recherches sur la Géographie, la Religion, la Langue, les Ecritures, et l'Histoire de l'Egypte avant l'invasion de Cambyse.* Paris, 1814; 2 vols.

BUNSEN, BARON, *Ægypten's Stelle in der Weltgeschichte.* Hamburg, 1845–57; 6 vols. 8vo. Translated into English under the title of *Egypt's Place in Universal History*, by COTTRELL and BIRCH. London, 1848–67; 5 vols. 8vo. Rather materials for history than history itself.

KENDRICK, *Ancient Egypt under the Pharaohs.* London, 1850; 2 vols. 8vo.

LEPSIUS, *Chronologie der Ægypter*, Einleitung und Erster Theil: Kritik der Quellen. Berlin, 1849; 4to.

POOLE, R. S., *Horæ Ægyptiacæ.* London, 1851; and article on *Egypt* in Dr. W. SMITH'S *Dictionary of the Bible*, vol. i.

WILKINSON, Sir G., *Historical Notice of Egypt* in RAWLINSON'S *Herodotus*, vol. ii. London, 1858–60.

PALMER, W., *Egyptian Chronicles, with a Harmony of Sacred and Egyptian Chronology, and an Appendix of Assyrian and Babylonian Antiquities.* London, 1861; 2 vols. 8vo.

BRUGSCH, H., *Histoire de l'Egypte des les premiers temps de son existence.* Leipzig, 1859; 4to, 1 vol. published; to be completed in 3 vols.

On the manners and customs of the Ancient Egyptians, the great work is—

WILKINSON, Sir G., *Manners and Customs of the Ancient Egyptians, including their Private Life, Government, Laws, etc., derived from a Comparison of the Paintings, Sculptures, and Ornaments still existing, with the Accounts of Ancient Authors.* London, 1837–41; 6 vols. 8vo.

The best general account of the country will be found in the

Description de l'Egypte, ou Recueil des Observations et des Recherches qui ont été faites en Egypte pendant l'Expédition de l'Armée Française. Paris, 1809–20. Text, 9 vols. folio; plates, 14 vols. folio.

Smaller works, suitable for the ordinary student, are—

WILKINSON, Sir G., *Modern Egypt and Thebes.* London, 1843; 2 vols. 8vo; and *Handbook for Egypt.* London, 1858; 2d edition, 8vo.

Antiquity of the Egyptian monarchy.

1. The early establishment of monarchical government in Egypt is indicated in Scripture by the mention of a Pharaoh as contemporary with Abraham. The full account which is given of the general character of the kingdom administered by Joseph suggests as the era of its foundation a date considerably more ancient than that of Abraham's visit. The priests themselves claimed for the monarchy, in the time of Herodotus, an antiquity of above 11,000 years. Manetho, writing after the reduction of his country by the Macedonians, was more moderate, assigning to the thirty dynasties which, according to him, preceded the Macedonian conquest, a number of years amounting in the aggregate to rather more than 5000. The several items which produce this amount may be correct, or nearly so; but, if their sum is assumed as measuring the duration of the monarchy, the calculation will be largely in excess; for the Egyptian monuments show that Manetho's dynasties were often reigning at the same time in different parts of the country. The difficulty of determining the true chronology of early Egypt arises from an uncertainty as to the extent to which Manetho's dynasties were contemporary. The

monuments prove a certain amount of contemporaneity. But it is unreasonable to suppose that they exhaust the subject, or do more than indicate a practice the extent of which must be determined, partly by examination of our documents, partly by reasonable conjecture.

Arrangement of Manetho's lists.

2. A careful examination of the names and numbers in Manetho's lists, and a laborious investigation of the monuments, have led the best English Egyptologers to construct, or adopt, the subjoined scheme, as that which best expresses the real position in which Manetho's first seventeen dynasties stood to one another.

About B.C.								
2700	1st Dynasty, Thinite.							
		3d Dynasty, Memphite.						
2500	2d Dynasty, Thinite.	4th Dynasty, Memphite.	5th Dynasty, Elephantine.					
2400								
2200		6th Dynasty, Memphite.		9th Dynasty, Heracleopolite.	11th Dynasty, Thebans.			
2100					12th Dynasty, Thebans.	14th Dynasty, Xoites.	15th Dynasty, Shepherds.	16th Dynasty, Shepherds.
2000					13th Dynasty, Thebans.			
1900								
1800		7th and 8th Dynasties, Memphite.						
				10th Dynasty, Heracleopolite.				
1700								
1600							17th Dynasty, Shepherds.	

3. It will be seen that, according to this scheme, there were in Egypt during the early period, at one time two, at another three, at another five or even six, parallel or contempora-

Contemporary kingdoms from B.C. 2700 -1525.

neous kingdoms, established in different parts of the country. For example, while the first and second dynasties of Manetho were ruling at This, his third, fourth, and sixth bore sway at Memphis; and, during a portion of this time, his fifth dynasty was ruling at Elephantine, his ninth at Heracleopolis, and his eleventh at Thebes or Diospolis. And the same general condition of things prevailed till near the close of the sixteenth century B.C., when Egypt was, probably for the first time, united into a single kingdom, ruled from the one centre, Thebes.

4. It is doubtful how far the names and numbers in Manetho's first and third dynasties are historical. The correspondence of the name, Menes (M'na), with that of other traditional founders of nations, or first men—with the Manes of Lydia, the Phrygian Manis, the Cretan Minos, the Indian Menu, the German Mannus, and the like—raises a suspicion that here too we are dealing with a fictitious personage, an ideal and not a real founder. The improbably long reign assigned to M'na (sixty or sixty-two years), and his strange death—he is said to have been killed by a hippopotamus—increase the doubt which the name causes. M'na's son and successor, Athothis (Thoth), the Egyptian Æsculapius, seems to be equally mythical. The other names are such as may have been borne by real kings, and it is possible that in Manetho's time they existed on monuments; but the chronology, which, in the case of the first dynasty, gives an average of thirty-two or thirty-three years to a reign, is evidently in excess, and can not be trusted.

Manetho's first and third dynasties perhaps unhistorical.

FIRST DYNASTY (THINITE).			THIRD DYNASTY (MEMPHITE).		
Kings.	Years.		Kings.	Years.	
	Euseb.	Afric.		Euseb.	Afric.
1. Menes	60	62	1. Necherophes	..	28
2. Athothis (his son)	27	57	2. Tosorthrus	..	29
3. Kenkenes (his son)	39	31	3. Tyreis	..	7
4. Uenephes (his son)	42	23	4. Mesochris	..	17
5. Usaphædus (his son)	20	20	5. Suphis	..	16
6. Miebidus (his son)	26	26	6. Tosertasis	..	19
7. Semempses (his son)	18	18	7. Aches	..	42
8. Bieneches (his son)	26	26	8. Sephuris	..	30
			9. Kerpheres	..	26
	258	263		298	214

5. With Manetho's second and fourth dynasties we reach

the time of contemporary monuments, and feel ourselves on sure historical ground. The tomb of Kœechus (Ke-ke-ou), the second king of the second dynasty, has been found near the pyramids of Gizeh; and Soris (Shurè), Suphis I. (Shufu), Suphis II. (Nou-shufu), and Mencheres (Men-ka-rè), the first four kings of the fourth, are known to us from several inscriptions. There is distinct monumental evidence that the second, fourth, and fifth dynasties were contemporary. The fourth was the principal one of the three, and bore sway at Memphis over Lower Egypt, while the second ruled Middle Egypt from This, and the fifth Upper Egypt from Elephantine. Probably the kings of the second and fifth dynasties were connected by blood with those of the fourth, and held their respective crowns by permission of the Memphite sovereigns. The tombs of monarchs belonging to all three dynasties exist in the neighborhood of Memphis; and there is even some doubt whether a king of the fifth, Shafrè, was not the true founder of the "Second Pyramid" near that city.

Real history begins with the fourth dynasty of pyramid builders and contemporary second and fifth dynasties.

6. The date of the establishment at Memphis of the fourth dynasty is given variously as B.C. 3209 (Bunsen), B.C. 2450 (Wilkinson), and B.C. 2440 (Poole). And the time during which it occupied the throne is estimated variously at 240, 210, and 155 years. The Egyptian practice of association is a fertile source of chronological confusion; and all estimates of the duration of a dynasty, so long as the practice continued, are mainly conjectural. Still the comparatively low dates of the English Egyptologers are on every ground preferable to the higher dates of the Germans; and the safest conclusion that can be drawn from a comparison of Manetho with the monuments seems to be, that a powerful monarchy was established at Memphis as early as the middle of the twenty-fifth century B.C., which was in some sort paramount over the whole country. The kings of this dynasty were the following:

The fourth dynasty.

1. Soris (Shurè), who reigned twenty-nine years according to Manetho, and built the northern pyramid of Abooseer, on the blocks of which his name has been found. 2. Suphis I. (Shufu), the Cheops of Herodotus and Chembes of Diodorus Siculus, the builder of the "Great Pyramid," to whom Manetho gives a reign of sixty-three years. 3. Suphis II. (Nou-shufu), his brother, who reigned conjointly with Suphis I., and took part in the construction of the "Great Pyramid." He outlived his brother by at least three years. 4. Men-

cheres (Men-ka-ré), the Mycerinus of Herodotus and Diodorus, perhaps the son of Suphis I., the builder of the "Third Pyramid," which contained his sarcophagus. He reigned, like Suphis I., sixty-three years. 5. Ratoises, twenty-five years. 6. Bicheris, twenty-two years. 7. Sebercheres, seven years. And 8. Thamphthis, nine years. Probable duration of the dynasty, about 220 years.

Advanced civilization of Egypt at this early time, about B.C. 2440–2220.

7. It is evident from the monuments that the civilization of Egypt at this early date was in many respects of an advanced order. A high degree of mechanical science and skill is implied in the quarrying, transporting, and raising into place of the huge blocks whereof the pyramids are composed, and considerable mathematical knowledge in the emplacement of each pyramid so as *exactly* to face the cardinal points. Writing appears in no rudimentary form, but in such a shape as to imply long use. Besides the hieroglyphics, which are well and accurately cut, a cursive character is seen on some of the blocks, the precursor of the later hieratic. The reed-pen and inkstand are among the hieroglyphics employed; and the scribe appears, pen in hand, in the paintings on the tombs, making notes on linen or papyrus. The drawing of human and animal figures is fully equal, if not superior, to that of later times; and the trades represented are nearly the same as are found under the Ramesside kings. Altogether it is apparent that the Egyptians of the Pyramid period were not just emerging out of barbarism, but were a people who had made very considerable progress in the arts of life.

Elaborate governmental system.

8. The governmental system was not of the simple character which is found in kingdoms recently formed out of village or tribe communities, but had a complicated organization of the sort which usually grows up with time. Egypt was divided into nomes, each of which had its governor. The military and civil services were separate, and each possessed various grades and kinds of functionaries. The priest caste was as distinct as in later times, and performed much the same duties.

Aggressive wars. Pyramids perhaps built by captives.

9. Aggressive war had begun to be waged. The mineral treasures of the Sinaitic peninsula excited the cupidity of the Memphitic kings, and Soris, the first king of the dynasty, seems to have conquered and occupied it. The copper mines of Wady Maghara and

Sarabit-el-Kadim were worked by the great Pyramid monarchs, whose operations there were evidently extensive. Whether there is any ground for regarding the kings in question as especially tyrannical, may perhaps be doubted. One of them was said to have written a sacred book, and another (according to Herodotus) had the character of a mild and good monarch. The pyramids may have been built by the labor of captives taken in war, in which case the native population would not have suffered by their erection.

CONTEMPORARY DYNASTIES FROM ABOUT B.C. 2440 TO 2220.

Branch Dynasty. II. Thinite.	Yrs.	Chief or Stem Dynasty. IV. Memphite.	Yrs.	Branch Dynasty. V. Elephantine.	Yrs.
1. Boëthus or Bochus	38	1. Soris	29	1. Usercheres (Osir-kef)	28
2. Kœechus (Ke-ke-ou)	39	2. Suphis I. } 3. Suphis II. (brother) }	66	2. Sephres (Shafré)	13
3. Binothris	47			3. Nephercheres (Nofr-ir-ke-re)	20
4. Tlas	17	4. Mencheres (son of Suphis I.)	63	4. Sisires (Osir-n-ré)	7
5. Sethenes	41				
6. Chæres	17	5. Ratoises	25	5. Cheres	20
7. Nephercheres	25	6. Bicheris	22	6. Rathures	44
8. Sesochris	48	7. Sebercheres	7	7. Mencheres	9
9. Cheneres	30	8. Thamphthis	9	8. Tancheres	44
				9. Onnus (U-nas)	33
	302		221		218

10. The fourth or "pyramid" dynasty was succeeded at Memphis by the sixth Manethonian dynasty, about B.C. 2220. The second and fifth still bore sway at This and Elephantine; while wholly new and probably independent dynasties now started up at Heracleopolis and Thebes. The Memphitic kings lost their pre-eminence. Egypt was broken up into really separate kingdoms, among which the Theban gradually became the most powerful.

The sixth and parallel dynasties.

CONTEMPORARY DYNASTIES FROM ABOUT B.C. 2220 TO 2080.

II. Thinite.	VI. Memphite.	Yrs.	V. Elephantine.	IX. Heracleopolite.	XI. Theban.
(Continuing under the last three kings.)	1. Othoës [2. Phios 3. Methosuphis 4. Phiops (Pepi) 5. Menthesuphis 6. Nitocris (Neit-akret)	30 53 7] 100 1 12	(Continuing.)	Achthoes (Muntopt I. Series of Enentefs. Muntopt II.).	Sixteen kings. 17. Ammenemes (Amun-m-hé).
		143			

11. The weakness of Egypt, thus parcelled out into five kingdoms, tempted foreign attack; and, about B.C. 2080, or a little later, a powerful enemy entered Lower Egypt from the north-east, and succeeded in destroying the Memphite kingdom, and obtaining possession of almost the whole country below lat. 29° 30′. These were the so-called HYK-sos, or Shepherd Kings, nomades from either Syria or Arabia, who exercised with extreme severity all the rights of conquerors, burning the cities, razing the temples to the ground, exterminating the male Egyptian population, and making slaves of the women and children. There is reason to believe that at least two Shepherd dynasties (Manetho's fifteenth and sixteenth) were established simultaneously in the conquered territory, the fifteenth reigning at Memphis, and the sixteenth either in the Delta, or at Avaris (Pelusium?). Native Egyptian dynasties continued, however, to hold much of the country. The ninth (Heracleopolite) held the Fáioom and the Nile valley southward as far as Hermopolis; the twelfth bore sway at Thebes; the fifth continued undisturbed at Elephantine. In the heart, moreover, of the Shepherd conquests, a new native kingdom sprang up; and the fourteenth (Xoite) dynasty maintained itself throughout the whole period of Hyksos ascendency in the most central portion of the Delta.

Invasion of the Hyksos. Lower Egypt conquered.

CONTEMPORARY DYNASTIES FROM ABOUT B.C. 2080 TO 1900.

V. ELEPHANTINE.	IX. HERACLEOPOLITE.	XII. THEBAN.	Yrs.	XIV. XOITE.	XV. SHEPHERDS.	Yrs.	XVI. SHEPHERDS.
(Continuing till about B.C. 1850.)	(Continuing.)	1. Sesonchosis, son of Ammenemes (Sesortasen I.)..	46	Seventy-six kings in 484 years.	1. Salatis...	19	Thirty kings in 518 years.
		2. Ammenemes II. (Amun-m-hé II.)	38		2. Bnon	44	
		3. Sesostris (Sesortasen II.)........	48		3. Apachnas	36	
		4. [La]mares (Amun-m-hé III.)...	8		4. Apophis.	61	
		5. Ameres..........	8		5. Jannas..	50	
		6. Ammenemes III. (Amun-m-hé IV.)	8				
		7. Skemiophris (his sister)..........	4		6. Asses....	49	
			160			259	
		XIII. THEBAN.					

12. Simultaneously with the irruption of the Shepherds

occurred an increase of the power of Thebes, which, under the monarchs of the twelfth dynasty, the Sesortasens and Amun-m-hés acquired a paramount authority over all Egypt from the borders of Ethiopia to the neighborhood of Memphis. The Elephantine and Heracleopolite dynasties, though continuing, became subordinate. Even Heliopolis, below Memphis, owned the authority of these powerful monarchs, who held the Sinaitic peninsula, and carried their arms into Arabia and Ethiopia. Amun-m-hé III., who seems to be the Maris (or Lamaris) of Manetho and the Mœris of Herodotus, constructed the remarkable work in the Faioom known as the Labyrinth. Sesortasen I. built numerous temples, and erected an obelisk. Architecture and the arts generally flourished; irrigation was extended; and the oppression of Lower Egypt under the rude Shepherd kings seemed for a considerable time to have augmented, rather than diminished, the prosperity of the Upper country.

The twelfth (Theban) dynasty holds the Hyksos in check.

13. But darker days arrived. The Theban monarchs of the thirteenth dynasty, less warlike or less fortunate than their predecessors, found themselves unable to resist the terrible "Shepherds," and, quitting their capital, fled into Ethiopia, while the invaders wreaked their vengeance on the memorials of the Sesortasens. Probably, after a while, the refugees returned and took up the position of tributaries, a position which must also have been occupied by all the other native monarchs who still maintained themselves, excepting possibly the Xoites, who may have found the marshes of the Delta an effectual protection. The *complete* establishment of the authority of the "Shepherds" may be dated about B.C. 1900. Their dominion lasted till about B.C. 1525. The seventh and eighth (Memphitic) dynasties, the tenth (Heracleopolite), and the seventeenth (Shepherd) belong to this interval. This is the darkest period of Egyptian history. "The Shepherds" left no monuments; and during nearly 300 years the very names of the kings are unknown to us.

The thirteenth (Theban) dynasty. The Hyksos conquer Upper Egypt.

14. A new day breaks upon us with the accession to power of Manetho's eighteenth dynasty, about B.C. 1525. A great national movement, headed by Amosis (Ames or Aahmes), king of the Thebaid, drove the

Revolt under Amosis.

foreign invaders, after a stout conflict, from the soil of Egypt, and, releasing the country from the incubus which had so long lain upon it, allowed the genius of the people free play. The most flourishing period of Egyptian history followed. The Theban king, who had led the movement, received as his reward the supreme authority over the whole country, a right which was inherited by his successors. Egypt was henceforth, until the time of the Ethiopic conquest, a single centralized monarchy. Contemporary dynasties ceased. Egyptian art attained its highest perfection. The great temple-palaces of Thebes were built. Numerous obelisks were erected. Internal prosperity led to aggressive wars. Ethiopia, Arabia, and Syria were invaded. The Euphrates was crossed; and a portion of Mesopotamia added to the empire.

Expulsion of the Hyksos. Most flourishing period of Egypt, B.C. 1525–1200, the eighteenth, nineteenth, and twentieth dynasties.

KINGS OF THE EIGHTEENTH DYNASTY:—1. Amos (Ames or Aahmes). Led the insurrection. Expelled the Shepherds. Reigned twenty-six years, B.C. 1525 to 1499. 2. Amunoph I. Married the widow of Amos. Reigned twenty-one years, B.C. 1499 to 1478. 3. Thothmes I. Warred in Ethiopia. On his death, Amen-set, his daughter, became regent for his infant sons, 4. Thothmes II., who died a minor, and 5. Thothmes III., who became full king, after Amen-set (Amensis of Manetho) had held office for twenty-two years. This monarch was one of the most remarkable of the dynasty. He warred in Ethiopia, Arabia, Syria, and Western Mesopotamia, and is thought to declare that he took tribute from Nineveh, Is (Hit), and Babylon. His temples and other buildings at Karnac, Thebes, Memphis, Heliopolis, Coptos, and other places are magnificent. He reigned at least forty-seven years, including the time of his minority, from about B.C. 1461 to 1414. 6. Amunoph II., his son, whom he associated shortly before his death, succeeded him. His reign was short and uneventful. He was followed by his son, 7. Thothmes IV. (Tuthmosis of Manetho), who cut the great sphinx near the Pyramids. He warred with the Libyans and the Ethiopians. His queen, Maut-m-va, appears to have been a foreigner. 8. Amunoph III., son of Thothmes IV. and Maut-m-va, succeeded about B.C. 1400. He was a great and powerful sovereign. Military expeditions were made in his reign against most of the countries previously attacked by Thothmes III. Many great buildings were erected. Agriculture was improved by the construction of tanks or reservoirs. The two large Colossi were made, one of which is known as "the vocal Memnon." Amunoph further introduced some religious changes, which are obscure, but which seem to have been very distasteful to his subjects. He reigned at least thirty-six years, about B.C. 1400 to 1364. 9. Horus, his son, succeeded as legitimate king; but at the same time pretenders started up, possibly among his brothers and sisters, and for about thirty years the country was distracted by the claims of various sovereigns. Horus, however, conquered or outlived his rivals, and in his later years obliterated their memorials. He warred successfully in Africa, and made additions to the buildings at Karnac, Luxor, and other places. His reign was reckoned at thirty-seven years, B.C. 1364 to 1327. 10. A king called Resitot (the Rathotis of Manetho) appears to have succeeded Horus, and to have brought the dynasty to a close. His relationship to Horus is uncertain. He reigned only a few years, B.C. 1327 to 1324.

KINGS OF THE NINETEENTH DYNASTY:—1. Ramesses I., founder of the dynasty (about B.C. 1324), derived his descent from Amos and Amunoph I., but not from any of the later kings. He reigned less than two years. 2. Seti, his son (the Sesostris of Herodotus and Diodorus, and the Sethos of Manetho), succeeded—a great and warlike monarch. He re-conquered Syria, which had revolted after the death of Amunoph III., and contended with the Arabs, the Hittites, the Tahai (Dai) on the borders of Cilicia, and the people of Western Mesopotamia. He built the Great Hall of Karnac, and constructed for himself the most beautiful of all the royal tombs. According to Manetho, he reigned upward of fifty years. 3. Ramesses II. (Ramessu-miamun), who had for many years ruled conjointly with his father, became sole king on his decease. He warred in the same regions and with the same people as his father, and also carried his arms deep into the African continent. The chief of his monuments is the Ramesseum (Memnonium) at Thebes. His *stelé*, engraved on the rocks at the Nahr-el-Kelb, is well known. Egyptian art reached its culminating point in his reign. He opened a canal from the Nile above Bubastis to the Red Sea, and maintained a fleet in those waters. In all, he reigned sixty-six years, from about B.C. 1311 to 1245. 4. Amenephthes (Menephthah), his son, succeeded. He is thought by some to be the Pharaoh of the Exodus. The length of his reign is uncertain. He was followed by his son, 5. Sethos II. (Seti), who was undistinguished, and had but a short reign.

KINGS OF THE TWENTIETH DYNASTY:—Ramesses III. (perhaps the Rhampsinitus of Herodotus, who was famous for his full treasury) ascended the throne about B.C. 1219. He was at once a great builder and a conqueror. He fought at sea with the Tokari (Carians?) and the Khairetana (Cretans?); and on land penetrated as far as Western Mesopotamia. His chief buildings, which are at Medinet-habu, though they are magnificent, indicate a certain decline of the arts. He was succeeded by four sons, who all bore the same name, Ramesses, and who were all equally undistinguished. Then came Ramesses VIII., the sixth king of the dynasty, who was more warlike than his predecessors, and made some successful foreign expeditions. Six or seven other kings of the same name followed, most of whom had short reigns. The dynasty seems to have come to an end about B.C. 1085.

Decline of the monarchy begins with the twentieth dynasty.

15. The decline of Egypt under the twentieth dynasty is very marked. We can ascribe it to nothing but internal decay—a decay proceeding mainly from those natural causes which are always at work, compelling nations and races, like individuals, after they have reached maturity, to sink in vital force,

to become debilitated, and finally to perish. Under the nineteenth dynasty Egypt reached her highest pitch of greatness, internal and external; under the twentieth she rapidly sank, alike in military power, in artistic genius, and in taste. For a space of almost two centuries, from about B.C. 1170 to 990, she scarcely undertook a single important enterprise; her architectural efforts during the whole of this time were mean, and her art without spirit or life. Subsequently, in the space between B.C. 990 and the Persian conquest, B.C. 525, she experienced one or two "revivals;" but the reaction on these occasions, being spasmodic and forced, exhausted rather than recruited her strength; nor did the efforts made, great as they were, suffice to do more than check for a while the decadence which they could not avert.

16. Among the special causes which produced this unusually rapid decline, the foremost place must be assigned to the spirit of caste, and particularly to the undue predominance of the sacerdotal order. It is true that *castes*, in the strict sense of the word, did not exist in Egypt, since a son was not absolutely compelled to follow his father's profession. But the separation of classes was so sharply and clearly defined, the hereditary descent of professions was so much the rule, that the system closely approximated to that which has been so long established in India, and which prevails there at the present day. It had, in fact, all the evils of caste. It discouraged progress, advance, improvement; it repressed personal ambition; it produced deadness, flatness, dull and tame uniformity. The priestly influence, which pervaded all ranks from the highest to the lowest, was used to maintain a conventional standard, alike in thought, in art, and in manners. Any tendency to deviate from the set forms of the old religion, that at any time showed itself, was sternly checked. The inclination of art to become naturalistic was curbed and subdued. All intercourse with foreigners, which might have introduced changes of manners, was forbidden. The aim was to maintain things at a certain set level, which was fixed and unalterable. But, as "non progredi est regredi," the result of repressing all advance and improvement was to bring about a rapid and general deterioration.

Causes of the decline.

Compare the accounts of the Egyptian castes, which are given by Herodotus, Plato, and Diodorus, with the remarks on the subject made by moderns. Herodotus represents the castes, or classes, as seven—viz., priests, warriors, cowherds, swineherds, tradesmen, interpreters, and boatmen; Plato as six—viz., priests, warriors, shepherds, artificers, husbandmen, and huntsmen; Diodorus as five—viz., priests, warriors, herdsmen, artificers, and husbandmen. Moderns lay it down that there were really five general classes—those of Diodorus—and that some of these were again subdivided, as is the case with some castes in India.

The twenty-first dynasty of priest-kings, B.C. 1085–990.

17. The growing influence of the priests, which seems to have reduced the later monarchs of the twentieth dynasty to *fainéants*, was shown still more markedly in the accession to power, about B.C. 1085, of the priestly dynasty of "Tanites," who occupy the twenty-first place in Manetho's list. These kings, who style themselves "High-priests of Amun," and who wear the priestly costume, seem to have held their court at Tanis (Zoan), in the Delta, but were acknowledged for kings equally in Upper Egypt. It must have been to one of them that Hadad fled when Joab slaughtered the Edomites, and in their ranks also must be sought the Pharaoh who gave his daughter in marriage to Solomon. According to Manetho, the dynasty held the throne for rather more than a hundred years; but the computation is thought to be in excess.

KINGS OF THE TWENTY-FIRST DYNASTY:—1. Smendes, who reigned twenty-six years. 2. Psusennes (Pisham I.). Reigned forty-one or forty-six years. 3. Nephercheres. Reigned four years. 4. Amenephthes (Menephthah II.). Reigned nine years. 5. Osochor (probably Pehor). Reigned six years. Left sculptures in a temple at Thebes. 6. Psinaches (Piônkh). Reigned nine years. 7. Psusennes II. (Pisham II.), his son. Left sculptures in the same temple as Pehor. Reigned fourteen (or thirty-five) years.

Slight revival under the twenty-second dynasty, B.C. 993–847.

18. With Sheshonk, the first king of the twenty-second dynasty, a revival of Egyptian power to a certain extent occurred. Though Sheshonk himself takes the title of "High-priest of Amun," having married the daughter of Pisham II., the last king of the sacerdotal (twenty-first) dynasty, yet beyond this no priestly character attaches to the monarchs of his house. Sheshonk resumes the practice of military expeditions, and his example is followed by one of the Osorkons. Monuments of some pretensions are erected by the kings of the line, at Thebes and at Bubastis in the Delta, which latter is the royal city of the time. The revival, however, is partial and

short-lived, the later monarchs of the dynasty being as undistinguished as any that had preceded them on the throne.

KINGS OF THE TWENTY-SECOND DYNASTY:—1. Sheshonk (the Shishak of Scripture, and probably the Asychis of Herodotus). Ascends the throne about B.C. 993, and reigns twenty-one years, B.C. 993 to 972. Receives Jeroboam at his court, and afterwards makes an expedition against Palestine, to establish Jeroboam in his kingdom. Invades Judæa, receives the submission of Rehoboam, and plunders Jerusalem. Succeeded by his son, 2. Osorkon I., who reigns fifteen years, from B.C. 972 to 957, and leaves the crown to his son, 3. Pehor, who holds it not more than a year or two, when he is succeeded, or superseded, by his brother-in-law, 4. Osorkon II., who was perhaps an Ethiopian prince, married to a daughter of Osorkon I. This king is probably the Zerach of Scripture, who made an unsuccessful expedition against Asia, about B.C. 942. He reigned twenty-three years, from B.C. 956 to 933. 5. Sheshonk II., his son, succeeded him; after whom the crown passed to a "prince of the Mashoash," 6. Takelot I., who was married to Keromama, a granddaughter of the third king, Pehor. He reigned (probably) twenty-three years, when he was succeeded by his son, 7. Osorkon III., who reigned at least twenty-eight years. He left the crown to his son, 8. Sheshonk III., who also reigned as much as twenty-eight or twenty-nine years. The dynasty ended with 9. Takelot II., son of Sheshonk III., the length of whose reign is quite uncertain. The probable duration of the dynasty was 146 years, B.C. 993 to 847.

19. The decline of the monarchy advanced now with rapid strides. On the death of Takelot II., a disintegration of the kingdom seems to have taken place. While the Bubastite line was carried on in a third Pisham (or Pishai) and a fourth Sheshonk, a rival line, Manetho's twenty-third dynasty, sprang up at Tanis, and obtained the chief power. The kings of this line, who are four in number, are wholly undistinguished.

Further decline. Twenty-third and parallel dynasties. B.C. 847–758.

KINGS OF THE TWENTY-THIRD DYNASTY:—1. Petubastes (Pet-su-pasht). Reigned forty years. 2. Osorko (Osorkon IV.). Reigned eight years. 3. Psammûs (Pse-mût). Reigned ten years. 4. Zet (probably Seti III.). Reigned thirty-one years. Duration of the dynasty, eighty-nine years, from B.C. 847 to 758.

20. A transfer of the seat of empire to Saïs, another city of the Delta, now took place. A king whom Manetho and Diodorus called Bocchoris (perhaps Pehor) ascended the throne. This monarch, after he had reigned forty-four years—either as an independent prince or as a tributary to Ethiopia—was put to death by Sabaco, an Ethiopian, who conquered Egypt and founded the twenty-fifth dynasty.

The twenty-fourth and twenty-fifth dynasties. Egypt conquered by Ethiopia, about B.C. 730.

KINGS OF THE TWENTY-FIFTH DYNASTY:—1. Sabaco I. (Shebek I.), the So or Seveh of Scripture. His treaty with Hoshea, the last king of Israel, must have been made about B.C. 724. Its conclusion shows that the encroachments of Assyria had begun to cause alarm. The first hostile contact between Assyria and Egypt occurred in his reign. Sargon, who was his adversary, defeated his troops, and made himself master of Philistia, about B.C. 719. 2. Sabaco II., the Sevechus of Manetho, succeeded, about B.C. 704. His reign of fourteen years terminated B.C. 690, when the third and greatest of the Ethiopian monarchs mounted the throne. This was 3. Tehrak—the Tirhakah of the Jews, and the Tarcus, Taracus, or Tearchon of the Greek writers—who contended successively with Sennacherib, Esarhaddon, and Asshur-bani-pal. Discomfiture of Sennacherib, about B.C. 698. Esarhaddon invades Lower Egypt, about B.C. 669, and breaks it up into a number of small kingdoms. Tirhakah re-establishes his authority, B.C. 668. Asshur-bani-pal, having succeeded, contends with Tirhakah for two years. Tirhakah is defeated and abdicates in favor of his son, who is driven out. Egypt is then once more broken up into petty kingdoms (compare the dodecarchy of Herodotus), and remains subject to Assyria, probably till the death of Asshur-bani-pal, about B.C. 647. Nechoh, the father of Psammetichus, is among the viceroys whom Asshur-bani-pal sets up.

21. Thus it appears that between B.C. 730 and 665 Egypt was conquered twice—first by the Ethiopians, and then, within about sixty years, by the Assyrians. The native Egyptian army had grown to be weak and contemptible, from a practice, which sprang up under the Sheshonks, of employing mainly foreign troops in military expeditions. There was also (as has been observed already) a general decline of the national spirit, which made submission to a foreign yoke less galling than it would have been at an earlier date.

Assyrian conquest of Egypt, B.C. 665.

22. It is difficult to say at what exact time the yoke of Assyria was thrown off. Psammetichus (Psamatik I.), who seems to have succeeded his father, Nechoh, or to have been associated by him, almost immediately after his (Nechoh's) establishment as viceroy by Asshur-bani-pal, counted his reign from the abdication of Tirhakah, as if he had from that time been independent and sole king. But there can be little doubt that in reality for several years he was merely one of many rulers, all equally subject to the great monarch of Assyria. The revolt which he headed *may* have happened in the reign of Asshur-bani-pal; but, more probably, it fell in that of his successor. Perhaps its true cause was the shattering of Assyrian power by the invasion of the

Re-establishment of Egyptian independence under the twenty-sixth (Saite) dynasty, about B.C. 630.

Scyths, about B.C. 632. Psammetichus, by the aid of Greek mercenaries, and (apparently) after some opposition from his brother viceroys, made himself independent, and established his dominion over the whole of Egypt. Native rule was thus restored after nearly a century of foreign domination.

KINGS OF THE TWENTY-SIXTH DYNASTY:—1. Psammetichus (Psamatik I.). Married an Ethiopian princess. Settled the Greek mercenaries in permanent camps near Bubastis. Offended the warrior caste, which deserted in great numbers to the Ethiopians. Encouraged art and constructed several great works. Besieged and took Ashdod. Bribed the Scythians to retire from Palestine without attacking Egypt. Was of an inquiring turn of mind, and tried many curious experiments. Reigned fifty-four years in all, from B.C. 664 to 610; but was probably not an independent monarch for more than twenty or thirty years. 2. Necholi, his son. Reigned sixteen years, from B.C. 610 to 594. Applied himself to naval and commercial matters. Built fleets in the Red Sea and the Mediterranean. Attempted to re-open the canal between the Red Sea and the Nile. Had Africa circumnavigated. Invaded Syria in his second year, B.C. 609; defeated Josiah at Megiddo, and conquered the whole tract between Egypt and Carchemish, on the Euphrates. Attacked by Nebuchadnezzar, B.C. 605; was defeated and forced to yield all his conquests. 3. Psammis (Psamatik II.), his son. Reigned only six years, from B.C. 594 to 588. Made an expedition into Ethiopia. 4. Apries (the Uaphris of Manetho, and the Pharaoh-hophra of Scripture), his son. Reigned nineteen years, from B.C. 588 to 569. Resumed the aggressive policy of his grandfather. Besieged Sidon, and fought a naval battle with Tyre. Assisted Zedekiah against Nebuchadnezzar, but ineffectually. Made an expedition against Cyrene, which ended ill. Deposed, either by a revolt on the part of his own subjects, or more probably by Nebuchadnezzar, B.C. 569. Succeeded by 5. Amasis (Ames or Aahmes), who probably held his crown at first under the Babylonian monarch. Having strengthened himself by marrying a niece of the late king, daughter of his sister, Nitocris, he after a while made himself independent. He adorned Saïs with grand buildings, and left monuments in all parts of the country. He encouraged Greek merchants to settle in Egypt, and was on friendly terms with Cyrene and other Greek States. The only expedition which he undertook was one against Cyprus, which submitted and became tributary. Fearing the growing power of Persia, he allied himself with Crœsus of Lydia and Polycrates of Samos; but nothing was gained by these prudential measures. After the death of Cyrus, Cambyses, his son, collected a great expedition against Egypt, and had probably commenced his march when Amasis died, having reigned forty-four years. The task of resisting this attack fell on his son, 6. Psammenitus (Psamatik III.), who met Cambyses near Pelusium, but was defeated and compelled to shut himself up in his capital, Memphis, which was shortly besieged and taken. Psammenitus was made prisoner after he had reigned six months, and soon afterwards, being suspected of an intention to revolt, was put to death, B.C. 525. Thus perished the Egyptian monarchy, after it had lasted, as a single united kingdom, for a thousand years.

Egypt conquered by Cambyses, B.C. 525.

23. The revolts of Egypt from Persia will necessarily come under consideration in the section on the Achæmenian Monarchy. Egypt was the most disaffected of all the Persian provinces, and was always striving after independence. Her antagonism to Persia seems to have been less political than polemical. It was no doubt fermented by the priests. On two occasions independence was so far achieved that native rulers were set up; and Manetho counts three native dynasties as interrupting the regular succession of the Persians. These form the twenty-eighth, the twenty-ninth, and the thirtieth of his series. The first of these consists of one king only, Amyrtæus, who revolted in conjunction with Inarus, and reigned from B.C. 460 to 455. The other two dynasties are consecutive, and cover the space from the revolt in the reign of Darius Nothus (B.C. 405) to the re-conquest under Ochus (B.C. 346).

Revolts, B.C. 460–455.

B.C. 405–346.

KINGS OF THE TWENTY-NINTH (MENDESIAN) DYNASTY:—1. Neferites (Nefaorot). Reigned six years, B.C. 405 to 399. 2. Achoris (Hakar). Reigned thirteen years, B.C. 399 to 386. 3. Psammuthis. Reigned one year, B.C. 386 to 385. 4. Nepherites II. Reigned four months, B.C. 384.

KINGS OF THE THIRTIETH (SEBENNYTIC) DYNASTY:—1. Nectanebo I. (Necht-nebef). Reigned eighteen years, B.C. 384 to 366. 2. Teos or Tachos. Reigned two years, B.C. 366 to 364. 3. Nectanebo II. (Necht-nebef). Reigned eighteen years, B.C. 364 to 346.

B. *History of Carthage from its Foundation to the Commencement of the Wars with Rome.*

SOURCES. It is unfortunate that we possess no native accounts of the History of Carthage. Native histories existed at the time of the Roman conquest, and were seen by Sallust; but no translation was made of them into the tongue of the conqueror. The Carthaginian inscriptions which modern research has discovered are in no instance historical. We have not even any description by a Greek or Latin writer of the general character or contents of the native histories. Nor is the deficiency of native records compensated by any exact or copious accounts from the pens of foreigners. Herodotus, who gives us monographs on the histories of so many ancient nations, is almost wholly silent about Carthage. Timæus, Ephorus, and Theopompus, the earliest Greek authors who treated of Carthaginian affairs at any length, were writers of poor judgment; and of their works, moreover, we have nothing but a few fragments. The earliest and most important notice of Carthage which has come down to us is Aristotle's account of the form of government (Pol. ii. 11). From this most valuable passage, combined with scattered notices in other writers, the constitutional history of the great commercial republic may be to some extent reconstructed. For the general course of her civil history, for her foundation and her earlier wars and conquests, we must have recourse to Justin, Diodorus, and Polybius. The later wars are treated at some length, but from a Roman point of view, by Polybius, Livy, and Appian. Herodotus has some important notices connected with the trade of the Carthaginians, on which further light is thrown by two translations of Carthaginian works, which are still extant. These are:

HANNO, *Periplus*, in C. MÜLLER'S *Geographi Græci Minores*. Paris, 1855; and ed. FALCONER. London, 1797.

FESTUS AVIENUS, *Ora Maritima* (i. 80–130; iv. 375–412), in HUDSON'S *Geographi Minores*, vol. iv. Oxford, 1698.

Modern works touching on the history of Carthage are the following:

BÖTTICHER, *Geschichte der Carthager nach den Quellen*, 8vo. Berlin, 1827.

HEEREN, *Ideen über die Politik*, etc., vol. iv. Translated into English, and published at Oxford by Talboys, 1832.

DAVIS, Dr. N., *Carthage and her Remains*. London, 1861. Containing an account of excavations on the site of Carthage made in the years 1857 and 1858.

The history of Carthage may be conveniently divided into three periods—the first extending from the foundation of the city to the commencement of the wars with Syracuse, B.C. 850 to 480; the next from the first attack on Syracuse to the breaking out of war with Rome, B.C. 480 to 264; and the third from the commencement of the Roman wars to their termination by the destruction of Carthage, B.C. 264 to 146. In the present place, only the first and second of these periods will be considered.

FIRST PERIOD.

From the Foundation of Carthage to the Commencement of the Wars with Syracuse, from about B.C. 850 *to* 480.

Foundation of Carthage and position of the city.

1. The foundation of Carthage, which was mentioned in the Tyrian histories, belonged to the time of Pygmalion, the son of Matgen, who seems to have reigned from about B.C. 871 to 824. The colony appears to have taken its rise, not from the mere commercial spirit in which other Tyrian settlements on the same coast had originated, but from political differences. Still, its relations with the mother city were, from first to last, friendly; though the bonds of union were under the Phœnician system of colonization even weaker and looser than under the Greek. The site chosen for the settlement was a

peninsula, projecting eastward into the Gulf of Tunis, and connected with the mainland towards the west by an isthmus about three miles across. Here were some excellent land-locked harbors, a position easily defensible, and a soil which was fairly fertile. The settlement was made with the good-will of the natives, who understood the benefits of commerce, and gladly let to the new-comers a portion of their soil at a fixed rent. For many years the place must have been one of small importance, little (if at all) superior to Utica or Hadrumetum; but by degrees an advance was made, and within a century or two from the date of her foundation, Carthage had become a considerable power, had shot ahead of all the other Phœnician settlements in these parts, and had acquired a large and valuable dominion.

Rapid advance.

2. The steps of the advance are somewhat difficult to trace. It would seem, however, that, unlike the other Phœnician colonies, and unlike the Phœnician cities of the Asiatic mainland themselves, Carthage aimed from the first at uniting a land with a sea dominion. The native tribes in the neighborhood of the city, originally nomades, were early won to agricultural occupations; Carthaginian colonies were thickly planted among them; intermarriages between the colonists and the native races were encouraged; and a mixed people grew up in the fertile territory south and south-west of Carthage, known as Liby-Phœnices, who adopted the language and habits of the immigrants, and readily took up the position of faithful and attached subjects. Beyond the range of territory thus occupied, Carthaginian influence was further extended over a large number of pure African tribes, of whom some applied themselves to agriculture, while the majority preserved their old nomadic mode of life. These tribes, like the Arabs in the modern Algeria, were held in a loose and almost nominal subjection; but still were reckoned as, in a certain sense, Carthaginian subjects, and no doubt contributed to the resources of the empire. The proper territory of Carthage was regarded as extending southward as far as the Lake Triton, and westward to the river Tusca, which divided Zeugitana from Numidia, thus nearly coinciding with the modern Beylik of Tunis.

3. But these limits were far from contenting the ambition

of the Carthaginians. From the compact and valuable territory above described, they proceeded to bring within the scope of their influence the tracts which lay beyond it eastward and westward. The authority of Carthage came gradually to be acknowledged by all the coast-tribes between the Tusca and the Pillars of Hercules, as well as by the various nomad races between Lake Triton and the territory of Cyrênê. In the former tract numerous settlements were made, and a right of marching troops along the shore was claimed and exercised. From the latter only commercial advantages were derived; but these were probably of considerable importance.

Extent of the land power.

4. In considering the position of the Carthaginians in Africa, it must not be forgotten that the Phœnicians had founded numerous settlements on the African mainland, and that Carthage was only the most powerful of these colonies. Utica, Hadrumetum, Leptis Magna, and other places, were at the first independent communities over which Carthage had no more right to exercise authority than they had over her. The dominion of Carthage seems to have been by degrees extended over these places; but to the last some of them, more especially Utica, retained a certain degree of independence; and, so far as these settlements are concerned, we must view Carthage rather as the head of a confederacy than as a single centralized power. Her confederates were too weak to resist her or to exercise much check upon her policy; but she had the disadvantage of being less than absolute mistress of many places lying within her territory.

Relations with other Phœnician colonies.

5. But the want of complete unity at home did not prevent her from aspiring after an extensive foreign dominion. Her influence was established in Western Sicily at an early date, and superseded in that region the still more ancient influence of Phœnicia. Sardinia was conquered, after long and bloody wars, towards the close of the sixth century B.C. The Balearic islands, Majorca, Minorca, and Ivica, seem to have been occupied even earlier. At a later time, settlements were made in Corsica and Spain; while the smaller islands, both of the Mediterranean and the Atlantic, Madeira, the Canaries, Malta, Gaulos (Gozo), and Cercina, were easily subjugated. By the close of the sixth century,

Colonies in the islands.

Carthaginian power extended from the greater Syrtis to the Fortunate Islands, and from Corsica to the flanks of Atlas.

6. To effect her conquests, the great trading city had, almost of necessity, recourse to mercenaries. Mercenaries had been employed by the Egyptian monarchs as early as the time of Psammetichus (B.C. 664), and were known to Homer about two centuries previously. Besides the nucleus of a disciplined force which Carthage obtained from her own native citizens and from the mixed race of Liby-Phœnices, and besides the irregulars which she drew from her other subjects, it was her practice to maintain large bodies of hired troops (μισθοφόρους), derived partly from the independent African nations, such as the Numidians and the Mauritanians, partly from the warlike European races with which her foreign trade brought her into contact—the Iberians of Spain, the Celts of Gaul, and the Ligurians of Northern Italy. The first evidence that we have of the existence of this practice belongs to the year B.C. 480; but there is sufficient reason to believe that it commenced considerably earlier.

Land force of mercenaries.

7. The naval power of Carthage must have dated from the foundation of the city; for, as the sea in ancient times swarmed with pirates, an extensive commerce required and implies the possession of a powerful navy. For several centuries the great Phœnician settlement must have been almost undisputed mistress of the Western and Central Mediterranean, the only approach to a rival being Tyrrhenia, which was, however, decidedly inferior. The officers and sailors in the fleets were mostly native Carthaginians, while the rowers were mainly slaves, whom the State bred or bought for the purpose.

Navy.

8. Towards the middle of the sixth century B.C., the jealousy of the Carthaginians was aroused by the intrusion, into waters which they regarded as their own, of Greek commerce. The enterprising Phocæans opened a trade with Tartessus, founded Massilia near the mouth of the Rhone, and sought to establish themselves in Corsica in force. Hereupon Carthage, assisted by Tyrrhenia, destroyed the Phocæan fleet, about B.C. 550. Soon afterwards quarrels arose in Sicily between the Carthaginians and the Greek settlements there, provoked apparently

Commercial rivalry between the Carthaginians and the Greeks.

by the latter. About the same time Rome, under the second Tarquin, became a flourishing kingdom, and a naval power of some consequence; and Carthage, accustomed to maintain friendly relations with the Italians, concluded a treaty with the rising State, about B.C. 508.

9. The constitution of Carthage, like that of most other great trading communities, was undoubtedly aristocratic. The native element, located at Carthage, or in the immediate neighborhood, was the sole depositary of political power, and governed at its will all the rest of the empire. Within this native element itself the chief distinction, which divided class from class, was that of wealth. The two Suffetes indeed, who stood in a certain sense at the head of the State, seem to have been chosen only from certain families; but otherwise all native Carthaginians were eligible to all offices. Practically what threw power into the hands of the rich was the fact that no office was salaried, and that thus the poor man could not afford to hold office. Public opinion was also strongly in favor of the rich. Candidates for power were expected to expend large sums of money, if not in actual bribery, yet at any rate in treating on the most extensive scale. Thus office, and with it power, became the heritage of a certain knot of peculiarly wealthy families.

Constitution of Carthage.

10. At the head of the State were two Suffetes, or Judges, who in the early times were Captains-general as well as chief civil magistrates, but whose office gradually came to be regarded as civil only and not military. These were elected by the citizens from certain families, probably for life. The next power in the State was the Council (σύγκλητος), a body consisting of several hundreds, from which were appointed, directly or indirectly, almost all the officers of the government—as the Senate of One Hundred (γερουσία), a Select Committee of the Council which directed all its proceedings; and the Pentarchies, Commissions of Five Members each, which managed the various departments of State, and filled up vacancies in the Senate. The Council of One Hundred (or, with the two Suffetes and the two High-priests, 104) Judges, a High Court of Judicature elected by the people, was the most popular element in the Constitution; but even its members were

The Suffetes, Council, and Senate of One Hundred.

The Council of One Hundred and Four.

practically chosen from the upper classes, and their power was used rather to check the excessive ambition of individual members of the aristocracy than to augment the civil rights or improve the social condition of the people. The people, however, were contented. They elected the Suffetes under certain restrictions, and the generals freely; they probably filled up vacancies in the Great Council; and in cases where the Suffetes and the Council differed, they discussed and determined political measures. Questions of peace and war, treaties, and the like, were frequently, though not necessarily, brought before them; and the aristocratical character of the Constitution was maintained by the weight of popular opinion, which was in favor of power resting with the rich. Through the openings which trade gave to enterprise any one might become rich; and extreme poverty was almost unknown, since no sooner did it appear than it was relieved by the planting of colonies and the allotment of waste lands to all who applied for them.

Revenue.

11. As the power of Carthage depended mainly on her maintenance of huge armies of mercenaries, it was a necessity of her position that she should have a large and secure revenue. This she drew, in part from State property, particularly mines, in Spain and elsewhere; in part from tribute, which was paid alike by the federate cities (Utica, Hadrumetum, etc.), by the Liby-Phœnices, by the dependent African nomades, and by the provinces (Sardinia, Sicily, etc.); and in part from customs, which were exacted rigorously through all her dominions. The most elastic of these sources of revenue was the tribute, which was augmented or diminished as her needs required; and which is said to have amounted sometimes to as much as fifty per cent. on the income of those subject to it.

Commerce.

12. The extent of Carthaginian commerce is uncertain; but there can be little doubt that it reached, at any rate, to the following places: in the north, Cornwall and the Scilly Islands; in the east, Phœnicia; towards the west, Madeira, the Canaries, and the coast of Guinea; towards the south, Fezzan. It was chiefly a trade by which Carthage obtained the commodities that she needed—wine, oil, dates, salt fish, silphium, gold, tin, lead, salt, ivory, pre-

cious stones, and slaves; exchanging against them her own manufactures—textile fabrics, hardware, pottery, ornaments for the person, harness for horses, tools, etc. But it was also to a considerable extent a carrying trade, whereby Carthage enabled the nations of Western Europe, Western Asia, and the interior of Africa to obtain respectively each other's products. It was in part a land, in part a sea traffic. While the Carthaginian merchants scoured the seas in all directions in their trading vessels, caravans directed by Carthaginian enterprise penetrated the Great Desert, and brought to Carthage from the south and the south-east the products of those far-off regions. Upper Egypt, Cyrênê, the oases of the Sahara, Fezzan, perhaps Ethiopia and Bornou, carried on in this way a traffic with the great commercial emporium. By sea her commerce was especially with Tyre, with her own colonies, with the nations of the Western Mediterranean, with the tribes of the African coast from the Pillars of Hercules to the Bight of Benin, and with the remote barbarians of South-western Albion.

SECOND PERIOD.

From the Commencement of the Wars with Syracuse to the breaking out of the first War with Rome, B.C. 480 *to* 264.

Views of Carthage upon Sicily. First great invasion, B.C. 480.

1. The desire of the Carthaginians to obtain complete possession of Sicily is in no way strange or surprising. Their prestige rested mainly on their maritime supremacy; and this supremacy was open to question, so long as the large island which lay closest to them and most directly opposite to their shores was mainly, or even to any great extent, under the influence of aliens. The settlement of the Greeks in Sicily, about B.C. 750 to 700, preceded the rise of the Carthaginians to greatness; and it must have been among the earliest objects of ambition of the last-named people, after they became powerful, to drive the Hellenes from the island. It would seem, however, that no great expedition had been made prior to B.C. 480. Till then Carthage had been content to hold the western corner of the island only, and to repulse intruders into that region, like Dôrieus. But in B.C. 480, when the expedition of Xerxes gave full occupation to the bulk of the

Greek nation, Carthage conceived that the time was come at which she might expect to attack the Greeks of Sicily with success, and to conquer them before they could receive succors from the mother country. Accordingly, a vast army was collected, and under Hamilcar, son of Mago, a great attack was made. But the victory of Gelo at Himera completely frustrated the expedition. Hamilcar fell or slew himself. The invading army was withdrawn, and Carthage consented to conclude an ignominious peace.

2. The check thus received induced the Carthaginians to suspend for a while their designs against the coveted island. Attention was turned to the consolidation of their African power; and under Hannibal, Hasdrubal, and Sappho, grandsons of Mago and nephews of Hamilcar, the native Libyan tribes were reduced to more complete dependence, and Carthage was released from a tribute which she had hitherto paid as an acknowledgment that the site on which she stood was Libyan ground. A contest was also carried on with the Greek settlement of Cyrênê, which terminated to the advantage of Carthage. Anticipated danger from the excessive influence of the family of Mago was guarded against by the creation of the Great Council of Judges, before whom every general had to appear on his return from an expedition.

Extension of the Carthaginian dominion in Africa, B.C. 480–409.

3. It was seventy years after their first ignominious failure when the Carthaginians once more invaded Sicily in force. Invited by Egesta to assist her against Selinus, they crossed over with a vast fleet and army, under the command of Hannibal, the grandson of Hamilcar, B.C. 409, destroyed Selinus and Himera, defeated the Greeks in several battles, and returned home in triumph. This first success was followed by wars (1) with Dionysius I., tyrant of Syracuse; (2) with Dionysius II. and Timoleon; and (3) with Agathocles.

Second invasion of Sicily, B.C. 409.

WAR WITH DIONYSIUS I., B.C. 405 to 368. Invasion of Sicily by Hannibal and Himilco. Capture of Agrigentum, Gela, and Camarina. Convention with Dionysius, B.C. 405. Convention broken by Dionysius, B.C. 397. His triumphant march. Camarina, Gela, Agrigentum, and Selinus recovered. Motya taken. Landing of Himilco, B.C. 396. Motya recovered. Messene taken. Victory of Mago off Catana. Siege of Syracuse. Pestilence, B.C. 395. Flight of Himilco and destruction of his deserted army. His suicide. Mago sent to Sicily, B.C. 393. Peace made the year following. Attempt of Dionysius to expel the Carthaginians from Sicily, B.C. 383, fails by his defeat at Cronium, B.C. 382. Peace made on terms favorable to Carthage. Renewed attempt of Dionysius, B.C. 368, again fails.

WAR WITH DIONYSIUS II., B.C. 346 to 340. Attempt of Carthage to take advantage of internal troubles at Syracuse after the death of Dion. Arrangement made with Hicetas. Danger of Syracuse. Timoleon sent from Corinth to its relief. Mago and Hicetas besiege Syracuse, B.C. 344. Distrust of the former; he suddenly retires. Timoleon attacks the Carthaginian towns, B.C. 341. Great armament sent from Carthage under Hasdrubal and Hamilcar defeated by Timoleon at the Crimêsus, B.C. 340. Another army sent under Gisco. Peace made on the old terms.

WAR WITH AGATHOCLES, B.C. 311 to 304. War begun by aggressions of Agathocles on Agrigentum. Victory of Hamilcar at the Himera, B.C. 310, followed by the siege of Syracuse. Resolution of Agathocles to transfer the war into Africa. He lands and burns his ships; is for some time successful, partly owing to the treachery of Bomilcar, but can not conquer Carthage. His son twice defeated during his absence in Africa, B.C. 305. On his return, he too is defeated, and flies. Peace made B.C. 304.

4. The result of these wars was not, on the whole, encouraging. At the cost of several hundreds of thousands of men, of large fleets, and of an immense treasure, Carthage had succeeded in maintaining possession of about one-third of Sicily, but had not advanced her boundary by a single mile. Her armies had generally been defeated, if they engaged their enemy upon any thing like even terms. She had found her generals decidedly inferior to those of the Greeks. Above all, she had learnt that she was vulnerable at home—that descents might be made on her own shores, and that her African subjects were not to be depended on. Still, she did not relinquish her object. After the death of Agathocles in B.C. 289, the Hellenic power in Sicily rapidly declined. The Mamertines seized Messana; and Carthage, resuming an aggressive attitude, seemed on the point of obtaining all her desires. Agrigentum was once more taken, all the southern part of the island occupied, and Syracuse itself threatened. But the landing of Pyrrhus at the invitation of Syracuse saved the city, and turned the fortune of war against Carthage, B.C. 279. His flight, two years later, did not restore matters to their former condition. Carthage had contracted obligations towards Syracuse in the war against Pyrrhus; and, moreover, a new contest was evidently impending. The great aggressive power of the West, Rome, was about to appear upon the

Result of the Sicilian wars.

scene; and, to resist her, Carthage required the friendly co-operation of the Greeks. A treaty was consequently made with Hiero; and Carthage paused, biding her time, and still hoping at no distant period to extend her domination over the entire island.

BOOK II.

HISTORY OF PERSIA FROM THE ACCESSION OF CYRUS TO THE DESTRUCTION OF THE EMPIRE BY ALEXANDER, FROM B.C. 558 TO 330.

SOURCES. First in importance (so far as they extend) are the native sources, consisting chiefly of inscriptions on rocks and buildings, which have been deciphered by the labors of Grotefend, Lassen, Burnouf, Westergaard, and Sir H. Rawlinson. These inscriptions cover the period from Cyrus, B.C. 550, to Artaxerxes Ochus, B.C. 350, but are unfortunately scanty, excepting for the space of about seven years, from the death of Cambyses to the full establishment of Darius I. in his kingdom. Among works on the inscriptions are the following:

RAWLINSON, Sir H., *The Persian Cuneiform Inscription at Behistun deciphered and translated*, with plates representing the exact condition of the original. Published in the Journal of the Asiatic Society, vol. x. (London, 1846–7), and followed by *Copies and Translations of the Persian Cuneiform Inscriptions of Persepolis, Hamadan, and Van.*

LASSEN, Prof., *Die Alt-Persischen Keilinschriften von Persepolis*, published in the *Zeitschrift für die Kunde des Morgenlandes*, vol. vi. Bonn, 1836.

BURNOUF, *Mémoire sur deux Inscriptions Cunéiformes, trouvées près d'Hamadan.* Paris, 1836.

SPIEGEL, *Die Alt-Persischen Keilinschriften*, 8vo; Leipzig, 1862. A transcript of the inscriptions in Roman characters, with a translation, a brief comment, and a valuable vocabulary.

Another valuable but scanty source of ancient Persian history consists of the Jewish writers, Daniel, Ezra, Nehemiah, and the anonymous author of Esther, who were contemporary with Persian kings, and lived under their sway. The book of Esther is especially important from the graphic representation which it gives us of the Persian court, and the habits and mode of life of the king.

We should possess, however, but a very slight knowledge of the history of Ancient Persia were it not for the labors of the Greeks. Four Greek writers especially devoted a large share of their attention to the subject; and of these two remain to us entire, of the third we possess by far the greater portion, while the fourth exists only in an epitome. These writers are (*a*) HERODOTUS, who traces the history of the empire from its foundation to the year B.C. 479. His work is valuable, as he had travelled in Persia, and derived much of his information from Persian informants. But these informants were not always trustworthy. (*b*) CTESIAS: he wrote a history of Persia from the accession of Cyrus to B.C. 398, and professed to have drawn the greater portion of his narrative from the Persian archives. But strong suspicions rest upon his good faith. His work is lost, and our knowledge of it rests almost entirely on an epitome made by the Patriarch Photius, about A.D. 880. (*c*) XENOPHON: his *Cyropædia* is a historical romance, on which a judicious criticism will place very slight reliance; but his *Anabasis* and *Hellenica* are of great value for the period and events of which they treat. (*d*) DIODORUS: his *Universal History* is the chief authority that we possess for the later Persian history, from Cunaxa to the expedition of Alexander. Other Greek writers who throw a light on portions of the history are—THUCYDIDES, for the period between B.C. 479 and 410; PLUTARCH, *Vitæ Cimonis, Artaxerxis, et Alexandri;* and ARRIAN, *Expeditio Alexandri Magni*, for the closing struggle, B.C. 334 to 330. Something may be gathered from the Latin writers, JUSTIN and Q. CURTIUS; but the latter, where he differs from ARRIAN, is untrustworthy.

The best modern works on Persian History are the following:

BRISSON, *De regio Persarum principatu.* Paris, 1590. A valuable compilation.

HEEREN, *Ideen*, etc., vol. i. (see p. 18).

RAWLINSON, G., *Five Great Monarchies*, vol. iv. (see p. 19).

Different opinions have been entertained as to the value of the modern Persian writers on the antiquities of their country. Some have seen in the poem of FIRDAUSI (the *Shahnameh*) and in the *Chronicle* of MIRKHOND, genuine history, a little embellished by romantic coloring and supernatural detail. But the best critics incline to regard the writings in question as pure romance, the events related as fictitious, and the personages as chiefly mythological.

Origin of the Persians.

1. THE Persians appear to have formed a part of a great Arian migration from the countries about the Oxus, which began at a very remote time, but was not completed till about B.C. 650. The line of migration was first westward, along the Elburz range into Armenia and Azerbijan, then south along Zagros, and finally south-east into Persia Proper. The chief who first set up an Arian monarchy in this last-named region seems to have been a certain Achæmenes (Hakhamanish), who probably ascended the throne about a century before Cyrus.

Tribes.

2. The nation was composed of two classes of persons—the settled population, which lived in towns or villages, for the most part cultivating the soil, and the pastoral tribes, whose habits were nomadic. The latter consisted of four distinct tribes—the Dai, the Mardi, the Dropici or Derbices, and the Sagartii; while the former comprised the six divisions of the Pasargadæ, the Maraphii, the Maspii, the Panthialæi, the Derusiæi, and the Germanii or Carmanians. Of these, the first three were superior; and a very marked precedency or pre-eminency attached to the

Pasargadæ. They formed a species of nobility, holding almost all the high offices both in the army and at the court. The royal family of the Achæmenidæ, or descendants of Achæmenes, belonged to this leading tribe.

Relations of subjection towards Media.

3. A line of native Persian kings held the throne from Achæmenes to Cyrus; but the sovereignty which they possessed was not, at any rate in the times immediately preceding Cyrus, an independent dominion. Relations of a feudal character bound Persia to Media; and the Achæmenian princes, either from the first, or certainly from some time before Cyrus rebelled, acknowledged the Median monarch for their suzerain. Cyrus lived as a sort of hostage at the court of Astyages, and could not leave it without permission. Cambyses, his father, had the royal title, and, practically, governed Persia; but he was subject to Astyages, and probably paid him an annual tribute.

Causes of the revolt.

4. The revolt of the Persians was not the consequence of their suffering any grievous oppression; nor did it even arise from any wide-spread discontent or dissatisfaction with their condition. Its main cause was the ambition of Cyrus. That prince had seen, as he grew up at Ecbatana, that the strength of the Medes was undermined by luxury, that their old warlike habits were laid aside, and that, in all the qualities which make the soldier, they were no match for his own countrymen. He had learnt to despise the *fainéant* monarch who occupied the Median throne. It occurred to him that it would be easy to make Persia an independent power; and this was probably all that he at first contemplated. But the fatal persistence of the Median monarch in attempts to reduce the rebels, and his capture in the second battle of Pasargadæ, opened the way to greater changes; and the Persian prince, rising to a level with the occasion, pushed his own country into the *imperial* position from which the success of his revolt had dislodged the Medes.

Its success and consequences.

Submission of the subjects of the Medes to Cyrus, B.C. 558. Rapid series of conquests. Defeat of Crœsus in Cappadocia and capture of Sardis, B.C. 554. Subjection of the Asiatic Greeks by Harpagus, B.C. 553. Conquest of the remote East—Hyrcania, Parthia, Bactria, Sacia, Chorasmia, Sogdiana, Aria, Drangiana, Arachosia, Sattagydia, Gandaria—about B.C. 553 to 540. Expedition against Babylon, commenced B.C. 539, terminates successfully, B.C. 538. Importance of the fall of Semitism.

Reign of Cyrus, B.C. 558–529.

5. The warlike prince who thus conquered the Persian empire did little to organize it. Professing, probably, a purer form of Zoroastrianism than that which prevailed in Media, where a mongrel religion had grown up from the mixture of the old Arian creed with Scythic element-worship, he retained his own form of belief as the religion of the empire. Universal toleration was, however, established. The Jews, regarded with special favor as monotheists, were replaced in their proper country. Ecbatana was kept as the capital, while Pasargadæ became a sacred city, used for coronations and interments. The civilization of the Medes, their art, architecture, ceremonial, dress, manners, and to some extent their luxury, were adopted by the conquering people. The employment of letters in inscriptions on public monuments began. No general system of administration was established. Some countries remained under tributary native kings; others were placed under governors; in some the governmental functions were divided, and native officers shared the administration with Persians. The rate of tribute was not fixed. Cyrus left the work of consolidation and organization to his successors, content to have given them an empire on which to exercise their powers.

Interest attaching to the Persian religion from its comparative purity. Religious sympathy between the Jews and Persians. Primitive religion of the Persians contained in the *Zendavesta*, more especially its earlier portions, the *Gâthas* and the *Vendidad*. The attention of European scholars was first called to the *Zendavesta* by ANQUETIL DU PERRON, whose *Zend-avesta, ouvrage de Zoroastre, traduit en Français sur l'original Zend*, was published at Paris in 1771. This work, which, though valuable at the time, was full of faults, is now superseded by the editions of Westergaard (1852–4) and Spiegel (1851–8), and the German translation of the latter writer. The best comments on the *Zendavesta* are—

BURNOUF, EUGENE, *Commentaire sur le Yaçna.* Paris, 1833: 4to.

HAUG, MARTIN, *Essays on the Sacred Language, Writings, and Religion of the Parsees.* Bombay, 1862.

SPIEGEL, F., *Commentar über das Avesta.* Leipzig, 1864.

Short accounts of the Zoroastrian religion, drawn from the best sources, will be found in Dr. PUSEY'S *Lectures on Daniel*, lectures viii. and ix., and in RAWLINSON'S *Five Great Monarchies*, vol. iii. ch. iv.

Last campaign and death of Cyrus.

6. The close of the reign of Cyrus is shrouded in some obscurity. We do not know why he did not carry out his designs against Egypt, nor what occupied him in the interval between B.C. 538 and

529. We can not even say with any certainty against what enemy he was engaged when he lost his life. Herodotus and Ctesias are here irreconcilably at variance, and though the authority of the former is greater, the narrative of the latter is in this instance the more credible. Both writers, however, are agreed that the Persian king was engaged in chastising an enemy on his north-eastern frontier, when he received the wound from which he died. Probably he was endeavoring to strike terror into the nomadic hordes who here bordered the empire, and so to secure his territories from their dreaded aggressions. If this was his aim, his enterprise was successful; for we hear of no invasion of Persia from the Turcoman country until after the time of Alexander.

Accession of Cambyses, B.C. 529. Death of Smerdis.

7. Cyrus left behind him two sons, Cambyses and Bardius, or (as the Greeks called him) Smerdis. To the former he left the regal title and the greater portion of his dominions; to the latter he secured the inheritance of some large and important provinces. This imprudent arrangement cost Smerdis his life, by rousing the jealousy of his brother, who very early in his reign caused him to be put to death secretly.

Submission of Phœnicia and Cyprus. Conquest of Egypt, etc.

8. The genius of Cambyses was warlike, like that of his father; but he did not possess the same ability. Nevertheless he added important provinces to the empire. First of all he procured the submission of Phœnicia and Cyprus, the great naval powers of Western Asia, which had not been subject to Cyrus. He then invaded Africa, B.C. 525, defeated Psammenitus in a pitched battle, took Memphis, conquered Egypt, received the submission of the neighboring Libyan tribes, and of the Greek towns of the Cyrenaïca, and proceeded to form designs of remarkable grandeur. But these projects all miscarried. The expedition against Carthage was stopped by the refusal of the Phœnicians to attack their own colony; that against the oasis of Ammon ended in a frightful disaster. His own march against Ethiopia was arrested by the failure of provisions and water in the Nubian desert; and the losses which he incurred by persisting too long in his attempt brought Egypt to the brink of rebellion. The severe measures taken to repress this revolt were directed especial-

ly against the powerful caste of the priests, and had the effect of thoroughly alienating the province, which thenceforth never ceased to detest and plot against its conquerors.

9. The stay of Cambyses in Egypt, imprudently prolonged, brought about a revolution at the Medo-Persian capital. A Magus, named Gomates, supported by his order, which was powerful in many parts of the empire, ventured to personate the dead Smerdis, and seized the throne in his name. His claim was tacitly acknowledged. Cambyses, when the news reached him in Syria on his march homeward, despairing of being able to make head against the impostor, committed suicide —B.C. 522—after having reigned eight years.

Usurpation of the pseudo-Smerdis. Suicide of Cambyses, B.C. 522.

The Magian revolution was religious rather than political. The subject is still to some extent obscure; but it seems certain that Magianism and Zoroastrianism were at this time two distinct and opposed systems. The pretender was a Magus, born in the eastern part of Persia; and the object of the revolution was to make Magianism the State religion. Its ill success re-established the pure religion of Zoroaster.

10. To conciliate his subjects, the pseudo-Smerdis began his reign by a three years' remission of tribute, and an exemption of the conquered nations from military service for the like space. At the same time, he adopted an extreme system of seclusion, in the hope that his imposture might escape detection, never quitting the palace, and allowing no communication between his wives and their relations. But the truth gradually oozed out. His religious reforms were startling in an Achæmenian prince. His seclusion was excessive and suspicious. Doubts began to be entertained, and secret messages between the great Persian nobles and some of the palace inmates converted these doubts into certainty. Darius, the son of Hystaspes, and probably heir-presumptive to the crown, headed an insurrection, and the impostor was slain after he had reigned eight months.

Reign of the pseudo-Smerdis.

Institution of the Magophonia, which continued to be observed down to the time of Artaxerxes Mnemon. Indication presented by this custom of a time when the Magi were not the Persian priests.

11. Darius I., who ascended the throne in January, B.C. 521, and held it for nearly thirty-six years, was the greatest of the Persian monarchs. He was at once a conqueror and

Accession of Darius I., B.C. 521. Series of revolts, B.C. 521–515.

an administrator. During the earlier part of his reign he was engaged in a series of struggles against rebellions, which broke out in almost all parts of the empire. Susiana, Babylonia, Persia Proper, Media, Assyria, Armenia, Hyrcania, Parthia, Margiana, Sagartia, and Sacia successively revolted. The satraps in Egypt and Asia Minor acted as though independent of his authority. The empire was shaken to its centre, and threatened to fall to pieces. But the military talent and prudence of the legitimate monarch prevailed. Within the space of six years the rebellions were all put down, the pretenders executed, and tranquillity generally restored throughout the disturbed provinces.

12. The evils of disorganization, which had thus manifested themselves so conspicuously, may have led Darius to turn his thoughts towards a remedy. At any rate, to him belongs the credit of having given to the Persian empire that peculiar organization and arrangement which maintained it in a fairly flourishing condition for nearly two centuries. He divided the whole empire into twenty (?) governments, called "satrapies," and established everywhere a uniform and somewhat complicated governmental system. Native tributary kings were swept away; and, in lieu of them, a single Persian official held in each province the supreme civil authority. A standing army of Medo-Persians, dispersed throughout the empire, supported the civil power, maintained tranquillity, and was ready to resist the attacks of foreigners. A fixed rate of tribute took the place of arbitrary exactions. "Royal roads" were established, and a system of posts arranged, whereby the court received rapid intelligence of all that occurred in the provinces, and promptly communicated its own commands to the remotest corners of the Persian territory.

Organization of the empire.

PECULIARITIES OF THE PERSIAN GOVERNMENTAL SYSTEM. (*a*) Limits of satrapies not always geographic, cognate tribes being grouped together, even though locally separate. (*b*) Elaborate system of checks established. The satrap properly only the civil governor. Military power wielded by the commandants and commanders of garrisons. Institution of royal secretaries, attached to the courts of the satraps as "King's Eyes" and "Ears"—with the right and duty of communicating directly with the Crown by the public post, and of keeping the king acquainted with all that occurred in their respective districts. (*c*) Visitation of provinces suddenly and without notice by royal commissioners, or by the king in person; overhauling of the administration and public hearing of complaints. (*d*) Institution of royal judges, perhaps confined to Persia Proper, but important as indicating the separation, in some cases at any rate, of judicial from administrative functions. (*e*) Fixity of the tribute levied by the State on the provinces, and division of it into—1, a money payment; and 2, a payment in kind; but indefinite power of exaction possessed by the satraps. Further revenue drawn by the State from—1. A water-rate; 2. Fisheries and the like; and 3. Presents. (*f*) Coinage of money, both gold and silver, on a large scale, and general circulation of both kinds of coin through the empire. Purity of the gold coinage extraordinary.

Weak points of the system, and tendency to gradual corruption. (*a*) System of checks tends to weaken authority, and is found inconvenient in times of danger. Practice of uniting offices, especially those of satrap and commandant, begins. The great increase of power thus obtained by the satraps leads naturally to formidable revolts. (*b*) Practical discontinuance of inspections by royal commissioners removes an important check upon misgovernment. (*c*) A tendency to make offices hereditary shows itself; and this limits the power of the Crown, and helps forward the process of disintegration. Detachment, partial or complete, of provinces from the empire. Provinces once lost not often recovered.

Military system.

13. The military system, established or inherited by Darius, had for its object to combine the maximum of efficiency against a foreign enemy with the minimum of danger from internal disaffection. The regular profession of arms was confined to the dominant race—or to that race and a few others of closely kindred origin—and a standing army, thus composed and amounting to several hundreds of thousands, maintained order throughout the Great King's dominions, and conducted the smaller and less important expeditions. But when danger threatened, or a great expedition was to be undertaken, the whole empire was laid under contribution; each one of the subject nations was required to send its quota; and in this way armies were collected which sometimes exceeded a million of men. In the later times, mercenaries were largely employed, not only in expeditions, but as a portion of the standing army.

Internal organization of the native standing army on a decimal system with six grades of officers. Three divisions of the service—infantry, cavalry, and chariots; but the last rarely used. Importance of the cavalry, which are either heavily armed, or exceedingly active and light. General goodness of the Persian troops, but worthlessness of the provincial levies.

14. The navy of the Persians was drawn entirely from the conquered nations. Phœnicia, Egypt, Cyprus, Cilicia, Asiatic

Navy.

Greece, and other of the maritime countries subject to Persia, furnished contingents of ships and crews according to their relative strength; and fleets were thus collected of above a thousand vessels. The ship of war ordinarily employed was the trireme; but lesser vessels were also used occasionally. The armed force on board the ships (ἐπιβάται or "marines") was Medo-Persian, either wholly or predominantly; and the fleets were usually placed under a Persian or Median commander.

Indian expedition of Darius.

15. The great king to whom Persia owed her civil, and (probably in part) her military organization, was not disposed to allow the warlike qualities of his subjects to rust for want of exercise. Shortly after the revolts had been put down, Darius I., by himself or by his generals, commenced and carried out a series of military expeditions of first-rate importance. The earliest of these was directed against Western India, or the regions now known as the Punjab and Scinde. After exploring the country by means of boats, which navigated the Indus from Attock to the sea, he led or sent a body of troops into the region, and rapidly reduced it to subjection. A valuable gold-tract was thus added to the empire, and the revenue was augmented by about one-third. Commerce also received an impulse from the opening of the Indian market to Persian traders, who thenceforth kept up a regular communication with the tribes bordering the Indus by coasting vessels which started from the Persian Gulf.

His invasion of Scythia, about B.C. 508.

16. The next great expedition was in the most directly opposite direction. It was undertaken against the numerous and warlike Scythian nation which possessed the vast plains of Southern Russia, extending between the Don and the Danube, the region now generally known as the Ukraine. The object of this expedition was not conquest, but the exhibition of the Persian military strength, the sight of which was calculated to strike terror into the Scythic hordes, and to prevent them from venturing to invade the territory of so powerful a neighbor. The *great* Persian kings, like the great Roman emperors, caused their own frontiers to be respected by overstepping them, and ravaging with fire and sword the countries of the fierce Northern barbarians.

Date of the expedition, probably about B.C. 508. Passage of the Bosphorus by a bridge of boats. Army marches through Thrace, while the fleet proceeds to bridge the Danube. Submission of the maritime Thracians. Resistance and conquest of the Getæ. Passage of the Danube and invasion of Scythia. Unresisted march of Darius through the country. His troops burn the inland town of Gelonus. He retires without loss, re-crosses the Danube, and returns to Asia in triumph.

Thrace and Pæonia conquered. Macedon submits, B.C. 507, 506.

17. The sequel of the Scythian expedition was the firm establishment of the Persian power on the European side of the straits, and the rapid extension of it over the parts of Thrace bordering on the Ægean, over the adjoining country of Pæonia, and even over the still more remote Macedonia. The Persian dominion now reached from the Indian desert to the borders of Thessaly, and from the Caucasus to Ethiopia.

Barca punished by Aryandes.

18. Simultaneously with the Scythic expedition, Aryandes, the satrap of Egypt, marched against the Greek town of Barca, in Africa, to avenge the murder of a king who was a Persian tributary. Barca was taken, and its inhabitants transplanted to Asia; but the hostility of the semi-independent nomades was aroused, and the army on its return suffered no inconsiderable losses.

Revolt of the Asiatic Greeks, B.C. 501.

Burning of Sardis, B.C. 500, and battle of Ephesus.

19. Not long afterwards the ambitious designs of Darius were violently interrupted by a revolt second in importance to scarcely any of those which had occupied his early years. The Greeks of Asia, provoked by the support which Darius lent to their tyrants, and perhaps rendered sensible of their power by the circumstances of the Scythic campaign, broke out into general rebellion at the instigation of Aristagoras of Miletus, murdered or expelled their tyrants, and defied the power of Persia. Two states of European Greece, Athens and Eretria, joined the rebels. Bold counsels prevailed, and an attack was made on the satrapial capital, Sardis. Unfortunately, the capture of the city was followed by its accidental conflagration; and the small knot of invaders, forced to retreat, were overtaken and defeated in the battle of Ephesus, whereupon the two European allies deserted the falling cause. On the other hand, numerous states, both European and Asiatic, excited by the news of the fall of Sardis, asserted independence; and the flames of rebellion were lighted along the entire Asiatic coast from the

Sea of Marmora to the Gulf of Issus. The Ionian, Æolic, and Hellespontine Greeks, the Carians and Caunians of the south-western corner of the peninsula, and the Cyprians, both Greek and native, made common cause; several battles were fought with varying success; but at last the power of Persia prevailed. The confederate fleet suffered defeat in the battle of Ladé, and soon afterwards Miletus was taken. The rebellious states were punished with great severity, and the authority of Darius was once more firmly established in all the revolted countries.

Battle of Ladé, B.C. 494.

Imprudent conduct of Athens at this juncture. Unless she was prepared to put forth all her strength, and give effectual aid to the insurrection, she had far better have taken no share in it. Would not it, however, have been true wisdom on her part to have made every effort in order to transfer the war, with which she was already threatened, into the enemy's country?

20. The honor of the Great King required that immediate vengeance should be taken on the bold foreigners who had intermeddled between him and his subjects. But, even apart from this, an expedition against Greece was certain, and could only be a question of time. The exploring voyage of Democedes, about B.C. 510, shows that even before the Scythian campaign an attack on this quarter was intended. An expedition was therefore fitted out, in B.C. 493, under Mardonius, which took the coast-line through Thrace and Macedonia. A storm at Athos, however, shattered the fleet; and the land-army was crippled by a night attack of the Brygi. Mardonius returned home without effecting his purpose; but his expedition was not wholly fruitless. His fleet reduced Thasos; and his army forced the Macedonians to exchange their positions of semi-independence for complete subjection to Persia.

First expedition against Greece under Mardonius fails.

21. The failure of Mardonius was followed within two years by the second great expedition against Greece—the first which reached it—that conducted by Datis. Datis proceeded by sea, crossing through the Cyclades, and falling first upon Eretria, which was besieged, and taken by treachery. A landing was then made at Marathon; but the defeat of the Persian host by Miltiades, and his rapid march to Athens immediately after the victory, frustrated the expedition, disappointing alike the commander and the Athenian ex-tyrant, Hippias, who had accompanied it.

Second expedition under Datis, B.C. 490. Battle of Marathon.

Importance of the victory at Marathon. First great check received by the Persians. The defeat showed how utterly powerless were the vast masses of an Oriental army against the disciplined valor of the Greeks. The whole history of the contest between Greece and Persia is but a repetition of this early lesson.

22. Undismayed by his two failures, Darius commenced preparations for a third attack, and would probably have proceeded in person against Athens, had not the revolt of Egypt first (B.C. 487), and then his own death (B.C. 486), intervened. Darius died after nominating as his successor, not his eldest son, Artobazanes, but the eldest of his sons by Atossa, daughter of Cyrus—a prince who had thus the advantage of having in his veins the blood of the great founder of the empire.

Third expedition stopped by Darius's death, B.C. 486.

23. Darius probably died at Susa; but he was buried in the vicinity of Persepolis, where he had prepared himself an elaborate rock tomb, adorned with sculptures and bearing a long inscription—all which remain to the present day. The great palace of Persepolis, in all its extent and grandeur, was his conception, if not altogether his work; as was also the equally magnificent structure at Susa, which was the ordinary royal residence from his time. He likewise set up the great rock inscription at Behistun (Bagistán), the most valuable of all the Persian monumental remains. Other memorials of his reign have been found, or are known to have existed, at Ecbatana, at Byzantium, in Thrace, and in Egypt. In the last-named country he re-opened the great canal between the Nile and the Red Sea, which the Ramessides had originally cut, and the Psamatiks had vainly endeavored to re-establish.

Great works of Darius I.

The best representations of the magnificent buildings at Persepolis will be found in the costly work of MM. FLANDIN and COSTE, entitled *Voyage en Perse*, 6 vols., large folio. Paris, 1845-50, published by the French Government. Nearly equal to this is a production of private enterprise, the work of the Baron TEXIER, called *Description de l'Arménie, de la Perse, et de la Mésopotamie*, 2 vols., folio. Paris, 1842-52.

Representations on a smaller scale, accompanied with much ingenious comment, will be found in the following works:

FERGUSSON, JAMES, *Palaces of Nineveh and Persepolis restored;* 8vo. London, 1851; and *History of Architecture*, vol. i. London, 1865, et seqq.

Students may also consult the chapter on "Persian Architecture," in RAWLINSON'S *Five Great Monarchies*, vol. iv. ch. v., and the account of Persepolis in VAUX'S *Nineveh and Persepolis;* 8vo. London, 1851.

The only authentic account yet given of the ruins of Susa is contained in

LOFTUS, W. K., *Travels and Researches in Chaldæa and Susiana;* 8vo. London, 1857.

Reign of Xerxes I., B.C. 486–465.

24. Xerxes I., who succeeded Darius, B.C. 486, commenced his reign by the reduction of Egypt, B.C. 485, which he intrusted to his brother, Achæmenes. He then provoked and chastised a rebellion of the Babylonians, enriching himself with the plunder of their temples. After this he turned his attention to the invasion of Greece.

Great expedition against Greece, B.C. 480.

25. Too much weight has probably been assigned to the cabals and intrigues of the Persian nobles, and the Greek refugees at Xerxes's court. Until failure checked the military aspirations of the nation, a Persian prince was almost under the necessity of undertaking some great conquest; and there was at this time no direction in which an expedition could so readily be undertaken as towards the west. Elsewhere high mountains, broad seas, or barren deserts skirted the empire—here only did Persian territory adjoin on a fruitful, well-watered, and pleasant region. The attempt to reduce Greece was the natural sequel to the conquests of Egypt, India, Thrace, and Macedon.

DETAILS OF THE EXPEDITION. Careful preparation for the space of four years, B.C. 484 to 481. Immense host collected. Question of its numbers. Excellent commissariat arrangements. Large and well-appointed fleet. March of the expedition in three columns along the coast, B.C. 480. Passage of the Hellespont on a double bridge of boats. Grand review at Doriscus. Advance through Thessaly unresisted. Fleet passes through canal of Athos. First disaster—loss of 400 ships by a storm off Cape Sepias. First encounter of land forces at Thermopylæ. Failure of the direct attack. Pass turned, and its defenders all slain. Sea-fights about the same time off Artemisium with indecisive result. Second disaster—loss of 200 ships off the coast of Eubœa. Advance through Phocis and Bœotia. Force detached against Delphi fails to take it. Invasion of Attica; Athens taken and burnt. General alarm. Greek naval force on the point of breaking up, is prevented by Themistocles, who brings about the battle of SALAMIS (Sept. 23, B.C. 480), which completes the destruction of the Persian fleet. Retreat of Xerxes. A picked Persian army under Mardonius winters in Thessaly, and resumes offensive operations in the spring, B.C. 479. Attica re-occupied. Negotiations opened with Argos. Sudden resolve of Sparta to take the offensive; large army gathered at the isthmus enters Attica. Retirement of Mardonius into Bœotia. Battle of Platæa, Sept. 25, B.C. 479, and complete destruction of the Persian host. Persians never again invade European Greece. Last remnant of the Persian fleet attacked by Leotychides at Mycalé. Protecting land force defeated, and ships burnt.

Aggressive attitude assumed by the Greeks. Battle of the Eurymedon, B.C. 466.

26. It was now the turn of the Greeks to retaliate on their prostrate foe. First under the lead of Sparta and then under that of Athens they freed the islands of the Ægean from the Persian yoke, expelled the Persian garrisons from Europe, and even ravaged the Asiatic coast and made descents on it at their pleasure. For twelve years no Persian fleet ventured to dispute with them the sovereignty of the seas; and when at last, in B.C. 466, a naval force was collected to protect Cilicia and Cyprus, it was defeated and destroyed by Cimon at the Eurymedon.

Weak character of Xerxes. Corruption of the court under him.

27. Soon after this Xerxes's reign came to an end. This weak prince, after the failure of his grand expedition, desisted from all military enterprise. No doubt his empire was greatly injured and exhausted by its losses in the Grecian war, and a period of repose was absolutely necessary; but it would seem to have been natural temperament, as much as prudence, that caused the unwarlike monarch to rest content under his discomfiture, and to make no effort to wipe out its disgrace. Xerxes, on his return to Asia, found consolation for his military failure in the delights of the seraglio, and ceased to trouble himself much about affairs of State. He was satisfied to check the further progress of the Greeks by corrupting their cleverest statesmen; and, submitting himself to the government of women and eunuchs, lost all manliness of character. His own indulgence in illicit amours caused violence and bloodshed in his family, and his example encouraged a similar profligacy in others. The bloody and licentious deeds which stain the whole of the later Persian history commence with Xerxes, who suffered the natural penalty of his follies and his crimes when, after reigning twenty years, he was murdered by the captain of his guard, Artabanus, and Aspamitres, his chamberlain.

His murder.

Probable identity of Xerxes with the Ahasuerus of Esther. The name Ahasuerus is the natural Semitic equivalent of the Arian Khshayarsha or Xerxes. Similarity of character. Agreement of the dates. Esther, however, can not be Amestris, if we accept the stories which Herodotus tells of that princess.

Reign of Artaxerxes I. Troubles of his first year, B.C. 465.

28. Artabanus placed on the throne the youngest son of Xerxes, Artaxerxes I., called by the Greeks *Macrocheir*, or "the Long-handed." The eldest son, Darius, accused by Artabanus of his father's assassination, was executed; the second, Hystaspes, who was satrap of Bactria, claimed the crown; and, attempting to enforce his claim, was defeated and slain in battle. About the same time the crimes of Artabanus were discovered, and he was put to death.

Revolt of Egypt, B.C. 460. Suppressed, B.C. 455.

29. Artaxerxes then reigned quietly for nearly forty years. He was a mild prince, possessed of several good qualities; but the weakness of his character caused a rapid declension of the empire under his sway. The revolt of Egypt was indeed suppressed after a while through the vigorous measures of the satrap of Syria, Megabyzus; and the Athenians, who had fomented it, were punished by the complete destruction of their fleet, and the loss of almost all their men. But the cruelty and perfidy shown in the execution of the captured Inarus must have increased Egyptian disaffection, while at the same time it disgusted Megabyzus and the better class of Persians, and became the cause of fresh misfortunes.

Revolt breaks out under Inarus, king of the Libyans, assisted by Amyrtæus, an Egyptian, B.C. 460. Battle of Papremis; Achæmenes defeated and slain. Persians shut up in Memphis. Aid of Athens asked, and 200 ships sent. Memphis taken, except the citadel (White-castle). Persian army enters Egypt under Megabyzus. Defeat of Inarus and relief of Memphis. Destruction of the Athenian squadron and capture of Inarus, B.C. 455. Amyrtæus maintains himself for six years more in the Delta, B.C. 455 to 449.

Battle of Cyprus and peace of Callias, B.C. 449.

30. Bent on recovering her prestige, Athens, in B.C. 449, dispatched a fleet to the Levant, under Cimon, which sailed to Cyprus and laid siege to Citium. There Cimon died; but the fleet which had been under his orders attacked and completely defeated a large Persian armament off Salamis, besides detaching a squadron to assist Amyrtæus, who still held out in the Delta.

Persia, dreading the loss of Cyprus and Egypt, consented to an inglorious peace. The independence of the Asiatic Greeks was recognized. Persia undertook not to visit with fleet or army the coasts of Western Asia Minor, and Athens agreed to abstain from attacks on Cyprus and Egypt. The Greek cities ceded by this treaty—the "peace of Callias"—to the Athenian confederacy included all those from the mouth of the Hellespont to Phaselis in Lycia, but did not include the cities on the shores of the Black Sea.

Revolt of Megabyzus, B.C. 447.

31. Scarcely less damaging to Persia was the revolt of Megabyzus, which followed. This powerful noble, disgusted at the treatment of Inarus, which was contrary to his pledged word, excited a rebellion in Syria, and so alarmed Artaxerxes that he was allowed to dictate the terms on which he would consent to be reconciled to his sovereign. An example was thus set of successful rebellion on the part of a satrap, which could not but have disastrous consequences. The prestige of the central government was weakened; and provincial governors were tempted to throw off their allegiance on any fair occasion that offered itself; since, if successful, they had nothing to fear, and in any case they might look for pardon.

Death of Artaxerxes I., B.C. 425.

32. The disorders of the court continued, and, indeed, increased, under Artaxerxes I., who allowed his mother Amestris, and his sister Amytis, who was married to Megabyzus, to indulge freely the cruelty and licentiousness of their dispositions. Artaxerxes died B.C. 425, and left his crown to his only legitimate son, Xerxes II.

Reigns of Xerxes II. and Secydianus.

33. Revolutions in the government now succeeded each other with great rapidity. Xerxes II., after reigning forty-five days, was assassinated by his half-brother, Secydianus or Sogdianus, an illegitimate son of Artaxerxes, who seized the throne, but was murdered in his turn, after a reign of six months and a half, by another brother, Ochus.

34. Ochus, on ascending the throne, took the name of Darius, and is known in history as Darius Nothus. He was married to Parysatis, his aunt, a daughter of Xerxes I., and reigned nineteen years, B.C. 424 to 405, under her tutelage. His reign, though checkered with some gleams of sunshine,

Accession of Darius II., B.C. 424. Rapid decline of the State. Revolts of satraps, B.C. 423–414.

was on the whole disastrous. Revolt succeeded to revolt; and, though most of the insurrections were quelled, it was at the cost of what remained of Persian honor and self-respect. Corruption was used instead of force against the rebellious armies; and the pledges freely given to the leaders in order to procure their submission were systematically disregarded. Arsites, the king's brother, his fellow-conspirator, a brother of Megabyzus, and Pissuthnes, the satrap of Lydia, were successively entrapped in this way, and suffered instant execution. So low had the feeling of honor sunk, that Pissuthnes's captor, Tissaphernes, instead of showing indignation, like Megabyzus (see § 31), accepted the satrapy of his victim, and thus made himself a participant in his sovereign's perfidy.

Relaxation of authority.

35. Still more dangerous to the State, if less disgraceful, were the practices which now arose of uniting commonly the offices of satrap and commander of the forces, and of committing to a single governor two, or even three, satrapies. The authority of the Crown was relaxed; satraps became practically uncontrolled; their lawless acts were winked at or condoned; and their governments tended more and more to become hereditary fiefs—the first step, in empires like the Persian, to disintegration.

National outbreaks. Attempt of the Medes, B.C. 408. Revolt of Egypt, B.C. 405.

36. The revolts of satraps were followed by national outbreaks, which, though sometimes quelled, were in other instances successful. In B.C. 408, the Medes, who had patiently acquiesced in Persian rule for more than a century, made an effort to shake off the yoke, but were defeated and reduced to subjection. Three years later, B.C. 405, Egypt once more rebelled, under Nepherites, and succeeded in establishing its independence. (See Book I., Part II., § 23.) The Persians were expelled from Africa, and a native prince seated himself on the throne of the Pharaohs.

Recovery of the Greek continental cities by Persia, in consequence of the Peloponnesian War, B.C. 412.

37. It was some compensation for this loss, and perhaps for others towards the north and north-east of the empire, that in Asia Minor the authority of the Great King was once more established over the Greek cities. It was the Peloponnesian War, rather than the peace of Callias, which had prevented any collision between the great powers of Europe

and Asia for thirty-seven years. Both Athens and Sparta had their hands full; and though it might have been expected that Persia would have at once taken advantage of the quarrel to reclaim at least her lost continental dominion, yet she seems to have refrained, through moderation or fear, until the Athenian disasters in Sicily encouraged her to make an effort. She then invited the Spartans to Asia, and by the treaties which she concluded with them, and the aid which she gave them, re-acquired without a struggle all the Greek cities of the coast. It was her policy, however, not to depress Athens too much—a policy which was steadily pursued, till the personal ambition of the younger Cyrus caused a departure from the line dictated by prudence.

Satraps of Asia Minor required to collect the tribute of the Greek cities, B.C. 413. Tissaphernes and Pharnabazus invite the Spartans to Asia. First treaty made by Sparta with Tissaphernes, B.C. 412. Second and third treaty in the same year. By the last *all Asia* expressly ceded to the king. Tissaphernes helps the Spartans, but cautiously. In disgust they quit him and accept the invitation of Pharnabazus. Rivalry of the satraps injurious to Persia. Pharnabazus, however, pursues the same policy as Tissaphernes, only more clumsily, till Cyrus appears upon the scene, B.C. 407, and, being anxious to obtain effectual aid from the Spartans, embraces their side of the quarrel heartily, and enables Lysander to bring the war to an end.

Corruption of the court.

38. The progress of corruption at court kept pace with the general decline which may be traced in all parts of the empire. The power of the eunuchs increased, and they began to aspire, not only to govern the monarch, but actually to seat themselves upon the throne. Female influence more and more directed the general course of affairs; and the vices of conscious weakness, perfidy and barbarity, came to be looked upon as the mainstays of government.

Reign of Artaxerxes II., B.C. 405–362.

39. Darius Nothus died B.C. 405, and was succeeded by his eldest son, Arsaces, who on his accession took the name of Artaxerxes. Artaxerxes II., called by the Greeks *Mnemon* on account of the excellence of his memory, had from the very first a rival in his brother Cyrus. Parysatis had endeavored to gain the kingdom for her younger son, while the succession was still open; and when her efforts failed, and Artaxerxes was named to succeed his father, she encouraged Cyrus to vindicate his

claim by arms. It would undoubtedly have been advantageous to Persia that the stronger-minded of the two brothers should have been victor in the struggle; but the fortune of war decided otherwise. Cyrus fell at Cunaxa, a victim to his own impetuosity; and Artaxerxes II. obtained undisputed possession of the throne, which he held for above forty years.

Attempt of Cyrus. Battle of Cunaxa, B.C. 401.

March of Cyrus from Sardis in the spring of B.C. 401. Passage of the Euphrates, about July. Battle of Cunaxa, about September. Treacherous massacre of the generals. Return of the Ten Thousand under Xenophon during the winter and the ensuing spring, B.C. 401 to 400.

40. The expedition of Cyrus produced a complete change in the relations between Persia and Sparta. Sparta had given Cyrus important assistance, and thereby irremediably offended the Persian monarch. The result of the expedition encouraged her to precipitate the rupture which she had provoked. Having secured the services of the Ten Thousand, she attacked the Persians in Asia Minor; and her troops, under Thimbron, Dercyllidas, and Agesilaüs, made the Persians tremble for their Asiatic dominion. Wisely resolving to find her enemy employment at home, Persia brought about a league between the chief of the secondary powers of Greece—Argos, Thebes, Athens, and Corinth—supplying them with the sinews of war, and contributing a contingent of ships, which at once turned the scale, and by the battle of Cnidus, B.C. 394, gave the mastery of the sea to the confederates. Agesilaüs was recalled to Europe, and Sparta found herself so pressed that she was glad to agree to the peace known as that of Antalcidas, whereby the Greeks of Europe generally relinquished to Persia their Asiatic brethren, and allowed the Great King to assume the part of authoritative arbiter in the Grecian quarrels, B.C. 387.

War between Sparta and Persia, B.C. 399-394.

Peace of Antalcidas, B.C. 387.

41. Glorious as the peace of Antalcidas was for Persia, and satisfactory as it must have been to her to see her most formidable enemies engaged in internecine conflict one with another, yet the internal condition of the empire showed no signs of improvement. The revolt of Evagoras, Greek tyrant of Salamis in Cyprus, was with difficulty put down, after a long and doubtful struggle, B.C. 391 to 379, in which disaffection was exhib-

Revolt of Evagoras, B.C. 391, who submits upon terms, B.C. 379.

ited by the Phœnicians, the Cilicians, the Carians, and the Idumæan Arabs. The terms made with Evagoras were a confession of weakness, since he retained his sovereignty, and merely consented to pay the Persian king an annual tribute.

Revolt of the Cadusians, B.C. 384.

42. The revolt of the Cadusians on the shores of the Caspian about this same period, B.C. 384, gave Artaxerxes II. an opportunity of trying his own qualifications for military command. The trial was unfavorable; for he was only saved from disaster by the skill of Tiribazus, one of his officers, who procured with consummate art the submission of the rebels.

Schemes of Artaxerxes. Occupation of Samos. Expedition against Egypt, B.C. 376.

43. Artaxerxes, however, proud of the success which might be said, on the whole, to have attended his arms, was not content with the mere recovery of newly-revolted provinces, but aspired to restore to the empire its ancient limits. His generals commenced the reduction of the Greek islands by the occupation of Samos; and in B.C. 375, having secured the services of the Athenian commander, Iphicrates, he sent a great expedition against Egypt, which was intended to reconquer that country. Iphicrates, however, and Pharnabazus, the Persian commander, quarrelled. The expedition wholly failed; and the knowledge of the failure provoked a general spirit of disaffection in the western satrapies, which brought the empire to the verge of destruction. But corruption and treachery, now the usual Persian weapons, were successful once more. Orontes and Rheomithras took bribes to desert their confederates; Datames was entrapped and executed. An attempt of Egypt, favored by Sparta, and promoted by Agesilaüs in person, B.C. 361, to annex Phœnicia and Syria, was frustrated by internal commotions, and the reign of Artaxerxes closed without any further contraction of the Persian territory.

Revolts.

Agesilaüs in Egypt, B.C. 361.

Disorders of the court.

44. The court continued during the reign of Artaxerxes II. a scene of horrors and atrocities of the same kind that had prevailed since the time of Xerxes I. Parysatis, the queen-mother, was its presiding spirit; and the long catalogue of her cruel and bloody deeds is almost without a parallel even in the history of Oriental despotisms. The members of the royal household became now

the special objects of jealousy to one another; family affection had disappeared; and executions, assassinations, and suicides decimated the royal stock.

Reign of Artaxerxes III., B.C. 359–338.

45. Ochus, the youngest legitimate son of Artaxerxes II., who had obtained the throne by the execution of his eldest and the suicide of his second brother, assumed on his accession (B.C. 359) the name of his father, and is known as Artaxerxes III. He was a prince of more vigor and spirit than any monarch since Darius Hystaspis; and the power, reputation, and general prosperity of the empire were greatly advanced under his administration. The court, however, was incurably corrupt; and Ochus can not be said to have at all improved its condition. Rather, it was a just Nemesis by which, after a reign of twenty-one years, B.C. 359 to 338, he fell a victim to a conspiracy of the seraglio.

Destruction of the royal stock.

46. The first step taken by the new king was the complete destruction of the royal family, or, at any rate, of all but its more remote branches. Having thus secured himself against rivals, he proceeded to arrange and execute some important enterprises.

Revolt of Artabazus, who flies to Philip of Macedon, B.C. 356–353.

47. The revolt of Artabazus in Asia Minor, fomented at first by Athens, and afterwards by Thebes, was important both as delaying the grand enterprise of Ochus, and as leading to the first betrayal of a spirit inimical to Persia on the part of Philip of Macedon. Philip received Artabazus as a refugee at his court, and thus provoked those hostile measures to which Ochus had recourse later in his reign—measures which furnished a ground of complaint to Alexander.

First expedition of Ochus against Egypt fails.

48. About B.C. 351, Ochus marched a large army into Egypt, bent on recovering that province to the empire. Nectanebo, however, the Egyptian king, met him in the field, defeated him, and completely repulsed his expedition. Ochus returned to Persia to collect fresh forces, and immediately the whole of the West was in a flame. Phœnicia reclaimed her independence, and placed herself under the government of Tennes, king of Sidon. Cyprus revolted, and set up nine native sovereigns. In Asia Minor a dozen petty chieftains assumed the airs of actual monarchs. Ochus, however,

Revolts.

nothing daunted, employed his satraps to quell or check the revolts, while he himself collected a second armament, obtained the services of Greek generals, and hired Greek mercenaries to the number of 10,000. He then proceeded in person against Phœnicia and Egypt, B.C. 346.

Second expedition against Phœnicia and Egypt, B.C. 346, which are recovered.

49. Partly by force, but mainly by treachery, Sidon was taken and Phœnicia reduced to subjection; Mentor, with 4000 Greeks, deserting and joining the Persians. Egypt was then a second time invaded; Nectanebo was defeated and driven from the country; and the Egyptian satrapy was recovered. The glory which Ochus thus acquired was great; but the value of his success, as an indication of reviving Persian vigor, was diminished by the fact that it was mainly owing to the conduct of Greek generals and the courage of Greek mercenaries. Still, to Bagoas, the eunuch, and to Ochus himself, some of the credit must be allowed; and the vigorous administration which followed on the Egyptian campaign gave promise of a real recovery of pristine force and strength. But this prospect was soon clouded by a fresh revolution in the palace, which removed the most capable of the later Achæmenian monarchs.

Period of vigor.

Ochus is murdered by Bagoas, B.C. 338. Reign of Arses.

50. A savage cruelty was one of the most prominent features in the character of Ochus; and his fierceness and violence had rendered him unpopular with his subjects, when the eunuch Bagoas, his chief minister, ventured on his assassination, B.C. 338. Bagoas placed Arses, the king's youngest son, upon the throne, and destroyed the rest of the seed royal. It was his object to reign as minister of a prince who was little more than a boy; but after two years he grew alarmed at some threats that Arses had uttered, and secured himself by a fresh murder. Not venturing to assume the vacant crown himself, he conferred it on a friend, named Codomannus—perhaps descended from Darius II.—who mounted the throne under the title of Darius III., and immediately put to death the wretch to whom he owed his elevation, B.C. 336.

Reign of Darius III., B.C. 336-330.

51. Superior morally to the greater number of his predecessors, Darius III. did not possess sufficient intellectual ability to enable him to grapple with the difficulties of the circumstances in which he was

placed. The Macedonian invasion of Asia, which had commenced before he mounted the throne, failed to alarm him as it ought to have done. He probably despised Alexander's youth and inexperience; at any rate, it is certain that he took no sufficient measures to guard his country against the attack with which it was threatened. Had Persia joined the European enemies of Alexander in the first year of his reign, the Macedonian conquest of Asia might never have taken place. Still, Darius was not wholly wanting to the occasion. An important native and mercenary force was collected in Mysia to oppose the invader, if he should land; and a large fleet was sent to the coast, which ought to have made the passage of the Hellespont a matter of difficulty. But the remissness and over-confidence of the Persian leaders rendered these measures ineffectual. Alexander's landing was unopposed, and the battle of the Granicus (B.C. 334), which might have been avoided, caused the immediate loss of all Asia Minor. Soon afterwards, the death of Memnon deprived Darius of his last chance of success by disconcerting all his plans for the invasion of Europe. Compelled to act wholly on the defensive, he levied two great armies, and fought two great battles against his foe. In the first of these, at Issus (B.C. 333), he no doubt threw away all chance of victory by engaging his adversary in a defile; but in the second all the advantages that nature had placed on the side of the Persians were given full play. The battle of ARBELA (Oct. 1, B.C. 331), fought in the broad plains of Adiabênê, on ground carefully selected and prepared by the Persians, fairly tested the relative strength of the two powers; and when it was lost, the empire of Persia came naturally to an end. The result of the contest might have been predicted from the time of the battle of Marathon. The inveterate tendency of Greece to disunion, and the liberal employment of Persian gold, had deferred a result that could not be prevented, for nearly two centuries.

Alexander invades Asia, B.C. 334.

Battle of Issus, B.C. 333.

Battle of Arbela, B.C. 331.

For the details of the Greek wars with Persia, see Book III., Third Period; and for those of the war between Darius and Alexander, see Book IV., First Period.

BOOK III.

HISTORY OF THE GRECIAN STATES FROM THE EARLIEST TIMES TO THE ACCESSION OF ALEXANDER.

Geographical Outline.

Shape, boundaries, and size of ancient Greece.

1. HELLAS, or Greece Proper, is a peninsula of moderate size, bounded on the north by Olympus, the Cambunian mountains, and an artificial line prolonged westward to the Acroceraunian promontory; on the west by the Adriatic or Ionian Gulf; on the south by the Mediterranean; and on the east by the Ægean Sea. Its greatest length from north to south, between the Cambunian mountains and Cape Tænarus, is about 250 English miles; its greatest width, between the Acroceraunian promontory and the mouth of the Peneus, or again between the coast of Acarnania and Marathon in Attica, is about 180 miles. Its superficial extent has been estimated at 35,000 square miles, which is somewhat less than the size of Portugal.

Chief characteristics: 1. Extent of sea-board. 2. Number of mountain-chains.

2. The geographical features which most distinctly characterize the Hellenic Peninsula are the number of its mountains and the extent of its sea-board. Numerous deep bays strongly indent the coast, while long and narrow promontories run out far into the sea on all sides, causing the proportion of coast to area to be very much greater than is found in any other country of Southern Europe. Excellent harbors abound; the tideless sea has few dangers; off the coast lie numerous littoral islands of great beauty and fertility. Nature has done her utmost to tempt the population to maritime pursuits, and to make them cultivate the art of navigation. Communication between most parts of the country is shorter and easier by sea than by land; for the mountain-chains which intersect the region in all directions are for the

most part lofty and rugged, traversable only by a few passes, often blocked by snow in the winter time.

General description of the mountain-system.

3. The MOUNTAIN-SYSTEM of Greece may best be regarded as an offshoot from the great European chain of the Alps. At a point a little to the west of the 21st degree of longitude (E. from Greenwich), the Albanian Alps throw out a spur, which, under the names of Scardus, Pindus, Corax, Taphiassus, Panachäicus, Lampea, Pholoë, Parrhasius, and Täygetus, runs in a direction a little east of south from the 42d parallel to the promontory of Tænarum. From this great *longitudinal* chain are thrown out, at brief intervals on either side, a series of lateral branches, having a general *latitudinal* direction; from which again there start off other cross ranges, which follow the course of the main chain, or backbone of the region, pointing nearly south-east. The latitudinal chains are especially marked and important in the eastern division of the country, between Pindus and the Ægean. Here are thrown off, successively, the Cambunian and Olympic range, which formed the northern boundary of Greece Proper; the range of Othrys, which separated Thessaly from Malis and Æniania; that of Œta, which divided between Malis and Doris; and that of Parnassus, Helicon, Cithæron, and Parnes, which, starting from near Delphi, terminated in the Rhamnusian promontory, opposite Eubœa, forming in its eastern portion a strong barrier between Bœotia and Attica. Of a similar character on the opposite side were Mount Lingus in Northern Epirus, which struck westward from Pindus at a point nearly opposite the Cambunians; together with Mount Tymphrestus in Northern, and Mount Bomius in Central Ætolia. In the Peloponnese, the main chain, which stretched from Rhium to Tænarum, threw off, on the west, Mount Scollis, which divided Achæa from Elis, and Mount Elæon, which separated Elis from Messenia; while, towards the east, the lateral branches were, first, one which, under the names of Erymanthus, Aroania, and Cyllene, divided Achæa from Arcadia, and which was then prolonged eastward to the Scyllæan promontory in Argolis; and, secondly, Mount Parthenium, which intervened between Argolis and Laconia. Of secondary longitudinal chains the only ones which need special mention are the range of Pelion and Ossa, which shut in Thessaly on the east;

that of Pentelicus, Hymettus, and Anhydrus, in Attica; and that of Parnon in the Peloponnese, which stretched from near Tegea to Malea.

The plains.

4. The MOUNTAIN-CHAINS of Greece occupy so large a portion of the area that but little is left for level ground or PLAINS. Still, a certain number of such spaces existed, and were the more valued for their rarity. The greater portion of Thessaly was a vast plain, surrounded by mountains, and drained by a single river, the Peneus. In Bœotia there were two large plains, one the marshy plain of the Cephissus, much of which was occupied by Lake Copaïs; and the other, the plain of Asopus, on the verge of which stood Thebes, Thespiæ, and Platæa. Attica boasted of three principal plains, that of Eleusis, adjoining the city of the name, that of Athens itself, and that of Marathon. In Western and Southern Peloponnese were the lowlands of Cava Elis on either side of the Peneus river, of Macaria, about the mouth of the Pamisus, and of Helos, at the embouchure of the Eurotas; in the central region were the high upland plains, or basins, of Tegea, Mantinea, Pheneus, and Orchomenus; while Eastern Peloponnese boasted the fertile alluvium of Argos, watered by the Chimarrhus, Erasinus, Phrixus, Charadrus, and Inachus.

The rivers.

5. The RIVERS of Greece were numerous, but of small volume, the majority being little more than winter torrents, and carrying little or no water in the summer-time. The only streams of any real magnitude were the Acheloüs, which rose in Epirus, and divided Ætolia from Acarnania; the northern Peneus, which drained the great Thessalian plain; and the Alpheus, the stream on whose banks stood Olympia. Among secondary rivers may be noticed the Thyamis, Oropus, and Arachthus, in Epirus; the Evenus and Daphnus, in Ætolia; the Spercheius, in Malis; the Cephissus and Asopus, in Bœotia; the Peneus, Pamisus, Eurotas, and Inachus, in the Peloponnese.

The Catabothra.

6. It is a characteristic of the Grecian rivers to disappear in *Catabothra* or subterraneous passages. The limestone rocks are full of caves and fissures, while the plains consist often of land-locked basins which present to the eye no manifest outlet. Here the streams commonly form lakes, the waters of which flow off through an under-

ground channel, sometimes visible, sometimes only conjectured to exist, to the sea. Instances of such visible outlets are those by which the Cephissus finds an egress from Lake Copaïs, in Bœotia (where art, however, has assisted nature), and those by which the superfluous waters are carried off from most of the lakes in the Peloponnese. Invisible channels are believed to give a means of escape to the waters of Lakes Hylicé and Trephia, in Bœotia.

The lakes.

7. The LAKES of Greece are numerous, but not very remarkable. The largest is Lake Copaïs, in Bœotia, the area of which has been estimated at forty-one square miles. Next in size to this is, probably, Bœbeïs, in Thessaly, formed mainly by the overflowings of the Peneus. To these may be added Lake Pambotis, in Epirus, on the southern shores of which was the oracular shrine of Dodona; Lakes Trichonis and Conopé, in Ætolia, between the Evenus and Acheloüs; Lake Nessonis, near Lake Bœbeïs, in Thessaly; Lake Xynias, in Achæa Phthiotis; the smaller Bœotian lakes, Hylicé and Trephia; and the Arcadian lakes of Pheneus, Stymphalus, Orchomenus, Mantinea, and Tegea.

The littoral islands.

8. It has been observed that the littoral islands of Greece were both numerous and important. The principal one was Eubœa, which lay as a great breakwater along the whole east coast of Attica, Bœotia, and Locris, extending in length rather more than 100 miles, with an average breadth of about fifteen miles. Very inferior to this in size, but nearly equal in importance, was Corcyra, on the opposite or western side of the peninsula, which had a length of forty, and a breadth varying from fifteen to five miles. Besides these, there lay off the west coast Paxos, Leucas or Leucadia, Ithaca, Cephallenia, and Zacynthus (now Zante); off the south, the Œnussæ and Cythera; off the east, Tiparenus, Hydria, Calauria, Ægina, Salamis, Cythnus, Ceos, Helené, Andros, Scyros, Peparethus, Halonnesus, and Sciathus. From the south-eastern shores of Eubœa and Attica, the Cyclades and Sporades extended in a continuous series, like a set of stepping-stones, across the Ægean Sea to Asia. On the other side, from Corcyra and the Acroceraunian promontory, the eye could see, on a clear day, the opposite coast of Italy.

9. The natural division of Greece is into NORTHERN, CEN-

TRAL, and SOUTHERN. Northern Greece extends from the north boundary-line to the point where the eastern and western shores are respectively indented by the Gulfs of Malis and Ambracia or Actium. Central Greece reaches from this point to the Isthmus of Corinth. Southern Greece is identical with the Peloponnese.

Natural divisions.

10. NORTHERN GREECE contained in ancient times two principal countries, Thessaly and Epirus, which were separated from each other by the high chain of Pindus. Besides these, there were, on the eastern side of the mountain barrier, Magnesia and Achæa Phthiotis; and in the mountain region itself, half-way between the two gulfs, Dolopia, or the country of the Dolopes.

NORTHERN GREECE.

11. Thessaly, the largest and most fertile country of Greece Proper, was almost identical with the basin of the Peneus. It was a region nearly circular in shape, with a diameter of about seventy miles. Mountains surrounded it on every side, from which descended numerous streams, all of them converging, and flowing ultimately into the Peneus. The united waters passed to the sea through a single narrow gorge, the celebrated vale of Tempé, which was said to have been caused by an earthquake. Thessaly was divided into four provinces:—(*a*) Perrhæbia on the north, along the skirts of Olympus and the Cambunians; (*b*) Histiæotis, towards the west, on the flanks of Pindus, and along the upper course of the Peneus; (*c*) Thessaliotis, towards the south, bordering on Achæa Phthiotis and Dolopia; and (*d*) Pelasgiotis, towards the east, between the Enipeus and Magnesia. Its chief cities were, in Perrhæbia, Gonni and Phalanna; in Histiæotis, Gomphi and Tricca; in Thessaliotis, Cierium and Pharsalus; in Pelasgiotis, Larissa and Pheræ.

Thessaly.

12. Epirus, the next largest country to Thessaly, was in shape an oblong square, seventy miles long from north to south, and about fifty-five miles across. It consisted of a series of lofty mountains, twisted spurs from Pindus, with narrow valleys between, along the courses of the numerous streams. The main divisions were—on the east, Molossis; chief cities, Dodona, Ambracia: to the north-west, Chaonia; cities, Phœnicé, Buthrotum, Cestria: to the south-west, Thesprotia; cities, Pandosia, Cassope, and in

Epirus.

later times, Nicopolis. Epirus, during the real historical period, was Illyrian rather than Greek.

13. Magnesia and Achæa Phthiotis are sometimes reckoned as parts of Thessaly; but, in the early times, at any rate, they were distinct countries. Magnesia was the coast-tract between the mouth of the Peneus and the Pagasæan Gulf, comprising the two connected ranges of Ossa and Pelion, with the country immediately at their base. It measured in length about sixty-five, and in width from ten to fifteen miles. Its chief cities were Myræ, Melibœa, and Casthanæa upon the eastern coast; Iolcus, in the Gulf of Pagasæ; and Bœbé, near Lake Bœbeïs, in the interior. Achæa Phthiotis was the tract immediately south of Thessaly, extending from the Pagasæan Gulf on the east to the part of Pindus inhabited by the Dolopes. It was a region nearly square in shape, each side of the square measuring about thirty miles. It consisted of Mount Othrys, with the country at its base. The chief cities were Halos, Thebæ Phthiotides, Itonus, Melitæa, Lamia, and Xyniæ, on Lake Xynias.

Magnesia.

Achæa Phthiotis.

14. Dolopia, or the country of the Dolopes, comprised a portion of the range of Pindus, together with the more western part of Othrys, and the upper valleys of several streams which ran into the Acheloüs. It was a small tract, not more than forty miles long by fifteen broad, and was very rugged and mountainous.

Dolopia.

15. Central Greece, or the tract intervening between Northern Greece and the Peloponnese, contained eleven countries; viz., Acarnania, Ætolia, Western Locris, Ænaniana, Doris, Malis, Eastern Locris, Phocis, Bœotia, Attica, and Megaris.

Central Greece.

16. Acarnania, the most western of the countries, was a triangular tract, bounded on the north by the Ambracian Gulf, on the east by the Acheloüs, and on the south-west by the Adriatic. Its sides measured respectively fifty, thirty-five, and thirty miles. Its chief cities were, in the interior, Stratus; on the coast, Anactorium, Solium, Astacus, and Œniadæ.

Acarnania.

17. Ætolia adjoined Acarnania on the east, and extended in that direction as far as Ænianía and Doris. On the north it was bounded by Dolopia; on the

Ætolia.

south by the Corinthian Gulf. In size it was about double Acarnania, and its area considerably exceeded that of any other country in this part of Hellas. It was generally mountainous, but contained a flat and marshy tract between the mouths of the Evenus and Acheloüs; and somewhat farther to the north, a large plain, in which were two great lakes, the Conopé and the Trichonis. Its chief cities were Pleuron, Calydon, and Thermon.

18. Western Locris, or the country of the Locri Ozolæ, lay on the coast of the Corinthian Gulf, immediately to the east of Ætolia. Its length along the coast was about thirty-seven miles, and its depth inland from about two miles to twenty-three. Its chief cities were Naupactus on the coast, and Amphissa in the interior.

Western Locris.

19. Ænianía, or Ætæa, as it was sometimes called, lay also east of Ætolia, but towards the north, whereas Locris adjoined it towards the south. Ænianía was separated from Ætolia by the continuation of Pindus southward, and was bounded on the north by Othrys and on the south by Œta. It lay thus on the course of the upper Spercheius River. It was an oval-shaped country, about twenty-seven miles long by eighteen broad. The chief town was Hypata.

Ænianía or Ætæa.

20. Doris intervened between Ænianía and Western Locris. This was a small and rugged country, inclosed between Mounts Parnassus and Callidromus, on the upper course of the Pindus River, a tributary of the Bœotian Cephissus. Its greatest length was about seventeen and its greatest width about ten miles. It contained the four cities of Pindus, Erineus, Bœum, and Cytinium, whence it was known as the Dorian Tetrapolis.

Doris.

21. Malis lay north of Doris, south of Achæa Phthiotis, and east of Ænianía. It was even smaller than Doris, which it resembled in shape. The greatest length was about fifteen and the greatest width about eight miles. The chief cities were Anticyra and Trachis; and, in later times, Heraclea. At the extreme eastern edge of Malis, between the mountains and the sea, was the pass of Thermopylæ.

Malis.

22. Eastern Locris lay next to Malis, along the shore of the Euripus or Eubœan channel. It was politically divided

Eastern Locris. into two parts, Epicnemidia and Opuntia; which, in later times, were physically separated by a small strip of ground, reckoned as belonging to Phocis. Epicnemidia extended about seventeen miles, from near Thermopylæ to near Daphnus, averaging about eight miles in width. Its chief town was Cnemides. Opuntia reached from Alôpé to beyond the mouth of the Cephissus, a distance of twenty-six miles. Its width was about equal to that of Epicnemidia. It derived its name from its chief city, Opus.

23. Phocis reached from Eastern Locris on the north to the Corinthian Gulf on the south. It was bounded on the west by Doris and Western Locris, on the east by Bœotia. It was squarish in shape, with an average length of twenty-five and an average breadth of twenty miles. The central and southern parts were extremely mountainous; but along the course of the Cephissus and its tributaries there were some fertile plains. The chief cities were Delphi, on the southern flank of Mount Parnassus, Elatæa, Parapotamii, Panopeus, Abæ, famous for its temple, and Hyampolis.

Phocis.

24. Bœotia was above twice the size of Phocis, having a length of fifty and an average breadth of twenty-three miles. It was generally flat and marshy, but contained the mountain range of Helicon on the south, and the lofty hills known as Ptoüs, Messapius, Hypatus, and Teumessus, towards the more eastern portion of the country. The lake Copaïs covered an area of forty-one square miles, or above one-thirtieth of the surface. There were also two smaller lakes between Copaïs and the Eubœan Sea, called respectively Hylicé and Trephia. The chief rivers of Bœotia were (besides the Cephissus, which entered it from Phocis) the Asopus, the Termessus, the Thespius, and the Oëroë. Bœotia was noted for the number and greatness of its cities. The chief of these was Thebes; but the following were also of importance: Orchomenus, Thespiæ, Tanagra, Coronæa, Lebadeia, Haliartus, Chæroneia, Leuctra, and Copæ.

Bœotia.

25. Attica was the foreland or peninsula which projected from Bœotia to the south-east. Its length, from Cithæron to Sunium, was seventy miles; its greatest width, from Munychia to Rhamnus, was thirty miles. Its

Attica.

area has been estimated at 720 square miles, or about one-fourth less than Bœotia. The general character of the tract was mountainous and infertile. On the north, Cithæron, Parnes, and Phelleus formed a continuous line running nearly east and west; from this descended three spurs: one, which divided Attica from the Megarid, known as Kerata; another, which separated the Eleusinian from the Athenian plain, called Ægaleos; and the third, which ran out from Parnes by Decelea and Marathon to Cape Zoster, named in the north Pentelicus, in the centre Hymettus, and near the south coast Anhydrus. The towns of Attica, except Athens, were unimportant. Its rivers, the two Cephissuses, the Ilissus, the Erasinus, and the Charadrus, were little more than torrent-courses.

Megaris.

26. Megaris, which adjoined on Attica to the west, occupied the northern portion of the Isthmus uniting Central Greece with the Peloponnese. It was the smallest of all the central Greek countries, excepting Doris and Malis, being about fourteen miles long by eleven broad, and containing less than 150 square miles. It had one city only, viz., Megara, with the ports Nisæa and Pegæ.

SOUTHERN GREECE.

27. SOUTHERN GREECE, or the Peloponnese, contained eleven countries—viz., Corinth, Sicyon, Achæa, Elis, Arcadia, Messenia, Laconia, Argolis, Epidauria, Trœzenia, and Hermionis.

Corinth.

28. The territory of Corinth adjoined Megaris, and included the larger portion of the Isthmus, together with a tract of somewhat greater magnitude in the Peloponnese. Its greatest length was twenty-five and its greatest width about twenty-three miles. Its shape, however, was extremely irregular; and its area can not be reckoned at more than 230 square miles. The only city of importance was Corinth, the capital, which had a port on either sea—on the Corinthian Gulf, Lechæum, and on the Saronic Gulf, Cenchreæ.

Sicyonia.

29. Sicyon, or Sicyonia, adjoined Corinth on the west. It lay along the shore of the Corinthian Gulf for a distance of about fifteen miles, and extended inland about twelve or thirteen miles. It contained but one city, viz., Sicyon.

30. Achæa came next to Sicyonia, and extended along the

coast a distance of about sixty-five miles. Its average width was about ten miles; and its area may be reckoned at 650 square miles. It contained twelve cities, of which Dymé, Patræ (now Patrás), and Pellené were the most important.

Achæa.

31. Elis lay on the west coast of the Peloponnese, extending from the mouth of the Larisus to that of the Neda, a distance of fifty-seven miles, and reaching inland to the foot of Erymanthus, about twenty-five miles. It was a more level country than was common in Greece, containing broad tracts of plain along the coast, and some tolerably wide valleys along the courses of the Peneus, Alpheus, and Neda rivers. Its chief cities were Elis, on the Peneus, the port Cyllênê, on the gulf of the same name, Olympia and Pisa, on the Alpheus, and Lepreum, in Southern Elis or Triphylia.

Elis.

32. Arcadia was the central mountain country—the Switzerland—of the Peloponnese. It reached from the mountain-chain of Erymanthus, Aroania, and Cyllênê in the north, to the sources of the Alpheus towards the south, a distance of about sixty miles. The average width was about forty miles. The area is reckoned at 1700 square miles. The country is for the most part a mountainous table-land, the rivers of which, excepting towards the west and the south-west, are absorbed in *catabothra*, and have no visible outlet to the sea. High plains and small lakes are numerous; but by far the greater part of the area is occupied by mountains and narrow but fertile valleys. Important cities were numerous. Among them may be named Mantinea, Tegea, Orchomenus, Pheneus, Heræa, Psophis, and, in the later times, Megalopolis.

Arcadia.

33. Messenia lay south of Elis and Western Arcadia, occupying the most westerly of the three forelands in which the Peloponnese terminates, and circling round the gulf between this foreland and the central one as far as the mouth of the Chœrius. Its length, from the Neda to the promontory of Acritas, was forty-five miles; its greatest width between Laconia and the western coast was thirty-seven miles. The area is estimated at 1160 square miles. Much of the country was mountainous; but along the course of the main river, the Pamisus, were some

Messenia.

broad plains, and the entire territory was fertile. The original capital was Stenyclerus; but afterwards Messênê, on the south-western flank of Mount Ithômê, became the chief town. Other important places were Eira on the upper Neda, Pylus (now Navarino), and Methônê, south of Pylus (now Modon).

34. Laconia embraced the two other Peloponnesian forelands, together with a considerable tract to the north of them. Its greatest length, between Argolis and the promontory of Malea, was nearly eighty miles, while its greatest width was not much short of fifty miles. The area approached nearly to 1900 square miles. The country consisted mainly of a single narrowish valley—that of the Eurotas—inclosed between two lofty mountain-ranges—those of Parnon and Taÿgetus. Hence the expression, "Hollow Lacedæmon." Sparta, the capital, lay on the Eurotas, at the distance of about twenty miles from the sea. The other towns were unimportant; the chief were Gythium and Thyrea on the coast, and Sellasia in the valley of the Ænus.

Laconia.

35. Argolis is a term sometimes applied to the whole tract projecting eastward from Achæa and Arcadia, with the exception of the small territory of Corinth: but the word will be here used in a narrower sense. Argolis Proper was bounded by Sicyonia and Corinthia on the north, by Epidaurus on the east, by Cynuria—a portion of Laconia—on the south, and by Arcadia on the west. Its greatest extent from north to south was about thirty, and from east to west about thirty-one miles. Its entire area did not exceed 700 square miles. Like the rest of the Peloponnese, it was mountainous, but contained a large and rich plain at the head of the Argolic Gulf. Its capital was, in early times, Mycenæ; afterwards Argos. Other cities of importance were Phlius, Cleonæ, and Tiryns. The port of Argos was Nauplia.

Argolis.

36. Epidauria lay east of Argolis, east and south of Corinthia. Its length from north to south was about twenty-three miles, and its breadth in the opposite direction about eight miles. It contained but one city of any note, viz., Epidaurus, the capital.

Epidauria.

37. Trœzenia adjoined Epidauria on the south-east. It comprised the north-eastern half of the Argolic foreland, to-

Trœzenia. gether with the rocky peninsula of Methana. Its greatest length was sixteen miles, and its greatest width, excluding Methana, nine miles. It contained two cities of note, Trœzen and Methana.

38. Hermionis adjoined Epidauria on the north and Trœzenia on the east. It formed the western termination of the Hermionis. Argolic foreland. In size it was about equal to Trœzenia. It contained but one town of any consequence, viz., Hermioné.

39. Besides the littoral islands of Greece, which have been already enumerated, there were several others, studding the Islands. Ægean Sea, which deserve notice; as particularly the following:—(*a*) In the Northern Ægean, Lemnos, Imbrus, Thasos, and Samothrace. (*b*) In the Central Ægean, besides Andros, Ceos, and Cythnus, which may be called littoral, Tenos, Syros, Gyarus, Delos, Myconus, Naxos, Paros, Siphnus, Melos, Thera, Amorgus, etc. (*c*) In the Southern Ægean, Crete. This last-named island was of considerable size. It extended from west to east a distance of 150 miles, and had an average width of about fifteen miles. The area considerably exceeded 2000 square miles. The chief cities were Cydonia and Gnossus on the north coast, and Gortyna in the interior. The whole island was mountainous but fertile.

On the character of the Greek Islands, see the work of

ROSS, L., *Reisen auf den Griechischen Inseln.* Stuttgart, 1840–52; 3 vols. 8vo.

On the general geography of Greece, the following may be consulted with advantage:

KRUSE, F. G. H., *Hellas.* Leipsic, 1825–27; 3 vols. 8vo. A general description of the geography of Greece from the best sources existing at the time. Still of value to the student.

CRAMER, J. A., *Geographical and Historical Description of Ancient Greece.* Oxford, 1828; 3 vols. 8vo.

LEAKE, Col., *Travels in Northern Greece.* London, 1835; 4 vols. 8vo.

" " *Travels in the Morea.* London, 1830; 3 vols. 8vo.

" " *Peloponnesiaca*, supplemental to the *Travels in the Morea.* London, 1846; 8vo.

CURTIUS, E., *Peloponnesus.* Gotha, 1851–2; 2 vols. 8vo.

CLARK, W. G., *Peloponnesus, Notes of Study and Travel.* London, 1858; 8vo.

NIEBUHR, B. G., *Lectures on the Ethnography and Geography of Ancient*

Greece, edited by L. SCHMITZ. London, 1853; 2 vols. 8vo; from the German edition of Dr. ISLER.

Concerning the Greek islands off the coast of Asia Minor, see Book I., Part I., A. (p. 29).

SKETCH OF THE HISTORY.

FIRST PERIOD.

The Ancient Traditional History, from the Earliest Times to the Dorian Occupation of the Peloponnese, about B.C. 1100 *to* 1000.

SOURCES. Native only. (*a*) HOMER. The two poems which pass under this venerable name, whatever their actual origin, must always continue to be, on account of their great antiquity, the prime authority for the early condition of things in Greece. Modern criticism agrees with ancient in viewing them as the earliest remains of Greek literature that have come down to us; and, if their actual date is about B.C. 850, as now generally believed, they must be regarded as standing apart on a vantage-ground of their own; for we have nothing else continuous or complete in Greek literature for nearly four centuries. (*b*) HERODOTUS. This writer, though the immediate subject of his history is the great Persian War, yet carries us back in the episodical portions of his work to very remote times, and is entitled to consideration as a careful inquirer into the antiquities of many nations, his own among the number. (*c*) THUCYDIDES. The sketch with which the history of Thucydides opens, a masterly production, gives the judgment of a shrewd and well-read Athenian of the fourth century B.C. on the antiquities of Greece. (*d*) DIODORUS SICULUS collected from previous writers, particularly Ephorus and Timæus, the early traditional history of Greece, and related it in his fourth, fifth, sixth, and seventh books; of these the fourth and fifth remain, while the other two are lost, excepting a few fragments. (*e*) Much interesting information on the early history of Greece is contained in the geographers, as particularly in Strabo, Pausanias, and Scymnus Chius. Of Plutarch's Lives one only, that of Theseus, belongs to the early period.

Among modern works treating of this time may be mentioned the following:

HEEREN, A. H. L., *Ideen über die Politik*, etc., vol. vi. Göttingen, 1826. Translated into English by TALBOYS. Oxford, 1830; 8vo.

NIEBUHR, B. G., *Vorträge über alte Geschichte.* Berlin, 1847; 3 vols. 8vo. Translated into English, with additions and corrections, by Dr. L. SCHMITZ. London, 1852.

MÜLLER, K. O., *Orchomenus und die Minyer.* Breslau, 1820; 8vo.

" " *Die Dorier.* Breslau, 1825; 2 vols. 8vo. Translated into English by Sir G. C. LEWIS. Oxford, 1830.

CLINTON, H. F., *Fasti Hellenici.* Oxford, 1830–41; 3 vols. 4to. The "Introduction" to the first volume bears particularly on this period.

THIRLWALL, Bp., *History of Greece*, vol. i. chaps. ii. to vii.

GROTE, G., *History of Greece*, vol. i. chaps. i. to xx.

The value to be placed on the general historical narrative belonging to these early times will depend, (1) on the view which is taken of the probability of oral traditions handing down correctly the general outline of events of national importance; and (2) on the question at what time historical events began to be contemporaneously recorded in inscriptions, or otherwise, by the Greeks. On the latter point, the student may compare the nineteenth chapter of Mr. GROTE's *History of Greece* with Mr. CLINTON's "Introduction," and with Col. MURE's *Remarks on two Appendices to* GROTE's *History of Greece.* London, 1851.

EARLIEST INHABITANTS OF GREECE.

1. THE Greeks of the historical times seem to have had no traditions of a migration from Asia. Their ancestors, they held, had always been in the country, though they had not always been called Hellenes. Greece had been inhabited from a remote age by races more or less homogeneous, and more or less closely allied with their own—Pelasgi, Leleges, Curêtes, Caucones, Aones, Dolopes, Dryopes, and the like. Of these, the Pelasgi had been the most important. The Hellenes proper had originally been but one tribe out of many cognate ones. They had dwelt in Achæa Phthiotis, or, according to others, near Dodona, and had originally been insignificant in numbers and of small account. In process of time, however, they acquired a reputation above that of the other tribes; recourse was had to them for advice and aid in circumstances of difficulty; other tribes came over to them, adopted their name, their form of speech, and the general character of their civilization. The growth and spread of the Hellenes was thus not by conquest but by influence; they did not overpower or expel the Pelasgi, Leleges, etc., but gradually assimilated them.

Pelasgi, etc.

Hellenes.

CHARACTERISTICS OF THE PELASGIC, OR ANTE-HELLENIC PERIOD. 1. Time of peace—golden age of the poets. 2. General pursuit of agriculture. 3. Architecture massive, and with little ornament. 4. Religion simple—no names of distinct gods. National sanctuary at Dodona.

Hellenic tribes: 1. Achæans. 2. Dorians.

2. The original Hellenic tribes seem to have been two only, the Dorians and the Achæans, of whom the latter preponderated in the more ancient times. Settled in Achæa Phthiotis from a remote antiquity, they were also, before the Dorian occupation, the leading race of

the Peloponnese. Here they are said to have had three kingdoms—those of Argos, Mycenæ, and Sparta—which attained to a considerable degree of prosperity and civilization. The Dorians were reported to have dwelt originally with the Achæans in Phthiotis; but their earliest ascertained locality was the tract on the Upper Pindus which retained the name of Doris down to Roman times. In this "small and sad region" they grew to greatness, increasing in numbers, acquiring martial habits, and perhaps developing a peculiar discipline.

Pelasgic tribes: 1. Ionians. 2. Æolians.

3. The most important of the Pelasgic tribes was that of the Ionians, which occupied in the earliest times the whole north coast of the Peloponnese, the Megarid, Attica, and Eubœa. Another (so-called) tribe (which is, however, perhaps, only a convenient designation under which to include such inhabitants of the country as were not Achæan, Dorian, or Ionian) was that of the Æolians, to which the Thessalians, Bœotians, Ætolians, Locrians, Phocians, Eleans, Pylians, etc., were regarded as belonging. These races having been gradually Hellenized, the entire four tribes came to be regarded as Hellenic, and a mythic genealogy was framed to express at once the ethnic unity and the tribal diversity of the four great divisions of the Hellenic people.

HELLEN.

DORUS.	XUTHUS.	ÆOLUS.
	ACHÆUS. ION.	

Foreign settlers in Greece. Benefits received from them. Letters.

4. According to the traditions of the Greeks, some important foreign elements were received into the nation during the period of which we are treating. Egyptians settled in Attica and Argolis; Phœnicians in Bœotia; and Mysians, or Phrygians, at Argos. The civilization of the settlers was higher than that of the people among whom they settled, and some considerable benefits were obtained from these foreign sources. Among them may be especially mentioned letters, which were derived from the Phœnicians, probably anterior to B.C. 1100. Although writing, for some centuries after its introduction, was not much used, yet its occasional employment, especially for public purposes, was an important check upon

the erratic tendencies of oral tradition. Inscriptions on the offerings in temples, and registers of the succession of kings and sacerdotal persons, were among the earliest of the Greek historical documents; and though there is no actual proof that they reached back as far as this "First Period," yet there is certainly no proof of the contrary, and many of the best critics believe in the *public* employment of writing in Greece thus early.

On this interesting question see, on the one side, Mr. FYNES CLINTON, in the "Introduction" to vol. i. of his *Fasti Hellenici*, and K. O. MULLER, *Dorians*, vol. i. pp. 147–156; and, on the other, Mr. GROTE, in his *History of Greece*, vol. i. chap. xix.

5. But, whatever benefits were derived by the Greeks from the foreigners who settled among them, it is evident that neither the purity of their race, nor the general character and course of their civilization, was much affected by extraneous influences. The incomers were comparatively few in number, and were absorbed into the Hellenic nation without leaving any thing more than a faint trace of themselves upon the language, customs, or religion of the people which received them into its bosom. Greek civilization was in the main of home growth. Even the ideas adopted from without acquired in the process of reception so new a stamp as to become almost original; and the Greek people must be held to have, on the whole, elaborated for themselves that form of civilization, and those ideas on the subjects of art, politics, morals, and religion, which have given them their peculiar reputation.

Greek civilization in the main of home growth.

Egyptian settlement at Athens traceable in the deities Athene (Neith) and Hephæstus (Phtha); in the early Athenian caste-tribes; and, perhaps, in the special religiousness (δεισιδαιμονία) of the Athenians. Phœnician settlement at Thebes traceable in the proper names, Cadmeians, Cadmeia, and Onca, and in such words as ἔρεβος, Ἐλιεύς, βάννα, ἀχάνη, σίδα, κ.τ.λ. Settlements of Danaus and Pelops in the Peloponnese not traceable.

6. History proper can scarcely be regarded as commencing until the very close of the period now under consideration, when we first meet with names which have some claim to be regarded as those of actual personages. But the general condition of the people at the period, and some of the movements of the races, and even their causes, may be laid down with an approach to certainty.

No history proper of this period.

7. The Homeric poems represent to us the general state of Greek society in the earliest times. The most noticeable features are:—(*a*) The predominance of the tribe or nation over the city, which exists indeed, but has nowhere the monopoly of political life. (*b*) The universality of kingly government, which is hereditary and based upon the notion of "divine right." (*c*) The existence of an hereditary nobility of a rank not much below that of the king, who form his council (βουλή) both in peace and war, but exercise no effectual control over his actions. (*d*) The existence of an assembly (ἀγορά) which is convened by the king, or, in his absence, by one of the chiefs, to receive communications, and witness trials, but not either to advise or judge. (*e*) The absence of polygamy and the high regard in which women are held. (*f*) Slavery everywhere established, and considered to be right. (*g*) Perpetual wars, not only between the Greeks and neighboring barbarians, but between the various Greek tribes and nations; preference of the military virtues over all others; excessive regard for stature and physical strength. (*h*) Wide prevalence of nautical habits combined with a disinclination to venture into unknown seas; dependence of the Greeks on foreigners for necessary imports. Piracy common; cities built at a distance from the sea from fear of pirates. (*i*) Strong religious feeling; belief in polytheism, in fate, in the divine Nemesis, and the punishment of heinous crimes by the Furies. Respect for the priestly character, for heralds, guests, and suppliants. Peculiar sanctity of temples and festival seasons.

General state of Greek society.

8. The religious sentiment, always strong in the Greek mind, formed in the early times one of the most important of the bonds of union which held men, and even tribes, together. Community of belief led to community of worship; and temples came to be frequented by all the tribes dwelling around them, who were thus induced to contract engagements with one another, and to form leagues of a peculiar character. These leagues, known as Amphictyonies, were not political alliances, much less confederations; they were, in their original conception, limited altogether to religious purposes; the tribes, or states, contracting them, bound themselves to protect certain sacred buildings, rites, and persons, but undertook no other

Religion a bond of union. Amphictyonies.

engagements towards one another. The most noted of these leagues was that whereof the oracular shrine of Delphi was the centre; which acquired its peculiar dignity and importance, not so much from the wealth and influence of the Delphic temple, as from the fact that among its twelve constituent members were included the two leading races of Greece.

Constitution of the Delphic Amphictyony. Its twelve members were the Thessalians, the Bœotians, the Dorians, the Ionians, the Perrhæbians, the Magnetes, the Locrians, the Œtæans or Ænianians, the Achæans of Phthia, the Phocians, the Dolopians, and the Malians. All the twelve members were equal. Meetings were held twice a year, once at Thermopylæ and once at Delphi. Deputies (called Pylagoræ and Hieromnemones) represented the tribes.

First great migratory movements caused by barbaric pressure.

9. Important movements of some of the principal races seem to have taken place towards the close of the early period. It may be suspected that these had their origin in the pressure upon North-western Greece of the Illyrian people, the parent (probably) of the modern Albanians. The tribes to the west of Pindus were always regarded as less Hellenic than those to the east; and the ground of distinction seems to have been the greater Illyrian element in that quarter. The Trojan War, if a real event, may have resulted from the Illyrian pressure, being an endeavor to obtain a vent for a population, cramped for room, in the most accessible part of Asia. To the same cause may be assigned the great movement which, commencing in Epirus (about B.C. 1200), produced a general shift of the populations of Northern and Central Hellas. Quitting Thesprotia in Epirus, the Thessalians crossed the Pindus mountain-chain, and descending on the fertile valley of the Peneus, drove out the Bœotians, and occupied it. The Bœotians proceeded southward over Othrys and Œta into the plain of the Cephissus, and driving out the Cadmeians and Minyans, acquired the territory to which they thenceforth gave name. The Cadmeians and Minyæ dispersed, and are found in Attica, in Lacedæmon, and elsewhere. The Dorians at the same time moved from their old home and occupied Dryopis, which thenceforward was known as Doris, expelling the Dryopians, who fled by sea and found a refuge in Eubœa, in Cythnus, and in the Peloponnese.

10. Not many years later a further, but apparently dis-

tinct, movement took place. The Dorians, cramped for room in their narrow valleys between Œta and Parnassus, having allied themselves with their neighbors, the Ætolians, crossed the Corinthian Gulf at its narrowest point, between Rhium and Antirrhium, and effected a lodgment in the Peloponnese. Elis, Messenia, Laconia, and Argolis were successively invaded, and at least partially conquered. Elis being assigned to the Ætolians, Dorian kingdoms were established in the three other countries. The previous Achæan inhabitants in part submitted, in part fled northward, and occupied the north coast of the Peloponnese, dispossessing the Ionians, who found a temporary refuge in Attica.

Second movement: migration of the Dorians.

11. A further result followed from the migrations and conquests here spoken of. The population of Greece, finding the continent too narrow for it, was forced to flow out into the islands of the Mediterranean and the shores to which those islands conducted. The Bœotian occupation of the plain of the Cephissus led to the first Greek settlements in Asia, those known as Æolian, in Lesbos and on the adjacent coast. The Achæan conquest of Ionia caused the Ionians, after a brief sojourn in Attica, to pass on through the Cyclades, to Chios, Samos, and the parts of Asia directly opposite. Finally, the success of the Dorians against the Achæans caused these last to emigrate, in part to Asia under Doric leaders, in part to Italy.

Consequences: settlements in the islands, in Asia, and in Italy.

For the history of these settlements, see the following section.

SECOND PERIOD.

From the Dorian Conquest of the Peloponnese (about B.C. 1100-1000) *to the Commencement of the Wars with Persia,* B.C. 500.

SOURCES. No extant Greek writer gives us the continuous history of this period, which has to be gathered from scattered notices in Herodotus, Thucydides, Strabo, Pausanias, Plutarch, and other authors. The books of Diodorus which treated of this period are lost. Some important light is thrown on it by the fragments which remain of contemporary poets, *e.g.*, Tyrtæus, Callinus, and Solon.

Among modern works embracing the period the most important are the *Histories* of THIRWALL and GROTE; to which may be added:

WACHSMUTH, *Hellenische Alterthumskunde.* Halle, 1826; 4 vols. 8vo.

TITTMANN, *Griechische Staatsverfassung.* Leipsic, 1822.

HERMANN, K. F., *Lehrbuch der Griechischen Staatsalterthümer*. Heidelberg, 1831; 8vo. Translated into English by TALBOYS. Oxford, 1836.

NIEBUHR, B. G., *Vorträge*, etc. Lectures xxiv. to xxxiv.

RAWLINSON, G., *History of Herodotus*. 4 vols. 2d edition. London, 1862. Two appendices to Book V. belong especially to this period.

PART I.

History of the principal Hellenic States in Greece Proper.

1. The history of the Hellenes subsequently to the Dorian occupation of the Peloponnese resolves itself into that of the several states. Still, a few general remarks may be made before proceeding to the special history of the more important cities and countries. (*a*) The progress of civilization was, for a time and to a certain extent, checked by the migrations and the troubles which they brought in their train. Stronger and more energetic but ruder races took the place of weaker but more polished ones. Physical qualities asserted a superiority over grace, refinement, and ingenuity. What the rough Dorians were in comparison with the refined Achæans of the Peloponnese, such were generally the conquering as compared with the conquered peoples. (*b*) But against this loss must be set the greater political vigor of the new era. War and movement, bringing out the personal qualities of each individual man, favored the growth of self-respect and self-assertion. Amid toils and dangers which were shared alike by all, the idea of political equality took its rise. A novel and unsettled state of things stimulated political inventiveness; and, various expedients being tried, the stock of political ideas increased rapidly. The simple hereditary monarchy of the heroic times was succeeded everywhere, except in Epirus, by some more complicated system of government—some system far more favorable to freedom and to the political education of the individual. (*c*) Another natural consequence of the new condition of things was the change by which the CITY acquired its special dignity and importance. The conquerors naturally settled themselves in some stronghold, and kept together for their greater security. Each such stronghold became a separate state, holding in subjection a certain tract of circumjacent country. At the

Consequences of the great migrations: 1. Check to civilization.

2. Increase of political vigor.

3. Importance acquired by Cities.

Number of separate states.

same time, the unconquered countries also, seeing the strength that resulted from unity, were induced in many cases to abolish their old system of village life and to centralize themselves by establishing capitals, and transferring the bulk of their population to them (συνοικίσεις). This was the case with Athens, Mantinea, Tegea, Dymé, etc. (*d*) In countries occupied by a single race, but broken up into many distinct states, each centralized in a single city, the idea of political confederation grew up, sometimes (it may be) suggested by a pre-existing amphictyony, but occasionally, it would seem, without any such preparative. The federal bond was in most cases weak; and in Bœotia alone was the union such as to constitute permanently a state of first-rate importance.

4. Formation of confederacies.

On the confederations of Greece, see Mr. E. A. FREEMAN'S *History of Federal Government*, vol. i. London, 1863.

2. The subdivision of Greece into a vast number of small states, united by no common political bond, and constantly at war with one another, did not prevent the formation and maintenance of a certain general Pan-Hellenic feeling—a consciousness of unity, a friendliness, and a readiness to make common cause against a foreign enemy. At the root of this feeling lay a conviction of identity of race. It was further fostered by the possession of a common language and a common literature; of similar habits and ideas; and of a common religion, of rites, temples, and festivals, which were equally open to all.

Unity of Greece: its causes.

Among the various unifying influences here mentioned, probably the most important were the common literature, more especially the poems of Homer, and the common festivals, more especially those known as the Great Games. Homer's grandest and most popular poem represented the Greeks as all engaged in a common enterprise against a foreign power. The Great Games gave to each Greek either one or two occasions in each year when he could meet all other Greeks in friendly rivalry, and join with them both in religious ceremonies and in amusements. On this subject consult MANSO, *Ueber den Antheil der Griechen an den Olympischen Spielen.* Breslau, 1772.

3. The first state which attained to political importance under the new condition of affairs in Greece was Argos. From Argos, according to the tradition, went forth the Dorian colonists, who formed settlements in Epidaurus, Trœzen, Phlius, Sicyon, and

History of Argos: her early pre-eminence.

Corinth; while from some of these places a further extension of Doric power was made, as from Epidaurus, which colonized Ægina and Epidaurus Limera, and from Corinth which colonized Megara. Argos, the prolific mother of so many children, stood to most of them in the relation of protectress, and almost of mistress. Her dominion reached, on the one hand, to the isthmus; on the other, to Cape Malea and the island of Cythera. For three or four centuries, from the Dorian conquest to the death of Pheidon (about B.C. 744), she was the leading power of the Peloponnese, a fact which she never forgot, and which had an important influence on her later history.

4. The government of Argos was at the first a monarchy of the heroic type, the supreme power being hereditary in the house of the Temenidæ, supposed descendants from Temenus the Heracleid, the eldest of the sons of Aristomachus. It was not long, however, before aspirations after political liberty arose, and, the power of the kings being greatly curtailed, a government, monarchical in form, but republican in reality, was established. This state of things lasted for some centuries; but about B.C. 780 to 770, on the accession of a monarch of more than ordinary capacity, a certain Pheidon, a reaction set in. Pheidon not only recovered all the lost royal privileges, but, exceeding them, constituted himself the first known Grecian "tyrant." A great man in every way, he enabled Argos to exercise something like a practical hegemony over the whole Peloponnese. Under him, probably, were sent forth the colonies which carried the Argive name to Crete, Rhodes, Cos, Cnidus, and Halicarnassus. The connection thus established with Asia led him to introduce into Greece coined money—a Lydian invention—and a system of weights and measures (*Φειδώνεια μέτρα*) believed to have been identical with the Babylonian.

Changes in government.

Reign of Pheidon, B.C. 780–744.

5. After the death of Pheidon, Argos declined in power; the ties uniting the confederacy became relaxed; the government returned to its previous form; and the history of the state is almost a blank. No doubt the development of Spartan power was the main cause of this decline; but it may be attributed also, in part, to the lack of eminent men, and in part to the injudicious severity

Decline of the Argive power.

with which Argos treated her periœcic cities and her confederates.

Petty wars of Argos with Sparta terminate (about B.C. 554) with the loss of the region called Cynuria, or the Thyreatis. Was the occupation by Sparta of the tract east of Parnon anterior or subsequent to this?

6. Among the other states of Greece, the two whose history is most ample and most interesting, even during this early period, are undoubtedly Sparta and Athens. Every "History of Greece" must mainly concern itself with the affairs of these two states, which are alone capable of being treated with any thing like completeness.

History of Sparta.

AUTHORITIES. Besides the general treatment of the subject in Histories of Greece, special works have been written on the History of Sparta, *e.g.*,

CRAGIUS, *De Republica Lacedæmoniorum libri quatuor.* Genevæ, 1593; 4to.

MEURSIUS, *De Regno Laconico libri duo.* Ultraj., 1687; 4to. And *Miscellanea Laconica.* Amstel., 1661; 4to.

MANSO, J. C. F., *Sparta; ein Versuch zur Aufklärung der Geschichte und Verfassung dieses Staates.* Leipsic, 1800; 3 vols. 8vo. By far the most important work on the subject. Excellent for the time at which it was written, and still of great value to the student.

ENGEL, C., *De Republica militari, sive comparatio Lacedæmoniorum, Cretensium, et Cosaccorum.* Göttingen, 1790.

History of Sparta. Long contest with Amyclæ.

7. The Dorians, who in the eleventh century effected a lodgment in the upper valley of the Eurotas, occupied at first a narrow space between Taÿgetus and Parnon, extending northward no farther than the various head-streams of the Eurotas and Ænus rivers, and southward only to a little beyond Sparta. This was a tract about twenty-five miles long by twenty broad, the area of which might be 400 square miles. In the lower valley, from a little below Sparta to the sea, the Achæans still maintained themselves, having their capital at Amyclæ, on the Eurotas, within two miles of the chief city of their enemies. Perpetual war went on between the two powers; but Sparta for the space of three centuries made little or no advance southward, Amyclæ commanding the valley, and the fortifications of Amyclæ defying her incessant attacks. Baffled in this quarter, she made attempts to reduce Arcadia, which failed, and even picked

Wars with Arcadia, Messenia, and Argos.

quarrels with her kindred states, Messenia and Argos, which led to petty wars of no consequence.

8. The government of Sparta during this period underwent changes akin to those which took place in Argos. The monarchs were at first absolute; but discontent soon manifested itself: concessions were made which were again revoked; and the whole period was one of internal struggle and disturbance. Nor were the differences between the kings and their Dorian subjects the only troubles of the time. The submitted Achæans, of whom there were many, were displeased at their treatment, murmured and even sometimes revolted, and being reduced by force of arms were degraded to a lower position.

Internal troubles.

Formation of the three classes into which the Lacedæmonians were divided throughout the whole of their subsequent history. 1. The Spartans, or free inhabitants of the capital, the sole possessors of political rights and privileges; Dorians by extraction, with few and unimportant exceptions, owners of the bulk of the soil, on the rent of which they lived in comfort and independence; 2. The Periœci, or free inhabitants of the country-towns and villages, citizens in a certain sense, but without franchise; possessors of the poorer lands, and the only class engaged in trade, commerce, and handicrafts; Achæans in blood for the most part, but with a slight Doric infusion. 3. The Helots, or slave population, composed of captives taken in war (ἁλωτοί), and of submitted rebels; Achæan mainly in blood till the Messenian wars, after which they may be regarded as Achæo-Dorians; chiefly employed in cultivating the lands of their Spartan masters, to whom they paid a fixed rent of one-half the produce. The third class was insignificant at first, but increased in number as Sparta extended her territory, and, upon the conquest of Messenia, became the preponderating element in the population.

Condition of the Helots not without its advantages, but rendered unhappy by the cruel institution of the Crypteia, a legalized system of assassination to which the government from time to time actually had recourse.

9. The double monarchy, which, according to the tradition, had existed from the time of the conquest, and which was peculiar to Sparta among all the Greek states, dated really, it is probable, from the time of struggle, being a device of those who sought to limit and curtail the royal authority. The two kings, like the two consuls at Rome, acted as checks upon each other; and the regal power, thus divided against itself, naturally became weaker and weaker. It had sunk, evidently, into a shadow of its former self, when Lycurgus, a member of the royal family, but not in the direct line of succession,

Legislation of Lycurgus, about B.C. 850.

gave to Sparta that constitution which raised her in a little while to a proud and wonderful eminence.

Difficulty of distinguishing how much of the Spartan constitution was original, and how much dated from Lycurgus. Tendency to exaggerate the extent of his innovations. Original constitution must have included the division into three tribes, Hyllæi, Dymanes, and Pamphyles, which was common to all Dorians, the monarchy, some sort of senate or council, and some kind of assembly. Doubtful whether the thirty *Obæ* were instituted by Lycurgus or no, and therefore doubtful whether he determined the number of the Senate. Chief object of his legislation to create and preserve a race of vigorous and warlike men. Hence, the introduction of his system of discipline was of primary importance; his constitutional changes were altogether secondary and by comparison trivial.

The LYCURGEAN CONSTITUTION may be briefly summed up as follows:—1. It maintained the double monarchy, but reduced the power of the kings, who became little more than presidents of the senate, with a right of proxy voting, and a casting vote if the senate was equally divided. 2. It maintained or established the senate of thirty members (twenty-eight and the two kings), representing the thirty Obæ, but, from the time of Lycurgus, elected by the general assembly of the citizens from among the Spartans who were more than sixty years of age. 3. It probably enlarged the powers of the assembly (ἀπέλλα), which had henceforth not only the right of electing the senate, but that of accepting or rejecting all laws, of deciding on peace and war, on alliances, etc. 4. It set up for the first time certain officers called Ephors, whose business it was to *watch over* the Lycurgean constitution and punish those who infringed it.

The LYCURGEAN DISCIPLINE comprised the following main points:—1. The decision in every case by state officials of the question whether a child should be reared or no. 2. The separation of all male children at the age of seven from their homes, and their training and education from that time by State educators. The usual branches of Greek education, letters, music, and gymnastics, were taught, but the literary part of the education was of least, and the gymnastic of far the greatest, account. The boy's time was chiefly passed in athletic exercises, then in hunting, and finally in drills, after which he was allowed to bear a part in military expeditions. He took his meals in public at the *syssitia*, his fare being both simple and scanty; he slept with his fellows in the public dormitories; at a certain age he was allowed no food except such as he could take without discovery. Every thing was done with the object of making him a perfectly efficient soldier. 3. The men had little more liberty than the boys. They too fed at the public messes (συσσίτια) on the plainest fare, and slept in the public barracks, only visiting their homes occasionally, and, as it were, by stealth. Their time was fully occupied by State duties, as drills, public hunting expeditions, superintendence and training of the boys, and actual warfare. They had no private life, and no time to employ in commerce, agriculture, or other profitable occupation. 4. The possession of gold and silver was forbidden, and no money allowed to circulate but a heavy iron coinage. 5. Girls were trained no less carefully than boys, in athletic exercises nearly similar; but separately, excepting on occasions, when their contests were witnessed by the males. 6. Marriage was superintended by the State. The citizen was forbidden to marry until he was of ripe age, and was then required to marry under a penalty. He chose his own wife; but if the marriage proved unprolific, he was bound to allow his wife to obtain issue by means of another. Other violations of the sanctity of marriage were also allowed under certain circumstances, as the bigamy both of men and women; but, excepting under State sanction, incontinency was forbidden and was rare.

Question of the division of the Lacedæmonian territory by Lycurgus. The division unknown to Herodotus, Thucydides, Xenophon, Isocrates, Plato, and Aristotle. Rests on the authority of Polybius and Plutarch. Intrinsically improbable. (Compare GROTE, *History of Greece*, part ii. chap. vi.)

10. The adoption of the Lycurgean system had the almost immediate effect of raising Sparta to the first place in Greece. Amyclæ fell in the next generation to Lycurgus; Pharis and Geronthræ submitted soon after. A generation later Helos was taken, and the whole valley of the Eurotas occupied. The Achæans submitted, or retired to Italy. Wars followed with Arcadia and Argos, the latter of whom lost all her territory south of Cynuria. Quarrels began with Messenia, which led on to a great struggle.

Rise of Sparta to power.

11. The conquest of Messenia by Sparta, which made her at once the dominant power of the Peloponnese, was the result of two great wars, each lasting about twenty years, and separated from each other by the space of about forty years. The wars seem to have been purely aggressive on the part of Sparta, and to have been prompted, in part, by the mere lust of conquest, in part by dislike of the liberal policy which the Dorians of Messenia had adopted towards their Achæan subjects. Despite the heroism of the Messenians and the assistance lent them by Arcadia and Argos, Sparta gained her object, in consequence of her superior military organization and training, joined to the advantage of her central position, which enabled her to strike suddenly with her full force any one of her three foes.

Conquest of Messenia, B.C. 743–668.

FIRST MESSENIAN WAR, B.C. 743 to 724. Long defense of Ithômé. Corinth assists Sparta in the war, while Argos, Arcadia, and Sicyon assist Messenia. Strength and resources of Messenia gradually exhausted. Ithômé evacuated, and resistance discontinued in the twentieth year after the war commenced. Many of the inhabitants quit the country, and fly to Arcadia and Argolis. Sparta reduces the remainder to the condition of Helots.

SECOND MESSENIAN WAR, B.C. 685 to 668. Standard of revolt raised by Aristomenes, who, assisted by Argos, Arcadia, Sicyon, and Pisatis, defeats the Spartans at the "Boar's Tomb," but is afterwards defeated and shut up in Eira. Prolonged defense of that fortress. The Spartans, encouraged by the Athenian poet Tyrtæus, at length successful. Eira taken. Aristomenes flies to Rhodes. The Messenians generally are once more reduced to the Helot condition; but the inhabitants of a few towns are admitted to the position of Periœci.

Changes in the constitution.

12. Closely connected with the Messenian wars were certain changes in the government and internal condition of Sparta, the general tendency of which was towards popularizing the constitution. The constant absence of the two kings from Sparta during the Messenian struggle increased the power of the Ephors, who, when no king was present, assumed that to them belonged the exercise of the royal functions. The loss of citizens in the wars led to the admission of new blood into the state, and probably caused the distinction into two classes of citizens (ὁμοιοὶ and ὑπομείονες), which is found to exist at a later date. The Ephors, elected annually by the entire body of the citizens, became the popular element in the government; and the gradual augmentation of their power was, in a certain sense, the triumph of the popular cause. At the same time it must be allowed that the constitutional changes made did not content the aspirations of the democratic party; and that the colony sent out to Tarentum at once indicated, and relieved, the dissatisfaction of the lower grade of citizens.

Are we to connect with the distinction of ὁμοιοὶ and ὑπομείονες the two ἐκκλησίαι at Sparta, the lesser (ἡ μικρά) and the greater (ἡ μεγάλη)? Is the former the assembly of the ὁμοιοὶ only, the latter that of the ὁμοιοὶ and ὑπομείονες together?

Wars with Pisatis, Arcadia, and Argos. Conquest of the Thyreatis.

13. The conquest of Messenia was followed by some wars of less importance, which tended, however, to increase the power of Sparta, and to render her still more decidedly the leading state of Greece. Pisatis and Triphylia were reduced directly after the close of the second Messenian war, and were handed over to the Eleans. Arcadia was then attacked, but made a vigorous resistance; and the sole fruit of a war which lasted three generations was the submission of Tegea. Argos about the same time lost the Thyreatis (about B.C. 554); and

Spartan influence was thus extended over, perhaps, two-thirds of the Peloponnese.

Recognition of Sparta as the leading power in Greece. Expeditions beyond the Peloponnese.

14. Hitherto the efforts and even the views of Sparta had been confined to the narrow peninsula within which her own territory lay; but the course of events now led her to a fuller recognition of her own greatness, and, as a natural consequence, to active exertions in a more extended sphere. The embassy of Crœsus in B.C. 555 was the first public acknowledgment which she received of her importance; and the readiness with which she embraced the offer of alliance, and prepared an expedition to assist the Lydian monarch, indicates the satisfaction which she felt in the new prospects which were opening out on her. Thirty years later (B.C. 525), she actually sent an expedition, conjointly with Corinth, to the coast of Asia, which failed, however, to effect its object, the deposition of Polycrates of Samos. Soon afterwards (B.C. 510), she assumed the right of interference in the internal affairs of the Greek states beyond the Peloponnese, and by her repeated invasions of Attica, and her efforts in favor of the Athenian oligarchs, sowed the seeds of that fear and dislike with which she was for nearly a century and a half regarded by the great democratic republic.

SPARTAN KINGS:—The personal history of the Spartan kings becomes interesting, and the dates of their several accessions may be fixed with tolerable certainty, from the time of Cleomenes and his colleague Demaratus. Of the previous monarchs we know little more than the names. These are—I. *Elder House of Agidæ.* 1. Eurysthenes; 2. Agis (his son?); 3. Echestratus (his son); 4. Labotas (his son); 5. Doryssus (his son); 6. Agesilaüs (his son); 7. Archelaus (his son); 8. Teleclus (his son); 9. Alcamenes (his son); 10. Polydorus (his son); 11. Eurycrates (his son); 12. Anaxander (his son); 13. Eurycratidas (his son); 14. Leon (his son); and 15. Anaxandridas (his son). II. *Younger House of Eurypontidæ.* 1. Procles; 2. Soüs (his son); 3. Eurypon (his son?); 4. Prytanis (his son); 5. Eunomus (his son); 6. Polydectes (his son); 7. Charilaüs (his son); 8. Nicander (his son); 9. Theopompus (his son); 10. Zeuxidamus (his grandson); 11. Anaxidamus (his son); 12. Archidamus I. (his son); 13. Agesicles (his son); and 14. Ariston (his son). These fifteen generations may probably have covered a space of nearly five centuries, from about B.C. 1000 to B.C. 520.

History of Athens.

AUTHORITIES. The History of Athens is best treated in the general works on Greek history enumerated above, pp. 137 seq. Besides these, however, many special works have been written on the History, Chronology, Constitution, and Finances of Athens. Among them the following are of importance:

CORSINI, *Fasti Attici.* Florence, 1744–56; 4 vols. 4to. The best work on the chronology.

SCHÖMANN, *De Comitiis Atheniensium.* Gryphisv., 1819; 8vo.

BOECKH, A., *Staatsaushaltung der Athener.* Berlin, 1817. Translated into English by Sir G. C. LEWIS, and published under the title, *Public Economy of Athens.* London, 1828; 2 vols. 8vo. An excellent work, quite exhaustive of its subject.

LEVESQUE, *Sur la constitution de la République d'Athènes,* in the fourth volume of the *Mémoires de l'Institut,* pp. 113 et seqq.

History of Athens: First, or Kingly, Period.

15. The traditional history of Athens commences with a Kingly Period. Monarchs of the old heroic type are said to have governed the country from a time considerably anterior to the Trojan War down to the death of Codrus, B.C. 1300 to 1050. The most celebrated of these kings was Theseus, to whom is ascribed the συνοικισμὸς, whereby Athens became the capital of a centralized monarchy, instead of one out of many nearly equal country towns. Another king, Menestheus, was said to have fought at Troy. Codrus, the last of the monarchs, fell, according to the tradition, in resisting a Dorian invasion, made from the recently conquered Peloponnese.

INSTITUTIONS OF THIS PERIOD. Among these must be placed, first of all, the division of the whole people into four tribes—Teleontes (or Geleontes), Hopletes, Ægicoreis, and Argadeis—which was, perhaps, common to the Athenians with all other Ionic peoples, and which appears to imply the early existence in Greece of the idea of *caste.* 2. The subdivisions of the tribes—first, into "Brotherhoods" (φρατρίαι) and "Clans" (γένη); and secondly, into "Thirdings" (τριττύες) and "Naucraries"—the former a division believed to rest, and probably actually resting, upon the basis of consanguinity; the latter an artificial arrangement made for certain State purposes, as taxation and military service. 3. The recognition of three classes in the community, viz., Nobles (εὐπατρίδαι), Farmers (γεωμόροι), and Artisans (δημιουργοί), the first of which alone possessed important political power, filling all offices of importance, and furnishing the senate or council (βουλή), which held its sittings on Mars' Hill (Areopagus). The "Farmers" and "Artisans" had no doubt the right of attending, and expressing assent or dissent, in the ἀγορά.

Second Period. Rule of the Archons for life.

16. The Kingly Period was followed at Athens by the gradual development of an aristocracy. The Eupatrids had acquired power enough under the kings to abolish monarchy at the death of Codrus, and to substitute for it the life-archonship, which, though con-

fined to the descendants of Codrus, was not a royal dignity, but a mere chief magistracy. The Eupatrids elected from among the qualified persons; and the archon was, at least in theory, responsible. Thirteen such archons held office before any further change was made, their united reigns covering a space of about three centuries, B.C. 1050 to 752.

In the earlier part of this period occurred the migration from Attica of the Ionians, Minyans, Pylians, and other refugees, who during the preceding time of disturbance had flocked into the Attic peninsula and there found an asylum. Otherwise, the whole of the period is devoid of historical incident.

Third Period. Rule of the Decennial Archons.

17. On the death of Alcmæon, the last archon for life, the Eupatrids made a further change. Archons were to be elected for ten years only, so that responsibility could be enforced, ex-archons being liable to prosecution and punishment. The descendants of Codrus were at first preserved in their old dignity; but the fourth decennial archon, Hippomanes, being deposed for his cruelty, the right of the Medontidæ was declared to be forfeited (B.C. 714), and the office was thrown open to all Eupatrids.

Fourth Period. Rule of the Nine Archons.

18. Finally, after seven decennial archons had held office, the supreme power was put in commission (B.C. 684). In lieu of a single chief magistrate, a board of nine archons, annually elected, was set up, the original kingly functions being divided among them. The aristocracy was now fully installed in power, office being confined to Eupatrids, and every office being open to all such persons, Eupatrids alone having the suffrage, and the Agora itself, or general assembly of the people, having ceased to meet, or become purely formal and passive.

Popular discontent. Legislation of Draco.

19. The full triumph of the oligarchy did not very long precede the first stir of democratic life. Within sixty years of the time of complete aristocratical ascendency, popular discontent began to manifest itself, and a *demand for written laws* arose, often the earliest cry of an oppressed people. Alarmed, but not intimidated, the nobles endeavored to crush the rising democratic spirit by an unsparing severity; their answer to the demands made on them was the legislation of Draco (B.C. 624), which, by making death the penalty for almost all crimes, placed the very lives of the citizens at the disposal of the ruling order. The increased dissatisfaction which this legislation caused

Insurrection of Cylon leads to Solon's legislation.

probably encouraged Cylon to make his rash attempt (B.C. 612), which was easily put down by the oligarchs; who, however, contrived to lose ground by their victory, incurring, as they did in the course of it, the guilt of sacrilege, and at the same time exasperating the people, who had hoped much from Cylon's effort. Under these circumstances, after a vain attempt had been made to quiet matters by the purification of Epimenides (B.C. 595), and after the political discontent had taken the new and dangerous shape involved in the formation of *local* factions (Pediæi, Parali, and Diacrii), Solon, an Eupatrid, but of so poor a family that he had himself been engaged in trade, was by common consent intrusted with the task of framing a new constitution, B.C. 594.

Chief Points of Solon's Legislation:—1. Main object, to substitute for the oppressive oligarchy a *moderate* government, which should admit all Athenian citizens to a share of power, but give a predominating influence to the higher orders. This was effected by (*a*) a division of the people for political purposes into four classes, according to the amount of their income; viz., the Pentacosiomedimni, or men whose income was of the yearly value of 500 medimni of corn; the Hippeis (knights), whose income was 300 such medimni; the Zeugitæ, whose income was 150; and the Thetes, whose income fell short of the last-named amount; of whom the last (the Thetes) had the suffrage only without elegibility to any office, while the highest office of all, the archonship, which was the only door of admission into the Council of the Areopagus, was confined to the Pentacosiomedimni. (*b*) The institution of a new council, which was in most respects to supersede the old Council of the Areopagus, to have the right of initiating legislation, and to form a portion of the executive. This council was to consist of 400 members, 100 from each of the old tribes, and was to be elected annually by the free votes of all the citizens. (*c*) The revival of a real *ἐκκλησία*, or assembly of the whole people, which was to elect the archons and councillors, to judge (*εὐθύνειν*) the former at the expiration of their year of office, and to accept or reject all the laws and decrees proposed by the council. (*d*) The institution of trial by jury, or the formation of popular law-courts, not indeed for the trial of offenses in the first instance, but for the hearing of appeals from other tribunals. (*e*) The retention of the old Council of the Areopagus, partly as a court of law, the highest tribunal in the State (compare the judicial functions of the English House of Lords), partly as a superintending body (compare the Ephoralty) charged with seeing to the observance of the laws, and empowered to prevent or punish any departure from them. 2. A secondary object of Solon's legislation was to remedy the existing evil of wide-spread poverty and distress. The rule of the oligarchy had impoverished the mass of the nation; and by the operation of a harsh and stern law of debt, the lands of the poorer cultivators had become mortgaged, and numbers of the citizens had sunk into the condition of slaves. Solon's remedies against these evils were the following:—(*a*) His σεισάχθεια, or abolition of debts—not, however, of all debts, but either those of a certain class, or those of persons proved insolvent. (*b*) A debasement of the currency, intended to be a reduction of one-fourth, or 25 per cent.; but accidentally a reduction of 27 per cent. (*c*) The abolition of servitude for debt, and the restoration to freedom of all former Athenian citizens not sold out of Attica. (*d*) The encouragement of industry by a provision that every father should teach his son a handicraft. It is uncertain how far these remedies would have had a permanent success. The rapid advance in the material prosperity of Athens, which followed quite independently of them, prevented the trial from being made, and at the same time rendered it unnecessary to recur again to such questionable expedients as cancelling debts and debasing the coin.

Struggle of parties terminated by the tyranny of Pisistratus.

20. The legislation of Solon, wise as it seems to moderns, was far from satisfying his contemporaries. Like most moderate politicians, he was accused by one party of having gone too far, by another of not having done enough. His personal influence sufficed for a time to restrain the discontented; but when this influence was withdrawn (about B.C. 570), violent contentions broke out. The *local* factions (see § 19) revived. A struggle commenced between a reactionary party under Lycurgus, a conservative party under the Alcmæonid Megacles, and a party of progress under Pisistratus, which terminated in the triumph of the last-named leader, who artfully turned his success to his own personal advantage by assuming the position of Dictator, or (as the Greeks called it) Tyrant, B.C. 560.

DYNASTY OF THE PISISTRATIDÆ:—1. Reign of Pisistratus. His first exaltation, B.C. 560. Flight of the Alcmæonidæ. Pisistratus in his turn driven into exile, about B.C. 554. Re-establishes himself by arrangement with Megacles, about B.C. 548. Offends Megacles, and is again forced to fly, about B.C. 547. Re-establishes himself by force of arms, about B.C. 537, and continues tyrant for the rest of his life. Reigns mildly, encourages the arts, and edits Homer. Dies, B.C. 527. Succeeded by his eldest son, Hippias. 2. Reign of Hippias, B.C. 527 to 510. Murder of Hipparchus, his brother, by Harmodius and Aristogeiton, B.C. 514. Intrigues of the exiled Alcmæonidæ, who bribe the Delphic oracle, and thereby induce the Spartans to dethrone Hippias. After the first attempt, under Anchimolius, had failed, Cleomenes, in B.C. 510, forces the Pisistratidæ to withdraw from the city.

Fresh troubles.

21. The expulsion of the tyrant was followed by fresh troubles. A contest for power arose between Isagoras, the friend of Cleomenes, and Clisthenes, the head of the Alcmæonid family, which terminated in favor

of the latter, despite the armed interference of Sparta. Clisthenes, however, had to purchase his victory by an alliance with the democratical party; and the natural result of his success was a further change in the constitution, which was modified in a democratic sense.

Constitution of Clisthenes.

CHIEF POINTS OF THE CONSTITUTION OF CLISTHENES:—(*a*) Admission to citizenship of all free inhabitants of Attica, whether members of the old tribes or not. (*b*) Supersession of the old tribes for political purposes by the new tribes, ten in number (each embracing ten demes, or country towns, with their adjacent districts), now for the first time established by the legislator. (*c*) Substitution of a council of five hundred, fifty from each of the ten tribes, for the Solonian council of four hundred. (*d*) Counteraction of the tendency to local factions by the inclusion within each tribe of demes remote from each other. (*e*) Fresh organization of the law courts (*δικαστήρια*), and extension of their functions. (*f*) Introduction of the Octracism. (*g*) Introduction of the principle of determining between the candidates for certain offices by lot. (*h*) Institution of the ten annual Strategi, who in a little time superseded the archons as the chief executive officers.

Military successes of Athens.

22. The establishment of democracy gave an impulse to the spirit of patriotism, which resulted almost immediately in some splendid military successes. Athens had for some time been growing in warlike power. Under Solon she had taken Salamis from Megara, and played an important part in the first Sacred War (B.C. 600 to 591). About B.C. 518, or a little earlier, she had accepted the protectorate of the Platæans. Now (B.C. 507) being attacked at one and the same time by Sparta, by Bœotia, and by the Chalcideans of Eubœa, she completely triumphed over the coalition. The Spartan kings quarrelled, and the force under their command withdrew without risking a battle. The Bœotians and Chalcideans were signally defeated. Chalcis itself was conquered and occupied. A naval struggle with Ægina, the ally of Bœotia, followed, during the continuance of which the first hostilities took place between Athens and Persia. Proud of her recent victories, and confident in her strength, Athens complied with the request of Aristagoras, and sent twenty ships to support the revolt which threatened to deprive the Great King of the whole sea-board of Asia Minor. Though the burning of Sardis was followed by the defeat of Ephesus, yet the Persian monarch deemed his honor involved in the further chastisement on her own soil of the audacious power which had pre-

sumed to invade his dominions. An attempt to conquer Greece would, no doubt, have been made even without provocation; but the part taken by Athens in the Ionic revolt precipitated the struggle. It was well that the contest came when it did. Had it been delayed until Athens had grown into a rival to Sparta, the result might have been different. Greece might then have succumbed; and European freedom and civilization, trampled under foot by the hordes of Asia, might have been unable to recover itself.

PART II.

History of the other Grecian States.

SOURCES. The data for the history of the other states are scanty. They consist chiefly of scattered notices in Herodotus, Thucydides, and the geographers. Light is occasionally thrown on the constitutional history of the states by Aristotle. Inscriptions also are, in many cases, of importance. Among the most valuable collections of these are:

CHISHULL, *Inscriptiones Asiaticæ.* London, 1728; folio.

BOECKH, *Corpus Inscriptionum Græcarum.* Berlin, 1828–43; 3 vols. folio. A magnificent work.

ROSE, *Inscriptiones Græcæ vetustissimæ.* Cambridge, 1825; 8vo.

The history of the smaller states will be most conveniently given under the five heads of (*a*) the Peloponnesian States; (*b*) the States of Central Greece; (*c*) those of Northern Greece; (*d*) those situated in the islands; and (*e*) those which either were, or were regarded as, colonies.

A. *Smaller Peloponnesian States.*

i. *Achæa.* The traditions said that when the Dorians conquered Sparta, the Spartan king Tisamenus, son of Orestes, led the Achæans northward, and, expelling the Ionians from the tract which lay along the Corinthian Gulf, set up an Achæan kingdom in those parts, which lasted for several generations. Ogygus, however, the latest of these monarchs, having left behind him sons of a tyrannical temper, the Achæans destroyed the monarchy, and set up a federal republic. Twelve cities composed the league, which were originally Pellênê, Ægeira (or Hyparesia), Ægæ, Bura, Helicé, Ægium, Rhypes, Patræ, Pharæ, Olenus, Dymé, and Tritæa, all situated on or near the coast except the last two, which were in the interior. The common place of meeting for the league was Helicé, where an annual festival was held, and common sacrifices were offered to Heliconian Neptune. The constitution of the several cities is said to have been democratic. The league was, no doubt, political as well as religious; but no details are known of it. According to Polybius it was admired for its fairness and equality, and was taken as a model by the cities of Magna Græcia in the early part of the fifth century. We may gather from Thucydides that it was of the loose type so common in Greece. The Achæans seem to have manifested in the early times a disposition to stay at home and to keep aloof from the quarrels of their neighbors. Hence the *history* of the country scarcely begins till the time of Antigonus, from which period the league formed a nucleus round which independent Greece rallied itself.

ii. *Arcadia.* The Arcadians were regarded as aboriginal inhabitants of their country. They called themselves προσέληνοι. The Dorian conquests in the Peloponnese left them untouched; and they retained to a late date, in their remote valleys and cold high mountain pastures, very primitive habits. The tradition makes the entire country form, in the old times, a single monarchy, which continues till B.C. 668; but it may be doubted whether there had really ever existed in Arcadia any thing more than an Amphictyonic union prior to Epaminondas. The whole country is physically broken up into separate valleys and basins, whose inhabitants would naturally form separate and distinct communities, while retaining a certain sense of ethnic relationship. The most important of these communities were Mantinea and Tegea, neighboring towns, between which there were frequent wars. Next to these may be placed Orchomenus, Pheneus, and Stymphalus towards the north-east; Cleitor and Heræa towards the west; and Phigaleia, on the north-western border, near Messenia. The Arcadians, however, loved villages rather than towns; and the numerous population was chiefly located in small hamlets scattered about the mountains. Arcadia was subject to constant aggressions at the hands of Sparta, which she sought to revenge upon fitting occasions. These aggressions began in the times previous to Lycurgus (see p. 147), and continued afterwards almost constantly. In retaliation, the Arcadians assisted Messenia throughout both the Messenian wars. Tegea, as the nearest state to Sparta, suffered most at her hands; and after a long struggle, it would seem that Arcadia generally (about B.C. 560) acknowledged the Lacedæmonian hegemony, placing her full military strength at the disposal of Sparta in her wars, but retaining her internal independence. Mantinea even, upon occasions, thwarted the policy of Sparta.

iii. *Corinth.* Corinth, a rich and famous city even in the times anterior to the Doric conquests, was occupied by Dorian settlers from Argos soon after the reduction of that state. A monarchy was established under kings who claimed descent from Hercules, twelve such rulers holding the throne during the space of 327 years. At the end of this time monarchy was exchanged for oligarchy, power remaining (as at Athens) in the hands of a branch of the royal family, the Bacchiadæ, who intermarried only among themselves, and elected each year from their own body a Prytanis, or chief magistrate. This state of things continued for ninety years, when a revolution was effected by Cypselus, who, having ingratiated himself with the people, rose up against the oligarchs, expelled them, and made himself tyrant. Cypselus reigned from B.C. 657 to 627, when he was succeeded by his son, Periander, who reigned from B.C. 627 to 587. A third monarch of the dynasty, Psammetichus, the nephew or grandson of Periander, mounted the throne, but was expelled, after a reign of three years, by the people, perhaps assisted by Sparta, B.C. 584. The time of the Cypselids was one of great material wealth and prosperity; literature and the arts flourished; commerce was encouraged; colonies were sent out; and the hegemony of the mother country over her colonies successfully asserted. (The chief Corinthian settlements were Corcyra, Ambracia, Leucas, Anactorium, Epidamnus, Apollonia, Syracuse, and Potidæa. Of these, Ambracia, Leucas, Anactorium, Epidamnus, Apollonia, and Potidæa were content to be subject. Corcyra generally asserted independence, but was forced to submit to the Cypselids. Syracuse must have been from the first practically independent.) After the downfall of the tyrants, who are said to have ruled harshly, a republic was established on a tolerably wide basis. Power was placed in the hands of the wealthy class; and even commerce and trade were no bars to the holding of office. Corinth became one of the richest of the Greek states; but, as she increased in wealth, she sank in political importance. Regard for her material interests induced her to accept the protection of Sparta, and from about B.C. 550 she became merely the second power in the Spartan league, a position which she occupied with slight interruptions till B.C. 394.

iv. *Elis.* The settlement of the Ætolo-Dorians under Oxylus (see p. 143) had been made in the more northern portion of the country, between the Larisus and the Ladon or Selleis. The region south of this as far as the Neda remained in the possession of the old inhabitants, and was divided into two districts, Pisatis, or the tract between the Ladon and the Alpheus, of which Pisa was the capital, and Triphylia, the tract between the Alpheus and the Neda, of which the chief city was Lepreum. The Eleans, however, claimed a hegemony over the whole country; and this claim gave rise to frequent wars, in which the Eleans had the advantage, though they never succeeded in completely absorbing even Pisatis. The chief importance of Elis was derived from the celebration within her territory of the Olympic Games, a festival originally Pisan, of which the direction was assumed by the Eleans, but constantly disputed by the Pisatans. Sparta in the early times supported the Elean claims; but in and after the Peloponnesian struggle it became her policy to uphold the independence of Lepreum. The Eleans dwelt chiefly in villages till after the close of the great Persian War, when the city of Elis was first founded, B.C. 477.

v. *Sicyon.* Sicyon was believed to have been one of the oldest cities in Greece, and to have had kings of its own at a very remote period. Homer, however, represents it as forming, at the time of the Trojan War, part of the dominions of Agamemnon. Nothing can be said to be really known of Sicyon until the time of the Doric immigration into the Peloponnese, when it was occupied by a body of Dorians from Argos, at whose head was Phalces, son of Temenus. A Heracleid monarchy was established in the line of this prince's descendants, which was superseded after some centuries by an oligarchy. Power during this period was wholly confined to the Dorians; the native non-Doric element in the population, which was numerous, being destitute of political privilege. But towards the beginning of the seventh century B.C. a change occurred. Orthagoras, a non-Dorian, said to have been by profession a cook, subverted the oligarchy, established himself upon the throne, and quietly transferred the predominance in the state from the Dorian to the non-Dorian population. He left his throne to his posterity, who ruled for above a hundred years. Clisthenes, the last monarch of the line, adding insult to injury, changed the names of the Dorian tribes in Sicyon from Hyllæi, Dymanes, and Pamphyli, to Hyatæ, Oneatæ, and Chæreatæ, or "Pig-folk," "Ass-folk," and "Swine-folk." He reigned from about B.C. 595 to 560. About sixty years after his death, the Dorians in Sicyon seem to have recovered their preponderance, and the state became one of the most submissive members of the Lacedæmonian confederacy.

B. *Smaller States of Central Greece.*

i. *Megaris.* Megaris was occupied by Dorians from Corinth, shortly after the great immigration into the Peloponnese. At first the colony seems to have been subject to the mother country; but this subjection was soon thrown off, and we find Corinth fomenting quarrels among the various Megarian towns—Megara, Heræa, Peiræa, Tripodiscus, and Cynosura—in the hope of recovering her influence. About B.C. 726 the Corinthians seem to have made an attempt at conquest, which was repulsed by Orsippus, the Olympian runner. Nearly at the same time commenced the series of Megarian colonies, which form so remarkable a feature in the history of this state. The first of these was Megara Hyblæa, near Syracuse, founded (according to Thucydides) in B.C. 728, from which was sent out a sub-colony to Selinus; then followed Chalcedon, in B.C. 674; Byzantium, in B.C. 657; Selymbria, in B.C. 662; Heraclea Pontica, in B.C. 559; and Chersonesus, near the modern Sebastopol, not long afterwards. The naval power of Megara must have been considerable; and it is not surprising to find that about this time (B.C. 600) she disputed with Athens the possession of Salamis. Her despot, Theagenes, was an enterprising and energetic monarch. Rising to power as the representative of the popular cause (about B.C. 630), he supported his son-in-law, Cylon, in his attempt to occupy a similar position at Athens. (See p. 155.) He adorned Megara with splendid buildings. He probably seized Salamis, and gained the victories which induced the Athenians for a time to put up with their loss. On his deposition by the oligarchs (about B.C. 600), the war was renewed—Nisæa was taken by Pisistratus, and Salamis recovered by Cylon. The oligarchs ruled without bloodshed, but still oppressively; so that shortly afterwards there was a second democratic revolution. Debts were now abolished, and even the return of the interest paid on them exacted (*παλιντοκία*). The rich were forced to entertain the poor in their houses. Temples and pilgrims are said to have been plundered. Vast numbers of the nobles were banished. At length the exiles were so numerous that they formed an army, invaded the country, and, reinstating themselves by force, established a somewhat narrow oligarchy, which ruled at least till B.C. 460.

ii. *Bœotia.* When the Bœotians, expelled from Arné by the Thessalians, settled in the country to which they henceforth gave name, expelling from it in their turn the Cadmæans, Minyæ, etc., they seem to have divided themselves into as many states as there were cities. What the form of government in the several states was at first is uncertain; we can only say that there is no trace of monarchy, and that as soon as we obtain a glimpse of the internal affairs of any of them, they are oligarchical republics. The number of the states seems to have been originally fourteen, but by the time of the Peloponnesian War it had dwindled to ten, partly by a process of absorption, partly by separation. Oropus, Eleutheræ, and Platæa had been lost to

Athens; Chæroneia had been incorporated with Orchomenus; the remaining ten states were Thebes, Orchomenus, Thespiæ, Lebadeia, Coroneia, Copæ, Haliartus, Tanagra, Anthedon, and perhaps Chalia. Between these states there had existed, probably from the first, an Amphictyony, or religious union, which had the temple of Itonian Athênê near Coroneia for its centre; and there took place once a year the celebration of the Pambœotia, or general festival of the Bœotians. By degrees, out of this religious association there grew up a federal union; the states recognized themselves as constituting a single political unit, and arranged among themselves a real federal government. The supreme authority was placed in the hands of a council (*βουλή*), which had a curious fourfold division; while the executive functions were exercised by eleven Bœotarchs (two from Thebes, one from each of the other cities), who were at once the generals of the league and its presiding magistrates. Though the place of meeting for the council seems to have been Coroneia, yet Thebes by her superior size and power obtained an undue predominance in the confederation, and used it in such a way as to excite the jealousy and disaffection of almost all the other cities. As early as B.C. 510, Platæa was driven to detach herself from the confederation, and to put herself under the protection of Athens. In later times Thespiæ made more than one attempt to follow the Platæan example, B.C. 423 and 414. The readiness of Athens to receive and protect revolted members of the league was among the causes of that hostility which Bœotia was always ready to display towards her; and the general tendency of members of the league to revolt was among the chief causes of that political weakness which Bœotia exhibits, as compared with Athens and Sparta.

iii. *Phocis.* There can be no doubt that Phocis was, like Bœotia, a confederation; but from the comparative insignificance of the state no details of the constitution have come down to us. The place of meeting for the deputies seems to have been an isolated building (*τὸ Φωκικόν*) on the route from Daulis to Delphi. No Phocian city had any such preponderance as belonged to Thebes among the cities of Bœotia, and hence the league appears to have been free from those perpetual jealousies and heartburnings which we remark in the neighboring country. Still certain secessions from the confederacy appear to have taken place, as that of Delphi, and, again, that of Cirrha, which was a separate state about B.C. 600. A constant enmity existed between Phocis and Thessaly, consequent upon the attempts made by the Thessalians from time to time to conquer the country. These attempts were successfully resisted; but they were so far injurious to the independence of Phocis, that they produced a tendency to lean on Bœotia and to look to her for aid. Still, the military history of Phocis down to the close of the Persian War is creditable to the nation, which frequently repulsed the invasions of the Thessalians, and which offered a brave resistance to the enormous host of Xerxes.

iv. *Locris.* There were three countries of this name; and though a certain ethnic connection between them may be assumed from the common appellation, yet politically the three countries appear to have been entirely separate and distinct. The Locri Ozolæ (the "stinking Locri") possessed the largest and most important tract, that lying between Parnassus and the Corinthian Gulf, bounded on the west by Ætolia. They probably formed a confederacy under the presidency of Amphissa. The Locri Epicnemidii, or Locrians of Mount Cnemis, and the Locri Opuntii, or those of Opus, were separated from their western brethren by the whole breadth of the territory of Phocis. They were also separated from each other, but only by a narrow strip or tongue of Phocian territory, which ran down to the Euripus at the town of Daphnus. Of the internal organization of the Epicnemidii we know nothing. The Opuntians were probably a confederacy under the hegemony of Opus.

v. *Ætolia.* Ætolia, the country of Diomed, though famous in the early times, fell back during the migratory period almost into a savage condition, probably through the influx into it of an Illyrian population which became only partially Hellenized. The nation was divided into numerous tribes, among which the most important were the Apodoti, the Ophioneis, the Eurytanes, and the Agræans. There were scarcely any cities, village life being preferred universally. No traces appear of a confederation of the tribes until the time of Alexander, though in times of danger they could unite for purposes of defense against the common enemy. The Agræans, so late as the Peloponnesian War, were under the government of a king: the political condition of the other tribes is unknown. It was not till the wars which arose among Alexander's successors that the Ætolians formed a real political union, and became an important power in Greece.

vi. *Acarnania.* The Acarnanians were among the more backward of the Greek nations in the historical times, but they were considerably more advanced than the Ætolians. They possessed a number of cities, among which the most important were Stratus, Amphilochian Argos, and Œniadæ. From a very remote date they had formed themselves into a federation, which not only held the usual assemblies for federal purposes (probably at Stratus), but had also a common Court of Justice (*δικαστήριον*) for the decision of causes, at Olpæ. There was great jealousy between the native Acarnanians and the colonies planted by the Corinthians on or near their coasts, Ambracia, Leucas, Anactorium, Sollium, and Astacus, which in the early times certainly did not belong to the league. The league itself was of the lax character usual in Greece, and allowed of the several cities forming their own alliances, and even taking opposite sides in a war.

C. *States of Northern Greece.*

i. *Thessaly.* The Thesprotian conquerors of Thessaly established a condition of things in that country not very unlike that which the Dorians introduced into Laconia. The conquerors themselves formed a noble class which claimed the ownership of most of the territory and confined to itself the possession of political power. The conquered were reduced to two very different positions: some retained their personal freedom and the right to their lands, but were made subject to tribute; others (the *Penestæ*) were reduced to the condition of serfs, cultivating the lands of their masters, but were protected in their holdings, could not be sold out of the country, and both might and did often acquire considerable property. The chief differences between the two countries were (1) that in Thessaly the intermediate class, Achæans, Magnetes, Perrhæbi, etc., instead of being scattered over the country and intermixed with the nobles and serfs, were the sole occupants of certain districts, retained their old ethnic name, their Amphictyonic vote, and their governmental organization; and (2) that the conquerors, instead of concentrating themselves in one city, took possession of several, establishing in each a distinct and separate government. The governments seem to have been originally monarchies, which merged in aristocracies, wherein one family held a quasi-royal position. The Aleuadæ at Larissa and Pharsalus (?) and the Scopadæ at Cranon correspond closely to the Medontidæ at Athens (see page 154). A federal tie of the weakest character united the several states of Thessaly in ordinary times; but upon occasions this extreme laxity was replaced by a most stringent centralization. A Tagus (Commander-in-Chief) of all Thessaly was appointed, who exercised powers little short of despotic over the whole country. Such, apparently, was the power wielded (about B.C. 510) by Cineas, and such beyond all question was the dominion of Jason of Pheræ, and his three brothers, Polydorus, Polyphron, and Alexander, B.C. 380 to 356. In the remoter times Thessaly was aggressive and menaced the independence of the states of Central Greece; but from the dawn of exact history to the time of Jason her general policy was peaceful, and, except as an occasional ally of Athens, she is not found to have taken any part in the internal quarrels of the Greeks. Her aristocracies were selfish, luxurious, and devoid of patriotic feeling: content with their position at home, they did not desire the glory of foreign conquest. Thus Thessaly plays a part in the history of Greece very disproportioned to her power and resources, not rising into any importance till very shortly before the Macedonian period.

ii. *Epirus.* Anterior to the Persian wars, and indeed until the time of Philip of Macedon, Epirus was a mere geographical expression, designating no ethnic nor political unity. The tract so called was parcelled out among a number of states, some of which were Greek, others barbarian. Of these the chief were: (1) the semi-barbarous kingdom of the Molossians, ruled over by a family which claimed descent from Achilles—a constitutional monarchy, where the king and people alike swore to observe the laws; (2) the kingdom of the Orestæ, barbarian; (3) the kingdom of the Parauæi, likewise barbarian; (4) the republic of the Chaonians, barbarian, administered by two annual magistrates chosen out of a single ruling family; (5) the republic of the Thesprotians, barbarian; and (6) the Ambracian republic, Greek, a colony and dependency of Corinth. By alliance with Philip of Macedon, the Molossian kings were enabled to bring the Epirotic states under their dominion, about B.C. 350. After their fall, B.C. 239, Epirus became a federal republic.

D. *Greek Insular States.*

i. *Corcyra.* Corcyra, the most western of the Greek islands, was colonized from Corinth about B.C. 730. From the fertility of the island, and the advantages of its situation, the settlement soon became important: a jealousy sprang up between it and the mother country, which led to hostilities as early as B.C. 670. During the rule of the Cypselid princes at Corinth, Corcyra was forced to submit to them; but soon after their fall independence was recovered. From this time till the commencement of the Peloponnesian War, the commerce and naval power of Corcyra went on increasing; so early as the time of the invasion of Xerxes (B.C. 480) their navy was the second in Greece, and just before the Peloponnesian War it amounted to 120 triremes. The government was a republic, which fluctuated between aristocracy and democracy; party spirit ran high; and both sides were guilty of grievous excesses. On the connection of Corcyra with Athens, see p. 203.

ii. *Cephallenia.* This island, though considerably larger than Corcyra, and exceedingly fertile, was politically insignificant. It contained four cities, each of which was a distinct state, Palé, Cranii, Samé, and Pronus or Pronesus. Probably the four were united in a sort of loose confederation. Palé seems to have been the most important of the cities.

iii. *Zacynthus*, which was originally peopled by Achæans from the Peloponnese, formed an independent state till the time of the Athenian confederacy. It had a single city, of the same name with the island itself, and is chiefly noted in the early ages as furnishing an asylum to fugitives from Sparta.

iv. *Ægina* is said to have been occupied by Dorian colonists from Epidaurus shortly after the invasion of the Peloponnese. It was at first completely dependent on the mother country; but, growing in naval power, it in a little time shook off the yoke, and became one of the most flourishing of the Grecian communities. The Æginetans early provoked the jealousy of Samos, and a war followed between the two powers, which had no very important consequences. About B.C. 500, Ægina found a more dangerous rival in her near neighbor, Athens, whose growing greatness she endeavored to check, in combination with Bœotia. A naval war, which lasted about twenty years, was terminated, B.C. 481, by the common danger which threatened all Greece from the armament collected by Xerxes. Ægina played an important part in the Persian struggle; but still it was one of the effects of the war to exalt her rival, Athens, to a very decided pre-eminence above all the other naval powers of Greece. Not content, however, with mere preponderance, Athens, on breaking with Sparta, B.C. 461, proceeded to crush Ægina, which resisted for four years, but in B.C. 457 became an Athenian dependency.

K. O. MÜLLER, *Ægineticorum liber.* Berlin, 1817; 8vo. This work contains, besides the political history, an account of Æginetan commerce and art.

COCKERELL, *Temples of Ægina and Bassæ.* London, 1860; folio. Contains a full account of the discoveries made in the island by the author and others in 1811 and 1812. The sculptures obtained by the exploring party are in the Glyptothek at Munich.

v. *Eubœa.* This large island contained a number of separate and independent states, whereof the two most important were Eretria and Chalcis. These cities rose to eminence at an early period, and contended together in a great war, wherein most of the Greeks of Europe, and even some from Asia, took part. The balance of advantage seems to have rested with Chalcis, which in the later times always appears as the chief city of the island. Chalcis sent out numerous and important colonies, as Cuma and Rhegium in Italy; Naxos, Leontini, Catana, and Zanclé in Sicily; Olynthus, Toroné, and many other places on the coast of Thrace. Its constitution was oligarchical, the chief power being lodged in the hands of the "Horse-keepers" (ἱπποβόται), or Knights. About B.C. 500, Chalcis was induced to join the Spartans and Bœotians in an attempt to crush Athens, which failed, and cost Chalcis its independence. The lands of the Hippobotæ were confiscated, and an Athenian colony established in the place. Chalcis, together with the rest of Eubœa, revolted from Athens in B.C. 445, but was again reduced by Pericles. In the Peloponnesian War, B.C. 411, better success attended a second effort.

vi. *The Cyclades.* These islands are said to have been originally peopled by Carians from Asia Minor; but about the time of the great migrations (B.C. 1200 to 1000) they were occupied by the Greeks, the more northern by Ionian, the more southern by Dorian adventurers. After a while an Ionian Amphictyony grew up in the northern group, having the islet of Delos for its centre, and the Temple of Apollo there for its place of meeting; whence the position occupied by Delos on the formation of the Athenian confederacy. The largest, and, politically speaking, most important of the Cyclades were Andros and Naxos; the former of which founded the colonies of Acanthus, Sané, Argilus, and Stageirus in Thrace, while the latter repulsed a Persian attack in B.C. 501, and contended against the whole force of Athens in B.C. 466. Paros, famous for its marble, may be placed next to Andros and Naxos. It was the mother city of Thasos, and of Pharos in Illyria. Little is known of the constitutional history of any of the Cyclades. Naxos, however, seems to have gone through the usual course of Greek revolutionary change, being governed by an oligarchy until the time of Lygdamis (B.C. 540 to 530), who, professing to espouse the popular cause, made himself king. His tyranny did not last long, and an oligarchy was once more established, which in its turn gave way to a democracy before B.C. 501.

vii. *Lemnos.* This island, which had a Thracian population in the earliest times and then a Pelasgic one, was first Hellenized after its conquest, about B.C. 500, by the great Miltiades. It was from this time regarded as an Athenian possession, and seems to have received a strong body of colonists from Athens. Lemnos contained two towns, Hephæstia and Myrina, which formed separate states at the time of the Athenian conquest. Hephæstia was at that time under a king.

viii. *Thasos*, which was peculiarly rich in minerals, was early colonized by the Phœnicians, who worked the mines very successfully. Ionians from Paros Hellenized it about B.C. 720 to 700, and soon raised it into a powerful state. Settlements were made by the Thasians upon the main-land opposite their northern shores, whereof the most important were Scapté-Hylé and Datum. The gold-mines in this quarter were largely worked, and in B.C. 492 the Thasians had an annual revenue of from 200 to 300 talents (£48,000 to £72,000). In B.C. 494, Histiæus of Miletus attempted to reduce the island, but failed; it was, however, in the following year forced to submit to the Persians. On the defeat of Xerxes, Thasos became a member of the Athenian confederacy, but revolting, B.C. 465, was attacked and forced to submit, B.C. 463. In the Peloponnesian War another revolt (B.C. 411) was again followed by submission, B.C. 408, and Thasos thenceforth continued, except for short intervals, subject to Athens.

ix. *Crete.* The population of Crete in the early times was of a very mixed character. Homer enumerates among its inhabitants Achæans, Eteocretes, Cydonians, Dorians, and Pelasgi. Of these the Eteocretes and Cydonians were even farther removed than the Pelasgi from the Hellenic type. In the early days the Cretans were famous pirates, whence probably the traditions of Minos and his naval power. Whether the Dorian population was really settled in the island from a remote antiquity, or reached Crete from the Peloponnese after the Dorian conquest of the Achæan kingdoms, is a disputed point; but the latter view is, on the whole, the more probable. In the historical times the Dorian element had a decided preponderance over all the rest, and institutions prevailed in all the chief cities which had a strong resemblance to those of Sparta. The Spartan division of the freemen into citizens and *periœci* existed only in Crete; and, though the latter country had no Helots, their place was supplied by slaves, public and private, who cultivated the lands for their masters. Among these last a system of *syssitia*, closely resembling the Spartan, was established; and a military training similar in character, though less severe. The island was parcelled out among a number of separate states, often at war with one another, but wise enough to unite generally against a common enemy. Of these states the most powerful were Gnossus and Gortyna, each of which aspired to exercise a hegemony over the whole island. Next in importance was Cydonia, and in later times Lyctus, or Lyttus. Originally the cities were ruled by hereditary kings; but ere long their place was taken by elected Cosmi, ten in each community, who held office for a certain period, probably a year, and were chosen from certain families. Side by side with this executive board, there existed in each community a senate (γερουσία), composed of all who had served the office of Cosmos with credit, and constituting really the chief power in the state. There was, further, an assembly (ἐκκλησία) comprising all the citizens, which accepted or rejected the measures submitted to it, but had no initiative, and no power of debate or amendment. Crete took no part in the general affairs of Greece till after the time of Alexander. It maintained a policy of abstinence during both the Persian and Peloponnesian Wars. The military character of the Cretans was, however, maintained, both by the frequent quarrels of the states one with another, and by the common practice of taking service as mercenaries.

The institutions and history of Crete have been made the subject of elaborate comment by several very laborious writers. The best works are those of

Meursius, *Creta, Cyprus, Rhodus.* Amsterdam, 1675; 4to. A most valuable collection of all that ancient writers have said on the subject.

Höck, *Kreta.* Göttingen, 1829; 3 vols. 8vo. Particularly ample in all that concerns the early, or mythological, history.

Neumann, K. F., *Rerum Creticarum specimen.* Göttingen, 1820.

x. *Cyprus.* This island seems to have been originally occupied by the Kittim, a Japhetic race, who left their name in the old capital, Citium (Κίτιον). Soon after the first development of Phœnician power, however, it passed into the possession of that people, who long continued the predominant race in the island. When Hellenic colonists first began to flow into it is doubtful; but there is evidence that by the time of Sargon (B.C. 720 to 700) a large portion of the island was Greek, and under Esarhaddon all the cities, except Paphos, Tamisus, and Aphrodisias, appear to have been ruled by Greek kings. Cyprus seems scarcely ever for any length of time to have been independent. It was held by the Phœnicians from about B.C. 1100 to 725, by the Assyrians from about B.C. 700 to 650, by the Egyptians from about B.C. 550 to 525, and by the Persians from B.C. 525 to 333. The most important of the cities, which, by whomsoever founded, eventually became Greek, were Salamis and Ammochosta (now Famagusta) on the eastern coast; Citium, Curium, and Paphos on the southern; Soli and Lapêthus on the northern; and Limenia, Tamasus, and Idalium in the interior. Amathus continued always Phœnician. The most flourishing of the Greek states was Salamis; and the later history of the island is closely connected with that of the Salaminian kings. Among these were: 1. Evelthon, contemporary with Arcesilaus III. of Cyrene, about B.C. 530; 2. Gorgus; and 3. Onesilus, contemporary with Darius Hystaspis, B.C. 520 to 500. The latter joined in the Ionian revolt, but was defeated and slain. 4. Evagoras I., contemporary with Artaxerxes Longimanus, B.C. 449. 5. Evagoras II., contemporary with Artaxerxes Mnemon, B.C. 391 to 370. This prince rebelled, and, assisted by the Athenians and Egyptians, carried on a long war against the Persians, but, after the Peace of Antalcidas, was forced to submit, B.C. 380, retaining, however, his sovereignty. 6. Protagoras, brother of Evagoras II., contemporary with Artaxerxes Ochus, B.C. 350. He banished Evagoras, son of Evagoras II., and joined the great revolt which followed Ochus's first and unsuccessful expedition against Egypt. This revolt was put down before B.C. 346, by the aid of mercenaries commanded by Phocion; and thenceforth Cyprus continued faithful to Persia, till Alexander's victory at Issus, when the nine kings of the island voluntarily transferred their allegiance to Macedon, B.C. 333.

The best and fullest account of the history of Cyprus will be found in the work of MEURSIUS, mentioned above. On the geography of the island the student may consult with profit—

ENGEL, *Kypros.* Berlin, 1841; 8vo.

ROSS, *Reisen nach Kos, Halicarnassus, Rhodos, und der Inseln Cypern.* Halle, 1852.

E. *Greek Colonies.*

The chief works treating the subject generally are the following:

RAOUL-ROCHETTE, *Histoire critique de l'établissement des Colonies Grècques.* Paris, 1815; 4 vols., 8vo. A most erudite and comprehensive work, but deficient in *critique.*

HEGEWISCH, D. H., *Geographische und historische Nachrichten, die Colonien der Griechen betreffend.* Altona, 1848; 8vo. Clear and concise.

ST. CROIX, *De l'état et du sort des Colonies des anciens peuples.* Philadelphia, 1779.

BOUGAINVILLE, J. P., *Quels étoient les droits des Métropoles Grècques sur les colonies; les devoirs des colonies envers les métropoles; et les engagements réciproques des unes et des autres?* Paris, 1745.

HERMANN, K. F., *Lehrbuch, etc.* (see p. 144), chap. iv. pp. 73-90. The best synopsis of the subject.

Hellenic colonies. Their number and wide diffusion.

1. The number of the Greek colonies, and their wide diffusion, are very remarkable. From the extreme recess of the Sea of Azov to the mouth of the Mediterranean, almost the entire coast, both of continents and islands, was studded with the settle-

ments of this active and energetic people. Most thickly were these sown towards the north and the north-east, more sparingly towards the south and west, where a rival civilization—the Phœnician—cramped, though it could not crush, Grecian enterprise. Carthage and Tyre would fain have kept exclusively in their own hands these regions; but the Greeks forced themselves in here and there, as in Egypt and in the Cyrenaïca; while of their own northern shore, except in Spain, they held exclusive possession, meeting their rivals in the islands of Corsica, Sardinia, Sicily, and Cyprus.

2. The main causes of the spread of the Greeks from their proper home in the Hellenic peninsula, over so many and such distant regions, were two in number. The race was prolific, and often found itself cramped for room, either from the mere natural increase of population, or from the pressure upon it of larger and more powerful nations. Hence arose movements which were, properly speaking, *migrations*, though the term "colonization" has been improperly applied to them. To this class belong the Æolian, Ionian, and Dorian settlements in Asia, and the Achæan in Italy. But the more usual cause of movement was commercial or political enterprise, the state which founded a settlement being desirous of extending its influence or its trade into a new region. Such settlements were *colonies* proper; and between these and the mother country there was always, at any rate at first, a certain connection, which was absent in the case of settlements arising out of migrations. Occasionally individual caprice or political disturbance led to the foundation of a new city; but such cases were comparatively rare, and require only a passing mention.

Origin of the settlements two-fold.

3. The colonies proper of the Greeks were of two kinds, ἀποικίαι and κληρουχίαι. In the former, the political connection between the mother country and the colony was slight and weak; in the latter, it was exceedingly close and strong. Ἀποικίαι were, in fact, independent communities, attached to the mother country merely by affection and by certain generally prevalent usages, which, however, were neither altogether obligatory nor very definite. The colony usually worshipped as a hero its original founder (οἰκιστής), and honored the same gods as the par-

Colonies proper. Their relation with their parent states.

ent city. It bore part in the great festivals of its *metropolis*, and contributed offerings to them. It distinguished by special honors at its own games and festivals the citizens of the parent community. It used the same emblems upon its coins. Its chief-priests were, in some instances, drawn continually from the mother state; and, if it designed to found a new settlement itself, it sought a leader from the same quarter. War between a parent city and a colony was regarded as impious, and a certain obligation lay on each to assist the other in times of danger. But the observance of these various usages was altogether voluntary; no attempt was ever made to enforce them, the complete political independence of the ἀποικία being always understood and acknowledged. In the κληρουχία the case was wholly different. There the state sent out a body of its citizens to form a new community in territory which it regarded as its own; the settlers retained all their rights as citizens of their old country, and in their new one were mainly a garrison intended to maintain the authority of those who sent them out. The dependence of κληρουχίαι on the parent state was thus entire and absolute. The cleruchs were merely citizens of their old state, to whom certain special duties had been assigned and certain benefits granted.

'Αποικίαι, how different from κληρουχίαι.

4. The Greek settlements of whatsoever kind may be divided geographically into the Eastern, the Western, and the Southern. Under the first head will come those of the eastern and northern shores of the Ægean, those of the Propontis, of the Black Sea, and of the Sea of Azov; under the second, those of Italy, Sicily, Gaul, Spain, and the adjacent islands; under the third, those of Africa. The order of this arrangement coincides, speaking broadly, with the chronological succession, and it will therefore be observed in the summary now to be given.

Geographical division of the settlements.

Colonies of the Eastern Group.

i. *On the East Coast of the Ægean.* These colonies are usually subdivided into the Æolian, the Ionian, and the Dorian, or those on the Mysian, those on the Lydian, and those on the Carian sea-board.

(*a*) *The Æolian Colonies.* The origin of these colonies is to be sought in the first of the two great migratory movements in Greece Proper. When the Bœotians driven out of Arné in Thessaly, dispossessed the Cadmeians,

Minyæ, and others of the tract thenceforward known as Bœotia, a portion of the inhabitants, including a number of refugees, quitted the country and proceeded in search of new homes under Bœotian (*i. e.*, Æolian) leaders. (See First Period, §§ 9 and 11.) Following the course of the Trojan expedition, these emigrants reached the north-western corner of Asia Minor, and there established themselves on the coast and in the islands. In Tenedos they founded a single city of the same name; in Lesbos they built five towns, Mytilênê, Methymna, Antissa, Eresus, and Pyrrha, all of them on the coast; upon the main-land they made twelve settlements, Smyrna, Cuma (or Phricônis), Myrina, Gryneium, and Pitanê, upon the coast, Temnus, Larissa, Neonteichos, Ægæ, certainly, and Cilla, Notium, and Ægiroëssa, probably in the interior. Of these cities Smyrna, which after a while joined the Ionian confederacy, and Cuma (or Cymê) were the most important. In Lesbos, Mytilênê obtained an ascendency over the other towns, having, however, always a jealous rival in Methymna. The Æolian power was spread considerably beyond its original limits by the colonizing efforts of Cuma and Lesbos. The tract between the Gulf of Adramyttium and the Hellespont became Æolian, its chief towns being Antandrus, Gargara, and Assus. Sestus, too, in the Chersonese, and Ænus on the coast of Thrace, were Æolian colonies. The Æolian towns seem in general to have been independent of one another; and there is no evidence that they formed at any time a confederacy, or even an Amphictyony. Their forms of government were various, and often suffered revolutionary changes. Mytilênê, in particular, suffered much from internal commotion, till Pittacus (about B.C. 600), as dictator (*αἰσυμνητής*), established tranquillity. Continental Æolis maintained its independence till the time of Crœsus (B.C. 568), when it was conquered together with Ionia and Doris. In B.C. 554 it passed under the sceptre of Persia. Lesbos continued free till somewhat later, but was subjected before the expedition of Cambyses against Egypt, B.C. 525. She took an important part in the Ionian revolt (B.C. 500 to 494), and was severely punished at its conclusion, B.C. 493. At the same time, Tenedos was subjugated. After the battle of Salamis, Lesbos recovered its independence, and in B.C. 477 became a member of the Athenian confederacy. For many years it was treated with special favor by Athens, but revolting early in the Peloponnesian War (B.C. 428), was conquered, and experienced great harshness. A second revolt, B.C. 412, was equally unsuccessful. After Ægos-potami (B.C. 404), Lesbos fell under Spartan influence, but was recovered to Athens in B.C. 390, and continued a dependency until its freedom was established by the Peace of Antalcidas, B.C. 387. In B.C. 334 it submitted to Alexander.

Special works on Lesbos, worthy of the student's attention, are—

PLEHN, S. L., *Lesbiacorum librer.* Berlin, 1826; 8vo.

LANDER, *Beiträge zur Kunde der Insel Lesbos.* Hamburg, 1827.

(*b*) *The Ionian Colonies.* The Ionian colonies were regarded by the Greeks as having been founded somewhat later than the Æolian. Their origin is to be sought in the second or great Dorian migration. An Ionian population, expelled from the northern coast of the Peloponnese by the fugitive Achæans, sought a refuge in Attica, where it was kindly harbored for a while; but the narrow, infertile, and already well-peopled Attica being insufficient for its needs, a migratory movement began across the Ægean Sea.

Ceos, Cythnus, Seriphus, Siphnus, Paros, Naxos, Syros, Andros, Tenos, Rheneia, Delos, and Myconus were successively occupied by Ionian colonists, who went out in some cases under Attic leaders. From the more eastern of these islands the passage was easy to Asia. Between B.C. 1000 and 800 a series of settlements were made on the Asiatic coasts and islands, directly below the settlements of the Æolians, by a stream of emigrants predominantly Ionian, though comprising also a great intermixture of races, as Abantes, Minyæ, Cadmeians, Dryopians, Phocians, Molossians, Arcadians, Epidaurian Dorians, and others. Twelve of these settlements were pre-eminent, and formed together an Amphictyony, which had its place of meeting at the Temple of Neptune, called the "Panionium," situated on the headland of Mycalé, opposite Samos. The twelve were Miletus, Myus, Priêné, Ephesus, Colophon, Lebedus, Teos, Erythræ, Clazomenæ, and Phocæa, upon the main-land, Samos and Chios upon islands. Of these by far the most important in the early times were Miletus, Phocæa, and Samos. Miletus was the first to develop into a powerful state. As early as B.C. 780 she began to send out that series of colonies which formed her chief glory, and gave her the name of Hecatompolis. The Hellespont, the Propontis, the Euxine, and the Sea of Azov, for the most part, received these settlements, of which an account will be given under other heads. About B.C. 600 Phocæa became distinguished. Her mariners were the first Greeks who explored the Adriatic Sea and the Western Mediterranean, and the only Greeks who are known to have ever adventured themselves beyond the pillars of Hercules into the Atlantic Ocean. They traded with Tartessus in Spain, founded Alalia in Corsica, Massilia on the coast of Gaul, and Elea, or Velia (Vela) in Italy. The rise of Samos to greatness was not much prior to B.C. 540. She owed her splendor chiefly to the tyrant Polycrates, the friend of Amasis of Egypt, under whom the arts flourished, commerce was developed, and the dominion of Samos extended over many of the Ægean Islands. The Ionian Greeks maintained their independence uninterruptedly till the rise of the Mermnad dynasty in Lydia, when they were made the object of a series of attacks by the Lydian kings, which led to their gradual subjection. Colophon was reduced by Gyges, about B.C. 700; Priêné by Ardys, about 650; Smyrna, after it had become Ionian, by Alyattes, about B.C. 620. Miletus, which had been attacked, successively, by every Mermnad king, was finally forced, with the rest of the Ionian towns, to submit to Crœsus, about B.C. 565. On the fall of the Lydian empire, B.C. 554, all the Ionian states, except Chios and Samos, passed under the yoke of Persia. Chios and Samos seem to have submitted to Cambyses, about B.C. 526. About this time it appears that most of the states were under the government of tyrants. The machinations of one of these, Histiæus of Miletus, and of his vicegerent, Aristagoras, led to the great revolt in the reign of Darius Hystaspis (B.C. 500), suppressed after six years of struggle with a severity which completely broke the power of Miletus and greatly reduced that of almost all the other states. Henceforth the most important states were Samos, Chios, and Ephesus. Samos, which invited the Greek fleet to Asia after Salamis (B.C. 479), and played an important part at Mycalé, entered readily into the Athenian confederacy, B.C. 477, and supported the measures by which Athens established her empire, but revolting in B.C. 440, was forcibly reduced by Pericles. She remained faithful to Athens throughout the Peloponnesian War, during the later part of which she was the head-quarters of Athenian power. Becoming free in B.C. 404, she was, about B.C. 380, recovered by Persia. Reconquered by Timotheus in B.C. 365, she passed into the number of Athenian *cleruchiæ*, and occupied this position till the time of Alexander. Chios, which revolted from Persia after Mycalé, became, like Samos, a member of the Athenian confederacy in B.C. 477, and continued faithful till B.C. 413, when it made alliance with the Spartans. The attempts of Athens to recover it by force of arms all failed; but in B.C. 378 it entered voluntarily into the restored Athenian confederation, in which it continued till B.C. 358, when, in conjunction with Cos, Rhodes, and Byzantium, it seceded. The "Social War" followed, by which Chios re-established her independence, B.C. 356. In B.C. 333 Chios was recovered to Persia by Memnon of Rhodes, but the next year it submitted to Alexander. Ephesus, insignificant during the early times, acquired the favor of the Persians by abstention from the Ionian revolt. Thenceforth it grew in power and wealth, succeeding apparently to the commercial position of Miletus and Phocæa. Its great glory was its Temple of Artemis, which was twice burnt—first by the Cimmerians, about B.C. 650, and again (B.C. 356) by Herostratus. In the Macedonian and Roman times, Ephesus was regarded as the first city of Asia Minor.

Several important works have been written on the history of Miletus. Among them may be noticed—

RAMBACH, F. E., *De Mileto ejusque coloniis.* Halle, 1790; 4to.

SOLDAN, G. T., *Rerum Milesiarum commentarius.* Darmstadt, 1829.

SCHRÖDER, A., *Rerum Milesiarum particula I.* Stralsund, 1827.

The best and fullest account of the history of Samos will be found in

PANOFKA, T., *Res Samiorum.* Berlin, 1822.

(*c*) *The Dorian Colonies.* These colonies issued from the Peloponnese during the time that the Dorians were gradually conquering it. The bulk of the colonists were often of some other race (as Achæans, Minyæ, etc.); but they went out under Doric leaders. The course taken by the emigrants was through the southern Cyclades, where Melos, Pholegandrus, Thera, Anaphé, and Astypalæa were reckoned as Dorian settlements. But the most important of the colonies were planted on the Asiatic coast and in the littoral islands. Three in Rhodes, Ialyssus, Lindus, and Cameirus; one in Cos, bearing the same name as the island; and two upon the main-land, Halicarnassus and Cnidus, formed originally an Amphictyony, which met at the Triopium, or Temple of Apollo Triopius, situated near the last-named city. But Halicarnassus, after a while, was excluded from the confederation. Other cities of Dorian origin, which did not, however, at any time belong to the Amphictyony, seem to have been Myndus, near Halicarnassus, and Phasêlis, on the coast of Lycia. The islands Calymna, Nisyrus, Telos, and Chalcia had also a Doric population. The Dorian colonies maintained their independence from their original foundation to the time of Crœsus, who reduced Halicarnassus, Myndus, and Cnidus. At the fall of the Lydian empire, these cities transferred their allegiance to Persia; and their example was followed by the island towns when Phœnicia submitted to Cambyses. The Dorians took no part in the Ionian revolt; and the cities were for the most part undistinguished until the time of Alexander. Halicarnassus, the birth-place of Herodotus, forms the only notable exception. Here, under the Persian kings, a dynasty of Hellenized Carians established itself, which held not only Halicarnassus, but most of Caria, together with Cos, Calymna, and Nisyrus. To this belonged, 1. A king, whose name is unknown, about B.C. 500, contemporary with Darius; 2. Artemisia, his widow, contemporary with and in the confidence of Xerxes, B.C. 480; 3. Pisindelis, her son, about B.C. 460; 4. Lygdamis, son of Pisindelis, about B.C. 450. Under him the monarchy came to an end, and Halicarnassus joined the Athenian confederacy. It was recovered by Persia after the Peace of Antalcidas, B.C. 387; and the old royal family seems to have been restored. We find, 5. Hecatomnus, king B.C. 380. He is succeeded, about B.C. 377, by 6. his son, Mausôlus, who is followed by his widow and sister, 7. Artemisia II., B.C. 353, the builder of the famous "Mausoleum." Artemisia dying, B.C. 351, the crown falls to 8. Idrieus, second son of Hecatomnus, who reigns seven years, and is succeeded by his widow and sister, 9. Ada. She is driven out, after reigning four years, by 10. her brother, Pixodarus, the third son of Hecatomnus, who dies after a reign of five years, B.C. 335; and is followed by 11. his son-in-law, Orontobates, king when the city is besieged by Alexander.

The sites of Cnidus and Halicarnassus have recently been very carefully explored. For a full account of the explorations, see the magnificently illustrated work of Mr. NEWTON, entitled *A History of Discoveries at Halicarnassus, Cnidus, and Branchidæ.* London, 1862; 2 vols. folio.

A good monograph on the subject of Cos was published in 1833 by KÜSTER. (*De Co insulâ.* Halle; 8vo.)

ii. *On the North Coast of the Ægean.* These settlements extended almost continuously along the entire coast from Methônê, in Pieria, to the Chersonese. They may be divided into western, central, and eastern.

(*a*) *Western Group.* This comprised Methônê, on the eastern coast of the Thermaic Gulf, which was a colony from Eretria, founded about B.C. 730, and the settlements of the Chalcidic peninsula, including those of the three long projections from it, Pallênê, Sithonia, and Actê, or the peninsula of Athos. The greater part of the settlements in this quarter were made by the town of Chalcis in Eubœa, but some were from Eretria, and several from Andros. Potidæa, the most important of them all in the early times, was a colony from Corinth. The cities of Chalcidian origin were chiefly in Sithonia; they included Torônê, Singus, Sermylê, Galepsus, and Mecyberna. Olynthus became a Chalcidian possession in B.C. 480. The colonies of Eretria were mainly in Pallênê. Among these the most important was Mendê. Andros founded Sanê, near the site of the canal of Xerxes, and Acanthus, Stageirus, and Argilus, on the coast between Athos and Amphipolis. Chalcidicê first became a power in the Peloponnesian War, when its cities, encouraged by Brasidas, revolted from Athens, B.C. 424. It joined the league headed by Argos after the Peace of Nicias, B.C. 421, and the restored Spartan confederacy in B.C. 418. Soon after the close of the Peloponnesian War, Olynthus acquired a preponderating influence in Chalcidicê, and became the head of a league which carried on war successfully with Macedon, B.C. 392 to 383; but, provoking by these successes the jealousy of Sparta, Olynthus was attacked by that state, and forced to become one of her subject allies.

Subsequently the power of the Olynthians was much curtailed by Athens, B.C. 368 to 363; and they were consequently unable to resist the attacks of Philip, even though assisted by Athens, who too late saw her error. Olynthus fell in B.C. 347, and Chalcidicé was swallowed up in Macedon.

(*b*) *Central Group.* This consisted of the cities from the Strymon to the Nestus, which were Amphipolis, Eïon, Myrcinus, Apollonia, Galepsus, Œsymé, Neapolis, Datum, Scapté-Hylé, and Crenides (afterwards Philippi). The earliest of these settlements seem to have been made from Thasos, after it had received its Parian colony; these were Datum, Scapté-Hylé, Œsymé, and Galepsus. Myrcinus, on the Strymonic Lake, was founded by Histiæus of Miletus about B.C. 508. Amphipolis, founded by Athens B.C. 465 (re-founded B.C. 437), grew at once into vast importance from the advantages of its site. It revolted from the Athenians B.C. 424, and, in alliance with Olynthus, resisted all their efforts to subdue it. In B.C. 358 it was taken and annexed by Philip.

(*c*) *Eastern Group.* Under this head come the settlements between the Nestus and the Hellespont, of which the chief were Abdera, founded by the Teians, when their city was threatened by Harpagus, about B.C. 553; Maroneia, a colony of Chios; Mesambria, of Samothrace; Cardia, of Miletus and Clazomenæ; Elæus, of Teos; Ænos, Alopeconnesus, and Sestos of Æolis. Of these Cardia, Elæus, Alopeconnesus, and Sestos were situated in the Chersonese, where were also the Greek cities of Madytus, Callipolis, and Pactya. The Chersonese became a single kingdom under the first Miltiades, about B.C. 560. He was succeeded, about B.C. 523, by his nephew, Stesagoras, who was followed, about B.C. 516, by his brother, the second Miltiades. The Persians conquered it in B.C. 493, and held it till B.C. 479. After this it was alternately subject to Athens and Sparta, till the battle of Chæroneia transferred the headship of Greece to Macedon.

iii. *Colonies of the Propontis.* On the Asiatic shores of the Propontis and the Bosphorus stood Lampsacus, a joint colony of the Phocæans and Milesians; Parium, a colony of Erythræ; Priapus, Artacé, Cyzicus, and Cius, colonies of Miletus; and Chalcedon, a colony of Megara. On the opposite or European shores were Bisanthé and Perinthus, colonies of the Samians, and Byzantium, like Chalcedon, a colony of the Megarians. In mid-sea was Proconnesus, a colony of the Milesians. Of these settlements Byzantium was, owing to its situation, by far the most important. It commanded the entrance to the Black Sea, and consequently controlled at its will the important trade which the Greeks carried on, chiefly for corn, with Thrace and Scythia. Cyzicus, Bisanthé, and Perinthus were also places of some consequence.

On early Byzantine history the student may consult with profit—

HEYNE'S *Antiquitates Byzantinæ; Commentationes duæ.* Göttingen, 1809; 8vo.

iv. *Colonies of the Euxine, the Cimmerian Bosphorus, and the Palus Mæotis.* These colonies were chiefly founded by Miletus; but a few of the most important proceeded from Megara. They extended almost continuously along the northern coast of Asia Minor and the eastern coast of Thrace, but were only occasional between the mouth of the Danube and that of the Phasis. We may subdivide them into (*a*) those in Thrace, (*b*) those in Scythia, and (*c*) those in Asia, south of the Caucasus.

(*a*) *Colonies on the East Coast of Thrace.* Proceeding northward from the Bosphorus, the most important settlements were Apollonia, Mesambria, Odessus, Callatis, Tomi, the scene of Ovid's exile, and Istria or Istropolis. Of these, Apollonia, Odessus, Callatis, Tomi, and Istria were Milesian settlements, while Mesambria was a colony of the Megarians. They were mostly founded in the course of the seventh century. Odessus, Tomi, Callatis, Mesambria, and Apollonia were at one time united in a league, the presidency of which belonged to Odessus. Commercially, the most important of the Thracian settlements seems to have been Istropolis.

(*b*) *Colonies on the Coast of Scythia.* The chief of these were Tyras, at the mouth of the Tyras (Dniester); Olbia, on the estuary of the Hypanis (Bog); Chersonesus Heracleiotica, near the site of the modern Sebastopol; Theudosia, on the site of Kaffa; Panticapæum (afterwards Bosporus), near the modern Kertch; Phanagoria, on the Asiatic coast opposite; and Tanais, in the extreme recess of the Palus Mæotis, at the mouth of the similarly-named river. With the single exception of Chersonesus Heracleiotica, these cities were all colonies of Miletus, founded chiefly in the eighth century. Chersonesus was a colony from Heracleia Pontica, on the opposite coast of Asia Minor, which was itself a colony from Megara. It was founded, probably, about the middle of the fifth century. In the early times, Olbia was the most important of the Scythian colonies; but about B.C. 480 Panticapæum became the great city of these parts. It was the capital of a Græco-Scythic kingdom, called that of the Bosporus, which extended westward beyond Theudosia, and eastward to the mouth of the Kouban, thus including both Theudosia and Phanagoria. A list of the kings is given by Diodorus 1. Spartacus I., reigned from B.C. 438 to 431. 2. Seleucus, reigned from B.C. 431 to 427. 3. Satyrus I., reigned from B.C. 407 to 393. 4. Leucon, his son, reigned from B.C. 393 to 353. 5. Spartacus II., his son, reigned from B.C. 353 to 348. 6. Parysades I., his brother, reigned from B.C. 348 to 310. 7. Satyrus II., his son, reigned nine months. 8. Prytanis, his brother, was deposed by 9. Eumêlus, also his brother, who reigned five years, from B.C. 309 to 304. He was succeeded by 10. Spartacus III., his son, who reigned twenty years, from B.C. 304 to 284. The kingdom seems to have remained after this in the same family till about B.C. 110, when it was handed over by Parysades II. to the great Mithridates. The kings of Bosporus, especially Satyrus I., and his son, Leucon, were on terms of close friendship with Athens, which depended mainly on Bosporus for its corn supplies.

(*c*) *Colonies of the Asiatic Coast, south of the Caucasus.* Commencing at the foot of the Caucasus, these were Dioscurias, in the modern Mingrelia, and Phasis, at the mouth of the Phasis, early colonies of the Milesians; Trapezus (Trebizond), Cerasus, and Cotyora, colonies of Sinôpé; Themiscyra; Amisus, a colony of Phocæa, or perhaps of Miletus; Sinôpé, undoubtedly a colony of Miletus; and Heracleia Pontica, a colony of Megara, founded about B.C. 560. Heracleia, Sinôpé, and Amisus were all cities of great importance. The first, situated in the territory of the Mariandyni, carried on an extensive trade with Scythia and Thrace, extended its dominion over the whole of the Mariandynian country, and at one time possessed the entire coast between the Sangarius and Parthenius rivers. The government was republican, but after contests of the usual character between the aristocratical and democratical parties, became a tyranny in the person of Clearchus, about B.C. 370. Clearchus was assassinated; but the crown continued to be held by his descendants down to the conquests of Alexander.—Sinôpé, founded by Miletus, probably about B.C. 780, was captured by the Cimmerians at the time of their great inroad, and made a sort of head-quarters from which they sent out their expeditions. After their expulsion it was recovered by the Milesians, about B.C. 630, and rose to great prosperity, becoming itself a colonizing power, and exercising a great influence over the neighboring barbarians. The tunny fishery of the Euxine, which it shared with Byzantium, was one of the great sources of its opulence.—Amisus, founded from Ionia about B.C. 600, received an Athenian colony about B.C. 450, and became shortly afterwards one of the most flourishing of the Black Sea settlements. It attained, however, its greatest prosperity under the kings of Pontus, B.C. 380 to 64, who sometimes made it their capital.

Colonies of the Western Group.

The colonies of the Western group include those on the Illyrian coast; those in Italy; those in Sicily; those on the coasts of Gaul and Spain; and those in Corsica and Sardinia.

i. *Colonies on the Coast of Illyria.* The two principal settlements in these parts were Apollonia and Epidamnus, the former a colony from Corinth, the latter from Corcyra. Epidamnus was founded about B.C. 625. It had a highly oligarchical constitution; but in course of time a democratical spirit arose, the state was revolutionized, and most of the oligarchs exiled. Hence arose the struggle which, as much as any thing, brought on the Peloponnesian War. Corinth assisted the oligarchs, Corcyra the democratic faction. The result is unknown to us; but it is probable that the Corcyræans were the victors. From about B.C. 312 Epidamnus was subject to attacks on the part of the Illyrians, which induced her, about B.C. 227, to place herself under the protection of the Romans. The Romans commonly called the city Dyrrhachium. Apollonia, founded by Periander, about B.C. 600, was comparatively insignificant until Roman times, when it became the seat of a university, and acquired a great reputation. Other Greek settlements on this coast were Oricus, near Apollonia; Lissus, north of Epidamnus, founded by the elder Dionysius; and Epidaurus, north-west of Lissus; but these were of small importance.

ii. *Colonies in Italy.* These settlements commenced in Iapygia, and were continued at brief intervals along the entire coast from the extreme eastern point of Italy to Campania on its western shores. The most important were Taras, or Tarentum, in the inner recess of the gulf bearing the same name; Metapontum, Sybaris, and Thurii, on the western coast of the same gulf; Croton, at its south-western extremity; Locri Epizephyrii, lower down, near the southern point of Bruttium; Rhegium, opposite Zanclé in Sicily; Laüs, at the mouth of the Laüs river; Elea, or Velia, on the coast of Lucania; Posidonia, afterwards Pæstum, near the mouth of the Silarus; Palæopolis and Neapolis, in the bay of Naples; and Cymé (Cumæ), beyond the northern extremity of the bay, near Lake Avernus. Of inferior importance were

Hydrus and Callipolis in Iapygia, dependencies of Tarentum; Heracleia and Siris, south of Metapontum, colonies respectively of Tarentum and Colophon; Caulonia, near Locri Epizephyrii, and Terina, on the opposite coast, colonies of Croton; Hipponium, south, and Temesa, north of Terina, colonies of Locri Epizephyrii; Pyxus (Buxentum), between Laüs and Velia, probably a colony of Siris; and Dicæarchia (Puteoli), near Baiæ, a colony of Cumæ. A special historical interest attaches to the following cities:

(*a*) *Taras*, or *Tarentum.* Founded from Sparta by the discontented Parthenii, about B.C. 708. At first overshadowed by the greatness of the Achæan cities, Metapontum, Sybaris, and Croton; but gradually raised to the first position among the Italic states by the excellence of its harbor and the vigor of its semi-Spartan people. Engaged in friendly commerce with Corinth as early as B.C. 600. Carried on successful wars with the Messapians and Peucetians, suffering, however, occasional defeat (as in B.C. 473). Resisted the foundation of Thurii, B.C. 443 to 433; but founded Heracleia in conjunction with the Thurians, B.C. 432. Held aloof from the struggle between Athens and Syracuse, B.C. 415 to 413. Raised to the head of the Italic confederacy against the Lucanians, about B.C. 350. Carried on long wars with frequent foreign aid, inviting successively Archidamus of Sparta, Alexander of Epirus, and Cleonymus of Sparta to its assistance. Came into hostile collision with Rome, B.C. 281, and invited Pyrrhus into Italy. Forced to submit to Rome, B.C. 273. Played an important part in the Second Punic War, B.C. 212 to 209, but after its capture by Fabius sank into a mere luxurious watering-place. The government of Tarentum was originally an aristocracy on the Spartan model, with kings presiding over it; but after the great defeat of the year B.C. 473, it became a decided democracy. The place of the king was taken by an annually elected Strategus; and the lot was introduced and extended to a full half of the magistrates. Archytas, the Pythagorean philosopher, held the office of Strategus for seven years in succession (about B.C. 370).

(*b*) *Metapontum.* Founded by Achæans from the Peloponnese, about B.C. 700 to 690, at the instance of Croton and Sybaris, which wished to be strengthened against Tarentum. Joined in a league with those two cities against the Ionian Siris, which effected the destruction of that place, about the middle of the sixth century B.C. Received Pythagoras on his expulsion from Crotona, about B.C. 520. Joined the Athenians in their attempt to conquer Sicily, B.C. 414. Made alliance with Alexander of Epirus, B.C. 332. Opposed Cleonymus, B.C. 303. Assisted Pyrrhus and Hannibal. Fell under the power of Rome, B.C. 207.

(*c*) *Sybaris.* The earliest of the Greek settlements in this part of Italy, was founded by the Achæans, about B.C. 720, and rapidly attained a great and extraordinary prosperity, which we must ascribe in part to the remarkable fertility of the territory, in part to the hold which the city obtained, through priority of settlement, on the Italian trade. Situated at a point where Italy is abnormally narrow, Sybaris was able to extend her dominion from sea to sea. She brought under several tribes of the Œnotrians, and planted colonies on the western coast of Italy, as especially Posidonia and Laüs. It was a peculiarity of her policy to admit strangers freely to her citizenship; and hence her population increased so enormously that, we are told, she could bring into the field 300,000 men. At the same time, luxury made rapid strides, and the Sybarites became proverbial for their refinement and their effeminate habits. Their trade was extensive. They had an important commerce with Miletus, and probably were for a time the chief carriers between the east and west, or at any rate divided with the Phœnicians this very profitable traffic. The most flourishing time of Sybaris was from B.C. 600 to 550. Its fall was caused by political dissensions. The old oligarchical government was succeeded, about B.C. 520, by a democracy, which was soon exchanged for a tyranny, one Telys obtaining the supreme power. Telys banished 500 of the oligarchs, who fled to Croton, and that city espousing their cause, a war followed, which terminated in the complete destruction of Sybaris, B.C. 510. Efforts were made to re-establish the fallen city, but they failed; and, instead of a new Sybaris, there arose near it the important city of Thurii. The Sybarites found a refuge in their colonies, Laüs and Scidrus.

(*d*) *Thurii.* This city was founded by Pericles, B.C. 443, and was no doubt intended by him to strengthen the Athenian interest in a part of the Grecian world which was almost wholly under the influence of Sparta. Its population was from the first of a mixed character, including a number of the old Sybarites, Greeks from various parts of the Peloponnese, Ionian Greeks, and others. Quarrels soon arose, especially between the Sybarites and the new-comers. The former were worsted and expelled. Fresh colonists were then invited from all parts of Greece; and the state was modelled anew on a democratic basis, but one in which the various ethnic elements were recognized and made the basis of the political organization. The legal code of Charondas was accepted. Thurii now grew in power, and, provoking the jealousy of Tarentum, was attacked by that state, but succeeded in maintaining its independence. In the Peloponnesian War, the Thurians, after some hesitation, joined the Athenians, B.C. 413, but revolted after the Sicilian disasters, and expelled the portion of the population which especially favored Athens. Soon after this, Thurii was attacked by the Lucanians; and a long war followed, generally to the disadvantage of the Thurians, who suffered one very signal defeat, B.C. 390. About B.C. 286 they implored the aid of the Romans, which brought upon them a new enemy in the Tarentines, who took and plundered the city, B.C. 283. Thurii was from this time a Roman dependency, occasionally wavering in its allegiance, as especially during the Second Punic War. It gradually declined in power, and at length, B.C. 194, received a Roman colony, and ceased altogether to be a distinct state.

(*e*) *Croton*, or *Crotona*, was founded by Achæans from the Peloponnese, shortly after the foundation of Sybaris, B.C. 710 probably. It rapidly rose to almost equal prosperity with its sister city, sending out colonies to Caulonia, near Locri, and to Terina on the opposite or western coast of Italy, and exercising a paramount authority over all the native races in its neighborhood. Less populous than Sybaris, but still able to bring into the field armies of 100,000 men and upward, it compensated for this inferiority by a special attention to athletic training, an attention evidenced by the number of Crotoniat victors at the Olympic Games. At the same time its citizens cultivated with success the science of medicine. The first war in which we find Croton engaged was one with the Locrians and Rhegines, who completely defeated her forces at the river Sagras, about B.C. 550. Soon after this she received the Samian refugee Pythagoras, who quickly acquired a great influence in the state by the secret society which he set up. The government was at the time a moderate oligarchy, power being in the hands of a Council of One Thousand, the descendants and representatives of the original settlers. The Pythagoreans were suspected of an intention to narrow the basis of the government, and were consequently expelled about B.C. 510, the constitution being at the same time revolutionized in a democratical sense. The Council of One Thousand was superseded by a new senate, taken by lot from the whole body of the citizens; and the principle was established that all magistrates should be accountable at the expiration of their term of office. This expulsion took place notwithstanding a signal military success gained during the Pythagorean ascendency, and attributable in great measure to the Pythagorean athlete, Milo. It was while the friends of Pythagoras were still in power that Croton received the banished Sybarites, rejecting the demand of Telys for their surrender (see § *c*), and met and defeated the Sybarite army on the banks of the river Traeis. Milo commanded in this battle, and the conquest of Sybaris was his doing. After these successes, Croton was without a rival in Italy, her power exceeding even that of Tarentum. She continued to flourish till the rise of the Sicilian tyrants, when she became subject to their attacks, and suffered much at their hands. Dionysius I., in B.C. 389, and Agathocles, in B.C. 299, took Croton. During the war with Pyrrhus, it passed into the possession of Rome, B.C. 277.

(*f*) *Locri Epizephyrii.* There can be little doubt that this city was, if not originally, yet at any rate ultimately and predominantly, a colony either of the Ozolian or the Opuntian Locrians, since no other probable account can be given of its name. Various dates are assigned to the settlement, which was probably not much later than B.C. 700. The legislation of Zaleucus, about B.C. 660, gave to Locri its chief celebrity. His laws, which continued in force for above two hundred years, were regarded as among the best in Greece; and the quiet and good government for which Locri was famous were in a great measure ascribed to them. It is uncertain whether Zaleucus framed the constitution, or found it already in existence. The said constitution was oligarchical, but on a tolerably broad basis. A hundred houses formed an exclusive nobility, but the chief power was in the hands of a council containing a thousand members, who are thought to have been elected freely from the people. Locri was in the early times subject to attacks on the part of Croton, but successfully resisted them and obtained an ample vengeance on its assailants by the important victory of the Sagras. (See the last section.) Though less populous, and on the whole less powerful than either Croton or Sybaris, she flourished longer than either, her prosperity continuing for more than three centuries, from B.C. 660 to 356. She was, during the greater part of this time, on terms of close friendship with Syracuse, which assisted her against Rhegium and Croton, enlarging her dominions at the expense of the latter. Her misfortunes, however, began from this quarter. Having admitted Dionysius II. into their city on his expulsion from Syracuse, the Locrians suffered grievous oppression at his hands during the space of six years, after which they were attacked by the Bruttians, who brought their power very low. Before the invasion of Pyrrhus they had submitted to the Romans; and, though they subsequently coquetted both with him and with Hannibal, yet they may be regarded as substantially a Roman dependency from about B.C. 280.

(*g*) *Rhegium.* Founded from Chalcis in Eubœa, about B.C. 725. Admitted from the first among its colonists a number of Messenian refugees, who were subsequently strengthened by accessions, and formed the ruling class in the community. The Council of One Thousand, which in Rhegium, as in Thurii and Croton, had the chief direction of affairs, was composed exclusively of Messenians; and from them were drawn the chief magistrates who administered the state. Cramped on the side of Italy by the near neighborhood of Locri, whose territory extended from sea to sea, and with whom she was almost constantly at war, Rhegium cultivated relations with Sicily, and aimed at extending her power in that direction. This purpose she accomplished under the despot Anaxilas, who made himself master of Zanclé, on the Sicilian coast, and changed its name to Messana. Anaxilas reigned from B.C. 494 to 476. He was succeeded by his two sons, minors, on behalf of whom ruled for nine years the regent Micythus, B.C. 476 to 467. The sons enjoyed the sovereignty for no more than six years, being expelled B.C. 461 by a revolution. Rhegium now, after a certain time of commotion, settled down into tranquillity, and, adopting the laws of Charondas, enjoyed a period of repose. This was disturbed by the ambitious projects of Dionysius I. of Syracuse, against whom the Rhegines declared war, B.C. 399, thus initiating the contest which broke their power and reduced them from a first-rate to a third-rate state. Rhegium was captured and destroyed by Dionysius in B.C. 387; and, though restored by the second Dionysius, never afterwards flourished. In the war with Pyrrhus, the Rhegines took the side of Rome, and received into their city, as a garrison, a body of Campanian troops, who, following the example of the Mamertines (see p. 185), murdered the inhabitants and seized the town, B.C. 280. After the close of the war, B.C. 270, the Romans executed these rebellious soldiers, and restored the city to the survivors of the massacre; but thenceforth Rhegium continued a mere dependency of Rome.

(*h*) *Elea* or *Velia.* This city was founded by the Phocæans, after their calamitous victory off the coast of Etruria over the combined Etruscan and Carthaginian fleets, about B.C. 550. Considerably removed from any other important Greek city, it flourished greatly, and became the seat of the famous Eleatic school of philosophy, whose teachers, Parmenides and Zeno, were among the masters of Grecian thought. It warred successfully with Posidonia, and resisted all the attempts made against its independence by the Lucanians. On its first contact with Rome, it was accepted into alliance, and remained for many years a *fœderata civitas*, but ultimately received the Roman franchise, probably by the Lex Julia, B.C. 90.

(*i*) *Cumæ* or *Cymé.* Tradition said that Cumæ was a colony from Chalcis in Eubœa, but placed its foundation at an era anterior to the colonizing period. It was probably founded really about the same time as Naxos in Sicily and Rhegium in Italy, i. e., towards the close of the eighth century. From the fertility and extent of its territory, it rapidly became a flourishing state. It planted the colonies of Misenum, Dicæarchia, Palæpolis, and Neapolis, on the Bay of Naples, and even joined its mother city, Chalcis, in founding the distant settlement of Zanclé, in Sicily. It extended its influence deeply into the interior of Campania, and is said to have occupied with colonies the two inland cities of Nola and Atella. Towards the close of the sixth century, its independence was threatened by Etruria; but the Cumæans, under Aristodemus, succeeded in defeating the immense host brought against them, and afterwards, by joining the Latins at Aricia, about B.C. 506, helped to break completely the Etruscan land power, and to drive the invader back across the Tiber. Aristodemus, thus a double victor, contrived shortly afterwards to effect a revolution, and to turn the previously existing oligarchy into a despotism. In B.C. 497 he gave a refuge to the last Tarquin, and six years afterwards detained the Roman corn-ships as a set-off against his claims on the property which Tarquinius had left at Rome. But the harshness of his rule brought about his downfall, and on his expulsion (about B.C. 486), the oligarchy was restored. Soon after, Etruria renewed her attacks, but this time came by sea. The Cumæans implored the aid of Hiero, king of Syracuse, whose victory (B.C. 474) over the Etruscan fleet completely delivered them from this danger. But a more dangerous foe was now approaching. The Samnites, about B.C. 425, began their attacks upon Campania, and rapidly overran it. Capua fell, B.C. 423; and Cumæ was able to resist only three years longer. The city was then taken by storm, the inhabitants massacred, and Cumæ sank into the condition of a second-rate Campanian town.

The best work on the Greek colonies in Italy is that of HEYNE, *Prolusiones XVI. de civitatum Græcarum per Magnam Græciam et Siciliam institutis et legibus.* Contained in the seventh volume of his *Opuscula.*

iii. *Colonies in Sicily.* The colonies in Sicily occupied almost the entire eastern and southern shores of the island, but were comparatively scanty on the north coast. They may best be divided under the two heads of (1) Dorian, and (2) Ionian. The chief Dorian settlements were Syracuse and Megara Hyblæa, on the east coast, and Gela, Camarina, Acragas or Agrigentum, and Selinus, on the south; while the chief Ionian were Naxos, Leontini, Catana, and Zanclé, in the east, and Himera in the north of the island. Among the settlements of minor importance may be named, Acræ and Casmenæ, colonies of Syracuse; Eubœa, a colony of Megara Hyblæa; Tauromenium, which succeeded to Naxos; Mylæ, a colony of Zanclé; Calacta, a colony from the Peloponnese; and Heracleia Minoa, a colony of Selinus. Of these Tauromenium and Calacta were comparatively late foundations.

(*a*) *Syracuse.* The history of Syracuse is, to a great extent, the history of Sicily. The colony was founded from Corinth, in or about B.C. 735, and retained its independence for a space of 523 years. This space may be subdivided into five lesser periods—viz., (1) from the foundation of the city to the commencement of the reign of Gelo, B.C. 736 to 484; (2) from the accession of Gelo to the expulsion of his brother Thrasybulus, B.C. 484 to 467; (3) from the expulsion of Thrasybulus to the accession of Dionysius I., B.C. 467 to 405; (4) from the accession of Dionysius I. to the expulsion of Dionysius II., B.C. 405 to 343; and (5) from the expulsion of Dionysius II. to the Roman conquest, B.C. 343 to 212. FIRST PERIOD, B.C. 736 to 484. Syracuse during this time did not rise to any great height of power, being overshadowed by the Italian cities Sybaris and Croton. Still, she founded the colonies of Acræ and Casmenæ, and established a settlement at Camarina, B.C. 601. About B.C. 555 Camarina endeavored to make herself independent, but was attacked and destroyed by the parent city. Sixty years later, Syracuse was in turn attacked by Hippocrates, tyrant of Gela, who defeated the Syracusans on the Helorus, and forced them to cede Camarina. Soon afterwards internal troubles broke out. The landed aristocracy (Gamori), who had hitherto held exclusive possession of political privileges, were driven out by the lower orders, assisted by the slaves. They took refuge at Casmenæ, and from thence called in the aid of Gelo, tyrant of Gela, who reinstated them, but while so doing established himself as despot of the town. SECOND PERIOD, B.C. 484 to 467. Dynasty of Gelo and his two brothers, Hiero and Thrasybulus. To Gelo is attributable the special greatness of Syracuse. Being lord of all eastern and south-eastern Sicily, he not only made Syracuse his capital, but vastly increased its size and population by transferring to it the inhabitants of various other Greek towns. The power of Gelo induced the Greeks of the continent, when threatened by Xerxes, B.C. 480, to solicit his aid; and it was not without reason that he required, as the condition on which he would grant it, the command of the allied forces either by land or sea. Although his offers were declined, he would still probably have taken part in the great Persian War, had it not been for the invasion of Sicily by the Carthaginians in the same year with Salamis. The victory of the Himera frustrated the Carthaginian attempt, and greatly augmented Gelo's glory and power. He reigned, however, only three years longer, dying B.C. 477. His brother, Hiero, then mounted the throne and reigned for ten years in great splendor. His naval victory over the Etruscans has been noticed under the head of Cumæ (supra, p. 181). He governed the Ionic cities under his sway with some severity, but was popular with his Dorian subjects, who were charmed with his brilliant court, his patronage of the arts, and his Olympic and other victories. He assisted the Agrigentines in throwing off the tyranny of Thrasidæus, B.C. 472; and, dying five years afterwards, left his throne to his brother Thrasybulus, B.C. 467. Thrasybulus, ruling tyrannically, was expelled from Sicily by a general rising of his subjects, after he had reigned eight months. THIRD PERIOD, B.C. 467 to 405. The fall of the Gelonian dynasty was followed by commotions in the other Greek towns of Sicily, and by struggles between the various claimants of the lands in the several states. The democracies, which were everywhere established, sometimes used their power harshly; and numerous civil wars were the consequence. However, in B.C. 461, a general congress was held; terms were arranged between the opposing parties, and tranquillity was restored. A flourishing time succeeded. The various Greek cities were all recognized as independent, and a general advance was made in opulence and splendor. Agrigentum especially rose to a great height of prosperity. In Syracuse some attempts at re-establishing tyranny were checked by the institution of petalism, B.C. 454, which, having served its purpose and becoming absurd, was soon afterwards discarded. The attempt of the Sicel prince Ducetius to establish a confederacy of the natives against the Greeks (B.C. 451) proved abortive, but had the unfortunate result of causing a quarrel between Syracuse and Agrigentum. A war followed between the first and second cities of Sicily, terminating in the humiliation of the latter, B.C. 446. Syracuse upon this revived her old schemes of a supremacy, and began to threaten the independence of the Chalcidic cities, Naxos, Catana, and Leontini. These, about B.C. 428, invoked the aid of Athens, which gladly sent them succors in B.C. 427. Alarmed at this interference, the Dorian cities called a congress in B.C. 424, which was attended by deputies from all the states, Ionic as well as Doric, and a general peace was agreed upon. The Athenians quitted the island, but soon found an excuse to return, and in B.C. 415 to 413 made their great and disastrous expedition. Scarcely was Sicily delivered from this danger, when another, and a worse, threatened it. Invited by the Egestæans, a Carthaginian army under Hannibal, the son of Gisco, invaded Sicily in B.C. 409, and took Selinus and Himera, completely defeating the combined forces of the Greeks. (See p. 99.) Three years afterwards the same commander took Agrigentum. FOURTH PERIOD, B.C. 405 to 343. Dynasty of the Dionysii. The advance of the Carthaginians after the sack of Agrigentum enabled Dionysius to obtain the supreme power at Syracuse. His reign commenced ominously by a defeat of his forces at Gela, followed by a mutiny of his troops. But a plague breaking out in the Carthaginian army, Himilco, who was now in command, consented to a peace, by which Carthage obtained almost the whole of the southern coast. Dionysius then turned his arms against the Ionian cities and the barbarians of the interior. Having reduced in succession Leontini, Naxos, and Catana, and established his power over most of the Sicel tribes, he (in B.C. 397) broke with Carthage; recovered, one after another, Camarina, Gela, Agrigentum, and Selinus; and even besieged and took the old Carthaginian settlement, Motya. But the next year the fortune of war turned against him. Himilco landed in Sicily with a vast army, recovered Motya, Selinus, and the other southern towns, took Messana, and even besieged Dionysius in Syracuse. But here again a plague spread itself in the Punic army (B.C. 395); the siege was raised; Himilco deserted his troops, and committed suicide. Hostilities, however, continued till B.C. 392, when peace was a second time concluded. Dionysius then for some years warred in Italy, forcing Rhegium and other places to submit to him, B.C. 387. In B.C. 383, and again in B.C. 368, he renewed his attempts to drive the Carthaginians from Sicily, but failed both times, and at his death, in B.C. 367, he left them in possession of full one-third of the island. Dionysius II. succeeded his father, a weak prince, at first kept under restraint by his uncle, Dio. Banishes Dio, B.C. 360. Troubles follow. Dio returns, B.C. 357, and rules till B.C. 353, when he is murdered by Calippus, who is driven out, B.C. 352, by Hipparinus. In B.C. 346, Dionysius returns and occupies Ortygia, while another aspirant to the supreme power, Hicetas, holds Achradina, and, to strengthen himself, calls in the Carthaginians. A patriotic party in the city applies to Corinth, which sends a body of troops under Timoleon, B.C. 344. Successes of Timoleon. Hicetas submits, and Dionysius II. goes into exile. FIFTH PERIOD, B.C. 343 to 212. Under the auspices of Timoleon, republican government was restored to Syracuse. War was renewed with the Carthaginians, B.C. 341; and the tyrants were put down in the Siceliot cities. A grand attempt of Carthage to establish her supremacy in B.C. 340 was frustrated by the victory of the Crimêsus; and peace was made on the old terms, which established the Halycus as the boundary between the two powers. A time of prosperity followed, B.C. 340 to 318; but in B.C. 317 the adventurer Agathocles made himself master of Syracuse and brought terrible calamities upon Sicily. Agathocles first extended his power over the Greek cities by the aid of Carthage, after which, turning against his allies, he strove to drive them from the island. But the decisive victory of Hamilcar at Ecnomus on the Himera (B.C. 310) upset all his plans; and nothing was left for him but to attempt a diversion by carrying the war into Africa. For four years, from B.C. 310 to 307, Carthage was made to tremble for her home dominion; but the over-bold effort could not be sustained. Though successful in several engagements, the Greek prince could make no impression on Carthage itself; and meanwhile Hamilcar continued the war in Sicily and several times assaulted Syracuse. In B.C. 307 Agathocles was forced to quit Africa, and shortly afterwards he concluded a peace, which left the Halycus still the boundary between the two nations. Agathocles now turned his attention to Italy; Croton was sacked and the Bruttii engaged and defeated. Important results might have followed; but in B.C. 289 Agathocles was murdered by Mænon, and with his death affairs in Sicily returned to a state of general confusion. Carthage took heart, and recommenced her aggressions. The mercenaries of Agathocles, under the name of Mamertini, seized Messana. The Syracusans, in alarm, invited over Pyrrhus from Italy, and thereby saved their city, but were obliged to submit for nearly three years (B.C. 278 to 276) to the authority of that imperious prince. The recall of Pyrrhus to the main-land left Syracuse once more free; and she wisely placed herself under the rule of Hiero II., said to have descended from one of the early Syracusan kings, who very soon restored her to her old position in Sicily. His war with the Mamertines, which he carried on at first single-handed, but afterwards in conjunction with Carthage, involved him for a time in hostilities with Rome, B.C. 264 to 263; but from this position he skillfully extracted himself by concluding a separate peace with the Romans in the last-named year, after which he continued throughout his reign their faithful and firm ally. His death, in B.C. 215, led to commotions which proved fatal to the independence of Syracuse. His grandson, Hieronymus, was murdered B.C. 214. Power was seized by Hippocrates and Epicydes. Syracuse deserted Rome, and espoused the side of Carthage. The siege by Marcellus followed, which, though protracted through the genius of Archimedes, terminated, B.C. 212, in the fall of the city and the absorption of the state into Rome.

The history of Syracuse is best given in the standard histories of Greece, especially THIRLWALL, chaps. xxii., xxv., xxvi., and GROTE, chaps. xliii., lvii.-lx., lxxxi.-lxxxv., and xcvii. Important works on its topography and antiquities have been written by

LETRONNE, *Essai critique sur la topographie de Syracuse.* Paris, 1812; 8vo.

GOELLER, F., *De situ et origine Syracusarum.* Lipsiæ, 1818; 8vo.

BONANNI, *Delle Antiche Siracuse.* Palermo, 1717; 2 vols. folio.

LEAKE, *Notes on Syracuse*, in the *Transactions of the Royal Society of Literature;* 2d series, vol. iii.

CAVALLARI, *Zur topographie von Syrakus.* Göttingen, 1845; 8vo.

(*b*) *Megara Hyblæa.* Founded from Megara, about B.C. 726. Sent out a colony to Selinus, about B.C. 626. Attacked and destroyed by Gelo, B.C. 481. Its inhabitants transferred to Syracuse.

(*c*) *Gela.* Founded from Rhodes and Crete, B.C. 690. Originally called Lindii. Sent out a colony to Agrigentum, B.C. 582. Appears first as an important state about B.C. 505, when the original oligarchy was subverted by Cleander, who succeeded in making himself despot, and reigned for seven years, from B.C. 505 to 498. He was succeeded by his brother, Hippocrates, an ambitious prince, who endeavored to make himself master of all the other Greek towns. He succeeded in conquering Leontini, Callipolis, Naxos, and Zanclé, which last he made over to the Samians; and he warred against the Syracusans with so much success that he compelled them to purchase peace by the cession of their colony, Camarina. His reign lasted from B.C. 498 to 491. At his death the supreme authority was seized by Gelo, who soon after (B.C. 485) conquered Syracuse and made it his capital. Gela now declined in power. Half its inhabitants were removed to Syracuse, and the remainder placed under the government of Hiero, Gelo's brother. The subjection of Gela to Syracuse continued till the expulsion of Thrasybulus, B.C. 466, when it recovered its independence, and grew strong enough to send out a colony to Camarina. A prosperous time now set in. Gela remained on terms of close friendship with the other Dorian cities, and was unmolested by any enemy. During the Athenian expedition it adhered steadily to the cause of Syracuse. At length, in B.C. 406, misfortune fell on the Geloans: the Carthaginians, in their advance along the southern coast, besieged and took the city, and the inhabitants, quitting their home, sought a refuge at Leontini. They were restored after the peace of B.C. 405, but as Carthaginian subjects; and henceforth Gela loses all its importance. It follows, for the most part, the fortunes of Syracuse; but owes its final ruin to its own colony, Agrigentum, whose tyrant, Phintias, destroyed its walls and buildings, B.C. 280, and removed its inhabitants to the city which he founded at the mouth of the Himera. (See under "Agrigentum.")

(*d*) *Camarinà.* This city was founded by the Syracusans, B.C. 601. About fifty years after the date of its foundation, it made an attempt to shake off the Syracusan yoke, but failing, was completely destroyed by the parent city. Some time after this, about B.C. 495, the site was ceded by Syracuse to Hippocrates of Gela, who rebuilt and repeopled the place. His successor, Gelo, once more destroyed the city, and transferred its inhabitants to Syracuse; after which the site was unoccupied till the downfall of Gelo's dynasty, B.C. 466, when the city received its third and final foundation at the hand of the Geloans. It now rose rapidly into power and importance, occupying a peculiar position among the Sicilian towns, since, though of Dorian origin, its jealousy and fear of its near neighbor, Syracuse, led it to take part with the Ionic cities, Naxos, Catana, and Leontini. When the Athenians first appeared in Sicily, B.C. 427, Camarina joined them; but in the great expedition, B.C. 415, it at first held aloof and then sided with Syracuse. A fatal blow was inflicted on it by the great Carthaginian invasion, B.C. 405, from which it never recovered. Attached generally to Syracuse in the wars which followed, it suffered much at the hands of the Carthaginians and the Mamertines. About B.C. 258 it finally passed into the possession of the Romans.

(*e*) *Agrigentum.* Agrigentum was, next to Syracuse, the most important city in Sicily. Founded from Gela, B.C. 582, it early surpassed its mother state, and about B.C. 570 to 540 attained to great power and prosperity under Phalaris, the first of the Sicilian tyrants. On the assassination of Phalaris it seems to have regained its freedom; but in B.C. 488 it fell again under a despot, one Thero, the son of Ænesidemus, who was descended from the destroyer of Phalaris. In alliance with Gelo, who married his daughter, this prince proceeded to make attacks on some of the Greek towns, as particularly Himera, which he conquered. The king of Himera, Terillus, called in the aid of Carthage; and the invasion followed which Gelo and Thero repulsed by the victory of B.C. 480. Thero ruled mildly, and left the crown to his son, Thrasydæus, whose cruelty caused his subjects to rebel, and to expel him, with the aid of Hiero, after he had reigned less than a year, B.C. 471. Agrigentum now established a democracy, under which it flourished greatly for nearly sixty years. Magnificent public buildings were erected; a vast trade was carried on, more especially with Africa and Gaul; and the wealth and luxury of the citizens became proverbial. Philosophy was cultivated, and the fame of the city was spread far and wide through the wisdom of Empedocles and the rhetorical ability of Polus. In her wars, Agrigentum generally fought on the side of Syracuse; but deeming herself aggrieved by the conduct of that state in the contest with the Sicel chief, Ducetius, she took up arms to avenge herself, but was completely defeated on the Himera (B.C. 446). The ill-feeling produced by this blow was probably the chief cause of her standing wholly aloof when her rival was threatened by Athens, B.C. 415 to 413. Eight years later the prosperity of Agrigentum came to an end, through her capture by the Carthaginians, who plundered and destroyed the city. A second Agrigentum arose, but never grew into very much importance. Enlarged and strengthened by Timoleon, about B.C. 340, she was able for a while to resist Agathocles, but was defeated by him on his return from Africa, B.C. 307, and compelled to sue for peace. The death of Agathocles enabled her to resume ambitious projects. Under a tyrant, named Phintias, she extended her dominion considerably, took and destroyed Gela, founded Phintias on the Southern Himera, and became mistress of a large portion of the interior. Pyrrhus, however, on his landing, found her submissive, B.C. 278; and at the commencement of the first Punic War, B.C. 264, she admitted a Carthaginian garrison. From this time for above fifty years the possession of Agrigentum was disputed between Carthage and Rome, to the latter of whom she remained permanently subject from her recovery by Lævinus, B.C. 210.

(*f*) *Selinus.* Founded from Megara Hyblæa, about B.C. 626. Had wars from a very early time with Egesta. Founded Heracleia Minoa before B.C. 520. Had fallen about this time under the sway of a tyrant, Peithagoras, who was put down by the Selinuntians, assisted by the Spartan Euryleon, one of the companions of Dorieus. Euryleon then seized the crown, but held it for a very short space, as the Selinuntians revolted and put him to death. According to Diodorus, Selinus joined the Carthaginians on their first invasion of Sicily, B.C. 480, and promised Hamilcar a contingent, but failed to send it. After the defeat of the Carthaginians and the downfall of the tyrants, Selinus participated in the general Sicilian prosperity. Her quarrels, however, continued with Egesta; and the appeals of the Egestæans, who were the weaker party, produced, first, the great Athenian expedition, B.C. 415, and then the Carthaginian invasion of B.C. 409. The first result of the latter was the siege and capture of Selinus, which thenceforth continued, with few and short intervals, subject to the Carthaginian authority. About B.C. 250 the Carthaginians destroyed it, and transferred its inhabitants to Lilybæm.

(*g*) *Naxos*, the earliest of the Greek settlements in Sicily, was founded from Chalcis, in Eubœa, B.C. 736. Its colonists were so numerous that in six years' time it was able to plant a settlement at Leontini, and soon afterwards one at Catana. Together with its daughter cities, it seems to have flourished until the rise of the great Geloan dynasty, when it lost its independence. Taken by Hippocrates, about B.C. 498, it passed under the rule of Gelo, and then of Hiero, the latter of whom removed its inhabitants to Leontini, and occupied Naxos with new settlers. It continued, however, Ionic and Chalcidian. Recovering independence on the fall of the dynasty of Gelo, it re-entered into close relations with its daughter cities; and from about B.C. 460, Naxos, Leontini, and Catana form an Ionic league, which is opposed to a Doric league under Syracuse. The preponderance of the Dorians forced the Ionians to look out for foreign aid, and Athens was invited in B.C. 427 and assisted in B.C. 415. The discomfiture of the Athenians was followed by war between the league and Syracuse, which continued till the menacing attitude of the Carthaginians in B.C. 409 suspended hostilities between the Greek States. Naxos bore her share in resisting the invaders; but on peace being made she was immediately attacked by Dionysius, who took and destroyed the town, and sold its inhabitants for slaves, B.C. 403. Tauromenium afterwards grew up near the site of Naxos, and being partly peopled by former Naxians was occasionally, but incorrectly, given the name.

(*h*) *Leontini*. The history of Leontini is closely connected with that of Naxos. It was founded from Naxos, B.C. 730, and itself founded the colony of Eubœa shortly afterwards. About B.C. 498 it fell under the sway of Hippocrates; and about B.C. 476 received the Naxians and Catanians who were removed from their homes by Hiero. It recovered independence, B.C. 466, on the fall of Thrasybulus. As the nearest neighbor to Syracuse of the three Chalcidic cities, it had to bear the brunt of her attacks. Hence it was the special danger of Leontini which caused the first invitation to be given to Athens; and the failure of the great Athenian expedition was followed rapidly by a Syracusan attack upon the city, B.C. 412, which resulted in its capture and annexation. Occasionally, indeed, during the troublous period—from B.C. 409 to 270—it asserted and even exercised independence; but the periods of autonomy were brief, and for the most part it was a mere dependency on Syracuse. It became Roman at the same time as that city, B.C. 212.

(*i*) *Catana*. Founded from Naxos. Date of the foundation uncertain, but probably earlier than B.C. 700. Charondas, about B.C. 550, gave Catana a code of laws. Hiero of Syracuse having conquered it, about B.C. 476, transferred its inhabitants to Leontini, replacing them by a body of 10,000 new citizens, and at the same time changing the name of the city to Ætna. But, at the downfall of Thrasybulus, these new citizens were expelled; and the former inhabitants, returning, brought back the old name. Leagued with Naxos and Leontini, Catana after this maintained her independence for more than half a century. In B.C. 415 she admitted the Athenians, and served as the basis for their earlier operations against Syracuse. After Dionysius I. had made peace with Carthage, B.C. 405, he took Catana, sold the inhabitants into slavery, and gave the city to some Campanian mercenaries. After this the place became politically insignificant; but its material prosperity was not much lessened, and it continued to be a wealthy and populous city, even under the Romans.

(*j*) *Zanclė*, afterwards Messana. The fortunes of Zanclé were very peculiar. Originally it was a Chalcidic city, being founded from Cumæ, in Italy, in conjunction with the mother state, Chalcis, in Eubœa, probably about B.C. 690 to 660. It early sent out a colony to Mylæ, on the north coast of the island, and in B.C. 648 it sent another still farther westward to Himera. In B.C. 494, desirous of filling up the gap between these two cities, Zanclé invited over a body of Samians, who wished to emigrate in consequence of the suppression of the Ionian revolt. The Samians consented; but, instead of carrying out the arrangement, they, at the instigation of Anaxilaüs of Rhegium, took violent possession of Zanclé. Soon afterwards, about B.C. 485, that monarch attacked and expelled them, supplying their place by a body of Rhegines, and at the same time changing the name of the city to Messana. The place continued dependent on Rhegium until B.C. 461, when it shook off the yoke and became free. From this time till B.C. 425 the Messanians flourished greatly, but in that year they were compelled to surrender to Athens, and became involved in the troubles which Athenian ambition brought upon Sicily. However, the lesson thus taught them was not without its use; since it induced them to preserve a strict neutrality at the time of the great Athenian expedition, B.C. 415 to 413. In the Carthaginian wars, Messana escaped injury till B.C. 396, when it was taken by Himilco and completely levelled with the ground. On the retirement of the Carthaginians, Dionysius restored it, and made great use of it in his wars with Rhegium. At his death Messana once more became free and rose in power; but in B.C. 312 it fell under the power of Agathocles, who treated it with extreme severity. Still worse calamities, however, came on it thirty years later, upon the death of the tyrant. His mercenary troops, chiefly Campanians, had agreed to quit Sicily, and were assembled at Messana, as the natural point of embarkation, when they suddenly turned against the inhabitants, massacred them, and, under the name of Mamertini, seized and held the city, which henceforth ceased to be a Greek state, about B.C. 282.

(*k*) *Himera* was founded from Zanclé, as above stated, in B.C. 648. In the early times it does not seem to have been very flourishing; and there is reason to believe that in the sixth century B.C. it fell under the dominion of the Agrigentine tyrant, Phalaris. Early in the fifth century, however (about B.C. 490), we find it once more independent; and about B.C. 490 to 485 it acquired importance under Terillus, a native despot, connected by alliance and intermarriage with Anaxilaüs of Rhegium. Terillus, attacked by Thero of Agrigentum, invited over the Carthaginians, B.C. 480, who came with a vast armament, evidently intending to conquer the island. The discomfiture of this host by Gelo and Thero (B.C. 480) left the latter in undisputed possession of Himera, which he placed under his son, Thrasydæus, a youth of a tyrannical disposition. Quarrels between Thrasydæus and his subjects followed, which induced Thero to banish vast numbers of the citizens and to supply their place with new settlers, chiefly Dorians, who made Himera into a Doric city, B.C. 476. On the expulsion of Thrasydæus, B.C. 472, with the help of Hiero, Himera became free, and shortly afterwards it helped the Syracusans to expel the tyrant Thrasybulus, B.C. 466. The exiles upon this returned, and such arrangements were made that the city never afterwards suffered from civil discord. In the Athenian war of B.C. 415 to 413 Himera gave a steady support to Syracuse; but five years after its close, the second Carthaginian invasion dealt it a fatal blow, the city being taken and destroyed by Hannibal, B.C. 408, and never afterwards rebuilt. Thermæ, sometimes called Thermæ Himerenses, which grew up at a short distance from the site of Himera, took its place, but never attained to any importance, remaining, with few and brief exceptions, subject to Carthage, until it passed into the possession of Rome, about B.C. 249. The Romans treated it with exceptional favor.

The work of HEYNE, mentioned (p. 182), is the best on the history of the Sicilian colonies generally. Good monographs have been written on some of the more important cities. Among these the following are best worthy of attention:

SIEFERT, O., *Akragas und sein Gebiet.* Hamburg, 1845; 8vo. *Zancle-Messana.*

REINGANUM, *Selinus und sein Gebiet.* Leipsic, 1827; 8vo.

On the antiquities of the island the following works may be consulted:

SERRA DI FALCO, *Antichità della Sicilia.* Palermo, 1834–39; 5 vols. folio.

BISCARI, *Viaggio per le antichità della Sicilia.* Palermo, 1817; 8vo.

TORREMUZZA, *Siciliæ urbium, populorum, regum quoque et tyrannorum numismata.* Palermo, 1781; folio.

CASTELLO, G. L., *Siciliæ et objacentium insularum veterum inscriptionum nova collectio.* Palermo, 1769; folio. Also

KEERL, J. H., *Siciliens vorzüglichste Münzen und Steinschriften aus dem Alterthume.* Gotha, 1802.

iv. *Colonies on the Coasts of Gaul and Spain.* By far the most important of these was Massilia (Marseilles), on the coast of Gaul, a colony of the Phocæans. It was probably founded about B.C. 600, when the coast was still in the occupation of the Ligurians. The relations of the colony with the natives were generally amicable; but we have an account of one attempt to surprise and destroy it, which terminated in failure. Massilia had a small territory, but one fertile in corn and wine. Her trade was large, and was carried on both by sea and land. Her merchants visited the interior of Gaul, and even obtained tin and lead by this overland route from the Scilly Islands. She extended her colonies eastward and westward along the coast of Gaul, and even planted some in Spain. The best known of these settlements were Olbia (near Hyeres), Antipolis (now Antibes), Nicæa (Nice), and Monœcus (Monaco). These all lay to the east. To the west were Agatha, Rhoda, Emporiæ, Hemeroscopeium, and Mænaca, the last named not far from Malaga. A special jealousy existed between Massilia and Carthage, which led often to hostilities; but the victory always remained with the little Greek state. More dangerous was the enmity of the Ligurians and Gauls, whose near neighborhood caused the Massiliots constant alarm. However, with the aid of the Romans, to whom Massilia allied herself as early as B.C. 218, these foes were kept in check, and Massilia preserved her freedom until the time of the Roman Civil Wars. Having then sided with Pompey, she was stormed by Cæsar, B.C. 49. Even after this she retained a nominal independence, being reckoned a "fœderata civitas" as late as the time of Pliny. The constitution of Massilia was an oligarchy. A council of six hundred members (τιμοῦχοι), how appointed we know not, but who held office for life, possessed the monopoly of political power. These deputed the administration to a committee of fifteen, of whom three were presidents.

Numerous works have been written on the history and constitution of Massilia; but they are not of very much value. The best are—

JOHANSEN, J. C., *Veteris Massiliæ res et instituta.* Kiel, 1818.

BRUCKNER, A., *Historia Reipublicæ Massiliensium.* Göttingen, 1826; 8vo.

v. *Colonies on the Coast of Africa.* The African colonies, like those on the coast of Gaul and Spain, all issued from one source. This was Cyrênê, founded by adventurers from Thera, at the instigation of the Delphic oracle, about B.C. 631. Cyrênê was at first governed by kings, viz.: 1. Battus I., the founder. Reigned forty years, from B.C. 631 to 591. Succeeded by his son, 2. Arcesilaüs I., who reigned sixteen years, from B.C. 591 to 575. Thus far Cyrênê was tranquil, but not particularly prosperous. 3. Battus II., surnamed "the Happy," succeeded. In his reign the Delphic oracle induced the stream of Greek colonization to set steadily towards Africa; and Cyrênê grew rapidly in population and importance. Fresh territory was occupied; and when the native tribes, robbed of their lands, called the Egyptians to their aid, Apries, the Egyptian monarch, was repulsed, and his army almost wholly destroyed, about B.C. 570. Battus II. was succeeded by his son, 4. Arcesilaüs II., who had dissensions with his brothers, which led to the founding of Barca, whither they betook themselves. The Libyans of the neighborhood preferring to attach themselves to Barca, Arcesilaüs attacked them, but suffered a severe defeat. Upon this he fell sick, and was murdered by his brother Learchus; who was in his turn put to death by Eryxo, the widow of Arcesilaüs, about B.C. 540. 5. Battus III., surnamed "the Lame," inherited the crown from his father. Under him the troubles of the state increased; and, appeal being made to Delphi, Demonax of Mantinea was called in to arrange affairs. He confined the royal authority within very narrow limits, and made a fresh division of the citizens into tribes upon an ethnic basis, about B.C. 538. 6. Arcesilaüs III., the son of Battus the Lame, succeeded, about B.C. 530. Submitted to the Persians B.C. 525. Claimed all the privileges of the early kings, and in the struggle that followed was forced to fly. Collected troops in Samos and effected his return; but, using his power cruelly, was murdered by his subjects at Barca. 7. Battus IV., his son, became king; but Pheretima, grandmother of this Battus, was, as it would seem, for some time regent, Battus being (it is probable) a minor. Flight of Pheretima to Egypt and expedition of Aryandes, about B.C. 514. Barca taken. Pheretima soon afterwards dies. Battus reigned till about B.C. 470, when he was succeeded by his son, 8. Arcesilaüs IV., who distinguished himself by his Pythian victories, and reigned probably till about B.C. 430. On his death, his son, another Battus, was expelled, and sought a refuge at the Cyrenæan colony of Euesperides. A democratic republic was now established, which seems, however, to have worked but ill. Violent party contests, from time to time, shook the state; and it fell more than once under the sway of tyrants. Still, in many respects, Cyrênê continued to flourish. Its trade, particularly in the celebrated *silphium*, remained great; its architecture was handsome; its sculpture far from contemptible; it took an important part in the favorite pursuit of the Greeks, philosophy, as the Cyrenaic School, founded by the Cyrenæan Aristippus, and the New Academy, founded by another Cyrenæan, Carneades, sufficiently show. Moreover, it contributed to Greek literature the poetry of Callimachus, and, in Christian times, the rhetoric of Synesius. It is uncertain when the dependence of Cyrênê on Persia ceased; but it can scarcely have continued later than the revolt of Egypt under Nepherites, B.C. 405. In B.C. 332, the Cyrenæans submitted to Alexander; and the whole of the Cyrenaïca became thenceforth a dependency of Egypt, falling successively to the Ptolêmies and the Romans.

The chief settlements in the Cyrenaïca, besides Cyrênê, were, 1. Barca. Founded, about B.C. 554, by seceders from Cyrênê in conjunction with native Libyans. Hence the city had always a semi-African character. Submitted to Cambyses, B.C. 525. Destroyed by Pheretima, aided by Aryandes, about B.C. 514, in revenge for the murder of her son. The inhabitants removed to Bactria. The new Barca, which grew up after this, was always an insignificant place. 2. Euesperides, or Hesperides. Founded by Arcesilaüs IV., about B.C. 450. Only important in the time of the Ptolemies, when it became Berenicê. 3. Tauchira, or Teuchira. Probably founded by Barca. Belonged, at any rate, to the Barcæans. Became Arsinoë under the Ptolemies. 4. Apollonia, the port of Cyrênê. This city, with the four previously mentioned, constituted the Cyrenaic "Pentapolis."

On the history of Cyrênê the student may consult with advantage the works of

HARDION, J., *Histoire de la ville de Cyrène*, in the *Mémoires de l'Académie des Inscriptions*, vol. iii. And

THRIGE, J. P., *Res Cyrenensium a primordiis inde civitatis*, etc. Hafniæ, 1828; 8vo.

Ample light has been thrown on the topography and antiquities by modern travellers. The best works are—

DELLA CELLA, *Viaggio da Tripoli di Barbaria alle Frontieri Occidentali dell' Egitto.* Genoa, 1819.

BEECHEY, *Expedition to Explore the North Coast of Africa.* London, 1828; 4to.

PACHO, F. R., *Relation d'un Voyage dans la Marmarique, la Cyrénaique*, etc. Paris, 1827; 4to.

HAMILTON, J., *Wanderings in North Africa.* London, 1856; 8vo.

BARTH, *Wanderungen durch das Punische und Kyrenaïsche Küstenland.* Berlin, 1849; 8vo. And the same writer's *Travels in North and Central Africa.* London, 1857–58; 5 vols. 8vo.

The settlement of Naucratis in Egypt was not, properly speaking, a Greek colony; but some mention of it may fitly be made here. Its position resembled that of Canton before the first Chinese war, or of Nagasaki and Jeddo at the present day. It was not relinquished to the Greeks, but was simply the place, and the only place, in Egypt where they were allowed to settle. A large Greek population was settled there after the time of Amasis, B.C. 569 to 525, composed chiefly of emigrants from the coasts and islands of Western Asia. The town boasted four Greek temples; and the Greeks had the free exercise of their religion, the appointment of their own magistrates, and the power of exacting customs and harbor-dues. The Naucratites manufactured porcelain and wreaths of flowers (artificial?). The place continued to flourish until the Alexandrine era, when it declined as Alexandria rose into greatness.

THIRD PERIOD.

From the Commencement of the Wars with Persia, B.C. 500, *to the Battle of Chæroneia*, B.C. 338.

SOURCES. For the first portion of this period, from B.C. 500 to 479, HERODOTUS (books v. to ix.) is our chief authority; but he may be supplemented to a considerable extent from PLUTARCH (*Vit. Themist.* and *Aristid.*) and NEPOS (*Vit. Miltiad.*, *Themist.*, *Aristid.*, and *Pausan.*). For the second portion of the period, from B.C. 479 to 431, the outline of THUCYDIDES (book i. chaps. 24 to 146) is of primary importance, especially for the chronology; but the details must be filled in from DIODORUS (book xi. and first half of book xii.), and, as before, from Plutarch and Nepos. (The latter has one "Life" only bearing on this period, that of Cimon; the former has two, those of Cimon and Pericles.) For most of the third portion of the period, the time of the Peloponnesian War—B.C. 431 to 404—we have the invaluable work of Thucydides (books ii. to viii.) as our single and sufficient guide; but, where the work of Thucydides breaks off, we must supplement his continuator, XENOPHON (*Hellenica*, books i. and ii.), by DIODORUS (last half of book xii.). For the fourth portion of the period, from the close of the Peloponnesian War to the battle of Mantineia—B.C. 404 to 362—Xenophon in his *Hellenica*, his *Anabasis*, and his *Agesilaus*, is our main authority: he is to be compared with Diodorus (books xiii. to xv.), Nepos (*Vit. Lysand.*, *Conon.*, *Pelop.*, *Epaminond.*, and *Ages.*), and Plutarch (*Vit. Pelop.*, *Artaxerxis*, and *Ages.*). For the remainder of the history—from B.C. 362 to 338—in default of contemporary writers, we are thrown primarily on the sixteenth book of Diodorus; but perhaps more real knowledge of the period is to be derived from the speeches of the orators, especially those of DEMOSTHENES and ÆSCHINES. The lives of Phocion and Demosthenes in Plutarch, and those of Iphicrates, Chabrias, Timotheus, and Datames in Nepos, further illustrate the period, which also receives some light from JUSTIN, PAUSANIAS, and a few other authors.

The most important modern works on the entire period from B.C. 500 to 338 are those to which reference has been already made under the "Sources" for the "First" and "Second Period." (See pp. 137 and 143.) But the following may be mentioned as specially illustrative of the "Third Period:"

BARTHELEMY, *Voyage du jeune Anacharsis en Grèce.* Paris, 1788; 4 vols. 4to. This work is one which will never become antiquated, combining, as it does, vast learning with remarkable refinement and good taste.

BECKER, W. A., *Charikles, Bilder alt-griechische Sitte.* Leipsic; 3 vols. 8vo. Translated into English by the Rev. F. METCALFE. London, 1845; 8vo.

BULWER, SIR E. L., *Athens, its Rise and Fall; with Views of the Literature, Philosophy, and Social Life of the Athenian People.* London, 1837; 2 vols. 8vo.

Magnificent works on the monuments of Greece, architectural and other, which belong chiefly to this period, have been published in the present century. Among these the following are the most remarkable:

STUART and REVETT, *The Antiquities of Athens Measured and Delineated.* London, 1762–1816; 4 vols. folio. The 2d Edition was published in 1825–27.

COCKERELL, SIR C., *Temples of Ægina and Bassæ.* (See p. 165.)

WORDSWORTH, CHRISTOPHER, *Greece; Pictorial, Descriptive, and Historical.* London, 1852; large 8vo.

CHOISEUL-GOUFFIER, *Voyage pittoresque de la Grèce.* Paris, 1782–1822; 2 vols. folio.

Tendency of the great Persian War to consolidate the Greek nation.

1. The tendency of the Greek States, in spite of their separatist leanings, towards consolidation and union round one or more centres, has been already noticed. (See p. 145.) Up to the date of the Persian War, Sparta was the state which exercised the greatest centralizing force, and gave the most promise of uniting under its leadership the scattered members of the Hellenic body. Events prior to the Persian War had been gradually leading up to the recognition of a Spartan headship. It required, however, the actual occurrence of the war to bring rapidly to maturity what hitherto had only existed in embryo—to place at once vividly before the whole race the consciousness of Hellenic unity, to drive Sparta to the assumption of leadership, and to induce the other Greek states to acquiesce calmly in the new position occupied by one of their number.

General recognition of *hegemonies.*

2. The beneficial influence of an extreme common danger was not limited to the time of its actual existence. The tendency towards consolidation, having once obtained a certain amount of strength, did not disappear with the cause which brought it into being. From the time of the Persian invasion, we notice a general inclination of the Greeks to gather themselves together into confederations under leaders. The chief states, Sparta, Athens, Bœotia, Argos, are recognized as possible holders of such a *hegemony;* and the history from this time thus possesses a character of unity for which we look in vain at an earlier period.

Immediate causes which led to the First Persian War. 1. Flight of Hippias to Sardis, and influence which he exercised over Artaphernes. 2. Revolt of the Ionians, and share taken by Athens and Eretria in the burning of Sardis, B.C. 500. (See p. 157.) 3. Treatment of the heralds of Darius by Athens and Sparta, B.C. 491. These causes, however, at the most hastened an attempt, which would in any case have been made, to extend the Persian dominion over continental Greece.

Expeditions of Mardonius, and of Datis—Battle of Marathon, B.C. 490.

3. The first expedition of Mardonius having been frustrated, in part by a storm, in part by the opposition of the Bryges, a tribe of Thracians, it was resolved, before a second expedition was sent out, to send heralds and summon the Greek states severally to surrender. The result of this policy was striking. The island states generally, and many of the continental ones, made their submission. Few, comparatively, rejected the overture. Athens and Sparta, however, marked their abhorrence of the proposal made them in the strongest possible way. In spite of the universally-received law, that the persons of heralds were sacred, they put the envoys of Darius to death, and thus placed themselves beyond all possibility of further parley with the enemy.

The submission of Ægina to Persia at this time is made a subject of complaint by Athens at Sparta. Punishment of Ægina by Cleomenes in consequence, and deposition of Demaratus, who attempts to thwart the expedition. Expedition of Datis and Artaphernes, B.C. 490. Occupation of Naxos. Capture of Eretria. Battle of Marathon, and failure of a subsequent attempt to surprise Athens. Tardy arrival of the Spartan succors. Unhappy end of Miltiades.

Great augmentation of the Athenian navy.

4. The victory of Marathon gave Greece a breathing-space before the decisive trial of strength between herself and Persia, which was manifestly impending. No one conceived that the danger was past, or that the Great King would patiently accept his defeat, without seeking to avenge it. The ten years which intervened between Marathon and Thermopylæ were years of preparation as much to Greece as to Persia. Athens especially, under the wise guidance of Themistocles, made herself ready for the coming conflict by the application of her great pecuniary resources to the increase of her navy, and by the training of her people in nautical habits. The war between this state and Ægina, which continued till B.C. 481, was very advantageous to the Grecian cause, by stimulating these naval efforts, and enabling Themistocles to persuade his countrymen to their good.

Influence of Themistocles at this time secured by the ostracism of his rival, Aristides, B.C. 482, probably.

Hellenic Congress meets at the Isthmus, B.C. 481.

5. The military preparations of Darius in the years B.C. 489 to 487, and those of Xerxes in B.C. 484 to 481, must have been well known to the Greeks, who could not doubt the quarter in which it was intended to strike a blow. Accordingly, we find the year B.C. 481 given up to counter-preparations. A general congress held at the Isthmus—a new feature in Greek history—arranged, or suppressed, the internal quarrels of the states attending it; assigned the command of the confederate forces, both by land and sea, to Sparta; and made an attempt to obtain assistance from distant, or reluctant, members of the Hellenic body—Argos, Crete, Corcyra, and Sicily. A resolution was at the same time taken to meet the invader at the extreme northern boundary of Greece, where it was thought that the pass of Tempé offered a favorable position for resistance.

Great invasion of Xerxes, B.C. 480. Battles of Thermopylæ, Salamis, Platæa, and Mycalé.

6. The force sent to Thessaly, finding the pass of Tempé untenable, withdraws at once; and the position of Thermopylæ and Artemisium is chosen for the combined resistance to the foe by sea and land. Though that position is forced, Attica overrun, and Athens taken and burnt, in revenge for Sardis, yet the defeat of his vast fleet at Salamis (B.C. 480) alarms Xerxes, and causes him to retire with all his remaining vessels and the greater part of his troops. Mardonius stays behind with 350,000 picked men, and the fate of Greece has to be determined by a land battle. This is fought the next year, B.C. 479, at Platæa, by the Spartan king, Pausanias, and the Athenian general, Aristides, who with 69,000 men completely defeat the Persian general, take his camp, and destroy his army. A battle at Mycalé (in Asia Minor), on the same day, effects the destruction of the remnant of the Persian fleet; and thus the entire invading armament, both naval and military, is swept away, the attempt at conquest having issued in utter failure.

DETAILS OF THE WAR. The Greeks evacuate Thessaly early in the year. Fresh deliberation at the Isthmus, and resolve to occupy Thermopylæ and Artemisium. Nine thousand men under Leonidas take post at Thermopylæ, and 271 vessels under Eurybiades guard the strait at Artemisium. Advance of Xerxes to Malis. Fruitless assaults on the Greek position during two days. Way of turning the position made known to the Persians by Ephialtes. Leonidas dismisses half his army. Gallant struggle of the remainder terminates in the complete destruction of all, except 400 Thebans, who are made prisoners. About the same time engagements take place between the Persian fleet of above 1000 vessels, and the very inferior Greek fleet at Artemisium, without any decisive advantage to either side; but the forcing of Thermopylæ by the Persian army induces Eurybiades to retire down the Euripus and bring his fleet to an anchor at Salamis. March of Xerxes through Phocis and Bœotia into Attica. Failure of attempt on Delphi. Burning of Athens. General alarm of the Greeks, and inclination of the fleet to disperse. Politic measures of Themistocles prevent the dispersal, and bring on a general engagement of the two fleets in the strait between Attica and Salamis, in which the Greeks with 380 sail completely vanquish and disperse the Persian fleet of 1207 triremes. Terror of Xerxes—his retreat. Mardonius winters in Thessaly, and in the summer of B.C. 479 resumes the offensive with 300,000 picked Asiatic troops, and 50,000 confederate Greeks. Negotiations follow between Persia and Argos. Persian troops re-occupy Attica and enter the Megarid. Long inaction of Sparta. Death of Cleombrotus and accession of Pausanias followed by a sudden change of policy. The full force of Sparta is levied; large contingents are demanded and obtained from the allies; and the Greeks take the field with above 100,000 men. Mardonius retires into Bœotia. The Greeks cross Cithæron and take up a position near Platæa. Manœuvres of Mardonius. He at length attacks the Greeks as they are executing a difficult movement, so that they have to engage with two-fifths of their army absent. Battle of Platæa. Complete rout of the Persians—only Artabazus, with a body of 40,000, retreats in good order. Double disaster at Mycalé a fit termination of the first act of the great historic drama.

The Greeks assume the offensive, B.C. 479.

7. The discomfiture of the assailing force which had threatened the liberties of Greece, while it was far from bringing the war to an end, entirely changed its character. Greece now took the offensive. Not content with driving her foe beyond her borders, she aimed at pressing Persia back from the advanced position which she had occupied in this quarter, regarding it as menacing to her own security. At the same time, she punished severely the Grecian states which had invited or encouraged the invader. Moreover, she vindicated to herself, as the natural consequence of the victories of Salamis and Mycalé, the complete command of the Levant, or Eastern Mediterranean, and the sovereignty over all the littoral islands, including Cyprus.

OPERATIONS AFTER MYCALÉ. Siege and capture of Sestos, B.C. 479. Expedition of Pausanias to Cyprus, and liberation of the island from the Persian yoke, B.C. 478. Siege of Byzantium, also conducted by Pausanias.

Byzantium taken. Siege and capture of Eïon, B.C. 477. Attempts on Doriscus.

8. The new position into which Greece had been brought by the course of events, a position requiring activity, enterprise, the constant employment of considerable forces at a distance from home, and the occupation of the Ægean with a powerful navy, led naturally to the great change which now took place in Grecian arrangements—the withdrawal of Sparta from the conduct of the Persian War, and the substitution of Athens as leader. No doubt Sparta did not see at once all which this change involved. The misconduct of Pausanias, who entered into treasonable negotiations with Xerxes, and the want of elasticity in her system, which unfitted her for distant foreign wars, made Sparta glad to retire from an unpleasant duty, the burden of which she threw upon Athens, without suspecting the profit and advantage which that ambitious state would derive from undertaking it. She did not suppose that she was thereby yielding up her claim to the headship of all Greece at home, or erecting Athens into a rival. She imagined that she could shift on to a subordinate responsibilities which were too much for her, without changing the attitude of that subordinate towards herself. This was a fatal mistake, so far as her own interests were concerned, and had to be redeemed at a vast cost during a war which lasted, with short interruptions, for the space of more than fifty years.

Sparta abdicates the leadership, B.C. 477.

9. On Athens the change made by the transference of the leadership had an effect which, if not really advantageous in all respects, seemed at any rate for a time to be extraordinarily beneficial. Her patriotic exertions during the war of invasion appeared to have received thereby their due reward. She had obtained a free vent for her superabundant activity, energy, and enterprise. She was to be at the head of a league of the naval powers of Greece, offensive and defensive, against Persia. The original idea of the league was that of a free confederation. Delos was appointed as its centre. There the Congress was to sit, and there was to be the common treasury. But Athens soon converted her acknowledged headship (ἡγεμονία) into a sovereignty (ἀρχή).

Assumption of the command by Athens. Commencement of the Athenian Empire.

First, the right of states to secede from the confederacy, which was left undecided by the terms of the confederation, was denied; and, upon its assertion, was decided in the negative by the unanswerable argument of force. Next, the treasury was transferred from Delos to Athens, and the meetings of the Congress were discontinued. Finally, the separate treasury of the league was merged in that of Athens; the money and ships of the allies were employed for her own aggrandizement in whatever way Athens pleased; and the various members of the league, excepting a few of the more powerful, were treated as Athenian subjects, compelled to model their governments in accordance with Athenian views, and even forced to allow all important causes to be transferred by appeal from their own local courts to those of the Imperial City. These changes, while they immensely increased the wealth and the apparent importance and power of Athens, did nevertheless, by arousing a deep and general feeling of discontent among her subject-allies, introduce an element of internal weakness into her system, which, when the time of trial came, was sure to show itself and to issue in disaster, if not in ruin.

Internal changes in the Athenian Constitution. Brilliant period of Athens.

10. Internal changes of considerable importance accompanied this exaltation of Athens to the headship of an Empire. The power of the Clisthenic *stratēgi* increased, while that of the old archons declined until it became a mere shadow. The democracy advanced. By a law of Aristides, B.C. 478, the last vestige of a property qualification was swept away, and every Athenian citizen was made eligible to every office. The law-courts were remodelled and systematized by Pericles, who also introduced the plan of paying the poorer citizens for their attendance. The old council of the Areopagus was assailed, its political power destroyed, and its functions made simply judicial. At the same time, however, certain conservative alterations were introduced by way of balance. The establishment of the Nomophylaces and the Nomothetæ, together with the institution of the Indictment for Illegality (γραφὴ παρανόμων), had a decided tendency to check the over-rapid progress of change. The practice of re-electing year after year a favorite *stratēgus* gave to the republic something of the stability of monarchy, and rendered fluc-

tuations in policy less frequent than they would otherwise have been, and less extreme. Meanwhile, the convenient institution of ostracism diminished the violence of party struggles, and preserved the state from all attempts upon its liberties. The sixty years which followed Salamis form, on the whole, the most brilliant period of Athenian history, and exhibit to us the exceptional spectacle of a full-blown democracy, which has nevertheless all the steadiness, the firmness, and the prudent self-control of a limited monarchy or other mixed government.

Ornamentation of the city. Athens the chief seat of literature and the arts.

11. Athens also during this period became the most splendid of Greek cities, and was the general resort of all who excelled in literature or in the arts. The Parthenon, the Theseium, the temple of Victory, the Propylæa were built, and adorned with the paintings of Polygnotus and the exquisite sculptures of Phidias and his school. Cimon and Pericles vied with each other in the beautifying of the city of their birth; and the encouragement which the latter especially gave to talent of every kind, collected to Athens a galaxy of intellectual lights such as is almost without parallel in the history of mankind. At the same time, works of utility were not neglected, but advanced at an equal pace with those whose character was ornamental. The defenses of Athens were rebuilt immediately after the departure of the Persians, and not long afterwards the fortifications were extended to the sea on either side by the "Long Walls" to the two ports of Piræus and Phalêrum. The triple harbor of Piræus was artificially enlarged and strengthened. New docks were made, and a town was laid out on a grand plan for the maritime population. A magnificent force of triremes was kept up, maintained always at the highest point of efficiency. Colonies were moreover sent out to distant shores, and new towns arose, at Amphipolis, Thurii, and elsewhere, which reproduced in remote and barbarous regions the splendor and taste of the mother city on a reduced scale.

Successes of Cimon, B.C. 475-463.

12. Although Aristides was the chief under whom Athens obtained her leadership, and Themistocles the statesman to whom she owed it that she was thought of for such a position, yet the guidance of the state on her new career was intrusted to neither the one

nor the other, but to Cimon. Aristides appears to have been regarded as deficient in military talent; and the dishonest conduct of Themistocles had rendered him justly open to suspicion. It was thus to the son of the victor at Marathon that the further humiliation of Persia was now committed.

CAMPAIGNS OF CIMON:—Siege and capture of Eïon, about B.C. 475. Occupation of Scyros, B.C. 470. Expedition to Asia, and victories of Cimon at the Eurymedon, B.C. 466. War with Thasos, B.C. 465, and attempt to found Amphipolis. Thasos reduced, B.C. 463. Contingent sent to aid the Spartans against their revolted Helots. Contingent dismissed, B.C. 461. Anger of the Athenians on this account.

Revolt of the Helots, B.C. 464. Cimon ostracized. Advent of Pericles to power.

13. The revolt of the Spartan Helots simultaneously with the siege of Thasos, B.C. 464, was an event the importance of which can scarcely be over-estimated. It led to the first actual rupture of friendly relations between Athens and Sparta; and it occupied the attention of Sparta so completely for ten years that she could do nothing during that time to check the rapid advance which Athens made, so soon as she found herself free to take whatever part she pleased in Grecian politics. It likewise caused the banishment of Cimon (B.C. 461), and the elevation of Pericles to the chief direction of affairs —a change of no small moment, being the substitution of a consummate statesman as chief of the state for a mere moderately skillful general.

Aims of Pericles.

14. The ambition of Pericles aimed at securing to Athens the first position in Greece both by land and sea. He understood that Sparta would not tolerate such pretensions, and was prepared to contest with that power the supremacy on shore. But he believed that ultimately, in such a country as Greece, the command of the sea would carry with it a predominant power over the land also. He did not design to withdraw Athens from her position of leader against Persia; but, treating the Persian War as a secondary and subordinate affair, he wished to direct the main energies of his country towards the acquisition of such authority and influence in central and northern Greece as would place her on a par with Sparta as a land power. At the same time, he sought to strengthen himself by alliances with such states of the Peloponnese as were jealous of Sparta; and he was willing, when danger threatened, to relinquish

the contest with Persia altogether, and to devote all his efforts to the establishment of the supremacy of Athens over Greece.

MILITARY HISTORY OF ATHENS UNDER PERICLES, from B.C. 461 to B.C. 447. Alliance made with Argos and Thessaly, B.C. 461. The Megarid annexed, and its capital connected by "Long Walls" with the sea. First Peloponnesian War, under the leadership of Corinth, B.C. 460 to 457. Double defeat of the Corinthians on the land, and victory gained by Athens over the Æginetans and their allies by sea. Siege of Ægina. Fleet of 200 vessels, dispatched to Cyprus against the Persians, proceeds to Egypt to assist Inarus. The Athenian "Long Walls" are begun. Effort made by Sparta to check her rival brings on the battle of Tanagra, B.C. 457, a Spartan victory, but one which left the field completely open to Athens. The victory of Myronidas at Œnophyta, sixty-two days after Tanagra (B.C. 456), lays Bœotia prostrate at her feet. Phocis and Opuntian Locris submit to her. Ægina surrenders, and joins the Athenian confederacy. Recall of Cimon, and completion of the "Long Walls." Triumphant cruise of Tolmidas round the Peloponnese, B.C. 455. Athenian expedition into Thessaly in the same year fails. Disasters overtake the ships sent to Egypt. Pericles in person makes an unsuccessful attempt on Œniadæ, B.C. 454. Warned by these continued disasters, and distrustful of the condition of Bœotia, Pericles, three years later, concludes a peace with Sparta for five years, B.C. 451. This enables him once more to dispatch a force against Persia, which is placed under the command of Cimon, who dies at the siege of Citium. The fleet, however, shortly afterwards gains a great victory off Salamis. Hereupon peace is made. Athens relinquishes to Persia Cyprus and Egypt, while Persia permits the independence of the Greek cities in Asia Minor, B.C. 450. A short pause occurs, and then the fabric of Athenian land empire is shattered by the rebellion of Bœotia and the defeat of Coroneia, B.C. 447, which involve the further immediate loss of Phocis and Locris, while they threaten still worse consequences.

15. The culminating period of Athenian greatness was the interval between Œnophyta and Coroneia, B.C. 456 to 447.

Athens reaches the height of her power, and begins to decline, B.C. 447.

Pericles, who at the outset appeared likely to succeed in all that he had planned, learned gradually by the course of events that he had overrated his country's powers, and wisely acquiesced in the inevitable. From about B.C. 454 his aim was to consolidate and conserve, not to enlarge, the dominion of Athens. But the policy of moderation came too late. Bœotia, Phocis, and Locris burned to be free, and determined to try the chance of arms, so soon as a convenient occasion offered. Coroneia came, and Athens was struck down upon her knees. Two years later, on the expiration of the five years' peace (B.C. 445), Sparta arranged a combination which threatened her rival with actual destruction. Megara on the one side and Eubœa on the other were stirred to revolt, while a Peloponnesian force under Pleistoanax and Cleandridas invaded Attica at Eleusis. But the crisis was met by Pericles with firmness and wisdom. The Spartan leaders were accessible to bribes, and the expenditure of a few talents relieved Athens from her greatest danger. Eubœa, the possession of which was of vital consequence to the unproductive Attica, received a severe punishment for her disaffection at the hands of Pericles himself. Megara, and a few outlying remnants of the land empire enjoyed from B.C. 456 to 447, were made the price of peace. By the cession of what it would have been impossible to retain, Athens purchased for herself a long term of rest, during which she might hope to recruit her strength and prepare herself to make another struggle for the supremacy.

Thirty years' peace concluded, B.C. 445. Authority of Pericles at its height. Ostracism of Thucydides, son of Melesias, B.C. 443. Great works of Pericles executed. Power of Athens nursed by extension of *cleruch* system (e. g., Hestiæa and Sinôpé), and by the judicious planting of colonies (e. g., Thurii, B.C. 443, and Amphipolis, B.C. 437). Good economy of Pericles, and flourishing condition of the treasury. The only interruption of peace during the thirteen years from B.C. 445 to 432 is caused by the defection of Samos, B.C. 440, which the Athenians provoke by interference in the local politics. Revolt put down, after a nine months' siege, by Pericles.

Commencement of differences between Corinth and Corcyra on account of Epidamnus, B.C. 436. Naval victory of the Corcyræans, B.C. 435. Great preparations of Corinth, and application of Corcyra to Athens, B.C. 433. Corcyra taken into alliance and effectually protected, B.C. 432.

In revenge, Corinth induces Potidæa to revolt from Athens, B.C. 432. Other Chalcidian cities join. Corinth assists the revolters. Perdiccas faithful to neither side. Athenians lay siege to Potidæa. Corinth appeals to Sparta, and, after fruitless negotiations, war is declared, B.C. 431.

The Peloponnesian War. B.C. 431–404.

16. The struggle which now commenced is known by the name of the "Peloponnesian War." It lasted twenty-seven years, from B.C. 431 to 404, and extended itself over almost the whole of the Grecian world, involving almost every state from Selinus at the extreme west of Sicily to Cnidus and Rhodes in the Ægean. Though in the main a war for supremacy between the two great powers of Greece, Athens and Sparta, it was also to a certain extent "a struggle of principles," and likewise, though to a lesser extent, "a war of races." Speaking gen-

erally, the Ionian Greeks were banded together on the one side, and made common cause with the Athenians; while the Dorian Greeks, with a few remarkable exceptions, gave their aid to the Spartans. But political sympathy determined, to a greater degree than race, the side to which each state should attach itself. Athens and Sparta were respectively in the eyes of the Greeks the representatives of the two principles of democracy and oligarchy; and it was felt that, according as the one or the other preponderated, the cause of oligarchical or democratical government was in the ascendant. The principle of non-intervention was unknown. Both powers alike were propagandist; and revolutionized, as occasion offered, the constitutions of their dependencies. Even without intervention, party spirit was constantly at work, and the triumph of a faction over its rival in this or that petty state might at any time disturb the balance of power between the two chief belligerents.

Contrast presented by the two chief belligerents.

17. These two belligerents offered a remarkable contrast to each other in many respects. Athens was predominantly a maritime, Sparta a land power. Athens had influence chiefly on the eastern side of Greece and in Asia; Sparta, on the western side of Greece, and in Italy and Sicily. Again, the position of Sparta with respect to her allies was very different from that of Athens. Sparta was at the head of a purely voluntary confederacy, the members of which regarded their interests as bound up in hers, and accepted her, on account of her superior military strength, as their natural leader. Athens was mistress of an empire which she had acquired, to a considerable extent, by force; and was disliked by most of her subject-allies, who accepted her leadership, not from choice, but from compulsion. Thus Sparta was able to present herself before men's minds in the character of "liberator of Greece;" though, had she obtained a complete ascendency over the rest of Greece, her yoke would probably have been found at least as galling as the Athenian.

ALLIES OF SPARTA. The allies on whom Sparta could count were the Corinthians, the Bœotians, the Megarians, the Phocians, the Locrians, the Ambraciots, the Leucadians, the Anactorians, the Arcadians, the Eleans, the Sicyonians, and the Achæans of Pellênê. In Ætolia the semi-barbarous inhabitants were inclined to be favorable to them; and in Italy and Sicily the

Dorian cities were their well-wishers, and might be expected, under certain circumstances, to lend them aid.

SUBJECT-ALLIES of ATHENS. These were Eubœa, Chios, Lesbos, Samos, the Cyclades and Sporades (except Melos and Thera, which were neutral), maritime Caria, all the Greek cities in Asia Minor and on the coast of Thrace, Platæa, Naupactus, Zacynthus, and Corcyra. The Thessalians and Acarnanians were friendly to them, and so were the Ionian cities in Sicily and Italy. Besides her allies, Athens held at this time, as parts of her own territory, Hestiæa, Ægina, Scyros, Lemnos, Imbrus, and the Chersonese.

18. Among the principal advantages which Athens possessed over Sparta at the commencement of the war was the better arrangement of her finance. Sparta can scarcely be said to have had a revenue at all. Her military expenses were met by extraordinary contributions, which she and her allies levied upon themselves, as occasion seemed to require. Athens, on the contrary, had an organized system, which secured her an annual revenue greatly exceeding her needs in time of peace, and sufficient to support the whole expense of a moderate war. When extraordinary efforts were required, she could fall back on her accumulations, which were large; or she could augment her income by requiring from her citizens an increased rate of property-tax.

Finances of Athens.

FINANCES of ATHENS. (i.) *Sources of her Revenue.* 1. The tribute paid by the subject-allies, which was originally fixed, by the rating of Aristides, at 460 talents (about £110,000) annually, but had been raised, by the substitution of money for ships, from that sum to 600 talents (£145,000). 2. The μετοίκιον, or direct tax paid by foreign residents. 3. The income derived from the public property of the state, especially from the mines, which about this time were very productive. 4. The customs—a 2 per cent. *ad valorem* duty on all exports and imports. 5. Harbor-dues—1 per cent. on the value of all cargoes brought into Athenian ports. 6. A duty on slaves, paid by their masters. 7. A tax on emancipated slaves, paid by themselves. 8. The εἰσφορά or property-tax—a resource on which the state could fall back, but which was not used in ordinary years. The entire revenue from all these sources put together has been estimated at 1000, and again at 2000 talents, i. e., at a quarter or half a million of our money. To complete the notion of the means of the state, we must add to these various sources of revenue the *liturgies*, which threw on individuals the duty of providing for various expenses that must otherwise have been defrayed by the state. (ii.) *Heads of Expenditure.* 1. The support of the navy, including building of ships and pay of men, was probably the largest head. 2. Next to this might come the expenditure on shows and sights (τὸ θεωρικόν). 3. The pay of soldiers in actual service would be a third head. 4. The dicasts', and at a later date the ecclesiasts' fees, would also be an important item. 5. In most years some money would be spent on public buildings. 6. Votes were likewise often passed for the reward of individuals, which must in some years have amounted to a large sum. 7. Finally, there was a kind of "secret-service money," which, though not large, was remarkable.

Athens began the war with an accumulation of coin to the amount of 6000 talents (nearly £1,500,000) in her treasury. She had likewise in her temples deposits and offerings of great value. The single statue of Athênê, in the Parthenon, is said to have had gold ornaments worth more than £125,000.

Three periods of the War.

19. The Peloponnesian War may be divided into three periods:—1st. From the commencement until the conclusion of the Peace of Nicias—ten years—B.C. 431 to 421. 2d. From the Peace of Nicias to its formal rupture by Sparta—eight years, B.C. 421 to 413. 3d. From the rupture of the Peace of Nicias to the capture of Athens—rather more than nine years—B.C. 413 to 404.

First Period, B.C. 431–421.

20. *First Period.*—The struggle was conducted for two years and a half by Pericles; then by Nicias, but under the check of a strong opposition led by Cleon. Athens was continually more and more successful up to B.C. 424, when the fortune of war changed. The rash expedition into Bœotia in that year lost Athens the flower of her troops at Delium; while the genius of the young Spartan, Brasidas, first saved Megara, and then, transferring the war into Thrace, threatened to deprive the Athenians of the entire mass of their allies in this quarter. The effort made to recover Amphipolis (B.C. 422) having failed, and Athens fearing greatly the further spread of disaffection among her subject-cities, peace was made on terms disadvantageous but not dishonorable to Athens—the general principle of the peace being the *statu quo ante bellum*, but certain exceptions being made with regard to Platæa and the Thracian towns, which placed Athens in a worse position than that which she held when the war began.

DETAILS OF THE WAR. B.C. 431. Attack on Platæa by Thebans. Invasion of Attica by Archidamus. Athenian fleet ravages the Peloponnesian coast, and brings over Cephallenia. First appearance of Brasidas, who saves Methônê. Athenians in full force ravage the Megarid. Alliance made by Athens with Sitalces, king of Thrace.—B.C. 430. Second invasion of Attica by Archidamus. Appearance of the plague. Athenian fleet, under Pericles, ravages Epidaurus and Trœzen. Plague carried to Potidæa. Spartans attempt to make alliance with Persia. Potidæa recovered.—B.C. 429. Spartans, under Archidamus, blockade Platæa, and under Cnemus attempt to reduce Acarnania. Failure of Cnemus, and naval victories of Phormio. Death of Pericles. Expedition of Sitalces.—B.C. 428. Third invasion of Attica, under Archidamus. Revolt of Mytilênê. Athenian fleet ravages the Peloponnese.—B.C. 427. Fourth invasion of Attica, under Cleomenes. Reduction and punishment of Mytilênê. Surrender of Platæa. Attempt of Peloponnesians to recover Corcyra by aid of the oligarchical party leads to a bloody revolution in that island. First Athenian expedition to Sicily.—B.C. 426. Earthquakes prevent the usual invasion of Attica. Failure of Nicias to take Melos. Unsuccessful expedition of Demosthenes into Ætolia. Foundation of Heracleia in Trachis by the Spartans. Defeat of Eurylochus at Olpæ by Demosthenes.—B.C. 425. Fifth invasion of Attica, under Agis. Occupation of Pylos, and blockade of Sphacteria. Attempt of Sparta to make peace frustrated by Cleon. Sphacteria captured by Cleon and Demosthenes. The Messenians settled at Pylos. Nicias, in command of the fleet, first attacks Corinth, but is beaten off, and then occupies Methana, in Epidauria. Fresh troubles in Corcyra. Anactorium taken. Chios suspected. —B.C. 424. Attica not invaded. Athenians under Nicias occupy Cythera, and take and burn Thyrea. Attempt to recover Megara fails, but results in capture of Nisæa. Disasters begin. The Greek cities in Sicily come to terms, and require the Athenians to quit the island. An invasion of Bœotia from two quarters completely fails, and the Athenians are signally defeated at Delium. Brasidas marches through Thessaly into Chalcidicé, and is received as a liberator by Acanthus, Argilus, Amphipolis, and other cities.—B.C. 423. A truce made for a year. Brasidas continues to receive into alliance such of the Chalcidic cities as revolt to him. His expedition, in conjunction with Perdiccas, against the Illyrians. Nicias recovers Mendé, besieges Scioné, and makes alliance with Perdiccas.—B.C. 422. Cleon, appointed to the command in Thrace, takes Torônê and Galepsus, and tries to recover Amphipolis, but is completely defeated by Brasidas, who, however, as well as Cleon, is slain in the battle. Hereupon peace is made, chiefly by the efforts of Nicias.

Second Period, B.C. 421–413. Rise of Alcibiades to power.

21. *Second Period.*—The continuance of hostilities during this period, while there was peace, and even for some time alliance, between the two chief belligerents, was attributable, at first, to the hatred which Corinth bore to Athens, and to the energy which she showed in forming coalitions against her detested rival. Afterwards it was owing also in part to the ambition and influence of Alcibiades, who desired a renewal of the war, hoping thereby to obtain a sphere suitable to his talents. Argos, during this period, rose for a time into consideration, her alliance being sought on all hands; but the battle of Mantinea, by destroying the flower of her troops, once more broke her power, and her final gravitation to the Athenian side was of no consequence.

DETAILS OF THE HISTORY. B.C. 421. Alliance, offensive and defensive, between Athens and Sparta. Defensive alliance between Argos, Corinth, Mantinea, Elis, and Chalcidicé. Alliance, offensive and defensive, between Sparta and Bœotia. — B.C. 420. Athens, offended hereat, makes alliance with Argos. Mantinea and Elis join this league. Sparta is rejoined by most of her old allies.—B.C. 419. Expedition of Alcibiades into the Peloponnese. War between Argos and Epidaurus. — B.C. 418. Sparta takes the field against Argos. Battle of Mantinea. Argos submits and joins the Peloponnesian league, but repents the next year, B.C. 417, and makes alliance with Athens.—B.C. 416. Athenian expedition against Melos.

22. Far more important than his Peloponnesian schemes was the project, which Alcibiades now brought forward, of conquering Sicily. The success of this attempt would have completely destroyed the balance of power in Greece, and have made Athens irresistible. The project, though perhaps somewhat over-bold, would probably have succeeded, had the task of carrying it through to the end been intrusted to the genius which conceived it. Unfortunately for Athens, she was forced to choose between endangering her liberties by maintaining Alcibiades in power and risking the failure of an expedition to which she was too far committed for her to be able to recede. The recall of Alcibiades was injurious to Athens in various ways. It deprived her of her best general, and of the only statesman she possessed who was competent to deal with all the peculiar difficulties of the expedition. It made Sparta fully acquainted with the Athenian schemes for the management of Sicilian affairs, and so enabled her to counteract them. Finally, it transferred to the enemy the most keen and subtle intellect of the time, an intellect almost certain to secure success to the side which it espoused. Still, if the choice lay (as probably it did) between accepting Alcibiades as tyrant and driving him into exile, we must hold Athens justified in the course which she took. There might easily be a rapid recovery from the effects of a disastrous expedition. Who could predict the time at which the state would recover from the loss of those liberties on which her prosperity had recently depended?

Project of conquering Sicily.

SICILIAN EXPEDITION. B.C. 415. First fleet and army sent out under the command of Nicias, Lamachus, and Alcibiades. Armament numbers 134 triremes, 5100 hoplites, and 1300 light-armed. Obtains possession of Naxos and Catana. Recall of Alcibiades, who escapes to Sparta. Desultory operations of Nicias.—B.C. 414. Siege of Syracuse commences. Death of Lamachus. Arrival of Gylippus.

23. *Third Period.*—The maintenance of the "Peace of Nicias" had long been rather nominal than real. Athens and Sparta had indeed abstained hitherto from direct attacks upon each other's territories; but they had been continually employed in plots against each other's interests, and they had met in conflict both in the Peloponnese and in Sicily. Now at length, after eight years, the worn-out fiction of a pretended amity was discarded; and the Spartans, by the advice of Alcibiades, not only once more invaded Attica, but made a permanent settlement at Deceleia within sight of Athens. The main theatre of the struggle continued, however, to be Sicily; where the Athenians clung with desperation to a scheme which prudence required them to relinquish, and lavishly sent fleet after fleet and army after army to maintain a conflict which was hopeless. Still the expedition might have re-embarked, without suffering any irreparable disaster, had it not been for an improvement in ship-building, devised by the Corinthians and eagerly adopted by the Syracusans, which deprived Athens of her command of the sea, and forced her armies to surrender at discretion. Thus the fatal blow, from which Athens never recovered, was struck by the hatred of Corinth, which, in the course of a few weeks, more than avenged the injuries of half a century.

Third Period, B.C. 413–404. Destruction of the Sicilian expedition, B.C. 413.

CONCLUSION OF THE WAR IN SICILY. Athens sends out a fresh armament under Demosthenes and Eurymedon. Night attack on the Syracusan works fails. Naval battles in the harbor of Syracuse result in defeat of Athens. Siege raised. Attempt of Nicias and Demosthenes to reach the south coast fails. Surrender of the two armies. Cruel treatment of the prisoners, B.C. 413.

24. The immediate result of the disasters in Sicily was the transference of the war to Asia Minor. Her great losses in ships and sailors had so crippled the naval power of Athens, that her command of the sea was gone; the more so, as her adversaries were strengthened by the accession to their fleet of a powerful Sicilian contingent. The knowledge of this entire change in the relative position of the two belligerents at sea, encouraged the subject-allies generally to shake off the Athenian yoke. Sparta saw the importance of encouraging this defection; and crossing the Ægean Sea in force, made the theatre of war Asia

Transfer of the War to Asia Minor, B.C. 412.

Minor, the islands, and the Hellespont. Here, for the first time, she was able to make the Persian alliance, which she had so long sought, of use to her. Persian gold enabled her to maintain a fleet equal or superior to that of Athens, and ultimately gave her the victory in the long doubtful contest.

Wonderful vigor of Athens.

25. What most surprises us, in the third and last period of the war, is the vigor of the Athenian defense; the elasticity of spirit, the energy, and the fertility of resource which seemed for a time to have completely surmounted the Sicilian calamity, and made the final issue once more appear to be doubtful. This wonderful recovery of strength and power was, no doubt, in a great measure due to the genius of one man—Alcibiades. But something must be attributed to the temper and character of the people. Athens, like Rome, is the greatest and most admirable in misfortune; it is then that her courage, her patience, and her patriotism deserve and command our sympathies.

DETAILS OF THE WAR TILL THE DISGRACE OF ALCIBIADES. B.C. 412. Revolt of Chios, Miletus, and other Ionian cities. Arrangements between Sparta and Tissaphernes. Samos preserved to Athens by a bloody revolution. Battle of Miletus. Naval victory of Astyochus. Cnidus and Rhodes revolt from Athens.—B.C. 411. War languishes. Finesse of Tissaphernes. Revolt of Abydos, Chalcedon, and Byzantium. Mindarus succeeds Astyochus, and transfers the war to the Hellespont, where he is supported by Pharnabazus. Recall of Alcibiades. Naval victory of Sestus gained by Thrasybulus. At home, the Athenians lose Eubœa.—B.C. 410. Great victory of Cyzicus gained by Alcibiades. Spartans make proposals of peace, which are rejected.—B.C. 409. Defeat of Thrasyllus, near Ephesus. Victory of Abydos. At home, loss of Nisæa and Pylos.—B.C. 408. Alcibiades recovers Chalcedon and Byzantium. Returns to Athens and is received with favor (B.C. 407); but, on the loss of the battle of Notium by his lieutenant in his absence, is disgraced, and goes into exile.

Arrival of the younger Cyrus gives the final victory to Sparta.

26. The arrival of the younger Cyrus in Asia Minor was of great advantage to Sparta, and must be regarded as mainly effective in bringing the war rapidly to a successful issue. Hitherto the satraps had pursued the policy which the interests of Persia required, had trimmed the balance, and contrived that neither side should obtain a decided preponderance over the other. But Cyrus had personal views, which such a course would not have subserved. He required the assistance of Greek troops and ships in the great enterprise that he was

meditating; and, to obtain such aid, it was necessary for him to make a real friend of one belligerent or the other. He chose Sparta, as best suited to furnish him the aid he required; and, having made his choice, he threw himself into the cause with all the energy of his nature. It was his prompt and lavish generosity which prevented the victory of Arginusæ from being of any real service to Athens, and enabled Lysander to undo its effects and regain the mastery of the sea, within the space of thirteen months, by the crowning victory of Ægos-potami. That victory *may* also have been in another way the result of Lysander's command of Persian gold; for it is a reasonable suspicion that some of the Athenian commanders were bribed, and that the negligence which lost the battle had been paid for out of the stores of Cyrus.

CLOSING YEARS OF THE WAR. Conon succeeds Alcibiades in the command, B.C. 406. Naval victory of Callicratidas. Conon is shut up in Mytilênê. Great efforts made to release him. Fresh armament sent out, and victory of the Athenians at Arginusæ. Condemnation of the generals for neglect of the men on board the disabled ships. Lysander sent as commander by Sparta, B.C. 405. At first, declines an engagement. Proceeds to the Hellespont. Takes Lampsacus. Destroys the Athenian fleet at Ægospotami, except the squadron of Conon. Blockades Athens by sea, while Pausanias and Agis invest it by land. The city surrenders after a five months' siege—April, B.C. 404. The long walls and the defenses of the Peiræus are destroyed; all ships of war except twelve are given up; Athens places herself under the leadership of Sparta, and the city is handed over to an oligarchy of thirty men.

27. The internal history of Athens during the third period of the Peloponnesian War is full of interest. The disastrous termination of the Sicilian expedition threw discredit upon democratical institutions; and immediately after the news of it reached Athens, the constitution was modified in an aristocratic direction, B.C. 412. The change, however, then made was not regarded as sufficient; and in B.C. 411 a more complete revolution was effected. Cowed by a terrorism which the political clubs knew well how to exercise, the Athenian democracy submitted to see itself abolished in a perfectly legal manner. A nominated Council of 400 succeeded to the elective βουλή; and a pretended committee of 5000 took the place of the time-honored ἐκκλησία. This government, which was practi-

Internal history of Athens during this period.

cally that of three or four individuals, lasted for about four months, when it was overthrown by violence, and the democracy was restored again under certain restrictions.

Triumph of Sparta. Oppressiveness of her leadership.

28. The triumph of Sparta was the triumph throughout Greece of oligarchical principles. At Athens the democracy was abolished, and the entire control of the government placed in the hands of a Board of Thirty, a board which has acquired in history the ominous name of "the Thirty Tyrants." Boards of Ten (δεκαρχίαι), chosen by himself, were set up by Lysander as the supreme authority in Samos and in other cities, while Spartan "harmosts," with indefinite powers, were established everywhere. The Greeks found that, instead of gaining by the change of masters, they had lost; they had exchanged the yoke of a power, which, if rapacious, was at any rate refined, civilized, and polished, for that of one which added to rapacity a coarse arrogance and a cruel harshness which were infinitely exasperating and offensive. Even in the matter of the tribute there was no relaxation. Sparta found that, to maintain an empire, she must have a revenue; and the contributions of her subject-allies were assessed at the annual rate of 1000 talents (£243,000).

TIME OF THE THIRTY TYRANTS AT ATHENS. Reign of Terror. Internal quarrels, and execution of Theramenes. Thrasybulus and the exiles seize Phylé; advance and occupy the Peiræus. Defeat and death of Critias. Interference of Lysander and Pausanias. Accommodation made with Sparta—deposition of the oligarchy, and return of the exiles. Restoration of the democracy as it stood before the capture of Athens, B.C. 403.

The condition of Athens under the Thirty may be regarded as a sample of what happened generally in the Greek cities which the fortune of war had placed at the mercy of Sparta.

Expedition of the Ten Thousand. Effects on Greek and Persian policy.

29. The expedition of the Ten Thousand, B.C. 401 to 400, belongs less to the history of Greece than to that of Persia (see p. 120); but it had some important consequences on the after course of Greek policy. The weakness of Persia was laid bare; it was seen that her capital might be reached, and that Greek troops might march in security from end to end of the Empire. Hitherto even the attacks of the Greeks on Persian territory had been in a measure defensive, having for their object the security of European Hellas, or the liberation of the Greek cities in Asia. Henceforth ideas of actu-

al conquest floated before the Grecian mind; and the more restless spirits looked to this quarter as the best field for their ambition. On the side of the Persians, alarm at the possible results of Greek audacity began to be felt, and a new policy was developed in consequence. The Court of Susa henceforth took an active part in the Greek struggles, allying itself continually with one side or the other, and employing the treasures of the state in defraying the cost of Greek armaments, or in corrupting Greek statesmen. Finally, Persia came to be viewed as the ultimate arbiter of the Greek quarrels; and rescripts of the Great King at once imposed peace on the belligerents, and defined the terms on which it should be concluded.

War of the Spartans with Persia, B.C. 399-394.

30. The immediate consequence of the Cyreian expedition was war between Persia and Sparta. Sparta was known to have lent her aid to Cyrus; and Tissaphernes had orders, on his return to the coast, to retaliate by severities on the Greek cities, which were now under the protection of the Spartans. The challenge thus thrown down was readily accepted; and for six years —B.C. 399 to 394—Sparta carried on war in Asia Minor, first under generals of no great talent, but, finally, under Agesilaus, who succeeded in making the Great King tremble for his empire. The consequences would probably have been serious, if Persia had not succeeded in effecting a combination against the Spartans in Greece itself, which forced them to recall Agesilaüs from Asia.

Attack of Tissaphernes on the Greek cities, B.C. 400. Command of Thimbron, and reinforcement of his army by the returned Ten Thousand, B.C. 399. Thimbron superseded by Dercyllidas—his successful campaigns. Agesilaüs crosses into Asia, B.C. 396, and takes the command. Victory of the Pactôlus, B.C. 395. Agesilaüs invades Phrygia and Paphlagonia. His recall, B.C. 394.

Corinthian War, B.C. 394, terminated by the "Peace of Antalcidas."

31. Instigated by the Persians, and jealous of the power of Sparta, Argos, Thebes, Corinth, and Athens formed an alliance against her in the year B.C. 395. A war of a checkered character followed. Sparta lost the command of the sea by the great victory of Conon at Cnidus, but maintained her superiority on land in the battles of Corinth, Coronæa, and Lechæum. Still she found the strain upon her resources so great, and the dif-

ficulty of resisting the confederation, supported as it was by the gold and the ships of Persia, so extreme, that after a few years she felt it necessary to procure peace at any cost. It was at her instance, and by her energetic exertions, that Persia was induced to come forward in the new character of arbitress, and to require the acceptance by the Greeks generally of the terms contained in the "Peace of Antalcidas" (see p. 120)—terms disgraceful to the Greeks, but advantageous to Sparta, as the clause establishing the independence of all the Greek states (πόλεις) injured Corinth and Thebes, while it left her own power untouched.

The Spartans invade Bœotia, and are defeated at Haliartus, B.C. 395. Lysander falls. Agesilaüs is recalled from Asia. Victory of Conon at Cnidus soon after his departure, B.C. 394. Battle of Corinth and Coronæa in the same year. Battle of Lechæum, B.C. 393. Conon and Pharnabazus with a Persian fleet ravage the Peloponnese and take Cythera. Long Walls of Athens restored. Revolutions at Corinth, B.C. 392, followed by a union with Argos. Successes of Iphicrates. Expeditions of Agesilaüs into Acarnania, B.C. 391, and of Agesipolis into Argolis, B.C. 390. Athenians assist the Cypriot rebel, Evagoras. Death of Thrasybulus. Teleutias plunders Piræus, B.C. 388. Acceptance of the "Peace of Antalcidas," B.C. 387.

32. The immediate consequences of the "Peace of Antalcidas" were the separation of Corinth from Argos, and the deposition of Thebes from her hegemony over the Bœotian cities. The re-establishment of Platæa followed, a judicious measure on the part of Sparta, tending to produce estrangement between Thebes and Athens. Sparta was now at the zenith of her power. Claiming the right of seeing to the execution of the treaty which she had negotiated, she extended her influence on all sides, nowhere meeting with resistance. But the intoxication of success had its usual effect in developing selfishness and arrogance—fatal defects in a ruling state, always stirring up sentiments of hostility, which sooner or later produce the downfall of the power that provokes them. The domineering insolence which dictated to Mantineia and Phlius, might indeed, if confined to those cities, or others like them, have had no ill results; but when, in time of peace, the citadel of Thebes was occupied, and the act, if not commanded, was at least approved and adopted by Sparta, the bitter enmity of one of the most powerful states of Greece was aroused, and

Effect of this "Peace."

Punishment of Mantineia and Phlius by Sparta.

Seizure of the Cadmeia, B.C. 382.

every other state was made to feel that, in its turn, it might by some similar deed be deprived of independence. But the aggressor was for the time triumphant; and having no open enemy now within the limits of Greece Proper, sought one on the borders of Thrace and Macedon, where, under the headship of Olynthus, a powerful confederacy was growing up, consisting in part of Greek, in part of Macedonian, cities. A war of four years, B.C. 382 to 379, sufficed to crush this rising power, and thus to remove from Northern Greece the only rival which Macedon had seriously to fear—the only state which, by its situation, its material resources, and its numerical strength, might have offered a considerable obstacle to the advance of the Macedonian kings to empire.

War with Olynthus, B.C. 382–379.

33. Thus far success had attended every enterprise of Sparta, however cruel or wicked; but at length the day of retribution came. Pelopidas and his friends effected a bloody revolution at Thebes, recovered the Cadmeia, expelling the Spartan garrison, and set about the restoration of the old Bœotian league. Athens, injured and insulted, declared war against her old rival, made alliance with Thebes, revived her old confederacy on fair and equitable terms, and recovered the empire of the seas by the victories of Naxos and Leucas. All the efforts of Sparta against her two antagonists failed, and after seven years of unsuccessful war she was reduced to make a second appeal to Persia, who once more dictated the terms on which peace was to be made. Athens, now grown jealous of Thebes, was content to sign, and her confederates followed her lead; but Thebes by the mouth of Epaminondas declined, unless she were recognized as head of Bœotia. As Sparta positively refused to admit this claim, Thebes was publicly and formally excluded from the Treaty of Peace.

Thebes recovers her independence.

War of Sparta against Thebes and Athens, B.C. 379–373.

Peace made with Athens.

Pelopidas and his brother exiles enter Thebes, murder the polemarchs, and induce the Spartan garrison to capitulate, B.C. 379. Expedition of Cleombrotus into Bœotia, and attempt of Sphodrias on the Piræus, B.C. 378. Acquittal of Sphodrias at Sparta causes Athens to declare war. Revival of the Athenian confederacy, but as a voluntary union, and with no fixed rate of tribute. New arrangement of the Athenian property-tax. Two expeditions of Agesilaüs against Thebes, B.C. 378 and 377. Attempt of Cleombrotus, B.C. 376. Sparta tries to reassert her command of the sea, but is defeated by

Chabrias near Naxos, B.C. 376, and by Timotheus off the peninsula of Leucas, B.C. 375. Victory of Pelopidas at Tegyra, B.C. 374, and recovery of all Bœotia by Thebes, except Orchomenus. Bœotian confederacy reorganized. Thebes attacks Phocis. Attempt of Sparta to take Corcyra fails, B.C. 373. Third embassy of Antalcidas to the court of Susa, and conclusion of peace at Sparta between all the belligerents except Thebes, B.C. 372.

Rise of Jason of Pheræ to power about this time. Application of Polydamas the Pharsalian to Sparta rejected, B.C. 374. Dionysius I. of Syracuse aids the Lacedæmonians, B.C. 373.

War of Sparta against Thebes. Battle of Leuctra, B.C. 371, and its consequences.

34. Sparta now, having only Thebes to contend with, imagined that her triumph was secure, and sent her troops into Bœotia under Cleombrotus, hoping to crush and destroy Thebes. But the magnificent victory of Epaminondas at Leuctra—the fruit at once of extraordinary strategic skill at the time, and of an excellent training of his soldiers previously—dashed all these hopes to the ground. Sparta fell, suddenly and forever, from her high estate. Almost all Central Greece joined Thebes. Arcadia rose and began to organize itself as a federation. The Lacedæmonian harmosts were expelled from all the cities, and the philo-Laconian party was everywhere put down. Epaminondas, moreover, as soon as the murder of Jason of Pheræ left him free to act, redoubled his blows. Entering the Peloponnese, he ravaged the whole Spartan territory at will, and even threatened the city; which Agesilaüs with some difficulty preserved. But these temporary losses and disgraces were as nothing compared with the permanent injuries which the prudent policy of the Theban leader inflicted on his foe, in the constitution of the Arcadian league and foundation of Megalopolis; and, still more, in the re-establishment of an independent Messenia and the building of Messênê. Henceforth Sparta was a second-rate rather than a first-rate power. She ceased to exercise a hegemony, and was territorially not much larger than Arcadia or Argos.

Invasion of Cleombrotus and battle of Leuctra, B.C. 371. Appearance on the scene of Jason of Pheræ, by whose advice the defeated army is allowed to retire. Great increase of Theban power alarms Athens. Assassination of Jason of Pheræ (B.C. 370) relieves Thebes from all apprehension of danger to her dominion at home. Invited by Arcadia, Epaminondas marches into the Peloponnese. Ravages Laconia and attacks Sparta itself. Founds Megalopolis as the centre of an Arcadian confederation. Builds Messênê, and re-constitutes Messenia as a state. Winters in Arcadia, and threatens a second attack on Sparta.

35. In her distress, Sparta makes appeal to Athens for aid; and an alliance is formed between these two powers on terms of equality, which is joined after a time by Achæa, Elis, and even by most of Arcadia, where a jealousy of Theban power and interference is gradually developed. Thebes, partly by mismanagement, partly by the mere circumstance of her being now the leading state, arouses hostility, and loses ground in the Peloponnese, which she endeavors to recover by obtaining and exhibiting a Persian rescript, declaring her the head of Greece, and requiring the other states to submit to her under pain of the Great King's displeasure. But missives of this character have now lost their force. The rescript is generally rejected; and the power of Thebes in the Peloponnese continues to decline.

Alliance of Athens with Sparta, B.C. 369.

36. Meanwhile, however, she was extending her influence in Northern Greece, and even beyond its borders. Her armies were sent into Thessaly, where they contended with Alexander of Pheræ, the brother of Jason, and, after some reverses, succeeded in reducing him to dependence. All Thessaly, together with Magnesia and Achæa Phthiotis, were thus brought under her sway. In Macedonia, she arbitrated between the different claimants of the throne, and took hostages, among whom was the young prince Philip. Her fleet about the same time proceeded to the coast of Asia.

Thessaly made subject to Thebes.

First expedition of Pelopidas against Alexander of Pheræ, B.C. 369. Alliance made with Alexander of Macedon.—Second expedition, B.C. 368. Pelopidas proceeds on into Macedonia, and receives hostages.—Third expedition, B.C. 366. Pelopidas seized by Alexander of Pheræ and cast into prison. First army sent to release him defeated. Second successful, under Epaminondas.—Fourth expedition, B.C. 363. Pelopidas slain.—Expedition of Malcitas and Diogeiton the same year. Alexander submits. Thessaly reduced.

37. But the honor of Thebes required that her influence should be re-established in the Peloponnese, and her friends there released from a situation which had become one of danger. Accordingly, in B.C. 362, Epaminondas once more took the field, and entering the Peloponnese, was within a little of surprising Sparta. Disappointed, however, of this prey by the activity of Agesilaüs, and of Mantineia by the sudden arrival of an Athenian

Thebes once more invades the Peloponnese, B.C. 362.

contingent, he brought matters to a decision by a pitched battle; in which, repeating the tactics of Leuctra, he once more completely defeated the Spartans and their allies, dying, however, in the arms of victory, B.C. 362. His death almost compensated Sparta for her defeat, since he left no worthy successor, and Thebes, which he and his friend Pelopidas had raised to greatness, sank back at once to a level with several other powers.

Exhaustion produced by the struggle.

38. The result of the struggle which Sparta had provoked by her seizure of the Theban citadel was the general exhaustion of Greece. No state was left with any decided predominance. The loss of all in men and money was great; and the battle of Mantineia deprived Greece of her ablest general. If profit was derived by any state from the war, it was by Athens, who recovered her maritime superiority (since the attempt of Epaminondas to establish a rival navy proved a failure), reconstituted her old confederacy, and even, by the occupation of Samos and the Chersonese, began to restore her empire. In Macedonia her influence to some extent balanced that of Thebes.

A general Peace made, from which Sparta alone excludes herself.

39. The general exhaustion naturally led to a peace, which was made on the principle of leaving things as they were. The independence of Messênê and the unification of Arcadia were expressly recognized, while the headship of Thebes and Athens over their respective confederacies was tacitly sanctioned. Sparta alone declined to sign the terms, since she would on no account forego her right to reconquer Messenia. She had no intention, however, of making any immediate appeal to arms, and allowed her king, Agesilaüs, to quit Sparta and take service under the native monarch of Egypt.

Death of Agesilaüs on his march from Egypt to Cyrênê, B.C. 361. His personal character stands, perhaps, as high as that of Epaminondas; but in military genius he was decidedly inferior to his Theban adversary.

Athens successful in several petty wars, B.C. 362-358.

40. The peace of B.C. 362 was not disturbed on the continent of Greece till after the lapse of six years. Meanwhile, however, hostilities continued at sea between Alexander of Pheræ and Athens, and, in the continental districts beyond the limits of Greece Proper, between Athens on the one hand, and

Amphipolis, Perdiccas of Macedon, and the Thracian princes, Cotys and his son Cersobleptes, on the other. Athens was intent on recovering her old dominion in these parts, while the Macedonian and Thracian kings were naturally jealous of her growing power. Nothing, however, as yet showed that any important consequences would arise out of these petty struggles. Macedonia was still one of the weakest of the states which bordered on Greece; and even when, on the death of Perdiccas, B.C. 359, his brother, Philip, who had escaped from Thebes, mounted the throne, it was impossible for the most sagacious intellect to foresee danger to Greece from this quarter.

41. The year B.C. 358 was the culminating-point of the second period of Athenian prosperity. Athens had once more made herself mistress of the Chersonese; she had recovered Eubœa, which had recently attached itself to Thebes; and she had obtained from Philip the acknowledgment of her right to Amphipolis, when the revolt of a considerable number of her more distant allies engaged her in the "Social War," the results of which injured her greatly. The war cost her the services of her three best generals, Chabrias, Timotheus, and Iphicrates; exhausted her treasury, and permanently diminished her resources. It likewise greatly tarnished her half-recovered reputation.

Social War, B.C. 358-355.

DETAILS OF THE WAR. Revolt begun—B.C. 358—by Rhodes, Cos, Chios, and Byzantium, which are afterwards joined by Sestus and other Hellespontine towns, and are assisted by Mausôlus, king of Caria. Unsuccessful siege of Chios by Chares and Chabrias, in which Chabrias falls, B.C. 358. Siege of Byzantium, B.C. 357. Unsuccessful sea-fight. Chares accuses Timotheus and Iphicrates, the former of whom is condemned and goes into exile, while the latter is disgraced, being never afterwards employed in any service.—Chares, Charidemus, and Phocion in command, B.C. 356, assist the revolted satrap, Artabazus, in order to obtain money to pay their sailors. Victory gained over Tithraustes. The Persian court threatens vengeance, and Athens hastily makes peace, B.C. 355, acknowledging the independence of the four rebel states.

42. The period of the "Social War" was also disastrous for Athens in another respect. So completely did the struggle with her allies occupy her attention, so incapable was she at this period of carrying on more than one war at a time, that she allowed Philip to absorb, one after another, Amphipolis, Pydna, Potidæa, and Methônê,

Losses of Athens to Philip.

and thus to sweep her from the Thermaic Gulf, almost without offering resistance. At first, indeed, she was cajoled by the crafty monarch; but, even when the mask was thrown off, she made no adequate effort, but patiently allowed the establishment of Macedonian ascendency over the entire region extending from the Peneus to the Nestus.

43. Before the "Social War" had come to an end, another exhausting struggle—fatal to Greece in its consequences—was begun in the central region of Hellas, through the vindictiveness of Thebes. Down to the battle of Leuctra, Phocis had fought on the Spartan side, and had thus provoked the enmity of Thebes, who now resolved on her destruction. The Amphictyonic assembly suffered itself to be made the tool of the oppressors; and, by condemning Phocis to a fine which she could not possibly pay, compelled her to fight for her existence. A war followed, in which Phocis, by the seizure and expenditure of the Delphic treasures, and the assistance, in some important conjunctures, of Achæa, Athens, and Sparta, maintained herself for eleven years against Thebes and her allies. At last, Thebes, blinded by her passionate hatred, called in Philip to her assistance, and thus purchased the destruction of her enemy at a cost which involved her own ruin and that of Greece generally.

Sacred War, B.C. 357-346.

Sentence of the Amphictyons against Phocis, B.C. 357. Philomêlus is made general; he seizes Delphi, and employs its treasures in raising mercenaries. After several victories, he is defeated and falls in battle, B.C. 354. Onomarchus, brother of Philomêlus, takes the command. He conquers Locris and Doris, invades Bœotia, and captures Orchomenus, B.C. 353. His aid is implored by Lycophron, tyrant of Pheræ, who is attacked by Philip. He enters Thessaly and joins Lycophron, engages the army of Philip, but is defeated and slain, B.C. 352. Phaÿllus succeeds him. Philip threatens Thermopylæ, which is saved by the promptitude of Athens. War continues with varied success, first under Phaÿllus, and after his death, B.C. 351, under Phalæcus, son of Onomarchus; but the Delphic treasures being exhausted, the power of Phocis wanes, and internal quarrels begin, B.C. 347. Thebes invokes the aid of Philip; Athens is cajoled into standing neutral; and Phalæcus is forced to surrender at discretion, B.C. 346. Philip passes Thermopylæ unopposed, crushes Phocis, and is rewarded by admission to the Amphictyonic Council in lieu of that state.

44. The ruin of Greece was now rapidly consummated. Within six years of the submission and punishment of Phocis, Philip openly declared war against Athens, the only power

in Greece capable of offering him any important opposition. His efforts at first were directed towards obtaining the command of the Bosphorus and Hellespont; but the second "Sacred War" gave him a pretext for marching his forces through Thermopylæ into Central Greece; and though Thebes and Athens joined to oppose him, the signal victory of Chæroneia (B.C. 338) laid Greece prostrate at his feet. All the states, excepting Sparta, at once acknowledged his supremacy; and, to mark distinctly the extinction of independent Hellas, and its absorption into the Macedonian monarchy, Philip was, in B.C. 337, formally appointed generalissimo of united Greece against the Persians. His assassination in the next year excited hopes, but produced no real change. The aspirations of the patriotic party in Greece after freedom were quenched in the blood which deluged revolted Thebes, B.C. 335; and assembled Greece at Corinth once more admitted the headship of Macedon, and conferred on the youthful Alexander the dignity previously granted to his father.

BOOK IV.

HISTORY OF THE MACEDONIAN MONARCHY.

Geographical Outline.

Macedonia—size and boundaries.

1. MACEDONIA PROPER was the country lying immediately to the north of Thessaly, between Mount Scardus on the one hand and the maritime plain of the Pierians and Bottiæans (Thracians) on the other. It was bounded towards the north by Pæonia, or the country of the Pæonians, from which it was separated by an irregular line, running probably a little north of the 41st parallel. Its greatest length from north to south was about ninety miles, while its width from east to west may have averaged seventy miles. Its area was probably not much short of 6000 square miles, or about half that of Belgium.

Character of the region.

2. The character of the tract comprised within these limits was multiform, but for the most part fertile. High mountain-chains, capped with snow during the greater part of the year, and very varied in the directions that they take, divide the territory into a number of distinct basins. Some of these have a lake in the centre, into which all the superfluous moisture drains; others are watered by rivers, which, with one exception, flow eastward to the Ægean. In both cases the basins are of large extent, offering to the eye the appearance of a succession of plains. The more elevated regions are for the most part richly wooded, and abound with sparkling rivulets, deep gorges, and frequent waterfalls; but in places this character gives way to one of dullness and monotony, the traveller passing for miles over a succession of bleak downs and bare hill sides, stony and shrubless.

Rivers and lakes.

3. The principal RIVERS of the region were the Lydias, or Ludias, now the Karasmak, and the Haliacmon, now the Vistritza. Besides these, there was a third stream of some importance, the Erigon, a tributary of the

Axius. The chief LAKES were those of Castoria, on a tributary of the Haliacmon, of Begorritis (Ostrovo ?) in the country of the Eordæans, and the Lydias Palus, near Pella.

Divisions.

4. Macedonia was divided into "Upper" and "Lower." Upper Macedonia comprised the whole of the broad mountainous tract which lay between Scardus and Bermius; while Lower Macedonia was the comparatively narrow strip along the eastern flank and at the foot of Bermius, between that range and the tracts known as Pieria and Bottiæa. Upper Macedonia was divided into a number of districts, which for the most part took their names from the tribes inhabiting them. The principal were, to the north, Pelagonia and Lyncestis, on the river Erigon; to the west, Orestis and Elymeia, on the upper Haliacmon; and in the centre, Eordæa, about Lake Begorritis.

A good sketch of Macedonian geography is given in Mr. GROTE's *History of Greece*, part ii. chap. xxv. The modern travellers who have best described the region are

LEAKE, Col., *Northern Greece*, vol. iii. (See p. 136.)
LEAR, E., *Journals of a Landscape Painter*. London, 1851; large 8vo.
PONQUEVILLE, *Voyage de la Grèce*. Paris, 1824; 4 vols. 8vo; 2d edition.
GRISEBACH, *Reisen durch Rumelien und Albanien*. Göttingen, 1843; 8vo.

HISTORICAL SKETCH.

FIRST PERIOD.

From the Commencement of the Monarchy to the Death of Alexander the Great, about B.C. 700 *to* B.C. 323.

SOURCES. For the first two centuries Macedonian history is almost a blank, nothing but a few names and some mythic tales being preserved to us in Herodotus. That writer is the best authority for the reigns of Amyntas I. and his son Alexander; but he must be supplemented from Thucydides (ii. 99) and Justin. Thucydides is the chief authority for the reign of Perdiccas. For the period from Archelaüs to Alexander we depend mainly on Justin and Diodorus. Philip's history, however, may be copiously illustrated from the Attic orators, especially Æschines and Demosthenes; but these partisan writers must not be trusted implicitly. On the history of Alexander the most trustworthy of the ancient authorities is ARRIAN (*Expeditio Alexandri*), who followed contemporary writers, especially Aristobulus and Ptolemy Lagi. Some interesting particulars are also furnished by Plutarch (*Vit. Alex.*), Nearchus (*Periplus*), and Diodorus (book xvii.). The biography of Q. Curtius is a rhetorical exercitation, on which it is impossible to place any dependence. (A good edition of the *Periplus* of NEARCHUS, the only writing of a companion of Alexander that has come down to us, is contained in C. MÜLLER's *Geographi Græci Minores.* Paris, 1855; 2 vols. tall 8vo.)

Among modern works specially treating the histories of Philip and Alexander the Great, the best are—

OLIVIER, *Histoire de Philippe, roi de Macédoine.* Paris, 1740; 2 vols. 8vo.

LELAND, *History of the Life and Reign of Philip, King of Macedon.* London, 1761; 4to.

WILLIAMS, *The Life and Actions of Alexander the Great;* originally published in the *Family Library.* London, 1830; 8vo.

DROYSEN, *Geschichte Alexander's des Grossen.* Hamburg, 1833; 8vo.

Macedonian kingdom founded about B.C. 700. Kings till Amyntas I.

1. ACCORDING to the tradition generally accepted by the Greeks, the Macedonian kingdom, which under Philip and Alexander attained to such extraordinary greatness, was founded by Hellenic emigrants from Argos. The Macedonians themselves were not Hellenes; they belonged to the barbaric races, not greatly differing from the Greeks in ethnic type, but far behind them in civilization, which bordered Hellas upon the north. They were a distinct race, not Pæonian, not Illyrian, not Thracian; but, of the three, their connection was closest with the Illyrians. The Argive colony, received hospitably, gradually acquired power in the region about Mount Bermius; and Perdiccas, one of the original emigrants, was (according to Herodotus) acknowledged as king. (Other writers mentioned three kings anterior to Perdiccas, whose joint reigns covered the space of about a century.) The period which follows is one of great obscurity, little being known of it but the names of the kings.

KINGS FROM PERDICCAS I. TO AMYNTAS I.:—1. Perdiccas I. Reigned nearly fifty years, from about B.C. 700 to 650. Succeeded by 2. Argæus, his son, who reigned about thirty years, B.C. 650 to 620. After him came his son, 3. Philip I., who also reigned about thirty years, B.C. 620 to 590. Philip was succeeded by his son, 4. Aëropus, whose reign lasted about twenty-five years, B.C. 590 to 565; and Aëropus by his son, 5. Alcetas, whose reign lasted twenty-eight or twenty-nine years, B.C. 565 to 537. Alcetas was followed by his son, 6. Amyntas I., who was king at the time of the expedition conducted by Megabazus, B.C. 507.

2. With Amyntas I., who was contemporary with Darius Hystaspis, light dawns upon Macedonian history. We find that by this time the Macedonian monarchs of this line

Time of conquest. Submission of Macedonia to Persia, B.C. 507.

had made themselves masters of Pieria and Bottiæa, had crossed the Axius and conquered Mygdonia and Anthemus, had dislodged the original Eordi from Eordia and themselves occupied it, and had dealt similarly with the Almôpes in Almopia, on the Rhœdias. But the advance of the Persians into Europe gave a sudden check to this period of prosperity. After a submission which was more nominal than real, in B.C. 507, the Macedonians, in B.C. 492, became Persian subjects, retaining, however, their own kings, who accepted the position of tributaries. Amyntas I., who appears to have died about B.C. 498, was succeeded by his son, Alexander I., king at the time of the great invasion of Xerxes, who played no unimportant part in the expedition, B.C. 480 to 470.

3. The repulse of the Persians set Macedonia free; and the career of conquest appears to have been at once resumed.

Career of conquest resumed.

Crestonæa and Bisaltia were reduced, and the Macedonian dominion pushed eastward almost to the Strymon. The authority of the monarchs of Pella was likewise extended over most of the inland Macedonian tribes, as the Lyncestæ, the Eleimiots, and others, who however retained their own kings.

Alexander, the son of Amyntas, is said to have reigned either forty-three or forty-four years, probably from about B.C. 498 to 454. Perdiccas, his son and successor, reigned probably forty-one years, from B.C. 454 to 413.

4. But Macedonia was about this time herself exposed to attacks from two unquiet neighbors. The maritime confed-

Wars of Perdiccas II. with Thrace and Athens.

eracy of Athens, which gave her a paramount authority over the Greek cities in Chalcidice, and even over Methônê in Pieria, brought the Athenians into the near neighborhood of Macedon, and necessitated relations between the two powers, which were at first friendly, but which grew to be hostile when Athens by her colony at Amphipolis put a check to the further progress of Macedon in that direction; and were still more embittered by the encouragement which Athens gave to Macedonian chiefs who rebelled against their sovereign. About the same time, a powerful Thracian kingdom was formed under Sitalces, B.C. 440 to 420, which threatened destruction to the far smaller Macedonian state with which it was conterminous. Macedonia, however, under the adroit Perdiccas, escaped both dangers; and, on the whole, increased in prosperity.

Commencement of differences with Athens, probably about B.C. 437, when Amphipolis was colonized. Support given to the brother of Perdiccas, Philip, and a chief named Derdas. Perdiccas retaliates by exciting the subject-allies of Athens to revolt, B.C. 432. Revolt of Potidæa, supported by Perdiccas, B.C. 432 to 430. Invasion of Sitalces, B.C. 429. Peace made by a marriage between Seuthes, nephew and heir of Sitalces, and Stratonicé, sister of Perdiccas. Invitation given by Perdiccas to Brasidas, B.C. 424, greatly damages Athens. War between Perdiccas and Athens continues, with intervals of peace, down to B.C. 416.

Brilliant reign of Archelaüs, B.C. 413-399.

5. The reign of Archelaüs, the bastard son of Perdiccas II., though short, was very important for Macedon, since this prince laid the foundation of her military greatness by the attention which he paid to the army, while at the same time he strengthened and improved the country by the construction of highways and of forts. He was also the first of the Macedonian princes who endeavored to encourage among his people a taste for Greek literature. Euripides the tragedian was welcomed to his court, as also was Plato the philosopher, and perhaps Hellanicus the historian. He engaged in wars with some of the Macedonian princes, as particularly with Arrhibæus; but he was relieved from all hostile collision with Athens by the Sicilian disaster. The character of Archelaüs was sanguinary and treacherous; in his habits he was licentious. After reigning fourteen years, he was assassinated by the victims of his lust, B.C. 399.

Forty years of disturbance, B.C. 399-359.

6. The murder of Archelaüs introduced a period of disturbance, both internal and external, which lasted till the accession of Philip, B.C. 359. During this interval the Macedonian court was a constant scene of plots and assassinations. The direct line of succession having failed, numerous pretenders to the crown sprang up, who at different times found supporters in the Illyrians, the Lacedæmonians, the Thebans, and the Athenians. Civil wars were almost perpetual. Kings were driven from their thrones and recovered them. There were at least two regencies. So violent were the commotions that it seemed doubtful whether the kingdom could long continue to maintain its existence; and, if the Olynthian league had been allowed to constitute itself without interference, it is

not unlikely that Macedon would have been absorbed, either by that confederacy or by the Illyrians.

KINGS AND REGENTS from B.C. 399 to 359:—1. Orestes, son of Archelaüs, a minor. Reigns four years under the guardianship of Aëropus, B.C. 399 to 395. 2. Aëropus, having murdered Orestes, reigns nearly two years as actual king, B.C. 395 to 394. He is succeeded by his son, 3. Pausanias, who reigns one year, when he is assassinated by Amyntas II., B.C. 393. 4. Amyntas II. has a reign which lasts, from its first year to its last, twenty-four years, B.C. 393 to 369; but during a part of this time he is expelled from his kingdom. 5. Argeus, the brother of Pausanias, reigns during the two years, B.C. 392 and 391. Amyntas then recovers his kingdom, and retains it to his death, in B.C. 369; but during these years he is several times reduced to the last extremity. At one time the Illyrians, at another the Olynthians, press him hard; and it is only by the aid of Sparta that he is able to maintain himself. 6. Alexander II., the son of Amyntas, succeeded him, and reigned between one and two years, when he was murdered by Ptolemy of Alôrus, who became regent for Perdiccas, the brother of Alexander II., B.C. 368, and was established in that position by Pelopidas. (See p. 217.) He held the supreme power for a little more than three years, and was then murdered in his turn by Perdiccas III., B.C. 364. 7. Perdiccas III. reigned five years, B.C. 364 to 359. The Athenians assisted him against the claims of a pretender named Pausanias; but shortly afterwards he fell in a war against the Illyrians, B.C. 359, leaving behind him an infant son, Amyntas. He was succeeded, however, on the throne by his brother, Philip II.

Accession of Philip, B.C. 359.

7. The reign of Philip is the turning-point in Macedonian history. Hitherto, if we except Archelaüs, Macedonia had not possessed a single king whose abilities exceeded the common average, or whose aims had about them any thing of grandeur. Notwithstanding their asserted and even admitted Hellenism, the "barbarian" character of their training and associations had its effect on the whole line of sovereigns; and their highest qualities were the rude valor and the sagacity bordering upon cunning which are seldom wanting in savages. But Philip was a monarch of a different stamp. In natural ability he was at least the equal of any of his Greek contemporaries; while the circumstances under which he grew to manhood were peculiarly favorable to the development of his talents. At the impressible age of fifteen, he was sent as a hostage to Thebes, where he resided for the greater part of three years (B.C. 368 to 365), while that state was at the height of its prosperity under Pelopidas and Epaminondas. He was thus brought into contact with those great men, was led to study their system, and emulate their ac-

tions. He learnt the great importance of military training, and the value of inventiveness to those who wish to succeed in war; he also acquired a facility of expressing himself in Greek, which was uncommon in a Macedonian.

Condition of Macedonian affairs. First successes of Philip.

8. The situation of Philip at his accession was one of extreme embarrassment and difficulty. Besides Amyntas, his nephew, for whom he at first professed to be regent, there were at least five pretenders to the throne, two of whom, Pausanias and Argæus, were supported by the arms of foreigners. The Illyrians, moreover, had recently gained a great victory over Perdiccas, and, flushed with success, had advanced into Macedonia and occupied most of the western provinces. Pæonia on the north, and Thrace upon the east, were unquiet neighbors, whose hostility might be counted on whenever other perils threatened. Within two years, however, Philip had repressed or overthrown all these enemies, and found himself free to commence those wars of aggression by which he converted the monarchy of Macedon into an empire.

Peace purchased from Thrace, B.C. 359. Negotiations with Athens. Amphipolis evacuated. Argæus defeated and captured. Pæonia invaded, B.C. 358. Great defeat of the Illyrians under Bardylis. Macedonian frontier pushed westward to Lake Lychnitis. Philip proclaimed king, B.C. 359.

Aggressions upon Athens, B.C. 358, 357.

9. Hitherto it had been the policy of Philip to profess himself a friend of the Athenians. Now, however, that his hands were free, it was his first object to disembarrass himself of these near neighbors, who blocked up his coast-line, watched his movements, and might seriously interfere with the execution of his projects. Accordingly, towards the close of B.C. 358, when Athens was already engaged in the "Social War," he suddenly laid siege to Amphipolis. Having taken the town, while he amused Athens with promises, he proceeded to attack and capture Pydna and Potidæa, actual Athenian possessions, making over the latter to Olynthus, to foment jealousy between her and Athens. He then conquered the entire coast district between the Strymon and the Nestus, thus becoming master of the important Thracian gold-mines, from which he shortly derived an annual revenue of a thousand talents!

Marriage of Philip with Olympias, B.C. 357. Foundation of Philippopolis, or Philippi, on the site of Crenides, for the protection of the gold-mines. Birth of Alexander, B.C. 356.

10. The year after these conquests we find Philip in Thessaly, where he interferes to protect the Aleuadæ of Larissa against the tyrants of Pheræ. The tyrants call in the aid of the Phocians, then at the zenith of their power, and Philip suffers certain reverses; but a few years later he is completely victorious, defeats and kills Onomarchus, and brings under his dominion the whole of Thessaly, together with Magnesia and Achæa Phthiotis. At the same time, he conquers Methônê, the last Athenian possession on the coast of Macedon, attacks Maroneia, and threatens the Chersonese. Athens, the sole power which could effectually have checked these successes, made only slight and feeble efforts to prevent them. Already Philip had found the advantage of having friends among the Attic orators; and their labors, backed by the selfish indolence which now characterized the Athenians, produced an inaction, which had the most fatal consequences.

Absorption of Thessaly, B.C. 352.

First expedition of Philip into Thessaly, B.C. 355. Conquest of Methônê, B.C. 354. Second expedition into Thessaly, B.C. 353. Philip twice defeated by Onomarchus. Third expedition; victory of Philip; Onomarchus slain, B.C. 352.

11. The victory of Philip over Onomarchus roused Athens to exertion. Advancing to Thermopylæ, Philip found the pass already occupied by an Athenian army, and did not venture to attack it. Greece was saved for the time; but six years later the folly of the Thebans, and the fears of the Athenians, who were driven to despair by the ill success of the Olynthian and Euboic wars, admitted the Macedonian conqueror within the barrier. Accepted as head of the league against the impious Phocians, Philip in a few weeks brought the "Sacred War" to an end, obtaining as his reward the seat in the Amphictyonic Council of which the Phocians were deprived, and thus acquiring a sort of right to intermeddle as much as he liked in the affairs of Central and even Southern Hellas.

Conduct of the "Sacred War."

Attempt to pass Thermopylæ fails, B.C. 352. Philip attacks Heræon-teichos. His navy damages the commerce of Athens, B.C. 351. Olynthian war commences, B.C. 350. Eubœa revolts from Athens, B.C. 349. Victory of Phocion at Tamynæ. Olynthian war ended by the capture and destruction of Olynthus and thirty-one other Chalcidic cities, B.C. 347. Despair of Athens. The Thebans invite Philip to conduct the war against the Phocians. Athens negotiates a peace, deserting the Phocians, who, as they can not hold Thermopylæ without the aid of the Athenian fleet, are compelled to make their submission, B.C. 346. Philip enters Phocis, reduces all the towns, and disperses the inhabitants into villages. Accepted into the Amphictyonic League, he necessarily becomes its head.

Causes of Philip's wonderful success.

12. The main causes of Philip's wonderful success were twofold: — (*a*) Bettering the lessons taught him by his model in the art of war, Epaminondas, he had armed, equipped, and trained the Macedonian forces till they were decidedly superior to the troops of any state in Greece. The Macedonian phalanx, invincible until it came to be opposed to the Romans, was his conception and his work. Nor was he content with excellence in one arm of the service. On every branch he bestowed equal care and thought. Each was brought into a state nearly approaching perfection. His cavalry, heavy and light, his peltasts, archers, slingers, darters, were all the best of their kind; his artillery was numerous and effective; his commissariat service was well arranged. (*b*) At the same time, he was a master of finesse. Taking advantage of the divided condition of Greece, and of the general prevalence of corruption among the citizens of almost every community, he played off state against state and politician against politician. Masking his purposes up to the last moment, promising, cajoling, bribing, intimidating, protesting, he advanced his interests even more by diplomacy than by force, having an infinite fund of artifice from which to draw, and scarcely ever recurring to means which he had used previously.

To these main causes must be added, (1) the extraordinary activity of the man, who scarcely ever rested a moment, and who seemed almost to possess the power of being in several places at once; and (2) the decline of patriotism, public spirit, and even courage in Greece—seen especially in the apathy of Athens, but really pervading the whole Hellenic world, which had passed its prime and was entering on the period of decay. A certain impetus was doubtless given to the general decline by the plunder of Delphi, which began by shocking and ended by depraving the national conscience; but the seat of the malady lay deeper; the precocious race was, in fact, prematurely exhausted, and under no circumstances could the pristine vigor have been recovered.

13. Philip had made peace with Athens in order to lay hold on Thermopylæ—a hold which he never afterwards re-

Hostilities in Eastern Thrace.

laxed. But it was far from his intention to maintain the peace an hour longer than suited his purpose. Having once more chastised the Illyrian and Pæonian tribes, he proceeded to invade Eastern Thrace, and to threaten the Athenian possessions in that quarter. At the same time, he aimed at getting into his hands the command of the Bosphorus, which would have enabled him to starve Greece into submission by stopping the importation of corn. Here, however, Persia (which had at last come to feel alarm at his progress) combined with Athens to resist him. Perinthus and Byzantium were saved, and the ambition of Philip was for the time thwarted.

The peace with Athens lasted, nominally, six years, B.C. 346 to 340. But Philip's aggressions recommenced as early as B.C. 343. He occupied Halonnesus, intrigued in Eubœa, and invaded the Chersonese, where Diopeithes opposed him with some success. In B.C. 341 Athens wrested Eubœa from his grasp; and in B.C. 340 war was declared formally on both sides. Philip laid siege in succession to Perinthus and Byzantium, but was foiled in both attacks, partly by Persian troops, partly by the fleet of Athens under Phocion. The credit of the Athenian successes at this time is due mainly to the counsels of Demosthenes.

Campaign on the Lower Danube, B.C. 339.

14. But the indefatigable warrior, balked of his prey, and obliged to wait till Grecian affairs should take a turn more favorable to him, marched suddenly northward and engaged in a campaign on the Lower Danube against a Scythian prince who held the tract now known as Bulgaria. Victorious here, he recrossed the Balkan with a large body of captives, when he was set upon by the Triballi (Thracians), defeated, and wounded in the thigh, B.C. 339. The wound necessitated a short period of inaction; but while the arch-plotter rested, his agents were busily at work, and the year of the Triballian defeat saw the fatal step taken, which was once more to bring a Macedonian army into the heart of Greece, and to destroy the last remaining chance of the cause of Hellenic freedom.

Disturbance at the Amphictyonic Congress of March, B.C. 339. Æschines procures a decree against the Locrians of Amphissa. Refusal of Athens and Thebes to join in the new crusade. Attempt to execute the decree fails. Aid of Philip invoked. He consents, and marches southward.

15. Appointed by the Amphictyons as their leader in a new "Sacred War," Philip once more passed Thermopylæ

Second expedition of Philip into Greece. Battle of Chæroneia, B.C. 338.

and entered Phocis. But he soon showed that he came on no trivial or temporary errand. The occupation of Nicæa, Cytinium, and more especially of Elateia, betrayed his intention of henceforth holding possession of Central Greece, and roused the two principal powers of the region to a last desperate effort. Thebes and Athens met him at Chæroneia in full force, with contingents from Corinth, Phocis, and Achæa. But the Macedonian phalanx was irresistible; and the complete defeat of the allies laid Greece at Philip's feet. The Congress of Corinth (B.C. 337), attended by all the states except Sparta, which proudly stood aloof, accepted the headship of Macedon; and the cities generally undertook to supply contingents to the force which he designed to lead against Persia.

Design to invade Persia. Philip assassinated, B.C. 336.

16. This design, however, was not executed. Great preparations were made in the course of B.C. 337; and early in B.C. 336 the van-guard of the Macedonian army was sent across into Asia. But, a few months later, the sword of Pausanias terminated the career of the Macedonian monarch, who fell a victim, in part to his unwillingness, or his inability to execute justice upon powerful offenders, in part to the quarrels and dissensions in his own family. Olympias certainly, Alexander probably, connived at the assassination of Philip, whose removal was necessary to their own safety. He died at the age of forty-seven, after a reign of twenty-three years.

Character of the Macedonian government.

17. It is difficult to say what exactly was the government of Macedonia under this prince. Practically, the monarch must have been nearly absolute; but it would appear that, theoretically, he was bound to govern according to certain long-established laws and customs; and it may be questioned whether he would have dared at any time to trangress, flagrantly and openly, any such law or usage. The Macedonian nobles were turbulent and free of speech. If accused of conspiracy or other crime, they were entitled to be tried before the public assembly. Their power must certainly have been to some extent a check upon the monarch. And after the formation of a great standing army, it became necessary for the monarch to consult the feelings and conform his acts to the wishes of the soldiers. But there seems to have been no such regular

machinery for checking and controlling the royal authority as is implied in *constitutional* government.

FLATHE, *Geschichte Makedoniens.* Leipzig, 1832–34; 2 vols. 8vo. Contains an overstatement of the constitutional character of the Macedonian government.

18. The reign of Alexander the Great has in the history of the world much the same importance which that of his father has in the history of Macedonia and of Greece. Alexander revolutionized the East, or, at any rate, so much of it as was connected with the West by intercourse or reciprocal influence. The results of a conquest effected in ten years continued for as many centuries, and remain in some respects to the present day. The Hellenization of Western Asia and North-eastern Africa, which dates from Alexander's successes, is one of the most remarkable facts in the history of the human race, and one of those most pregnant with important consequences. It is as absurd to deny to the author of such a revolution the possession of extraordinary genius as to suppose that the Iliad could have been written by a man of no particular ability.

Reign of Alexander the Great, B.C. 336–323.

See, on the Hellenization of Asia, in part by Alexander, in part by his successors, the important work of DROYSEN, *Geschichte des Hellenismus oder der Bildung des Hellenistischen Staaten Systemes.* Hamburg, 1843; 8vo.

19. The situation of Alexander, on his accession, was extremely critical; and it depended wholly on his own energy and force of character whether he would retain his father's power or lose it. His position was far from assured at home, where he had many rivals; and among the conquered nations there was a general inclination to test the qualities of the new and young prince by the assertion of independence. But Alexander was equal to the occasion. Seizing the throne without a moment's hesitation, he executed or drove out his rivals. Forestalling any open hostility on the part of the Greeks, he marched hastily, at the head of a large army, through Thessaly, Phocis, and Bœotia, to Corinth, and there required, and obtained, from the deputies whom he had convened to meet him, the same "hegemony," or leadership, which had been granted to his father. Sparta alone, as she had done before, stood aloof. From Corinth, Alexander retraced his steps to Macedon,

His early difficulties. He is appointed to the leadership of Greece.

Campaigns in Thrace and Illyria.

and thence proceeded to chastise his enemies in the North and West, invading Thrace, defeating the Triballi and the Getæ, and even crossing the Danube; after which he turned southward, and attacked and defeated the Illyrians under Clitus and Glaucias.

Revolt and destruction of Thebes, B.C. 335.

20. Meanwhile, in Greece, a false report of Alexander's death induced Thebes to raise the standard of revolt. A general insurrection might have followed but for the promptness and celerity of the young monarch. Marching straight from Illyria southward, he appeared suddenly in Bœotia, stormed and took Thebes, and, after a wholesale massacre, punished the survivors by completely destroying their city and selling them all as slaves. This signal vengeance had the effect intended. All Greece was terror-struck; and Alexander could feel that he might commence his Asiatic enterprise in tolerable security. Greece was now not likely to rebel, unless he suffered some considerable reverse.

Passage of the Hellespont. Battle of the Granicus, B.C. 334.

21. In the spring of B.C. 334 Alexander passed the Hellespont with an army numbering about 35,000 men. The usual remissness of the Persians allowed him to cross without opposition. A plan of operations, suggested by Memnon the Rhodian, which consisted in avoiding an engagement in Asia Minor, and carrying the war into Macedonia by means of the overwhelming Persian fleet, was rejected, and battle was given to Alexander, on the Granicus, by a force only a little superior to his own. The victory of the invader placed Asia Minor at his mercy, and Alexander with his usual celerity proceeded to overrun it. Still, he seems to have been unwilling to remove his army very far from the Ægean coast, so long as Memnon was alive. But the death of that able commander, in the spring of B.C. 333, left him free to act; and he at once took the road which led to the heart of the Persian empire.

Battle of Issus, November, B.C. 333. Conquests of Tyre, Gaza, and Egypt.

22. The conflict at Issus between Alexander and Darius himself was brought on under circumstances peculiarly favorable to the Macedonian monarch. Darius had intended to fight in the plain of Antioch, where his vast army would have had room to act. But, as Alexander did not come to meet him, he grew

impatient, and advanced into the defiles which lie between Syria and Cilicia. The armies met, almost without warning, in a position where numbers gave no advantage. Under such circumstances the defeat of the Persians was a matter of course. Alexander deserves less credit for the victory of Issus than for the use he made of it. It was a wise and far-seeing policy which disdained the simple plan of pressing forward on a defeated foe, and preferred to let him escape and reorganize his forces, while the victory was utilized in another way. Once possessed of the command of the sea, Alexander would be completely secure at home. He therefore proceeded from Issus against Tyre, Gaza, and Egypt. Twenty months sufficed for the reduction of these places. Having possessed himself of all the maritime provinces of Persia, Alexander, in B.C. 331, proceeded to seek his enemy in the heart of his empire.

The foundation of Alexandria in the most favorable situation for commerce that Egypt offers, indicated that Alexander was no vulgar conqueror, but one with far-sighted aims and projects. Alexandria, as the capital of a separate kingdom, may have grown to be more than its founder ever intended; but it could under no circumstances have failed to become a great city. Alexander deserves credit both for conceiving the idea of changing the capital, and for fixing on so excellent a site.

23. In the final conflict, near Arbela, the relative strength of the two contending parties was fairly tried. Darius had collected the full force of his empire, had selected and prepared his ground, and had even obtained the aid of allies. His defeat was owing, in part, to the intrinsic superiority of the European over the Asiatic soldier; in part, and in *great* part, to the consummate ability of the Macedonian commander. The conflict was absolutely decisive, for it was impossible that any battle should be fought under conditions more favorable to Persia. Accordingly, the three capitals, Babylon, Susa, and Persepolis, surrendered, almost without resistance; and the Persian monarch became a fugitive, and was ere long murdered by his servants.

Battle of Arbela, B.C. 331.

Surrender of Babylon, Susa, and Persepolis.

Agis, the Spartan king, heads an insurrection in Greece; but is attacked and defeated by Antipater, B.C. 330.

24. The most remarkable part of Alexander's career now commences. An ordinary conqueror would have been sat-

Conquest of the north-eastern provinces, and invasion of India.

isfied with the submission of the great capitals, and would have awaited, in the luxurious abodes which they offered, the adhesion of the more distant provinces. But for Alexander rest possessed no attractions. So long as there were lands or men to conquer, it was his delight to subjugate them. The pursuit of Darius and then of Bessus, drew him on to the north-eastern corner of the Persian Empire, whence the way was open into a new world, generally believed to be one of immense wealth. From Bactria and Sogdiana, Alexander proceeded through Affghanistan to India, which he entered on the side whence alone India is accessible by land, viz., the north-west. At first he warred with the princes who held their governments as dependencies of Persia; but, when these had submitted, he desired still to press eastward, and complete the subjugation of the continent, which was believed to terminate at no great distance. The refusal of his soldiers to proceed stopped him at the Sutlej, and forced him to relinquish his designs, and to bend his steps homeward.

DETAILS OF THE MARCH TO BACTRIA AND INDIA. Advance to Ecbatana, B.C. 330. March thence to Rhages. Murder of Darius by Bessus. Flight of Bessus. Conquest of Hyrcania, Aria, and Drangiana. Trial and execution of Philotas. Execution of Parmenio. Invasion of Bactria and capture of Bessus, B.C. 329. March to the Jaxartes. Conquest of Bactria and Sogdiana, B.C. 328–7. Murder of Clitus. Execution of Callisthenes. March to the Indus, B.C. 326. Defeat of Porus. Advance to the Hyphasis (Sutlej)—refusal of the troops to proceed farther. Descent of the Indus, B.C. 326–5.

25. It was characteristic of Alexander, that, even when compelled to desist from a forward movement, he did not retrace his steps, but returned to the Persian capital by an entirely new route. Following the course of the Indus in ships built for the purpose, while his army marched along the banks, he conquered the valley as he descended, and, having reached the ocean, proceeded with the bulk of his troops westward through Gedrosia (Beloochistan) and Carmania into Persia. Meanwhile his admiral, Nearchus, sailed from the Indus to the Euphrates, thus reopening a line of communication which had probably been little used since the time of Darius Hystaspis. Alexander, in his march, experienced terrible difficulties; and the losses incurred in the Gedrosian desert exceeded those of all the rest of the expedition. Still

he brought back to Persepolis the greater portion of his army, and found himself in a position, not only to maintain his conquests, but to undertake fresh ones, for the purpose of rounding off and completing his empire.

The voyage of Nearchus lasted five months, from the end of September, B.C. 325, to the end of February, B.C. 324. Alexander's land march from the Indus to Persepolis, the greatest feat that he ever performed, occupied about the same period. We must ascribe to the prestige of his previous successes the fact that he was not attacked and crushed on this return march through trackless and utterly desert regions.

Nearchus's voyage was treated, in the last century, by VINCENT, whose work, *The Voyage of Nearchus from the Indus to the Euphrates* (London, 1797; 4to), was very creditable to the author. A better comment on the text will, however, be found in the *Geographi Græci Minores* of Mons. C. MÜLLER. (See p. 224.)

26. It was the intention of Alexander, after taking the measures which he thought advisable for the consolidation of his empire, and the improvement of his intended capital, Babylon, to attempt the conquest of the peninsula of Arabia —a vast tract inconveniently interposed between his western and his eastern provinces. A fleet, under Nearchus, was to have proceeded along the coast, whilst Alexander, with an immense host, traversed the interior. But these plans were brought to an end by the sudden death of their projector at Babylon, in the thirteenth year of his reign and the thirty-third of his age, June, B.C. 323. This premature demise makes it impossible to determine whether, or no, the political wisdom of Alexander was on a par with his strategic ability—whether, or no, he would have succeeded in consolidating and uniting his heterogeneous conquests, and have proved the Darius as well as the Cyrus of his empire. Cut off unexpectedly in the vigor of early manhood, he left no inheritor, either of his power or of his projects. The empire which he had constructed broke into fragments soon after his death; and his plans, whatever they were, perished with him.

The policy of Alexander, so far as appears, aimed at complete fusion and amalgamation of his own Græco-Macedonian subjects with the dominant race of the subjugated countries, the Medo-Persians. He felt the difficulty of holding such extensive conquests by garrisons of Europeans, and therefore determined to associate in the task of ruling and governing the Asiatic race which had shown itself most capable of those high functions. Ultimately, he would have fused the two peoples into one by translations of populations and intermarriages. Meanwhile, he united the two in the military and civil services, incorporating 20,000 Persians into his phalanx, appointing many Persians to satrapies, and composing his court pretty equally of Persian and Macedonian noblemen. His scheme had the merits of originality and intrinsic fairness. Its execution would undoubtedly have elevated Asia to a point which she has never yet reached. But this advantage could not have been gained without some counterbalancing loss. The mixed people which it was his object to produce, while vastly superior to ordinary Asiatics, would have fallen far below the Hellenic, perhaps even below the Macedonian type. It is thus not much to be regretted that the scheme was nipped in the bud, and Hellenic culture preserved in tolerable purity to exercise a paramount influence over the Roman, and so over the modern, world.

The death of Alexander has been ascribed by some to poison, by others to habitual drunkenness. But the hardships of the Gedrosian march and the unhealthiness of the Chaldæan marshes sufficiently account for it.

SECOND PERIOD.

From the Death of Alexander the Great to the Battle of Ipsus,
B.C. 323 *to* 301.

SOURCES. The main authority for this period is DIODORUS, books xviii. to xx. He appears to have followed, in this portion of his History, the contemporary author, HIERONYMUS of Cardia, who wrote an account of Alexander and his successors, about B.C. 270. PLUTARCH's lives of Eumenes, Demetrius, and Phocion are also of considerable value; for, though he draws generally from DIODORUS, yet occasionally he has recourse to independent authorities, e. g., DURIS of Samos, who wrote a Greek and also a Macedonian History, about B.C. 280. The thirteenth book of JUSTIN's History and the fragments of ARRIAN and DEXIPPUS should also be consulted. For these fragments, see the *Fragmenta Historicorum Græcorum* of C. MÜLLER, vol. iii.

Among modern works especially treating of the period, the best is

DROYSEN, *Geschichte der Nachfolger Alexander's des Grossen.* Hamburg, 1836–43; 2 vols. 8vo.

The student will do well to consult also chapters xcv. and xcvi. of Mr. GROTE's *History of Greece*, and chapters lvi.-lix. of Bishop THIRLWALL's work on the same subject.

Troubles consequent on Alexander's death.

1. The circumstances under which Alexander died led naturally to a period of convulsion. He left at his death no legitimate issue, and designated no successor. The Macedonian law of succession was uncertain; and, of those who had the best title to the throne, there was not one who could be considered by any unprejudiced person worthy of it. The great generals of the deceased king became thus, almost of necessity, aspirants to the regal dignity; and it was scarcely possible that their

rival claims could be settled without an appeal to arms and a long and bloody struggle. For a time, the fiction of a united Macedonian Empire under the sovereignty of the old royal family was kept up; but from the first the generals were the real depositaries of power, and practically a division of authority took effect almost from Alexander's death.

Alexander left behind him an illegitimate son, named Hercules, a boy ten or twelve years old. He also left Roxana pregnant. The other living members of the royal family were Arrhidæus, his half-brother, a bastard son of Philip, who was grown up; Cleopatra, Cynané, and Thessalonica, his sisters; and Eurydicé, his niece, daughter of Cynané and Amyntas, son of Perdiccas III. Olympias also, the widow of Philip and mother of Alexander, was still living.

Settlement of the succession—regents.

2. The difficulty with respect to the succession was terminated without bloodshed. The claims of Hercules being passed over, Arrhidæus, who was at Babylon, was proclaimed king under the name of Philip, and with the understanding that he was to share the empire with Roxana's child, if she should give birth to a boy. At the same time, four guardians, or regents, were appointed—Antipater and Craterus in Europe, Perdiccas and Leonnatus (for whom was soon afterwards substituted Meleager) in Asia. But the murder of Meleager by Perdiccas shortly reduced the number of guardians to three.

Great power of Perdiccas. He distributes the provinces.

3. The sole command of the great army of Asia, assumed by Perdiccas on the death of Meleager, made his position vastly superior to that of his European colleagues, and enabled him to take the entire direction of affairs on his own side of the Hellespont. But, to maintain this position, it was necessary for him to content the other great military chiefs, who had lately been his equals, and who would not have been satisfied to remain very much his inferiors. Accordingly, a distribution of satrapies was made within a few weeks of Alexander's death; and each chief of any pretensions received a province proportioned to his merits or his influence.

In this partition, Ptolemy Lagi, reputed an illegitimate son of Philip, received Egypt; Pithon, Media; Antigonus, Phrygia, Lycia, and Pamphylia; Eumenes the Cardian, Cappadocia, which remained, however, still to be conquered; Leonnatus, Mysia; Lysimachus, Macedonian Thrace; Menander, Lydia; Asander, Caria; Philotas, Cilicia; and Laomedon, Syria. Nearchus, Alexander's admiral, received the government of Lycia and Pamphylia, as sub-satrap under Antigonus; and Cleomenes remained in a similar position under Ptolemy Lagi. The other provinces continued under the governors appointed by Alexander.

Insubordination of the provincial governors.

4. It was not the intention of Perdiccas to break up the unity of Alexander's empire. Roxana having given birth to a boy, the government was carried on in the name of the two joint kings. Perdiccas's own office was that of vizier or prime minister. The generals who had received provinces were viewed by Perdiccas as mere governors intrusted with their administration, and answerable to the kings for it. He himself, as prime minister, undertook to give commands to the governors as to their courses of action. But he soon found that they declined to pay his commands any respect. The centrifugal force was greater than the centripetal; and the disintegration of the empire was not to be avoided.

Leonnatus and Antigonus, required by Perdiccas to put Eumenes in possession of Cappadocia, make light of his orders. Antigonus does nothing. Leonnatus schemes to marry Cleopatra and supplant Antipater in Macedon; but wishing first to put down the insurrection of the Greeks, he marches into Thessaly, where he falls. Ptolemy Lagi puts Cleomenes to death, and acts as independent prince in Egypt. Perdiccas has to undertake the Cappadocian war in person, defeats Ariarathes, and installs Eumenes. In another part of the empire, Pithon plans to make himself independent by the help of those discontented colonists who had been settled by Alexander along his northeastern frontier; he is balked, however, by the foresight and prompt cruelty of the vizier.

Ambition of Perdiccas. League of the satraps against him.

5. It was probably the uncertainty of his actual position, and the difficulty of improving it without some violent step, that led Perdiccas to entertain the idea of removing the kings, and himself seizing the empire. Though he had married Nicæa, the daughter of Antipater, he arranged to repudiate her, and negotiated a marriage with Cleopatra, Alexander's sister. Such a union would have given to his claims the color of legitimacy. The opposition which he had chiefly to fear was that of his colleagues in the regency, Antipater and Craterus, and of the powerful satraps, Ptolemy Lagi and Antigonus. The former he hoped to cajole, while he crushed the latter. But his designs were penetrated. Antigonus fled to Macedonia, B.C. 322, and warned Craterus and Antip-

ater of their danger. A league was made between them and Ptolemy; and thus, in the war which followed, Perdiccas and his friend Eumenes were engaged on the one side against Antipater, Craterus, Antigonus, and Ptolemy Lagi on the other.

First war among the "Successors," B.C. 321. Death of Perdiccas.

6. Perdiccas, leaving Eumenes to defend Asia, marched in person against Ptolemy. His army was from the first disaffected; and, when the military operations with which he commenced the campaign failed, they openly mutinied, attacked him, and slew him in his tent. Meanwhile Eumenes, remaining on the defensive in Asia Minor, repulsed the assaults made upon him, defeated and slew Craterus, and made himself a great reputation.

Antipater sole regent, B.C. 320.

7. The removal of Perdiccas from the scene necessitated a new arrangement. Ptolemy declining the regency, it was conferred by the army of Perdiccas on Pithon and Arrhidæus, two of their generals, who with difficulty maintained their position against the intrigues of Eurydicé, the young wife of the mock monarch, Philip Arrhidæus, until the arrival of Antipater in Syria, to whom they resigned their office. Antipater, now became sole regent, silenced Eurydicé, and made a fresh division of the provinces at Triparadisus, in Northern Syria, B.C. 320.

By this division, while Ptolemy Lagi and Antigonus retained their old governments, Clitus received Lydia, and Arrhidæus Mysia or the Hellespontine Phrygia; Seleucus was made satrap of Babylon, and Antigonus satrap of Susiana. The care and custody of the two kings was at first intrusted to Antigonus, but afterwards assumed by Antipater himself. To Antigonus was assigned the conduct of the war with Eumenes. Cassander, the son of Antipater, was made second in command under Antigonus, with the title of *chiliarch*.

Wars of Antigonus with Eumenes, and of Ptolemy with Laomedon.

8. A war followed between Antigonus and Eumenes. Defeated in the open field through the treachery of Apollonides, whom Antigonus had bribed, Eumenes took refuge in the mountain fastness of Nora, where he defended himself successfully against every attack for many months. Antigonus turned his arms against other so-called rebels, defeated them, and became master of the greater part of Asia Minor. Meanwhile, Ptolemy picked a quarrel with Laomedon, satrap of Syria, sent an army into his province, and annexed it.

9. The death of the regent Antipater in Macedonia produced a further complication. Overlooking the claims of his son, Cassander, he bequeathed the regency to his friend, the aged Polysperchon, and thus drove Cassander into opposition. Cassander fled to Antigonus; and a league was formed between Ptolemy, Cassander, and Antigonus on the one hand, and Polysperchon and Eumenes on the other; the two latter defending the cause of unity and of the Macedonian monarchs, the three former that of disruption and of satrapial independence.

Death of Antipater. Regency of Polysperchon.

10. Antigonus began the war by absorbing Lydia and attacking Mysia. He was soon, however, called away to the East by the threatening attitude of Eumenes, who had collected a force in Cilicia, with which he menaced Syria and Phœnicia. The command of the sea, which Phœnicia might have given, would have enabled Eumenes and Polysperchon to unite their forces and act together. It was the policy of Antigonus to prevent this. Accordingly, after defeating the royal fleet, commanded by Clitus, near Byzantium, he marched in person against Eumenes, who retreated before him, crossed the Euphrates and Tigris, and united his troops with those of a number of the Eastern satraps, whom he found leagued together to resist the aggressions of Seleucus and Pithon. Antigonus advanced to Susa, while Eumenes retreated into Persia Proper. Two battles were fought with little advantage to either side; but at last the Macedonian jealousy of a foreigner and the insubordination of Alexander's veterans prevailed. Eumenes was seized by his own troops, delivered up to Antigonus, and put to death, B.C. 316.

War of the Satraps against Polysperchon and Eumenes. B.C. 319–316. Death of Eumenes.

11. Meanwhile, in Europe, Cassander had proved fully capable of making head against Polysperchon. After counteracting the effect of Polysperchon's proceedings in Attica and the Peloponnese, he had marched into Macedonia, where important changes had taken place among the members of the royal family. Eurydicé, the young wife of Philip Arrhidæus, had raised a party, and so alarmed Polysperchon for his own power that he had determined on making common cause with Olympias, who returned from Epirus to Macedon on his invitation. Eurydicé

Successes of Cassander.

found herself powerless in the presence of the more august princess, and, betaking herself to flight, was arrested, and, together with her husband, put to death by her rival, B.C. 317. But Cassander avenged her the next year. Entering Macedonia suddenly, he carried all before him, besieged Olympias in Pydna, and, though she surrendered on terms, allowed her to be killed by her enemies. Roxana and the young Alexander he held as prisoners, while he strengthened his title to the Macedonian throne by a marriage with Thessalonica, the daughter of King Philip.

Ambition of Antigonus. League formed against him, B.C. 315.

12. Thus the rebellious satraps had everywhere triumphed over the royalists, and the Macedonian throne had fallen, though Roxana and the young Alexander were still living. But now the victors fell out among themselves. Antigonus, after the death of Eumenes, had begun to let it be seen that nothing less than the entire empire of Alexander would content him. He slew Pithon, drove Seleucus from Babylonia, and distributed the Eastern provinces to his creatures. He then marched westward, where important changes had occurred during his absence. Cassander had made himself complete master of Macedonia and Greece; Lysimachus had firmly established himself in Thrace; and Asander, satrap of Caria, had extended his dominion over Lycia and Cappadocia. These chiefs, fearing the ambition of Antigonus, entered into a league with Ptolemy Lagi and Seleucus, now a fugitive at his court; and when the terms which they proposed were rejected, made preparations for war.

First War of Antigonus with the Satraps, B.C. 314-311.

13. The war of Antigonus against Ptolemy, Cassander, Seleucus, Asander (or the Carian Cassander), and Lysimachus lasted for three years. Antigonus had the assistance of his son Demetrius in Asia, and (at first) of Polysperchon and his son Alexander in Europe. He was, on the whole, moderately successful in Syria, Asia Minor, and Greece; but the recovery of Babylonia by Seleucus, and the general adhesion to his cause of the Eastern provinces, more than counterbalanced these gains.

DETAILS of the WAR. Antigonus, anxious to obtain the mastery of the sea, begins by attacking Syria and Phœnicia, B.C. 314. Ptolemy Lagi makes but a poor defense; and the fall of Tyre, after a siege of fifteen months, places Phœnicia at Antigonus's disposal. At the same time, most of Asia Minor is recovered to Antigonus by his nephew, Ptolemy. Antigonus then, leaving Demetrius in Phœnicia, proceeds in person against Asander—B.C. 313—and succeeds in crushing him. He menaces both Lysimachus and Cassander, but is recalled to Syria by the ill success of Demetrius, whom Ptolemy has defeated at Gaza, B.C. 312. This victory encourages Seleucus to attempt the recovery of Babylon. He marches thither and is well received, defeats Nicanor, governor of Media, and becomes master of Babylonia, Media, Susiana, and Persia. Demetrius is sent against him as soon as his successes are known; but he effects little, and returns to his father. Meanwhile, Antigonus recovers Syria, but receives a check in an attempt against the Arabs of Petra. Cassander, on the whole, loses ground in Greece; and the desire for a breathing-space induces the greater number of the belligerents to consent to a peace in B.C. 311, which none of them intend to be lasting.

Peace of B.C. 311.

14. The terms of the peace negotiated in B.C. 311 were, (1) That each should keep what he possessed; (2) That the Greek cities should be independent; (3) That Cassander should retain his power till the young Alexander came of age. Seleucus was no party to the treaty, and was not mentioned in it. It was probably thought that he could well hold his own; though had he been seriously menaced, the treaty would have been at once thrown to the winds. As it was, only a few months passed before there was a renewal of hostilities.

The murder of Roxana and the young Alexander by the orders of Cassander was a natural consequence of the third article of the treaty, and was no doubt expected by Antigonus. He gladly saw these royal personages removed out of his way; while it suited him that the odium of the act should attach to one of his adversaries.

Second War of Antigonus with the Satraps, B.C. 310-301.

15. Hostilities recommenced in the year following the treaty, B.C. 310. They were precipitated by the breach which took place between Antigonus and his nephew Ptolemy, who had been employed by him against Cassander in Greece. Ptolemy Lagi was the first to take up arms. Complaining that Antigonus had not withdrawn his garrisons from the Greek cities of Asia Minor, he undertook to liberate them. Antigonus, on his side, complained that Cassander did not withdraw his garrisons from the cities of European Greece. Thus the war was renewed, nominally for the *freedom of Greece*. In reality, the contest was for supremacy on the part of Antigonus, for independence on that of the satraps; and the only

question with respect to Greece was, who should be her master.

DETAILS OF THE STRUGGLE. Ptolemy ousts the garrisons of Antigonus from the maritime towns of Cilicia, but receives a check from Demetrius, B.C. 310. Polysperchon puts forward Hercules as heir to the Macedonian throne, but soon afterwards consents to his murder. Ptolemy assumes the offensive, crosses the Ægean, and occupies Sicyon and Corinth. A marriage is arranged between him and Cleopatra, Alexander's sister, the last survivor of the Macedonian royal house; but Antigonus prevents it by having Cleopatra assassinated, B.C. 308. Demetrius restores Athens to a nominal freedom, B.C. 307. Adulation of the Athenians. Antigonus recalls Demetrius to Asia, and orders him to reduce Cyprus, which was now wholly under Ptolemy, B.C. 306. Siege of Salamis. Arrival of Ptolemy. Great sea-fight off Salamis, one of the most bloody in history. Defeat of Ptolemy, who escapes with only eight ships—17,000 prisoners taken. Antigonus now assumes the diadem and the royal title; on which his example is followed by Ptolemy, Cassander, Lysimachus, and Seleucus. Attempt of Antigonus in the same year to reduce Egypt fails. Expedition of Demetrius against Rhodes, B.C. 305. Gallant defense of the Rhodians secures their neutrality. Demetrius henceforth known as Poliorcetes, the "Besieger." During the absence of Demetrius in Rhodes, Cassander and Polysperchon had gained ground in Greece. As soon, therefore, as peace was made with the Rhodians, he crossed the Ægean, defeated Cassander, recovered Bœotia and Attica, and re-entered Athens, where he passed the winter of B.C. 304 to 303 in gross debauchery and impiety. The next spring, B.C. 303, he invades the Peloponnese; takes Sicyon and Corinth; recovers Achæa, Arcadia, and Argolis; arranges affairs in Western Greece; and prepares to invade Macedonia. Cassander and Lysimachus, perceiving their danger, concert measures and implore the aid of Seleucus and Ptolemy. While Cassander meets Demetrius in Thessaly, Lysimachus invades Asia Minor, B.C. 302. Imprudent inaction of Demetrius. Lysimachus conquers Mysia, Lydia, and part of Phrygia; but, when Antigonus advances to meet him, retreats into Bithynia, and there stands on the defensive. Antigonus summons Demetrius to his aid from Europe. Ptolemy recovers Syria, but does not venture to proceed any farther. Seleucus, at the head of all the forces of the East, advances from Babylon, and is allowed to effect a junction with Lysimachus. The combined armies give battle to Antigonus and Demetrius at Ipsus in Phrygia, and completely defeat them. Antigonus is slain. Demetrius escapes and takes refuge in Greece, but is not allowed to enter Athens.

Division of the Empire after the Battle of Ipsus.

16. The conquerors at Ipsus, Seleucus and Lysimachus, divided the dominions of Alexander afresh. As was natural, they took to themselves the lion's share. The greater part of Asia Minor was made over to Lysimachus. Seleucus received Cappadocia, part of Phrygia, Upper Syria, Mesopotamia, and the valley of the Euphrates. Cilicia was given to Cassander's brother, Pleis-

tarchus. Neither Cassander himself nor Ptolemy received any additions to their dominions.

General condition of Greece and the East at the close of the struggle.

17. War had now raged over most of the countries conquered by Alexander for the space of twenty years. The loss of lives and the consumption of treasure had been immense. Greece, Asia Minor, Cyprus, and Syria, which had been the chief scenes of conflict, must have suffered especially. Nowhere had there been much attempt at organization or internal improvements, the attention of the rulers having been continually fixed on military affairs. Still, the evils of constant warfare had been, out of Greece at any rate, partly counterbalanced, (1) by the foundation of large and magnificent cities, intended partly as indications of the wealth and greatness of their founders, partly as memorials to hand down their names to after ages; (2) by the habits of military discipline imparted to a certain number of the Asiatics; and (3) by the spread of the Greek language and of Greek ideas over most of Western Asia and North-eastern Africa. The many dialects of Asia Minor died away and completely disappeared before the tongue of the conqueror; which, even where it did not wholly oust the vernacular (as in Egypt, in Syria, and in Upper Asia), stood beside it and above it as the language of the ruling classes and of the educated, generally intelligible to such persons from the shores of the Adriatic to the banks of the Indus, and from the Crimea to Elephantiné. Knowledge rapidly progressed; for not only did the native histories of Egypt, Babylon, Phœnicia, Judæa, and other Eastern countries become now for the first time really known to the Greeks, but the philosophic thought and the accumulated scientific stores of the most advanced Oriental nations were thrown open to them, and Greek intelligence was able to employ itself on materials of considerable value, which had hitherto been quite inaccessible. A great advance was made in the sciences of mathematics, astronomy, geography, ethology, and natural history, partly through this opening up of Oriental stores, partly through the enlarged acquaintance with the world and its phenomena which followed on the occupation by the Greeks of vast tracts previously untrodden by Europeans. Commerce, too, in spite of the unsettled state of the newly-occupied countries, ex-

tended its operations. On the other hand, upon Greece itself familiarity with Asiatic ideas and modes of life produced a debasing effect. The Oriental habits of servility and adulation superseded the old free-spoken independence and manliness; patriotism and public spirit disappeared; luxury increased; literature lost its vigor; art deteriorated; and the people sank into a nation of pedants, parasites, and adventurers.

THIRD PERIOD.

History of the States into which the Macedonian Monarchy was broken up after the Battle of Ipsus.

PART I.

History of the Syrian Kingdom of the Seleucidæ, B.C. 312 *to* 65.

SOURCES. The original authorities for the history of Syria during this period are two books (xix., xx.), and the fragments of several lost books, of DIODORUS (lib. xxi.-xxxiv.), the epitome of JUSTIN, some books and fragments of POLYBIUS (especially books v., vii., and viii.), the *Syriaca* of APPIAN, LIVY (books xxxi. to xlv.), the Books of Maccabees, and the *Antiquities* of JOSEPHUS. None of these works contain a continuous or complete account of the whole period; and the history has to be constructed by piecing together the different narratives. The chronology of the later kings depends mainly upon the dates which appear on their coins.

Of modern works on the subject the most important are—

FOY-VAILLANT, J., *Imperium Seleucidarum sive historia regum Syriæ.* Paris, 1681; 4to. The 2d edition, published at the Hague in 1732, is the best.

FROELICH, E., *Annales compendiarii rerum et regum Syriæ, numis veteribus illustrati.* Vienna, 1744; folio. A 2d edition followed in 1754.

DROYSEN, *Geschichte der Nachfolger Alexander's des Grossen.* Hamburg, 1836-43; 2 vols. 8vo.

The period has also been well treated by B. G. NIEBUHR in his *Vorträge über alte Geschichte*, vol. iii., Lectures 88-112.

1. The kingdom of the Seleucidæ was originally established in Inner Asia. It dates from the year B.C. 312, when its founder, Seleucus Nicator, or "the Conqueror," taking advantage of the check which Antigonus had received by the victory of Ptolemy Lagi over Demetrius, near Gaza, returned to the province from which he had been a few years earlier expelled by his great adversary, and, re-establishing himself without much difficulty, assumed the diadem. At first, the kingdom consisted merely of Babylonia and the adjacent regions, Susiana,

Foundation of the kingdom, B.C. 312.

Reign of Seleucus.

Media, and Persia; but, after the unsuccessful expedition of Demetrius (B.C. 311), the Oriental provinces generally submitted themselves, and within six years from the date of his return to Babylon, Seleucus was master of all the countries lying between the Indus and Euphrates on the one hand, the Jaxartes and the Indian Ocean on the other.

Expedition against India.

2. Shortly afterwards he undertook a great campaign against Sandracottus (Chandragupta), an Indian monarch, who bore sway in the region about the western head streams of the Ganges. After a brief struggle, he concluded a peace with this powerful prince, who furnished him with 500 elephants, and threw India open to his traders. It is probable that he purchased the good-will of Sandracottus by ceding to him a portion of his own Indian possessions.

Battle of Ipsus, B.C. 301.

3. In the year B.C. 302 Seleucus, whose aid had been invoked by Lysimachus and Cassander, set out from Babylon for Asia Minor, and, having wintered in Cappadocia, effected a junction with the forces of Lysimachus early in the spring of B.C. 301. The battle of Ipsus (see p. 245) followed. Antigonus was defeated and slain, and his dominions shared by his conquerors. To the kingdom of Seleucus were added Cappadocia, part of Phrygia, Upper Syria, and the right bank of the middle Euphrates.

Enlargement of the kingdom.

Removal of the capital to Antioch.

4. By this arrangement the territorial increase which the kingdom received was not large; but the change in the seat of empire, which the accession of territory brought about, was extremely important. By shifting his capital from Babylonia to Syria, from the Lower Tigris to the Orontes, Seleucus thought to strengthen himself against his rivals, Lysimachus and Ptolemy. He forgot, apparently, that by placing his capital at one extremity of his long kingdom he weakened it generally, and, in particular, loosened his grasp upon the more eastern provinces, which were the least Hellenized and the most liable to revolt. Had Babylon or Seleucia continued the seat of government, the East might probably have been retained; the kingdom of the Parthians might never have grown up. Rome, when she interfered in the affairs of Asia, would have found a great Greek Empire situated beyond the Euphrates, and so almost inaccessible to

her arms; the two civilizations would have co-existed, instead of being superseded the one by the other, and the history of Asia and of the world would have been widely different.

The followers of Alexander inherited from their master a peculiar fondness for the building of new cities, which they called after themselves, their fathers, or their favorite wives. Cassander built Thessalonica on the bay of the name, and Cassandreia in the peninsula of Pallêné. Lysimachus fixed his seat of government at a new town, which he called Lysimacheia, on the neck of the Chersonese. Antigonus was building Antigoneia, on the Orontes, when he fell at Ipsus. His son, Demetrius, made his capital Demetrias, on the gulf of Pagasæ. Seleucus, even before he transferred the seat of government to Antioch, had removed it from Babylon to his city of Seleucia, on the Tigris. Ptolemy alone maintained the capital which he found established on his arrival in Egypt. The numerous Antiochs, Laodiceias, Epiphaneias, and Seleuceias, with which Asia became covered, attest the continuance of the taste in the successors of Nicator.

5. Though Seleucus had come to the rescue, on the invitation of Ptolemy, Cassander, and Lysimachus, yet he was well aware that he could place no dependence on the continuance of their amity. His success made them jealous of him, and induced them to draw nearer to each other, and unite their interests by intermarriages. Seleucus, therefore, cast about for an ally, and found one in Demetrius, the son of Antigonus, his late adversary, whom he attached to himself in the same way. Demetrius, who had escaped from Ipsus with a considerable force, was a personage of importance; and, by supporting him in his quarrels with Cassander, and then Lysimachus, Seleucus was able to keep those princes employed.

Alliance of Seleucus with Demetrius, B.C. 299.

Marriage of Lysimachus with Arsinoë, daughter of Ptolemy Lagi, B.C. 301. Of Seleucus with Stratonicé, daughter of Demetrius, B.C. 299. Of Antipater, second son of Cassander, with Eurydicé, daughter of Lysimachus; and of Alexander, Cassander's third son, with Lysandra, daughter of Ptolemy, soon afterwards. Attempt at a match between Demetrius and Ptolemaïs, daughter of Ptolemy, furthered by Seleucus, who seems to have been at this time really desirous of peace. Marriage of Lysandra, after Alexander's death, with Agathocles, the eldest son of Lysimachus.

6. In Asia a period of tranquillity followed the marriage of Seleucus. Cassander and Lysimachus were occupied with wars in Europe raised by the ambition of Demetrius. Ptolemy by himself was too weak to effect any thing, and, having been allowed to retain

Tranquil period. Organization of the empire.

Lower Syria and Palestine, had no ground of complaint. Seleucus employed the interval (about twelve years, B.C. 299 to 287) in building his capital, Antioch; enlarging and beautifying its port, Seleuceia; and consolidating, arranging, and organizing his vast empire. The whole territory was divided into seventy-two satrapies, which were placed under the government of Greeks or Macedonians, not of natives. A large standing army was maintained, composed mainly of native troops, officered by Macedonians or Greeks. After a while, Seleucus divided his empire with his son Antiochus, committing to him the entire government of all the provinces beyond the Euphrates—a dangerous precedent, though one which can scarcely be said to have had actual evil consequences. At the same time, Seleucus yielded to Antiochus the possession of his consort, Stratonicé, with whom that prince had fallen desperately in love.

Invasion of Asia by Demetrius, B.C. 287. His death.

7. The first disturbance of the tranquillity was caused by the wild projects of Demetrius. That hare-brained prince, after gaining and then losing Macedonia, plunged suddenly into Asia, where he hoped to win by his sword a new dominion. Unable to make any serious impression on the kingdom of Lysimachus, he entered Cilicia and became engaged in hostilities with Seleucus, who defeated him, took him prisoner, and kept him in a private condition for the rest of his life.

Rupture with Lysimachus. Conquest of Asia Minor, B.C. 281. Murder of Seleucus.

8. Shortly afterwards, B.C. 281, occurred the rupture between Seleucus and Lysimachus, which led to the death of that aged monarch and the conquest of great part of his dominions. Domestic troubles, caused by Arsinoë, paved the way for the attack of Seleucus, who found his best support in the disaffection of his enemy's subjects. The battle of Corupedion cost Lysimachus his life; and gave the whole of Asia Minor into the hands of the Syrian king. It might have been expected that the European provinces would have been gained with equal ease, and that, with the exception of Egypt, the scattered fragments of Alexander's empire would have been once more reunited. But an avenger of Lysimachus appeared in the person of the Egyptian exile, Ptolemy Ceraunus, the eldest son of Ptolemy Lagi; and as Seleucus was proceeding to take possession of Lysimacheia, his late

rival's capital, he was murdered in open day by the Egyptian adventurer, who thereupon became king of Macedon.

9. Antiochus I. (Soter) succeeded to his father's dominions, B.C. 280, and shortly became engaged in hostilities with Zipœtes and Nicomedes, native kings of Bithynia, the former of whom had successfully maintained his independence against Lysimachus. Nicomedes (B.C. 278), finding his own resources insufficient for the struggle, availed himself of the assistance of the Gauls, who had been now for some years ravaging Eastern Europe, and had already aided him against his brother Zipœtes. With their help he maintained his independence, and crippled the power of Antiochus, who lost Northern Phrygia, which was occupied by the Gauls and became Galatia, and North-western Lydia, which became the kingdom of Pergamus. Antiochus succeeded in inflicting one considerable defeat on the Gauls, B.C. 275, whence his cognomen of "Soter" (Saviour); otherwise his expeditions were unfortunate; and the Syrian empire at his death had declined considerably below the point of greatness and splendor reached under Nicator.

Reign of Antiochus I. (Soter), B.C. 280–261.

Unsuccessful expedition against Egypt, B.C. 264, undertaken to support the rebel king of Cyrênê, Magas, who had espoused Apamê, a daughter of Antiochus. Failure of an attempt to recover Pergamus, B.C. 263. Antiochus defeated near Sardis by Eumenes. Defeat and death of Antiochus in a battle with the Gauls near Ephesus, B.C. 261.

10. Antiochus II. surnamed Θεός, "the God," succeeded his father. He was a weak and effeminate prince, sunk in sensuality and profligacy, who allowed the kingdom to be ruled by his wives and male favorites. Under him the decline of the empire became rapid. The weakness of his government tempted the provinces to rebel; and the Parthian and Bactrian kingdoms date from his reign. The only success which attended him was in his war with Egypt, at the close of which he recovered what he had previously lost to Philadelphus in Asia Minor.

Reign of Antiochus II. (Theus), B.C. 261–246.

Details of this Reign. Marriage of Antiochus with Laodicê, daughter of Achæus. Her influence, and that of his sister Apamê, wife of Magas, engage him in a war with Ptolemy Philadelphus, B.C. 260, which is terminated, B.C. 252, by a marriage between Antiochus and Berenicê, Ptolemy's daughter. Soon after the close of this war, B.C. 255, Parthia and Bactria revolt and establish their independence. On the death of Philadelphus, B.C. 247, Antiochus repudiates Berenicê and takes back his former wife Laodicê, who, however, doubtful of his constancy, murders him to secure the throne for her son Seleucus, B.C. 246.

11. Seleucus II., surnamed Callinicus, became king on the assassination of his father. Throughout his reign, which lasted rather more than twenty years, B.C. 246 to 226, he was most unfortunate, being engaged in wars with Ptolemy Euergetes, with Antiochus Hierax, his own brother, and with the Parthian king, Arsaces II., in all of which he met with disasters. Still, it is remarkable that, even when his fortunes were at the lowest ebb, he always found a means of recovering himself, so that his epithet of Callinicus, "the Victorious," was not wholly inappropriate. The kingdom must have been greatly weakened and exhausted during his reign; but its limits were not seriously contracted. Portions of Asia Minor were indeed lost to Ptolemy and to Attalus, and the Parthians appear to have made themselves masters of Hyrcania; but, excepting in these two quarters, Seleucus recovered his losses, and left the territories which he had inherited to his son, Seleucus Ceraunus.

Reign of Seleucus II. (Callinicus), B.C. 246-226.

Ptolemy Euergetes invades Syria, B.C. 245, to avenge the murder of his sister, Berenicé, and her infant son, who had been put to death by Laodicé, with the consent of Callinicus. In the war which follows, he carries every thing before him. All Asia within the Euphrates, excepting some parts of Lydia and Phrygia, submits to him. He then proceeds across the Euphrates, and adds to his dominion Mesopotamia, Babylonia, Susiana, Media, and Persia. His exactions, however, make him unpopular; and on the occurrence of a revolt in Egypt he loses almost all his conquests. Callinicus once more rules from the Indus to the Ægean. But an intestine war is soon afterwards provoked by the ambition of his brother. Antiochus, surnamed *Hierax*, "the Hawk," at the age of fourteen revolts against Callinicus, and, aided by his uncle Andromachus and a body of Gallic mercenaries, obtains important successes. Meanwhile, the Parthians had gained advantages in Upper Asia, and Callinicus undertook an expedition against them, about B.C. 237, but was defeated in a great battle. The war between the brothers was then renewed, and continued till B.C. 229, when Antiochus was completely defeated and became a fugitive. It was probably during this contest that Attalus became master of most of Asia Minor. Seleucus died through a fall from his horse, B.C. 226.

12. Seleucus III.—surnamed Ceraunus, "the Thunderbolt"—had a reign which lasted only three years. Assisted by his cousin, the younger Achæus, he prepared a great expedition against the Pergamene mon-

Reign of Seleucus III. (Ceraunus).

arch, Attalus, whose dominions now reached to the Taurus. His ill-paid army, however, while on the march, became mutinous; and he was assassinated by some of his officers, B.C. 223.

13. On the death of Seleucus III., Antiochus III., surnamed "the Great," ascended the throne. His long reign, which exceeded thirty-six years, constitutes the most eventful period of Syrian history. Antiochus did much to recover, consolidate, and in some quarters enlarge, his empire. He put down the important rebellions of Molo and Achæus, checked the progress of the Parthians and Bactrians, restored his frontier towards India, drove the Egyptians from Asia, and even at one time established his dominion over a portion of Europe. But these successes were more than counterbalanced by the losses which he sustained in his war with the Romans, whom he needlessly drew into Asia. The alliance between Rome and Pergamus, and the consequent aggrandizement of that kingdom, were deeply injurious to Syria, and greatly accelerated her decline. Antiochus was unwise to provoke the hostility of the Romans, and foolish, when he had provoked it, not to take the advice of Hannibal as to the mode in which the war should be conducted. Had he united with Macedonia and Carthage, and transferred the contest into Italy, the Roman power might have been broken or checked. By standing alone, and on the defensive, he at once made his defeat certain, and rendered its consequences more injurious than they would have been otherwise.

Reign of Antiochus III. (the Great), B.C. 223–187.

DETAILS OF THIS REIGN. At first, the cruel and crafty Carian, Hermeias, is all-powerful with the young prince. At his instigation Antiochus makes war upon Egypt, B.C. 223, while he sends his generals to put down the revolt of Molo. When his generals, however, are defeated, he proceeds in person against the rebels, defeats and crushes them, B.C. 220, makes a successful expedition into Atropatênê, and, having caused Hermeias to be put to death, returns in triumph to Syria. Achæus during his absence had assumed the diadem and the title of king. Antiochus remonstrates, but does not march against his rebellious relation, preferring to resume his schemes against Egypt. An important war follows with Ptolemy Philopator, B.C. 219, in which Antiochus is at first completely successful; but the battle of Raphia, B.C. 217, deprives him of all his conquests, except the maritime Seleuceia, which he retains. Antiochus, having made peace with Egypt, turns his arms next against Achæus, B.C. 216, and, assisted by Attalus, defeats him, besieges him in Sardis, and finally obtains possession of his person by treachery, B.C. 214.

War then followed with Parthia, which had assumed an aggressive attitude under Arsaces III., and was threatening Media. Antiochus led his army from Ecbatana across the desert to Hecatompylos, the capital of Parthia, which he took, B.C. 213, and then crossed the mountains into Hyrcania, where a battle seems to have been fought, the issue of which was so far doubtful that Antiochus was induced to make peace with Arsaces, allowing him the title of king, and confirming him in the possession of Parthia and Hyrcania. He then turned his arms against Bactria; but, after gaining certain advantages, he admitted Euthydemus also, the Bactrian king, to terms, negotiated a marriage between one of his daughters and Demetrius, the king's son, and left him in possession of Bactria and Sogdiana. He then crossed the Hindoo Koosh into Affghanistan, and renewed the old Syrian alliance with the Indian kingdom of those parts, which was now ruled by a monarch who is called Sophagasenus. Finally, Antiochus returned home through Arachosia, Drangiana, and Carmania (Candahar, Seistan, and Kerman), where he wintered, and from which he undertook a naval expedition against the Arabs on the west shore of the Persian Gulf, whom he punished for their piracies.

Return of Antiochus from the East, B.C. 205, and resumption of his Egyptian projects. A treaty is made with Philip of Macedon for the partition of the kingdom of the Ptolemies between the two powers. War in Cœlé-Syria, Phœnicia, and Palestine, with varied success, terminated by a great victory over Scopas near Panias, B.C. 198. Marriage of Cleopatra, daughter of Antiochus, with Ptolemy V. (Epiphanes). Cœlé-Syria and Palestine promised as a dowry, but not delivered.

The conquests of Antiochus in Asia Minor and Europe, B.C. 197 to 196, bring him into contact with the Romans, who require him to evacuate the Chersonese and restore the Greek cities in Asia Minor to freedom. He indignantly rejects their demands, and prepares for war. Flight of Hannibal to his court, B.C. 195. Antiochus makes alliance with the Ætolians, and in B.C. 192 crosses into Greece, lands at Demetrias, and takes Chalcis. Great battle at Thermopylæ between the Romans, under Acilius Glabrio, and the allied forces of Antiochus and the Ætolians. Antiochus, completely defeated, quits Europe and returns to Asia, B.C. 191. His fleet has orders to protect the shores and prevent the Romans from landing. But the battle of Corycus ruins these hopes. The Romans obtain the mastery of the sea; and their army, having crossed the Hellespont without opposition, gains under the two Scipios the great victory of Magnesia, which places Antiochus at their mercy, B.C. 190. He purchases peace by ceding all Asia Minor except Cilicia, and by consenting to pay a contribution of 12,000 talents. The ceded provinces are added by the Romans to the kingdom of Pergamus, which is thus raised into a rival to Syria.

The defeat of Magnesia is followed by the revolt of Armenia, B.C. 189, which henceforth becomes independent. It leads also to the death of Antiochus, who, in order to pay the war contribution imposed upon him by the Romans, is driven to the plunder of the Oriental temples. Hence a tumult in Elymaïs, wherein the king is killed, B.C. 187.

14. Antiochus was succeeded by his son, Seleucus IV.,

who took the name of Philopator, and reigned eleven years, B.C. 187 to 176. This period was wholly uneventful. The fear of Rome, and the weakness produced by exhaustion, forced Seleucus to remain quiet, even when Eumenes of Pergamus seemed about to conquer and absorb Pontus. Rome held as a hostage for his fidelity, first, his brother, Antiochus, and then his son, Demetrius. Seleucus was murdered by Heliodorus, his treasurer (B.C. 176), who hoped to succeed to his dominions.

Reign of Seleucus IV. (Philopator), B.C. 187–176.

15. On the death of Seleucus, the throne was seized by Heliodorus; but it was not long before Antiochus, the brother of the late king, with the help of the Pergamene monarch, Eumenes, recovered it. This prince, who is known in history as Antiochus IV., or (more commonly) as Antiochus Epiphanes, was a man of courage and energy. He engaged in important wars with Armenia and Egypt; and would beyond a doubt have conquered the latter country, had it not been for the interposition of the Romans. Still, the energy of Epiphanes was of little benefit to his country. He gained no permanent advantage from his Egyptian campaigns, since the Romans deprived him even of Cyprus. He made no serious impression on Armenia, though he captured Artaxias, its sovereign. On the other hand, his religious intolerance raised him up an enemy in the heart of his empire, whose bitter hostility proved under his successors a prolific source of weakness. The Jews, favored by former kings of Syria, were driven to desperation by the mad project of this self-willed monarch, who, not content with plundering the Temple to satisfy his necessities, profaned it by setting up in the Holy of Holies the image of Jupiter Olympius. His luxury and extravagance also tended to ruin his empire, and made him seek to enrich himself with the plunder of other temples besides that at Jerusalem. An attempt of this kind, which was baffled, in Elymaïs, is said to have been followed by an access of superstitious terror, which led to his death at Tabæ, B.C. 164.

Reign of Antiochus IV. (Epiphanes), B.C. 176–164.

DETAILS OF THIS REIGN. Antiochus, assisted by Eumenes, drives out Heliodorus, and obtains the throne, B.C. 176. He astonishes his subjects by an affectation of Roman manners. His good-natured profuseness. Threatened with war by the ministers of Ptolemy Philometor, who claim Cœlé-Syria and Palestine as the dowry of Cleopatra, the late queen-mother, Antiochus marches against Egypt, and in four campaigns—B.C. 171 to 168—reduces it to such straits, that the aid of Rome is invoked, and Antiochus is haughtily required by Popillius to relinquish forthwith all his conquests. He obeys unwillingly, and vents his rage by cruelties on the Jews, whose temple he plunders and desecrates. After this we find him holding a magnificent festival at Daphne, which is attended by thousands from all parts of Greece, B.C. 166. His expedition against Armenia and capture of Artaxias probably took place in the next year, B.C. 165, and in the year following, B.C. 164, he died, as above stated, at Tabæ.

Reign of Antiochus V. (Eupator), B.C. 164–162.

16. Epiphanes was succeeded by Antiochus V., surnamed Eupator, a boy not more than twelve years old. The chief power during his reign was in the hands of Lysias, whom Epiphanes had left as regent when he quitted Antioch. Lysias attempts to reduce the rebel Jews, but allows himself to be diverted from the war by the attitude of his rival Philip, whom he attacks, defeats, and puts to death. He takes no steps, however, to resist the Parthians when they overrun the Eastern provinces, or the Romans when they harshly enforce the terms of the treaty concluded after the battle of Magnesia. The position of affairs, which we can well understand the Romans favoring, was most injurious to the power of Syria, which, in the hands of a minor and a regent, was equally incapable of maintaining internal order and repelling foreign attack. It was an advantage to Syria when Demetrius, the adult son of Seleucus Philopator, escaped from Rome, where he had been long detained as a hostage, and, putting Lysias and Eupator to death, himself mounted the throne.

The war between Lysias and Philip, which allowed the Parthians to spread unresisted over the fairest of the Eastern provinces, was caused by the imprudence of Epiphanes, who had left his young son, Antiochus, to the care of Lysias on quitting Antioch, but upon his death-bed appointed a new guardian in the person of Philip. Philip, who had the support of a part of the army, seized Antioch, where he was defeated and slain, B.C. 162.

Reign of Demetrius I. (Soter), B.C. 162–151.

17. Demetrius, having succeeded in obtaining the sanction of Rome to his usurpation, occupied himself for some years in attempts to reduce the Jews. He appears to have been a vigorous administrator, and a man of considerable ambition and energy; but he could not arrest the decline of the Syrian state. The Romans compelled him to desist from his attacks on the Jews; and when he ventured on an expedition into Cappadocia, for the pur-

pose of expelling the king Ariarathes, and giving the crown to Orophernes, his bastard brother, a league was formed against him by the neighboring kings, to which the Romans became parties; and a pretender, Alexander Balas, an illegitimate son of Epiphanes, was encouraged to come forward and claim the throne. So low had the Syrian power now sunk, that both Demetrius and his rival courted the favor of the despised Jews; and their adhesion to the cause of the pretender probably turned the scale in his favor. After two years of warfare and two important battles, Demetrius was defeated, and lost both his crown and life.

The friendship of Demetrius with the historian Polybius gives an interest to his reign which the Syrian history rarely possesses. Polybius advised and aided his escape from Rome, and records its circumstances with great minuteness. We have more details too of this king's private character and tastes than of most others. It appears that he was addicted to hunting (whence the symbols on his coins), and was also an intemperate drinker.

Reign of Alexander Balas, B.C. 151–146.

18. Alexander Balas, who had been supported in his struggle with Demetrius by the kings of Pergamus and Egypt, was given by the latter the hand of Cleopatra, his daughter. But he soon proved himself unfit to rule. Committing the management of affairs to an unworthy favorite, Ammonius, he gave himself up to every kind of self-indulgence. Upon this, Demetrius, the eldest son of the late king, perceiving that Balas had become odious to his subjects, took heart, and, landing in Cilicia, commenced a struggle for the throne. The fidelity of the Jews protected Alexander for a while; but when his father-in-law, Ptolemy Philometor, passed over to the side of his antagonist, the contest was decided against him. Defeated in a pitched battle near Antioch, he fled to Abæ in Arabia, where he was assassinated by his own officers, who sent his head to Ptolemy.

First reign of Demetrius II. (Nicator), B.C. 146–140.

19. Demetrius II., surnamed Nicator, then ascended the throne. He had already, while pretender, married Cleopatra, the wife of his rival, whom Ptolemy had forced Balas to give up. On obtaining full possession of the kingdom, he ruled tyrannically, and disgusted many of his subjects. The people of Antioch having risen in revolt, and Demetrius having allowed his Jewish body-guard to plunder the town, Diodotus of Apamea set up

a rival king in the person of Antiochus VI., son of Alexander Balas, a child of two years of age, who bore the regal title for three or four years (B.C. 146 to 143), after which Diodotus removed him, and, taking the name of Trypho, declared himself independent monarch (*αὐτοκράτωρ*). After vain efforts to reduce his rivals for the space of about seven years, Demetrius, leaving his wife, Cleopatra, to maintain his interests in Syria, marched into his Eastern provinces, which were in danger of falling a prey to the Parthians. Here, though at first he gained such advantages as enabled him to assume the title of "Conqueror" (*νικάτωρ*), his arms soon met with a reverse. Defeated by the Parthian monarch, Arsaces VI., in the year B.C. 140, he was taken prisoner, and remained a captive at the Parthian court for several years.

The acknowledgment of Jewish independence by Demetrius shortly before his expedition to the East, B.C. 142, was an event of some importance in the history of the Jewish nation. Though it may be true that at a later period they again fell under the dominion of the Syrian kings, yet it seems certain that they dated their independence from the grant of Demetrius.

20. During the absence of Demetrius in the remote East, his wife, Cleopatra, unable to make head against Tryphon, looked out for some effectual support, and found it in Antiochus of Sida (Sidetes), her husband's brother, who, joining his arms with hers, attacked Tryphon, and after a struggle, which seems to have lasted nearly two years, defeated him and put him to death. Antiochus Sidetes upon this became sole monarch of Syria, B.C. 137, and contracted a marriage with Cleopatra, his captive brother's wife, who considered herself practically divorced by her husband's captivity and marriage with a Parthian princess. His first step, after establishing his authority, was to reduce the Jews, B.C. 135 to 133. A few years later, B.C. 129, he undertook an expedition into Parthia for the purpose of delivering his brother, and gained some important successes; but was finally defeated by the Parthian monarch, who attacked his army in its winter-quarters, and destroyed it with its commander.

Reign of Antiochus VII. (Sidetes), B.C. 137–129.

21. Meanwhile Demetrius II., having been released from captivity by the Parthian monarch, who hoped by exciting troubles in Syria to force Antiochus to retreat, had reached Antioch and recovered

Second reign of Demetrius II., B.C. 129–126.

his former kingdom. But he was not suffered to remain long in tranquillity. Ptolemy Physcon, the king of Egypt, raised up a pretender to his crown in the person of Alexander Zabinas, who professed to be the son of Balas. A battle was fought between the rivals near Damascus, in which Demetrius was completely defeated. Forced to take flight, he sought a refuge with his wife at Ptolemaïs, but was rejected; whereupon he endeavored to throw himself into Tyre, but was captured and slain, B.C. 126.

22. War followed between Zabinas and Cleopatra, who, having put to death Seleucus, her eldest son, because he had assumed the diadem without her permission, associated with herself on the throne her second son, Antiochus, and reigned conjointly with him till B.C. 121. Zabinas maintained himself in parts of Syria for seven years; but, having quarrelled with his patron, Ptolemy Physcon, he was reduced to straits, about B.C. 124, and two years afterwards was completely crushed by Antiochus, who forced him to swallow poison, B.C. 122. Soon afterwards—B.C. 121—Antiochus found himself under the necessity of putting his mother to death in order to secure his own life, against which he discovered her to be plotting.

Parallel reigns of Alexander II. (Zabinas), Antiochus VIII. (Grypus), and Cleopatra.

23. Syria now enjoyed a period of tranquillity under Antiochus VIII., for the space of eight years, B.C. 122 to 114. The Eastern provinces were, however, completely lost, and no attempt was made to recover them. The Syrian kingdom was confined within Taurus on the north, the Euphrates on the east, and Palestine on the south. Judæa had become wholly independent. The great empire, which had once reached from Phrygia to the Indus, had shrunk to the dimensions of a province; and there was no spirit in either prince or people to make any effort to regain what had been lost. The country was exhausted by the constant wars, the pillage of the soldiers, and the rapacity of the monarchs. Wealth was accumulated in a few hands. The people of the capital were wholly given up to luxury. If Rome had chosen to step in at any time after the death of the second Demetrius, she might have become mistress of the whole of Syria almost without a struggle. At first her domestic troubles, and then her contest with Mith-

Sole reign of Antiochus VIII., B.C. 122-114.

ridates, hindered her, so that it was not till half a century later that the miseries of Syria were ended by her absorption into the Roman empire.

Revolt of Antiochus Cyzicenus. Parallel reigns of Cyzicenus and Grypus, B.C. 114–96.

24. The tranquillity of Antiochus VIII. was disturbed in B.C. 114 by the revolt of his half-brother, Antiochus Cyzicenus, the son of Cleopatra by Antiochus Sidetes, her third husband. A bloody contest followed, which it was attempted to terminate at the close of three years, B.C. 111, by a partition of the territory. But the feud soon broke out afresh. War raged between the brothers for nine years, B.C. 105 to 96, with varied success, but with no decided advantage to either, while the disintegration of the empire rapidly proceeded. The towns on the coast, Tyre, Sidon, Seleuceia, assumed independence. Cilicia revolted. The Arabs ravaged Syria on the one hand, and the Egyptians on the other. At length, amid these various calamities, the reign of Antiochus VIII. came to an end by his assassination, in B.C. 96, by Heracleon, an officer of his court.

Reign of Seleucus V. (Epiphanes), B.C. 96–95.

25. Heracleon endeavored to seize the crown, but failed. It fell to Seleucus V. (Epiphanes), the eldest son of Grypus, who continued the war with Antiochus Cyzicenus, and brought it to a successful issue in the second year of his reign, B.C. 95, when Cyzicenus, defeated in a great battle, slew himself to prevent his capture. But the struggle between the two houses was not yet ended. Antiochus Eusebes, the son of Cyzicenus, assumed the royal title, and attacking Seleucus drove him out of Syria into Cilicia, where he perished miserably, being burnt alive by the people of Mopsuestia, from whom he had required a contribution.

Reigns of Philip and Tigranes, B.C. 95–69.

26. Philip, the second son of Antiochus Grypus, succeeded, and carried on the war with Eusebes for some years, in conjunction with his brothers, Demetrius, and Antiochus Dionysus, until at last Eusebes was overcome and forced to take refuge in Parthia. Philip and his brothers then fell out, and engaged in war one against another. At length the Syrians, seeing no end to these civil contests, called to their aid the king of the neighboring Armenia, Tigranes, and putting themselves under his rule, obtained a respite from suffering for about fourteen

years, B.C. 83 to 69. At the close of this period, Tigranes, having mixed himself up in the Mithridatic war, was defeated by the Romans, and forced to relinquish Syria.

Reign of Antiochus Asiaticus, B.C. 69-65.

27. The Syrian throne seems then to have fallen to Antiochus Asiaticus, the son of Eusebes, who held it for four years only, when he was dispossessed by Pompey, and the remnant of the kingdom of the Seleucidæ was reduced into the form of a Roman province, B.C. 65.

PART II.

History of the Egyptian Kingdom of the Ptolemies, B.C. 323 *to* 30.

SOURCES. The sources for the Egyptian history of this period are for the most part identical with those which have been mentioned at the head of the last section (p. 247) as sources for the history of the Seleucidæ; but on the whole they are scantier and less satisfactory. As the contact between Judæa and Egypt during this period was only occasional, the information furnished by JOSEPHUS and the *Books of Maccabees* is discontinuous and fragmentary. Again, there is no work on Egypt corresponding to the *Syriaca* of APPIAN. The chronology, moreover, is in confusion, owing to the fact that the Ptolemies adopted no era, only dating their coins in some instances by their regnal years; so that the exactness which an era furnishes is wanting. Some important details with respect to foreign conquests and to the internal administration are, however, preserved to us in INSCRIPTIONS, of which the chief are—

The INSCRIPTION OF ADULE, seen by COSMAS INDOPLEUSTA, about A.D. 520, and preserved to us in his work, which MONTFAUCON has edited in his *Collectio nova patrum et scriptorum Græcorum.* Paris, 1706; 2 vols. folio. The inscription itself was first published by LEO ALLATIUS in a small pamphlet entitled *Ptolemæi Euergetis monumentum Adulitanum.* Romæ, 1631. It has since been edited by FABRICIUS in his *Bibliotheca Græca*, vol. ii.; by CHISHULL in his *Antiquitates Asiaticæ* (London, 1728; folio); by BOECKH in his *Corpus Inscriptionum Græcarum*, vol. iii., and by others. Mr. SALT was the first to point out that it consisted of two entirely distinct documents belonging to very different ages. (See his *Narrative* in Lord VALENTIA's *Voyages and Travels to India, Ceylon*, etc. London, 1809; 3 vols. 4to.) This conclusion has since been adopted by NIEBUHR, HEEREN, LETRONNE, BOECKH, and most scholars.

The ROSETTA STONE, interesting not merely as a key to the decipherment of the hieroglyphics, but also as a document throwing considerable light on the internal administration of Egypt. The stone itself is in the British Museum. The inscription, which belongs to about the year B.C. 196 or 197, has been carefully edited by several scholars, among whom may be noticed especially—

AMEILHON, *Eclaircissemens sur l'inscription Grecque du monument trouvé à Rosette.* Paris, 1803; 8vo.

LETRONNE, *Inscription Grecque de Rosette; texte et traduction littérale, accompagnée d'un commentaire critique, historique, et archéologique.* Paris, 1841; 8vo.

BOECKH, in his *Corpus Inscriptionum Græcarum*, vol. iii. pp. 334–342.

Among modern works on the History of Egypt under the Ptolemies the most important are—

FOY-VAILLANT, *Historia Ptolemæorum Ægypti regum ad fidem numismatum accommodata.* Amstel. 1701; folio.

CHAMPOLLION-FIGEAC, *Annales des Lagides, ou Chronologie des Rois Grecs d'Egypte, successeurs d'Alexandre le Grand.* Paris, 1819; 2 vols. 8vo.

LETRONNE, *Recherches pour servir à l'histoire de l'Egypte pendant la domination des Grecs et des Romains, tirées des inscriptions Grecques et Latines, relatives à la chronologie, à l'état des arts, aux usages civiles et religieux de ce pays.* Paris, 1828; 8vo.

The subject is also treated, in connection with the other history of the time, by DROYSEN, in his *Geschichte der Nachfolger Alexanders* (supra, p. 238); and by NIEBUHR in his *Vorträge über alte Geschichte* (supra, p. 137). A good analysis of the chronology is contained in the third volume of the *Fasti Hellenici* of CLINTON (pp. 379–400), and a valuable summary in the *Corpus Inscriptionum Græcarum* of BOECKH, vol. iii. p. 288.

Flourishing condition of the kingdom.

1. The kingdom of the Ptolemies, which owed its origin to Alexander the Great, rose to a pitch of greatness and prosperity which, it is probable, was never dreamt of by the Conqueror. His subjection of Egypt was accomplished rapidly; and he spent but little time in the organization of his conquest. Still, the foundation of all Egypt's later greatness was laid, and the character of its second civilization determined, by him, in the act by which he transferred the seat of government from the inland position of Memphis to the maritime Alexandria. By this alteration not only was the continued pre-eminence of the Macedo-Greek element secured, but the character of the Egyptians themselves was modified. Commercial pursuits were adopted by a large part of the nation. Intercourse with foreigners, hitherto checked and discouraged, became common. Production was stimulated; enterprise throve; and the stereotyped habits of this most rigid of ancient peoples were to a large extent broken into. In language and religion they still continued separate from their conquerors; but their manners and tone of thought underwent a change. The stiff-necked rebels against the authority of the Persian crown became the willing subjects of the Macedonians. Absorbed in the pursuits of industry, or in the novel employment of literature, the Egyptians forgot their

old love of independence, and contentedly acquiesced in the new regime.

The history of Egypt during this period is, in the main, the history of Alexandria, the capital. Here, and here alone, were the Macedo-Greeks settled in any considerable numbers. Here dwelt the Court; and here was to be seen that remarkable contrast of three widely differing elements—the Greek, the Jewish, and the native Egyptian—which gave to the Ptolemaic kingdom its peculiar character. The Jews were granted by the first Ptolemy great privileges in the new capital; and these they retained to the time of the Roman conquest. They formed a distinct community in Alexandria, which had its own organization, and was governed by its own officers. The Macedo-Greeks were, of course, the sole full citizens. They were divided into tribes (*φυλαί*), and into wards (*δημοί*), and had no doubt a *βουλή*, or municipal council. The native Egyptians would be without any such privileges. A judge, probably nominated by the monarch, was placed at their head, who was answerable for their tranquillity. On the government and topography of ancient Alexandria the student may consult—

MEINEKE, *Analecta Alexandrina.* Berlin, 1843; 8vo.

BONAMY, *Description de la ville d'Alexandrie* in the *Mémoires de l'Académie des Inscriptions*, vol. ix.

MANSO, *Briefe über alt-Alexandrie*, in his *Vermischte Schriften*, vol. i.; and the article on Alexandria in Dr. W. SMITH's *Dictionary of Greek and Roman Geography.*

2. In the history of nations much depends on the characters of individuals; and Egypt seems to have been very largely indebted to the first Ptolemy for her extraordinary prosperity. Assigned the African provinces in the division of Alexander's dominions after his death (B.C. 323), he proceeded at once to his government, and, resigning any great ambition, sought to render his own territory unassailable, and to make such additions to it as could be attempted without much risk. It was among his special aims to make Egypt a great naval power; and in this he succeeded almost beyond his hopes, having after many vicissitudes established his authority over Palestine, Phœnicia, and Cœlé-Syria; and also possessed himself of the island of Cyprus. Cilicia, Caria, and Pamphylia were open to his attacks, and sometimes subject to his sway. For a time he even held important positions in Greece, e. g., Corinth and Sicyon; but he never allowed the maintenance of these distant acquisitions to entangle him inextricably in foreign wars, or to endanger his home dominions. Attacked twice in his own province, once

Reign of Ptolemy I. (Soter), B.C. 323-283.

He conquers Palestine, Phœnicia, part of Syria, and Cyprus.

by Perdiccas (B.C. 321), and once by Demetrius and Antigonus (B.C. 306), he both times repulsed his assailants and maintained his own territory intact. Readily retiring if danger threatened, he was always prompt to advance when occasion offered. His combined prudence and vigor obtained the reward of ultimate success; and his death left Egypt in possession of all the more important of his conquests.

It was essential to the plans of Ptolemy Lagi (Soter) to possess himself of Palestine and Phœnicia; for, in order that Egypt might be a great naval power, she required both the timber of those countries and the services of their sea-faring population. Ptolemy first occupied them B.C. 320, almost immediately after repulsing the attack of Perdiccas, when he took Laomedon, the Syrian satrap, prisoner, placed garrisons in the Phœnician towns, and annexed the whole region as far as the Taurus range. Six years later, B.C. 314, in the war of the satraps with Antigonus, on the siege and fall of Tyre, all was again lost; and though the battle of Gaza, B.C. 312, enabled Ptolemy once more to advance and recover his ground to some extent, yet in the peace of B.C. 311 the whole of the disputed territory was ceded. It was partially recovered in B.C. 302, after the attack of Antigonus on Egypt had failed, and he was threatened by Lysimachus and Seleucus. By the peace which followed the battle of Ipsus, B.C. 301, Ptolemy was left in possession of what he had regained, which included Palestine, Phœnicia, and perhaps a part of Cœlé-Syria; but not Upper Syria, which fell to Seleucus.

At what time Ptolemy first occupied Cyprus is uncertain; but as early as B.C. 314 it was the scene of conflict between his forces and those of Antigonus. Two years later, B.C. 312, it was completely subjugated by the Egyptian monarch, who placed it under the government of an officer, called Nicocreon, allowing, however, a certain subordinate authority to the native kings. One of these, Nicocles, king of Paphos, having intrigued with Antigonus, was, in B.C. 309, put to death. In B.C. 306 occurred the expedition of Demetrius against Cyprus, the siege of Salamis, and the great naval defeat of Ptolemy (see p. 245), which gave Cyprus over to Antigonus and Demetrius. Even after Ipsus the island remained faithful to the last-named prince; and it was not till B.C. 294 or 293, when Demetrius was engaged in Macedonia, that Ptolemy once more led an expedition into the island and re-established his authority over it. From this time Cyprus remained an undisputed possession of the Egyptian crown. It was regarded as the most valuable of all the foreign dependencies, on account of its position, its mineral wealth, and its large stores of excellent timber. The Ptolemies governed it by means of a viceroy, who was always a nobleman of the first rank, and united in his person the military, civil, and sacerdotal authority, his title in inscriptions being *στρατηγὸς καὶ ναύαρχος καὶ ἀρχιερεὺς ὁ κατὰ τὴν νῆσον.*

3. In one quarter alone did Ptolemy endeavor to extend his African dominion. The flourishing country of the Cyrenaïca, which lay not far from Egypt upon the west, had welcomed Alexander as a deliverer from the power of Persia,

Reduction of the Cyrenaïca and the Libyan tribes between it and Egypt.

and been accepted by him into alliance. Ptolemy, who coveted its natural wealth, and disliked the existence of an independent republic in his neighborhood, found an occasion in the troubles which at this time fell upon Cyrênê, to establish his authority over the whole region. At the same time he must have brought under subjection the Libyan tribes of the district between Egypt and the Cyrenaïca, who in former times had been dépendent upon the native Egyptian monarchy, and had submitted to the Persians when Egypt was conquered by Cambyses.

Details of the Conquest. Invasion of the Cyrenaïca by Thimbron with a body of mercenaries. He seizes the port of Cyrênê and attacks the town, B.C. 320. The Cyrenians accept a position of dependence; but soon afterwards revolt, and, while Thimbron is engaged in repelling their attack upon his Barcæan allies, they recover their port. Both sides having received reinforcements, a great battle takes place, in which Thimbron is victorious. Disturbances follow in Cyrênê, and the nobles, being expelled by the people, fly to Egypt and persuade Ptolemy to reinstate them; which he does by his general, Ophellas, who then subdues the entire region. After remaining subjects of Egypt for seven years, the Cyrenians revolted, B.C. 313, but were reduced by Ptolemy's general, Agis. After this, however, Ophellas seems to have made himself practically independent; and Egypt might have lost her dependency altogether, if his ambition had not prompted him to accept the specious proposals of Agathocles, who needed his support against Carthage. When Ophellas fell a victim to the treachery of the Sicilian adventurer, B.C. 308, Ptolemy seized the opportunity, and, once more occupying the country, placed it under the government of his son, Magas.

Governmental system; treatment of native Egyptians.

4. The system of government established by Ptolemy Lagi, so far as it can be made out, was the following. The monarch was supreme, and indeed absolute, having the sole direction of affairs and the sole appointment of all officers. The changes, however, made in the internal administration were few. The division of the whole country into nomes was maintained; and most of the old nomes were kept, a certain number only being subdivided. Each was ruled by its nomarch, who received his appointment from the crown, and might at any time be superseded. The nomarchs were frequently, perhaps even generally, native Egyptians. They administered in their provinces the old Egyptian laws, and maintained the old Egyptian religion. It was from first to last a part of the established policy of the Lagid monarchs to protect and

honor the religion of their subjects, which they regarded as closely akin to their own, and of which they ostentatiously made themselves the patrons. Ptolemy Lagi began the practice of rebuilding and ornamenting the temples of the Egyptian gods, and paid particular honor to the supposed incarnations of Apis. The old privileges of the priests, and especially their exemption from land-tax, were continued; and they were allowed everywhere the utmost freedom in the exercise of every rite of their religion. In return for these favors the priests were expected to acknowledge a quasi-divinity in the Lagid monarchs, and to perform certain ceremonies in their honor, both in their lifetime and after their decease.

Privileges of the Græco-Macedonians.

5. At the same time many exclusive privileges were reserved for the conquering race. The tranquillity of the country was maintained by a standing army composed almost exclusively of Greeks and Macedonians, and officered wholly by members of the dominant class. This army was located in, comparatively, a few spots, so that its presence was not much felt by the great bulk of the population. As positions of authority in the military service were reserved for Græco-Macedonians, so also in the civil service of the country all offices of any importance were filled up from the same class. This class, moreover, which was found chiefly in a small number of the chief towns, enjoyed full municipal liberty in these places, electing its own officers, and, for the most part, administering its own affairs without interference on the part of the central government.

DISPOSITION OF THE STANDING ARMY. Alexander stationed the troops with which he garrisoned Egypt at two places only, Pelusium and Memphis; the latter being the native capital—the Moscow of the Egyptians—and the former the key of Egypt on the only side on which it is open to a land attack. In later times, Ptolemaïs in the Thebaïd, Elephantiné, and Parembolé in Nubia were likewise made military stations; and an important body of troops was also maintained at Alexandria, where they guarded the person of the monarch.

Encouragement of learning and science.

6. One of the chief peculiarities of the early Lagid kingdom—a peculiarity for which it was indebted to its founder—was its encouragement of literature and science. Ptolemy Lagi was himself an author; and, alone among the successors of Alexander,

inherited the regard for men of learning and research which had distinguished his great patron. Following the example of Aristotle, he set himself to collect an extensive library, and lodged it in a building connected with the royal palace. Men of learning were invited by him to take up their residence at Alexandria; and the "Museum" was founded, a College of Professors, which rapidly drew to it a vast body of students, and rendered Alexandria the university of the Eastern world. It was too late in the history of the Greek race to obtain, by the fostering influence of judicious patronage, the creation of masterpieces; but exact science, criticism, and even poetry of an unpretentious kind, were produced; and much excellent literary work was done, to the great benefit of the moderns. Euclid, and Apollonius of Perga, in mathematics; Philetas, Callimachus, and Apollonius of Rhodes, in poetry; Aristophanes of Byzantium, and Aristarchus, in criticism; Eratosthenes in chronology and geography; Hipparchus in astronomical science; and Manetho in history—adorned the Lagid period, and sufficiently indicate that the Lagid patronage of learning was not unfruitful. Apelles, too, and Antiphilus produced many of their best pictures at the Alexandrian court.

Four lines of study, corresponding to the modern "faculties," were chiefly pursued by academical students at Alexandria—viz., Poetry, Mathematics, Astronomy, and Medicine, criticism being included under poetry. The "Museum," or university building, comprised chambers for the Professors; a common hall where they took their meals together; a long corridor for exercise and ambulatory lectures; a theatre for scholastic festivals and public disputations; a botanical garden; and a menagerie. It has been well said, that the services rendered by the "Museum" to learning are probably greater than those of any "Academy" in modern Europe. Further details on this interesting subject will be found in

GEIER, *De Ptolemæi Lagidis vita, et commentariorum fragmentis commentatio.* Halæ Sax., 1838; 4to.

HEYNE, *De Genio sæculi Ptolemæorum*, in his *Opuscula Academica.* Göttingen, 1785–8; 3 vols. 8vo.

MATTER, *Essai historique sur l'école d'Alexandrie.* Paris, 1820; 2d edition, 1840.

PARTHEY, *Das Alexandrinische Museum.* Berlin, 1838; 8vo.

7. The character of Ptolemy Lagi was superior to that of most of the princes who were his contemporaries. In an age of treachery and violence, he appears to have remained faithful to his engagements, and to have

Character of Ptolemy Lagi.

been rarely guilty of any bloodshed that was not absolutely necessary for his own safety and that of his kingdom. His mode of life was simple and unostentatious. He was a brave soldier, and never scrupled to incur personal danger. The generosity of his temper was evinced by his frequently setting his prisoners free without ransom. In his domestic relations he was, however, unhappy. He married two wives, Eurydicé, the daughter of Antipater, whom he divorced, and Berenicé, her companion. By Eurydicé he had a son, Ptolemy Ceraunus, who should naturally have been his successor; but Berenicé prevailed on him in his old age to prefer her son, Philadelphus; and Ptolemy Ceraunus, offended, became an exile from his country, and an intriguer against the interests of his brother and his other relatives. Enmity and bloodshed were thus introduced into the family; and to that was shortly afterwards added the crime of incest, a fatal cause of decay and corruption.

8. Ptolemy Lagi adorned his capital with a number of great works. The principal of these were the royal palace, the Museum, the lofty Pharos, upon the island which formed the port, the mole or causeway, nearly a mile in length (Heptastadium), which connected this island with the shore, the Soma or mausoleum, containing the body of Alexander, the temple of Serapis (completed by his son, Philadelphus), and the Hippodrome or great racecourse. He likewise rebuilt the inner chamber of the grand temple at Karnak, and probably repaired many other Egyptian buildings. After a reign of forty years, having attained to the advanced age of eighty-four, he died in Alexandria, B.C. 283, leaving his crown to his son, Philadelphus, the eldest of his children by Berenicé, whom he had already two years before associated with him in the kingdom.

His great works.

His death.

The nomination of Philadelphus by Ptolemy Lagi has been paralleled with that of Xerxes by Darius, and supposed to have rested on the same right (Niebuhr); but, practically, the *reign* of the Egyptian monarch had commenced before his marriage with Eurydicé. The real resemblance is that in both cases the younger son owed his advancement to the influence of his mother over a father already in his dotage.

9. Ptolemy II., surnamed Philadelphus, was born at Cos, B.C. 309, and was consequently twenty-six years of age at the

Reign of Ptolemy II. (Philadelphus), B.C. 283–247.

commencement of his sole reign. He inherited his father's love for literature and genius for administration, but not his military capacity. Still, he did not abstain altogether even from aggressive wars, but had an eye to the events which were passing in other countries, and sought to maintain by his arms the balance of power established in his father's lifetime. His chief wars were with the rebel king of Cyrênê, his half-brother, Magas; with Antiochus I. and Antiochus II., kings of Syria; and with Antigonus Gonatas, king of Macedon. They occupied the space of about twenty years, from B.C. 269 to 249. Philadelphus was fairly successful in them, excepting that he was forced, as the result of his struggle with Magas, to acknowledge the independence of that monarch.

His wars.

DETAILS OF THESE WARS. (*a*) MACEDONIAN WAR:—As early as B.C. 269 Philadelphus seems to have sent aid to the Spartan king, Areus, who was threatened by Antigonus. Shortly afterwards he dispatched a fleet under Patroclus to assist and protect the Athenians, B.C. 247 (?). In B.C. 251 he gave pecuniary help to Aratus when that patriot first formed the project of raising up a counterpoise to Macedon in the famous "Achæan League." Some years later he became an actual ally of the League. (*b*) CYRENÆAN and SYRIAN WARS:—These two wars were closely connected. It is uncertain in what year Magas asserted his independence, but in B.C. 266, not content with the kingdom of Cyrênê, he marched against Egypt, attacked and took Parætonium, and was proceeding farther eastward when a revolt of the Marmaridæ, a native African tribe, recalled him. Two years later, B.C. 264, having made a treaty with Antiochus I. (whose daughter, Apame, was his wife), he undertook a second expedition, and once more occupied Parætonium. Philadelphus, however, found means to frustrate the efforts of both his antagonists. Antiochus was kept employed at home, and Magas without his ally was unable to make any progress. After a while a partial peace was made. Magas was recognized as independent monarch of the Cyrenaïca, and his daughter, Berenicé, was betrothed to the eldest son of Philadelphus, Ptolemy (Euergetes), B.C. 259. Hostilities continued with Syria, where Antiochus II. had succeeded his father; but in B.C. 249 this war also was terminated by a marriage, Antiochus receiving the hand of Berenicé, Philadelphus's daughter. It was probably during the Syrian War that Philadelphus possessed himself of the coast, at any rate, of Caria, Lycia, Pamphylia, and Cilicia, and also of many of the Cyclades.

10. The home administration of Ptolemy Philadelphus was in all respects eminently successful. To him belongs the credit of developing to their fullest extent the commercial advantages which the position of Egypt throws open

His home administration. Encouragement of commerce.

to her, and of bringing by these means her material prosperity to its culminating point. By reopening the canal uniting the Red Sea with the Nile—a construction of the greatest of the Ramesside kings (see p. 85)—and building the port of Arsinoë on the site of the modern Suez, he united the East and West, allowing the merchandise of either region to reach the other by water carriage. As this, however, owing to the dangers of the Red Sea navigation, was not enough, he constructed two other harbors, and founded two other cities, each called Berenicé, on the eastern African coast, one nearly in lat. 24°, the other still farther to the south, probably about lat. 13°. A high-road was opened from the northern Berenicé to Coptos on the Nile (near Thebes), and the merchandise of India, Arabia, and Ethiopia flowed to Europe for several centuries chiefly by this route. The Ethiopian trade was particularly valuable. Not only was ivory imported largely from this region, but the elephant was hunted on a large scale, and the hunters' captures were brought alive into Egypt, where they were used in the military service. Ptolemaïs, in lat. 18° 40′, was the emporium for this traffic.

Other steps taken by Philadelphus with a view to the extension or security of commerce were, (1) his suppression of the banditti which infested Upper Egypt at the very outset of his reign; (2) his exploration of the western or Arabian coast of the Red Sea, by means of a naval expedition under Satyrus; and (3) his dispatch of an ambassador named Dionysius to India, on a mission to the native princes.

On the trade of Alexandria see the treatise of DE SCHMIDT, *Opuscula quibus res antiquæ precipue Ægyptiacæ explanantur.* Carolsruh., 1765; 8vo.

11. The material prosperity of Egypt which these measures insured was naturally accompanied by a flourishing condition of the revenue. Philadelphus is said to have derived from Egypt alone, without counting the tribute in grain, an annual income of 14,800 talents (more than three and a half millions sterling), or as much as Darius Hystaspis obtained from the whole of his vast empire. The revenue was raised chiefly from customs, but was supplemented from other sources. The remoter provinces, Palestine, Phœnicia, Cyprus, etc., seem to have paid a tribute; but of the mode of its assessment we know nothing.

Revenue.

12. The military force which Philadelphus maintained is

said to have amounted to 200,000 foot and 40,000 horse, besides elephants and war-chariots. He had also a fleet of 1500 vessels, many of which were of extraordinary size. The number of rowers required to man these vessels must have exceeded, rather than fallen short of, 600,000 men.

Land and sea forces.

13. The fame of Philadelphus depends, however, far less upon his military exploits, or his talents for organization and administration, than upon his efforts in the cause of learning. In this respect, if in no other, he surpassed his father, and deserves to be regarded as the special cause of the literary glories of his country. The library which the first Ptolemy had founded was by the second so largely increased that he has often been regarded as its author. The minor library of the Serapeium was entirely of his collection. Learned men were invited to his court from every quarter; and literary works of the highest value were undertaken at his desire or under his patronage. Among these the most important were the translation of the Hebrew Scriptures into the Greek language (which was commenced in his reign and continued under several of his successors), and the "History of Egypt," derived from the native records, which was composed in Greek during his reign by the Egyptian priest Manetho. Philadelphus also patronized painting and sculpture, and adorned his capital with architectural works of great magnificence.

Patronage of learning.

Among the galaxy of literary and scientific names which adorned the court of Philadelphus the most remarkable are the poets THEOCRITUS and CALLIMACHUS, ZENODOTUS the grammarian, EUCLID, the philosophers HEGESIAS and THEODORUS, and the astronomers TIMOCHARIS, ARISTARCHUS of Samos, and ARATUS. Of these, first Zenodotus, and then Callimachus held the office of Librarian.

On the subject of the Alexandrian Library, or Libraries, the student may consult with advantage

BECK, *Specimen historiæ bibliothecarum Alexandrinarum.* Lipsiæ, 1810; 4to.

DEDEL, G., *Historia critica bibliothecæ Alexandrinæ.* Lugd. Bat. 1823; 4to.

RITSCHEL, *Die Alexandrinischen Bibliotheken unter der ersten Ptolemäern.* Breslau, 1838; 8vo.

14. In his personal character, Philadelphus presents an unfavorable contrast to his father. Immediately upon at-

Character of Philadelphus. His death.

taining the throne he banished Demetrius Phalereus, for the sole offense that he had advised Ptolemy Lagi against altering the succession. Shortly afterwards he put to death two of his brothers. He divorced his first wife Arsinoë, the daughter of Lysimachus, and banished her to Coptos in Upper Egypt, in order that he might contract an incestuous marriage with his full sister, Arsinoë, who had been already married to his half-brother Ceraunus. To this princess, who bore him no children, he continued tenderly attached, taking in reference to her the epithet "Philadelphus," and honoring her by giving her name to several of the cities which he built, and erecting to her memory a magnificent monument at Alexandria, which was known as the Arsinoëum. Nor did he long survive her decease. He died in B.C. 247, of disease, at Alexandria, having lived sixty-two years, and reigned thirty-eight, or thirty-six from the death of his father.

The gold coins of Philadelphus and his wife Arsinoë are numerous, and exceedingly beautiful.

Reign of Ptolemy III. (Euergetes), B.C. 247-222. His wars and conquests.

15. Ptolemy III., surnamed Euergetes ("the Benefactor"), the eldest son of Philadelphus by his first wife, succeeded him. This prince was the most enterprising of all the Lagid monarchs; and under him Egypt, which had hitherto maintained a defensive attitude, became an aggressive power, and accomplished important conquests. The greater part of these were, it is true, retained for only a few years; but others were more permanent, and became real additions to the empire. The empire obtained now its greatest extension, comprising, besides Egypt and Nubia, the Cyrenaïca, which was recovered by the marriage of Berenicé, daughter and heiress of Magas, to Euergetes; parts of Ethiopia, especially the tract about Adulé; a portion of the opposite or western coast of Arabia; Palestine, Phœnicia, and Cœlé-Syria; Cyprus, Cilicia, Pamphylia, Lycia, Caria, and Ionia; the Cyclades; and a portion of Thrace, including the city of Lysimacheia in the Chersonese.

WARS OF EUERGETES. (*a*) *With Syria.* First War. The wrongs of his sister, Berenicé, who was first divorced by Antiochus, and then murdered by Laodicé, with the consent of Seleucus Callinicus (see p. 252), provoked Euergetes to invade Syria, B.C. 245. Having taken Antioch, he crossed the Euphrates and reduced Mesopotamia, Babylonia, Susiana, Media, and Persia. The Eastern provinces to the borders of Bactria submitted to him. At the same time, his fleet ravaged the coasts of Asia Minor and Thrace, reducing all the maritime tracts to subjection. Recalled to Egypt by a threatening of troubles, about B.C. 243, he rapidly lost his Eastern conquests, which were recovered by Seleucus; but those in Asia Minor and in Europe, which depended on his command of the sea, continued subject to him. The first war was terminated, B.C. 241, by a truce for ten years, after it had raged for four years over almost the whole of Western Asia.—Second War. A quarrel having broken out between Seleucus and his brother, Antiochus Hierax, Euergetes sided with the latter. After numerous alternations, success rested with Seleucus; and Antiochus fled to Egypt, where Ptolemy kept him a prisoner. At the same time he made peace with Seleucus, B.C. 229. (*b*) *War with Macedonia.* Euergetes followed his father's policy in this quarter, supporting Aratus and the Achæan league until they came to terms with Antigonus, and then supporting Cleomenes of Sparta against the confederates. In the course of the struggle, his admirals engaged the fleet of Antigonus off Andros, and completely defeated it. (*c*) *War with Ethiopia.* Towards the close of his reign, Euergetes turned his arms against his southern neighbors, and made himself master of the coast about Adulé, where he set up his famous inscription. (See p. 261.)

16. Friendly relations had been established with Rome by Ptolemy Philadelphus, as early as B.C. 273. Euergetes continued this policy, but declined the assistance which the great republic was anxious to lend him in his Syrian wars. It would seem that the ambitious projects of Rome and her aspirations after universal dominion were already, at the least, suspected.

Relations with Rome.

17. Like his father and grandfather, Euergetes was a patron of art and letters. He added largely to the great library at Alexandria, collecting the best manuscripts from all quarters, sometimes by very questionable means. The poet, Apollonius Rhodius, the geographer and chronologist, Eratosthenes, and the grammarian, Aristophanes of Byzantium, adorned his court. Alexandria does not seem to have owed to him many of her buildings; but he gratified his Egyptian subjects by important architectural works, as well as by the restoration of various images of their gods, which he had recovered in his Eastern expedition.

Patronage of learning.

Large additions were made by Euergetes to the great temple at Thebes. He also erected an entirely new one at Esné; and dedicated one to Osiris at Canôpus in the name of himself and his wife, Berenicé.

18. After a reign of twenty-five years, during which he had enjoyed almost uninterrupted success, and had raised

Death of Ptolemy Euergetes.

Egypt to perhaps the highest pitch of prosperity that she ever attained, Euergetes died, according to the best authority, by a natural death; though there were not wanting persons to ascribe his decease to the machinations of his son. He left behind him three children —Ptolemy, who succeeded him, Magas, and Arsinoë, who became the wife of her elder brother.

Termination of the brilliant period of Lagid history.

19. The glorious period of the Macedo-Egyptian history terminates with Euergetes. Three kings of remarkable talent, and of moderately good moral character, had held the throne for a little more than a century (101 years), and had rendered Egypt the most flourishing of the kingdoms which had arisen out of the disruption of Alexander's empire. They were followed by a succession of wicked and incapable monarchs, among whom it is difficult to find one who has any claim to our respect or esteem. Historians reckon nine Ptolemies after Euergetes. Except Philometor, who was mild and humane, Lathyrus, who was amiable but weak, and Ptolemy XII. (sometimes called Dionysus), who was merely young and incompetent, they were all, almost equally, detestable.

Reign of Ptolemy IV. (Philopator), B.C. 222-205.

20. Ptolemy IV., who assumed the title of Philopator to disarm the suspicions which ascribed to him the death of his father, was the eldest son of Euergetes, and ascended the throne B.C. 222. His first acts, after seating himself upon the throne, were the murder of his mother, Berenicé, who had wished her younger son to obtain the succession; of his brother, Magas; and of his father's brother, Lysimachus. He followed up these outrages by quarrelling with the Spartan refugee Cleomenes, and driving him into a revolt, which cost him and his family their lives. He then contracted an incestuous marriage with his sister, Arsinoë, and abandoning the direction of affairs to his minister, Sosibius, the adviser of these measures, gave himself up to a life of intemperance and profligacy. Agathoclea, a professional singer, and her brother, Agathocles, the children of a famous courtesan, became his favorites, and ruled the court, while Sosibius managed the kingdom. To gratify these minions of his pleasures, Philopator, about B.C. 208, put to death his wife, Arsinoë, after she had borne him an heir to the empire.

His weakness and debauchery.

21. The weakness of Philopator, and the mismanagement of the State by Sosibius, who was at once incapable and wicked, laid the empire open to attack; and it was not long before the young king of Syria, Antiochus III., took advantage of the condition of affairs to advance his own pretensions to the possession of the long-disputed tract between Syria Proper and Egypt. It might have been expected that, under the circumstances, he would have been successful. But the Egyptian forces, relaxed though their discipline had been by Sosibius, were still superior to the Syrians; and the battle of Raphia (B.C. 217) was a repetition of the lessons taught at Pelusium and Gaza. The invader was once more defeated upon the borders, and by the peace which followed, the losses of the two preceding years were, with one exception, recovered.

War of Philopator with Antiochus the Great.

DETAILS OF THE WAR. Antiochus commenced, B.C. 219, by besieging Seleuceia, the port of Antioch, which had remained in the hands of the Egyptians since the great invasion of Euergetes. Being joined by Theodotus, the Egyptian governor of Cœlé-Syria, he invaded that country, took Tyre and Ptolemaïs (Acre), and advanced to the frontiers of Egypt. The next year, B.C. 218, an Egyptian army under Nicolaüs was sent to oppose him; but this force was completely defeated near Porphyreon. In the third year of the war, B.C. 217, Philopator marched out from Alexandria in person, with 70,000 foot, 5000 horse, and 73 elephants. Antiochus advanced to give him battle, and the two armies met at Raphia, on the eastern edge of the desert. After a vain attempt on the part of Theodotus to assassinate Philopator in his camp, an engagement took place, and Antiochus was completely defeated. He then made peace, relinquishing all his conquests but Seleuceia.

22. The Syrian war was only just brought to a close when disaffection showed itself among Philopator's Egyptian subjects. The causes of their discontent are obscure; and we are without any details as to the course of the struggle. But there is evidence that it lasted through a considerable number of years, and was only brought to a close after much effusion of blood on both sides.

Revolt of the native Egyptians.

23. Notwithstanding his inhumanity and addiction to the worst forms of vice, Philopator so far observed the traditions of his house as to continue their patronage of letters. He lived on familiar terms with the men of learning who frequented his court, and espe-

Philopator's patronage of literature.

cially distinguished with his favor the grammarian Aristarchus. To show his admiration for Homer, he dedicated a temple to him. He further even engaged, himself, in literary pursuits, composing tragedies and poems of various kinds.

24. Worn out prematurely by his excesses, Philopator died at about the age of forty, after he had held the throne for seventeen years. He left behind him one only child, a son, named Ptolemy, the issue of his marriage with Arsinoë. This child, who at the time of his father's death was no more than five years old, was immediately acknowledged as king. He reigned from B.C. 205 to 181, and is distinguished in history by the surname of Epiphanes. The affairs of Egypt during his minority were, at first, administered by the infamous Agathocles, who, however, soon fell a victim to the popular fury, together with his sister, his mother, and his whole family. The honest but incompetent Tlepolemus succeeded as regent; but in the critical circumstances wherein Egypt was now placed by the league of Antiochus with Philip of Macedon (see Book IV., § 13), it was felt that incompetency would be fatal; and the important step was taken of calling in the assistance of the Romans, who sent M. Lepidus, B.C. 201, to undertake the management of affairs. Lepidus saved Egypt from conquest; but was unable, or unwilling, to obtain for her the restoration of the territory whereof the two spoilers had deprived her by their combined attack. Antiochus succeeded in first deferring and then evading the restoration of his share of the spoil, while Philip did not even make a pretense of giving back a single foot of territory. Thus Egypt lost in this reign the whole of her foreign possessions except Cyprus and the Cyrenaïca—losses which were never recovered.

His death. Reign of Ptolemy V. (Epiphanes), B.C. 205–181. Regency of Agathocles—of Tlepolemus.

Regency of Lepidus.

For the details of the war between Epiphanes and his assailants, see Book IV., Per. III., Part I., § 13, and Per. III., Part III., § 25.

25. Lepidus, on quitting Egypt, B.C. 199, handed over the administration to Aristomenes, the Acarnanian, a man of vigor and probity, who restored the finances, and put fresh life into the administration. But the external were followed by internal troubles. A revolt of the Egyptians, and a conspiracy on the part of the general, Scopas, showed the danger of a long minority, and induced

Regency of Aristomenes.

the new regent to curtail his own term of office. At the age of fourteen, Epiphanes was declared of full age, and assumed the reins of government, B.C. 196.

To this occasion belongs the famous "Rosetta stone," which contains a decree of the priests at the time of the coronation of Epiphanes, establishing the manner in which he was to be worshipped thenceforth in all the temples. Incidentally, there is an enumeration of all the benefits supposed to have been conferred by the monarch during his minority, which throws some light on the internal administration of Egypt, and also on the events of the earlier portion of Epiphanes's reign.

26. But little is known of Epiphanes from the time of his assuming the government. His marriage with Cleopatra, the daughter of Antiochus the Great, which had been arranged in B.C. 199 as a portion of the terms of peace, was not celebrated till B.C. 193, when he had attained the age of seventeen. Shortly after this the monarch appears to have quarrelled with his minister and late guardian, Aristomenes, whom he barbarously removed by poison. A certain Polycrates then became his chief adviser, and assisted him to quell a second very serious revolt on the part of the native Egyptians. Towards the close of his reign he formed designs for the recovery of Cœlé-Syria and Palestine, which he proposed to wrest from Seleucus, who had succeeded his father, Antiochus. But before he could carry his designs into effect, he was murdered by his officers, whom he had alarmed by an unguarded expression, B.C. 181.

Actual reign of Epiphanes, B.C. 196–181.

27. By his marriage with Cleopatra, Epiphanes had become the father of three children, two sons, both of whom received the name of Ptolemy, and a daughter, called after her mother. The eldest of these children, who took the surname of Philometor, succeeded him,* and reigned as Ptolemy VI. His age at his accession was only seven, and during his early years he remained under the regency of his mother, whose administration was vigorous and successful. At her death, in B.C. 173, the young prince fell under far inferior guardianship—that of Eulæus the eunuch and Lenæus, ministers at once

Reign of Ptolemy VI. (Philometor), B.C. 181–146.

* Lepsius interposes at this point a Ptolemy Eupator, whom he calls Ptolemy VI. His relationship to the kings who precede and follow him is not apparent.

corrupt and incapable. These weak men, mistaking audacity for vigor, rashly claimed from Antiochus Epiphanes the surrender of Cœlé-Syria and Palestine, the nominal dowry of the late queen-mother, and, when their demand was contemptuously rejected, flew to arms. Their invasion of Syria quickly brought upon them the vengeance of Antiochus, who defeated their forces at Pelusium, B.C. 170, and would certainly have conquered all Egypt, had it not been for the interposition of the Romans, who made him retire, and even deprived him of all his conquests.

His Syrian War.

DETAILS OF THE WAR WITH ANTIOCHUS. After his victory at Pelusium, Antiochus advanced to Memphis, and having obtained possession of the young king's person, endeavored to use him as his tool for effecting the entire reduction of the country. But the Alexandrians set up Philometor's brother, Ptolemy Physcon, as king, and successfully defended their city, till Antiochus raised the siege. Threatened by the Romans, he evacuated Egypt, except Pelusium, leaving Philometor as king at Memphis. But Philometor now refused to be a tool any more. Having come to terms with Physcon, B.C. 169, agreeing to reign jointly with him, and having married his sister, Cleopatra, he re-entered Alexandria and prepared for war. Antiochus, upon this, invaded Egypt a second time, while he also dispatched an expedition against Cyprus, B.C. 168, and was completely successful in both places. Cyprus was conquered, and Alexandria would undoubtedly have fallen, had not the Romans interposed. Popillius ordered the conqueror to retire from Egypt, and to restore Cyprus to the Egyptians; and Antiochus, though with extreme reluctance, obeyed both commands, B.C. 168.

28. By the timely aid thus given, Rome was brought into a new position with respect to Egypt. Hitherto she had merely been a friendly ally, receiving more favors than she conferred. Henceforth she was viewed as exercising a sort of protectorate; and her right was recognized to interfere in the internal troubles of the kingdom, and to act as arbiter between rival princes. The claims of such persons were discussed before the Roman Senate, and the princes themselves went to Rome in person to plead their cause. The decision of the Senate was not, indeed, always implicitly obeyed; but still Rome exercised a most important influence from this time, not only over the external policy but over the dynastic squabbles of the Egyptians.

New relations between Rome and Egypt.

29. The joint reign of the two kings, Philometor and Physcon, which commenced in B.C. 169, continued till B.C. 165, when the brothers quarrelled and Philometor was driven

War of Philometor with his brother, Physcon, B.C. 164-154.

into exile. Having gone to Rome and implored assistance from the Senate, he was re-instated in his kingdom by Roman deputies, who arranged a partition of the territory between the brothers, which might have closed the dispute, could Physcon have remained contented with his allotted portion. But his ambition and intrigues caused fresh troubles, which were, however, quelled after a time by the final establishment of Physcon as king of Cyrênê only.

At the division of territory made in B.C. 164, Physcon received Cyrênê and Libya. Discontented with this allotment, he went to Rome in the next year, and obtained the further grant of Cyprus, which Philometor was expected to give up. He, however, refused; and Physcon was preparing to go to war when Cyrênê revolted and engaged his attention for some considerable time. In B.C. 154 he went for the second time to Rome, and received a squadron of five ships, to help him to obtain Cyprus. With these he proceeded to the island and endeavored to conquer it, but was defeated and made prisoner by his brother, who, however, not only spared his life, but re-established him as king of Cyrênê.

30. During the continuance of the war between the two brothers, Demetrius I., who had become king of Syria, B.C.

Wars of Philometor with Demetrius I. and Alexander Balas, B.C. 151-146.

162, had made an attempt to obtain possession of Cyprus by bribing the governor, and had thereby provoked the hostility of Philometor. No sooner, therefore, was Philometor free from domestic troubles than, resolving to revenge himself, he induced Alexander Balas to come forward as a pretender to the Syrian crown, and lent him the full weight of his support, even giving him his daughter, Cleopatra, in marriage, B.C. 150. But the ingratitude of Balas, after he had obtained the throne by Ptolemy's aid, alienated his patron. The Egyptian king, having with some difficulty escaped a treacherous attempt upon his life, passed over to the side of the younger Demetrius, gave Cleopatra in marriage to him, and succeeded in seating him upon the throne. In the last battle, however, which was fought near Antioch, he was thrown from his horse, and lost his life, B.C. 146.

31. Ptolemy Philometor left behind him three children, the issue of his marriage with his full sister, Cleopatra, viz., a son,

Brief reign of Ptolemy VII. (Eupator).

Ptolemy, who was proclaimed king, under the name of Eupator (or Philopator, according to Lepsius), and two daughters, both called Cleopatra, the elder married first to Alexander Balas and then to Demetrius II., the younger still a virgin. Eupator, after reigning a few days, was deposed and then murdered by his uncle, Physcon, the king of Cyrênê, who claimed and obtained the throne.

Reign of Ptolemy VIII. (Physcon), B.C. 146–117. His cruelties.

32. Ptolemy Physcon, called also Euergetes II., acquired the throne in consequence of an arrangement mediated by the Romans, who stipulated that he should marry his sister Cleopatra, the widow of his brother, Philometor. Having become king in this way, his first act was the murder of his nephew. (See the last section.) He then proceeded to treat with the utmost severity all those who had taken part against him in the recent contest, killing some and banishing others. By these measures he created such alarm, that Alexandria became half emptied of its inhabitants, and he was forced to invite new colonists to repeople it. Meanwhile he gave himself up to gluttony and other vices, and became bloated to an extraordinary degree, and so corpulent that he could scarcely walk. He further repudiated Cleopatra, his sister, though she had borne him a son, Memphitis, and took to wife her daughter, called also Cleopatra, the child of his brother, Philometor. After a while his cruelties and excesses disgusted the Alexandrians, who broke out into frequent revolts. Several of these were put down; but at last Physcon was compelled to fly to Cyprus, and his sister Cleopatra was made queen, B.C. 130.

His flight to Cyprus.

War followed for three years between the brother and sister. The murder of Memphitis, his own son, in order to grieve the mother, and the barbarous act of sending her the head and hands of his victim, so exasperated the Alexandrians that at first they supported the cause of Cleopatra with spirit. But her imprudent application for aid to Demetrius II. alarmed their patriotism, and induced them to recall Physcon, B.C. 127. Cleopatra took refuge in Syria.

Re-establishment of Physcon in his kingdom.

33. On the re-establishment of Physcon in his kingdom, he resolved to revenge himself on Demetrius for the support which he had given to Cleopatra. He therefore brought forward the pretender Alexander Zabinas, and lent him such support that he shortly became king of Syria, B.C. 126. But Zabinas, like his reputed father, Balas, proved ungrateful; and the offended Physcon

proceeded to pull down the throne which he had erected, joining Antiochus Grypus against Zabinas, and giving him his daughter, Tryphæna, in marriage. The result was the ruin of Zabinas, and the peaceful establishment of Grypus, with whom Physcon lived on friendly terms during the remainder of his life.

The expulsion of Physcon from his kingdom seems to have taught him a lesson. No cruelties are recorded of him in the later portion of his reign. It was probably at this time that he showed himself a patron of letters, and composed the works which gave him some repute as an author.

34. Physcon died in B.C. 117, and was succeeded by his eldest son, Ptolemy IX., commonly distinguished by the epithet of Lathyrus. Egypt now lost the Cyrenaïca, which was bequeathed by Physcon to his natural son, Apion, who at his death made it over to the Romans. The ties which bound Cyprus to Egypt also became relaxed, for Lathyrus, and his brother, Alexander, alternately held it, almost as a separate kingdom. The reign of Lathyrus, which commenced B.C. 117, did not terminate till B.C. 81, thus covering a space of thirty-six years; but during one-half of this time he was a fugitive from Egypt, ruling only over Cyprus, while his brother took his place at Alexandria. We must divide his reign into three periods—the first lasting from B.C. 117 to 107, a space of ten years, during which he was nominal king of Egypt under the tutelage of his mother; the second, from B.C. 107 to 89, eighteen years, which he spent in Cyprus; and the third, from B.C. 89 to 81, eight years, during which he ruled Egypt as actual and sole monarch.

Reign of Ptolemy IX. (Lathyrus), B.C. 117–81.

Three periods.

DETAILS OF THIS REIGN.—FIRST PERIOD. Lathyrus, recalled from Cyprus, is forced to divorce his sister, Cleopatra, and to marry his other sister, Selênê, who is more devoted to the interests of the queen-mother. He rules quietly, his mother having the real power, and his brother Alexander reigning in Cyprus, till B.C. 107, when, having offended his mother by pursuing a policy adverse to hers in Syria, he is driven out, and has to change places with Alexander.—SECOND PERIOD. Lathyrus not only maintains himself as king of Cyprus against the attempts of his mother to dispossess him, but takes a part in the Syrian troubles, opposing the power of the Jews, and supporting Antiochus Cyzicenus and his son Demetrius. Meanwhile Cleopatra and Ptolemy Alexander rule Egypt conjointly, until at last they also quarrel; Alexander, fearing his mother's designs, puts her to death; and, the Alexandrians rising against him, he is expelled, and Lathyrus summoned from Cyprus to resume

Reign of Cleopatra and Ptolemy X. (Alexander I.).

the sovereignty.—THIRD PERIOD. Lathyrus defeats an attempt of Alexander to re-establish himself at Cyprus. Death of Alexander. Revolt and three years' siege of Thebes in Upper Egypt, terminates in its capture and ruin, B.C. 86. Lathyrus then reigns quietly till B.C. 81.

Reigns of Berenicé and Ptolemy XI. (Alexander II.), B.C. 80.

35. Lathyrus left behind him one legitimate child only, Berenicé, his daughter by Selêné, who succeeded him upon the throne, and remained for six months sole monarch. She was then married to her first cousin, Ptolemy Alexander II., the son of Ptolemy Alexander I., who claimed the crown of Egypt under the patronage of the great Sulla. It was agreed that they should reign conjointly; but within three weeks of his marriage, Alexander put his wife to death. This act so enraged the Alexandrians that they rose in revolt against the murderer and slew him in the public gymnasium, B.C. 80.

Time of confusion.

36. A time of trouble followed. The succession was disputed between two illegitimate sons of Lathyrus, two legitimate sons of Selêné, the sister of Lathyrus, by Antiochus Eusebes, king of Syria, her third husband, and probably other claimants. Roman influence was wanted to decide the contest, and Rome for some reason or other hung back. A further disintegration of the empire was the consequence. The younger of the two sons of Ptolemy Lathyrus seized Cyprus, and made it a separate kingdom. The elder seems to have possessed himself of a part of Egypt. Other parts of Egypt appear to have fallen into the power of a certain Alexander, called by some writers Ptolemy Alexander III., who was driven out after some years, and, flying to Tyre, died there and bequeathed Egypt to the Romans.

Reign of Ptolemy XII. (Auletes), B.C. 80–51.

37. Ultimately the whole of Egypt passed under the sway of the elder of the two illegitimate sons of Lathyrus, who took the titles of *Neos Dionysos* ("the New Bacchus"), Philopator, and Philadelphus, but was most commonly known as Auletes, the "Flute-player." The years of his reign were counted from B.C. 80, though he can scarcely have become king of all Egypt till fifteen years later, B.C. 65. It was his great object during the earlier portion of his reign to get himself acknowledged by the Romans; but this he was not able to effect till B.C.

59, the year of Cæsar's consulship, when his bribes were effectual. But his orgies and his "fluting" had by this time disgusted the Alexandrians; so that, when he increased the weight of taxation in order to replenish his treasury, exhausted by the vast sums he had spent in bribery, they rose against him, and, after a short struggle, drove him from his kingdom. Auletes fled to Rome; and the Alexandrians placed upon the throne his two daughters, Tryphæna and Berenicé, of whom the former lived only a year, while the latter retained the crown till the restoration of her father, B.C. 55. He returned under the protection of Pompey, who sent Gabinius at the head of a strong Roman force to reinstate him. The Alexandrians were compelled to submit; and Auletes immediately executed Berenicé, who had endeavored to retain the crown and had resisted his return in arms. Auletes then reigned about three years and a half in tolerable peace, under the protection of a Roman garrison. He died B.C. 51, having done as much as in him lay to degrade and ruin his country.

The chronological difficulties of the period between the deaths of Lathyrus and Auletes have been treated with great skill by CLINTON in his *Fasti Hellenici*, vol. iii., Appendix, chap. 5, § 8, 9. A somewhat different view is taken by BOECKH (*Corp. Ins. Græc.*, vol. iii. p. 288).

38. Ptolemy Auletes left behind him four children—Cleopatra, aged seventeen; a boy, Ptolemy, aged thirteen; another boy, called also Ptolemy; and a girl, called Arsinoë. The last two were of very tender age. He left the crown, under approval of the Romans, to Cleopatra and the elder Ptolemy, who were to rule conjointly, and to be married when Ptolemy was of full age. These directions were carried out; but the imperious spirit of Cleopatra ill brooked any control, and it was not long ere she quarrelled with her boy-husband, and endeavored to deprive him of the kingdom. War followed; and Cleopatra, driven to take refuge in Syria, was fortunate enough to secure the protection of Julius Cæsar, whom she fascinated by her charms, B.C. 48. With his aid she obtained the victory over her brother, who perished in the struggle. Cleopatra was now established sole queen, B.C. 47, but on condition that she married in due time her other brother, the younger son of Auletes. Observing the letter of this agreement, Cleopa-

Reign of Cleopatra, B.C. 51-30.

tra violated its spirit by having her second husband, shortly after the wedding, removed by poison, B.C. 44. The remainder of Cleopatra's reign was, almost to its close, prosperous. Protected by Julius Cæsar during his lifetime, she succeeded soon after his decease in fascinating Antony, B.C. 41, and making him her slave for the rest of his lifetime. The details of this period belong to Roman rather than to Egyptian history; and will be treated in the last book of this Manual. It will be sufficient to note here that the latest descendant of the Ptolemies retained the royal title to the end, and showed something of the spirit of a queen in preferring death to captivity, and perishing upon the capture of her capital, B.C. 30.

PART III.

History of Macedonia, and of Greece, from the Death of Alexander to the Roman Conquest, B.C. 323 *to* 146.

SOURCES. The sources for this history are nearly the same as those which have been cited for the contemporary history of Syria and Egypt. (See pp. 247, 261.) The chief ancient authorities are DIODORUS SICULUS (books xix.–xxxii., the first two of which only are complete), POLYBIUS, JUSTIN, PLUTARCH (*Vitæ Demetrii, Pyrrhi, Æmilii Paulli, Agidis, Cleomenis, Arati, Philopœmonis et Flaminini*), and LIVY (books xxvi.–xlv., and Epitomes of books xlvi.–lii.). To these may be added, for the Macedonian chronology, EUSEBIUS (*Chronicorum Canonum liber prior*, c. xxxviii.), and for occasional facts in the history, PAUSANIAS.

Of modern works treating of, or touching, the period, the most important are DROYSEN, *Nachfolger*, etc. (supra, p. 247), FLATHE, *Geschichte Makedoniens* (supra, p. 233), and FREEMAN, *History of Federal Governments* (supra, p. 145, chaps. v.–ix.). The third volume of NIEBUHR'S *Lectures*, and the last volume of Bp. THIRLWALL'S *History of Greece*, are also very worthy of the student's attention. SCHORN'S *Geschichte Griechenlands* (see p. 298), indicates also a careful study of the period.

State of Greece during Alexander's conquests.

1. Grecian history had been suspended during the time of Alexander's career of conquest. A slight disturbance of the general tranquillity had indeed occurred, when Alexander plunged into the unknown countries beyond the Zagros range, by the movement against Antipater, which the Spartan king, Agis, originated in B.C. 330. But the disturbance was soon quelled. Agis was defeated and slain; and from this time the whole of Greece remained perfectly tranquil until the news came of Alexander's premature demise during the summer of B.C.

323. Then, indeed, hope rose high; and a great effort was made to burst the chains which bound Greece to the footstool of the Macedonian kings, Athens, under Demosthenes and Hyperides, taking, as was natural, the lead in the struggle for freedom. A large confederacy was formed; and the Lamian War was entered upon in the confident expectation that the effect would be the liberation of Greece from the yoke of her oppressor. But the result disappointed these hopes. After a bright gleam of success, the confederate Greeks were completely defeated at Crannon, B.C. 322, and the yoke of Macedonia was riveted upon them more firmly than ever.

Great revolt. Lamian War. B.C. 323–321.

DETAILS OF THE LAMIAN WAR. The league included Athens, Argos, Epidaurus, Trœzen, Elis, Messenia, Sicyon, Carystus in Eubœa, Phocis, Locris, Doris, Dolopia, Ænianía, the Ætolians, the Acarnanians, Leucas, part of Epirus, most of Thessaly, and the greater number of the Malians, Ætæans, and Achæans of Phthiôtis. Athens furnished a worthy leader in Leosthenes, who defeated Antipater near Thermopylæ, and forced him to seek a refuge within the walls of Lamia. Antipater sent urgent entreaties for aid to the Macedonian leaders in Asia, while Leosthenes pressed the siege, but without result, receiving in the course of it, unfortunately for the Greek cause, a wound, from the effects of which he died, B.C. 323. The command fell to Antiphilus, who, early in B.C. 322, met and defeated the Macedonian general, Leonnatus, in Thessaly, as he was bringing succor to Antipater, but was in his turn beaten by the combined forces of Craterus and Antipater at Crannon in Thessaly; after which the league fell to pieces, and the several states concluded separate treaties of peace with the conqueror, who granted favorable terms to all excepting Athens and Ætolia. Towards Athens extreme severity was shown. Twelve thousand out of the 21,000 citizens were actually deported from the city and removed to Thrace, Illyria, Italy, or the Cyrenaïca. The 9000 richest citizens—the "party of order" headed by Phocion—were left in exclusive possession of the state. A Macedonian garrison was at the same time placed in Munychia; and the leaders of the anti-Macedonian party, Demosthenes, Hyperides, and others, were proscribed. Their deaths soon followed; and marked the complete extinction of Athenian autonomy. Ætolia was then threatened with a fate even worse than that which had befallen Athens. But the Ætolians resisted; their country was a difficult one; and, the ambition of Perdiccas having about this time alarmed Antipater for his own safety, the Macedonian forces were withdrawn from Ætolia, and peace concluded, B.C. 321.

2. The position of Antipater, as supreme ruler of Macedonia, was far from being safe and assured. The female members of the Macedonian royal family—Olympias, the widow of Philip; Cleopatra, her daughter; Cynané, daughter of Philip by an Illyrian moth-

Difficult position of Antipater in Macedonia.

er; and Eurydicé, daughter of Cynané by her husband Amyntas (himself a first cousin of Alexander)—were, one and all, persons of ability and ambition, who saw with extreme dissatisfaction the aggrandizement of the generals of Alexander and the low condition into which the royal power had fallen, shared between an infant and an imbecile. Dissatisfied, moreover, with their own positions and prospects, they commenced intrigues for the purpose of improving them. Olympias first offered the hand of Cleopatra to Leonnatus, who was to have turned against Antipater, if he had been successful in his Grecian expedition. When the death of Leonnatus frustrated this scheme, Olympias cast her eyes farther abroad, and fixed on Perdiccas as the chief to whom she would betroth her daughter. Meanwhile, Cynané boldly crossed over to Asia with Eurydicé, and offered her in marriage to Philip Arrhidæus, the nominal king. To gratify Olympias, who hated these members of the royal house, Perdiccas put Cynané to death; and he would probably have likewise removed Eurydicé, had not the soldiers, exasperated at the mother's murder, compelled him to allow the marriage of the daughter with Philip. Meanwhile, he consented to Olympias's schemes, prepared to repudiate his wife, Nicæa, the daughter of Antipater, and hoped, with the aid of his friend, Eumenes, to make himself master of the whole of Alexander's empire. (See Second Period, § 5.)

Intrigues of the Macedonian princesses.

3. The designs of Perdiccas, and his intrigues with Olympias, having been discovered by Antigonus, and the life of that chief being in danger from Perdiccas in consequence, he fled to Europe in the course of B.C. 322, and informed Antipater and Craterus of their peril. Fully appreciating the importance of the intelligence, those leaders at once concluded a league with Ptolemy, and in the spring of B.C. 321 invaded Asia for the purpose of attacking their rival. Here they found Eumenes prepared to resist them; and so great was the ability of that general, that, though Perdiccas had led the greater portion of his forces against Egypt, he maintained the war successfully, defeating and killing Craterus, and holding Antipater in check. But the murder of Perdiccas by his troops, and their fraternization with their opponents, changed the

Rupture between Antipater and Perdiccas. Antipater in Asia, B.C. 321.

whole face of affairs. Antipater found himself, without an effort, master of the situation. Proclaimed sole regent by the soldiers, he took the custody of the royal persons, re-distributed the satrapies (see Second Period, § 7), and, returning into Macedonia, held for about two years the first position in the empire. He was now, however, an old man, and his late campaigns had probably shaken him; at any rate, soon after his return to Europe, he died, B.C. 318, leaving the regency to his brother officer, the aged Polysperchon.

Death of Antipater.

Antipater's conduct in passing over his two sons, Cassander and Philip, is certainly remarkable. Did he think them incapable, or was he only anxious to spare them the risks of great political exaltation?

4. The disappointment of Cassander, the elder of the two surviving sons of Antipater, produced the second great war between the generals of Alexander. Cassander, having begun to intrigue against Polysperchon, was driven from Macedonia by the regent, and, flying to Antigonus, induced him to embrace his cause. The league followed between Antigonus, Ptolemy, and Cassander on the one hand, and Polysperchon and Eumenes on the other (see Second Period, § 9), Antigonus undertaking to contend with Eumenes in Asia, while Cassander afforded employment to Polysperchon in Europe.

Regency of Polysperchon.

Flight of Cassander.

5. In the war which ensued between Cassander and Polysperchon, the former proved eventually superior. Polysperchon had on his side the influence of Olympias, which was great; and his proclamation of freedom to the Greeks was a judicious step, from which he derived considerable advantage. But neither as a soldier nor as a statesman was he Cassander's equal. He lost Athens by an imprudent delay, and failed against Megalopolis through want of military ability. His policy in allowing Olympias to gratify her hatreds without let or hindrance was ruinous to his cause, by thoroughly alienating the Macedonians. Cassander's triumph in B.C. 316 reduced him to a secondary position, transferring the supreme authority in Macedonia to his rival.

War of Polysperchon with Cassander, B.C. 318-316.

DETAILS OF THE WAR. The rupture commenced with the seizure by Nicanor, one of Cassander's partisans, of the chief command at Munychia, B.C. 318. Polysperchon sent his son, Alexander, to negotiate with the Athenians, and, if possible, recover the fortress. At the same time, he published his edict, recalling the Greek exiles generally. The old citizens flocked back to Athens, and, espousing the cause of Polysperchon, endeavored to induce Nicanor to withdraw. He, however, so far from yielding to their request, by a sudden attack occupied Piræus, and cut off Athens from the sea. This was done with the connivance of Phocion, who leaned very decidedly towards Cassander. Presently, Polysperchon, finding that Alexander made no progress, advanced upon Athens in person; whereupon the Athenians took heart, rose up against Phocion and his friends, and, having condemned and executed them, re-established a democratic constitution. Polysperchon should now have marched straight into Attica; but, suffering minor matters to delay him, he allowed Cassander to sail in, occupy Piræus, and deprive him of the whole advantage of the revolution. After a vain attempt to reduce Piræus by siege, he left Athens to her fate, and invaded Peloponnese, where he was for the most part fairly successful, but failed completely against Megalopolis. Meanwhile Athens came to terms with Cassander, accepting his rule, and submitting to receive as governor his nominee, Demetrius Phalereus, B.C. 317. Polysperchon having withdrawn into Epirus, Cassander now entered the Peloponnese and won back most of the cities. Hereupon Polysperchon played his last stake. Joining his cause with that of Olympias, he invited her to accompany him into Macedonia, to the alarm and indignation of Philip Arrhidæus and his consort, who thereupon sought the aid of Cassander. But Olympias was too quick for this combination to take effect. Entering Macedonia in the autumn of B.C. 317, she encountered no opposition. Philip's soldiers passed over to her camp, and both he and his consort found themselves at her mercy. Olympias was not apt to spare. Philip Arrhidæus, his wife, Eurydicé, Nicanor, the brother of Cassander, and one hundred other leading Macedonians, were put to death. But the day of retribution was at hand. In the spring of B.C. 316, Cassander quitted Peloponnese, and entering Macedonia from Thessaly, besieged Olympias in Pydna. The attempts made by Polysperchon to relieve her failed; and after a few months she was forced to surrender herself, and to give over all Macedonia into Cassander's power. Soon after, Cassander, though he had promised to spare her life, caused her to be executed, after a pretended trial by a public assembly of the Macedonians.

Reign of Cassander, B.C. 316–296.

6. The reign of Cassander over Macedonia, which now commenced, lasted from B.C. 316 to 296, a period of twenty years. The talents of this prince are unquestionable, but his moral conduct fell below that of even the majority of his contemporaries, which was sufficiently reprehensible. His bad faith towards Olympias was followed, within a few years, by the murders of Roxana and the infant Alexander, by complicity in the murder of Hercules, the illegitimate son of Alexander the Great, and by treachery towards Polysperchon, who was first seduced into crime and then defrauded of his reward. Cas-

sander, however, was a clever statesman, a good general, and a brave soldier. His first step on obtaining possession of Macedonia was to marry Thessalonica, the sister of Alexander the Great, and thus to connect himself with the family of the conqueror. Next, fearing the ambition of Antigonus, who, after his victory over Eumenes, aspired to rule the whole empire (see Second Period, § 12), he entered into the league of the satraps against that powerful commander, and bore his part in the great war, which commencing B.C. 315, on the return of Antigonus from the East, terminated B.C. 301, at the battle of Ipsus. In this war Cassander, though he displayed unceasing activity, and much ability for intrigue, was on the whole unsuccessful; and he would probably have lost Greece and Macedonia to his powerful adversary, had not the advance of Seleucus from Babylon and the defeat of Antigonus at Ipsus saved him.

DETAILS OF THE WAR IN EUROPE. The war is divided into two portions by the peace of the year B.C. 311, which, practically, was a mere truce for a year.—FIRST PORTION, B.C. 315 to 312. Antigonus, having made alliance with Polysperchon and his son, Alexander, sends Aristodemus of Miletus to their assistance, B.C. 314. Cassander wins Alexander to his side, and, after his murder, is supported by his widow, Cratesipolis. He makes, however, no great impression on the Peloponnese, and in B.C. 313 turns his arms against the Ætolian confederacy, which now first appears as an important power, in league with Antigonus. Cassander, and his general, Philip, obtain successes in this quarter, whereupon Antigonus sends a second expedition into Greece (B.C. 312) under his nephew, Ptolemy, and deprives Cassander of all his gains, turning the scale decidedly in his own favor. The peace of B.C. 311 follows, after which the war is renewed.—SECOND PORTION, B.C. 310 to 301. Cassander having murdered the remaining legitimate monarch, Alexander, together with his mother, Roxana, gives an opportunity to Polysperchon to bring forward Hercules as rightful king of Macedonia, B.C. 310. The Macedonians inclining towards this young prince, Cassander finds himself in considerable peril; whereupon he negotiates with Polysperchon, and induces him to assassinate his *protégé*, by the promise of establishing him in the government of Peloponnesus, a promise never executed. Hercules having been removed, B.C. 309, Polysperchon marches southward, but has to fight his way, Southern Greece being greatly disorganized, and Cassander's influence over it but slight. This condition of affairs encourages Ptolemy Lagi, hitherto an ally of Cassander's, to make an expedition into these parts on his own account, and to occupy Corinth and Sicyon, B.C. 308. Cassander unwillingly acquiesces in this intrusion of a rival. The next year he suffers a more important loss. Antigonus sends his son Demetrius (Poliorcetes) into Greece, and orders him to proclaim the autonomy of the Greek cities, B.C. 307. Athens receives him with open arms. He captures Munychia and Megara, held by Macedonian garrisons, enters Athens in triumph, and formally proclaims it free. The exigencies of the general struggle summoning Demetrius to other scenes (Rhodes, Cyprus, etc.), no further progress is made till the year B.C. 302, when he returns to Athens and is once more enthusiastically received. All Southern Greece joins him, and in the spring of B.C. 301, he advances into Thessaly at the head of an army of 56,000 men, with which he threatens Cassander in Macedonia. But at this point Cassander is saved by the danger of Antigonus in Asia. Demetrius being recalled by his father, a peace is formally concluded, and Demetrius quitting Europe leaves Greece at the mercy of his antagonist.

7. Cassander did not live long to enjoy the tranquillity which the defeat and death of Antigonus at Ipsus brought him. He died B.C. 298, three years after Ipsus, leaving the crown to the eldest of his three sons by Thessalonicé, Philip. This prince was carried off by sickness before he had reigned a year; and the Macedonian dominions at his death fell to Thessalonicé, his mother, who made a division of them between her two surviving sons, Antipater and Alexander, assigning to the latter Western, and to the former Eastern Macedonia.

Death of Cassander. Reign of Philip, B.C. 298-297.

8. Antipater, who regarded himself as wronged in the partition, having wreaked his vengeance on his mother by causing her to be assassinated, applied for aid to his wife's father, Lysimachus; while Alexander, fearing his brother's designs, called in the help of Pyrrhus the Epirote and of Demetrius, B.C. 297. Demetrius, after the defeat of Ipsus, had still contrived to maintain the position of a sovereign. Rejected at first by Athens, he had besieged and taken that city, had recovered possession of Attica, the Megarid, and great portions of the Peloponnese, and had thus possessed himself of a considerable power. Appealed to by Alexander, he professed to embrace his cause; but ere long he took advantage of his position to murder the young prince, and possess himself of his kingdom. Antipater was about the same time put to death by Lysimachus, B.C. 294.

Reigns of Antipater II. and Alexander, B.C. 297-294.

9. The kingdom of Demetrius comprised, not only Macedonia, but Thessaly, Attica, Megaris, and the greater part of the Peloponnese. Had he been content with these territories, he might have remained quietly in the possession of them, for the families of Alexander the Great and of Antipater were extinct, and the

Reign of Demetrius Poliorcetes, B.C. 294-287.

connection of Demetrius with Seleucus, who had married his daughter (see Third Period, Part I., § 5), would have rendered his neighbors cautious of meddling with him. But the ambition of Demetrius was insatiate, and his self-confidence unbounded. After establishing his authority in Central Greece and twice taking Thebes, he made an unprovoked attack upon Pyrrhus, B.C. 290, from whom he desired to wrest some provinces ceded to him by the late king, Alexander. In this attempt he completely failed, whereupon he formed a new project. Collecting a vast army, he let it be understood that he claimed the entire dominion of his father, Antigonus, and was about to proceed to its recovery, B.C. 288. Seleucus and Lysimachus, whom this project threatened, were induced, in consequence, to encourage Pyrrhus to carry his arms into Macedonia on the one side, while Lysimachus himself invaded it on the other. Placed thus between two fires, and finding at the same time that his soldiers were not to be depended upon, Demetrius, in B.C. 287, relinquished the Macedonian throne, and escaped secretly to Demetrias, the city which he had built on the Pagasean Gulf and had made a sort of capital. From hence he proceeded on the expedition, which cost him his liberty, against Asia. (See Third Period, Part I., § 7.)

First reign of Pyrrhus, B.C. 287–286.

10. On the flight of Demetrius, Pyrrhus of Epirus became king of the greater part of Macedonia; but a share of the spoil was at once claimed by Lysimachus, who received the tract adjoining his own territories. A mere share, however, did not long satisfy the Macedonian chieftain. Finding that the rule of an Epirotic prince was distasteful to the Macedonians, he contrived after a little while to pick a quarrel with his recent ally, and having invaded his Macedonian territories, forced him to relinquish them and retire to his own country, after a reign which lasted less than a year.

Reign of Lysimachus, B.C. 286–281.

11. By the success of Lysimachus, Macedonia became a mere appendage to a large kingdom, which reached from the Halys to the Pindus range, its centre being Thrace, and its capital Lysimacheia in the Chersonese. These circumstances might not by themselves have alienated the Macedonians, though they could scarcely have failed after a time to arouse discontent; but

when Lysimachus, after suffering jealousy and dissension to carry ruin into his own family, proceeded to acts of tyranny and violence towards his nobles and other subjects, these last called on Seleucus Nicator to interfere for their preservation; and that monarch, having invaded the territories of his neighbor, defeated him in the battle of Corupedion, where Lysimachus, fighting with his usual gallantry, was not only beaten but slain.

Battle of Corupedion.

The domestic relations of Lysimachus, which led to this unhappy result, were somewhat complicated. He was married to Arsinoë, a daughter of Ptolemy Lagi by his second wife, Berenicé, while his eldest son, Agathocles, the issue of an earlier marriage, was married to Lysandra, a daughter of Ptolemy by his first wife, Eurydicé. Arsinoë, hating her half-sister, persuaded her husband that Agathocles was plotting against him, whereupon Lysimachus put him to death. The widowed Lysandra fled to Seleucus, accompanied by Ptolemy Ceraunus, her brother, who had quitted Egypt through fear of Berenicé.

12. By the victory of Corupedion, Seleucus Nicator became master of the entire kingdom of Lysimachus, and, with the exception of Egypt, appeared to have reunited almost the whole of the dominions of Alexander. But this union was short-lived. Within a few weeks of his victory, Seleucus was murdered by Ptolemy Ceraunus, the Egyptian refugee whom he had protected; and the Macedonians, indifferent by whom they were ruled, accepted the Egyptian prince without a murmur.

Brief reign of Seleucus Nicator, B.C. 281.

13. The short reign of Ptolemy Ceraunus (B.C. 281 to 279) was stained by crimes and marked by many imprudences. Regarding the two sons of Lysimachus by Arsinoë, his half-sister, as possible rivals, he persuaded her into a marriage, in order to get her children into his power; and, having prevailed with the credulous princess, first murdered her sons before her eyes, and then banished her to Samothrace. Escaping to Egypt, she became the wife of her brother, Philadelphus, and would probably have induced him to avenge her wrongs, had not the crime of Ceraunus received its just punishment in another way. A great invasion of the Gauls—one of those vast waves of migration which from time to time sweep over the world—occurring just as Ceraunus felt himself in secure possession of his kingdom,

Reign of Ptolemy Ceraunus, B.C. 281–279.

Great irruption of the Gauls into Greece.

disturbed his ease, and called for wise and vigorous measures of resistance. Ceraunus met the crisis with sufficient courage, but with a complete absence of prudent counsel. Instead of organizing a united resistance to a common enemy, or conciliating a foe whom he was too weak to oppose singly, he both exasperated the Gauls by a contemptuous message, and refused the proffers of assistance which he received from his neighbors. Opposing the unaided force of Macedon to their furious onset, he was completely defeated in a great battle, B.C. 279, and, falling into the hands of his enemies, was barbarously put to death. The Gauls then ravaged Macedonia far and wide; nor was it till B.C. 277 that Macedonia once more obtained a settled government.

The INVASION OF THE GAULS is one of the most interesting events of the post-Alexandrine history. It had permanent effects on Eastern Europe and Western Asia, producing among other results the new country of Galatia. We may connect the migration to a certain extent with the great movement of about a century earlier, which destroyed the Etruscan power in the plain of the Po, created Gallia Cisalpina, and caused such great calamities to Rome and to most of Italy. Ever since the first lodgment of the Gauls in Northern Italy, a migration had been continually in progress. Tribe after tribe crossed the Pennine Alps and sought new homes in the sunny South. For a time Italy sufficed for the flood of emigrants; but after a while it was found that no further impression could be made on the stubborn Etruscan, Latin, and Samnite nations, and the stream was forced to find a new vent. The Alps were recrossed where they curve round the top of the Adriatic; and Gallic tribes occupied the plain of the Danube and its tributaries, dispossessing the previous inhabitants, and becoming known either by the general name of Celts, or as Scordisci, Cimbri, etc. Probably the battle of Sentinum, B.C. 295, by finally closing Italy against Gallic adventure, gave a fresh impulse to the eastward flow of the migratory current. At any rate, by the end of the year B.C. 280 a large mass of hungry immigrants had accumulated in Northern Illyria, and in the regions about Mounts Scomius and Scardus. This mass, in B.C. 279, rolled forward in three waves, which took three different directions. One, under Cerethrius, took a north-easterly course against the Triballi and the Thracians; another, under Brennus and Acichorius, proceeded due east against the Pæonians; the third, under a chief named Belgius, marched south-east and fell upon Macedonia. It was with this last leader and his troops that Ptolemy Ceraunus came into contact. Warned by the Dardanian king of the impending danger, and offered by him a contingent of 20,000 men, Ceraunus proudly rejected the overture, confiding in his own strength. Summoned by the Gallic chief to save his kingdom from invasion by an assignment of land and a money payment, he made an indignant reply, utterly rejecting the proposition. Invasion followed as a matter of course, and in the first battle Ceraunus lost both his crown and his life. The Gauls then ravaged Macedonia at their will, until they were checked by Sosthenes, who had succeeded to the chief authority, after Meleager, the brother of Ceraunus, and Antipater, a nephew of Cassander, had each held the throne for a few weeks. In the following year, B.C. 278, a second and still more formidable irruption of the Gauls took place. Brennus, having first invaded Macedonia and defeated Sosthenes, marched into Southern Greece, forced the pass of Thermopylæ in the same way as the Persians under Xerxes, and endeavored to sack Delphi, but was repulsed and forced to retreat. His demoralized army broke up; and the Gallic hordes generally were shattered into mere bands of marauders, which perished by cold, famine, or the sword. In Thrace, however, a body contrived to establish a kingdom; and in Asia Minor, the hordes which had crossed over on the invitation of Nicomedes, native king of Bithynia (see Period III., Part I., § 9), made themselves masters of Northern Phrygia, B.C. 277, which was thenceforward known as Galatia. Other bodies of Gauls took service under the various European and Asiatic princes, who found them useful as mercenaries, and employed them in the wars which they waged one against another.

First reign of Antigonus Gonatas, B.C. 277-273.

14. On the retirement of the Gauls, Antipater, the nephew of Cassander, came forward for the second time, and was accepted as king by a portion, at any rate, of the Macedonians. But a new pretender soon appeared upon the scene. Antigonus Gonatas, the son of Demetrius Poliorcetes, who had maintained himself since that monarch's captivity as an independent prince in Central or Southern Hellas, claimed the throne once filled by his father, and, having taken into his service a body of Gallic mercenaries, defeated Antipater and made himself master of Macedonia. His pretensions being disputed by Antiochus Soter, the son of Seleucus, who had succeeded to the throne of Syria, he engaged in war with that prince, crossing into Asia and uniting his forces with those of Nicomedes, the Bithynian king, whom Antiochus was endeavoring to conquer. To this combination Antiochus was forced to yield: relinquishing his claims, he gave his sister, Phila, in marriage to Antigonus, and recognized him as king of Macedonia. Antigonus upon this fully established his power, repulsing a fresh attack of the Gauls, and recovering Cassandreia from the cruel tyrant, Apollodorus.

Expulsion of Antigonus by Pyrrhus.

15. But he was not long left in repose. In B.C. 274, Pyrrhus finally quitted Italy, having failed in all his schemes, but having made himself a great reputation. Landing in Epirus with a scanty force, he found the condition of Macedonia and of Greece favorable to his ambition. Antigonus had no hold on the affec-

tions of his subjects, whose recollections of his father, Demetrius, were unpleasing. The Greek cities were, some of them, under tyrants, others occupied against their will by Macedonian garrisons. Above all, Greece and Macedonia were full of military adventurers, ready to flock to any standard which offered them a fair prospect of plunder. Pyrrhus, therefore, having taken a body of Celts into his pay, declared war against Antigonus, B.C. 273, and suddenly invaded Macedonia. Antigonus gave him battle, but was worsted owing to the disaffection of his soldiers, and, being twice defeated, became a fugitive and a wanderer.

The frequent changes of this period must be ascribed to two principal causes. 1. The old royal family of the Macedonians having become extinct, none of the new houses had as yet obtained a hold on the respect or affections of the bulk of the people. One house was regarded as very little better than another. None had reigned long enough to obtain any *prestige*. 2. Mercenaries had come to form the main strength of armies; and mercenaries are at all times ready to change sides and desert the leader of to-day, if they fancy that they see in his rival a more generous or a more fortunate commander. The Macedonian nation, dispersed over the world, had become weakened; and its fate was now settled for it by Gauls, Thracians, and Illyrians.

Second reign of Pyrrhus, B.C. 273-271. His death.

16. The victories of Pyrrhus, and his son Ptolemy, placed the Macedonian crown upon the brow of the former, who might not improbably have become the founder of a great power, if he could have turned his attention to consolidation, instead of looking out for fresh conquests. But the arts and employments of peace had no charm for the Epirotic knight-errant. Hardly was he settled in his seat, when, upon the invitation of Cleonymus of Sparta, he led an expedition into the Peloponnese, and attempted the conquest of that rough and difficult region. Repulsed from Sparta, which he had hoped to surprise, he sought to cover his disappointment by the capture of Argos; but here he was still more unsuccessful. Antigonus, now once more at the head of an army, watched the city, prepared to dispute its occupation, while the lately threatened Spartans hung upon the invader's rear. In a desperate attempt to seize the place by night, the adventurous Epirote was first wounded by a soldier and then slain by the blow of a tile, thrown from a house-top by an Argive woman, B.C. 271.

CHARACTER OF PYRRHUS. Amid the blood-thirsty, treacherous, and dissolute princes of the post-Alexandrine times, the character of Pyrrhus stands out as something by comparison admirable. He was not really either a good or a great man. His conduct was often stained with cruelty, and occasionally with an insincerity that approached perfidiousness. His aims were purely selfish, and show no trace of patriotism. Though his military talent was remarkable, his courage great, and circumstances on the whole fairly favorable to him, he effected nothing permanent, nothing even grand or considerable. His talents strike us as misapplied, and his life as wasted. With a little more solidity and singleness of purpose he might have effected much. As it was, his powers were frittered away upon unconnected and often ill-judged enterprises.

Second reign of Antigonus Gonatas, B.C. 271-239.

17. On the death of Pyrrhus the Macedonian throne was recovered by Antigonus, who commenced his second reign by establishing his influence over most of the Peloponnese, after which he was engaged in a long war with the Athenians (B.C. 268 to 263), who were supported by Sparta and by Egypt. These allies rendered, however, but little help; and Athens must have soon succumbed, had not Antigonus been called away to Macedonia by the invasion of Alexander, son of Pyrrhus. This enterprising prince carried, at first, all before him, and was even acknowledged as Macedonian king; but ere long, Demetrius, the son of Antigonus, having defeated Alexander near Derdia, re-established his father's dominion over Macedon, and, invading Epirus, succeeded in driving the Epirotic monarch out of his paternal kingdom. The Epirots soon restored him; but from this time he remained at peace with Antigonus, who was able once more to devote his undivided attention to the subjugation of the Greeks. In B.C. 263, he took Athens, and rendered himself complete master of Attica; and, in B.C. 244, nineteen years afterwards, he contrived by a treacherous stratagem to obtain possession of Corinth. But at this point his successes ceased. A power had been quietly growing up in a corner of the Peloponnese which was to become a counterpoise to Macedonia, and to give to the closing scenes of Grecian history an interest little inferior to that which had belonged to its earlier pages. The Achæan League, resuscitated from its ashes about the time of the invasion of the Gauls, B.C. 280, had acquired in the space of thirty-seven years sufficient strength and consistency to venture on defying the puissant king of Macedon and braving his extreme displeasure. In

His relation with the Achæan League.

B.C. 243, Aratus, the general of the League and in a certain sense its founder, by a sudden and well-planned attack surprised and took Corinth; which immediately joined the League, whereto it owed its freedom. This success was followed by others. Megara, Trœzen, and Epidaurus threw off their allegiance to Antigonus and attached themselves to the League in the course of the same year. Athens and Argos were threatened; and the League assumed an attitude of unmistakable antagonism to the power and pretensions of Macedon. Antigonus, grown timorous in his old age, met the bold aggressions of the League with no overt acts of hostility. Contenting himself with inciting the Ætolians to attack the new power, he remained wholly on the defensive, neither attempting to recover the lost towns, nor to retaliate by any invasion of Achæa.

RISE AND GROWTH OF THE ACHÆAN LEAGUE. The old confederacy of the twelve Achæan cities, which has been already spoken of (see Book III., Period II., Part II., § A), appears to have been dissolved soon after the death of Alexander, by the influence of the Macedonian princes, especially Cassander and Demetrius—about B.C. 300 to 290. It was not long wholly in abeyance. About B.C. 280, the cities began to draw together again, a league being formed between Patræ and Dymé, which was joined almost immediately by Pharæ and Tritæa. Five years later, B.C. 275, Ægium, Bura, and Ceryneia came in, expelling their Macedonian garrisons or their tyrants; and soon afterwards the other three surviving cities of the original twelve, Ægeira, Pellêné, and Leontium (Helicé and Olenus had ceased to exist) were recovered; and the whole of Achæa was thereby once more united into a single political unit. Thus far the movement had no great importance, being simply the re-formation of an old community which had never previously played an important part in Grecian affairs. A new character was given to the League, and the foundation of its greatness laid in B.C. 251, when Aratus, the liberator of Sicyon from tyranny, induced that wholly separate and indeed alien state to ask, and the Achæans to grant, its admission into the confederacy. By adopting the principle that foreign states might be received into the League, and become members of it on terms of equality with the several Achæan towns, an indefinite power of expansion was given to the union, which became in principle, and might become in fact, Pan-Hellenic. These consequences were not, perhaps, at once generally seen; but when, in B.C. 243, Aratus, the general of the League, threw down the gauntlet to Antigonus, captured his town of Corinth, and induced it to join the confederation, and further proceeded to accept as additional members the revolted cities of Megara, Epidaurus, and Trœzen, the existence of a new and formidable power in Southern Greece was fully revealed, and only the willfully blind would fail to perceive it. The aftergrowth of the League, its extension to Cleônæ, Cynætha, Stymphalus, Cleitor, Pheneus, Caphyæ, Heræa, Telphusa, Megalopolis, Ægina, Hermioné, Argos, Phlius, was the natural result of the principle asserted in B.C. 251, a principle new to Greece at the time, and of the greatest importance to her, since its general adoption might have saved her from annihilation. Unfortunately, the old love of separate independence, and the old spirit of jealousy and rivalry, prevented the adoption of the principle from being general; and its partial acceptance could not avail greatly. Still, even this partial acceptance deferred for a time the absorption of Greece by a foreign power; and it shed a glory around the period of her decline and fall, which recalls in some degree the splendor of those days when she rose to greatness.

CHIEF FEATURES OF THE CONSTITUTION. 1. Equality of the federated cities, each of which had one vote only in the Federal Congress. 2. Complete internal independence of the several states, which had the exclusive ordering of their own domestic affairs and appointment of their own local magistrates and governors. 3. Management of the affairs of the League by a General Congress, which met regularly twice a year at some city of the League (at first Ægium, afterwards Corinth or Argos), and might be summoned to hold extraordinary meetings by the chief magistrate at other times. This congress consisted, not of deputies from the states, but of all the citizens of the states who chose to attend. It appointed the Council (*βουλή*), a committee of its own body, who prepared measures previously to their submission to the General Congress, received and conferred with ambassadors, and the like; it also appointed the ten Ministers (*δημιουργοί*), who formed the council of the head of the state; and the head of the state himself (*στρατηγός*), who united the chief military with the chief civil authority. 4. Constitution in theory democratic; but practical tendency towards an aristocracy of wealth, in consequence of offices being unpaid, and the citizens having to travel at their own expense in order to attend the general meetings of the Congress. 5. Great power of the Strategus or General, who not only had the entire direction of the armed force, but in practice for the most part guided the whole policy of the League. Restriction on his re-election, which could only take place, legally, every other year.

The following works on the subject of the Achæan League are deserving of attention:

MERLEKER, C. F., *Achaicorum libri tres.* Darmstadt, 1837; 8vo.

SCHORN, *Geschichte Griechenlands von der Entstehung des Ætolischen und Achäischen Bundes bis auf die Zerstörung Korinths.* Bonn, 1833; 8vo.

HELWING, *Geschichte des Achäischen Bundes.* Lemgo, 1829; 8vo.

FREEMAN, E. A., *History of Federal Government*, vol. i. chaps. v.–ix.

18. Antigonus Gonatas died B.C. 239, at the age of eighty, having reigned in all thirty-seven years. He left his crown to his son, Demetrius II., who inherited his ambition without his talents. The first acts of Demetrius were to form a close alliance with Epirus, now under the rule of Olympias, Alexander's widow; to accept the hand of her daughter Phthia, whereby he offended his queen, Stratonicé, and through her Seleucus, the

Reign of Demetrius II., B.C. 239–229.

Syrian king; and to break with the Ætolians, who were seeking at this time to deprive Olympias of a portion of her dominions. The Ætolians, alarmed, sought the alliance of the Achæan League; and in the war which followed, Demetrius was opposed by both these important powers. He contrived, however, to defeat Aratus in Thessaly, to reduce Bœotia, and to re-establish Macedonian ascendency as far as the Isthmus. But this was all that he could effect. No impression was made by his arms on either of the great Leagues. No aid was given to Epirus, where the royal family was shortly afterwards exterminated. Demetrius was perhaps recalled to Macedonia by the aggressive attitude of the Dardanians, who certainly attacked him in his later years, and gave him a severe defeat. It is thought by some that he perished in the battle. But this is uncertain.

The assertion of Porphyry in Eusebius, that Demetrius II. conquered Libya and Cyrênê, is untrue, and arises from a confusion between him and one of his uncles. Macedonia was far too weak at this time for any such enterprise.

First interference of ROME in Grecian affairs.

The most important fact of this period was the interference, *now for the first time*, of the Romans in the affairs of Greece. The embassy to the Ætolians, warning them against interference with Acarnania, belongs probably to the year B.C. 238; that to the Ætolians and Achæans, announcing the success of the Roman arms against the Illyrians, belongs certainly to B.C. 228. In the same year, or the year preceding, Corcyra, Apollonia, and Epidamnus became Roman dependencies.

Regency of Antigonus Doson, B.C. 229-220.

19. Demetrius left an only son, Philip, who was but eight years old at his decease. He was at once acknowledged king; but owing to his tender age, his guardianship was undertaken by his kinsman, Antigonus, the son of his father's first cousin, Demetrius "the Handsome." It was, consequently, this prince who directed the policy of Macedonia during the period which immediately followed on the death of Demetrius II.—who, in fact, ruled Macedonia for nine years, from B.C. 229 to 220. The events of this period are of first-rate interest, including, as they do, the last display of patriotism and vigor at Sparta, and the remarkable turn of affairs whereby Macedonia, from being the deadly foe of the Achæan League, became its friend, ally, and protector.

CONDITION OF SPARTA at this period. The Spartan constitution had remained unchanged in form from the time of the Messenian Wars (see pp. 150, 151) to the period which we have now reached—a space of above four centuries. A project of revolution, conceived by Cinadon, B.C. 399, had been discovered before it could be put in execution, and had proved abortive. But, though no formal or violent change had occurred, a subtle gradual alteration had destroyed the ideal of Lycurgus. The chief points of this alteration were the following:— (*a*) Diminution of the number of the citizens, by the operation of the laws which always cause an aristocracy, that does not recruit itself from without, to become more and more contracted. (*b*) Further and still more striking diminution of the number of *full* citizens, by the operation of the Lycurgean law limiting citizenship to Spartans of independent means. (*c*) Concentration of wealth, and especially of landed property, in a few hands, partly by the practice of marrying heiresses to wealthy men, partly by the permission to deal freely with landed estates by gift, sale, or will obtained by the law of Epitadeus. (*d*) Constant encroachment of the Ephors on the power of the kings, and final reduction of the latter to mere ciphers. (*e*) Relaxation of the Lycurgean discipline. Abandonment by the citizens generally of the old simple and frugal rule of life, and adoption by the wealthy of habits of luxury. (*f*) Contraction of heavy debts by the poorer members of the state, who were thus placed at the mercy of a small class of wealthy capitalists. The result of the whole was that the entire number of adult male Spartans did not exceed 700; and of these not more than 100 were in possession of the full rights of citizens. This narrow oligarchy was occupied almost exclusively with the difficulties of its own position; and Sparta consequently stood aloof from Grecian politics, and had done so since the attempt of Agis III., in B.C. 330. Even insults were tamely submitted to; and when Illyrian pirates ravaged the coast, or Ætolian marauders the interior, no vengeance was exacted. Under these circumstances the idea of a reform arose. It was proposed to increase the number of citizens to 4500 by admitting Periœci and foreigners; to *redivide the land* of the state in equal allotments to these persons and to 15,000 selected Laconians; to *abolish debts;* and to re-establish the *syssitia* and the rest of the Lycurgean discipline. A first attempt to carry out the reform, made by Agis, B.C. 244 to 241, met with only partial success, being frustrated by the treachery of the Ephor Agesilaüs, and the open opposition of the other king, Leonidas, who returned from the exile into which Agis had driven him, and placed himself at the head of the counter-revolution. Agis fell a martyr to his reforming zeal; and the old state of things was re-established B.C. 241. But five years later Leonidas died, and was succeeded by his son, Cleomenes, B.C. 236, who had married Agis's widow, Agiatis. Under her influence the young monarch revived the projects of Agis, and, having first acquired a great military reputation in a war with the Achæan League, succeeded in effecting their accomplishment, B.C. 226. At the same time, he abolished the Ephoralty, modified the character of the Senate (γερουσία), and practically destroyed the double monarchy by making his own brother, Euclides, second king. A glorious period for Sparta followed. Not only were the forces of the Achæan League defeated, but Argos, the ancient rival of Sparta, submitted to her; Corinth, revolting from

Changes at Sparta since the time of Theopompus.

Reforms proposed by Agis.

Carried out by Cleomenes.

Wars of Cleomenes.

the Achæans, placed herself under Spartan protection; Epidaurus, Hermioné, Trœzen, and most of Arcadia did the same; and even Pellêné, one of the ten Achæan towns, was occupied, and received a Lacedæmonian garrison, B.C. 224 to 223. But the tide soon after turned. The animating spirit of the Achæan League, Aratus, in his jealousy of Cleomenes, took the traitorous step of calling in Antigonus to his aid, and agreed to reinstate him in the possession of the Acrocorinthus. The result was fatal at once for Greece and for Cleomenes. The Achæan League lost its character as the defender of Greek liberty, and to a great extent broke up. Cleomenes, forced to stand upon the defensive, was attacked and defeated at Sellasia, B.C. 221, and became a fugitive at the court of Ptolemy. The reaction triumphed at Sparta, and her last chance of recovering her ancient glory was lost. Macedonia was once more supreme over almost all Greece, the only parts unsubdued being Ætolia, Messenia, and Elis. All the efforts of Aratus to raise up a power in Greece which might counterbalance Macedon, and of Agis and Cleomenes to regenerate their country and make her the fitting head of a free Hellas, had ended in simply delivering Greece up, bound hand and foot, into the power of her great enemy.

Battle of Sellasia, B.C. 221.

20. The other wars of Antigonus Doson were comparatively unimportant. He repulsed an attack of the Dardanians, who had defeated his predecessor, suppressed an insurrection in Thessaly, and made an expedition by sea against South-western Asia Minor, which is said to have resulted in the conquest of Caria. It was impossible, however, that he should long hold this distant dependency, which shortly reverted to Egypt, the chief maritime power of this period. Soon after his return from Greece, Antigonus died of disease, having held the sovereignty for the space of nine years. He was succeeded by the rightful heir to the throne, Philip, the son of Demetrius II., in whose name he had carried on the government.

Minor wars of Antigonus Doson.

21. Philip, who was still no more than seventeen years old, was left by his kinsman to the care of tutors and guardians. He seemed to ascend the throne at a favorable moment, when Macedonia, at very little expenditure of either men or money, had recovered Greece, had repulsed her Illyrian adversaries, and was released, by the death of Ptolemy Euergetes, from her most formidable enemy among the successors of Alexander. But all these advantages were neutralized by the rash conduct of the king himself, who first allied himself with Hannibal against Rome, and then with Antiochus against Egypt. No doubt Philip saw, more clearly than most of his contempo-

Reign of Philip III., B.C. 220-179.

raries, the dangerously aggressive character of the Roman power; nor can we blame him for seeking to form coalitions against the conquering republic. But, before venturing to make Rome his enemy, he should have consolidated his power at home; and, when he made the venture, he should have been content with no half measures, but should have thrown himself, heart and soul, into the quarrel.

War of the Leagues.

22. The first war in which the young prince engaged was one that had broken out between the Achæans and Ætolians. The Ætolians, who now for the first time show themselves a really first-rate Greek power, had been gradually growing in importance, from the time when they provoked the special anger of Antipater in the Lamian War (supra, p. 285), and were threatened with transplantation into Asia. Somewhat earlier than this they had organized themselves into a Federal Republic, and had thus set the example which the Achæans followed half a century afterwards. Some account of their institutions, and of the extent of their power, is requisite for the proper understanding both of their strength and of their weakness.

Character of the Ætolian League.

The rise of the League belongs probably to the reign of Alexander, when the various tribes, who had previously only acted together upon certain occasions, formed a permanent union, with a view (probably) of maintaining their independence. The union, which was originally one of *tribes*, not of cities, involved (*a*) the institution of the "Pan-Ætolicum" or General Assembly of all Ætolians, which met regularly once a year—commonly at Thermon—for the discussion of business and election of officers, and might also be convened, as often as was thought to be desirable, by the chief magistrate; (*b*) the nomination of a select council (ἀπόκλητοι), consisting seemingly of 1000 members, no doubt appointed by the Assembly, which performed the ordinary functions of a Greek council or senate; (*c*) the creation of a chief of the League, a federal head, who was elected annually by the Assembly at its regular meeting, and of two other great officers, elected in the same way, a commander of cavalry (ἱππάρχης), and a Secretary (γραμματεύς); and (*d*) the election of certain officers called "Synedri" and "Nomographi," whose duties are uncertain. After the League had existed for some little time, it began to be aggressive and to spread itself. Œniadæ was annexed while Alexander was engaged in Asia;

Extent of the League.

Heracleia in Trachis, at the time of the great Gallic invasion (supra, p. 293). Afterwards Acarnania, Western Locris, Doris, Southern Thessaly, Achæa Phthiotis, several cities of Arcadia, Cius on the Propontis, and the islands of Teos and Cephallenia joined the League voluntarily, or were forced into it; and it even at one time had relations with Bœotia which almost amounted to incorporation. It thus stretched across

Central Greece from the Ionian to the Ægean Sea, comprising also islands in both seas, and other still more remote dependencies. It was not, however, the principle of the League to admit, generally, foreign states on terms of equality. This may have been done in some instances; but usually the relation established was one of inequality—inequality varying in degree from mere inferiority of dignity to absolute subjection. This is one of the most marked differences between the Ætolian League and that of Achæa. Another difference is to be traced in the wilder character and inferior Hellenism of the Ætolians, who never quite emerged out of the state of barbarity described by Thucydides, but continued a robber nation to the end. Ætolia had at no time any patriotic aims—she wished simply her own aggrandizement. In her wars, what she mainly sought was plunder, and her expeditions were generally raids for the sake of carrying off spoil. To gain her ends, she was ready to wink at any infringement of international law and to ally herself with any power. On two occasions only did she do good service to Greece, in the Lamian War and at the great Gallic inroad, her conception of her own interests on these occasions happening to coincide with the interests of Hellas. She joined with Epirus to crush Acarnania, and was ready to join with Macedon to partition Achæa. Finally, she brought the Romans in upon Greece by a formal treaty of alliance, entering into a treasonable partnership with the foreign power which the Greeks had most to fear, and obtaining the aid of Roman fleets and armies to help her against her Hellenic adversaries. It is further remarkable that Ætolia never produced a great man. While Achæa had her Aratus, her Lydiades, and her Philopœmen, all of them men who would have been remarkable at any period of Grecian history, Ætolia could produce nothing higher than a Dorimachus or a Scopas, successful robbers on a par with Philomelus and Onomarchus, but with no pretensions to the character of either generals or statesmen.

Contrasts of the Ætolian and Achæan Leagues.

BRANDSTAETER, F. A., *Geschichte des ätolischen Landes und Volkes.* Berlin, 1844; 8vo.

23. The war of the Ætolians and Achæans was provoked by the former, who thought they saw in the accession of so young a prince as Philip to the throne of Macedon a favorable opportunity for advancing their interests after their own peculiar method. It commenced with the invasion of Messenia, and would probably have been ruinous to Achæa, had Philip allowed himself to be detained in Macedonia by apprehensions of danger from his Illyrian neighbors, or had he shown less vigor and ability in his proceedings after he entered Greece. Though thwarted by the treachery of his minister and guardian, Apelles, who was jealous of the influence of Aratus, and but little aided by any of his Greek allies, he gained a series of brilliant successes, overrunning most of

Successful part taken by Philip in the Ætolo-Achæan War.

Ætolia, capturing Thermon, the capital, detaching from the League Phigaleia in Arcadia and the Phthian Thebes, and showing himself in all respects a worthy successor of the old Macedonian conquerors. But after four years of this successful warfare, he allowed himself to be diverted from what should have been his first object, the *complete* reduction of Greece, by the prospect which opened upon him after Hannibal's victory at Lake Thrasimene. At the instance of Demetrius of Pharos he concluded a peace with the Ætolians on the principle of *uti possedetis*, and, retiring into Macedonia, entered upon those negotiations which involved him shortly afterwards in a war with Rome.

DETAILS OF THE ÆTOLO-ACHÆAN WAR. Incursion of the Ætolians through Achæa into Messenia under Scopas and Dorimachus, and plundering expeditions by sea at the same time against Acarnania and Epirus, B.C. 220. Defeat of Aratus at Caphyæ. The Ætolians capture Cynætha. Advance of Philip, B.C. 219. He invades Ætolia and captures Pæanium and Œniadæ, but is recalled to Macedon by a rumored incursion of the Dardanians. Having terrified the Dardanians into submission, he returns during the winter into Greece, enters Peloponnese, defeats the Ætolian general, Euripidas, takes Psophis, overruns Elis, receives the submission of Phigaleia, and finally rests his army for the remainder of the winter at Argos, B.C. 218. In the early spring, having collected a fleet, he sails to Cephallenia and besieges Palé, but fails to take it owing to the treachery of Apelles. Crossing to Acarnania, he invades Ætolia from the north-west, and, marching into the very centre of the country, takes and destroys Thermon, the capital, defeats every force which attempts to oppose him, and proceeding to Corinth, enters the Peloponnese and ravages the whole territory of Sparta, as far as Malea and Tænarum. On his return, he defeats Lycurgus, the Spartan king, near Sparta. Winter approaching, he returns to Macedonia, and captures Bylazora in Pæonia, a city commanding the passes into Macedonia from the country of the Dardanians. In the spring of B.C. 217, he advances into Thessaly, besieges and takes Phthian Thebes, and thence proceeds to Argos to be present at the Nemean Games. Here the news of the battle of Lake Thrasimene reaches him, and he consents to peace.

The history of this war has been written by MERLEKER. See his *Geschichte des Ætolisch-Achäischen Bundesgenossen Krieges, nach den Quellen dargestellt.* Königsberg, 1831; 8vo.

It is also given in considerable detail by THIRLWALL, *History of Greece*, vol. viii. chap. lxiii.

First war of Philip with the Romans, B.C. 214–207.

24. The negotiations opened by Philip with Hannibal, B.C. 216, interrupted by the capture of his ambassadors, were brought to a successful issue in B.C. 215; and in the ensuing year Philip began his first war with Rome by the siege of Apollonia, the chief Roman

port in Illyricum. By securing this place, he expected to facilitate the invasion of Italy on which he was bent, and to prepare the way for that complete expulsion of the Romans from the eastern coast of the gulf, which was one of the objects he had most at heart. But he soon learned that the Romans were an enemy with whom, under any circumstances whatever, it was dangerous to contend. Defeated by M. Valerius, who surprised his camp at night, he was obliged to burn his ships and make a hasty retreat. His schemes of invasion were rudely overthrown; and, three years later, B.C. 211, the Romans, by concluding a treaty with Ætolia and her allies (Elis, Sparta, the Illyrian chief, Scerdilaidas, and Attalus, king of Pergamus), gave the war a new character, transferring it into Philip's own dominions, and so occupying him there that he was forced to implore aid from Carthage instead of bringing succor to Hannibal. After many changes of fortune, the Macedonian monarch, having by the hands of his ally, Philopœmen, defeated the Spartans at Mantineia, induced the Ætolians to conclude a separate peace; after which the Romans, anxious to concentrate all their energies on the war with Carthage, consented to a treaty on terms not dishonorable to either party.

DETAILS OF THE FIRST ROMAN WAR. The Romans (B.C. 211) conquer Zacynthus, Œniadæ, and Nesos, and deliver them over to the Ætolians. Philip is engaged with wars at home against the Illyrians and Thracians. The next year (B.C. 210) the Romans take Anticyra in Locris, and the island of Ægina, and hand them over in like manner. Philip advances to Malis, and besieges Echinus, which he takes, despite an attempt of the Romans and Ætolians to relieve it. In B.C. 209, Philopœmen appears upon the scene and commences those reforms by which he gave new life and vigor to Achæa. On the other side Attalus arrives from Asia, and co-operates with the Romans and Ætolians. Philip now marches southward, and, entering the Peloponnese, defeats a Roman detachment in Achæa, and invades Elis, but is there defeated by Sulpicius Galba and narrowly escapes with his life. The operations of the next year, B.C. 208, were unimportant. The chief event was the recall of Attalus, who was forced to return to Asia in order to repel an attack made upon his kingdom by his neighbor, Prusias of Bithynia. Nearly of equal importance was the appointment of Philopœmen to the headship of Achæa, which produced in the year following, B.C. 207, the victory of Mantineia, and placed Philip on that vantage-ground which enabled him to dictate terms to the Achæans, and to conclude his peace with the Romans on conditions which were fairly equal.

25. Philip had now a breathing-space, and might have em-

ployed it to consolidate his power in Macedonia and Greece, before the storm broke upon him which was manifestly impending. But his ambition was too great, and his views were too grand, to allow of his engaging in a work so humble and unexciting as consolidation. The Macedonian monarch had by this time disappointed all his earlier promise of virtue and moderation. He had grown profligate in morals, criminal in his acts, both public and private, and strangely reckless in his policy. Grasping after a vast empire, he neglected to secure what he already possessed, and, while enlarging the bounds, he diminished the real strength of his kingdom. It became now his object to extend his dominion on the side of Asia, and with this view he first (about B.C. 205) concluded a treaty with Antiochus the Great for the partition of the territories of Egypt, and then (B.C. 203) plunged into a war with Attalus and the Rhodians. His own share of the Egyptian spoils was to comprise Lysimacheia and the adjoining parts of Thrace, Samos, Ephesus, Caria, and perhaps other portions of Asia Minor. He began at once to take possession of these places. A war with Attalus and Rhodes was almost the necessary result of such proceedings, since their existence depended on the maintenance of a balance of power in these parts, and the instinct of self-preservation naturally threw them on the Egyptian side. Philip, moreover, took no steps to disarm their hostility: on the contrary, before war was declared, he burnt the arsenal of the Rhodians by the hands of an emissary; and in the war itself, one of his opening acts was to strengthen Prusias, the enemy of Attalus, by making over to him the Ætolian dependency, Cius. The main event of the war was the great defeat of his fleet by the combined squadrons of the two powers off Chios, B.C. 201, a defeat ill compensated by the subsequent victory of Ladé. Still Philip was, on the whole, successful, and accomplished the main objects which he had in view, making himself master of Thasos, Samos, Chios, of Caria, and of many places in Ionia. Unassisted by Egypt, the allies were too weak to protect her territory, and Philip obtained the extension of dominion which he had desired, but at the cost of provoking the intense hostility of two powerful naval states, and the ill-will of Ætolia, which he had injured by his conquest of Cius.

War with Egypt, Attalus and the Rhodians, B.C. 203-200.

26. These proceedings of Philip in the Ægean had, moreover, been well calculated to bring about a rupture of the peace with Rome. Friendly relations had existed between the Romans and Egypt from the time of Ptolemy Philadelphus (supra, p. 273), and even from an earlier date Rhodes and Rome had been on terms of intimacy. Attalus was an actual ally of Rome, and had been included in the late treaty. It is therefore not surprising that in B.C. 200 Rome remonstrated, and, when Philip rejected every demand, declared the peace at an end and renewed the war.

Rupture with Rome, B.C. 200.

27. The Second War of Philip with Rome is the turning-point in the history of Ancient Europe, deciding, as it did, the question whether Macedon and Rome should continue two parallel forces, dividing between them the general direction of European affairs, or whether the power of the former should be completely swept away, and the dominion of the latter over the civilized West finally and firmly established. It is perhaps doubtful what the result would have been, if Philip had guided his conduct by the commonest rules of prudence; if, aware of the nature of the conflict into which he was about to be plunged, he had conciliated instead of alienating his natural supports, and had so been able to meet Rome at the head of a general confederacy of the Hellenes. As it was, Greece was at first divided, the Rhodians, Athenians, and Athamanians siding with Rome; Ætolia, Epirus, Achæa, and Sparta being neutral; and Thessaly, Bœotia, Acarnania, Megalopolis, and Argos supporting Philip; while in the latter part of the war, after Flamininus had proclaimed himself the champion of Grecian freedom, almost the entire force of Hellas was thrown on the side of the Romans. Rome had also the alliance of the Illyrian tribes, always hostile to their Macedonian neighbors, and of Attalus, king of Pergamus. Philip was left at last without a friend or ally, excepting Acarnania, which exhibited the unusual spectacle of a grateful nation firmly adhering to its benefactor in his adversity.

Second War of Philip with Rome, B.C. 200–197.

Allies of either party.

DETAILS OF THE SECOND ROMAN WAR. Sulpicius Galba lands in Epirus, B.C. 200, and early the next year, in concert with the Dardanians and Illyrians, attacks Macedonia on the land side, while the Roman fleet, with the contingents of Attalus and the Rhodians, threatens the sea-board. Galba gains some advantages, but makes no very serious impression. The fleet takes

Andros and Oreus in Eubœa. Towards winter Ætolia joins the Roman side, and her troops invade Thessaly, where they are defeated by Philip near Pharcadon. In B.C. 198 the consul Villius, landing in Epirus late in the year, effects nothing, but T. Quinctius Flamininus, his successor, defeats Philip on the Aous, and, proclaiming liberty to the Greeks, proceeds through Thessaly into Phocis, besieging only the towns held by Macedonian garrisons. The fleet takes Eretria and Carystus in Eubœa. Achæa and Bœotia join the Romans. Philip makes alliance with Nabis, and gives him Argos. In B.C. 197, Flamininus, having wintered at Thebes, invaded Thessaly and met Philip at Cynocephalæ, where he completely defeated him. This battle decided the war, and with it the fate of Macedonia. Philip at once consented to terms of peace.

Battle of Cynocephalæ, B.C. 197.

28. The terms of peace agreed to by Philip after the battle of Cynocephalæ were the following:—(1) He was to evacuate all the Greek cities which he held, whether in Europe or Asia, some immediately, the others within a given time. (2) He was to surrender his state-galley and all his navy except five light ships. (3) He was to restore all the Roman prisoners and deserters; and (4) he was to pay to the Romans 1000 talents, 500 at once, the rest in ten annual installments. He was also to abstain from all aggressive war, and to surrender any claim to his revolted province, Orestis. These terms, though hard, were as favorable as he had any right to expect. Had the Ætolians been allowed to have their way, he would have been far more severely treated.

Terms of peace granted to Philip.

29. The policy of Rome in proclaiming freedom to the Greeks, and even withdrawing her garrisons from the great fortresses of Demetrias, Chalcis, and Corinth—the "fetters of Greece"—was undoubtedly sound. Greek freedom could not be maintained excepting under her protection; and, by undertaking the protectorate, she attached the bulk of the Greek people to her cause. At the same time, the establishment of *universal* freedom prevented any state from having much power; and in the quarrels that were sure to ensue Rome would find her advantage.

Settlement of Greece, B.C. 194.

The chief features of the settlement of Greece made by Flamininus, B.C. 194, were the subdivision of states and the establishment of separate independence. Perrhæbia, Dolopia, and Magnesia were detached from Thessaly and erected into independent communities. In Eubœa, Oreus, Eretria, and Carystus were made free towns. Argos was detached from Sparta, and became once more her own mistress. The Leagues of Achæa and Ætolia were not, however, dissolved, but were left to balance each other. Achæa even received back some of her lost states, as Corinth, Heræa, and Triphylia. Greece generally seems to have been content with the arrangement made, but it wholly failed to satisfy the Ætolians.

War of Rome with Ætolia, B.C. 194–190.

30. War broke out in Greece in the very year of Flamininus's departure, B.C. 194, by the intrigues of the Ætolians, who encouraged Nabis to attack the Achæans, then murdered Nabis, and finally invited Antiochus over from Asia. The defeat of Antiochus at Thermopylæ, B.C. 191 (supra, p. 254), left the Ætolians to bear the brunt of the war which they had provoked, and after the battle of Magnesia, B.C. 190, there was nothing left for them but complete submission. Rome curtailed their territory, and made them subject-allies, but forbore to crush them utterly, since they might still be useful against Macedonia.

Growth of the Achæan League.

31. The degradation of Ætolia was favorable to the growth and advancement of the Achæan League, which at one and the same time was patronized by Rome, and seemed to patriotic Greeks the only remaining rallying-point for a national party. The League at this time was under the guidance of the able and honest Philopœmen, whose efforts for its extension were crowned with remarkable success. After the murder of Nabis by the Ætolians, Sparta was induced to join the League, B.C. 192; and, a year later, the last of the Peloponnesian states which had remained separate, Messênê and Elis, came in. The League now reached its widest territorial extent, comprising all the Peloponnese, together with Megara and other places beyond its limits.

The annexation of Sparta, though legally effected, was an injudicious measure; and its compulsory retention in the League, after it had shown plainly its wish to secede, was a fatal mistake. Messênê, on the other hand, though by the murder of Philopœmen it seemed to be intensely hostile, was rightly retained, since there the opponents of union were a mere faction.

Troubles of Philip's closing years.

32. After the conclusion of his peace with Rome, Philip for some years remained quiet. But having assisted the Romans in their struggle with Antiochus and the Ætolians, he was allowed to extend his dominions by wars not only with Thrace, but also with the Dolopians, Athamanians, and even the Thessalians and

Magnesians. When, however, his assistance was no longer needed, Rome required him to give up all his conquests and retire within the limits of Macedonia. Prolonged negotiations followed, until at last (B.C. 183) the Senate was induced to relax in their demands by the mediation of Demetrius, Philip's second son, long a hostage at Rome, for whom they professed to have a warm regard. The favor openly shown towards this prince by the Roman government was not perhaps intended to injure him; but it naturally had that result. It roused the suspicion of his father and the jealousy of his elder brother, Perseus, and led to the series of accusations against the innocent youth, which at length induced his father to consent to his death, B.C. 181. It may have been remorse for his hasty act which brought Philip himself to the grave within two years of his son's decease, at the age of fifty-eight.

Accession of the last king, Perseus, B.C. 179.

33. It is said that Philip had intended, on discovering the innocence of Demetrius, and the guilt of his false accuser, Perseus, to debar the latter from the succession. He brought forward into public life a certain Antigonus, a nephew of Antigonus Doson, and would, it is believed, have made him his heir, had he not died both prematurely and suddenly. Antigonus being absent from the court, Perseus mounted the throne without opposition; but he took care to secure himself in its possession by soon afterwards murdering his rival.

Preparations for the final struggle with Rome.

34. It had been the aim of Philip, ever since the battle of Cynocephalæ, and it continued to be the aim of Perseus, to maintain the peace with Rome as long as might be feasible, but at the same time to invigorate and strengthen Macedonia in every possible way, and so to prepare her for a second struggle, which it was hoped might terminate differently from the first. Philip repopulated his exhausted provinces by transplantations of Thracians and others, recruited his finances by careful working of the mineral treasures in which Macedonia abounded, raised and disciplined a large military force, and entered into alliances with several of the Northern nations, Illyrian, Celtic, and perhaps even German, whom he hoped to launch against Rome, when the proper time should arrive. Perseus, inheriting this policy, pursued it diligently for eight

years, allying himself by intermarriages with Prusias of Bithynia and Seleucus of Syria, winning to his cause Cotys the Odrysian, Gentius the Illyrian, the Scordisci, the Bastarnæ, and others. Even in Greece he had a considerable party, who thought his yoke would be more tolerable than that of Rome. Bœotia actually entered into his alliance; and the other states mostly wavered and might have been won, had proper measures been taken. But as the danger of a rupture drew near, Perseus's good genius seemed to forsake him. He continued to pursue the policy of procrastination long after the time had arrived for vigorous and prompt action. He allowed Rome to crush his friends in Greece without reaching out a hand to their assistance. Above all, by a foolish and ill-timed niggardliness, he lost the advantage of almost all the alliances which he had contracted, disgusting and alienating his allies, one after another, by the refusal of the subsidies which they required before setting their troops in motion. He thus derived no benefit from his well-filled treasury, which simply went to swell the Roman gains at the end of the war.

War of Perseus with Rome, B.C. 171–169.

Battle of Pydna.

35. The Romans landed in Epirus in the spring of B.C. 171, and employed themselves for some months in detaching from Perseus his allies, and in putting down his party in the Greek states. They dissolved the Bœotian League, secured the election of their partisans in various places, and obtained promises of aid from Achæa and Thessaly. Perseus allowed himself to be entrapped into making a truce during these months, and the Romans were thus able to complete their preparations at their leisure. At length, towards autumn, both armies took the field—Perseus with 39,000 foot and 4000 horse, the Romans with an equal number of horse, but with foot not much exceeding 30,000. In the first battle, which was fought in Thessaly, Perseus was victorious; but he made no use of his victory, except to sue for peace, which was denied him. The war then languished for two years; but in B.C. 168, the command being taken by L. Æmilius Paullus, Perseus was forced to an engagement near Pydna (June 22), which decided the fate of the monarchy. The defeated prince fled to Samothrace, carrying with him 6000 talents—a sum the judicious expenditure of which might

have turned the scale against the Romans. Here he was shortly afterwards captured by the prætor Octavius, and, being carried to Rome by the victorious consul, was led in triumph, and within a few years killed by ill usage, about B.C. 166.

According to some accounts, Perseus voluntarily starved himself to death; but the more general statement is that he was killed by his guards, who had orders to prevent him from sleeping. The exact date of his death is uncertain.

36. The conquered kingdom of Macedonia was not at once reduced into the form of a Roman province, but was divided up into four distinct states, each of them, it would seem, a kind of federal republic, which were expressly forbidden to have any dealings one with another. Amphipolis, Thessalonica, Pella, and Pelagonia were made the capitals of the four states. To prevent any outburst of discontent at the loss of political status, the burdens hitherto laid upon the people were lightened. Rome was content to receive in tribute from the Macedonians one-half the amount which they had been in the habit of paying to their kings.

Treatment of Macedonia.

37. In Greece, the immediate effect of the last Macedonian War was the disappearance of four out of the five Federal Unions, which had recently divided almost the whole of the Hellenic soil among them. The allegiance of Ætolia had wavered during the struggle; and at its close the Romans either formally dissolved the League, or made it simply municipal. Acarnania, which went over to Rome in the course of the war, was nominally allowed to continue a confederacy, but practically vanishes from Grecian history from this moment. Bœotia having submitted, B.C. 171, was formally broken up into distinct cities. Epirus was punished for deserting the Roman side by desolation and depopulation, the remnant of her people being handed over to the rule of a tyrant. The only power remaining in Greece which possessed at once some strength and a remnant of independence, was Achæa, whose fidelity to Rome during the whole course of the war made it impossible even for the Roman Senate to proceed at once to treat her as an enemy.

Effect of the war on Greece.

38. Achæa, nevertheless, was doomed from the moment

that Macedonia fell. The policy of Rome was at this time not guided by a sense of honor, but wholly by a regard for her own interests. Having crushed Macedonia and mastered all Greece except Achæa, she required for the completion of her work in this quarter that Achæa should either become wholly submissive to her will, or be conquered. It was at once to test the submissiveness of the Achæan people, and to obtain hostages for their continued good behavior, that Rome, in B.C. 167, required by her ambassadors the trial of above a thousand of the chief Achæans on the charge of having secretly aided Perseus; and, when the Achæan Assembly did not dare to refuse, carried off to Italy the whole of the accused persons. All the more moderate and independent of the Achæans were thus deported, and the strong partisans of Rome, Callicrates and his friends, were left in sole possession of the government. For seventeen years the accused persons were kept in prison in Etruscan towns without a hearing. Then, when their number had dwindled to three hundred, and their unjust detention had so exasperated them that a rash and reckless policy might be expected from their return to power, Rome suddenly released the remnant and sent them back to their country.

Proceedings of the Romans in Achæa. Deportation of one thousand chief citizens.

Their return.

39. The natural consequences followed. Power fell into the hands of Diæus, Critolaüs, and Damocritus, three of the exiles who were most bitterly enraged against Rome; and these persons played into the hands of their hated enemies by exciting troubles intended to annoy the Romans, but which really gave them the pretext — which was exactly what they wanted—for an armed interference. The rebellion of Andriscus, a pretended son of Perseus, in Macedonia (B.C. 149 to 148), caused a brief delay; but in B.C. 146, four years after the return of the exiles, war was actually declared. Metellus first, and then Mummius, defeated the forces of the League; Critolaüs fell in battle; Diæus slew himself; Corinth, where the remnant of the Achæan army had taken refuge, was taken and sacked, and the last faint spark of Grecian independence was extinguished. Achæa was not, indeed, at once reduced into a province; and, though the

Last War of the Achæans against Rome, ends B.C. 146.

League was formally dissolved, yet, after an interval, its nominal revival was permitted; but the substance of liberty had vanished at the battle of Leucopetra, and the image of it which Polybius was allowed to restore was a mere shadow, known by both parties to be illusory. Before many years were past, Achæa received, like the other provinces, her proconsul, and became an integral part of the great empire against which she had found it vain to attempt to struggle.

DETAILS OF THE LAST ACHÆAN WAR. Interference of the League between Athens and Oropus, and also between Sparta and Megalopolis, B.C. 150. Appeal of Sparta to Rome, answered by an ambiguous rescript, B.C. 149. Defeat of the Spartans by Damocritus, B.C. 148. Interference of Metellus. Dissolution of the League demanded. In return, the Roman envoys are insulted at Corinth. After fruitless negotiations, which consume most of the year B.C. 147, war is finally declared in B.C. 146, Critolaüs being Achæan general, and Metellus the commander on the Roman side. Heracleia having revolted from the League, Critolaüs proceeds to reduce it, but is forced to raise the siege by Metellus, who completely defeats him at Scarpheia, near Thermopylæ. Death of Critolaüs. Final effort made by Diæus. He collects a force at Corinth; gains a slight advantage over the Romans under Mummius, and then fights the pitched battle of Leucopetra, in which he is completely beaten. Corinth falls. Mummius plunders and destroys it.

PART IV.

History of the Smaller States and Kingdoms formed out of the Fragments of Alexander's Monarchy.

SOURCES. Besides most of the ancient writers mentioned above as authorities for the history of the Syrian, Egyptian, and Macedonian kingdoms, the following are of value:—(*a*) The fragments of MEMNON of Heracleia Pontica, published in the *Fragmenta Historicorum Græcorum* of C. MÜLLER. Paris, 1849; vol. iii. (*b*) The *Parthica* of ARRIAN, contained in the *Bibliotheca* of PHOTIUS (ed. BEKKER. Berolini, 1824; 2 vols. 4to). (*c*) The great work of the Jewish historian FL. JOSEPHUS, entitled *Antiquitatum Judaicarum libri xx.* (ed. K. E. RICHTER. Lipsiæ, 1825–7; 4 vols. 8vo). (*d*) AMMIANUS MARCELLINUS, *Historia Romana* (ed. WAGNER et ERFURDT. Lipsiæ, 1808; 3 vols. 8vo). And, especially for the Jewish history, (*e*) The Books of *Maccabees.*

Modern works on this portion of Ancient History treat, in general, only some branch of it, and will therefore find their most fitting place under the heads of the various states and kingdoms.

Besides the three main kingdoms of Syria, Egypt, and Macedonia, which were formed out of the great empire of

Rise of smaller states out of the fragments of Alexander's empire.

Alexander, there arose in the East at this time, partly out of Alexander's dominions, partly out of unconquered portions of the Persian territory, a number of independent lesser states, mostly monarchies, which played an important part in Oriental history during the decline of the Macedonian and the rise of the Roman power, and of which therefore some account must be given in a work like the present. The principal of these were, first, in Asia Minor, Pergamus, Bithynia, Paphlagonia, Pontus and Cappadocia; secondly, in the region adjoining, Greater and Lesser Armenia; thirdly, in the remoter East, Bactria and Parthia; and, fourthly, in the tract between Syria and Egypt, Judæa.

Our information on the subject of these kingdoms is very scanty. No ancient writer gives us any continuous or separate history of any of them. It is only so far as they become implicated in the affairs of the greater kingdoms that they attract the ancient writers' attention. Their history is thus very incomplete, and sometimes quite fragmentary. Much, however, has been done towards making out a continuous narrative, in some cases, by a skillful combination of scattered notices, and a judicious use of the knowledge derived from coins.

I. KINGDOM OF PERGAMUS.

Kingdom of Pergamus: its rise and general features.

1. In Western Asia the most important of the lesser kingdoms was that of Pergamus, which arose in the course of the war waged between Seleucus Nicator and Lysimachus. (See p. 250.) Small and insignificant at its origin, this kingdom gradually grew into power and importance by the combined military genius and prudence of its princes, who had the skill to side always with the stronger party. By assisting Syria against the revolted satrap Achæus, and Rome against Macedon and Syria, the kings of Pergamus gradually enlarged their dominion, until they were at length masters of fully half Asia Minor. At the same time, they had the good taste to encourage art and literature, and to render the capital of their kingdom a sort of rival to Alexandria. They adorned Pergamus with noble buildings, the remains of which may be seen at the present day. They warmly fostered the kindred arts of painting and sculpture. To advance literature, they established an extensive public library, and attracted to their capital a considerable number of learned men. A grammat-

ical and critical school grew up at Pergamus only second to the Alexandrian; and the Egyptian papyrus was outdone, as a literary material, by the *charta Pergamena* (parchment).

2. The founder of the kingdom was a certain Philetærus, a eunuch, whom Lysimachus had made governor of the place and guardian of his treasures. On the death of Lysimachus at the battle of Corupedion, Philetærus maintained possession of the fortress on his own account, and, by a judicious employment of the wealth whereof he had become possessed, in the hire of mercenaries and otherwise, he succeeded in establishing his independence, and even in transmitting his principality and treasure to his nephew, Eumenes, the son of Eumenes, his brother.

Reign of Philetærus, B.C. 281–263.

3. Eumenes I., the successor of Philetærus, was attacked, very shortly after his accession, by Antiochus I., the son and successor of Seleucus, but defeated him in a pitched battle near Sardis, and obtained an increase of territory by his victory. He reigned twenty-two years, and died from the effects of over-drinking, B.C. 241, bequeathing Pergamus to his first cousin, Attalus—the son of his father's brother, Attalus, by Antiochis, the daughter of Achæus.

Reign of Eumenes I., B.C. 263–241.

4. Attalus I. distinguished himself early in his reign (about B.C. 239) by a great victory over the Gauls, who had been now for above thirty years settled in Northern Phrygia (Galatia), whence they made continual plundering raids upon their neighbors. On obtaining this success, he for the first time assumed the title of "king," having previously, like his two predecessors, borne only that of "dynast." From this time we hear nothing of him for the space of about ten years, when we find him engaged in a war with Antiochus Hierax, the brother of Seleucus Callinicus, who was endeavoring to make himself king of Asia Minor. Having defeated this ambitious prince, and driven him out of Asia, Attalus succeeded in vastly enlarging his own dominions, which, about B.C. 226, included most of the countries west of the Halys and north of Taurus. But the Syrian monarchs were not inclined to submit to this loss of territory. First Seleucus Ceraunus (B.C. 226), and then Antiochus the Great, by his general Achæus (B.C. 223), made war upon Attalus, and by the year B.C. 221 his

Reign of Attalus I., B.C. 241–197.

conquests were all lost, and his dominions once more reduced to the mere Pergamene principality. But in B.C. 218 the tide again turned. By the help of Gallic mercenaries Attalus recovered Æolis; and two years later he made a treaty with Antiochus the Great against Achæus, who had been driven into revolt, which led to his receiving back from Antiochus, after Achæus's defeat and death, B.C. 214, most of the territory whereof he had been deprived seven years previously. Three years after this, B.C. 211, by joining the Ætolians and Romans against Philip, he laid the foundation of the later prosperity of his kingdom, which depended on its enjoying the favor and patronage of Rome. In vain Philip, after peace had been made, B.C. 204, turned upon Attalus, invading and ravaging his territory, and endeavoring to sweep his fleet from the sea. Attalus, in alliance with Rhodes, proved more than a match for this antagonist; and the battle of Chios, B.C. 201, avenged the desolation of Pergamus. In the second war between Rome and Philip, B.C. 199, the Pergamene monarch, though he was seventy years of age, took again an active part, supporting the Romans with his fleet, and giving them very valuable aid. But the exertion proved too much for his physical strength: he was seized with illness as he pleaded the cause of Rome in an assembly of the Bœotians, B.C. 197, and, having been conveyed to Pergamus, died there in the course of the same year. He left behind him four sons by his wife Apollonias, viz., Eumenes, Attalus, Philetærus, and Athenæus.

The encouragement of art and literature by the Pergamene monarchs dates from this reign. Already were the temples raised so noted for their magnificence and rare workmanship. The cordial reception of Attalus at Athens was no doubt in part owing to the character of a patron of learning which attached to him.

5. Eumenes II., the eldest of the sons of Attalus, succeeded him. He was a prudent and warlike prince, the inheritor at once of his father's talents and his policy. In the wars which Rome waged with Philip, with Antiochus, and with Perseus, he threw his weight on the Roman side, only on one occasion showing some slight symptoms of wavering, when in B.C. 169 he held some separate correspondence with Perseus. In return for the aid which he furnished against Antiochus, Rome, after the bat-

Reign of Eumenes II., B.C. 197–159.

tle of Magnesia, made over to him the greater part of the territory whereof she had deprived the Syrian king. Not only were Mysia, Lydia, Phrygia, Lycaonia, Pamphylia, and portions of Caria and Lycia, acknowledged now by the authority of Rome to be integral parts of the kingdom of Pergamus, but even the Chersonese, with its capital Lysimacheia, and the adjacent parts of Thrace, were attached to it. The Pergamene monarchy became in this way one of the greatest kingdoms of the East; and in the war which followed with Prusias of Bithynia, B.C. 183, it was still further enlarged by the addition of the Hellespontine Phrygia. In those waged with Pharnaces of Pontus, B.C. 183 to 179, and with the Gauls, about B.C. 168, it was, however, the object of Eumenes to maintain, rather than to enlarge, his boundaries. Towards the close of his long reign he seems to have become suspicious of the increasing power of the Romans, and to have been inclined to counteract their influence, so far as he dared. Hence the Romans distrusted him, and were disposed to support against him his brother Attalus, who was more thoroughly attached to their interests. It was perhaps fortunate for Eumenes that he died when he did: otherwise, he might have had to contend for the possession of his kingdom with his own brother, supported by all the power of Rome.

The patronage of art and literature, commenced by the first Attalus, was carried yet farther by Eumenes. He founded the great library at Pergamus, which was regarded as rivalling that of Alexandria, and adorned his capital with a vast number of splendid buildings. Crates of Mallus began to teach at Pergamus in his reign.

Reign of Attalus II. (Philadelphus), B.C. 159–138.

6. Though Eumenes left behind him a son, called Attalus, yet, as this Attalus was a mere boy, the crown was assumed by his uncle, Attalus, who took the surname of Philadelphus. Philadelphus reigned twenty-one years, from B.C. 159 to 138. In the earlier part of his reign he was actively engaged in various wars, restoring Ariarathes to his kingdom, about B.C. 157, helping Alexander Bala against Demetrius, B.C. 152, assisting the Romans to crush Andriscus, the pseudo-Philip, B.C. 149 to 148, and, above all, engaging in a prolonged contest with Prusias II., who would undoubtedly have conquered him and annexed Pergamus to Bithynia, if Attalus had not called in the aid

of Ariarathes of Cappadocia and Mithridates of Pontus, and also that of the Romans. The threats of Rome forced Prusias to abstain, and even to compensate Attalus for his losses. Attalus, nevertheless, was glad when, B.C. 149, an opportunity offered itself of exchanging Prusias for a more peaceful and friendly neighbor. With this view he supported Nicomedes in his rebellion against his father, and helped to establish him in his kingdom. A quiet time followed, which Attalus devoted to the strengthening of his power by the building of new cities, and to the encouragement of literature and art. Becoming infirm as he approached his eightieth year, he devolved the cares of the government on his minister, Philopœmen, who became the real ruler of the country. Finally, at the age of eighty-two, Philadelphus died, leaving the crown to his nephew and ward, Attalus, the son of Eumenes II., who must have been now about thirty years old.

Among the cities built by Philadelphus were Eumeneia in Phrygia, Philadelpheia in Lydia, and Attaleia in Pamphylia. He is said to have given 100 talents (nearly £25,000) for a picture, and to have offered for another 600,000 sesterces (£4375). He greatly augmented the library commenced by his predecessor. Crates of Mallus belongs mainly to his reign.

Reign of Attalus III. (Philometor), B.C. 138-133.

7. Attalus III., the son of Eumenes II., on ascending the throne took the name of Philometor, in honor of his mother, Stratonicé, the daughter of Ariarathes, king of Cappadocia. He reigned five years only, from B.C. 138 to 133; yet into this short space he crowded more crimes and odious actions than are ascribed to all the other kings of his house put together. He condemned to death without trial all the old counsellors and friends of his father and uncle, and at the same time destroyed their families. He then caused to be assassinated almost all those who held any office of trust in the kingdom. Finally, he turned against his own relations, and even put to death his mother, for whom he had professed a warm affection. At length remorse seized him, and he abandoned the cares of state, devoting himself to painting, sculpture, and gardening, on which last subject he wrote a work. He died of a fever, brought on, it is said, by a sun-stroke; and, by a will as strange as his conduct, left the Roman People his heir.

8. Rome readily accepted the legacy; but Aristonicus, a bastard son of Eumenes II., boldly disputed the prize with them, claiming the kingdom as his natural inheritance. He compelled the cities to acknowledge him, which had at first refused through fear of the Romans; and when Licinius Crassus was sent to take forcible possession of the country, Aristonicus defeated him, and took him prisoner, B.C. 131. In the year following, however, Aristonicus was himself defeated and made prisoner by Peperna; and the kingdom of Pergamus became shortly afterwards a Roman province.

Reign of Aristonicus, B.C. 133–130.

On the history of Pergamus, see the Essay of the Abbé SEVIN, *Recherches sur les Rois de Pergame*, in the *Mémoires de l'Académie des Inscriptions*, vol. xii. Paris, 1729; 4to. And CLINTON's *Kings of Pergamus*, in his *Fasti Hellenici*, vol. iii. Appendix, chap. vi.

On the remains of the ancient town, see CHOISEUL-GOUFFIER, *Voyage Pittoresque de la Grèce*. Paris, 1782–1809; 2 vols. folio; and ARUNDELL, *Visit to the Seven Churches in Asia*. London, 1828; 8vo.

II. KINGDOM OF BITHYNIA.

1. Though Bithynia was conquered by Crœsus (supra, p. 52), and submitted readily to Cyrus, when he absorbed the Lydian empire into his own dominions, yet we find, somewhat early in the Persian period, that the country is governed by native kings, who are not unfrequently at war with the satraps of Asia Minor. The first of these semi-independent monarchs is Dydalsus, who must have been contemporary with the earlier part of the Peloponnesian War. He was succeeded by Boteiras, probably the opponent of Pharnabazus (about B.C. 400), who left the crown to his son, Bas, B.C. 376. This king, the last under the Persians, held the throne for the long term of fifty years, and thus saw the commencement of the new state of things under the Macedonians.

Semi-independent kings under the Persians, B.C. 430–333.

2. With the dissolution of the Persian empire, which Alexander's conquests brought about, Bithynia acquired complete independence. Bas successfully resisted the attempts which Alexander made by his general Carantus (Caranus?) to reduce him, and at his death, in B.C. 326, he left to his son, Zipœtes, a flourishing and wholly autonomous kingdom.

Reign of Bas, B.C. 376–326.

3. Zipœtes, the son and successor of Bas, successfully maintained the independence, which he had inherited, against the attacks of Lysimachus and Antiochus Soter, while he threatened the Greek cities in his neighborhood, Heracleia Pontica, Astacus, and Chalcedon. He reigned forty-eight years, from B.C. 326 to B.C. 278, and left behind him four sons, Nicomedes, Zipœtes, and two others.

Reign of Zipœtes, B.C. 326–278.

Following the example of the contemporary Macedonian monarchs, Zipœtes built himself a new capital, which he called after his own name—Zipœtium under Mount Lyperus.

4. It would seem that, at the death of Zipœtes, a dispute concerning the succession arose between two of his sons. The eldest of them, Nicomedes, finding himself in danger of losing the kingdom to Zipœtes, his younger brother, invited the Gauls to cross over from Europe to his assistance, and by their aid defeated his brother and fully established his authority. He repelled by the same aid an attack on his independence made by Antiochus I. Nothing more is known of Nicomedes, except that he founded Nicomedeia on the Gulf of Astacus, and that he married two wives, Ditizelé and Etazeta, by the former of whom he had a single son, Zeïlas, while by the latter he had three children, Prusias, Tibœtes, and Lysandra, to whom, for their mother's sake, he desired to leave his kingdom.

Reign of Nicomedes I., B.C. 278 to about 248.

5. Zeïlas, who was living as an exile in Armenia, having obtained the services of a band of Gauls, entered Bithynia, and established his authority by a war in which he frequently defeated the partisans of his half-brothers. Very little is known of his history; but we may gather from some passages that he carried on successful wars with Paphlagonia and Cappadocia, in both of which countries he founded cities. He reigned about twenty years, and finally perished in an attempt which he made to destroy by treachery a number of Gallic chiefs at a banquet. He was succeeded by his son, Prusias.

Reign of Zeïlas, about B.C. 248–228.

6. Prusias I., known as "Prusias the Lame," ascended the throne probably about B.C. 228, and held it at least forty-five years. The earlier years of his reign were uneventful; but, from about B.C. 220 nearly to his death, he was engaged in a series of important

Reign of Prusias I., about B.C. 228–180.

wars, and brought into contact with some of the chief powers of Asia and Europe. By his unceasing energy he extended his dominions in several directions, and would have raised Bithynia into one of the most important of the Asiatic kingdoms, had he not unfortunately given offense to the Romans, first, by attacking their ally, Eumenes of Pergamus, and, secondly, by sheltering Hannibal. Not content with extorting the consent of Prusias to the surrender of the Carthaginian refugee, who was thereby driven to put an end to his own life, Rome, under the threat of war, compelled the Bithynian monarch to cede to Eumenes the whole of the Hellespontine Phrygia. He compensated himself to some extent by attacking Heracleia Pontica; but here he received the wound from which he derived his surname of "the Lame," and shortly after this he died, leaving the crown to a son called, like himself, Prusias.

DETAILS OF THIS REIGN. Prusias assists Rhodes against Byzantium, B.C. 220. Tibœtes, his uncle, is moved to assert his claims to the Bithynian crown; but, while on his way to do so, dies, B.C. 219. Prusias sends rich presents to the Rhodians after the destruction of their city by an earthquake, B.C. 217. Gains a great victory over the Gauls, B.C. 216. Joins Philip of Macedon in his first war against Rome, and attacks the territories of Attalus, who is thereby forced to return to Asia, B.C. 208. Between the first and second Macedonian War joins Philip in the siege of Cius, which he takes and keeps, changing its name to Prusa. At the same time, B.C. 203, he takes Myrleia and calls it Apameia, after his wife. From the second Macedonian War, and from the war between Rome and Antiochus the Great, he stands aloof; but after the Romans have withdrawn, B.C. 188, he ventures to attack, and, by Hannibal's help, defeats Eumenes. Rome hereupon interposes, demands Hannibal, B.C. 183, and makes Prusias compensate Eumenes by the cession of a province. Prusias then goes to war with Heracleia Pontica, and takes Cierus and Tius, but is wounded and soon afterwards dies, about B.C. 180.

Reign of Prusias II., B.C. 180-149.

7. Prusias II., the son and successor of Prusias I., was the most wicked and contemptible of the Bithynian monarchs. Though he had married, at his own request, the sister of the Macedonian king, Perseus, yet, when that monarch was attacked by the Romans, he lent him no aid, only venturing once, B.C. 169, to intercede for his brother-in-law by an embassy. When victory declared itself on the Roman side, he made the most abject submission, and thus obtained the assent of Rome to his retention of his kingdom. Like his father, he

lived on bad terms with Eumenes; and, when that king died and was succeeded by Attalus II., he ventured to begin a war, B.C. 156, which would certainly have been successful, had the Romans abstained from interference. They, however, by threats induced Prusias to consent to a peace, by which he relinquished the fruits of his victories, and even engaged to pay to Attalus the sum of 500 talents. Meanwhile, he had alienated the affections of his subjects by his cruelties and impieties, while Nicomedes, his son, had conciliated their regard. Viewing, therefore, his son as a rival, Prusias first sent him to Rome, and then gave orders that he should be assassinated. But his emissary betrayed him; and Nicomedes, learning his danger, with the connivance of the Senate, quitted Rome and returned as a pretender to his own country. There, being openly supported by Attalus, and known to have the good wishes of the Romans, he was received with general favor; and, having besieged his father in Nicomedeia, obtained possession of his person and put him to death, B.C. 149.

Reign of Nicomedes II., B.C. 149-91.

8. Nicomedes II., who now mounted the throne, followed the example of the Syrian and Egyptian kings in assuming the title of "Epiphanes," or "Illustrious." He reigned fifty-eight years, from B.C. 149 to 91, and took an active part in the wars which at this time desolated Asia Minor. It was his object to stand well with the Romans, and hence he willingly sent a contingent to their aid when they warred with Aristonicus of Pergamus (see p. 320), B.C. 133 to 130, and, professedly at any rate, rendered obedience to the various commands which they addressed to him. Still he made several attempts, all of them more or less displeasing to Rome, at increasing the power and extent of his kingdom. In B.C. 102 he attacked Paphlagonia in combination with Mithridates the Great, and took possession of a portion of it. Required by Rome to restore his conquest to the legitimate heir, he handed it over to one of his own sons, whom he pretended to be a Paphlagonian prince, and made him take the name of Pylæmenes. Shortly afterwards, B.C. 96, when Mithridates endeavored to annex Cappadocia, and Laodicé, the widow of the late king, fled to him, he married her, and, warmly espousing her cause, established her as queen in Cappadocia; whence, however, she

was shortly expelled by Mithridates. Finally, in B.C. 93, after the deaths of the two sons of Laodicé, he brought forward an impostor, who claimed to be also her son, and endeavored to obtain for him the crown of Cappadocia. Here, however, he overreached himself. The imposture was detected; and Rome not only refused to admit the title of his *protégé* to the Cappadocian crown, but required him likewise to abandon possession of Paphlagonia, which was to be restored to independence. Soon after this, the long reign of Nicomedes II. came to an end. His age at his decease can not have been much less than eighty.

9. Nicomedes II. left behind him two sons, Nicomedes and Socrates, who was surnamed "the Good" (Χρηστός). Nicomedes, who was the elder of the two, succeeded, and is known as Nicomedes III. He took the titles of "Epiphanes" and "Philopator." Scarcely was he seated on the throne when, at the instigation of Mithridates, his brother Socrates, accusing him of illegitimacy, claimed the kingdom, and, with the aid of an army which Mithridates furnished, drove Nicomedes out, and assumed the crown. Rome, however, in the next year, B.C. 90, by a simple decree reinstated Nicomedes, who proceeded, in B.C. 89, to retaliate upon Mithridates by plundering incursions into his territories. Thus provoked, Mithridates, in B.C. 88, collected a vast army, defeated Nicomedes on the Amneius, and drove him with his Roman allies out of Asia. The first Mithridatic War followed; and at its close, in B.C. 84, Nicomedes was restored to his kingdom for the second time, and had a tranquil reign after this for the space of ten years. Dying without issue, in B.C. 74, he left by will his kingdom to the Romans—a legacy which brought about the third and greatest "Mithridatic War."

Reign of Nicomedes III., B.C. 91–74.

The history of the kings of Bithynia has been treated of separately by several writers. Among them may be noticed:

SEVIN, *Recherches sur les Rois de Bithynie*, in the *Mémoires de l'Académie des Inscriptions*, vol. xv.

FOY-VAILLANT, J., *Regum Bithyniæ Historia*, in his *Achæmenidarum Imperium*. Paris, 1725; 4to.

CLINTON, H. F., *Kings of Bithynia*, in his *Fasti Hellenici*, vol. iii., Appendix, chap. vii.

III. KINGDOM OF PAPHLAGONIA.

1. Like Bithynia, Paphlagonia became semi-independent under the Achæmenian monarchs. As early as B.C. 400, the rulers of the country are said to have paid very little regard to the Great King's orders; and in B.C. 394 we find the monarch, Cotys, allying himself with Agesilaüs against Persia. Thirty or forty years later another king is mentioned as reduced by the Persian satrap, Datames. On the dissolution of the Persian empire, Paphlagonia was attached to his dominions by Mithridates of Pontus, and it continued for a considerable time to be a portion of the Pontic kingdom.

Kings during the Persian period.

EARLY PAPHLAGONIAN KINGS:—1. Corylas, about B.C. 400, allows the Ten Thousand to pass through his country. 2. Cotys, or Otys, makes alliance with Agesilaüs, and assists him in his war with Pharnabazus, B.C. 394. 3. Thyus, or Thys, noted for the magnificence of his entertainments, is attacked by Datames, at the command of Artaxerxes Mnemon, made prisoner, and carried to the court, where he continues to live in extraordinary splendor, about B.C. 375 to 365.

2. The circumstances under which, and the time when, Paphlagonia regained its independence, are unknown to us; but, soon after B.C. 200, we find the throne once more occupied by native monarchs, who are entangled in the wars of the period. These princes have a difficulty in maintaining themselves against the monarchs of Pontus on the one hand, and those of Bithynia on the other; but they nevertheless hold the throne till B.C. 102, when, the last native king, Pylæmenes I., dying without issue, Mithridates the Great and Nicomedes II. conjointly seize the country, and the latter establishes on the throne one of his own sons, who rules for about eight years, when Mithridates expels him and takes possession of the whole territory.

LATER PAPHLAGONIAN KINGS:—1. Morzes or Morzias, fights against the Romans in the Gallo-Grecian War, B.C. 189. Is attacked and conquered by Pharnaces, about B.C. 181, but reinstated in his dominions and compensated in B.C. 179. 2. Pylæmenes I. assists the Romans in their war against Aristonicus of Pergamus, B.C. 131. Said to have bequeathed his kingdom to Mithridates. 3. Pylæmenes II., the son of Nicomedes II., of Bithynia. Placed on the throne by his father, B.C. 102. Forced to retire, about B.C. 90.

IV. KINGDOM OF PONTUS.

1. The satrapy of Cappadocia appears to have been conferred by Darius Hystaspis as an hereditary fief on Otanes, one of the seven conspirators, who was descended from the ancient Arian kings of Cappadocia. It continued to form a single province of the empire, and to be governed by satraps descended from Otanes, till the year B.C. 363, when Ariobarzanes, the son of the Mithridates who was satrap in the time of Xenophon, rebelled, and made himself king of the portion of Cappadocia which lay along the coast, and which was thence called "Pontus" by the Greeks. Inland Cappadocia continued to be a province of Persia. Ariobarzanes reigned twenty-six years, from B.C. 363 to 337, when he was succeeded by his son, Mithridates I. (commonly called Mithridates II.), who held the kingdom at the time of the Macedonian invasion.

Foundation of the kingdom by Ariobarzanes I., B.C. 363.

2. Mithridates I., who ascended the throne B.C. 337, seems to have remained neutral during the contest between Darius Codomannus and Alexander. On the reduction of Cappadocia by Perdiccas, B.C. 322, he was, however, compelled to submit to the Macedonians, after which he enjoyed for a time the favor of Antigonus and helped him in his wars. But Antigonus, growing jealous of him, basely plotted his death; whereupon he returned to Pontus and resumed a separate sovereignty, about B.C. 318. In B.C. 317 he supported Eumenes against Antigonus; and in B.C. 302 he was about to join the league of the satraps against the same monarch, when Antigonus, suspecting his intention, caused him to be assassinated.

Reign of Mithridates I., B.C. 337–302.

3. Mithridates II., the son of Mithridates I., succeeded. He added considerably to his hereditary dominions by the acquisition of parts of Cappadocia and Paphlagonia, and even ventured to conclude an alliance with the Greeks of Heracleia Pontica, B.C. 281, whom he undertook to defend against Seleucus. According to Diodorus, he reigned thirty-six years, from B.C. 302 to 266. He left the crown to his son, Ariobarzanes.

Reign of Mithridates II., B.C. 302–266.

4. Ariobarzanes II., who appears to have reigned about twenty-one years, from B.C. 266 to 245, did little to distin-

Reign of Ariobarzanes II., B.C. 266 to about 245.

guish himself. He repulsed an attack of Ptolemy (Euergetes?) by the assistance of the Gauls, but afterwards quarrelled with that fickle people, whose close neighborhood was very injurious to his kingdom. He also obtained possession of the town of Amastris upon the Euxine, which was surrendered to him by Eumenes, its dynast. On his death he was succeeded by his son, Mithridates, who was a minor.

Reign of Mithridates III., about B.C. 245–190.

5. Mithridates III., the most distinguished of the earlier Pontic monarchs, made it his object to strengthen and augment his kingdom by alliances with the other monarchs and princes of Asia, rather than by warfare. As soon as he had attained to manhood, he married a sister of Seleucus Callinicus, with whom he received the province of Phrygia as a dowry. In B.C. 222, he gave his daughter, Laodicé, in marriage to Antiochus the Great, the son of Callinicus, and at the same time married another daughter, called also Laodicé, to Achæus, the cousin of Antiochus. He did not allow these connections, however, to fetter his political action. In the war between Seleucus Callinicus and Antiochus Hierax, he sided with the latter, and on one occasion he inflicted a most severe defeat upon his brother-in-law, who lost 20,000 men. In B.C. 220, he turned his arms against the Greeks of Sinôpé, but this town, which was assisted by the Rhodians, appears to have maintained itself against his efforts. It is uncertain how long Mithridates III. reigned, but the conjecture is reasonable that he died about B.C. 190.

Reign of Pharnaces I., about B.C. 190–160.

6. He was succeeded on the throne by his son, Pharnaces, who conquered Sinôpé, and made it the royal residence, about B.C. 183. This king soon afterwards involved himself in a war with Eumenes of Pergamus (see p. 318), of whose greatly augmented power he had naturally become jealous. Rome endeavored to hinder hostilities from breaking out, but in B.C. 181 Pharnaces took the field, overran Paphlagonia, expelling the king, Morzes or Morzias, and poured his troops into Cappadocia and Galatia. At first, he met with considerable success; but after a while the tide turned, and in B.C. 179 he was glad to make peace on condition of giving up all his conquests except the town of Sinôpé. After this we hear nothing

more of him; but he seems to have lived some considerable time longer, probably till about B.C. 160.

7. Pharnaces I. was succeeded by his son, Mithridates, who took the name of "Euergetes," and reigned about forty years, from near B.C. 160 to 120. He entered into alliance with Attalus II., king of Pergamus, and lent him important assistance in his wars with Prusias II. of Bithynia, B.C. 154. A few years later he made alliance with Rome, and sent a contingent to bear a part in the Third Punic War, B.C. 150 to 146. He likewise assisted Rome in the war against Aristonicus, B.C. 131, and at its close received the Greater Phrygia as the reward of his services. His end was tragical. About B.C. 120, his own immediate attendants conspired against him, and assassinated him at Sinôpé, where he held his court.

Reign of Mithridates IV., about B.C. 160–120.

8. Mithridates, the elder of his two sons, succeeded, and took the title of "Eupator," for which, however, modern historians have generally substituted the more high-sounding epithet of "the Great." He was undoubtedly the most able of all the Pontic kings, and will bear comparison with any of the Asiatic monarchs since Darius Hystaspis. Ascending the throne while he was still a minor, and intrusted to guardians whom he suspected, it was not till about B.C. 112 that he could undertake any important enterprise. But the interval of about eight years was well employed in the training of his own mind and body—the former by the study of languages, whereof he is said to have spoken twenty-five; the latter by perpetual hunting expeditions in the roughest and most remote regions. On reaching the age of twenty, and assuming the conduct of affairs, he seems to have realized at once the danger of his position as ruler of a petty kingdom, which must, by its position upon her borders, be almost immediately attacked by Rome, and could not be expected to make any effectual resistance. Already, during his minority, the grasping republic had seized his province of Phrygia; and this was felt to be merely a foretaste of the indignities and injuries with which, so long as he was weak, he would have to put up. Mithridates therefore determined, not unwisely, to seek to strengthen his kingdom, and to raise it into a condition in which it might be a match for Rome.

Reign of Mithridates V. (the Great), B.C. 120–64.

With this object, in B.C. 112, he boldly started forth on a career of Eastern conquest. Here Rome could not interfere with him; and in the space of about seven years he had added to his dominions the Lesser Armenia, Colchis, the entire eastern coast of the Black Sea, the Chersonesus Taurica, or kingdom of the Bosporus (the modern Crimea), and even the whole tract westward from that point to the Tyras, or Dniester. Having thus enlarged his dominions, and having further strengthened himself by alliances with the wild tribes on the Danube, Getæ, Sarmatæ, and others, whom he hoped one day to launch upon Italy, he returned to Asia Minor, and commenced a series of intrigues and intermarriages, calculated to give him greater power in this quarter.

His conquests.

Marriage of Mithridates's sister, Laodicé, to Ariarathes VI., king of Cappadocia, probably in the early part of his reign, about B.C. 120 to 115. Marriage of his daughter, Cleopatra, to Tigranes, king of the Greater Armenia, about B.C. 96. Alliance with Nicomedes II. of Bithynia, for the partition of Paphlagonia, B.C. 102. Occupation of Galatia the same year. First seizure of Cappadocia, and consequent war with Nicomedes (see p. 323), B.C. 96. Nicomedes defeated, and Ariarathes VII., son of Ariarathes VI. and Laodicé, set up. Quarrel picked with this prince by Mithridates, who invites him to a conference and murders him, about B.C. 94. Attempt to establish his own son on the Cappadocian throne fails, B.C. 93. Attempt to place Socrates on the throne of Bithynia, B.C. 90, also fails.

9. Although it must have been evident, both to the Romans and to Mithridates, that peace between them could not be maintained much longer, yet neither party was as yet prepared for an actual rupture. The hands of Rome were tied by the condition of Italy, where the "Social War" impended; and Mithridates regarded it as prudent to temporize a little longer. He therefore submitted, in B.C. 92, to the decree of the Roman Senate, which assigned Cappadocia to a native monarch, Ariobarzanes, and in B.C. 90 to another decree which reinstated Nicomedes on the throne of Bithynia. When, however, in the following year, Nicomedes, encouraged by the Romans, proceeded to invade the Pontic kingdom, and the demand which Mithridates made for redress produced no result, it seemed to him that the time was come when he must change his policy, and, laying aside all pretense of friendliness, commence the actual struggle.

Rupture with Rome, and First War, B.C. 88–84.

FIRST ROMAN WAR. The war began, B.C. 88, with the invasion of Cappadocia by Mithridates, who took possession of the country and drove out Ariobarzanes. Bithynia was then invaded, and the forces of Nicomedes were completely routed on the Amneius. His Roman allies also suffered a severe defeat. Mithridates overran Galatia, Phrygia, and even the Roman province of Asia, becoming master of all Asia Minor except a few towns in Lycia and Ionia. Having taken up his winter-quarters at Pergamus, he gave the fatal order that all Romans and Italians in Asia should on one day be massacred—an order which was generally obeyed, and which caused the death of 80,000 persons. The next year, B.C. 87, Mithridates sent his general, Archelaüs, with a powerful fleet and army, into Greece; and in B.C. 86 he sent a second army to reinforce the first under Taxilas. But the Romans under Sulla totally defeated the entire combined force at Chæroneia in the same year, and Mithridates had to send over a third army, which he placed under the command of Dorylaüs. Hitherto the Pontic prince had been the assailant, and had kept the war in the enemy's country, but now a change occurred. A second Roman army under Fimbria, a Marian partisan, took the field, and carrying the war into Asia, made Mithridates tremble for his own territory. His generals lost a great battle in Bithynia, B.C. 85, and he himself, forced to become a fugitive, with difficulty avoided falling into his enemies' hands. Soon afterwards Archelaüs and Dorylaüs suffered a severe reverse in Greece; and Mithridates felt himself obliged to sue for peace. The first negotiation was unsuccessful; but in B.C. 84 terms were agreed upon. The Pontic prince surrendered all his conquests, agreed to pay a sum of 2000 talents (nearly half a million sterling) to indemnify Rome for the cost of the war, and also delivered into the victor's hands a fleet of seventy ships. Nicomedes and Ariobarzanes were restored to their kingdoms, and the Roman authority was re-established in the province of "Asia."

Revolts, and Second Roman War, B.C. 83–82.

10. The disasters suffered by Mithridates in the Roman War encouraged the nations which he had subjected in the East to revolt. The kingdom of the Bosporus threw off its allegiance, the Colchians rebelled, and other nations in the same quarter showed symptoms of disaffection. Mithridates proceeded to collect a large fleet and army for the reduction of the rebels, when his enterprise had to be relinquished on account of a second and wholly unprovoked Roman War. Murena, the Roman commander in Asia, suddenly attacked him, almost without a pretext, B.C. 83; and it was not till the close of the following year that peace was re-established.

SECOND ROMAN WAR. Murena invades Pontus at the instigation of Archelaüs, who, having incurred the suspicion of ill-faith, had fled from the court of his master and been received with honor by the Romans. Mithridates makes no resistance, but sends to Rome to complain, B.C. 83. The Senate by a legate commands Murena to desist; but, disregarding the injunction, he prepares for a second invasion. Mithridates meets him on the banks of the Halys, and gains a complete victory. Murena escapes with difficulty into Phrygia, while Cappadocia is occupied by Mithridates. The Senate now sends a second legate, and peace is restored, Mithridates once more evacuating Cappadocia, B.C. 82.

Preparations for the final struggle.

11. The conclusion of the Second Roman War allowed Mithridates to complete the reduction of his revolted subjects, which he accomplished without much difficulty between the years B.C. 81 and 74. He suffered, however, during this interval, some heavy losses in an attempt which he made to subdue the Achæans of the Caucasus. But it was not so much in wars as in preparations for war that the Pontic monarch employed the breathing-space allowed him by the Romans after the failure of the attack of Murena. Vast efforts were made by him to collect and discipline a formidable army; troops were gathered from all quarters, even from the banks of the Danube; the Roman arms and training were adopted; fresh alliances were concluded or attempted; the fleet was raised to the number of 400 triremes; nothing was left undone that care or energy could accomplish towards the construction of a power which might fairly hope to hold its own when the time for a final trial of strength with Rome should arrive.

Alliance of Mithridates with Sertorius, about B.C. 75. Renewal of the alliance with Tigranes. Attempts to conclude treaties with Phraates, king of Parthia, and with various Scythic chiefs. Sarmatians, Scyths, and Bastarnæ are induced to serve in the Pontic army.

Breaking out of the Third Roman War, B.C. 74.

12. The armed truce might have continued some years longer, for Mithridates still hoped to increase his power, and Rome was occupied by the war in Spain against the rebel Sertorius, had not the death of Nicomedes III., king of Bithynia, in B.C. 74, brought about a crisis. That monarch, having no issue, followed the example of Attalus, king of Pergamus, in leaving his dominions by will to the Roman people. Had Mithridates allowed Rome to take possession, the Pontic kingdom would have been laid open to attack along the whole of its western border; Rome would have been brought within five days' march of Sinôpé; and thus the position of Pontus, when war broke out, would have been greatly weakened. Mithridates therefore resolved to seize Bithynia before Rome could occupy it. But this act was equivalent to a declaration of war, since the

honor of the great republic could not allow of her tamely submitting to the seizure of what she regarded as her own property.

General sketch of the war. Causes of the success of the Romans.

13. The Third War of Mithridates with Rome, which broke out in B.C. 74, was protracted to B.C. 65, and thus lasted nearly nine years. The scene of the war was Asia. Its result was scarcely doubtful from the first, for the Asiatic levies of Mithridates, though armed after the Roman fashion and disciplined to a certain extent, were no match for the trained veterans of the Roman legions. The protraction of the war was owing, in the first place, to the genius and energy of the Pontic monarch, who created army after army, and who gradually learnt the wisdom of avoiding pitched battles, and wasting the power of the enemy by cutting off his supplies, falling on his detachments, entangling him in difficult ground, and otherwise harassing and annoying him. It was further owing to the participation in it of a new foe, Tigranes, who brought to the aid of his neighbor and connection a force exceeding his own, and very considerable resources. Rome was barely capable of contending at one and the same time with two such kingdoms as those of Pontus and Armenia; and up to the close of B.C. 67, though her generals had gained many signal victories, she had made no great impression on either of her two adversaries. The war, if conducted without any change of plan, might still have continued for another decade of years, before the power of resistance possessed by the two kings would have been exhausted. But the genius of Pompey devised a scheme by which an immediate and decisive result was made attainable. His treaty with Phraates, king of Parthia, brought a new power into the field—a power fully capable of turning the balance in favor of the side whereto it attached itself. The attitude of Phraates at the opening of the campaign of B.C. 66 paralyzed Tigranes; and the Pontic monarch, deprived of the succors on which he had hitherto greatly depended, though he still resisted, and even fought a battle against his new antagonist, was completely and manifestly overmatched. Defeated near the Armenian border by the Romans under Pompey, and forbidden to seek a refuge in Armenia by his timid and suspicious brother-in-law, he had no choice but to yield

his home dominions to the victor, and to retire to those remote territories of which he had become possessed by conquest. Even Pompey shrank from following his beaten foe into these inhospitable regions, and with the passage of Mithridates across the river Phasis, his third war with Rome came to an end.

DETAILS OF THE WAR. B.C. 74. Advance of Mithridates through Bithynia. His victory over Cotta. Sieges of Chalcedon and Cyzicus.—B.C. 73. Siege of Cyzicus abandoned. Great losses of Mithridates. His army defeated by Lucullus. Double defeat of his fleet. He, however, takes Heracleia Pontica, and, returning to his capital, raises a fresh army, and takes up a position at Cabeira.—B.C. 72. Lucullus besieges Amisus, but when Mithridates does not move to its relief, he raises the siege and marches upon Cabeira. Numerous partial encounters follow. At length Mithridates determines to move his camp, whereupon a panic ensues; his army is attacked and routed, and he himself with difficulty escapes and flies to Tigranes, in Armenia.—B.C. 71 to 70. A pause in the war now occurs, while the Romans endeavor to persuade Tigranes to surrender Mithridates. On his final refusal, B.C. 70, he too is declared a public enemy, and the war is transferred into his territories.—B.C. 69. Great victory of Lucullus over Tigranes, near Tigranocerta, and capture of that city. Ineffectual appeal of Mithridates to the Parthian king, Phraates.—B.C. 68. Second victory of Lucullus over Tigranes and Mithridates at Artaxata. Siege of Nisibis. Mithridates returns with an army to Pontus, defeats Fabius, and shuts him up in Cabeira.—B.C. 67. Great victory of Mithridates over Triarius: 7000 Romans slain. Action of Lucullus paralyzed by the disaffection of his soldiers. Mithridates and Tigranes recover Pontus and Cappadocia.—B.C. 66. Lucullus recalled, and Pompey sent into Asia. Treaty of friendship and alliance made with Phraates. Tigranes devotes all his efforts to the defense of his southern frontier. Mithridates retreats before Pompey, but is compelled to fight at great disadvantage, and loses almost his whole army. He flies to Synoria, where he once more collects a force, and prepares to move into Armenia; but Tigranes declines to receive him, and he therefore retreats eastward, crosses the Phasis and winters at Dioscurias, in the modern Mingrelia. The war now comes to an end, though no peace is made, Mithridates having practically relinquished his kingdom and withdrawn to regions whither Rome does not care to follow him.

14. Mithridates, in B.C. 65, retreated from Dioscurias to Panticapæum, and established himself in the old kingdom of the Bosporus. Such a principality was, however, too narrow for his ambition. Having vainly attempted to come to terms with Pompey, he formed the wild design of renewing the struggle with Rome by attacking her in a new quarter. It was his intention to proceed westward round the European side of the Black Sea, and to throw himself upon the

Roman frontier, perhaps even to march upon Italy. But neither his soldiers nor his near relatives were willing to embark in so wild a project. Its announcement caused general disaffection, which at last ended in conspiracy. His own son, Pharnaces, headed the malcontents; and the aged monarch, finding no support in any quarter, caused himself to be dispatched by one of his guards, B.C. 63. The bulk of Pontus became a Roman province, though a portion continued till the time of Nero to be ruled by princes belonging to the old royal stock.

Among works on the kingdom of Pontus may be mentioned the following:

FOY-VAILLANT, J., *Reges Ponti*, in his *Achæmenidarum Imperium* (see p. 324).

WOLTERSDORF, J. E., *Commentatio vitam Mithridatis Magni per annos digestam sistens.* Gottingæ, 1812.

CLINTON, H. F., *Kings of Pontus*, in his *Fasti Hellenici*, vol. iii., Appendix, chap. viii.

V. KINGDOM OF CAPPADOCIA.

1. After the division of the Cappadocian satrapy into two provinces, a northern and a southern (see p. 326), the latter continued subject to Persia, the government being, however, hereditary in a branch of the same family which had made itself independent in the northern province. The Datames and Ariamnes of Diodorus held this position, and are not to be regarded as independent kings. It was only when the successes of Alexander loosed the bands which held the Persian empire together (B.C. 331) that the satrap, Ariarathes, the son of Ariamnes, assumed the airs of independence, and, resisting the attack of Perdiccas, was by him defeated, made a prisoner, and crucified, B.C. 322.

Independence assumed by Ariarathes I., B.C. 331.

2 Perdiccas, having subjected Cappadocia, made over his conquest to Eumenes, who continued, nominally at any rate, its ruler until his death in B.C. 316. Cappadocia then revolted under Ariarathes II., the nephew of Ariarathes I., who defeated and slew the Macedonian general, Amyntas, expelled the foreign garrisons, and reestablished the independence of his country. No attempt seems to have been made to dispossess him either by Antigonus or Seleucus; and Ariarathes left his crown to the eldest of his sons, Ariamnes, probably about B.C. 280.

Reign of Ariarathes II., about B.C. 315–280.

3. The next two kings, Ariamnes, and his son, Ariarathes

III., are little heard of in history: they appear to have reigned quietly but ingloriously. A friendly connection between the royal houses of Cappadocia and Syria was established in the reign of the former, who obtained as a wife for his much-loved son, Stratonicé, the daughter of Antiochus Theus. The two reigns of Ariamnes and Ariarathes III. appear to have covered a space of about sixty years, from B.C. 280 to 220. Ariarathes III. left the crown to a son, bearing the same name, who was at the time of his father's death an infant.

Reigns of Ariamnes and Ariarathes III., about B.C. 280–220.

4. The reign of Ariarathes IV. is remarkable as being that which ended the comparative isolation of Cappadocia, and brought the kingdom into close relation with the other monarchies of Asia Minor, and not only with them, but also with the great republic of the West. The history of Cappadocia is henceforth inextricably intermixed with that of the other kingdoms of Western Asia, and has been to a great extent anticipated in what has been said of them. Ariarathes IV., who was the first cousin of Antiochus the Great, married in B.C. 192 his daughter Antiochis, and, being thus doubly connected with the Seleucid family, entered into close alliance with the Syrian king, assisted him in his war against Rome, and bore his part in the great battle of Magnesia by which the power of the Syrian empire was broken, B.C. 190. Having thus incurred the hostility of the Romans, and at the same time become sensible of the greatness of their power, Ariarathes proceeded, in B.C. 188, to deprecate their wrath, and by an alliance with the Roman *protégé*, Eumenes, which was cemented by a marriage, succeeded in appeasing the offended republic and obtained favorable terms. Ariarathes then assisted Eumenes in his war with Pharnaces of Pontus, B.C. 183 to 179, after which he was engaged in a prolonged quarrel with the Gauls of Galatia, who wished to annex a portion of his territory. He continued on the most friendly terms with Rome from the conclusion of peace in B.C. 188 till his death in the winter of B.C. 163–2. His reign lasted fifty-eight years.

Reign of Ariarathes IV., B.C. 220–162.

Ariarathes IV. must have been married at least twice. By his first wife he had a daughter, married to Eumenes of Pergamus, in B.C. 188. By his second, Antiochis, the daughter of Antiochus the Great, he had a son, Mithridates, who took the name of Ariarathes at his accession. He had also two other reputed sons by Antiochis, Ariarathes, and Holophernes or Orophernes, supposititious children whom Antiochis had imposed upon him when she thought herself barren.

Reign of Ariarathes V., B.C. 162–131.

5. Ariarathes V., surnamed "Philopator" from the affection which he bore his father, maintained the alliance between Cappadocia and Rome with great fidelity. Solicited by Demetrius Soter to enter into alliance with him and to connect his family with that of the Seleucidæ once more by a marriage, he declined out of regard for Rome. Angered by his refusal, Demetrius set up against him the pretender, Orophernes, B.C. 158, and for a time deprived him of his kingdom. The Romans, however, with the help of Attalus II., restored him in the year following. After this Ariarathes lent Attalus important aid in his war with Prusias of Bithynia, B.C. 156 to 154, and when Aristonicus attempted to resist the Roman occupation of that province, B.C. 133, he joined the Romans in person, and lost his life in their cause, B.C. 131.

The character of Ariarathes V. stands out in remarkable contrast to those of almost all his contemporaries. He was a student of philosophy, and made Cappadocia a residence of learned men. Out of respect for his father he would accept no share in the government during his lifetime. When Artaxias of Armenia suggested to him an iniquitous appropriation of a neighboring kingdom, he not only declined the overture, but was indignant that it had been made to him. No cruel or perfidious deed of his doing is upon record. He conciliated the affection of his subjects and commanded the respect of his neighbors. The history of the three centuries after Alexander shows us no other monarch who led so pure and blameless a life.

Regency of Laodicé, and reign of Ariarathes VI., B.C. 131–96.

6. Ariarathes V. seems to have left behind him as many as six sons, none of whom, however, had reached maturity. Laodicé, therefore, the queen-mother, became regent; and, being an ambitious and unscrupulous woman, she contrived to poison five out of her six sons before they were of age to reign, and so kept the government in her own hands. One, the youngest, was preserved, like the Jewish king, Joash, by his near relatives; and, after the death of Laodicé, who fell a victim to the popular indignation, he ascended the throne under the name of Ariarathes VI. Little is known of this king, except that he made alliance with Mithridates the Great, and married a sister of that monarch, named also Laodicé, about B.C. 115. By her he had two sons, both named Ariarathes. He was mur-

dered by an emissary of Mithridates, B.C. 96, when his sons were just growing into men.

7. On the removal of Ariarathes VI. his dominions were seized by his brother-in-law, Mithridates, who designed to assume the rule of them himself; but Laodicé, the widow of the late king, having called in the aid of Nicomedes II., king of Bithynia, whom she married, Mithridates, in order to retain his hold on Cappadocia, found it necessary to allow the country its own monarch, and accordingly set up as king, B.C. 96 or 95, Ariarathes VII., elder son of Ariarathes VI., and consequently the legitimate monarch. This prince, however, showing himself too independent, Mithridates, in B.C. 94, invited him to a conference and slew him; after which he placed on the throne a son of his own, aged eight years, whose name he changed to Ariarathes. But the Cappadocians rose in rebellion against this attempt, and raised to the throne another Ariarathes, the son of Ariarathes VI., and the younger brother of Ariarathes VII., who endeavored to establish himself, but was driven out by Mithridates and died shortly afterwards. By the death of this prince the old royal family of Cappadocia became extinct; and though pretenders to the throne, claiming a royal descent, were put forward both by Mithridates and Nicomedes, yet, as the nullity of these claims was patent, Rome permitted the Cappadocians to choose themselves a new sovereign, which they did in B.C. 93, when Ariobarzanes was proclaimed king.

Reigns of Ariarathes VII., and Ariarathes VIII., B.C. 96–93.

8. Ariobarzanes had scarcely ascended the throne when he was expelled by Tigranes, king of Armenia, and forced to fly to Rome for protection. The Romans reinstated him in the next year, B.C. 92; and he reigned in peace for four years, B.C. 92 to 88, when he was again ejected, this time by Mithridates, who seized his territories, and retained possession of them during the whole of his first war with the Romans. At the peace, made in B.C. 84, Ariobarzanes was once more restored. He now continued undisturbed till B.C. 67, when Mithridates and Tigranes in combination drove him from his kingdom for the third time, after which, in B.C. 66, he received his third restoration at the hands of Pompey. About two years later he abdicated in favor of his son, Ariobarzanes.

Reign of Ariobarzanes I., B.C. 93–64.

9. Ariobarzanes II., the friend of Cicero, began to reign probably in B.C. 64. He took the titles of "Eusebes" (the Pious) and "Philorhomæus" (lover of the Romans), and appears to have aimed steadily at deserving the latter appellation. It was difficult, however, to please all parties in the civil wars. Ariobarzanes sided with Pompey against Cæsar, and owed it to the magnanimity of the latter that he was not deprived of his kingdom after Pharsalia, but forgiven and allowed an increase of territory. In the next civil war he was less fortunate. Having ventured to oppose the "Liberators," he was seized and put to death by Cassius, B.C. 42, after he had reigned between twenty-one and twenty-two years.

Reign of Ariobarzanes II., B.C. 64–42.

10. After Philippi, Antony conferred the crown of Cappadocia on Ariarathes IX., the son (apparently) of the last king. It was not long, however, before this prince lost his favor, and, in B.C. 36, he was put to death by Antony's orders, who wanted his throne for Archelaüs, one of his creatures. Archelaüs, the grandson of Mithridates's general of the same name, ruled Cappadocia from B.C. 36 to A.D. 15, when he was summoned to Rome by Tiberius, who had been offended by the circumstance that Archelaüs paid him no attention when he was in voluntary exile at Rhodes. Archelaüs in vain endeavored to excuse himself: he was retained at Rome by the tyrant, and died there, either of a disease, or possibly by his own hand, about A.D. 17. His kingdom was then reduced into the form of a Roman province.

Reigns of Ariarathes IX. and Archelaüs.

On the Cappadocian history, see CLINTON'S *Kings of Cappadocia*, in his *Fasti Hellenici*, vol. iii., Appendix, chap. ix.

VI. KINGDOM OF THE GREATER ARMENIA.

1. Armenia, which, from the date of the battle of Ipsus, B.C. 301, formed a portion of the empire of the Seleucidæ, revolted on the defeat of Antiochus the Great by the Romans, B.C. 190, and became split up into two kingdoms, Armenia Major and Armenia Minor, the latter lying on the west bank of the Euphrates. The first king of Armenia Major was Artaxias, who had been a general of Antiochus. He built Artaxata, the capital, and

Independence established, B.C. 190. Early monarchs.

reigned probably about twenty-five years, when he was attacked, defeated, and made prisoner by Antiochus Epiphanes, about B.C. 165, who recovered Armenia to the Syrian empire. How long the subjection continued is uncertain; but about B.C. 100 we find an Armenian king mentioned, who seems to be independent, and who carries on war with the Parthian monarch, Mithridates. This king, who is called by Justin Ortoadistes, appears to have been succeeded, B.C. 96, by the greatest of the Armenian monarchs, Tigranes I., who took the part already described (supra, p. 332) in the great war between Mithridates of Pontus and the Romans.

Reign of Tigranes I., B.C. 96-55. His early wars.

2. Tigranes I., who was a descendant of Artaxias, raised Armenia from the condition of a petty kingdom to a powerful and extensive empire. Compelled in his early years to purchase a peace of the Parthians by a cession of territory, he soon afterwards, about B.C. 90 to 87, not only recovered his provinces, but added to his dominions the important countries of Atropatênê and Gordyênê (or Upper Mesopotamia), chastising the Parthian monarch on his own soil, and gaining for himself a great reputation. He then determined to attack the Syrian kingdom, which was verging to its fall under Philip, son of Grypus. Having crossed the Euphrates, he easily made himself master of the entire Syrian territory, including the province of Cilicia; and for fourteen years, B.C. 83 to 69, his dominions reached across the whole of Western Asia, from the borders of Pamphylia to the shores of the Caspian. It was during these years that he founded his great capital of Tigranocerta, and gave grievous offense to Rome by his conduct towards her *protégé*, Ariobarzanes of Cappadocia, whose territory he ravaged, B.C. 75, carrying off more than 300,000 people. Soon afterwards he added to the offense by receiving and supporting Mithridates, and thus he drew the Roman arms upon himself and his kingdom.

War with the Romans, B.C. 69-66.

WAR OF TIGRANES WITH ROME. B.C. 69. Tigranes invades Lycaonia. Lucullus proceeds into Armenia, defeats Mithrobarzanes, and threatens Tigranocerta. Tigranes marches to the relief of his capital. Great battle between the two armies. Tigranes completely defeated. Tigranocerta falls. Defection of Syria, which is given to Antiochus Asiaticus, the son of Eusebes.—B.C. 68. Tigranes, accompanied by Mithridates, retreats to the Armenian highlands, whither they are followed by Lucullus. Battle near Artaxata, another Roman victory. Disaffection of the troops of Lucullus prevents any further successes. Lucullus quits Armenia, and marches southward into Mesopotamia. Siege and fall of Nisibis.—B.C. 67. Tigranes and Mithridates take the offensive; the latter recovers Pontus; the former reoccupies Cappadocia, and invades Armenia Minor. The movements of Lucullus are paralyzed by the disaffection of his troops.—B.C. 66. Command of Pompey, who allies himself with the Parthian king, Phraates. Rebellion of the young Tigranes, who is supported by Phraates against his father. Invasion of Armenia by Phraates. Second invasion, later in the year, by Pompey. Submission of Tigranes. Terms granted him.

Later years of Tigranes.

3. The result of the war with Rome was the loss by Tigranes of all his conquests. He retained merely his original kingdom of the Greater Armenia. The fidelity, however, which he showed towards Pompey led to the enlargement of his dominions, B.C. 65, by the addition of Gordyênê; and the Roman alliance was otherwise serviceable to him in the war which he continued to wage with Parthia. He appears to have died about B.C. 55, eleven years after the conclusion of his peace with Rome, and one year before the expedition of Crassus.

Reign of Artavasdes I., B.C. 55–34.

4. Tigranes was succeeded by his son, Artavasdes I., who began his reign by following out the later policy of his father, and endeavoring to keep on good terms with the Romans. He bore a part in the great expedition of Crassus against the Parthians, B.C. 54; and it was only when Orodes, the Parthian king, advanced against him, and he was unable to obtain any assistance from Rome, that he consented to a Parthian alliance, and gave his daughter in marriage to Orodes's son, Pacorus. This led him, when Pacorus invaded Syria, B.C. 51, to take up an attitude of hostility to the Romans. But, at a later date, when Antony threatened the Parthians, B.C. 36, he again espoused the Roman side, and took part in that general's expedition into Media Atropatênê, which turned out unfortunately. Antony attributed his repulse to Artavasdes deserting him in his difficulties, and therefore invaded his country, in B.C. 34, obtained possession of his person, and carried him into captivity. Cleopatra afterwards, B.C. 30, put Artavasdes to death.

It is worth remark that there was a considerable degree of culture in Armenia at this period. Its character was Greek. Tigranes I. struck coins with a Greek legend. Artavasdes I. wrote speeches, tragedies, and even historical works in the Greek language.

5. On the captivity of Artavasdes, the Armenians conferred

the royal dignity on Artaxias II., his son. At first the Romans, in conjunction with Artavasdes of Atropatênê, drove him out; but during the struggle between Octavius and Antony he returned, defeated the Atropatênian monarch, and took him prisoner. At the same time, he gave command for a massacre of all the Romans in Armenia, which accordingly took place. He reigned from B.C. 34 to 19, when he was murdered by his relations.

Reign of Artaxias II., B.C. 34–19.

6. The Romans now brought forward a candidate for the throne in the person of Tigranes, the brother of Artaxias II., who was installed in his kingdom by Tiberius at the command of Augustus, and ruled the country as Tigranes II. From this time Armenian independence was really at an end. The titular monarchs were mere puppets, maintained in their position by the Roman emperors or the Parthian kings, who alternately exercised a preponderating influence over the country. At length Armenia was made into a Roman province by Trajan, B.C. 114.

A general *History of Armenia* from the earliest times to his own day was written in the Armenian language by MOSES CHORENENSIS, about A.D. 430 to 450. It embodies the national traditions, and possesses thus a certain amount of interest; but it is contradicted by classical writers, contemporary with the events, on so many points that it can not be regarded as possessing more than a very slight historical value. This work was translated into Latin by WHISTON, and published in a single 4to volume. London, 1736.

Lists of the Armenian kings from Artaxias downward have been collected by FOY-VAILLANT, in his *Arsacidarum Imperium* (Appendix, *Elenchus regum Armeniæ Majoris*), by BROTIER in his notes to Tacitus (vol. i. pp. 426 to 428), and others.

VII. KINGDOM OF ARMENIA MINOR.

The kingdom of Armenia Minor was founded by Zariadras, a general of Antiochus the Great, about the same time that Artaxias founded the kingdom of Armenia Major, i. e., about B.C. 190. It continued a separate state, governed by the descendants of the founder, till the time of Mithridates of Pontus, when it was annexed to his dominions by that ambitious prince. Subsequently it fell almost wholly under the power of the Romans, and was generally attached to one or other of the neighboring kingdoms, until the reign of Vespasian, when it was converted into a Roman province. The names of the

Duration of the kingdom, from B.C. 190 to A.D. 73.

early kings after Zariadras are unknown. Among the later were a Cotys, contemporary with Caligula, A.D. 47, and an Aristobulus, contemporary with Nero, A.D. 54. The latter prince belonged to the family of the Herods.

VIII. KINGDOM OF BACTRIA.

1. The Bactrian satrapy was for some time after the death of Alexander only nominally subject to any of the so-called "Successors." But, about B.C. 305, Seleucus Nicator in his Oriental expedition received the submission of the governor; and from that date till the reign of his grandson, Antiochus Theus, Bactria continued to be a province of the Syrian empire. Then, however, the personal character of Antiochus Theus, and his entanglement in a war with Ptolemy Philadelphus, which taxed his powers to the utmost, encouraged the remoter provinces to revolt; and about B.C. 255 Diodotus, satrap of Bactria, declared himself independent, and became the founder of the Bactrian kingdom.

Origin of the kingdom, about B.C. 255.

2. Little is known of Diodotus I. beyond the date of his accession, and the fact of the continuance of his reign from about B.C. 255 to 237. It is possible that about B.C. 244 he (nominally at any rate) submitted to Ptolemy Euergetes; and probable that when Seleucus Callinicus made his first attack on Parthia, Diodotus lent him assistance, and obtained in return an acknowledgment of his independence. He appears to have died during the expedition of Callinicus, which is assigned probably to the year B.C. 237. At his death he left the crown to a son of the same name.

Reign of Diodotus I., about B.C. 255–237.

It is to be borne in mind that the Bactrian kingdom was in its origin purely Greek, and that thus it stands in marked contrast with the Parthian. The coins of Diodotus I. are excellent in type; they have wholly Greek legends.

3. Diodotus II., who succeeded Diodotus I. about B.C. 237, pursued a policy quite different from that of his father. Instead of lending aid to Callinicus, he concluded a treaty with Arsaces II. (Tiridates), the Parthian king, and probably assisted him in the great battle by which Parthian independence was regarded as finally established.

Reign of Diodotus II.

Nothing more is known of this king; nor can it even be determined whether it was he or his son who was removed by Euthydemus, when that prince seized the crown, about B.C. 222.

4. Euthydemus, the third known Bactrian king, was a Greek of Magnesia, in Asia Minor. The circumstances under which he seized the crown are unknown to us; but it appears that he had been king for some considerable time when Antiochus the Great, having made peace with Arsaces, the third Parthian monarch, turned his arms against Bactria with the view of reducing it to subjection. In a battle fought on the Arius (Heri-Rud), Euthydemus was defeated; but Antiochus, who received a wound in the engagement, shortly after granted him terms, promised to give one of his daughters in marriage to Demetrius, Euthydemus's son, and left him in quiet possession of his dominions, B.C. 206. The Indian conquests of Demetrius seem to have commenced soon afterwards, while his father was still living. They were on the south side of the Paropamisus, in the modern Candahar and Cabul.

Reign of Euthydemus, about B.C. 222–200.

5. Demetrius, who is proved by his coins to have been king of Bactria, no doubt succeeded his father. He engaged in an important series of conquests—partly as crown prince, partly as king—on the southern side of the Paropamisus, which extended probably over the greater portion of Affghanistan, and may even have embraced some districts of the Punjab region. The city of Demetrias in Arachosia, and that of Euthydemeia on the Hydaspes, are with reason regarded as traces of these conquests. While Demetrius was thus employed, a rebel named Eucratides seems to have supplanted him at home; and the reigns of these monarchs were for some time parallel, Demetrius ruling on the south and Eucratides on the north side of the mountains.

Reign of Demetrius, about B.C. 200–180.

The dates for the accession and death of Demetrius are exceedingly doubtful. The best authorities assign him, conjecturally, the space from about B.C. 200 to 180.

6. After the death of Demetrius, Eucratides appears to have reigned over both kingdoms. He was a monarch of considerable vigor and activity, and pushed his conquests deep into the Punjab re-

Reign of Eucratides, about B.C. 180–160.

gion. He lost, however, a portion of his home territory to the Parthian princes. On his return from an Indian expedition he was waylaid and slain by his own son, whom he had previously associated in the kingdom. His reign must have lasted from about B.C. 180 to 160.

7. The son of Eucratides, who after his murder became sole monarch of Bactria, appears to have been a certain Heliocles, who took the title of Δίκαιος, "the Just," and reigned over Bactria probably from about B.C. 160 to 150. Nothing is known in detail of the circumstances of his reign; but there is reason to believe that Bactria now rapidly declined in power, being pressed upon by the Scythian nomades towards the north, and by the Parthians on the west and south, and continually losing one province after another to the invaders. It was in vain that these unhappy Greeks implored in their isolation the aid of their Syrian brethren against the constant encroachments of the barbarians. The expedition of Demetrius Nicator, undertaken for their relief, B.C. 142, terminated in his defeat and capture. Hellenic culture and civilization proved in this quarter no match for barbaric force, and had of necessity to give way and retreat. After the reign of Heliocles, we have no further indication of Greek rulers to the north of the Paropamisus. On the southern side of the mountain-chain somewhat more of tenacity was shown. In Cabul and Candahar Greek kingdoms, offshoots of the Bactrian, continued to exist down to about B.C. 80, when the last remnant of Hellenic power in this quarter was swept away by the Yue-chi and other Scythic, or Tatar, races.

Reign of Heliocles, about B.C. 160–150.

Decline of Bactrian power.

To these Indian, rather than Bactrian, kingdoms belong the names of Lysias (about B.C. 160), Antimachus (same date), Apollodotus (same date), Menander (B.C. 140), Philoxenes (same date), Anticleides, Archebius, Diomedes (about B.C. 100), Hermæus (same date), and others, whose coins, which have Greek legends, show them to have reigned in these regions. No great historical interest attaches to any of these kings except Menander. Menander was a powerful monarch, who held his court probably at the city of Cabul, and ruled over the whole tract extending from the Paropamisus on the north to the Indian Ocean towards the south, and from the neighborhood of Herat on the one side, to the Jumna, a tributary of the Ganges, on the other. His coins are found in the Hazarah country, west of Cabul, at Cabul itself, at Peshawur, and on the banks of the Jumna. In the first century after Christ they were current on the coast of Guzerat, and about the mouths of the Indus. There is reason therefore to believe that Strabo did not exaggerate his power, which probably lasted for about a quarter of a century in the regions mentioned.

On the Græco-Bactrian history, see the following works:

BAYER, T. S., *Historia regni Græcorum Bactriani.* Petropol., 1738; 4to. The earliest, and, so far as the notices of the ancients go, the most complete work on the subject.

WILSON, Prof. H. H., *Ariana Antiqua* (chap. iv.). London, 1841; 4to. Contains a full and excellent account and representation of the Græco-Bactrian coins.

LASSEN, Prof., *Indische Alterthumskunde.* Bonn, 1849; 2 vols. tall 8vo. See particularly the section entitled *Geschichte der Griechisch-Baktrischen Könige*, vol. ii. pp. 277 to 344.

Special works on the Coins of Bactria and the adjoining countries are numerous. Among them the following deserve attention:

RAOUL-ROCHETTE, *Notice sur quelques médailles grecques inédites, appartenant à des rois inconnus de Bactriane et de l'Inde*, published in the *Journal des Savants* for 1834; pp. 328 et seqq.

GROTEFEND, C. L., *Die Münzen der griechischen, parthischen, und indoskythischen Könige von Baktrien und den Ländern am Indus.* Hanover, 1839.

IX. KINGDOM OF PARTHIA.

Parthian kingdom, from B.C. 256 to A.D. 226.

The Parthian kingdom is said to have been founded nearly at the same time with the Bactrian, during the reign of Antiochus Theus in Syria, about B.C. 255 or 256. It originated, however, not in the revolt of a satrap, but in the uprising of a nation. Reinforced by a kindred body of Turanians from beyond the Jaxartes, the Parthi of the region lying south-east of the Caspian rose in revolt against their Grecian masters, and succeeded in establishing their independence. From a small beginning they gradually spread their power over the greater part of Western Asia, being for a considerable period lords of all the countries between the Euphrates and the Sutlej. As the Parthian kingdom, though a fragment of the empire of Alexander, was never absorbed into that of the Romans, but continued to exist side by side with the Roman empire during the most flourishing period of the latter, it is proposed to reserve the details of the history for the next Book, and to give only this brief notice of the general character of the monarchy in the present place.

X. KINGDOM OF JUDÆA.

Importance of Jewish history.

1. Though the Jewish kingdom, which came into being midway in the Syrian period, originating in the intolerable cruelties and oppressions of the Syrian kings, was geographically of such small extent as scarcely to claim distinct treatment in a work which must needs omit to notice many of the lesser states and kingdoms, yet the undying interest which attaches to the Jewish people, and the vast influence which the nation has exercised over the progress of civilization, will justify, it is thought, in the present place, not only an account of the kingdom, but a sketch of the general history of the nation from the time when, as related in the first Book (p. 69), it was carried into captivity by Nebuchadnezzar to the period of the re-establishment of independence. This history naturally divides itself into two periods:—1. From the Captivity to the fall of the Persian empire, B.C. 586 to 323; and, 2. From the fall of the Persian empire to the re-establishment of an independent kingdom, B.C. 323 to 168. The history of the kingdom may also be most conveniently treated in two portions:—1. The Maccabee period, from B.C. 168 to 37; and, 2. The period of the Herods, B.C. 37 to A.D. 44, when Judæa became finally a Roman province. Thus the entire history will fall under four heads.

Periods.

First Period, B.C. 586–323. Return from captivity.

2. FIRST PERIOD. About fifty years after the completion of the Captivity by Nebuchadnezzar, and nearly seventy years after its commencement, a great change was effected in the condition of the Jewish people by Cyrus. That monarch, having captured Babylon in the year B.C. 538, found among his new subjects an oppressed race, in whose religion he recognized a considerable resemblance to his own, and in whose fortunes he therefore took a special interest. Learning that they had been violently removed from their own country two generations previously, and finding that numbers of them had a strong desire to return, he gave permission that such as wished might go back and re-establish themselves in their country. Accordingly, a colony, numbering 42,360 persons, besides their servants, set out from Babylonia, and made their way to Jerusalem; in or near which the greater num-

ber of them settled. This colony, at the head of which was Zerubbabel, a descendant of the old line of kings, was afterwards strengthened by two others, one led by Ezra, in B.C. 458, and the other by Nehemiah, in B.C. 445. Besides these known accessions, there was probably also for many years a continual influx of individuals, or families, who were attracted to their own land, not only by the love of country, which has always been so especially strong in the Jews, but also by motives of religion. Still great numbers of Jews, probably half the nation, remained where they had so long resided, in Babylonia and the adjoining countries.

3. The exiles who returned under Zerubbabel belonged predominantly, if not exclusively, to three tribes, Judah, Levi, and Benjamin. It was their first object to rebuild their famous Temple on its former site, and to re-establish the old Temple-service. But in this work they were greatly hindered by their neighbors. A mixed race, partly Israelite, partly foreign—including Babylonians, Persians, Elamites, Arabs, and others—had repeopled the old kingdom of Samaria, and established there a mongrel worship, in part Jehovistic, in part idolatrous. On the first arrival of the Jewish colony, this mixed race proposed to join the new-comers in the erection of their Temple, and to make it a common sanctuary open both to themselves and the Jews. But such a course would have been dangerous to the purity of religion; and Zerubbabel very properly declined the offer. His refusal stirred up a spirit of hostility among the "Samaritans;" which showed itself in prolonged efforts to prevent the rebuilding of the Temple and the city—efforts which were for a while successful, considerably delaying, though they could not finally defeat, the work.

The Temple rebuilt, B.C. 535–515.

Building of Temple commenced about B.C. 535. Work stopped by a rescript of the pseudo-Smerdis (Artaxerxes of Ezra iv. 7–23), about B.C. 522. Resumed, B.C. 519, in consequence of a decree of Darius Hystaspis. Completion of Temple, B.C. 515.

4. The favor of Darius Hystaspis allowed the Jews to complete their Temple, and to establish themselves firmly in the country of their ancestors, despite the ill-will of the surrounding nations and tribes. But in the reign of his successor, Xerxes, a terrible danger was incurred. That weak

Danger of the Jews. Projected massacre averted by the interposition of Esther, about B.C. 473.

prince allowed his minister, Haman (Omanes?), to persuade him that it would be for the advantage of his empire, if the Jews, who were to be found in various parts of his dominions, always a distinct race, not amalgamating with those among whom they lived, could be quietly got rid of. Having obtained the monarch's consent, he planned and prepared a general massacre, by which on one day the whole race was to be swept from the earth. Fortunately for the doomed nation, the inclination of the fickle king had shifted before the day of execution came, the interposition of the wife in favor at the time, who was a Jewess, having availed for the preservation of her people. Instead of being taken unawares by their enemies, and massacred unresistingly, the Jews were everywhere warned of their danger and allowed to stand on their defense. The weight of the government was thrown on their side; and the result was that, wherever they were attacked, they triumphed, and improved their future position by the destruction of all their most bitter adversaries.

The "Ahasuerus" of the Book of Esther has been identified by writers of repute with Darius Hystaspis and with Artaxerxes Longimanus, as well as with Xerxes. But the notes of time, character, and name, which all point to Xerxes, have produced among moderns almost a *consensus* in his favor. The historical character of the narrative is proved by the institution of the feast of Purim, which is still kept by the Jews, and of which no other account can be given.

5. Though the Jews had thus escaped this great danger, and had strengthened their position by the destruction of so many of their enemies, yet their continued existence as a separate nation was still far from secure. Two causes imperilled it. In spite of the refusal to allow foreigners, even though partially allied in race, to take part in the rebuilding of the Temple, a tendency showed itself, as time went on, towards a fusion with the surrounding peoples. The practice of intermarriage with these peoples commenced, and had gained a great head when Ezra brought his colony from Babylon in the seventh year of Longimanus, B.C. 458. By the earnest efforts, first of Ezra, and then of Nehemiah, about B.C. 434, this evil was checked.

Tendency to intermixture with foreigners checked by Ezra and Nehemiah.

6. The other peril was of a different kind. Jerusalem,

though rebuilt on the old site by the colony of Zerubbabel, was without walls or other defenses, and thus lay open to attack on the part of any hostile neighbor. The authority of Persia was weak in the more remote provinces, which not unfrequently revolted, and remained for years in a state bordering on anarchy. It was an important gain to the Jews when, in the twentieth year of Artaxerxes, Nehemiah came down from the court with authority to refortify the city, and effected his purpose despite the opposition which he encountered, B.C. 445.

Fortification of Jerusalem, B.C. 445.

7. It was a feature of the Persian system to allow the nations under their rule a good deal of self-government and internal independence. Judæa was a portion of the Syrian satrapy, and had no doubt to submit to such requisitions as the Syrian satrap made upon it for men and money. But, so long as these requisitions were complied with, there was not much further interference with the people, or with their mode of managing their own affairs. Occasionally a local governor (Tirshatha), with a rank and title below those of a satrap, was appointed by the Crown to superintend Judæa, or Jerusalem; but these officers do not appear to have succeeded each other with regularity, and, when they were appointed, it would seem that they were always natives. In default of a regular succession of such governors, the High-priests came to be regarded as not merely the religious but also the political heads of the nation, and the general direction of affairs fell into their hands.

Method of administration under the Persians.

LINE OF HIGH-PRIESTS from the commencement to the close of the Persian period:—1. Jeshua, B.C. 536 to 515. Contemporary with Zerubbabel, Haggai, and Zechariah. 2. Joiakim, son of Jeshua, about B.C. 500 to 460. 3. Eliashib, son of Joiakim, B.C. 458 to 434. Contemporary with Ezra and Nehemiah. 4. Joiada, son of Eliashib, about B.C. 430 to 400. Contemporary with Darius Nothus. 5. Jonathan, son of Joiada, about B.C. 400 to 360. Contemporary with Artaxerxes Mnemon. Murders his brother Jeshua. 6. Jaddua, son of Jonathan, about 360 to 330. Contemporary with Darius Codomannus. After the fall of Tyre, yields Jerusalem to Alexander the Great.

8. SECOND PERIOD. In the partitions which were made of Alexander's dominions at Babylon and at Triparadisus (see pp. 239 and 241), the Syrian satrapy, which included Palestine, was consti-

Judæa under the Ptolemies, B.C. 320-203.

tuted a separate government. But a very little time elapsed before Ptolemy Lagi annexed the satrapy, the southern division of which continued thenceforward, except during short intervals, a portion of the kingdom of Egypt, until the reign of Ptolemy Epiphanes. It is uncertain whether Alexander assigned the Jews any special privileges in the great city which he founded in Egypt; but there can be no doubt that the early Ptolemies highly favored this class of their subjects, attracting them in vast numbers to their capital, encouraging their literature, and granting them many privileges. The subjection of Judæa to Egypt lasted from B.C. 320 to B.C. 203; and though the country was during this space ravaged more than once by the forces of contending armies, yet on the whole the time must be regarded as one of general peace and prosperity. The high-priests continued to be at the head of the state, and ruled Judæa without much oppressive interference from the Egyptians.

The HIGH-PRIESTS during this period were—1. Onias I., the son of Jaddua, about B.C. 330 to 300. 2. Simon the Just, the son of Onias, about B.C. 300 to 290. 3. Eleazar, brother of Simon the Just, about B.C. 290 to 265. 4. Manasseh, also a brother of Simon, about B.C. 265 to 240. 5. Onias II., son of Simon, B.C. 240 to 226. Nearly brought about a rupture with Egypt from his refusal to pay the customary tribute. 6. Simon II., son of Onias II., B.C. 226 to 198.

Judæa voluntarily places herself under the Seleucidæ, B.C. 203.

9. Towards the close of the Ptolemaic period, the Jews began to have serious cause of complaint against their Egyptian rulers. The fourth Ptolemy (Philopator), a weak and debauched prince, attempted to violate the sanctity of the Jewish Temple by entering it, and, when his attempt was frustrated, sought to revenge himself by punishing the Alexandrian Jews, who had done him no injury at all. It was the natural result of these violent proceedings that the Jews, in disgust and alarm, should seek a protector elsewhere. Accordingly, when Antiochus the Great, in the infancy of Ptolemy Epiphanes, determined to attack Egypt, and to annex, if possible, to his own dominions the valuable maritime tract extending from his province of Upper Syria to the Sinaitic Desert, the Jews voluntarily joined him; and though Ptolemy's general, Scopas, recovered most of what had been lost, yet Antiochus, by the victory of Paneas, B.C. 198, was left in final possession

of the whole region, which thenceforth, though often disputed by Egypt, became a possession of the Syrian kings.

Ill-treatment of the Jews by the Seleucidæ leads to revolt, B.C. 168.

10. Under Antiochus the Great, and for a time under his elder son, Seleucus Philopator, the Jews had no reason to repent the exchange they had made. Both Antiochus, and Seleucus for a while, respected the privileges of the nation, and abstained from any proceedings that could give umbrage to their new subjects. But towards the close of the reign of Seleucus, an important change of policy took place. The wealth of the Jewish Temple being reported to the Syrian monarch, and his own needs being great, he made an attempt to appropriate the sacred treasure, which was however frustrated, either by miracle, or by the contrivance of the High-priest Onias. This unwarrantable attempt of Seleucus was followed by worse outrages in the reign of his brother and successor, Antiochus Epiphanes. Not only did that monarch sell the office of High-priest, first to Jason and then to Menelaüs, but he endeavored to effect by systematic proceedings the complete Hellenization of the Jews, whereto a party in the nation was already sufficiently inclined. Further, having, by his own iniquitous proceedings in the matter of the high-priesthood, given occasion to a civil war between the rival claimants, he chose to regard the war as rebellion against his authority, and on his return from his second Egyptian campaign, B.C. 170, took possession of Jerusalem, and gave it up to massacre and pillage. At the same time he plundered the Temple of its sacred vessels and treasures. Nor was this all. Two years afterwards, B.C. 168, he caused Jerusalem to be occupied a second time by an armed force, set up an idol altar in the Temple, and caused sacrifice to be offered there to Jupiter Olympius. The Jews were forbidden any longer to observe the Law, and were to be Hellenized by main force. Hence the rising under the Maccabees, and the gradual re-establishment of independence.

HIGH-PRIESTS UNDER THE SYRIANS:—1. Onias III., son of Simon II., B.C. 198 to 175. Frustrates the attempt made to plunder the Temple by Heliodorus at the command of Seleucus Philopator. Deprived of the priesthood by Antiochus Epiphanes at the instigation of Jason. 2. Jason, brother of Onias III., B.C. 175 to 172. Buys the office of Antiochus. Introduces Greek customs. Sends an offering to Hercules at Tyre. Supplanted by his emissary Menelaüs. 3. Menelaüs (according to Josephus, brother of Jason), B.C. 172 to 163. Buys the office. Civil war between him and Jason. Put to death by Antiochus Eupator.

Judæa under the Maccabees, B.C. 168-37.

11. THIRD PERIOD. At first the patriots who rose up against the attempt to annihilate the national religion and life were a scanty band, maintaining themselves with difficulty in the mountains against the forces of the Syrian kings. Jerusalem, which was won by Judas Maccabæus, was lost again at his death; and it was not till about B.C. 153, fourteen years after the first revolt, that the struggle entered on a new phase in consequence of the contentions which then began between different pretenders to the Syrian throne. When war arose between Demetrius and Alexander Balas, the support of the Jews was felt to be of importance by both parties. Both, consequently, made overtures to Jonathan, the third Maccabee prince, who was shortly recognized not only as prince, but also as high-priest of the nation. From this time, as there were almost constant disputes between rival claimants of the crown in Syria, the Jews were able to maintain themselves with comparative ease. Once or twice, during a pause in the Syrian contest, they were attacked and were forced to make a temporary submission. But the general result was that they maintained, and indeed continually enlarged, their independence. For some time they did not object to acknowledge the Syrian monarch as their suzerain, and to pay him an annual tribute; but after the death of Antiochus VII. (Sidetes) all such payments seem to have ceased, and the complete independence of the country was established. Coins were struck bearing the name of the Maccabee prince, and the title of "King." Judæa was indeed from this time as powerful a monarchy as Syria. John Hyrcanus conquered Samaria and Idumæa, and thus largely extended the Jewish boundaries, exactly at the time when those of Syria were undergoing rapid contraction. (See p. 259.)

Commencement of subjection to Rome, B.C. 63.

12. The deliverance of the state from any further fear of subjection by Syria was followed almost immediately by internal quarrels and dissensions, which led naturally to the acceptance of a position of subordination under another power. The Pharisees and Sadducees, hitherto mere religious sects, became transformed

into political factions. Civil wars broke out. The members of the royal family quarrelled among each other, and the different pretenders to the crown appealed for assistance to foreign nations. About B.C. 63 the Romans entered upon the scene; and for the last twenty-six years of the Maccabee period—B.C. 63 to 37—while feeble princes of the once mighty Asmonæan family still nominally held the throne, the Great Republic was really supreme in Palestine, took tribute, and appointed governors, or sanctioned the rule of kings, at her pleasure. It is the change of dynasty, and not any change in the internal condition of the country, that causes the year B.C. 37 to be taken as that at which to draw the line between the close of one period and the commencement of another.

LIST OF THE ASMONÆAN PRINCES:—1. Mattathias, a priest, leader of the revolt, B.C. 168 to 167. 2. Judas Maccabæus, his third son. After some small successes, defeats Apollonius at Beth-horon, B.C. 167. Gains a victory at Emmaus over the forces of Lysias, B.C. 166, and defeats Lysias himself at Beth-sura, B.C. 165. Occupies all Jerusalem except the citadel, and purifies the Temple. Jerusalem besieged by Lysias, B.C. 163. Expedition of Nicanor, B.C. 161. Judas defeats him at Capharsalama and at Adasa. Invasion of Bacchides. Judas is defeated and falls at Eleasa, "the Jewish Thermopylæ." Jerusalem recovered by the Syrians. 3. Jonathan, a younger brother of Judas, maintains the war for eight years with fair success in the mountains north-east of Jerusalem, inflicting several defeats upon Bacchides. The invasion of Syria by Alexander Balas, B.C. 153, entirely changes his position. Both parties court him. Demetrius puts him in possession of Jerusalem. Alexander nominates him to the high-priesthood, and obtains his assistance in the war which follows. At his death, B.C. 146, Demetrius II. makes terms with the Jews, but fails to fulfill them, in consequence of which Jonathan joins the party of Antiochus VI., the son of Alexander Balas, and lends it efficient aid, till his murder by the conspirator Tryphon, B.C. 144. 4. Simon, the last remaining son of Mattathias, succeeded his brother Jonathan, and to avenge his death made common cause with Demetrius II. against Tryphon, B.C. 143, stipulating, however, at the same time for the complete independence of his country. The first Jewish coins are now struck. The Syrian garrison is expelled from the citadel of Jerusalem. Simon is practically king of the Jews. At the same time he holds the high-priesthood. The Jews continue undisturbed and prosperous for some years; and when, in B.C. 138, Antiochus Sidetes, having reduced Tryphon to extremities, resolves to make an attempt to reconquer the country, his general, Cendebæus, is defeated, and Simon once more triumphs. Soon afterwards, however, B.C. 135, he is assassinated by his own son-in-law, Ptolemæus, who attempts to seize the kingdom. 5. John Hyrcanus, son of Simon, obtains the government; but before he is well settled in his kingdom, Sidetes renews his enterprise, and after a war which lasts two years, B.C. 135 to 133, he forces Hyrcanus to acknowledge his authority, to dismantle Jerusalem, and to renew the payment of tribute. But on the death of Sidetes in the Parthian War, B.C. 129, Hyrcanus throws off the yoke, and takes advantage of the troubles which break out anew in Syria to enlarge his dominions by the conquest of Idumæa and Samaria, B.C. 109. From this time the authority of Syria is at an end. John Hyrcanus dies in peace, B.C. 106, leaving the government to his eldest son, Aristobulus. 6. Aristobulus reigns one year only, during which he shows a cruel disposition. He is succeeded by his brother, 7. Alexander Jannæus, who reigns from B.C. 105 to 78. In this reign the quarrels between the Pharisees and Sadducees come to a head and disturb the peace of the country. Alexander is a Sadducee; and, the Pharisees having induced the people to insult him, a war breaks out, which rages for six years (B.C. 95 to 89), Jannæus being finally the victor. An attempt is subsequently made to dethrone him by the aid of Demetrius Eucærus of Syria. (See p. 260.) Success again rests with Jannæus, who once more severely punishes his adversaries. After this he reigns for some years peacefully, and is allowed to leave his crown to his widow, 8. Alexandra, who joins the party of the Pharisees, and is maintained on the throne by their influence. At her death, in B.C. 70, her two sons, 9. Hyrcanus, the high-priest, and, 10. Aristobulus, quarrelled for the possession of the throne, and engaged in a civil war, which lasted till Pompey, in B.C. 63, took Jerusalem, carried off Aristobulus, and established Hyrcanus, who then reigned quietly from B.C. 63 to 57. In B.C. 57, Aristobulus, having escaped from Rome, raised fresh troubles, which were quelled by the Roman commander, Gabinius, who deposed Hyrcanus, and established a species of oligarchy, which lasted ten years, B.C. 57 to 47. Hyrcanus was then restored to power by Julius Cæsar, whom he had aided in the Egyptian campaign of B.C. 48, and remained at the head of affairs till B.C. 40, when he was deposed and mutilated by the last Asmonæan prince, 11. Antigonus, who, having obtained a Parthian force, took Jerusalem, and held the government for three years, B.C. 40 to 37, when he was forced to yield to Herod, assisted by the Romans.

Judæa under the Herods, B.C. 37 to A.D. 44.

13. FOURTH PERIOD. During the fourth period Roman influence was, not only practically, as during much of the third period, but professedly predominant over the country. The Herods, who owed their establishment in authority wholly to the Romans, had no other means of maintaining themselves than by preserving the favor of their patrons. Obnoxious, except to a small fraction of the nation, from their Idumæan descent, they were hated still more as the minions of a foreign power, a standing proof to the nation of its own weakness and degraded condition. On the other hand, there were no doubt some who viewed the rule of the Herods as, in a certain sense, a protection against Rome, a something interposed between the nation and its purely heathen oppressors, saving the nation-

al life from extinction, and offering the best compromise which circumstances permitted between an impossible entire independence and a too probable absorption into the empire. Such persons were willing to see in Herod the Great, and again in Herod Agrippa, the Messiah—the king foredoomed to save them from the yoke of the foreigner, and to obtain for them the respect, if not even the obedience, of the surrounding peoples.

14. But these feelings, and the attachment to the dynasty which grew out of them, must have become weaker as time went on. The kingdom of the Herods gradually lost instead of gaining in power. Rome continually encroached more and more. As early as A.D. 8, a portion of Palestine, and the most important portion in the eyes of the Jews, was formally incorporated into the Roman empire; and though the caprice of an emperor afterwards revoked this proceeding, and restored another Herod to the throne of his grandfather, yet from the moment when the first Procurator levied taxes in a Jewish province all but the willfully blind must have seen what was impending. The civil authority of the last native prince over Judæa came to an end in A.D. 44; and the whole of Palestine, except a small district held as a kingdom by Agrippa II., was from that time absorbed into the empire, being appended to the Roman province of Syria and ruled wholly by Roman Procurators. The national life was consequently at the last gasp. As far as political forms went, it was extinct; but there remained enough of vital energy in the seeming corpse for the nation once more to reassert itself, and to show by the great "War of Independence" that it was not to be finally crushed without a fearful struggle, the issue of which at one time appeared almost doubtful.

Period of Roman encroachments, A.D. 8-44.

LINE OF JEWISH GOVERNORS from B.C. 37 to A.D. 44:—1. Herod the Great. Obtains his crown by the favor of Antony, B.C. 37. Marries Mariamné, the Asmonæan princess, the same year. His dominions increased by Augustus, after Actium, B.C. 30. Rebuilds the Temple with great magnificence, but also rebuilds that on Mount Gerizim, and at Cæsarea erects heathen temples. Maintains a body-guard of foreign mercenaries. Cruel and suspicious, especially towards the members of his own family. Puts to death Mariamné, her grandfather Hyrcanus, her two sons Aristobulus and Alexander, Antipater, his eldest son, and others. Dies B.C. 4 (according to the received chronology). 2. Archelaüs, 3. Antipas, and 4. Philip, inherit portions of their father's dominions, Archelaüs having Idumæa, Judæa, and Samaria; Antipas, Galilee and Peræa; and Philip, Ituræa and Trachonitis. Archelaüs rules oppressively, and is deposed by the Romans, A.D. 8, who add his dominions to the province of Syria, but assign the actual government to Procurators. These were, 5. Coponius; 6. M. Ambivius; 7. Annius Rufus; 8. Valerius Gratus, A.D. 14 to 25; 9. Pontius Pilate, A.D. 25 to 36; 10. Marcellus. Antipas ruled in Galilee from B.C. 4 to A.D. 39, when he was deposed; and Philip in Trachonitis, from B.C. 4 to A.D. 37, when he died. As these principalities became vacant they were conferred by the favor of Caligula on 11. Herod Agrippa I., the son of Aristobulus, who in A.D. 41 received from Claudius the further addition to his kingdom of Samaria and Judæa, and thus united under his sway all Palestine. He died, after commencing a persecution of the Christians, A.D. 44; whereupon the Romans placed Palestine once more under the government of Procurators. Those of Judæa were, 12. Caspius Fadus, A.D. 44 to 48; 13. Ventidius Cumanus, A.D. 48 to 49; 14. Antonius Felix, A.D. 49 to 55; 15. Porcius Festus, A.D. 55 to 59; 16. Albinus, A.D. 62 to 65; and 17. Gessius Florus, under whom the Jews broke out into open rebellion. Parallel with this later line of Procurators was the government of 17. Herod Agrippa II., first in Chalcis, and then in Abilêné and Trachonitis, from A.D. 50 to 70, when his principality was swallowed up in the new arrangements consequent upon the revolt of the Jews and their reduction. Agrippa assisted the Romans in the Jewish War; and at its close retired to Rome, where he lived till the third year of Trajan, A.D. 100.

Tyranny of the Procurators, B.C. 44–66. Revolts put down. Destruction of Jerusalem, B.C. 70.

15. The proximate cause of the great Jewish revolt and of the "War of Independence" was the oppression of the Procurators, and especially of Gessius Florus. But, even had the Roman governors ruled mildly, it is probable that a rebellion would sooner or later have broken out. The Roman system was unlike those of the foreign powers to which Judæa had in former times submitted. It was intolerant of differences, and aimed everywhere, not only at absorbing, but at assimilating the populations. The Jews could under no circumstances have allowed their nationality to be crushed otherwise than by violence. As it was, the tyranny of Gessius Florus precipitated a struggle which must have come in any case, and made the contest fiercer, bloodier, and more protracted than it might have been otherwise. From the first revolt against his authority to the capture of the city by Titus was a period of nearly five years, B.C. 66 to 70. The fall of the city was followed by its destruction, partly as a punishment for the desperation of the resistance, but more as a precaution to deprive the Jews, now felt to be really formi-

dable, of their natural rallying-point in any future rebellion.

Works upon the history of the Jews are numerous, and many of them are extremely valuable. The more important have been already noticed. (See p. 59.) But the following also deserve attention:

BASNAGE, *Histoire des Juifs depuis Jésus Christ jusqu'à present.* La Haye, 1716; 15 vols. 12mo. Parts i. and ii. belong to this period.

PRIDEAUX, *The Old and New Testament connected in the History of the Jews and Neighboring Nations.* London, 1714; 2 vols. 8vo. Much of this treatise is now antiquated; but it has not been wholly superseded by any later English work on the subject.

JOST, J. M., *Geschichte der Israeliten seit der Zeit der Makkabäer bis auf unsere Tage.* Berlin, 1828–47; 10 vols. 8vo.

HERZFELD, C., *Geschichte des Volkes Israel von Vollendung des zweiten Tempel bis zur Einsetzung des Makkabäers Schimon zum hohen Priester.* Leipzig, 1863; 2 vols. 8vo. An excellent sketch of the history is also contained in the valuable work of DOLLINGER, J. J. T., *Der Heide und der Jude.* München, 1857. An authorized translation of this work has been published under the title of *The Gentile and the Jew in the Courts of the Temple of Christ.* From the German by N. DARNELL. London, 1862; 2 vols. 8vo.

BOOK V.

HISTORY OF ROME FROM THE EARLIEST TIMES TO THE FALL OF THE WESTERN EMPIRE, A.D. 476, AND PARALLEL HISTORY OF PARTHIA.

PART I.—HISTORY OF ROME.

Preliminary Remarks on the Geography of Ancient Italy.

1. THE Italian Peninsula is the smallest of the three tracts which project themselves from the European continent southward into the Mediterranean. Its greatest length between the Alps and Cape Spartivento is 720 miles, and its greatest width between the Little St. Bernard and the hills north of Trieste is 330 miles. The ordinary width, however, is only 100 miles; and the area is thus, even including the littoral islands, not much more than 110,000 square miles. The peninsula was bounded on the north and north-west by the Alps, on the east by the Adriatic, on the south by the Mediterranean, and on the west by the Tyrrhenian Sea (*Mare Tyrrhenum*).

Italy—size and boundaries.

2. The LITTORAL EXTENT of Italy is, in proportion to its area, very considerable, chiefly owing to the length and narrowness of the peninsula; for the main coasts are but very slightly indented. Towards the west a moderate number of shallow gulfs, or rather bays, give a certain variety to the coast-line; while on the east there is but one important headland, that of Gargano; and but one bay of any size, that of Manfredonia. Southward, however, the shore has two considerable indentations in what would otherwise be but a short line, viz., the deep Gulf of Taranto and the shallower one of Squillace. A character generally similar attaches to the coasts of the Italian islands, Sardinia, Sicily, and Corsica; and hence, though a nautical tendency belongs naturally to the Italian people, the tendency is not so distinct and pronounced as in the neighboring country of Greece.

Extent of the sea-board.

3. The MOUNTAINS of Italy consist of the two famous chains of the Alps and the Apennines. (*a*) The Alps, which bound Italy along the whole of its northern and a part of its western side, form a lofty barrier naturally isolating the region from the rest of Europe. Nowhere less along the entire boundary-line than 4000 feet in height, and varying from that minimum to a maximum of 15,000 feet, they are penetrable by no more than ten or twelve difficult passes, even at the present day. Their general direction is from east to west, or, speaking more strictly, from N.E. by E. to S.W. by W.; but, at a certain point in their course, the point in which they culminate, this direction ceases, and they suddenly change their course and run nearly due north and south. Mont Blanc stands at the corner thus formed, like a gigantic buttress at the angle of a mighty building. The length of the chain from Mont Blanc southward to the coast is about 150 miles; the length eastward, so far as the Alps are Italian, is about 330 miles. Thus this huge barrier guards Italy for a distance of 480 miles with a rampart which in ancient time could scarcely be scaled. (*b*) From the point where the Alps, striking southward from Mont Blanc, reach most nearly to the sea, a secondary chain is thrown off, which runs at first from west to east, almost parallel with the shore, to about the longitude of Cremona (10° east from Greenwich, nearly), after which it begins to trend south of east, and passing in this direction across about three-fourths of the peninsula, it again turns still more to the south, and proceeds in a course which is, as nearly as possible, due south-east, parallel to the two coasts of the peninsula, along its entire length. This chain is properly the Apennines. In modern geography its more western portion bears the name of "The Maritime Alps;" but as the chain is really continuous from a point a little north-east of Nice to the neighborhood of Reggio (Rhegium), a single name should be given to it throughout; and, for distinction's sake, that name should certainly not be "Alps" but "Apennines." The Apennines in Northern Italy consist of but a single chain, which throws off twisted spurs to the right hand and to the left; but, when Central Italy is reached, the character of the range becomes more complicated. Below Lake Fucinus the chain

The mountain system. The Alps.

The Apennines.

bifurcates. While one range, the stronger of the two, pursues the old south-easterly direction, another of minor elevation branches off to the south, and approaching the south coast very closely in the vicinity of Salernum, curves round and rejoins the main chain near Compsa. The range then proceeds in a single line nearly to Venusia, when it splits once more; and while one branch runs on nearly due east to the extreme promontory of Iapygia, the other proceeds almost due south to Rhegium.

4. The most marked feature of Italian geography is the strong contrast in which Northern stands to Southern Italy.

Contrast between Northern and Southern Italy.

Northern Italy is almost all plain; Southern almost all mountain. The conformation of the mountain ranges in the north leaves between the parallel chains of the Swiss Alps and the Upper Apennines a vast tract—from 100 to 150 miles in width, which (speaking broadly) may be called a single plain—"the Plain of the Po," or "the Plain of Lombardo-Venetia." In Southern Italy, or the Peninsula proper, plains of more than a few miles in extent are rare. The Apennines, with their many-twisted spurs, spread broadly over the land, and form a continuous mountain region which occupies at least one half of the surface. But this is not all. Where the chain is sufficiently narrow to allow of the interposition, between its base and the shore, of any tolerably wide tract—as in Etruria, in Latium, and in Campania—separate systems of hills and mountains, volcanic in character, exist, and prevent the occurrence of any really extensive levels. The only exception to this general rule is in Apulia, where an extensive tract of plain is found about the Candelaro, Cervaro, and Ofanto rivers.

5. The RIVERS of Italy are exceedingly numerous; but only one or two are of any considerable size. The great river is the Po (Padus), which, rising at the foot of

The rivers.

Monte Viso, in lat. 44° 40′, long. 7°, nearly, drains almost the whole of the great northern plain, receiving above a hundred tributaries, and having a course which, counting only main windings, probably exceeds 400 miles. The chief of its tributaries are the Duria (Dora Baltea), the Ticinus (Ticino), the Addua (Adda), the Ollius (Oglio), and the Mincius (Mincio), from the north; from the south, the Tanarus

(Tanaro), the Trebia (Trebbia), the Tarus (Taro), the Secia (Secchia), the Scultenna (Panaro), and the Rhenus (Reno). The next most important of the Italian rivers is the Athesis, or Adige, which, rising in the Tyrolean Alps, flows southward nearly to Verona; after which, curving round, it runs parallel with the Po into the Adriatic. Both these rivers are beyond the limits of the Peninsula proper. Within those limits the chief streams are the Arnus, Tiber, Liris, Vulturnus, and Silarus on the western side of the Apennines; the Æsis, Aternus, Tifernus, Frento, Cerbalus, and Aufidus to the east of those mountains.

The lakes.

6. Italy possesses a fair number of LAKES. Most of these lie towards the north, on the skirts of the Alps, at the point where the mountains sink down into the plain. The chief are the Benacus (Lago di Garda), between Lombardy and Venetia, the Sevinus (Lago d' Iseo), the Larius (Lago di Como), the Ceresius (Lago di Lugano), the Verbanus (Lago Maggiore), and the Lago d' Orta, which is unnoticed by the ancients. There is one important lake, the Lacus Fucinus, in the Central Apennine region. In Etruria are the Trasimenus (Lago di Perugia), the Volsiniensis (Lago di Bolsena), and the Sabatinus (Lago di Bracciano). Besides these, there are numerous lagoons on the sea-coast, especially in the neighborhood of Venice, and several mountain tarns of small size, but of great beauty.

The islands.

7. The Italian ISLANDS are, from their size, their fertility, and their mineral treasures, peculiarly important. They constitute nearly one-fourth of the whole area of the country. Sicily is exceedingly productive both in corn and in wine of an excellent quality. Sardinia and Corsica are rich in minerals. Even the little island of Elba (Ilva) is valuable for its iron. Sicily and the Lipari isles yield abundance of sulphur.

Chief divisions.

8. The only NATURAL DIVISION of Italy is into Northern and Southern—the former comprising the plain of the Po and the mountains inclosing it, so far as they are Italian; the latter coextensive with the Peninsula proper. It is usual, however, to divide the peninsula itself artificially into two portions by a line drawn across it from the mouth of the Silarus to that of the Tifernus. In this way a triple division of Italy is produced: and the three

parts are then called NORTHERN, CENTRAL, and SOUTHERN. It will be convenient to enumerate the countries into which Italy was anciently parcelled out under the three heads furnished by this latter division.

9. NORTHERN ITALY contained, in the most ancient times to which history goes back, the three countries of Liguria, Upper Etruria, and Venetia. After a while, part of Liguria and almost the whole of Upper Etruria were occupied by Gallic immigrants; and, the boundary-lines being to some extent changed, there still remained in this large and important tract three countries only, viz., Liguria, Venetia, and Gallia Cisalpina; the last-named having, as it were, taken the place of Upper Etruria.

NORTHERN ITALY.

10. Liguria was the tract at the extreme west of Northern Italy. Before the Gallic invasion it probably reached to the Pennine and Graian Alps; but in later times it was regarded as bounded on the north by the Po, on the west by the Alps from Monte Viso (Vesulus) southward, on the south by the Mediterranean, and on the east by the river Macra. It was a country almost entirely mountainous; for spurs from the Alps and Apennines occupy the whole tract between the mountain-ranges and the river Po, as far down as long. 9°. Liguria derived its name from its inhabitants, the Ligures or Ligyes, a race who once occupied the entire coast from below the mouth of the Arno to Massilia. Its chief towns were Genua (Genoa), Nicæ (Nice), and Asta (Asti).

Liguria.

11. Venetia was at the opposite side, or extreme east, of North Italy. It is difficult to say what were its original or natural limits. From the earliest times of which we have any knowledge, the Veneti were always encroached upon, first by the Etruscans and then by the Gauls, until a mere corner of North Italy still remained in their possession. This corner lay between Histria on the one side, and the Lesser Meduacus upon the other; southward it extended to the Adriatic Sea, northward to the flanks of the Alps. It was a tract of country for the most part exceedingly flat, well watered by streams flowing from the Alps, and fertile. The chief city in ancient times was Patavium, on the Lesser Meduacus; but this place was afterwards eclipsed by Aquileia.

Venetia.

12. The Etruscan state, which the Gauls conquered, was a confederacy of twelve cities, whose territory reached from the Ticinus on the west to the Adriatic and the mouths of the Po upon the east. Among its cities were Melpum, Mediolanum (Milan), Mantua, Verona, Hatria, and Felsina or Bononia. Northward it was bounded by the Alps, southward by the Apennines and the course of the Utis, or perhaps by that of the Rubicon. When the Gauls made their conquests they overstepped these boundaries, taking from the Ligurians all their territory north of the Padus, and perhaps some to the south, about Placentia and Parma, encroaching on the Veneti towards the east, and southward advancing into Umbria. Thus Gallia Cisalpina had larger limits than had belonged to North Etruria. It was bounded on the north and west by the Alps; on the south by Liguria, the main chain of the Apennines, and the Æsis river; on the east by the Adriatic and Venetia. The whole tract, except in some swampy districts, was richly fertile. While it remained Gallic, it was almost without cities. The Gauls lived, themselves, in open unwalled villages, and suffered most of the Etruscan towns to fall to decay. Some, as Melpum, disappeared. A few maintained themselves as Etruscan, in a state of semi-independence; e. g., Mantua and Verona. In Roman times, however, the country was occupied by a number of most important cities, chiefly Roman colonies. Among these were, in the region south of the Po, Placentia, Parma, Mutina (now Modena), Bononia (now Bologna), Ravenna, and Ariminium (now Rimini); and across the river to the north of it, Augusta Taurinorum (Turin), Ticinum (Pavia), Mediolanum (Milan), Brixia (Brescia), Cremona, Mantua, Verona, and Vincentia (now Vicenza).

Gallia Cisalpina.

13. CENTRAL ITALY, or the upper portion of the Peninsula proper, comprised six countries—Etruria, Latium, and Campania towards the west; Umbria, Picenum, and the Sabine territory (which had no general name) towards the east. These countries included the three most important in Italy, viz., Latium, Etruria, and the territory of the Sabines.

CENTRAL ITALY.

14. Etruria, or Tyrrhenia (as it was called by the Greeks), was the tract immediately south and west of the northern Apennines, interposed between that chain and the Medi-

Etruria. terranean. It was bounded on the north by Liguria and Gallia Cisalpina; on the east by Umbria and the old Sabine country; on the west by the Mediterranean Sea; and on the south by Latium. The line of separation between it and the rest of the continent was very marked, being first the strong chain of the Apennines, and then, almost from its source, the river Tiber. Etruria was watered by two main streams, the Arnus (Arno), and the Clanis (Chiana), a tributary of the Tiber. It was for the most part mountainous, consisting in its northern and eastern portions of strong spurs thrown off from the Apennines, and in its southern and western, of a separate system of rocky hills, ramifying irregularly, and reaching from the valleys of the Arnus and Clanis very nearly to the coast. The little level land which it contained was along the courses of the rivers and near the sea-shore. The soil was generally rich, but in places marshy. The country contained three important lakes. (See § 6.) The original Etrurian state consisted of a confederacy of twelve cities, among which were certainly Volsinii, Tarquinii, Vetulonium, Perusia, and Clusium; and probably Volaterræ, Arretium, Rusellæ, Veii, and Agylla or Cære. Other important towns were Pisæ (Pisa), and Fæsulæ (Fiesole), north of the Arnus; Populonia and Cosa, on the coast between the Arnus and the Tiber; Cortona in the Clanis valley; and Falerii near the Tiber, about eighteen miles north of Veii.

15. Latium lay below Etruria, on the left bank of the Tiber. It was bounded on the north by the Tiber, the Anio, and the Upper Liris rivers; on the west and south by the Mediterranean; on the east by the Lower Liris and a spur of the Apennines. These, however, were not its original limits, but those whereto it ultimately attained. Anciently many non-Latin tribes inhabited portions of the territory. The Volsci held the isolated range of hills reaching from near Præneste to the coast at Tarracina or Anxur. The Æqui were in possession of the Mons Algidus, and of the mountain-range between Præneste and the Anio. The Hernici were located in the valley of the Trerus, a tributary of the Liris. On the Lower Liris were established the Ausones. The nation of the Latins formed, we are told, a confederacy of thirty cities, Alba having origi-

nally the pre-eminency. Among the thirty the most important were the following:—Tibur, Gabii, Præneste, Tusculum, Velitræ, Aricia, Lanuvium, Laurentum, Lavinium, Ardea, Antium, Circeii, Anxur or Tarracina, Setia, Norba, and Satricum. Latium was chiefly a low plain, but diversified towards the north by spurs from the Apennines, in the centre and towards the south by two important ranges of hills. One of these, known as "the Volscian range," extends in a continuous line from near Præneste to Tarracina; the other, which is quite separate and detached, rises out of the plain between the Volscian range and the Tiber, and is known as "the Alban range," or the "Mons Algidus." Both are in the western part of the country. The eastern is comparatively a flat region. Here were Anagnia, the old capital of the Hernici, Arpinum, Fregellæ, Aquinum, Interamna ad Lirim; and, on the coast, Lantulæ, Fundi, Formiæ, Minturnæ, and Vescia.

Campania.

16. Campania in its general character very much resembled Latium, but the isolated volcanic hills which here diversified the plain were loftier and placed nearer the coast. To the extreme south of the country a strong spur ran out from the Apennines terminating in the promontory of Minerva, the southern protection of the Bay of Naples. Campania extended along the coast from the Liris to the Silarus, and reached inland to the more southern of the two Apennine ranges, which, separating a little below Lake Fucinus, reunite at Compsa. The plain country was all rich, especially that about Capua. Among the principal Campanian towns were Capua, the capital, Nola and Teanum in the interior, and upon the coast Sinuessa, Cumæ, Puteoli, Parthenopé, or Neapolis, Herculaneum, Pompeii, Surrentum, Salernum, and Picentia.

Umbria.

17. Umbria lay east of Etruria, from which it was separated, first by the range of the Apennines, and then by the river Tiber. It was bounded on the north by Gallia Cisalpina; on the east and south-east by Picenum and the Sabine country; on the south-west and west by Etruria. Before the invasion of the Gauls it reached as far north as the Rubicon, and included all the Adriatic coast between that stream and the Æsis; but after the coming of the Senones this tract was lost, and Umbria was shut

out from the sea. The Umbrian territory was almost wholly mountainous, consisting, as it did, chiefly of the main chain of the Apennines, together with the spurs on either side of the chain, from the source of the Tiber to the junction with the Tiber of the Nar. Some rich plains, however, occurred in the Tiber and Lower Nar valleys. The chief towns of Umbria were Iguvium, famous for its inscriptions; Sentinum, the scene of the great battle with the Gauls and Samnites; Spoletium (now Spoleto); Interamna (now Terni); and Narnia (Narni), which, though on the left bank of the Nar, was still reckoned to Umbria.

Picenum.

18. Picenum extended along the coast of the Adriatic from the Æsis to the Matrinus (Piomba) river. It was composed mainly of spurs from the Apennines, but contained along the coast some flat and fertile country. The chief towns were Ancona, on the coast, Firmum (Fermo), Asculum Picenum (Ascoli), and Hadria (Atri), in the interior.

The Sabine territory.

19. The territory of the Sabine races, in which Picenum ought perhaps to be included, was at once the most extensive and the most advantageously situated of all the countries of Central Italy. In length, from the Mons Fiscellus (Monte Rotondo) to the Mons Vultur (Monte Vulture), it exceeded 200 miles; while in breadth it reached very nearly from sea to sea, bordering the Adriatic from the Matrinus to the Tifernus rivers, and closely approaching the Mediterranean in the vicinity of Salernum. In the north it comprised all the valleys of the Upper Nar and its tributaries, together with a portion of the valley of the Tiber, the plain country south and east of Lake Fucinus, and the valleys of the Suinus and Aternus rivers. Its central mass was made up of the valleys of the Sagrus, Trinius, and Tifernus, together with the mountain-ranges between them; while southward it comprised the whole of the great Samnite upland drained by the Vulturnus, and its tributaries. The territory had many distinct political divisions. The north-western tract, about the Nar and Tiber, reaching from the main chain of the Apennines to the Anio, was the country of the old Sabines (Sabini), the only race to which that name is applied by the ancient writers. East and south-east of this region, the tract about Lake Fucinus, and

the valleys of the Suinus and Aternus rivers, were in the possession of the League of the Four Cantons, the Marsi, Marrucini, Peligni, and Vestini, who probably were Sabine races. Still farther to the east, the valleys of the Sagrus and Trinius, and the coast tract from Ortona to the Tifernus, formed the country of the Frentani. South and south-east of this was Samnium, comprising the high upland, the main chain of the Apennines, and the eastern flank of that chain for a certain distance. The chief of the Sabine towns were Reate on the Velinus, a tributary of the Nar; Teate and Aternum on the Aternus; Marrubium on Lake Fucinus; and Beneventum and Bovianum in Samnium.

SOUTHERN ITALY.

20. SOUTHERN ITALY, or the tract below the Tifernus and Silarus rivers, contained four countries—on the west, Lucania and Bruttium; on the east, Apulia and Messapia, or, as it was sometimes called, Iapygia. The entire number of distinct countries in ancient Italy was thus thirteen.

Lucania.

21. Lucania extended along the west coast of Italy from the Silarus to the Laüs river. Its boundary on the north was formed by the Silarus, the chain of the Apennines from Compsa to the Mons Vultur, and the course of the Bradanus (Brandano). Eastward, its border was the shore of the Tarentine Gulf; southward, where it adjoined Bruttium, the line of demarkation ran from the Lower Laüs across the mountains to the Crathis, or river of Thurii. The country was both picturesque and fertile, diversified by numerous spurs from the Apennine range, and watered by a multitude of rivers. It had few native cities of any importance; but the coasts were thickly occupied by Grecian settlements of great celebrity. Among these were, on the west coast, Posidonia or Pæstum, Elea or Velia, Pyxus or Buxentum, and Laüs; on the east, Metapontum, Heracleia, Pandosia, Siris, Sybaris, and Thurii. (See pp. 177–182.)

Bruttium.

22. Bruttium adjoined Lucania on the south, and was a country very similar in character. Its chief native city was Consentia, in the interior, near the sources of the Crathis river. On the western coast were the Greek towns of Temesa, Terina, Hipponium, and Rhegium; on the eastern those of Croton, Caulonia, and Locri.

23. Apulia lay entirely on the eastern coast, adjoining

Samnium upon the west, and separated from the country of the Frentani by the Tifernus river. The range of the Apennines, extending from the Mons Vultur eastward as far as long. 17° 40′, divided it from Iapygia. Apulia differed from all the other countries of the Peninsula proper in being almost wholly a plain. Except in the north-west corner of the province, no spurs of any importance here quit the Apennines, but from their base extends a vast and rich level tract, from twenty to forty miles wide, intersected by numerous streams, and diversified towards its more eastern portion by a number of lakes. The tract is especially adapted for the grazing of cattle. Among its rivers are the Aufidus, on the banks of which Cannæ was fought, the Cerbalus, and the river of Arpi. The only mountainous part of Apulia is the north and north-west, where the Apennines send down to the coast two strongly-marked spurs, one between the Tifernus and the Frento rivers, the other, east of the Frento, a still stronger and more important range, which running towards the north-east reaches the coast, and forms the well-known rocky promontory of Garganum. The chief cities of Apulia were Larinum, near the Tifernus; Luceria, Sipontum, and Arpi, north of the Cerbalus; Salapia, between the Cerbalus and Aufidus; and Canusium, Cannæ, and Venusia, south of that river. It was usual to divide Apulia into two regions, of which the north-western was called Daunia, the south-eastern Peucetia.

Apulia.

24. Messapia, or Iapygia, lay south and east of Apulia, comprising the entire long promontory which has been called the "heel" of Italy, and a triangular tract between the east Apennine range and the river Bradanus. Towards the east it was low and flat, full of numerous small lakes, and without important rivers; westward it was diversified by numerous ranges of hills, spurs from the Apulian Apennines, which sheltered it upon the north and rendered it one of the softest and most luxurious of the Italian countries. The most important of the Iapygian cities was Taras, or Tarentum, the famous Lacedæmonian colony. (See p. 177.) Other Greek settlements were Callipolis (now Gallipoli), and Hydrus or Hydruntum (now Otranto). The chief native town was Brundusium.

Iapygia.

25. The geography of Italy is incomplete without a de-

scription of the principal islands. These were three in number, Sicily, Sardinia, and Corsica. There were also numerous islets along the western and a few off the eastern coast, which will require a very brief notice.

ISLANDS.

26. Sicily, which is estimated to contain about ten thousand square miles, is an irregular triangle, the sides of which face respectively the north, the east, and the south-west. None of the coasts is much indented; but of the three, the northern has the most noticeable bays and headlands. Here are the gulfs of Castel-a-Mare, Palermo, Patti, and Milazzo; the headlands of Trapani (Drepanum), Capo St. Vito, Capo di Gallo, Capo Zaffarana, Capo Orlando, Capo Calava, and Capo Bianco. The south-western, and most of the eastern, shores run in smooth lines; but towards the extreme south-east of the island there is a fair amount of indentation. Good harbors are numerous. The most remarkable are those of Messana and Syracuse, the former protected by a curious curved strip of land, resembling a sickle, whence the old name of Zanclé; the latter rendered secure in all winds by the headland of Plemmyrium and the natural breakwater of Ortygia. There are also excellent ports at Lilybæum and Panormus (Palermo). The mountain system of Sicily consists of a main chain, the continuation of the Bruttian Apennines (Aspromonte), which traverses the island from east to west, beginning near Messina (Messana) and terminating at Cape Drepanum. This main chain, known in its different parts by various names, throws off, about midway in its course, a strong spur, which strikes south-east and terminates in Cape Pachynus (Passaro). Thus the island is divided by its mountain system into three tracts of comparative lowland—a narrow tract facing northward between the main chain and the north coast; a long and broad tract facing the south-west, bounded on the north by the western half of the main chain, and on the east by the spur; and a broad but comparatively short tract facing the east, bounded on the west by the spur, and on the north by the eastern half of the main chain. In none of these lowlands, however, is there really much flat country. Towards the north and towards the south-west, both the main chain and the spur throw off numerous branches, which occupy almost the

Sicily.

whole country between the rivers; while towards the east, where alone are there any extensive plains, volcanic action has thrown up the separate and independent mountain of Etna, which occupies with its wide-spreading roots almost one-third of what should naturally have been lowland. Thus Sicily, excepting in the tract between Etna and Syracuse, where the famous "Piano di Catania" extends itself, is almost entirely made up of mountain and valley, and, in a military point of view, is an exceedingly strong and difficult country. Its chief rivers are the Simæthus on the east, which drains nearly the whole of the great plain; the Himera and Halycus on the south; and the Hypsa, near the extreme south-west corner. The only important native town was Enna, nearly in the centre of the island; all the other cities of any note were settlements of foreigners; Eryx and Egesta, or Segesta, of the Trojans (?); Lilybæum, Motya, Panormus, and Soloeis, or Soluntum, of the Carthaginians; Himera, Messana, Tauromenium, Naxos, Catana, Megara Hyblæa, Syracuse, Camarina, Gela, Agrigentum, and Selinus, of the Greeks. (On the history of the Greek settlements, see pp. 181–190.)

Sardinia.

27. Sardinia, which modern surveys show to be larger than Sicily, has an area of probably about 11,000 square miles. It is an oblong parallelogram, the sides of which may be viewed roughly as facing the four cardinal points, though in reality the south side has a slight inclination towards the east, and the north side a stronger one towards the west. Though less mountainous than either Sicily or Corsica, Sardinia is traversed by an important chain which runs parallel with the eastern and western shores, but nearer the former, from Cape Lungo-Sardo on the north to Cape Carbonara at the extreme south of the island. This chain throws out numerous short branch ranges on either side, which cover nearly the whole of the eastern half of the island. The western half has three separate mountain-clusters of its own. One, the smallest, is at the extreme north-west corner of the island, between the Gulfs of Asinara and Alghero; another, three or four times larger, fills the south-western corner, reaching from Cape Spartivento to the Gulf of Oristano. Both these are, like the main range, of primary (granitic) formation. The third

cluster, which is interposed between the two others, occupying the whole tract extending northward from the Gulf of Oristano and the river Tirso to the coast between the Turrilano and Coguinas rivers, is much the largest of the three, and is of comparatively recent volcanic formation. These mountain-clusters, together with the main range, occupy by far the greater portion of the island. They still, however, leave room for some important plains, as especially that of Campidano on the south, which stretches across from the Gulf of Cagliari to that of Oristano; that of Ozieri on the north, on the upper course of the Coguinas; and that of Sassari in the north-west, which reaches across the isthmus from Alghero to Porto Torres. Sardinia is fairly fertile, but has always been noted for its malaria. Its chief river was the Thyrsus (Tirso). The principal cities were Caralis (Cagliari), on the south coast, in the bay of the same name; Sulci, at the extreme south-west of the island, opposite the Insula Plumbaria; Neapolis, in the Gulf of Asinara; and Olbia, towards the north-eastern end of the island. There was no city of any importance in the interior.

Corsica.

28. Corsica, situated directly to the north of Sardinia, was more mountainous and rugged than either of the other two great islands. A strong mountain-chain ran through the island from north to south, culminating towards the centre in the Mons Antæus (Monte Rotondo). Numerous branch ranges intersected the country on either side of the main chain, rendering the entire region one of constant mountain and valley. Streams were numerous; but the limits of the island were too narrow for them to attain any considerable size. The chief town was Alalia (afterwards Aleria), a colony of the Phocæans. Besides this, the only places of any importance were Mariana, on the east coast, above Alalia, Centurimum (now Centuri), on the west side of the northern promontory, Urcinium on the west coast (now Ajaccio), and Talcinum (now Corte) in the interior.

Islets.

29. The lesser islands adjacent to Italy were Ilva (Elba), between northern Corsica and the main-land; Igilium (Giglio) and Dianium (Giannuti), opposite the Mons Argentarius in Etruria; Palmaria, Pontia, Sinonia, and Pandataria, off Anxur; Pithecussa (Ischia), Prochyta (Procida), and Capreæ (Capri), in the Bay of Naples;

Strongyle (Stromboli), Euonymus (Panaria), Lipara (Lipari), Vulcania (Volcano), Didymé (Salina), Phœnicussa (Felicudi), Ericussa (Alicudi), and Ustica, off the north coast of Sicily; the Ægates Insulæ, off the western point of the same island; the Chœrades Insulæ, off Tarentum; and Trimetus (Tremiti) in the Adriatic, north of the Mons Garganus.

On the geography of Italy, the most important works are—

CLUVERIUS, *Italia Antiqua.* Lugd. Bat., 1624; 2 vols. folio.

ROMANELLI, *Antica Topografia istorica del Regno di Napoli.* Napoli, 1815; 3 vols. 4to.

MANNERT, K., *Geographie der Griechen und Römer aus ihren Schriften dargestellt.* Leipzig, 1801–29; 10 vols. 8vo.

SWINBURNE, H., *Travels in the Two Sicilies in the Years* 1777–80. London, 1783–85; 2 vols. 4to.

DENNIS, G., *Cities and Cemeteries of the Etruscans.* London, 1848; 2 vols. 8vo.

ABEKEN, *Mittel-Italien vor den Zeiten Römischer Herrschaft.* Stuttgart, 1843; 8vo.

CRAMER, *Geographical and Historical Description of Ancient Italy.* Oxford, 1826; 2 vols. 8vo.

A comprehensive work on the subject, combining local knowledge with advanced scholarship and a good knowledge of the ancient authorities, is still a desideratum.

SKETCH OF THE HISTORY.

FIRST PERIOD.

The Ancient Traditional History from the Earliest Times to the Commencement of the Republic, B.C. 508.

SOURCES. 1. *Native.* A few fragments of the *Fasti Triumphales* belong to this early period; but such knowledge of it as we possess is derived mainly from the works of historians. Among these the first place must be assigned to the fragments of the early Annalists, especially of Q. FABIUS PICTOR, many of which are preserved in DIONYSIUS of Halicarnassus. The most copious native writer on the period is LIVY, who delivers an account of it in his First Book. Other native authorities are CICERO, who has sketched the constitutional history of the period in his treatise *De Republica* (book ii.), and FLORUS, who has briefly epitomized it. The portion of VELLEIUS PATERCULUS which treated of the time is almost entirely lost. No lives of NEPOS touch on it. Many allusions to it are contained, however, in the works of the poets and grammarians, as OVID (*Fasti*), VIRGIL (*Æneid,* book vi.), SERVIUS (*ad Æneid.*), FESTUS, and others. 2. *Foreign.* The Greek writers are fuller on the early history than the Roman. The most important of them is DIONYSIUS of Halicarnassus, in whose work (*Archæologia Ro-*

mana; ed. REISKE. Lipsiæ, 1774–77; 6 vols. 8vo) the ante-regal and regal periods occupy the first four books. Next to DIONYSIUS may be placed PLUTARCH, whose Lives of Romulus, Numa, and Poplicola bear upon this portion of the history. The part of DIODORUS SICULUS which treated of the time (books vii.–x.) is lost, with the exception of a few brief fragments.

On the value of these sources the most diametrically opposite opinions continue to be held after a controversy which has lasted more than a century. The negative criticism, which was begun by Perizonius, Bayle, and Beaufort, received a strong impulse, early in the present century, from the great work of

NIEBUHR, B. G., *Römische Geschichte.* Berlin, 1826–32; 3 vols. 8vo. (First and second volumes translated by JULIUS HARE and BP. THIRLWALL, Cambridge, 1831–32; third volume translated by Dr. W. SMITH, and Dr. L. SCHMITZ. London, 1842; 8vo); which was followed in England by the very popular work of

ARNOLD, Dr. T., *History of Rome.* London, 1838–43; 3 vols. 8vo; and in Germany, after an interval of a quarter of a century, by that of

SCHWEGLER, A., *Römische Geschichte.* Tübingen, 1853–58; 3 vols. 8vo. Written in the true spirit of the Tübingen School.

The doubts of the last-named writer, falling on congenial soil in this country, produced an elaborate, but intensely skeptical work, which has probably exhausted all that can be said on the negative side of the subject, viz.:

LEWIS, Sir G. C., *On the Credibility of the Early Roman History.* London, 1855; 2 vols. 8vo.

On the opposite side of the question some important treatises have been published recently. Note especially the following:

AMPÈRE, J. J., *L'Histoire Romaine à Rome.* Paris, 1862–64; 4 vols. 8vo. The writer argues that the discoveries made by recent excavations with regard to the original Rome strongly confirm the early traditional history.

DYER, T. H., *History of the City of Rome.* London, 1865; 8vo; and the same writer's *History of the Kings of Rome.* London, 1868; 8vo. It is Mr. Dyer's object to show, first, that authentic materials for the early history existed in the times of the first Annalists, B.C. 220 to 200; and, secondly, that the internal difficulties and discrepancies are not such as to render the history that has come down to us incredible.

Works of a more dogmatic and less argumentative character, embracing the early period, or distinctly written upon it, worthy of the reader's attention, are the following:

NEWMAN, F., *Regal Rome; an Introduction to Roman History.* London, 1852; 12mo.

MOMMSEN, TH., *Römische Geschichte.* 3d edition. Berlin, 1861; 3 vols. 8vo. The value of this very original work is greatly diminished by the almost entire absence of references. (Translated by W. P. DICKSON. London, 1862; 3 vols. small 8vo.)

KEIGHTLEY, T., *History of Rome.* London, 1836. A useful compendium.

KORTUEM, F., *Römische Geschichte.* Heidelberg, 1843; 8vo.

LIDDELL, H. G., *History of Rome from the Earliest Times to the Establishment of the Empire.* London, 1855; 2 vols. 8vo.

GREGOROVIUS, F., *Geschichte der Stadt Rom.* Stuttgart, 1859–62; 4 vols. 8vo.

PETER, C., *Geschichte Roms.* Halle, 1865–67; 3 vols. 8vo.

1. ITALY was inhabited, at the earliest times to which our knowledge carries us back, by five principal races. These were the Ligurians, the Venetians, the Etruscans, the Italians proper, and the Iapygians. The Ligurians and Venetians may have been branches of one stock, the Illyrian; but there is no sufficient evidence to prove this connection. They were weak and unimportant races, confined to narrow regions in the north, and without any influence on the general history of Italy. Setting them aside, therefore, for the present, we may confine our attention to the three other races.

Chief races of ancient Italy.

2. The Iapygians were probably among the earliest settlers. The heel of Italy, which stretches out towards Greece, invites colonization from that quarter; and it would seem that at a very remote date a stream of settlers passed across the narrow sea from the Hellenic to the Italic peninsula, and landing on the Iapygian promontory spread themselves northward and westward over the greater portion of the foot of Italy. The language of the race in question remains in numerous inscriptions which have been discovered in the Terra di Otranto, and shows them to have been nearly connected with the Greeks. Their worship of Greek gods, and the readiness with which, at a later date, they became actually Hellenized, point in the same direction. We have reason to conclude that a race kindred with the Greeks held in the early times the greater part of Southern Italy, which was thus prepared for the later more positively Hellenic settlements. To this stock appear to have belonged the Messapians, Peucetians, Œnotrians, the Chaones or Chones, and perhaps the Daunii.

The Iapygians.

It is supposed by some that the Iapygian migration took place by land, the settlers passing round the coast of the Adriatic Sea, and being pushed southward by later immigrants. This is possible; but migration by sea may be accomplished even by a very primitive people.

3. The Italians proper, who in the historical times occupy with their numerous tribes almost the whole of Central Italy, appear to have been later in-comers than the Iapygians, to have proceeded from the north, and

The Italians proper.

to have pressed with great weight on the semi-Greek population of the southern regions. They comprised, apparently, four principal subordinate races; viz., the Umbrians, the Sabines, the Oscans, and the Latins. Of these the Umbrians and Oscans were very closely connected. The Latins were quite distinct. The Sabines are suspected to have been nearly allied to the Osco-Umbrians.

The Sabine race was remarkable for its numerous subdivisions. It comprised the Sabini proper, the Samnites, the Picentes (probably), the Marsi, Marrucini, Peligni, and Vestini, the Frentani, the Campani, and the Lucani. The Samnites had also subdivisions of their own, e. g., the Caraceni, the Pentri, and the Hirpini.

There were also a considerable number of Oscan tribes; as the Volsci, Æqui, Hernici (?), Aurunci, Ausones, and Apuli. These names seem, however, to be chiefly variants of the general ethnic title.

The Etruscans.

4. The Tuscans or Etruscans, the most powerful nation of the north, differed in race *completely* from all the other inhabitants of Italy. It appears to be, on the whole, most probable that they were Turanians, of a type similar to that which is found in various parts of Europe—Lapps and Finns in the extreme north, Esthonians on the Baltic, Basques in Spain—remnants of a primitive population that once, we may suppose, overspread the whole of Europe. The original seat of the race, so far as it is traceable, seems to have been Rhætia, or the country about the head-streams of the Rhine, the Inn, and the Adige. Their native name was RAS; and this name, changed by the Italians into Rhæsi or Rhæti, was long attached to the mountain region from which their hordes had issued. These hordes at a very remote time spread themselves over the plain of the Po from the Ticinus to beyond the Adige, and formed there, as we are told, a confederacy of twelve cities. (See p. 363.) After having flourished in this tract for an indefinite period, they overflowed the mountain barrier to the south, and occupying the region between the northern Apennines and the Tiber, formed there a second, quite separate, confederacy, consisting, like the northern one, of twelve distinct states. Subsequently, but probably later than the period now under consideration, they passed the Tiber and established temporarily a dominion in Campania, where Capua and Nola were cities founded by them.

CHARACTERISTICS OF THE ETRUSCANS. Physically, they were a brawny, stout race, short in stature, with large heads and thick arms, offering a strong contrast to the graceful and slender Italians. Their religious ideas were gloomy and strange. They delighted in auguries, in the mystical handling of numbers, and in the exact observance of a minute and manifold ritual. There can be no doubt that they had made a considerable advance in the arts; but it is still a question how far the works of art found in their tombs are of native production, how far mere imports from Greece. They were certainly the best architects of all the early Italian races, and the only race that showed a marked inclination to maritime pursuits. Tuscan corsairs covered the Western Mediterranean from a very early time; and Agylla had, before B.C. 550, an important trade.

Among the most important works on the interesting subject of the language and art of the Etruscans are—

INGHIRAMI, *Monumenti Etruschi.* Fiesole, 1821–26; 7 vols. 4to.

LANZI, *Saggio di Lingua Etrusca e di altre antiche d'Italia.* Roma, 1789; 8vo. The edition of Florence, 1824–25, is the best.

DENNIS, G., *Cities and Cemeteries of the Etruscans.* (See p. 372.)

MÜLLER, K. O., *Die Etrusker.* Breslau, 1828; 2 vols. 8vo.

MICALI, *Storia degli Antichi Popoli Italiani.* Firenze, 1832; 3 vols. 8vo.

Origin of the Romans: the Trojan colony.

5. There can be no doubt that the Romans belonged, at any rate predominantly, to the second of the three races who seem in the early times to have divided the peninsula among them—the race which has been here termed, κατ' ἐξοχήν, "Italic." They had, indeed, a tradition which connected them with a body of immigrants who were thought to have come by sea into Italy from the distant city of Troy, at a date which preceded by nearly 500 years the building of the city. And this tradition was brought out into great prominence by writers of the Imperial times. But, whatever amount of truth we may suppose to be contained in the "story of Æneas," it is evident that the crews of a few vessels landing on a thickly-peopled coast, and belonging to a race not much more civilized than that to which they came, could make but a very slight impression on the previous population, in which they would be sure to be very soon swallowed up and absorbed. The Trojan colony to Latium is therefore, whether true or false, a matter of small consequence—it had no part in determining the ethnic character of the Roman people.

The Romans really Latins.

6. Nor is there much difficulty in deciding to which of the branch races included here under the general name of "Italic," the Romans belonged. Language is the most certain indication of race, and the language

which the Romans spoke was Latin. Their own traditions connected the early city in a special way with Lavinium and Alba Longa; and these cities were universally allowed to have been two of the thirty Latin towns. To whatever extent the Romans were a mixed people—and that they were so to some extent is admitted by all—it is impossible to doubt that they were predominantly and essentially—not Oscans, not Sabines, much less Umbrians—but Latins.

Rome probably a colony of Alba Longa.

7. It is, however, far from easy to determine in what exact position the original Rome stood to the Latin stock. It is clear that she was not a mere Latin town, not one of the thirty. She stands in the early times of the monarchy quite outside the confederacy; and a peculiar character belongs to her which is not simply and wholly Latin. The tradition which makes her foundation the spontaneous act of a band of adventurous young men, whose affection for the locality leads them to set up a new town, which is also a new state, on the spot where they have been wont to pasture their flocks, is at variance with the condition of Italy at the time, which was not a wilderness, with abundant waste land, whereon the first comer might settle, but a thickly-peopled country, where every inch of ground had an owner, or was disputed between neighboring tribes. If there be any truth at all in the account which has come down to us of the original settlement, that account must be a poeticized version of a very ordinary occurrence. The Latin towns were in the habit of extending or defending their territories by the establishment of colonies. Nothing is more easily conceivable than that the original Rome should have been a colony from Alba Longa, planted in a strong though unhealthy position at the extreme verge of the territory, where it was threatened by the Tuscans upon the west and still more by the advancing Sabines towards the north. Rome herself was afterwards accustomed to plant her colonies in exactly such positions. Among the various conjectures which critics have formed on the subject of the origin of Rome, that which regards her as a colony from Alba appears to be the most worthy of acceptance.

The list of the Alban kings can not be regarded as in any sense belonging to Roman history, for the history of a colony dates from its foundation.

Were the list genuine, it would be an important record for early *Italian* history, as distinct from Roman. But the catalogue has all the appearance of being a forgery.

Rome independent. The *synœcismus* with the Sabines.

8. But if Rome was originally a mere Alban dependency, it is certain that she did not long continue such. The first clearly marked fact in her history is her entrance into voluntary union with the natives of an adjacent Sabine settlement, an act which implies independence and the assertion of sovereignty. The colony must either previously have shaken off the yoke of the mother-city, or else must, in the very act of uniting herself with an alien people, have asserted autonomy. From the date of the *συνοικισμός*, if no earlier, Rome was, it is clear, a self-governing community. No power exercised control over her. She stood aloof from the Latin league, on terms which were at first rather hostile than friendly. Her position was unique among the states and cities of the period. The amalgamation of two bloods, two civilizations, two kindred, but still somewhat different, religious systems, produced a peculiar people—a people stronger than its neighbors, possessing wider views and sympathies, and more varied tastes—a people better calculated than its neighbors to form a nucleus round which the various tribes of the Italic stock might gather themselves.

Earliest history constitutional, not personal.

9. While the history of individuals at this remote period is wholly wanting—for such names as Romulus, Remus, Celer, Titus Tatius, and the like, can not be regarded as having any thing more of historic substance than their parallels, Hellen, Dorus, Ion, Amyclas, Hoples, etc., the *heroes eponymi* of Greek legend—it is not impossible to trace out the early character of the government, the chief features of the constitution, the principal divisions and subdivisions of classes within the community, and the rights and privileges attaching to each. Tradition is a trustworthy guide for certain main features; analogy and analysis may be allowed to furnish others; for the laws of the growth of states are sufficiently well known and sufficiently uniform to make it possible in most cases, where we have before us a full-grown constitution, to trace it back to its foundations, and gather a fair knowledge of its history from the form and character of its several parts.

10. The known points of the early constitution are the following:—(*a*) The form of government was monarchical. A chief, called "rex," i. e., "ruler," or "director," stood at the head of the state, exercising a great, though not an absolute, power over the citizens. (*b*) The monarchy was not hereditary, but elective. When the king died, there was an "interregnum." The direction of affairs was taken by the Senate or Council, whose ten chief men ("Decem Primi") exercised the royal authority, each in his turn, for five days. It belonged to the Senate to elect, and to the people to confirm the king. (*c*) Under the king was, first of all, an hereditary nobility ("patricii"), members of certain noble families, not deriving their nobility from the king, but possessing it by immemorial descent. These noble families or "houses" ("gentes") were, prior to the *συνοικισμός*, one hundred in number; after the *συνοικισμός*, two hundred. Each was represented by its chief in the council of the king ("senatus"); and thus the senators were originally one hundred, afterwards two hundred. All the members of a "house" had one name ("nomen gentilitium"); all might participate in certain sacred rites ("sacra gentilitia"); and all had certain rights of property in common. (*d*) All the males of full age belonging to the nobility possessed the right of attending the public Assembly ("comitia"), where they voted in ten bodies ("curiæ"), each composed of the members of ten "houses." Each *curia* had its chief, called "curio;" and the Assembly was presided over by the chief of the ten *curiones*, who was called "Curio Maximus." (*e*) Every change of law required the consent of both the Senate and the Assembly. The Senate had the right of discussing and voting, but the Assembly had the right of voting only. The Assembly was also privileged to determine on peace or war; and if one of its members appealed to it from the sentence of the king, or of a judge, it determined the appeal and condemned or acquitted at its pleasure. (*f*) In addition to the members of the "gentes," the early Roman state contained two other classes. These were the Clients and the Slaves. The Slaves resembled persons of their class in other communities; but the Clients were a peculiar institution. They were dependents upon the noble "houses," and personally free, but pos-

Chief points of the early constitution.

The king, the Patres, and the Clients.

sessed of no political privileges, and usually either cultivated the lands of their "patrons," or carried on a trade under their protection. They resembled to a considerable extent the "retainers" of the Middle Ages.

Division of the monarchy between the Latin and Sabine Romans.

11. Under this constitution, Rome flourished for a period which is somewhat vague and indefinite, without the occurrence of any important change. According to one tradition, a double monarchy was tried for a short time, in order that the two elements of the state—the Roman and the Sabine (or the Ramnes and the Tities)—might each furnish a ruler from their own body. But the experiment was not tried for very long. In lieu of it, we may suspect that for a while the principle of alternation was employed, the Romans and the Sabines each in their turn furnishing a king to the community.

This seems to be implied in the ordinary narrative, which gives, as the first four kings—1. Romulus (Latin from Alba); 2. Numa (Sabine); 3. Tullus (Latin from Medullia); and 4. Ancus (Sabine—grandson of Numa).

Traces of the two nationalities in the religion.

12. The duplication of the community, which was thus perceptible through all ranks, affected also to a considerable extent the national religion. Not only was there a duplication of the chief religious officers in consequence of the *synœcismus*, but sometimes the duplication extended to the objects of worship, the deities themselves. Quirinus, for instance, seems to have been the Sabine Mars, worshipped, like the Latin Mars, by his own "Flamen" and college of "Salii." Juno was perhaps the Sabine equivalent of the Latin Diana, another form of the same name, but in the popular belief a different goddess. In the ranks of the hierarchy the duplication was more marked. It can be traced in the college of the Pontifices, in that of the Augurs, in that of the Vestal Virgins, in the priesthoods of Mars, and (probably) in the priesthood of Hercules.

CHARACTER OF THE ROMAN RELIGION. (*a*) Less imaginative and more matter-of-fact than the Greek. (*b*) Consisted mainly in the recognition of certain obligations (religiones); viz., (i.) the obligation to worship each of the state gods with sacrifices of a stated kind at stated times, and to keep certain festivals; (ii.) the obligation on the part of the *paterfamilias* to make daily offerings to the "Lares" of his own household; (iii.) the obligation to perform vows and to make occasional thank-offerings; (iv.) the obligation to abstain from business on "dies nefasti." (*c*) Though mainly of home growth, contained a certain number of foreign elements, derived chiefly from contact with the Greeks. The most important of these was belief in the value of oracles, shown in the practice of consulting the Sibylline books.

Reign of Tullus Hostilius. Personal history begins.

13. The names which tradition assigned to the early Roman monarchs seem to be fictitious. Romulus, Titus Tatius, and Numa Pompilius are personifications rather than personages. We first touch on personal history in the Roman records when we come to the name of Tullus Hostilius, the fourth, or, omitting Tatius, the third traditional king. There is every reason to believe that this monarch actually lived and reigned; his name was the first that was handed down to posterity, owing to the fact that he was the first king who effected an important conquest, and raised Rome from a humble position to one of dignity and eminence. It is the great glory of Tullus that he conquered Alba Longa, the chief of the Latin cities, the mother-city of Rome itself. His conquest probably doubled, or even tripled, the Roman territory; it prepared the way for that hegemony of Rome over all Latium to which she owed her subsequent greatness; and it largely increased the population of Rome, and the military strength of the nation. For Tullus was not content with a simple conquest. Following up the principle of *synœcismus*, which had already been found to answer, he destroyed Alba, except its temples, and transferred the inhabitants to his own capital. He thus greatly strengthened the Latin element in the Roman state, and made the Sabines a mere modifying influence in a community essentially Latin.

INTERNAL CHANGES consequent on the destruction of Alba. The Alban nobles (Luceres?) being added to the Patrician body on the plan already adopted upon the junction of the primitive Romans, or Ramnes, with the Sabines (Tities), the tribes became three, the *curiæ* thirty, and the "houses" three hundred. The Senate, however, continued at its former number of two hundred, the privilege of sending their representatives into it not being at first conceded to the Alban houses. No change was made in the chief sacred offices—those of the Flamens, Pontifices, and Augurs—but as the *home* of the Alban race was now transferred to Rome, the college of Vestal Virgins was increased from four to six.

Reign of Ancus Martius. Rise of the "Plebs."

14. The next Roman king whose name has descended to us is Ancus Martius, who is said to have belonged to the Sabines or Tities. This monarch appears to have been regarded by the later Romans as the founder of the Plebeian order. He pursued the policy

of Tullus both in making war on neighboring Latin towns, and in using his victories for the aggrandizement of his capital by transferring to Rome the populations of the conquered states. A portion of the new settlers undoubtedly became Clients; but the richer and more independent would decline to take up this relationship, and would be content with the protection of the king. Hence would come a sudden augmentation of that free commonalty, which must always grow up—out of various elements—in all states which commence, like Rome, with a privileged class of nobles, and a wholly unprivileged class of retainers or dependents.

ELEMENTS OF A "PLEBS" OR COMMONALTY. (*a*) Free settlers; either political refugees, mercenary soldiers, or traders. The first-named would be numerous in a time of so much disturbance as that in which Rome grew up. (*b*) Forced settlers. To this class would belong the whole of the conquered populations, except such as were either formally admitted into the Patrician body, or voluntarily attached themselves as retainers to a noble house. (*c*) Clients, whose "family," or, at any rate, whose "gens," died out and became extinct. (*d*) The issue of marriages of inequality, i. e., of all cases in which a Patrician took to wife a person of a class which did not possess the right of intermarriage with the noble houses ("jus connubii"). This last element would be small but very important.

The "Plebs" recognized by Ancus. He assigns it the Aventine.

15. The time at which it becomes necessary, or expedient, in such a community as the Roman, to recognize the existence of the commonalty in a formal way, by the grant of political or municipal rights, varies with circumstances within very wide limits. At Rome the recognition took place early, matters coming rapidly to a head in consequence of the quick growth of the territory, and especially of the practice, which the kings pursued, of removing large masses of the conquered populations to their capital. If, as we are told, Ancus gave up the entire Aventine Hill, previously uninhabited, to his new settlers, thus assigning to their exclusive occupation a distinct quarter of the capital, municipal institutions must have been at the same time granted, for a whole quarter of a town can not be surrendered to anarchy. The "Plebs" must at once have had "ædiles," if not "tribunes;" and a machinery must have been established for their election, since nomination by the monarch is not to be thought of. But of the details of Ancus's regulations, whatever they were, we have no knowl-

edge, the later arrangements of Servius having not only superseded but obliterated them.

Other acts of Ancus.

16. Among the other acts assigned to Ancus Martius, the most important are, the extension of the Roman territory to the sea, and the establishment of the port of Ostia; the construction of salt-pans (*salinæ*) in its neighborhood; the erection of the "pons sublicius," or "bridge of piles," across the Tiber, and the occupation of the Janiculan Hill by a strong fort, or *tête du pont;* the draining of some of the low land about the Seven Hills by the "Fossa Quiritium," and the construction of the first prison. It would seem that civilization was advancing with both its advantages and its drawbacks—trade, manufactures, and engineering skill on the one hand; on the other, crime and its repression.

The curious notion of a modern historian, that Rome was from the first differentiated from the rest of the Latin nation by a peculiarly *commercial* character, is remarkably at variance with the tradition, that she obtained her first access to the sea in the reign of Ancus.

Reign of Tarquinius Priscus. His constitutional changes.

17. The next known king of Rome is L. Tarquinius Priscus. According to the tradition, he was a refugee from the Etruscan town of Tarquinii; according to the evidence furnished by his name and by his acts, he was a Latin, probably belonging to one of the noble "houses" from Alba. Two important constitutional changes are attributed to him. (*a*) He raised the ideal number of the Senate from two hundred to three hundred, by adding to it the representatives of the "Gentes Minores," or "Younger Houses"—who can scarcely be different from the "houses" adopted into the Patrician body from among the nobles of Alba. If he were himself a member of one of these "houses," his act would, it is clear, have been thoroughly natural. (*b*) He "doubled the equestrian centuries," or, in other words, the *actual* number of the Patrician "houses." The "houses" had, apparently, so dwindled, that instead of the ideal number of three hundred, the actual number was but one hundred and fifty, or thereabouts. Tarquin proposed to add one hundred and fifty new "houses" from among the nobles who had settled at Rome after the addition of the Albans; these he proposed to add in three new tribes, which were to stand side by side with the three

old tribes of the Ramnes, Tities, and Luceres. Opposed by the Patricians, who put forward the augur, Attus Navius, as objector, he yielded so far as to create no new tribes; but still he added the new "houses" in three new half-tribes, attaching them to the old Ramnes, Tities, and Luceres, but on terms of slight inferiority.

According to Cicero, the distinction of "Gentes Majores" and "Gentes Minores" applied to the "houses" anterior to, and the "houses" constituted by Tarquinius Priscus; but Livy and Dionysius regard the distinction as established earlier.

18. The wars of Tarquinius Priscus were also of importance. He repulsed a fierce attack of the Sabines, who had crossed the Anio and threatened Rome itself. He then attacked the Latin towns on the Upper Tiber and in the angle between the Tiber and the Anio, and reduced all of them except Nomentum. Antemnæ, Crustumerium, Ficulea or Ficulnea, Medullia, Cænina, Corniculum, and Cameria were among his conquests. After this, towards the close of his reign, he engaged in a war, on the other side of the Tiber, with the Etruscans, and gained important successes.

His wars.

19. Tarquinius Priscus was distinguished among the kings of Rome for the number and the character of his great works. To him is ascribed by the best authorities the Cloaca Maxima, the most remarkable monument now existing of the regal period, a construction of the grandest and most massive description. Connected with the Cloaca, and undoubtedly the work of the same builder, was a strong and solid quay along the left bank of the Tiber, which checked the natural inclination of the river to flow off on that side and to inundate the low lands about the Palatine and Capitoline Hills. Tarquin further constructed for the entertainment of the people a "Circus," or race-course, known as the "Circus Maximus;" and he also designed and commenced the great Temple of Jove, on the Capitoline Hill, which was completed by the last monarch.

His great works.

Is there any reason for regarding these massive works as "Etruscan" in character? Was not the early architecture of the Latins just as massive as that of their neighbors across the Tiber, and indeed very similar to it in all respects? The remains at Præneste, Tibur, Tarracina, and other Latin towns are as massive as any in Etruria.

20. Tarquinius Priscus appears to have been succeeded in the kingdom by Servius Tullius. According to the account which has most verisimilitude, Servius was an Etruscan, one of a body of mercenaries whom Tarquin had employed and had settled in his capital. He took advantage of his position about the monarch's person to conceal his death for a time, and act in his name; after which he boldly threw off the mask, and openly usurped the throne. Having gained considerable successes against the Etruscans, he felt himself strong enough to devise and carry through a complete change of the constitution. Hitherto, the whole political power, except that wielded by the king, had been engrossed by the noble "Houses." Servius determined to admit all ranks of freemen to the franchise. Taking the existing arrangements of the army as a groundwork, he constructed a new Assembly ("comitia centuriata"), in which all free Romans found a place. Dividing the citizens into "classes" according to the amount of their property, he then subdivided the "classes" into a larger or smaller number of "centuries" according to the aggregate of the property possessed by the "class;" and to each century, whatever the number of the persons composing it, he gave a single vote. The result was that a decidedly preponderating power was given to the richer classes; but if they differed among themselves, the poorer classes came in and decided the point in dispute.

Reign of Servius Tullius. His Etruscan War.

His arrangement of the "Comitia centuriata."

DETAILS OF THE COMITIA CENTURIATA. With regard to the main points, the three great authorities, Cicero, Livy, and Dionysius, are agreed; but with respect to minor points there is a good deal of discrepancy. *Main Points:* (*a*) The first place in the Assembly was given to the *equites* (horsemen), who formed eighteen centuries, six of which (*sex suffragia, sex centuriæ*) were exclusively Patrician, while the remaining twelve were mixed, being composed indifferently of Patricians, Plebeians, and (perhaps) Clients. A property qualification, amount unknown, separated off this class from the rest. (*b*) The bulk of the citizens below the "equites" were divided into five "classes," according as their property amounted to 100,000, 75,000, 50,000, 25,000, and 12,500 (Dionys.), or 11,000 (Livy) asses. The first class furnished 80 centuries, the second, third, and fourth 20 each, and the fifth 30. The number of individuals in the century rose as the property qualification sank. If (as is thought probable) a century of the first class contained 75 men, then one of the second contained 100, of the third 150, of the fourth 300, of the fifth 600. (*c*) There were a certain small number of centuries of professionals—artillerymen, and musicians—to which no property qualification attached. (*d*) The remainder of the free population, below the "classes," formed also a certain small number of centuries, not more at any rate than four, in the lowest of which were included even those who had nothing. (*e*) Finally, whatever the exact details, the arrangement was undoubtedly such, that, if the "equites" and the centuries of the first class were unanimous, the matter was determined; a majority was obtained, and, in that case, the votes of the remaining centuries were not taken.

His institution of the local tribes.

21. Another important institution ascribed by good authority to the reign of Servius is that of the local tribes. Hitherto the only "tribes" in Rome had been those of the Patrician order—the Ramnes, Tities, and Luceres—which were hereditary, and had no connection with localities. Servius divided the city into four, and the territory probably into twenty-six districts, and formed the land-owners within every such district into a tribe. Each tribe had the right of meeting and appointing its own "tribunus," its "ædilis," and probably its "judex" or "judices." It is doubtful whether the whole body of the tribes had at first the right of meeting together in one place; but ultimately the right was asserted and exercised, the meeting-place for the whole body being the forum at Rome. Here were held the "comitia tributa," which were not, perhaps, exclusively Plebeian, but which came to be so regarded from the great preponderance of the Plebeians in the class of land-owners. The original object of Servius in creating this organization was perhaps, as much as any thing, the assessment and collection of the property-tax (*tributum*), which the tribunes had to levy, collect, and pay into the treasury. He may also, however, have aimed at contenting the mass of the Plebeians, by intrusting them to a considerable extent with the power of self-government.

The four city tribes were called the Palatine, the Colline, the Esquiline, and the Suburran. Of the original country tribes the names of fifteen only are known. They are the Æmilian, the Camilian, the Cluentian, the Cornelian, the Fabian, the Galerian, the Horatian, the Lemonian, the Menenian, the Papirian, the Papinian, the Romilian, the Sergian, the Veturian, and the Voltinian. There is an evident connection between these names and those of the Patrician "houses."

His allotment of lands.

22. Servius is also said to have made an allotment of land out of the public domain to needy Plebeians—an act which greatly exasperated the Patricians, who

had hitherto enjoyed all the advantage to be derived from such land by means of their right of occupation (*possessio*). The land allotted appears to have lain on the right bank of the Tiber, consisting of tracts which had been ceded by the Etruscans after their defeat. (See § 20.)

23. According to some authors, it was likewise this king who raised Rome externally into a new and most important position, getting her to be acknowledged as actual head of the entire Latin confederacy, or at any rate of all but few recalcitrant towns, such as Gabii. This position was undoubtedly held by Rome at the close of the monarchy; and it may have been first assumed in the reign of Servius. The position was not exactly that which had been occupied by Alba. Alba had been one of the thirty cities, exercising a presidency over her sister states, which gave her a superiority of rank and dignity, but no real control over the federation. Rome was never one of the Latin cities. Her position was that of a "separate state, confronting the league," equal to it, or even superior to it in power, and when accepted as a close ally, necessarily exercising a protectorate. By the terms of the treaty, equality between Rome and Latium was jealously insisted upon; but, practically, Rome was paramount, and directed the policy of the league at her pleasure.

His league with the Latins.

24. An extension of the city of Rome accompanied this advance in her territorial influence and in her dignity. The original "Roma quadrata" was confined to a single hill, the Palatine, of which perhaps it occupied only the north-western half. From this centre the town spread to the neighboring heights, the Esquiline on the north-east, and the Cœlian on the south-east, whereon suburbs grew up, perched upon eminences, which together with the Palatine were seven in number, and constituted the primitive "Septimontium." The Rome which had these limits was confronted by a separate settlement, probably Sabine, on the hills ("colles") directly to the north, the Capitoline, Quirinal, and Viminal. But after a while the two communities coalesced; and the Rome of Tullus probably included the houses both of the "Montani" and the "Collini," or those of the "Mount-men" and the "Hill-men." Ancus added a settlement on the Aventine, so completing

His extension and fortification of the city.

the later "Septimontium." It remained, however, for Servius to inclose the various eminences, and a considerable space between and beyond them, within a single continuous line of wall. It is significative of the greatness of the Roman state at this time, that the "walls of Servius" sufficed for the city down to the time of Aurelian.

Many excellent works have been written on the topography of Rome, especially in recent times. The best are—

GELL, Sir W., *Topography of Rome and its Vicinity.* London, 1846. 2d edition.

BUNSEN, Baron, *Beschreibung der Stadt Rom.* Stuttgart, 1829–49; 3 vols. 8vo. With Atlas.

BECKER, W. A., *Handbuch der Römischen Alterthümer.* Leipzig, 1843–64; 3 vols. 8vo.

CANINI, L., *Indicazione topografica di Roma antica.* Roma, 1850. 4th edition, 8vo. And the same writer's *Edifizj di Roma antica.* Roma, 1840; 4 vols. folio.

DYER, T., *The History of the City of Rome.* (See p. 373.)

His intention to abdicate. His death.

25. It is said that Servius, towards the close of a long reign, began to fear for the stability of his institutions, and planned measures which would, he hoped, secure their continuance. He intended to abdicate, before doing so presiding at the election of two magistrates by the free votes of the people assembled in their centuries (*comitia centuriata*), who should be understood to be appointed to their office, not for life, but only for a single year. It should be their business, before the end of the year, to hold an assembly for the election of their successors; and thus the state would have passed, without violence or revolution, under the government of popular annual magistrates. The office of chief magistrate was, it is probable, to be open to both orders. But the members of the "houses," disgusted at this prospect, frustrated the monarch's plans by anticipating them. Before Servius could effect the changes which he had designed, they broke out in open revolt, murdered the aged monarch in the Senate-house, and placed a Tarquin, the son of the former king of the same name, on the throne.

26. L. Tarquinius Superbus, the last king of Rome, having gained his crown by the sole favor of the Patricians, acted no doubt in some respects oppressively towards the other order. He set aside at once the whole constitution of Ser-

Reign of Tarquinius Superbus. His treatment of the commonalty.

vius, and restored that which had existed under the earlier kings. But it may be questioned whether his oppression of the commonalty ever proceeded farther than this. Some writers represent him as grinding down the people by task-work of a grievous and distasteful kind, and then, when they murmured, banishing them from Rome to distant colonies. But the works which seem to be rightfully assigned to the second Tarquin are not of such a character as to imply servile or grinding labor. Their object was most probably the contentation of the poorer classes, who obtained by means of them constant employment at good wages. And the planting of colonies was always a popular measure, involving, as it did of necessity, an allotment of fresh lands to needy persons. Again, the "cloacæ" of Superbus, and his construction of permanent stone seats in the Circus Maximus, were for the advantage of the lower classes of the citizens.

His tyranny over the Patricians, and his expulsion.

27. The real "tyranny" of Superbus was over the Patricians. It can not have commenced very early in his reign. When, however, he felt himself securely settled upon the throne, when he had made himself fairly popular with the bulk of the community, when, by the vigor of his external administration, he had acquired a reputation, and perhaps an amount of military strength which made him careless of offending the "houses," he ceased to respect the rights of the privileged class, and, dispensing with their assistance in the government, took the complete direction of affairs into his own hands. Perhaps this was not much more than earlier monarchs had done, when they felt themselves fairly established. But the spirit of the nobles was higher than it had formerly been. They had recently slain one king and set up another. They viewed Tarquin as their creature, and were indignant that he should turn against them. Still, had the tyranny of the monarch been merely political; had their persons and the honor of their families remained secure, it is quite possible that no outbreak would have occurred. But Tarquin, suspicious of their intentions, commenced a series of prosecutions. He had charges brought against the most powerful Patricians, and took cognizance of them himself. Disallowing the right of appeal, he punished numbers by death or exile. Finally,

the outrage upon a noble Patrician matron woke the smouldering discontent into a flame. Rebellion broke out; and, the monarch having sought safety in flight, the Patrician order, with the tacit acquiescence of the Plebeians, revolutionized the government.

The vigor of Tarquin's administration to the last is indicated by the "Treaty with Carthage," which he must have been negotiating at the time of his dethronement. The story of his dealings with Turnus Herdonius seems to indicate that he held a position of more authority with respect to the Latin league than had been occupied by Servius. And the terms used with respect to the Latins in the treaty above mentioned confirm this view. The conquest of Gabii in his reign is probably a fact, though the circumstances of the conquest may be fictitious.

The great works of Tarquin were the Capitoline Temple, the branch *cloacæ* which drained into the Cloaca Maxima, the seats in the Circus Maximus, and perhaps the Cyclopian wall still existing at Signia.

Chronology of the regal period.

28. The chronology of the kingly period at Rome is extremely uncertain. Traditionally the period was reckoned at either 240 or 244 years. To Romulus were assigned 37 years; to Numa, 39 (or 43); to Tullus, 32; to Ancus, 24; to Tarquin I., 38; to Servius, 44; to Tarquin II., 25; and an "interregnum" of a year was counted between Romulus and Numa. It has been pointed out that the average duration of the reigns (35 years nearly) is improbably long; and that the numbers bear in many points the appearance of artificial manipulation. On the earlier numbers in the list, and therefore upon the total, no dependence at all can be placed; for neither Romulus nor Numa can be regarded as real personages. There is reason to believe that the "regifugium" took place in or about the year B.C. 508. Perhaps we may accept the traditions with respect to the later kings so far as to believe that the reigns of the last three monarchs covered the space of about a century, and those of the two preceding them the space of about half a century. The time that the monarchy had lasted before Tullus was probably unknown to the Romans at the period when history first began to be written.

See on this subject the work of ALGAROTTI, *Saggio sopra la durata de' regni de' rè di Roma*, in his *Opere* (Venezia, 1791–4; 17 vols. 8vo); and compare NIEBUHR, *Roman History*, vol. i. pp. 238–257, and LEWIS, *Credibility of the Early Roman History*, vol. i. pp. 411–546.

SECOND PERIOD.

From the Foundation of the Republic to the Commencement of the Samnite Wars, B.C. 508 *to* 340.

SOURCES. The most copious authorities are, as before, LIVY (books ii.–vii.), and DIONYSIUS (books v.–xi. and fragments of books xii.–xx.); to which may be added PLUTARCH, in his lives of *Poplicola*, *Coriolanus*, and *Camillus;* DIODORUS SICULUS (books xi.–xvi.); and the fragments of APPIAN, and DIO CASSIUS. Occasional notices of the period, mostly of great value, are also found in POLYBIUS. For the chronology, the best authority is the important monument dug up on the site of the Forum, and generally known as the *Fasti Capitolini* (see p. 20), which, so far as it goes, is invaluable.

The period is scantily treated in the history of MOMMSEN, copiously in those of NIEBUHR, ARNOLD, and PETER. Mommsen, however, has published an important work on the chronology, entitled *Die Römische Chronologie bis auf Cæsar.* 2d edition, Berlin, 1859; 8vo.

1. The interest of the Roman history during the whole of this period belongs mainly to the internal affairs of the Republic, the struggle between the orders, the growth of the constitution and of the laws; secondarily only, and by comparison, slightly, to the external affairs, wars, treaties, alliances, and conquests. With the three exceptions of the first Latin War, the Veientine contest, and the great attack of Gauls, the wars are uneventful and unimportant. The progress made is slight. It may be questioned whether at the close of the period Terminus has advanced in any direction beyond the point which it had reached under the kings. The relations of Rome to Latium are certainly less close and less to the advantage of Rome at the close of the period than at its commencement; and thus far, the power of the Roman state is diminished rather than augmented.

Wars of this period unimportant.

2. The internal changes during the period are, on the contrary, of the highest interest and importance. They include the establishment of the Plebeian Tribunate, the Decemviral constitution and legislation, the institution of the Censorship, the experiments of the First and Second Military Tribunates, the re-establishment of the Consulship with the proviso that one consul should be a Plebeian, the infringement of the proviso, and the whole series of the early agrarian enactments and disturbances. There is no portion of the constitutional history

High interest of the internal history.

of any ancient state which has a deeper interest than this—none from which lessons of greater value can be learnt. A certain amount of obscurity rests, indeed, upon many points, on which we should be glad to have clearer and more certain knowledge; but, despite this drawback, the history is in the highest degree instructive, and will well reward the study of all those who love both order and freedom.

Constitution of B.C. 508. Its fairness towards the Plebeians.

3. The constitution established on the expulsion of Tarquin was, in part, the actualization of the ideal of Servius, in part an enlargement of that ideal, conceived in the same spirit. Servius had designed to intrust the government of the state to two annual magistrates elected by the free voice of the centuries, and had made the centuries, in which all freemen were enrolled, the recognized Assembly of the Roman people. He had given the non-burghers generally the rights of municipal self-government; of the election of their own "tribunes," "ædiles," and "judges;" and of the assessment and collection of their own taxes. But this, so far as appears, was all. The leaders of the revolution of B.C. 508 went farther. They restored the constitution of Servius, and they added to it. Two "prætors," or "consuls," were elected by the free voice of the centuries, according to a form of proceedings which Servius had left behind him in writing; and one of the first pair of consuls was a non-burgher or Plebeian. The Senate, which had dwindled under the later kings, partly from natural causes, partly by the deliberate policy of the tyrant, was completed to its ideal number of 300, by the addition of 164 life-members ("conscripti"), chosen from the richest of the "equites," of whom a considerable number were Plebeians. The right of appeal, suspended under the last king, was revived, and was so enlarged as to include all freemen. Thus, at the outset, the new constitution wore the appearance, at any rate, of equality. No sharp line of demarkation was drawn between the two orders in respect of personal freedom, or admissibility to political privilege; and it is not too much to say that, if the spirit which animated the Patrician body in B.C. 508 had continued to prevail, contentions and struggles between the two orders would never have arisen.

4. But this fair prospect was soon clouded over. The Patricians had been induced to make the concessions above

Commencement of Patrician oppression.

enumerated to the other Order, not from any sense of justice, but through fear of Tarquin and his partisans, who were laboring to bring about a restoration. Of this there was for a time considerable danger. There was a royalist party among the Patricians themselves; and both the Etruscans and the Latins were inclined to espouse the quarrel of the deposed king. When, however, this peril was past, when the chiefs of the royalist faction were banished or executed, when the Etruscans had met a resistance which they had not counted on, and the Latins had sustained the complete defeat of the Lake Regillus, the policy of the Patricians changed. No Plebeian was allowed to enjoy the consulship after Brutus, and by degrees it grew to be forgotten that any but Patricians had ever been regarded as eligible. No plan was adopted by which Plebeians could obtain regular entrance into the Senate; and, as their life-members died off, the council of the nation was once more closed to them. The whole power of the government was engrossed by the Patrician order; which, finding itself free from any check, naturally became overbearing and oppressive.

The Dictatorship.

The imminent danger of a restoration at one time is indicated by the story, which Livy tells, of the origin of the Dictatorship. Such an office was evidently no part of the original idea of the constitution; but was exactly what might naturally have been devised to meet an emergency. If the circumstances were such as Livy mentions, the first Dictator must have been named by the Senate. In after-times it is certain that the Senate claimed the right of nomination, though practically they were generally satisfied to select the consul who should nominate.

Operation of the law of debt.

5. The loss of political privilege would not, it is probable, by itself, have called forth any active movement on the part of the commonalty. It required the stimulus of personal suffering to stir up the law-loving Roman to offer any resistance to constituted authority. This stimulus was found in the harsh enforcement, not long after the commencement of the Republic, of the law of debtor and creditor—a law which, under the circumstances of the time, pressed heavily on vast numbers of the community, and threatened to deprive them of their personal freedom, if not even of their lives.

NATURE OF THE ROMAN LAW OF DEBT. Distinction between debts arising from money lent and ordinary debts; in the former case, both the property and the person answerable; in the latter, the property only. Process of attaching the person troublesome and tedious. Rights of creditor, when the process was complete, extreme; including certainly the right to use, or sell, the debtor as a slave, and probably the right to put him to death. At any rate, several creditors, by proceeding at once, obtained the right to put to death. Nature of the *nexus*, doubtful; but no reasonable doubt that the practice grew up of persons, when they borrowed money, contracting to work out their debt by the performance of tasks set them by their creditors. Thus, practically, there were four classes of debtors:—(1) Persons who had borrowed under no special contract, and were still at liberty, proceedings not having been commenced against them; (2) persons who had borrowed under a contract to work out their debts, who consequently spent the day, *like* slaves, but not *as* slaves, in the workshops (*ergastula*) of their masters; (3) persons against whom the law of debt was in course of enforcement, who were kept in custody by their creditors, but could not be compelled by them to do work of any kind; and (4) persons against whom the law had been fully enforced, and who, having been assigned to their creditors (*addicti*), were their actual slaves.

Causes of the general poverty: (1) Defection of the Latins; (2) Conquest of Porsenna; (3) Incursions of the Sabines and Oscans.

6. The operation of the law of debt acquired political importance chiefly from the large number of the debtors at this period of the history; and it is therefore necessary to inquire what were the circumstances which caused the wide prevalence of indebtedness at the time—a prevalence which threatened revolution. Now, in the first place, nothing is more clear than that the change from the Monarchy to the Republic was accompanied by a diminution in the power and prestige of Rome, which sank from a position of pre-eminence among the central Italian nations to one of comparative insignificance. The Latins profited by the occasion to reclaim their complete independence; the Etruscans assumed an aggressive attitude, and an Etruscan monarch, Lars Porsenna, appears to have actually for a term of years held Rome in subjection. This yoke was indeed shaken off after a while; but a permanent result of the subjection remained in the loss of almost all the territory on the right bank of the Tiber. The Romans whose lands lay on that side of the river thus lost them; while at the same time the separation between Rome and Latium laid the Roman territory on the south side of the river open to incursions. The Sabines and Oscans plundered and ravaged freely; the crops were ruined, the farm buildings and imple-

ments destroyed, the cattle carried off. A general impoverishment was the natural consequence; and this would of course be felt most by the poorest classes, and especially by those whose small plots of land were their sole means of sustenance.

Aggravations of the poverty.

7. The poverty thus produced was further aggravated, 1. By the exaction of taxes, which by the Roman system were assessed upon individuals, not for a single year, but for a term of five years, and had to be paid for that term, whether the property on which they were levied remained in the possession of the individual or not; 2. By the high rate of interest, which, under the peculiar circumstances of the time, rose probably from the normal rate of 10 per cent. (*unciarium fœnus*) to such rates as 30, 40, or perhaps even 50 per cent.; 3. By the non-payment of the rents due to the treasury from the *possessores*, the withholding of which caused the property-tax (*tributum*) to become a serious burden; 4. By the cessation of the system of allotments (*divisio agrorum*) instituted by Servius, which was intended to compensate the Plebeians for their exclusion from the right of *possessio*.

The first secession, B.C. 492.

8. When the sufferings of the poorer classes had reached to a certain height from the cruel enforcement of the laws concerning debt, murmurs and indignant outcries began to be heard. At first, however, the opposition of the discontented took a purely legal shape. The Roman was a volunteer army, not a conscription; and the Plebeians had been wont, at the call of the consuls, freely to offer their services. Now they declined to give in their names unless upon the promise of a redress of grievances. Promises to this effect were made and broken. The Plebeians then, driven to despair, "seceded"—that is to say, they withdrew from Rome in a body, and proceeded to prepare for themselves new abodes across the Anio, intending to found a new city separate from the burgesses, where they might live under their own sole government. Such a step was no doubt revolutionary; it implied the complete disruption of the state; but it was revolution of a kind which involved no bloodshed. The burghers, however, seeing in the step taken the ruin of both orders—for Rome divided against herself must have speedily succumbed to some one or other

of her powerful neighbors—felt compelled to yield. The Plebs required as the conditions of their return, 1. That all debts of persons who could prove themselves insolvent should be cancelled; 2. That all persons in the custody of their creditors on account of debt should be set at liberty; and 3. That certain guardians of the Plebeian order should be annually elected by the nation at large, whose persons should be sacred, who should be recognized as magistrates of the nation, and whose special business should be to defend and protect from injury all Plebeians appealing to them. These were the famous "Tribuni Plebis," or "Tribunes of the Commons," who played so important a part in the later history of the Republic. Their original number is uncertain; but it would seem to have been either five or two.

System of allotments the true remedy against the poverty.

9. It is evident that the economical portion of this arrangement very insufficiently met the difficulty of the existing poverty; and there can be little doubt that, besides the formal provisos above mentioned, there was an understanding that the Plebeian grievances should be redressed by an equitable system of allotments. Such a system was advocated shortly afterwards, B.C. 484, by Sp. Cassius, one of the consuls under whom the Plebs returned from their secession, but was violently opposed by the bulk of the Patrician order, and cost its advocate his life. Still, from time to time, concessions of this kind were made, to keep the Plebeians in good humor; and gradually, as the territory once more grew in size, considerable portions of it were parcelled out to small proprietors.

In B.C. 468, Ti. Æmilius and L. Valerius brought forward an agrarian law, which was opposed by Ap. Claudius, and perhaps not passed. In B.C. 465 the same Æmilius and Q. Fabius were more successful, providing for 1000 needy Plebeians by their colony to Antium. In B.C. 415, and again in B.C. 392, small allotments were made. In B.C. 390, after the fall of Veii, an allotment was made of seven *jugera* to all who wished, in the Veientine territory. Eight years later, B. C. 382, 2000 Plebeians received small allotments at Satricum; and two years after this Plebeian colonies were settled at Nepete (in Etruria) and in the Pontine marsh district.

10. But a new character was given to the struggle between the orders by the tribunate, which enabled the wealthier Plebeians, whose especial grievance was their exclusion from the chief offices in the state, to turn the efforts of their

Struggle for equal rights commences. Law of Publilius Volero, B.C. 470.

order to the obtaining of equal political privileges and thus to initiate a contest which lasted for above a century. The first step taken in advance was by the law of Publilius Volero (B.C. 470), the main importance of which was that it assumed the initiative in legislation, hitherto exclusively in the hands of the other order. When the attempt thus made to legislate in a matter of public importance succeeded, when, by the sanction of the Senate and Patricians, the *rogatio Publilia* became law, the contest was virtually decided; a door was opened by means of which an entrance might be effected into the very citadel of the constitution; all that was necessary was sufficient patience and perseverance, a determination in spite of all obstacles to press steadily forward to the required end, and to consent permanently to no compromise that should seriously interfere with the great principle of equal rights.

11. The Plebeians, victorious in this first struggle, did not long rest upon their oars. In B.C. 460 the tribune, C. Terentilius Harsa, brought forward a proposition, the real object of which was a complete change of the constitution. He proposed the creation of a board of commissioners, half Patrician, half Plebeian, whose duties should be to codify the existing laws, to limit and define the authority of the consuls, and to establish a constitution just and equitable to both orders. The proposition was opposed with the utmost determination and violence. Even at the last, it was not formally carried; but, after ten years of the most vehement strife, after Rome, through the contentions between the orders, had several times been nearly taken by the Volscians, and had once been actually occupied by a band of adventurers under a Sabine named Appius Herdonius, called in by some of the more violent of the Patrician body, the nobles virtually yielded—they agreed that that should be done which the law proposed, but required that it should be done in another way. The nation, assembled in its centuries, should freely choose the ten commissioners to whom so important a task was to be intrusted, and who would, moreover, constitute a provisional government, superseding for the time all other magistrates. The Plebeians consented; and the natural conse-

Law of Terentilius Harsa leads to the appointment of the first Decemvirs.

quence was that ten Patricians were chosen—Patricians, however, mostly of known moderation, who might be expected to perform their task prudently and justly.

Work accomplished by the first Decemvirs. Code of Laws.

12. The First Decemvirs did not disappoint the expectations formed of them. In their codification of the laws they did little but stereotype the existing practice, putting, for the most part, into a written form what had previously been matter of precedent and usage. In some matters, however, where the law was loose and indeterminate, they had to give it definiteness and precision by expressing for the first time its provisions in writing. The code of the Twelve Tables—"*fons omnis publici privatique juris*"—which dates from this time, was a most valuable digest of the early Roman law, and, even in the fragmentary state in which it has come down to us, deserves careful study.

The fragments of the code have been published by several writers, as by HAUBOLD in his *Institutionum juris Romani privati Lineamenta*, Lipsiæ, 1826; and by DIRKSEN in his *Uebersicht der bisherigen Versuche zur Kritik und Herstellung des Textes der Zwölf-Tafel-Fragmente*, Leipzig, 1824. The subject has been well treated by ARNOLD in his *Roman History*, vol. i., chap. xiv. The following are the Tables, as given by DIRKSEN, the original form of the language being only partially preserved:

LAWS OF THE TWELVE TABLES.

FIRST TABLE.

SI. IN. IVS. VOCAT. NI. IT. ANTESTATOR. IGITVR. EM. CAPITO.

SI. CALVITVR. PEDEMVE. STRVIT. MANVM. ENDOIACITO.

SI. MORBVS. AEVITASVE. VITIVM. ESCIT. QVI. IN. IVS. VOCABIT. IVMENTVM. DATO. SI. NOLET. ARCERAM. NE. STERNITO.

ASSIDVO. VINDEX. ASSIDVVS. ESTO. PROLETARIO. QVOI. QVIS. VOLET. VINDEX. ESTO.

REM. VBI. PAGVNT. ORATO.

NI. PAGVNT. IN. COMITIO. AVT. IN. FORO. ANTE. MERIDIEM. CAVSAM. CONIICITO. QVOM. PERORANT. AMBO. PRAESENTES.

POST. MERIDIEM. PRAESENTI. STLITEM. ADDICITO.

SOL. OCCASVS. SVPREMA. TEMPESTAS. ESTO.

—VADES.—SVBVADES.—

SECOND TABLE.

MORBVS.—SONTICVS.—STATVS. DIES. CVM. HOSTE.—QVID. HORVM. FVIT. VNVM. IVDICI. ARBITROVE. REO. VE. DIES. DIFFISVS. ESTO.

CV. TESTIMONIVM. DEFVERIT. IS. TERTIIS. DIEBVS. OB. PORTVM. OBVAGVLATVM. ITO.

THIRD TABLE.

AERIS. CONFESSI. REBVSQVE. IVRE. IVDICATIS. TRIGINTA. DIES. IVSTI. SVNTO.

POST. DEINDE. MANVS. INIECTIO. ESTO. IN. IVS. DVCITO.

NI. IVDICATVM. FACIT. AVT. QVIPS. ENDO. EM. IVRE. VINDICIT. SECVM. DVCITO. VINCITO. AVT. NERVO. AVT. COMPEDIBVS. QVINDECIM. PONDO. NE. MAIORE. AVT. SI. VOLET. MINORE. VINCITO.

SI. VOLET. SVO. VIVITO. NI. SVO. VIVIT. QVI. EM. VINCTVM. HABEBIT. LIBRAS. FARRIS. ENDO. DIES. DATO. SI. VOLET. PLVS. DATO.

TERTIIS. NVNDINIS. PARTIS. SECANTO. SI. PLVS. MINVSVE. SECVERVNT. SE. FRAVDE. ESTO.

ADVERSVS. HOSTEM. AETERNA. AVCTORITAS.

FOURTH TABLE.

SI. PATER. FILIVM. TER. VENVM. DVIT. FILIVS. A. PATRE. LIBER. ESTO.

FIFTH TABLE.

VTI. LEGASSIT. SVPER. PECVNIA. TVTELAVE. SVAE. REI. ITA. IVS. ESTO.

SI. INTESTATO. MORITVR. CVI. SVVS. HERES. NEC. SIT. ADGNATVS. PROXIMVS. FAMILIAM. HABETO.

SI. AGNATVS. NEC. ESCIT. GENTILIS. FAMILIAM. NANCITOR.

SI. FVRIOSVS. EST. AGNATORVM. GENTILIVMQUE. IN. EO. PECVNIAQVE. EIVS. POTESTAS. ESTO.—AST. EI. CVSTOS. NEC. ESCIT.

EX. EA. FAMILIA.......IN. EAM. FAMILIAM.

SIXTH TABLE.

CVM. NEXVM. FACIET. MANCIPIVMQVE. VTI. LINGVA. NVNCVPASSIT. ITA. IVS. ESTO.

SI. QVI. IN. IVRE. MANVM. CONSERVNT.

TIGNVM. IVNCTVM. AEDIBVS. VINEAEQVE. ET. CONCAPET. NE. SOLVITO.

QVANDOQVE. SARPTA. DONEC. DEMPTA. ERVNT.

SEVENTH TABLE.

—HORTVS.—HEREDIVM.—TVGVRIVM.—

— —SI. IVRGANT.—

— —SI. AQVA. PLVVIA. NOCET.—

EIGHTH TABLE.

SI. MEMBRVM. RVPIT. NI. CVM. EO. PACIT. TALIO. ESTO.

SI. INIVRIAM. FAXIT. ALTERI. VIGINTI. QVINQVE. AERIS. POENAE. SVNTO.

—RVPITIAS.—SARCITO.

—QVI. FRVGES. EXCANTASSIT.—NEVE. ALIENAM. SEGETEM. PELLEXERIS.—

SI. NOX. FVRTVM. FACTVM. SIT. SI. IM. OCCISIT. IVRE. CAESVS. ESTO.

SI. ADORAT. FVRTO. QVOD. NEC. MANIFESTVM. ESCIT.—

PATRONVS. SI. CLIENTI. FRAVDEM. FECERIT. SACER. ESTO.

QVI. SE. SIERIT. TESTARIER. LIBRIPENSVE. FVERIT. NI. TESTIMONIVM. FARIATVR. IMPROBVS. INTESTABILISQVE. ESTO.

QVI. MALVM. CARMEN. INCANTASSET.— —MALVM. VENENVM.

. . . .

TENTH TABLE.

HOMINEM. MORTVVM. IN. VRBE. NE. SEPELITO. NEVE. VRITO.

HOC. PLVS. NE. FACITO.—ROGVM. ASCIA. NE. POLITO.

MVLIERES. GENAS. NE. RADVNTO. NEVE. LESSVM. FVNERIS. ERGO. HABENTO.

HOMINI. MORTVO. NE. OSSA. LEGITO. QVO. POST. FVNVS. FACIAT.

QVI. CORONAM. PARIT. IPSE. PECVNIAVE. EIVS. VIRTVTIS. ERGO. DVITOR. EI.
NEVE. AVRVM. ADDITO. QVOI. AVRO. DENTES. VINCTI. ESCVNT. AST. IM. CUM. ILLO. SEPELIRE. VREREVE. SE. FRAVDE. ESTO.

. . . .

TWELFTH TABLE.

SI. SERVVS. FVRTVM. FAXIT. NOXIAMVE. NOCVIT.—
SI. VINDICIAM. FALSAM. TVLIT......SI. VELIT. IS.......TOR. ARBITROS. TRES. DATO. EORVM. ARBITRIO......FRVCTVS. DVPLIONE. DAMNVM. DECIDITO.

13. But the main work of the Decemvirs was the constitution which they devised and sought to establish. In lieu of the double magistracy, half Patrician and half Plebeian, which had recently divided the state, and had threatened actual disruption, the Decemvirs instituted a single governmental body—a board of ten, half Patrician and half Plebeian, which was to supersede at once the consulate and the tribunate, and to be the sole Roman executive. The centuries were to elect; and the Patrician assembly was, probably, to confirm the election. It is suspected that the duration of the office was intended to exceed a year; but this is perhaps uncertain.

New Constitution. Second Decemvirate.

14. Fairly as this constitution was intended, and really liberal as were its provisions, as a practical measure of relief it failed entirely. One member of the board, Appius Claudius, obtained a complete ascendency over his colleagues, and persuaded them, as soon as they came into office, to appear and act as tyrants. The abolition of all the other high magistracies had removed those checks which had previously restrained consuls, tribunes, and even dictators; there was now no power in the state which could legally interfere to prevent an abuse of authority, unless it were the Senate; and the Senate was on the whole inclined to prefer a tyranny which did not greatly affect its own members, to the tumults and disorders of the last forty years. Rather than see the tribunate restored, the Patricians, and their representatives the senators, were prepared to bear much; and thus there was small hope of redress from this quarter.

The second Decemvirate becomes a tyranny, B.C. 449.

15. It was on the Plebeians that the yoke of the Decemvirs pressed most heavily. It was supposed that, as they had now no legal mode of even making their complaints heard, since there were no tribunes to summon the tribes to

Revolt breaks out. The Plebs secede for the second time. The Decemvirs abdicate, B.C. 448.

meet, they at any rate might be oppressed and insulted with absolute impunity. Accordingly, they were subjected to every kind of wrong and indignity—the Decemvirs and their partisans plundered them, outraged their persons, heaped contumely upon them, and finally attacked them in the tenderest of all points—the honor of their families. Then at length resistance was aroused. As the wrongs of Lucretia had armed the Patricians against Tarquin, so those of Virginia produced a rising of the Plebeians against Appius. The armies, which were in the field, revolted: the commons at home rose; and, when the Senate still declined to take any active steps against the Decemvirs, the whole mass of the Plebeians once more occupied the Mons Sacer. The walls of a new city began to rise; the Roman state was split in two; its foreign enemies, seeing their opportunity, assumed a threatening attitude; destruction was imminent; when at last the Senate yielded. Appius and his colleagues were required by a decree (*senatusconsultum*) to resign their offices, and, having now no physical force on which they could fall back, they submitted, and went through the formalities of abdication.

Re-establishment of the consulate and tribunate of the Plebs.

16. Forced hurriedly to extemporize a government, the state fell back upon that form which had immediately preceded the establishment of the First Decemvirate. It was adopted, however, with certain modifications. Prior to the Decemvirate for above thirty years, the Patricians had claimed and exercised the right of appointing by their own exclusive assembly one of the two consuls. It was impossible at the present conjuncture to maintain so manifestly unfair an usurpation. The free election of both consuls was consequently restored to the centuries. The tribunate of the Plebs was re-established exactly as it had existed before the Decemvirate. But the position of the other Plebeian magistrates was improved. The Plebeian "ædiles" and judges were allowed the "sacrosanct" character; and the former were made custodians of all decrees passed by the Senate, which it henceforth became impossible for the magistrates to ignore or falsify. Further, a distinct recognition was made of the right of the tribunes to consult the tribes on matters of public concern, and thus initiate legislation—a right

hitherto resting merely upon grounds of reason and prescription.

The law of Valerius and Horatius, "*ut quod tributim plebs jussisset populum teneret*," could not at this time have meant more, than that *plebiscita* should be binding, if they received the sanction of the Senate and Curies. This is further rendered evident by the later history of the Publilian and Hortensian laws.

Constitution of B.C. 442. The consulship superseded by the combined censorship and military tribunate.

17. In relinquishing temporarily their claim to a share in the supreme magistracy for the purpose of securing at any cost the restoration of the much-valued tribunate, the Plebeians were far from intending to profess themselves satisfied with the exclusive possession of high office by the other party. They expected, perhaps, that some proposition for giving them a certain share in the government would emanate from the Patricians themselves, who were not universally blind to the justice of their claims. But, as time went on and no movement in this direction was made, the Plebeian leaders once more took up the question, and in B.C. 442, C. Canuleius, one of the tribunes, brought forward two separate but connected laws, one opening the consulship to the Plebeian order, the other legalizing intermarriage between Patricians and Plebeians, and providing that the children should follow the rank of the father. Both laws encountered a strenuous opposition; and, according to one authority, no concession was made until the Plebs once more seceded, this time across the Tiber to the Janiculan Hill, when the "Intermarriage Law" (*lex de connubio*) was passed, and, in lieu of the other, a compromise was effected between the orders. It was agreed to put the consulate in commission, substituting for the double rule of two equal magistrates, which had hitherto prevailed, a board of (probably) five persons* of unequal rank, among whom the consular powers were to be parcelled out. The duties with respect to the revenue, and the arrangement of the roll of the Senate, of the knights, and of the citizens generally in the centuries, which had hitherto been exercised by the consuls, were

* Mommsen says "eight"—two censors, and *six* military tribunes; but there is no instance of a board of six military tribunes till B.C. 402, forty years later; after which time there is no instance of a board containing less than six.

separated off and made over to two "Censors" elected by the centuries from among the nobles only. The remaining duties of the consuls were consigned to three "military tribunes," also elected by the centuries, but from the Patricians and Plebeians indifferently. The latter officers were to be annual; the former were to hold office for a term of five years.

It is probable that the constitution of B.C. 442 was intended to supersede altogether that which preceded it, and to rule the elections year after year regularly. But the Patricians contrived to throw a doubt on this intention; and the practice grew up of the Senate formally determining towards the close of the year whether the ensuing election should be one of military tribunes or of consuls. In the latter case the Patricians were secure of the two seats without a struggle; in the former there was danger that one or more Plebeians might be elected.

Unsatisfactory working of this constitution.

18. The working of this constitution was extremely unsatisfactory to the Plebeians. By means of the irregular alternation of the consulate with the military tribunate, at least half the supreme magistracies were monopolized by the nobles without the Plebeians being able even to be candidates. With respect to the other half, it might have been thought that they could have avenged themselves. But practically it was found that only on rare occasions, under circumstances of peculiar excitement, could the centuries be induced to elect a Plebeian candidate. The Patricians by their own votes and those of their clients in the centuries of the first class (see p. 385) had almost the complete control of the elections; and during nearly forty years, at the most *three* Plebeians obtained a place in the college. Even then their position was insecure. The colleges of sacred lore might be called upon to inquire whether some accidental informality at the election had not rendered it invalid. Of the three Plebeian tribunes elected under the constitution of B.C. 442, one was made to resign in his third month of office, because the augural tent had not been pitched rightly.

Illiberal treatment of the Plebeians in other respects.

19. Nor were the Plebeians compensated for their disappointment with respect to the constitution of B.C. 442 by mild or liberal treatment in other respects during the forty years that it lasted (B.C. 442 to 402). The dignity of the censorship was indeed lessened by the Æmilian law, which diminished the dura-

tion of the office from five years to eighteen months; but any advantage which the Plebeians might seem to have gained in this respect was counterbalanced by the elevation of the prefect of the city, an exclusively Patrician officer, to the position of a colleague of the military tribunes when there were no censors in office. A demand which the Plebeians made for a share of the quæstorship was practically eluded in the way which had now come to be fashionable, by throwing the office open to both orders. Requests for allotments of land were either wholly rejected, or answered by niggardly assignments of two "jugera" to a man in portions of the territory very open to attack on the part of an enemy. The state-rents were generally withheld by the "possessores;" and, to make up the deficiency in the revenue, the property-tax was unduly augmented. The demand of the tribunes, that the soldiers should receive pay during the time that they were on active service, was not complied with; nor was any thing done to alleviate the pressure caused by the high rate of interest.

Modification of the military tribunate. Constitution of B.C. 402.

20. Thus the Plebeians, though, by the letter of the constitution, they had made certain not inconsiderable gains since the abolition of the Decemvirate, were scarcely better contented with their position in the state than they had been when Terentilius or when Canuleius commenced their agitations. And the Patricians were quite aware of their feelings. Accordingly, when, about B.C. 403, the military position of Rome among her neighbors had become such as to justify the nation in entering upon a more important war than any hitherto waged by the Republic, and it was clear that success would depend very much upon the heartiness and unanimity with which the whole nation threw itself into the struggle, the Patricians themselves came forward with proposals for a change in the military tribunate, and probably one also in the censorship, which had for their object the better contentation of the other order. A new constitution was framed; and at the same time it was agreed that the state-rents should be carefully collected, and from the money thus obtained regular pay should be given to the soldiers, who were now to be called upon to serve the whole, or nearly the whole, of the year.

CONSTITUTION OF B.C. 402. (*a*) The number of the military tribunes is raised from three to six, one of whom, however, is the "præfectus urbis," and so necessarily a Patrician—perhaps even elected by the Patrician assembly. The other five are elected by the centuries freely from either order. (*b*) The censorship is, like the military tribunate, thrown open to both orders. (*c*) It is agreed that this constitution shall operate permanently; or, in other words, that the consulate shall be wholly given up, and military tribunes hold office every year.

Wars of the Republic from its commencement to B.C. 402.

21. The wars of the Republic had hitherto been of minor importance. After the yoke of Porsenna was thrown off (see § 6) a short and sharp struggle had supervened with the Latins, who were compelled by Sp. Cassius (B.C. 491), if not to renew their old treaty, at any rate to enter into a league, offensive and defensive, with the Romans. The Hernicans of the Upper Liris country were soon afterwards (B.C. 484) forced by the same general to join the alliance. The special object of the league was to resist the encroachments of the Oscan nations, particularly the Æqui and Volsci, who were now at the height of their power. A long struggle with these nations, attended with very varying success, had followed. Rome had at times been reduced to great straits. Many Latin cities had been taken and occupied by the Volscians. But, after above half a century of almost perpetual contest, the power of the Oscans began to wane. The confederated Romans, Latins, and Hernicans recovered most of their lost ground. Tarracina was reoccupied, B.C. 403. At the same time, the pressure of the Sabines upon Rome, constant in the earlier years of the Republic, had ceased. A great victory, gained by the consul Horatius, in B.C. 446, had relieved Rome of this enemy, whose superabundant energies found for many years an ample scope in Southern Italy. Under these circumstances of comparative freedom from any pressing danger, Rome felt that the time was come when she might make a fresh start in the race for power. She was cramped for room towards the north and west by the near vicinity of an important but not very formidable state, Veii. Having first tested her adversary's strength in a contest for the possession of that single post which the Etruscans still held south of the Tiber, namely, Fidenæ, and having after some difficulty been successful so far (B.C. 423), Rome proceeded in B.C. 402 to enter upon a fresh war with Veii, dis-

tinctly intending to effect, if she could, a permanent conquest.

22. The war with the Veientines, commenced in this spirit, lasted, according to the tradition, ten years—B.C. 402 to 392. Rome now for the first time maintained in the field continuously an armed force, thus laying the foundation of that "standing army" to which she ultimately owed most of her greatness. She made her attack on the powerful Etruscan state at a fortunate time. Almost contemporaneously with her first serious aggressions upon the southernmost city of the confederacy began that terrible inroad from the North which utterly shattered and broke up the Etruscan power in the plain of the Po, and first alarmed and then seriously crippled the strength of the Cis-Apennine league. Had not the Gallic invasion occupied the whole attention of the Northern Etruscans, it is probable that they would have made common cause with the threatened Veii, in which case the war would scarcely have terminated as it did in the capture and ruin of the city.

War with Veii, B.C. 402-392, terminates in its capture and ruin.

DETAILS OF THE LAST WAR WITH VEII. B.C. 402 to 401. The Romans occupy various posts in the Veientine territory, and offer battle, which is declined.—B.C. 400. The siege of Veii is commenced—attempt at circumvallation. The Veientines destroy the works, which are, however, restored late in the year.—B.C. 399. Aid brought to the Veientines by the people of Falerii and Capena. The Roman works are carried and the besieging army is driven off.—B.C. 398. Roman armies invade the territories of Falerii and Capena. No great impression made.—B.C. 397. Siege of Veii re-formed.—B.C. 396. Second attempt of the Falisci and Capenates to relieve their neighbor fails.—B.C. 394. Attempt of the people of Tarquinii equally unsuccessful.—B.C. 392. Veii stormed by Camillus.

23. The successful issue of the war with Veii encouraged the Romans to fresh efforts in the same direction. Capena was conquered and her territory absorbed in the year after Veii fell. Then Falerii was attacked and forced to cede some of her lands. The neighboring towns of Nepete and Sutrium submitted at the same time, and became Roman dependencies. Finally, war was declared against the Volsinians, and the Roman arms were carried beyond the Ciminian mountains. Here victory was again with the aggressors; but the success failed to bring any increase of territory.

Further gains in Etruria.

24. But now the progress of Rome received a sudden and terrible check. The Gallic hordes, which had begun to swarm across the Alps about B.C. 400, and had conquered Northern Etruria nearly at the time when the Romans took Veii, after a brief pause crossed the Apennines, and spread like a flood over Central Italy. Whether Rome gave them any special provocation, or no, is doubtful. At any rate, they poured down the valley of the Tiber in irresistible force, utterly defeated the entire armed strength of the Romans upon the Allia, captured the city, and burnt almost the whole of it, except the Capitol. The Capitol itself was besieged for months, but still held out, when the Gauls, weary of inaction and alarmed for the safety of their conquests in the plain of the Po, consented, on the payment of a large sum of money, to retire.

Attack of the Gauls. Rome burnt, B.C. 387.

It is questionable whether the destruction of Rome was so complete as generally alleged. The Gauls would have wished to save a portion of the buildings as a shelter to themselves against heat and wet. And these they would not have been likely to destroy at their departure under its circumstances. The town would probably have contained many solid stone buildings calculated to resist a rapid conflagration. And the Capitol, with its temples and other public edifices, was, we know, untouched.

The question concerning the credibility of the early Roman history depends to a considerable extent upon the amount of devastation committed by the Gauls. But it is also, in part, independent of that question, turning upon the further one, which of the existing monuments were likely to have been usually kept in the Capitol, or to have been removed to it before the siege began.

25. It might have been expected that this fearful blow would have been fatal to the supremacy of Rome among the Italic nations. But the result was otherwise. At first, indeed, consequences followed which brought the Republic into serious danger, and seemed to menace its existence. The Latins and Hernicans, who had been united in the closest possible league with the Romans, the former for above, the latter for not much less than a century, took the opportunity of Rome's defeat to declare the league dissolved. The Oscan nations, the Volsci especially, renewed their attacks. The Etruscans took the offensive. Rome was saved from immediate destruction by the genius of Camillus, and then gradually rose again to power and preponderance by her own inherent energy. To

Effect of the Gallic inroads. Military history of Rome from B.C. 387-355.

account for the slightness of the check which the Gallic conquest gave to her external prosperity, we must bear in mind that the attack of the Gauls was not really upon Rome alone, or even upon Rome specially and peculiarly. The first burst of their fury had fallen on the Etruscans, and had permanently weakened that important people. Their later irruptions injured the Italic nations generally, not Rome in particular. The Umbrians, Sabines, Latins, Æqui, and Volsci all suffered, perhaps about equally. Thus Rome, on the whole, succeeded in maintaining her place among the Italian states; and, the same causes which had previously given her a preponderance continuing to work, she gradually lifted herself up once more above her neighbors. She warred successfully with the Volscians, and with several cities of the Latins, which were now leagued with them. She held her own in Etruria. After an interval of about a generation she induced the Latins and compelled the Hernicans to resume their old position of confederates (B.C. 355) under her hegemony. Within five-and-thirty years of the destruction of the city, Rome had fully recovered from all the effects of the blow dealt by the Gauls; and, if we take into account the general weakness caused by the Gallic ravages, had relatively improved her position.

Internal history. Failure of the constitution of B.C. 402. Recurrence of general poverty.

26. While Rome thus, on the whole, prospered externally, her internal condition was also gradually improving. The second military tribunate was not, indeed, very much more successful than the first, failing equally to content the aspirations of the Plebeian order. Though it gave them a larger proportion of the high offices, the proportion was still so small—not so much as one-twelfth—that their dissatisfaction, not unreasonably, continued. They never obtained the military tribunate excepting under abnormal circumstances; and on the single occasion on which they gained the censorship (B.C. 376), it was wrested from them under a religious pretext. The Patricians could still, ordinarily, command the votes of the centuries; and, if a Plebeian obtained office, it was by Patrician sufferance or contrivance. Excepting under peculiar circumstances, the nobles were inclined to grasp as much power as they could; and hence the Plebeians felt that they had no firm hold on the constitution, no security

for the continuance of even that small share of office which had practically fallen to them. They would probably have set themselves to obtain a change in the constitution many years before the Licinio-Sextian laws were actually brought forward, had not the Gallic invasion produced such an extent of poverty and debt as effectually cramped for a time all Plebeian aspirations, changing the struggle for equal rights into a struggle for existence.

CAUSES OF THE GENERAL POVERTY at this period. (*a*) Loss of property—farm-buildings, implements, crops, cattle, even seed-corn—in consequence of the Gallic inroad. (*b*) Necessity of borrowing money in order to rebuild the demolished houses and re-stock the plundered farms. (*c*) High rate of interest, owing to the necessary suspension of the Decemviral enactment. (*d*) Probable forfeiture of the security given to the State for the completion of the houses in a year. (*e*) Rise in the amount of property-tax, owing partly to the number of public buildings which required to be rebuilt or repaired, and partly to the non-payment of the state-rents. (*f*) Difficulty of providing allotments at a time when Rome was not making much advance territorially.

The second item might have been in great part spared, if Rome had been deserted and its population had removed to Veii. But the moral grounds against such a transfer of the capital far outweighed all the material ones in its favor.

Affair of M. Manlius, B.C. 381.

27. The first important result of the general prevalency of distress among the Plebeians was the attempt of M. Manlius. Less pure and disinterested than his prototype, Spurius Cassius, he made the Plebeian wrongs the stalking-horse of his own ambition. Partly tempted, partly goaded into crime, he is entitled to our pity even though we condemn him. His intentions were probably at the first honest, and the means that he designed to use legal; but the opposition which he encountered drove him to desperate measures, and he became in the end a dangerous conspirator. Well would it have been for Rome had she possessed a method, like that which Athens enjoyed in the ostracism, of securing her own liberties by the temporary banishment, rather than the death, of a great citizen!

Slight attempts to relieve the poverty.

28. During the Manlian struggle, and immediately after it, some slight efforts were made by the government to relieve the general destitution. In B.C. 382 two thousand Plebeians received allotments of two and a half *jugera* at Satricum. Two years later, colonies

were sent out to Nepete in Etruria and to the Pontine marsh district. But these were mere palliatives, and in no way met or grappled with the disease. It was necessary, if the bulk of the Plebeian order was not to be swept away from the state, becoming the slaves of the Patricians or of foreigners, that measures should be taken on a large scale, both to meet the present distress, and to prevent such crises from recurring.

29. Great difficulties call for, and seem in a way to produce, great men. Fourteen years after the distress had become considerable owing to the Gallic inroad, two Plebeians of high rank and great ability, C. Licinius Stolo and L. Sextius, came forward with a scheme of legislation skillfully framed so as to cover all the various heads of Plebeian grievance, and to provide at once a remedy for the actually existing evils and security against future oppression. Considering that there were two kinds of evil to remedy, political inequality and want, they framed their measures against both. For the immediate relief of the needy, they brought forward their "*lex de œre alieno*," which provided that whatever had been paid on any debt in the way of interest should be counted as a repayment of the principal and deducted from the amount due; and that the balance remaining, if any, should be demandable only in installments, which should be spread over the space of three years. For the prevention of the poverty in future, they proposed their "*lex agraria*"—which, in the first place, threw open the right of occupying the public land to the Plebeians; in the second, affixed a limit beyond which occupation should not be carried; and in the third, required all occupiers to employ in the cultivation of their farms a certain definite proportion of free labor. For the establishment of the principle of political equality, they proposed the restoration of the consulship, with the proviso that one of the two consuls should each year be a Plebeian (*lex de consulatu*); and the equal division of a sacred office, that of the keepers of the Sibylline books, between the two orders (*lex de decemviris sacrorum*).

Grand scheme of Licinius and Sextius.

30. The importance of these laws was immense. They established fully the principle of the equality of the two orders, both as respected sacred and civil office—a principle

Importance of the Licinio-Sextian legislation. Its acceptance, B.C. 364.

which, once admitted, was sure to work itself out to the full in course of time. They greatly alleviated the existing poverty, and by the two provisions for extending the right of occupation to Plebeians, and compelling the employment of a large amount of free labor on the public lands, they made considerable provision against extreme poverty in the future. Above all, they secured to the Plebeians a succession of champions in the highest offices of the State, who would watch over their interests and protect them against unfair treatment. Naturally, therefore, being so important, the laws were opposed with the utmost determination by the other order. The struggle, according to some authorities, was of eleven years' duration. It was probably not until a "secession" had begun, or at any rate was threatened, that the Patricians yielded, the laws received the sanction of both the Senate and the Assembly of the nobles, and a Plebeian consul, L. Sextius, was elected, B.C. 363.

Two new offices arose in connection with the Licinio-Sextian legislation—the Prætorship (exclusively Patrician) and the Curule Ædileship (alternately Patrician and Plebeian). The Prætorship is perhaps best viewed as an office formed by detaching from the rest some of the old consular powers, and so as a sort of compensation to the Patricians for their loss of one consulship. (Compare the origin of the Censorship.) The Curule Ædileship was probably an old office newly arranged—the Patrician Ædileship being new-cast, because of the admission of the Plebeians into the nation.

Time of reaction. The Licinio-Sextian constitution set aside illegally.

31. It might have seemed that the struggle between the orders would now have come to a close—that when the highest civil, and one of the highest religious, offices had been once opened to the Plebeian order, there remained nothing which the other order could regard as worth fighting for. But the fact was otherwise. Not only were there, now as ever, among the Patricians those who would not yield without a struggle even the last "rag of privilege;" but there existed in the body at this time a party disinclined to view the recent defeat as decisive, or to accept it as final. During the quarter of a century which followed on the passage of the Licinio-Sextian laws, it was uncertain whether or no the Plebeian advance could be maintained. A certain amount of reaction set in. For the space of fourteen years—from B.C. 352 to B.C.

339—the regular operation of the Licinio-Sextian constitution was set aside. Instead of Plebeian consuls following each other in regular succession year after year, the Fasti show during the fourteen years seven Plebeian names only, while there are twenty-one Patrician.

It is uncertain by what means this illegal system was introduced or maintained; but there are grounds for suspecting that it was very mainly through the defection of a portion of the Plebeian nobility from the cause of their order. Four Plebeians, C. Marcius Rutilus, M. Popillius Lænas, C. Pœtelius, and C. Plautius, seem to have become Patrician partisans, and as a reward for their services to have received through the influence of the Patricians an accumulation of high offices. These men and their party among the Plebeians connived at the Patrician usurpations, which were the less sensibly felt by the mass of the Order, as they affected directly only the interests of the comparatively few wealthy families.

Discontent of the Plebeians.

32. The illegal setting aside of the Licinio-Sextian constitution could not fail to produce among the more prudent and far-seeing of the Plebeians violent discontent. If a party in the State is once allowed to begin the practice of setting the law at nought, there is no saying where it will stop. The old champions of the Plebeian cause—the Licinii, Genucii, Publilii, etc.—must have been violently angered; and as time went on and the illegality continued, the bulk of the Order must have become more and more disgusted with their own renegades and with the Patrician usurpers. These last must have felt, during the whole time of the usurpation, that they walked upon a hidden volcano—that a fire might at any moment burst forth which would imperil the very existence of the community.

Measures taken to keep down the discontent.

33. It was probably with the view of pacifying and soothing the discontented, that the Patricians granted during this interval many boons to the poorer classes. The re-establishment of the uncial rate of interest (10 per cent.) in B.C. 351, and the subsequent reduction of the rate by one-half in B.C. 344, were popular measures, evidently designed to gratify the lower orders. The tax on the manumission of slaves (B.C. 354) would also please them, since it would fall wholly upon the wealthy. Of a still more popular character were the general liquidation of debts, in B.C. 349, by means of a Commission empowered to make

advances from the treasury to all needy persons who could offer a fair security; and the suspension of the property-tax, and spread of the debts over the space of three years, which were among the measures of relief adopted in B.C. 344. The practical opening to the Plebeians without a struggle of the civil offices parallel with the Consulate—the Dictatorship and the Mastership of the Knights (B.C. 353)—may also be regarded as among the politic concessions of this period, made for the sake of keeping the Plebeians in good humor, and preventing an outbreak.

Fear of an outbreak produces a peace policy.

34. But, though these boons and blandishments effected something, it was felt nevertheless that the state of affairs was unsettled, and that, on the occurrence of any convenient opportunity, there would probably be a rising. Accordingly the government determined, so far as in it lay, to avoid furnishing an opportunity; and hence, for almost the first time in the history of the Roman State, we find a policy of peace adopted and steadily maintained for a series of years. Between the years B.C. 355 and 347, treaties of peace were concluded with all the important powers of Central Italy; and Rome left herself no enemy against whom she could legitimately commence a war excepting the shattered remnants of the Oscan nations and perhaps the Sabines of the tract beyond the Anio.

Peace and alliance were made with the Latins, B.C. 355; with the Hernicans in the same year; with the Samnites, B.C. 351; with Cære, B.C. 350; with Tarquinii and Falerii, in B.C. 348. It is not impossible that a treaty was made with the Gauls after the campaign of B.C. 346, after which they are never again found in Latium. A commercial treaty with the Carthaginians was made in B.C. 345; but this would not belong to the "peace policy" here spoken of, since there was at this time no possibility of a war with Carthage.

The peace policy given up. War with Samnium.

35. At length, in B.C. 340, twelve years after the Licinio-Sextian constitution had been set aside, an occasion offered which tempted the government to depart from its peace policy, and to run the risk of internal trouble which was well known to be implied in the commencement of a great and important war. The temptation, one which it was impossible to resist, was the offer of the Campanians to become Roman subject-allies, if Rome would protect them against the Samnites. To accept this offer was

to more than double the Roman territory; to reject it was greatly to strengthen the Samnites, already the chief power of the south of Italy. The government, which though Patrician, was still Roman, was too patriotic to hesitate. Campania was therefore received into alliance, and the First Samnite War was the immediate consequence.

36. The military operations of the war will be described in the next portion of this book (Per. III., § 2); but its effect on the civil history is too closely connected with the period of which we are now treating to admit of separation from it. The Roman army, having carried on a successful campaign, wintered in Campania; and the soldier-citizens, having thus had an opportunity of consulting together, determined to mutiny. Some were for a "secession" to Capua, but the majority were for enforcing their will upon the usurping government at Rome. In vain the consuls, perceiving what was afloat, tried to disperse the army little by little before an outbreak should come. Their intention was perceived, and the mutiny took place at once. The army marched upon Rome and made its demands—the government met it with a hasty levy, but these troops refused to fight. Long negotiations followed. At length, a tribune of the Plebs, a Genucius, proposed and carried through a series of laws, which were accepted on both sides as terms of reconciliation. The Licinian constitution was practically re-established; but it was enacted, as a just penalty on the Patricians for their repeated usurpation of both consulships, that, though both consuls might never legally be Patricians, it should be allowable for both of them to be Plebeians. To prevent any future seduction of a Plebeian party by the temptation of accumulated offices, it was enacted that no Plebeian should henceforth hold the same office twice within ten years, or two offices in the same year. To alleviate the remaining pressure of debt, there was an absolute abolition of all outstanding claims, and a law was passed making the lending of money upon interest illegal. Some military grievances were at the same time redressed, provision being made that no soldier should be dismissed the service without cause shown, and that no petty officer should be degraded to the ranks. On these conditions peace was re-

Mutiny of the soldiers.

Restoration of the Licinio-Sextian constitution and passing of the Genucian laws, B.C. 339.

established; and domestic tranquillity being attained, Rome was once more ready to devote her whole strength to the forwarding of her interests abroad.

For a full account of this interesting period of Roman history, see an article contributed by the present writer to the *Oxford and Cambridge Review* for April, 1846; pp. 241–257.

THIRD PERIOD.

History of Rome from the breaking out of the First Samnite War, B.C. 340, *to the Commencement of the Wars with Carthage*, B.C. 264.

SOURCES. (*a*) *Authors.* LIVY and DIODORUS are the chief authorities for the earlier portion of this period; but the latter writer fails us after B.C. 302. The fragments of APPIAN'S *Samnitica* are of some value. For the war with Pyrrhus, PLUTARCH'S *Life* of that hero is the main source; but his narrative must be supplemented from the fragments of DIO CASSIUS, DIONYSIUS, and APPIAN, and from the continuous narratives of JUSTIN, OROSIUS, and ZONARAS. For the period following the departure of Pyrrhus from Italy (B.C. 275 to 264) these latter writers are almost our sole authorities. We may consult however with advantage the *Epitomes* of LIVY and the brief abstract of FLORUS. (*b*) *Inscriptions.* The *Fasti Capitolini* are full and tolerably continuous for the greater portion of this period. There belong also to it a certain number of sepulchral and other inscriptions, which will be found in—

ORELLI, J. C., *Inscriptionum Latinarum selectarum amplissima collectio.* Turici, 1828; 2 vols. 8vo; and in

MOMMSEN, TH., *Inscriptiones Latinæ antiquissimæ ad Cæsaris mortem.* Berolini, 1863; folio.

The modern writers best worth consulting on this period are those already mentioned (supra, p. 283) as authorities on the history of Period II.

External history of this period chiefly important.

1. The Third Period of Roman History is that of the great wars in Italy, whereby Rome succeeded in making herself mistress of the entire Peninsula proper. It comprises the four Samnite Wars, the great Latin War, the war with Pyrrhus, a war with the Gauls, and several minor wars terminating in the conquest of the other lesser Italian nations. The external history of the period is thus of the highest interest; while the internal history is, comparatively speaking, scanty and unimportant.

First war of Rome with Samnium, B.C. 340–338.

2. When Rome determined to accept the Campanians as subject-allies, she broke her treaty with Samnium, and practically made a declaration of war. Campania was a Samnite dependency which had revolted, and which the Samnites were bent on subjuga-

ting. The interposition of Rome in the quarrel resembled that of Athens in the contest between Corinth and Corcyra (supra, p. 203). Morally, it could not be justified; but, as a matter of policy, it could not be impugned. Rome already saw that her most formidable Italian rival was Samnium, and that it was with Samnium she would have to contend for the first place in Italy. A step which at once strengthened herself and weakened her antagonist could not but be expedient; and we can not be surprised that, despite its injustice, the step was taken.

DETAILS OF THE WAR. B.C. 340. Rome sends two consular armies into Campania, one of which enters Samnium from the west, while the Latins invade the country of the Peligni and threaten Samnium on the north. The Roman invading army gets into difficulties, but is extricated by the courage and conduct of a Decius. The Latins make no serious impression. The other Roman army, however, which remains in Campania, gains two victories, one at Mount Gaurus, near Naples, and the other at Suessula. Both Roman armies winter in Campania.—B.C. 339. Mutiny of the Roman troops. The whole management of the war is left to the Latins, who carry it on successfully, protecting Campania, and more than once defeating the Samnites.—B.C. 338. The Romans and Latins invade Samnium separately. Rome, perceiving that Latium has assumed an independent attitude, hastily makes peace with the Samnites, and determines to attempt the subjugation of Latium.

Great Latin War, B.C. 337-335.

3. Rome, about to engage in a war for supremacy with Latium, strengthened herself by an alliance with the knot of Sabine communities known as "the Marsian League." Latium obtained the adhesion of the Campanians, Sidicinians, and Volscians. Samnium was an active ally to neither party, but took the opportunity, which the contest offered, to advance her frontier on the side of the Volscian territory. The struggle between the two main belligerents was begun and concluded within the space of three years, and, indeed, was virtually decided by the events of the first campaign. The battles of Vesuvius and Trifanum (B.C. 337) were stoutly contested by the Latins, but nevertheless were very decided Roman victories. Their effect was to break up the confederacy. Many states at once submitted. Others continued a desultory and ineffectual resistance; but by the end of B.C. 335 the last Latin town had made its submission; and Rome, having effected the conquest, proceeded to the work of pacification.

PACIFICATION OF LATIUM. The principles of the pacification were isolation and separation of interests. The federal meetings at the *lucus Ferentinus* were of course abolished. The rights of intermarriage between the citizens of the different states, and of holding lands in each others' territories, were suspended. Some cities, as Velitræ and Antium, were occupied by Roman colonies. Others, as Tibur and Præneste, forfeited a large portion of their territory. One town, Tusculum, was simply restored to its former condition of a Roman "municipium." The same position was assigned to Aricia, Nomentum, and Pedum. Lanuvium was received into full citizenship. Laurentum, which had taken no part in the war, was allowed a nominal independence.

Pause of twelve years' duration, B.C. 335-323.

4. The conclusion of the great struggle with Latium is followed by a pause of twelve years, during which Rome undertook nothing but trivial and unimportant wars, and those chiefly wars which were forced upon her. Her action was paralyzed by two causes, one internal, the other external. Her internal danger was from the subjected Latins, who were known to be discontented with their treatment, and might be expected to revolt the moment Rome should enter upon any important contest. The external cause of alarm was the invasion of Alexander of Epirus, uncle of Alexander the Great, who landed in Italy, B.C. 331, at the invitation of the Tarentines. Alexander's quarrel was mainly with the Samnites and their dependent allies; but, if he had been successful against them, he would probably have attempted the conquest of Italy. Rome, doubtful of the result, protected herself by a treaty with the invader, and then nursed her strength and prepared herself to resist him if he should attack her.

MINOR WARS OF THIS PERIOD. In B.C. 333 and 332 Rome attacks and reduces the Ausonians. The year after their reduction, she makes war on the Sidicini. In B.C. 327 Privernum and Fundi revolt under Vitruvius Vaccus. Fundi speedily submits. Privernum is reduced, B.C. 326. In the same year an attack of the Gauls is met and repulsed.

Aggressions of Rome upon Samnium.

5. The reverses which befell Alexander of Epirus, about B.C. 325, encouraged the Romans to resume their old policy of aggression, and to take steps which led naturally and almost necessarily to the renewal of the struggle with Samnium. By founding the colony of Fregellæ on land conquered by the Samnites from the Volscians, a challenge was flung down to Samnium, which she could scarcely refuse to take up. This was followed by an attack on Palæopolis, an independent Greek city, which

had long been under Samnite protection. War ensued as a matter of course. The time had, in fact, come when Rome was prepared to contest, with the power which she recognized as her great rival, the mastery of Southern Italy. Mistress of Latium and Campania, and secured by treaties from any early Etruscan attack, she felt herself equal to a vast effort; and she therefore determined to seize the occasion for a war which should decide whether the hegemony of the peninsula, or at any rate of its southern portion, should belong to herself or to the Samnites.

Second War with Samnium, B.C. 323–303.

6. The Second Samnite War—the duel between the two chief races of Italy—covered a space of twenty-one years, from B.C. 323 to 303, inclusive. It divides itself naturally into three portions. During the first, from B.C. 323 to 319, the war languished, neither party apparently putting forth its full strength. During the second, from B.C. 319 to 312, the issue was really determined by the three great battles, of the Caudine Forks, of Lautulæ, and of Cinna. The third period, from B.C. 312 to 303, was again one of languid hostilities, the war being unduly spun out, partly by the stubborn resistance of the beaten party, partly through the desultory attacks which were made upon Rome during these years by various enemies.

Details of the War. First Period, B.C. 323 to 319. Rome obtains allies among the Lucanians and Apulians, and prepares to attack Samnium from the south; but the Samnites crush the Roman party in Lucania, B.C. 323. Rome then makes war on the Vestini and the other members of the Marsian League, defeats them and establishes a line of communication with Apulia through their territories, B.C. 322. The next year the war is transferred into Apulia, with such effect that in B.C. 320 the Samnites make proposals for peace. These, however, are rejected, and the war continues. Second Period, B.C. 319 to 312. The great victory of the Caudine Forks is gained by C. Pontius, B.C. 319. Half the Roman army is destroyed. The rest surrenders, but is released from captivity, on the signature of a peace by the consuls and two tribunes of the Plebs. The authorities, however, having recovered their men, refuse to be bound by the treaty, which they declare informal. The war continues without any very important event till the year B.C. 313, when the battle of Lautulæ is fought. This is a second great Samnite victory, and seems to promise them complete success in the war. Campania revolts from Rome. The Ausonians join the Samnites. The Volscians of Sora go over to them, massacring the Roman colonists. Luceria, one of the chief towns of Apulia, deserts the Roman alliance. There is a general expectation that the Samnites are going to carry all before them, and a wide-spread defection from the Roman cause. But in the ensuing year all is reversed. By a vast effort Rome succeeds in bringing into the field an army larger and better appointed than that which had been lost; the Samnites are once more met in the field; and the Romans gain the victory of Cinna, defeating their enemy with such loss that there is no after-recovery from the blow. THIRD PERIOD, B.C. 311 to 303. The Romans carry the war into Samnium, which they ravage year after year. Only two battles of any importance are fought. In B.C. 308 the Samnites make a last effort, defeat the Romans under C. Marcius Rutilus, but are in their turn defeated by L. Papirius Cursor. The war is prolonged in consequence of the efforts which are made to help Samnium by other powers, as by the Etruscans, in B.C. 309 and 308; by the Umbrians, in the latter year; by the Marsi and Peligni, in B.C. 307; by the Sallentini, in B.C. 306; and by the Æqui and Hernici, in B.C. 305. Could the efforts of these various nations have been concentrated into one great attack, Rome, if she had not succumbed, might have received a serious check. But the want of union among her foes gave her an easy triumph: every attack was repulsed; and in the year B.C. 303, Samnium, in despair, submitted, becoming politically subject to the Romans, but retaining its internal independence.

Revolt and final pacification of Latium, B.C. 322.

7. The Second Samnite War brought the disaffection of the Latins very rapidly to a head. In B.C. 322, the second year of the war, there was beyond a doubt a great Latin revolt. Tusculum, Velitræ, and Privernum, three of the cities which had experienced the harshest treatment, took the lead. A night attack seems to have been made on Rome, and great alarm caused. The Roman government, however, met the danger with its usual wisdom. While some recommended measures of extreme violence, the Senate adopted a policy of conciliation. Terms were made with the rebels, some of whom were given, others promised, full citizenship. The discontented part of Latium was, in fact, incorporated into Rome. To mark the completeness and reality of the union, L. Fulvius, the leader of the revolt, became consul for the year, B.C. 321. Henceforth Latium was satisfied with its position, and continued faithful through all the later troubles and rebellions.

Interval between Second and Third Samnite Wars, B.C. 303–298.

8. An interval of five years only—B.C. 303 to 298—separates the Second from the Third Samnite War. Rome utilized it by completely reducing the remnant of the Æquian people, by bringing the four nations forming the Marsian League into the position of her subject-allies, by making alliances with the Frentani and Picentini, and by seizing and occupying the

strong position of Nequinum (Narnia) in Umbria. She also during this period sent aid to the Lucanians, who were attacked by Cleonymus of Sparta. Samnium probably negotiated, during the pause, with the Etruscans, Umbrians, and Gauls, taking steps towards the formation of that "League of Italy" which she brought to bear against Rome in the ensuing war.

Third Samnite War. General outline.

9. The Third Samnite War is the contest of confederated Italy against the terrible enemy whose greatness was now seen to threaten every power in the peninsula. Its turning-point, which well deserves its place among the ten or twelve "Decisive Battles of the World," was the battle of Sentinum. After two years of comparatively petty warfare, Samnium, in B.C. 296, brought the projected alliance to bear. Gellius Egnatius marched, with the flower of the Samnite force, across Central Italy into Etruria. The Gauls and Umbrians joined; and in B.C. 295, the confederate army of the four nations advanced upon Rome, which appeared to be on the brink of destruction. But a bold step taken by the Romans saved them. Instead of standing merely on the defensive, they met the invaders with one army under the consuls Fabius and Decius, while they marched another into the heart of Etruria. On hearing this, the selfish Etruscans, deserting their confederates, drew off to protect their own country. The Samnites and Gauls retired across the Apennines to Sentinum, losing the Umbrians on the way, who remained to protect their own towns. Rome followed the retreating force, and after a desperate struggle defeated it, thus really deciding the war. The confederation was broken up. The Gauls took no further part in the contest. Rome carried it on separately with Etruria on the one side and Samnium on the other, till the exhaustion of both powers compelled them to make peace. Samnium was forced to submit unconditionally, was mulcted in a portion of its territory, and became a subject-ally of Rome.

Battle of Sentinum.

DETAILS OF THE WAR. FIRST PERIOD, B.C. 298 to 297. The Samnites, B.C. 298, form alliances with the Lucanians and Apulians. Roman armies invade Etruria and Samnium, defeat the Etruscans at Volaterra, and take Bovianum and Aufidena in Northern Samnium.—B.C. 297. Fabius defeats the Samnites and Decius the Apulians. Lucania compelled to submit to

Rome. SECOND PERIOD, B.C. 296 to 295. Gellius Egnatius marches into Etruria.—B.C. 296. The whole Roman force being collected to meet him, Samnium invades Campania, which, however, Rome recovers towards the close of the year.—B.C. 295. The Gauls and Umbrians join the Etruscans and Samnites. Advance of the allied army. Destruction of a Roman legion at Clusium. Romans invade Etruria. Allies retreat. Battle of Sentinum. The Gauls withdraw from the alliance. THIRD PERIOD, B.C. 294 to 290. War carried on by the Romans separately in Etruria and Samnium. Desperate resistance of the Samnites. Great effort made in B.C. 292. Defeat of Fabius Gurges by C. Pontius, followed by the defeat and capture of Pontius by Fabius Maximus. Pontius led in triumph and put to death, B.C. 291. The Samnites submit, B.C. 290.

Interval between the Third Samnite war and the war with Pyrrhus, B.C. 290–280.

10. Ten years intervened between the close of the Third Samnite War and the commencement of the next great struggle in which Rome was engaged. Much obscurity rests upon this interval, in which we lose the guidance of Livy without obtaining that of Plutarch. It appears, however, that shortly after the close of the Third Samnite War troubles broke out afresh in Southern Italy in consequence of a war between the Lucanians and the Greeks of Thurii, B.C. 288. Rome interfered to protect Thurii, whereupon the Lucanians effected a union against Rome of the Gauls (Senones), Etruscans, Umbrians, Samnites, Lucanians, Bruttians, and Tarentines, which, in the year B.C. 283, menaced the Republic with destruction. But, though brought into serious danger, Rome triumphed over her difficulties. Fabricius defeated the combined Lucanians and Bruttians, relieved Thurii, and received the submission of almost all the Greek towns of the neighborhood except Tarentum. Dolabella avenged on the Senonian Gauls the defeat of Metellus at Arretium, by seizing their country and driving them beyond its borders. The Etruscans, and their allies, the Boii (Gauls), were defeated with great slaughter at Lake Vadimon. Tarentum alone remained unpunished. It was probably to inflict damage on this covert enemy, with whom as yet there had been no actual contest, that a Roman fleet was sent in B.C. 282, contrary to the terms of an existing treaty, to cruise round the heel of Italy. This fleet having been attacked and sunk by the Tarentines, who also took possession of Thurii, Rome in B.C. 281 declared war against Tarentum, which, accustomed to lean on Greece for support, invited over the

Epirote prince Pyrrhus, who had already made himself a name by his victory over Demetrius Poliorcetes, and his first brief reign over Macedonia. (See p. 291.)

War with Pyrrhus, B.C. 280–274.

11. The war with Pyrrhus lasted six years, from B.C. 280 to 274. It was the first trial of strength between Macedonized Greece and Rome. Pyrrhus brought with him into Italy an army of 22,500 foot and 3000 horse, disciplined in the Macedonian fashion, and also 20 elephants. At the outset he obtained no troops from any Italians but the Tarentines, whose services were almost worthless. Nevertheless, in his first battle on the Siris, though with an army inferior in number, he completely defeated the Romans, chiefly by the help of his elephants, which disconcerted the Roman cavalry. All Lower Italy then joined him; and, in the remainder of the contest, he had the assistance of the Italian Greeks generally, of the Lucanians, the Bruttians, and, above all, the Samnites. But neither after his first victory, near Heracleia, nor after his second, at Ausculum (Ascoli), was he able to effect any thing. The battles which he gained were stoutly contested, and cost him, each of them, several thousands of men, whom he could not replace and could ill spare. His power necessarily waned as time went on. His allies, except the Samnites, were of little value. His Greek troops harmonized ill with the Italians. Above all, while he fought for glory, the Romans fought for their existence; and their patriotism and patient courage proved more than a match for the gallantry and brilliant strategy of their opponent. It was as much from disgust at his ill success, so far as the general ends of the war were concerned, as from the attraction of a tempting offer, that Pyrrhus, in B.C. 278, quitted Italy for Sicily, accepted the Protectorate of the Greeks, and engaged in a war with the Carthaginians which threw them on the Roman side. Successful in this quarter to a certain extent, but, with his usual restlessness, leaving his conquest uncompleted, the Epirote prince returned to Italy with difficulty; and, having lost Sicily almost at the moment of his departure, engaged the Romans in a third battle near Beneventum, and being there completely defeated, gave up the war, and returned with the almost entire loss of his army, but with heightened reputation, to his native country.

CHRONOLOGY OF THE WAR. Pyrrhus lands in Italy early in B.C. 280. Defeats Lævinus near Heracleia in the autumn of the same year. Attempt to conclude peace fails. Advance of Pyrrhus into Apulia, B.C. 279. Battle of Ausculum. Pyrrhus invited into Sicily. Second attempt at a peace, B.C. 278. Pyrrhus, leaving garrisons in Tarentum and Locri, sails to Syracuse. The Romans recover all Southern Italy except Tarentum. Return of Pyrrhus from Sicily, B.C. 276. Battle of Beneventum. Pyrrhus quits Italy.

Consolidation of the Roman power in peninsular Italy, B.C. 276–265.

12. The departure of Pyrrhus was followed rapidly by the complete subjugation of Southern Italy. Tarentum surrendered B.C. 272. Lucania and Bruttium submitted in the same year. Rhegium was stormed, B.C. 270. In Samnium a guerrilla warfare was maintained till B.C. 269, when resistance finally ceased. The Sallentines and Messapians were conquered in B.C. 266. At the same time Rome extended and consolidated her power in the North. A quarrel was picked with Picenum in B.C. 268. War and subjection followed; and, to prevent future resistance, half the nation was torn from its native land and transplanted to the opposite coast, where it received settlements on the Gulf of Salernum. In B.C. 266, Umbria was forced to make its submission; and in the year following, Volsinii, the chief of the Etruscan towns, was besieged, taken, and razed to the ground. At the close of the year B.C. 265, Rome reigned supreme over the length and breadth of Italy, from the Macra to Tarentum and Rhegium.

System of colonies.

13. The chief means by which Rome established and secured her power was her system of colonies, with its supplement, her military roads. The foundation of colonies began, if we may believe the Roman historians, under the kings. At any rate, it is certain that early in the struggle between the combined Romans, Latins, and Hernici on the one hand and the Oscan nations on the other, the plan of establishing colonies, as garrisons, in towns taken from the enemy, was very widely adopted. Such colonies were made up, in equal or nearly equal proportions, of citizens of the three nations, who together formed the burgher or Patrician body in the city where they took up their abode, the previous inhabitants counting only as a "Plebs." The system, thus employed by Rome in conjunction with her allies, was afterwards made use of copiously in the conquests which she effected for her own sole advantage. As Terminus advanced, either colonies of Roman citizens (*colo-*

nicæ civium Romanorum), who retained all their civic rights, or "Latin colonies" (*coloniæ Latinæ*), consisting of Romans who by becoming colonists lost their rights of voting in the Roman "comitia" and of aspiring to honors (*jus suffragii et honorum*), but retained the rest of their citizenship, were planted far and wide over Italy. These colonists, being Romans, having many Roman rights, and being planted in an invidious position among aliens, naturally clung to the mother-city, and were the great bulwarks of Roman power throughout the peninsula.

The following places are said to have been founded as colonies under the kings:—Antemnæ and Crustumerium, ascribed to Romulus; Ostia, to Ancus; Signia and Circeii, to Tarquinius Superbus. Among the joint colonies of the Romans, Latins, and Hernici, were probably Signia, founded B.C. 493; Velitræ, founded B.C. 492; Norba, founded B.C. 490; Cora and Suessa Pometia, founded probably about the same time; Antium, founded B.C. 465, afterwards recovered by the Volscians; Ardea, founded B.C. 439; Lavici, founded B.C. 415; Circeii, re-founded B.C. 391; Vitellia, founded before B.C. 390; Satricum, founded B.C. 382; and Setia, founded B.C. 379, strengthened B.C. 376. Among Roman colonies, mostly, however, with Latin rights, were Sutrium, founded about B.C. 383; Nepete, founded B.C. 380; Antium, founded B.C. 335; Cales, founded B.C. 332; Anxur or Tarracina, founded B.C. 326; Fregellæ, founded B.C. 325; Luceria, founded B.C. 312; Suessa Aurunca and Pontiæ, founded B.C. 311; Casinum and Interamna, founded B.C. 310; Saticula, founded probably about the same time; Sora and Alba Fucentia, founded B.C. 302; Carseoli, founded B.C. 301; Narnia, founded B.C. 299; Minturnæ and Sinuessa, founded B.C. 296; Venusia, founded B.C. 291—20,000 colonists sent there; Hatria in Picenum, founded B.C. 289; Sena, founded B.C. 283; Pæstum and Cosa, founded B.C. 273; Beneventum and Ariminum, founded B.C. 268; Firmium and Castrum Novum, founded B.C. 264; and Æsernia, founded B.C. 263. Of these by far the greater number were *coloniæ Latinæ;* but Ostia, Circeii, and the maritime colonies generally, were *coloniæ civium Romanorum.*

14. Closely connected with the Roman colonial system was that of the military roads. The genius of Appius Claudius Cæcus first conceived the idea of connecting Rome with her newly-annexed dependency, Campania, by a solid paved road of excellent construction (B.C. 310 to 306). This road, which issued from the Porta Capena (Gate of Capua), passed through Aricia, Velitræ, Setia, Tarracina, Minturnæ, Sinuessa, and Casilinum to Capua; whence it was carried, probably as early as B.C. 291, to Venusia, and later to Brundusium. Much of the work still remains, and attracts the admiration of travellers.

Military roads.

It is doubtful whether any other of the great *viæ* belong to this period. The "Via Valeria" probably took its name from the censor of B.C. 305, M. Valerius Maximus; but it is not likely that any part of the real solid *via* was made by him.

On the general subject of the Roman Roads, see the work of BERGIER, *Histoire des grands chemins de l'Empire Romaine* (Paris, 1622, 4to); and NIBBY, *Delle Vie degli Antichi dissertazione*, in the 4th volume of the 4th Roman edition of NARDINI'S *Roma Antica* (Roma, 1818–20; 4 vols. 8vo).

On the colonial system of the Romans, see MADVIG, J. N., *De Jure et Conditione Coloniarum Populi Romani.* Hauniæ, 1832; 4to.

Relations of Rome to the subject communities.

15. The mode in which Rome, having attained her supremacy, administered the government of Italy, was exceedingly complicated. It is impossible in a work like the present to do more than point out the main features of the system, and distinguish, one from another, the principal classes into which the population of the state was divided. Broadly, we may say that the Roman Republic bore sway in Italy over a host of minor republics. Self-government was most widely spread. Every colony was a sort of independent community, electing its own officers and administering its own affairs. Every foreign city under their rule was recognized by the Romans as a separate state, and was placed on a certain definite footing with regard to the central community. The most highly favored were the *fœderatæ civitates*—states that had submitted to Rome upon terms varying of course in different cases, but in all implying the management of their own affairs, the appointment of their own governors, and the administration of their own laws. Next to these in advantage of position were the *municipia*, foreign states which had received all the burdens together with some or all of the rights of Roman citizenship. Last of all came the *dedititii*, natives of communities which had surrendered themselves to Rome absolutely, and which had all the burdens without any of the rights of citizens. Roman law was administered in these communities by a governor (*præfectus*) appointed by Rome.

Besides the classes above enumerated, and occupying a still lower position, were, (1) the *native* inhabitants of the cities occupied by Roman or Latin colonies, who were almost without rights; and (2) the Slaves, who were the absolute property of their masters.

16. Rome reserved to herself three principal rights, whereby she regarded her sovereignty as sufficiently guarded. (*a*)

Rights of sovereignty reserved to herself by Rome.

She alone might make peace or declare war; (*b*) she alone might receive embassies from foreign powers; and (*c*) she alone might coin money. She had also undoubtedly the right (*d*) of requiring from her subject-allies such contingents of troops as she needed in any war; which involved a further right (*e*) of indirect taxation, since the contingents were armed and paid by the community which furnished them. She did not, like Athens, directly tax her subject-allies; but she derived nevertheless an important revenue from them. On the conquest of a state, Rome always claimed to succeed to the rights of the previously existing government; and, as each Italian state had a public domain of some kind or other, Rome, as she pushed her conquests, became mistress of a vast amount of real property of various kinds, as especially mines, forests, quarries, fisheries, salt-works, and the like. Further, generally, when a state submitted to her after a war, she required, beyond all these sources of revenue, the cession of a tract of arable or pasture land, which she added to her old "ager publicus." Thus the domain of Rome was continually increasing; and it was (at least in part) to collect the revenue from the domain throughout Italy that, in B.C. 267, the four "Italian quæstors" were appointed, "the first Roman functionaries to whom a residence and a district out of Rome were assigned by law."

Constitutional changes in Rome itself. Equalization of the Orders.

17. The constitutional changes in Rome itself during the period under consideration were not very numerous or important. They consisted mainly in the carrying out to their logical result of the Licinio-Sextian enactments—in the complete equalization, that is, of the two Orders. By the laws of Publilius Philo, of Ovinius, and of the Ogulnii, the last vestiges of Patrician ascendency were removed, and the Plebeians were placed in all important respects on a complete equality with the Patricians. Admitted practically to a full moiety of the high governmental offices, they acquired by degrees, through the operation of the Ovinian law, an influence fully equal to that of the Patricians in the Senate. By the tribunate, which remained exclusively theirs, they had even an advantage over the other Order. The strong-hold of the exclusive party, which last yielded itself, was, naturally, that of relig-

ious privilege. But when the Pontificate and the Augurship were fairly divided between the Orders, the struggle between the "houses" and the commons was over, and there was nothing left for the latter to desire.

Legislation of Publilius Philo, B.C. 339. One place in the censorship secured to the Plebeians. Prætorship (probably) thrown open. Right of the Patrician Assembly to interfere with legislation abolished, or made a mere form. Law of Ovinius (date uncertain) gives all ex-consuls, prætors, and curule ædiles a *right* to seats in the Senate. Ogulnian Law, B.C. 300, enlarges the colleges of Pontiffs and Augurs, and gives half the places in each to the Plebeians.

18. But the termination of the internal struggle which had hitherto occupied the commonwealth, and secured it against the deadly evil of political stagnation, was not complete before a new agitation manifested itself, an agitation of a far more dangerous character than that which was now just coming to an end. Hitherto the right of suffrage at Rome, at any rate in the more important of the two popular assemblies—the tribes (*comitia tributa*)—had rested upon the double basis of free birth and the possession of a plot of freehold land. About B.C. 312, the class which these qualifications excluded from the franchise began to exhibit symptoms of discontent. Appius Claudius Cæcus, one of the boldest of political innovators, perceiving these symptoms, and either regarding them as a real peril to the State or as indicating an occasion which he might turn to his own personal advantage, being censor in the year above mentioned, came forward as the champion of the excluded classes, and, after vainly attempting to introduce individuals belonging to them into the Senate, enrolled the entire mass both in the centuries and in the tribes. Nor was this all. Instead of assigning the new voters to the city tribes, within whose local limits they for the most part dwelt, Appius spread them through all, or a majority, of the tribes, and thus gave them practically an absolute control over the elections. Their power was soon seen, (1) in the election of a freedman, Cn. Flavius, to the curule ædileship, which gave him a seat in the Senate for the remainder of his life; and (2) in the election of tribunes who enabled Appius to prolong his term of office illegally to the close of the fourth year. This was the inauguration of a

New agitation. Premature attempt of Appius Claudius Cæcus to establish the democracy.

real ochlocracy, a government in which the preponderating weight belonged to the lowest class of the people. Evil consequences would no doubt have been rapidly developed, had not the work of Appius been to a great extent undone—the sting extracted from his measures—by the skill and boldness of two most sagacious censors. When Q. Fabius Maximus and P. Decius Mus, B.C. 304, removed all who were without landed qualification and all the poorer freedmen from the country tribes, and distributed them among the four city tribes only, the revolutionary force of Ap. Claudius's proceedings was annulled, and nothing remained but a very harmless, and almost nominal enfranchisement of the lower orders. When the "factio forensis" could command the votes of four tribes only out of thirty-one, or ultimately of thirty-five, it was rendered powerless in the *comitia tributa*. In the centuries it was of course even weaker, since there wealth had a vast preponderance over mere numbers.

Moderate arrangement made by Q. Fabius Maximus.

19. The pressure of poverty still continued to be felt at Rome for many years after the Licinian, and even after the Genucian legislation. An insurrection, proceeding to the length of a secession, occurred in B.C. 287 in consequence of the wide-spread distress. An abolition of debts was found to be once more a State necessity, and was submitted to with a view to peace and the contentation of the poorer classes. But the tide of military success, which soon afterwards set in, put a stop for a long term of years to this ground of complaint and disturbance. The numerous and large colonies which were continually being sent out from B.C. 232 to 177, were an effectual relief to the proletariate, and put an end for the time to any thing like extreme poverty among Roman citizens. At the same time the farming of the revenue largely increased the wealth of the more opulent classes. It is not till about B.C. 133 that we find the questions of debt and of the relief of poverty once more brought into prominence and recognized as matters which require the attention of statesmen.

Relief of poverty by means of colonies.

FOURTH PERIOD.

From the Commencement of the First War with Carthage to the Rise of the Civil Broils under the Gracchi, B.C. 264 *to* 133.

SOURCES. The most important of the ancient authorities for this period is POLYBIUS, the earliest writer in whom we see fully developed the true spirit of historical criticism. If the great work of this author (see p. 17) had come down to us in a complete form, we should no more have needed any other authority for the period treated in it, than we need any work, besides that of Thucydides, for the history of the Peloponnesian War, from B.C. 431 to 411. Unfortunately, the complete books descend no lower than B.C. 216; and even the fragments fail us from the year B.C. 146. Consequently, after B.C. 216 we have to depend very much upon other writers, as especially LIVY, whose "Second Decade" covers the space from B.C. 218 to 166, thus taking up the history almost exactly where the complete books of Polybius break off. Next to Polybius and Livy may be placed APPIAN, whose *Punica*, *Bellum Hannibalicum*, and *Iberica* belong to this period and occasionally throw important light upon the course of events. The epitome of FLORUS is not here of much value. The biographer, PLUTARCH, on the other hand, is a considerable help, his "Lives" of *Fabius Maximus*, *P. Æmilius*, *Marcellus*, *M. Cato*, and *Flamininus* falling, all of them, within this brief space of one hundred and thirty years. The short *Life of Hannibal* by CORN. NEPOS possesses also some interest; and occasional aid may be derived from DIODORUS, and ZONARAS.

Of modern writers on this portion of Roman History, besides those already noticed (supra, pp. 373 and 374), the following should be consulted:

MONTESQUIEU, Marquis de, *Considérations sur les causes de la grandeur des Romains et de leur décadence.* Amsterdam, 1734; 8vo.

Fourth Period. Special interest of the external history.

1. In the "Fourth Period" of Roman History, as in the "Third" (see p. 415), and even more decidedly, the interest attaches itself to the external relations of the people rather than to their internal condition. The interval comprises the long struggle with Carthage, the Gallic War and conquest of the plain of the Po, the three Macedonian Wars, the war with Antiochus of Syria, the conquest of Greece, the Numantine War, and the reduction of most of the Spanish Peninsula. At the commencement of the period the dominion of Rome was confined to the mere peninsular portion of Italy; at its close she bore sway over the whole of Southern Europe from the shores of the Atlantic to the straits of Constantinople, over the chief Mediterranean islands, and over a portion of North Africa; while, further, her influence was paramount throughout the East, where Pergamus and Egypt were her

dependents, and Syria existed merely by her sufferance. In B.C. 264, she had just reached a position entitling her to count among the "Great Powers" of the world, as it then was; to rank, i. e., with Carthage, Macedonia, and Syria; in B.C. 134, she had absorbed two of these "Great Powers," and made the third a dependency. She was clearly the sole "Great Power" left; or, if there was a second, it was the newly-formed empire beyond the Euphrates—that of the Parthians—which rose up as Syria declined, and which ultimately remained the only counterpoise to the Roman state through the whole period of its greatness.

Commencement of jealousy between Rome and Carthage.

2. The circumstances of the struggle with Pyrrhus, and the Southern Italians, had forced Rome to become to some extent a maritime power. As she gradually mastered Italy, it became necessary to protect her coasts, exposed as they were to attack from Epirus, from Sicily, from Carthage, even from Greece, as experience showed. Accordingly, a fleet began to be formed as early as B.C. 338, which received constant additions, and had by the year B.C. 267 acquired such importance that four "quæstors of the fleet" (*quæstores classici*) were then appointed, and stationed at different ports of Italy, with the special object of guarding the coasts and keeping the marine in an efficient condition. But this new tendency on the part of the great Italian state could not fail to provoke the jealousy of the chief maritime power of the Western Mediterranean, Carthage, whose policy it had always been to oppose the establishment of any naval rival in the waters which she regarded as her own. Thus, unfriendly feelings, arising out of a consciousness of clashing interests, had for some time been growing up between Carthage and Rome. Temporarily suspended during the height of the Pyrrhic War, when a common danger for a while drew the two states together, they burst out at its close in greater force than ever; and nothing was needed but a decent pretext, in order that the two lukewarm allies should become open and avowed enemies.

First Punic War, B.C. 264-241.

3. The pretext was not long wanting. The Mamertines, a body of Campanian mercenaries who had seized Messana, being threatened with destruction by the combined Carthaginians and Syracusans, applied

for help to Rome, and were readily received into her alliance. Rome invaded Sicily, and by an act of treachery made herself mistress of the disputed post. War with Carthage necessarily followed, a war for the possession of Sicily, and for maritime supremacy in the Mediterranean. The most remarkable feature of the war was the rapid development of the Roman naval power during its course—a development which is without a parallel in the history of the world. With few and insignificant exceptions, the Romans were landsmen till B.C. 262. In that year they began to form a powerful fleet. Only two years later, B.C. 260, they completely defeated, under Duilius, the whole naval force of the Carthaginians; and the supremacy thus acquired they succeeded in maintaining by the later victories of Regulus and Lutatius. Their victories by sea emboldened them to send an army across to Africa, and to attack their enemy in his own country. Success at first attended the efforts of Regulus; but after a little while he was involved in difficulties, and his entire army was either slain or captured. But notwithstanding this and numerous other disasters, the indomitable spirit of the Romans prevailed. After twenty-three years of perpetual warfare, Carthage felt herself exhausted, and sued for peace. The terms which she obtained required her to evacuate Sicily and the adjacent islands, to pay to Rome a war contribution of 2200 talents, to acknowledge the independence of Hiero, king of Syracuse, and bind herself not to make war on him or his allies.

DETAILS OF THE WAR. Invasion of Sicily by the Romans, B.C. 264. Occupation of Messana. The Carthaginians and Hiero attempt its recovery, but fail. Hiero deserts the Carthaginian side and becomes an ally of Rome, B.C. 263. His example is followed by the Greek towns generally. The Romans besiege Agrigentum, which is defended by Hannibal, son of Gisgo, B.C. 262. Attempt to raise the siege fails, and Agrigentum falls. First efforts of Rome to construct a powerful fleet. Fleet of 120 sail launched, B.C. 260. Victory of Duilius at Mylæ, due to the invention of boarding bridges. Corsica attacked, B.C. 259. Aleria taken. Indecisive combat off Cape Tyndaris, B.C. 257. Great victory of Ecnomus, B.C. 256, and invasion of Africa by M. Atilius Regulus, who is successful at first, but in B.C. 255 suffers a complete defeat, and falls into the enemy's hands. The Romans evacuate Africa. Destruction of their fleet by storms. Great despondency at Rome, B.C. 253. The war confined to Sicily, where Thermæ is taken, B.C. 252, and Eryx, B.C. 249. Lilybæum, however, and Drepana still hold out; and in an attempt to take the latter, B.C. 249, the Roman fleet is completely destroyed.

Six years of petty warfare follow, B.C. 248 to B.C. 242, the advantage remaining on the whole with the Carthaginians, who, under Hamilcar Barca, recover some of their lost ground in Sicily, and at the same time infest the Roman coasts with their privateers. At last, however, in B.C. 241, Rome once more makes a great effort. A number of the citizens from their private resources build and man a fleet of 200 sail, which they present to the nation; and with this fleet the consul, C. Lutatius, gains a great victory at the Ægates Insulæ, which completely breaks the spirit of the Carthaginians, and induces them to consent to a peace on the terms above mentioned.

Importance of the war.

4. The great importance of this war was, that it forced Rome to become a first-rate naval power. Though the Romans did not during its course obtain the complete mastery of the sea, they showed themselves fully a match for the Carthaginians on the element of which they had scarcely any previous experience. Their land force being much superior to that of Carthage, and their resources not greatly inferior, it became tolerably apparent that success would ultimately rest with them. Their chief deficiency was in generalship, wherein their commanders were decidedly surpassed, not only by the Carthaginian patriot Hamilcar, but even the mercenary Xanthippus. Here the Roman system was principally to blame, whereby the commanders were changed annually, and the same person was expected to be able to command equally well both by land and by sea. Carthage continued her commanders in office, and had separate ones for the land and the sea service. Even Carthage, however, was unwise enough to deprive herself of the services of many an experienced captain by the barbarous practice of putting to death any general or admiral who experienced a reverse.

Further progress of Rome. Seizure of Sardinia and Corsica.

5. An interval of twenty-three years separated the First from the Second Punic War. It was employed by both sides in energetic efforts to consolidate and extend their power. Rome, in B.C. 238, taking advantage of the position in which Carthage was placed by the revolt of her mercenaries, made herself mistress of the island of Sardinia, and when, upon the submission of the mercenaries, Carthage required its restoration, played the part of the wolf in the fable, declared herself injured by her victim, and threatened a renewal of the war. Exhausted Carthage had to purchase her forbearance by the cession of the island, and the payment of a fine

amounting to 1200 talents, B.C. 237. Rome then proceeded to annex Corsica; and soon afterwards (B.C. 227) she laid the foundation of her provincial system by the establishment of her first "Proconsuls," one to administer her possessions in Sicily, the other to govern Sardinia and Corsica.

CHIEF POINTS OF THE PROVINCIAL SYSTEM OF ROME. The Proconsul unites in his own person the supreme military and civil functions. He is at once commander-in-chief, governor, and supreme judge. The revenue, however, is administered by quæstors responsible to the Senate. Native authorities are to a great extent tolerated; and different degrees of privilege are conferred on different portions of a province. No regular contingent of troops is required: but in lieu of this burden, one-tenth of the produce of the whole land is claimed by Rome as hers, and a tax of 5 per cent. is levied on all imports and exports.

War with the Boii, B.C. 238–236.

6. About the same time that she seized Sardinia, Rome was engaged in a war with the Boii (Gauls) and Ligures in North Italy, in which the Boii are said to have been the aggressors. Unsuccessful in their attempts during the campaigns of B.C. 238 and 237, these barbarians, in B.C. 236, invited the aid of their kindred tribes from beyond the Alps; but the allies after a little while fell out, and the Boii and Ligures were glad to buy peace of Rome by the cession of some of their lands.

Suppression of Illyrian piracy. Lodgment effected in Greece.

7. Rome, soon afterwards, showed herself for the first time on the eastern coast of the Adriatic, and took part in the affairs of Greece. The decay of Grecian power had allowed the piratical dispositions of the Illyrians to have free course; and the commerce of the Adriatic, the coasts of Epirus and Corcyra, and perhaps even that of Italy to some extent, suffered from the constant attacks of Illyrian cruisers. Entreated to protect them by the unhappy Greek cities, the Romans, in B.C. 230, sent an embassy to Scodra, to require the cessation of the piracies. Their ambassadors were murdered; and a war necessarily followed. Rome, in B.C. 229, with a fleet of 200 ships, cleared the Adriatic, made the Illyrians of Scodra tributary, established Demetrius of Pharos as dependent dynast over the coasts and islands of Dalmatia, and accepted the protectorate of the Greeks of Apollonia, Epidamnus, and Corcyra. In return the Greeks acknowledged the Romans as their kin, and admitted them to participation in the Isthmian games and the Eleusinian mysteries. Thus Rome ob-

tained a hold upon the opposite side of the Adriatic, and a right of interference in the affairs of Greece.

8. A still more important war soon followed. Rome, before engaging in any further enterprises beyond the limits of Italy, was anxious to extend her dominion to its natural boundary upon the north, the great chain of the Alps which shuts off Italy from the rest of Europe. With this view, she proceeded, about B.C. 232, to make large assignments of land, and plant new and important colonies, in the territory of the Senones, thus augmenting her strength towards the north and preparing for a great contest with the Gauls. These last, finding themselves threatened, at once flew to arms. Obtaining aid from their kindred tribes in and beyond the Alps, they crossed the Apennines in B.C. 225, and spread themselves far and wide over Etruria, advancing as far as Clusium, and threatening Rome as in the days of Brennus. Three armies took the field against them, and though one, composed of Etruscans, was completely defeated, the two others, combining their attack, gained a great victory over the invaders near Telamon, and forced them to evacuate Etruria. Rome then carried the war into the plain of the Po. Having allied herself with the Veneti, and even with the Gallic tribe adjoining them, the Cenomani, she was able in a little time to reduce the whole tract to subjection. The Boii and Lingones submitted in B.C. 224; the Anari in B.C. 223; the Insubres were conquered after a fierce struggle, which occupied the years B.C. 223 and 222. Mediolanum and Comum, the last towns which held out, submitted in the last-named year, and Roman dominion was at length extended to the great barrier of the Alps.

Conquest of Cisalpine Gaul, B.C. 225–222.

To establish herself firmly in the valuable tract thus conquered, Rome planted it thickly with colonies. Of these the most important were Placentia (Piacenza), Cremona, and Mutina (Modena); to which were added afterwards Parma, Mediolanum, Brixia, Comum, Verona, and Mantua. The newly-conquered tract was at the same time attached to the capital by the "Flaminian Way," which was carried to Narnia about B.C. 300, to Spoletium in B.C. 240, and to Ariminium in B.C. 220.

9. These conquests were scarcely effected when fresh troubles broke out in Illyria. Demetrius of Pharos, dissatisfied with the position accorded him by the Romans, de-

War with Demetrius of Pharos, B.C. 219.

clared himself independent, attacked the Roman allies, and encouraged the Illyrians to resume the practice of piracy. Allied with Antigonus Doson (see p. 299), he thought himself strong enough to defy the Roman power. But Antigonus dying, B.C. 220, and Philip, his successor, being a mere boy, a Roman army, in B.C. 219, chastised Demetrius, destroyed his capital, and drove him from his kingdom.

Growth of the Carthaginian power in Spain, B.C. 236–220.

10. It was ill-judged in Rome to allow this petty quarrel to draw her attention to the East, when in the West an enemy had arisen, against whom her utmost efforts were now needed. From the moment that Carthage was not only robbed of Sardinia, but forced to pay a fine for having ventured to remonstrate against the wrong done her, the determination to resume the struggle with Rome at the first convenient opportunity became a fixed national sentiment. There was indeed a peace party in the Punic community; but it had little weight or force. The advocates of war, who had found their fitting leaders in the warriors of the Barcine family—Hamilcar, his sons, and son-in-law—were all-powerful in the government; and under them it became and remained the one sole object of Carthage to bring herself into a position in which she could hope to renew her contest with her hated antagonist on such terms as might promise her a fair prospect of success. No sooner was the revolt of the mercenaries put down (B.C. 237) by the judicious efforts of Hamilcar Barca, than the project was formed of obtaining in Spain a compensation, and more than a compensation, for all that had been lost in Sicily, Sardinia, and the lesser islands. Hamilcar, in the last nine years of his life, B.C. 236 to 228, established the Carthaginian power over the whole of Southern and South-eastern Spain, the fairest portion of the peninsula. His work was carried on and completed in the course of the next eight years, B.C. 227 to 220, by his son-in-law, Hasdrubal. Andalusia, Murcia, and Valencia were occupied. A warlike population, Iberic and Celtic, was reduced and trained to arms under Carthaginian officers. Towns were built; trade prospered; agriculture flourished. Above all, the rich silver-mines near Carthagena (Carthago Nova) were discovered and skillfully worked; Spain more than

paid her expenses; and the home-treasury was amply provided with those "sinews of war" without which a sustained military effort is impossible.

Passive attitude of Rome.

11. The indifference with which Rome saw this extension of the Carthaginian power is very surprising. She did indeed make alliance with the semi-Greek communities of Saguntum (Zacynthus) and Emporiæ about B.C. 226, and at the same time obtained a promise from Hasdrubal that he would not push his conquests beyond the Ebro; but otherwise she appeared unobservant or careless of her rival's acquisitions. Probably she thought that the designs of Carthage were in the main commercial, and regarded an invasion of Italy from the side of Spain as simply an impossibility. Perhaps she thought her enemy's strength so much reduced, and her own so much increased, as to render it inconceivable that the struggle should ever be renewed, unless she chose at her own time to force a contest. As she remained mistress of the sea, and Carthage did not even make any effort to dispute her maritime supremacy, it seemed difficult for her rival to attack her in any quarter, while it was easy for her to carry the war into any portion of the Carthaginian territory.

Plans of Hannibal.

12. But Hannibal, sworn from his boyhood to eternal hatred of Rome, had determined, as soon as he succeeded to the command (B.C. 220), on the mode and route by which he would seek to give vent to his enmity, to save his own nation and at the same time destroy her foe. Fully appreciating the weakness of Carthage for defense, it was his scheme to carry the war without a moment's unnecessary delay into the enemy's country, to give the Romans ample employment there, and see if he could not exhaust their resources and shatter their confederacy. The land route from Spain to Italy had for him no terrors. He could count on the good dispositions of most of the Celtic tribes, who looked on him as the destined deliverer of Cisalpine Gaul from the iron gripe of Rome. He probably knew but little of the dangers and difficulties of crossing the Alps; but he was well aware that they had been often crossed by the Gauls, and that he would find in the Alpine valleys an ample supply of friendly and experienced guides. Arrived in Cisalpine Gaul, he would have the whole population with

him, and he would be able, after due consideration, to determine on his further course. With the veteran army which he brought from Spain, and with his own strategic ability, he trusted to defeat any force that Rome could bring into the field against him. For ultimate success he depended on his power of loosening the ties which bound the Italic confederacy together, of raising up enemies to Rome in Italy itself, and at the same time of maintaining his army in such efficiency that it might be distinctly recognized as master of the open field, incapable of being resisted unless behind walls, or by defensive guerrilla warfare. With these views and objects, Hannibal, in B.C. 219, commenced the Second Punic War by laying siege to Saguntum.

Second Punic War: its general course.

13. The issue of the Second Punic War was determined by the dauntless resolution and the internal vigor of Rome. She had opposed to her the most consummate general of antiquity; a state as populous and richer in resources than her own; a veteran army; a possible combination of various powerful allies; above all, an amount of disaffection among her own subjects, the extent of which could not be estimated beforehand, but which was at any rate sure to be considerable. Three battles showed that Hannibal was irresistible in the field, and taught the Romans to avoid general engagements. The third was followed by a wide-spread defection of the Roman subject-allies—all Italy from Samnium and Campania southward passed over to the side of Hannibal. But the rest of the federation stood firm. Not a Latin deserted to the enemy. Central Italy from sea to sea held to Rome. She had the resources of Etruria, Umbria, Picenum, Sabina, Latium, to draw upon, besides her own. By immense efforts, including the contraction of a large National Debt, she contrived to maintain her ground, and gradually to reduce Hannibal to the defensive. The alliances, by which Hannibal sought to better his position, with Syracuse, B.C. 215, and with Philip of Macedon, B.C. 216, did him scant service, Rome in each case meeting the new enemy on his own ground, and there keeping him fully employed. The hopes of a successful issue to Carthage then rested upon the junction of the second army of Spain, under Hasdrubal, with the reduced force of Hannibal in Italy, a junction frustrated by the battle of the

Metaurus, which was thus the turning-point of the war. After this reverse, the transfer of the war into Africa was a matter of course; and this transfer rendered necessary the recall of Hannibal from Italy and the relinquishment of all the great hopes which his glorious enterprise had excited. There remained just a possibility that in a last pitched battle on his native soil, Hannibal's genius might re-establish the superiority of the Carthaginian arms. But the battle of Zama removed this final chance. Hannibal met in Scipio Africanus a general, not indeed his equal, but far superior to any of those with whom he had been previously engaged; and, his troops being mostly of inferior quality, he suffered, through no fault of his own, the great defeat which rendered further resistance impossible. Carthage, after Zama, became a dependent Roman ally.

DETAILS OF THE WAR. The Second Punic War may be divided into three periods—a first period of three years, from the fall of Saguntum to Cannæ, a period of uninterrupted Carthaginian victory, B.C. 218 to 216; a second period of nine years, from Cannæ to the battle of the Metaurus, a time of alternate victory and reverse, during which there was still a good hope that the great enterprise of the Carthaginian general might be crowned with ultimate success, B.C. 215 to 207; and a third period of six years, a time of constant Roman advance and progress, when the termination of the war in favor of Rome was certain, and the only question was how long resistance could be protracted, B.C. 206 to 201.

FIRST PERIOD, B.C. 218 to 216.—B.C. 218. Passage of the Pyrenees, and the Rhone. Encounter with the army of P. Cornelius Scipio on the left bank of the river. March to the Alps, and passage of the great chain, probably by the Little St. Bernard, in the month of September. Capture of Turin. The Ligurians, and the Celts generally, declare for Hannibal. Scipio defeated in a cavalry engagement on the Ticino. Great battle of the Trebia in the same year (December) makes Hannibal master of the whole of Northern Italy.—B.C. 217. Passage of the Apennines, and march through the marshes of Northern Etruria. Hannibal loses an eye. Great victory on the shores of Lake Trasimene. Alarm at Rome. Q. Fabius Maximus made dictator. A siege expected. Hannibal marches through Umbria into Picenum, where he rests and reorganizes his army. He then proceeds along the coast into Southern Italy, hoping to produce insurrection among the Roman allies, who, however, remain faithful. The dictator, Fabius (Cunctator), keeps an army in the field, but avoids an engagement. Hannibal winters in Apulia.—B.C. 216. Great effort made by Rome to crush the invader terminates in the terrible disaster of Cannæ, where Rome loses from 70,000 to 80,000 men. Accession of Philip of Macedon and of Syracuse to the Carthaginian alliance. General defection of the Southern Italians, and especially of Capua. Noble attitude of Rome in her hour of greatest danger. Resolve to continue the war and, while maintaining the struggle both in Spain and Italy, to attack Macedonia and Syracuse.

The question of the pass by which Hannibal crossed the Alps has been a matter of much controversy, and can scarcely be said even now to be settled; but the weight of modern authority is decidedly in favor of the Little St. Bernard. The chief works on the subject are:

WHITAKER, Rev. J., *The Course of Hannibal over the Alps ascertained.* London, 1794; 2 vols. 8vo. This writer argues in favor of the Great St. Bernard.

CRAMER (Dean) and WICKHAM, G.L., *Dissertation on the Passage of Hannibal over the Alps.* Oxford, 1820; 8vo.

LONG, H. L., *The March of Hannibal from the Rhone to the Alps.* London, 1831; 8vo.

ELLIS, Rev. R., *A Treatise on Hannibal's Passage of the Alps, in which his route is traced over the Little Mt. Cenis.* Cambridge, 1854. And the same writer's *Inquiry into the Ancient Routes between Italy and Gaul; with an Examination of the Theory of Hannibal's Passage of the Alps by the Little St. Bernard.* Cambridge, 1867; 8vo.

LAW, W. J., *The Alps of Hannibal.* London, 1866; 8vo.

SECOND PERIOD, B.C. 215 to 207. The Second period of the war is devoid of any great battles, until the one with which it closes, and is (comparatively speaking) uninteresting. Hannibal, having to protect the Southern Italians, who have come over to him, is reduced to the defensive. As he can not detach the Latins, or the Northern Italians, from the Roman confederacy, he needs some great accession of force in order to bring the war to a successful issue. For such an accession he long continues to hope; but it never arrives. Philip of Macedon is kept employed in Illyricum and Greece from B.C. 214 to 207, when peace is made with him. (See p. 305.) Syracuse is besieged by Marcellus, B.C. 214, and taken, B.C. 212. Hasdrubal is detained in Spain year after year, first by the brothers Cn. and P. Cornelius Scipio, and then by the young Publius (afterwards known as Africanus), until B.C. 208, when, at the sacrifice of a portion of his army, he makes his way to the northward, crosses the Pyrenees, and, wintering in Gaul, proceeds the next spring by the route which his brother had followed, across the Alps, into Italy. The Gauls and Ligurians join him. Etruria and Umbria waver in their allegiance. Rome seems to be brought into greater danger than ever. But once more her constancy and courage assert themselves. Every man capable of bearing arms is called out to fight. Twenty-three legions are enrolled. Above all, by a masterly manœuvre, the consul, Claudius Nero, deceives Hannibal, and marching away to the north with half his army, concentrates the great bulk of the Roman strength against Hasdrubal, and crushes him on the Metaurus, before he can effect a junction with his long-expectant brother, B.C. 207. With the defeat of Hasdrubal disappears the last ray of hope for Carthage, which has no further reserve that can be brought into play with any prospect of affecting the general issue.

THIRD PERIOD, B.C. 206 to 201. It is surprising that the Romans did not carry the war into Africa in the year following the battle of the Metaurus. Nothing more was to be feared from Hannibal, who had retreated into the farther corner of Bruttium. Much less was the expedition of Mago to

North Italy, B.C. 205, a real danger. It would seem that the Senate hesitated owing to the want of any general of sufficient ability, who at the same time was sufficiently popular to call forth a national effort. Thus it was not till B.C. 204 that an expedition was actually sent into Africa, under the young Scipio, who had recently returned from Spain with a deservedly high reputation. Scipio, having landed, besieged Utica, but was shortly driven back to the coast, and wintered on a promontory, where he intrenched himself. The next year, however, B.C. 203, he assumed an aggressive attitude; defeated the Carthaginian levies in two battles; took Syphax prisoner; and forced the Punic government, as a last resource, to recall Hannibal. That general arrived from Italy in B.C. 202, and after a vain attempt at negotiation, made a last effort to turn the scale in favor of his country at the battle of Zama, where, however, he suffered defeat, though a defeat without dishonor. Negotiations were then renewed, and a peace was concluded (B.C. 201) on the terms which follow:—(1) The relinquishment by Carthage of all her territory beyond the limits of Africa; (2) an engagement on her part not to engage in war out of Africa, nor even in Africa without permission from the Romans; (3) the payment to Rome of an annual contribution of 200 talents (£48,800) for the next fifty years; (4) the surrender of all their ships except ten, and all their elephants; and (5) the restoration to Masinissa of all that had belonged to himself or to his ancestors. These terms were, on the whole, moderate and fair under the circumstances; and it is creditable to Scipio that he had the clemency to propose, and to Hannibal that he had the wisdom to accept, them.

The History of the Hannibalic, or Second Punic War, has been particularly well written by Dr. ARNOLD. See his *History of Rome*, vol. iii., pp. 63 to 455.

Gains of Rome by the war.

14. The gains of Rome by the Second Punic War were, in the first place, the complete removal of Carthage from the position of a counterpoise and rival to that of a small dependent community, powerless for good or evil; secondly, the addition to the Roman land dominion of the greater part of Spain, which was formed into two provinces, Citerior and Ulterior; thirdly, the absorption of the previously independent state of Syracuse into the Roman province of Sicily; fourthly, the setting up of a Roman protectorate over the native African tribes; and fifthly, the full and complete establishment of Roman maritime supremacy over the whole of the Western Mediterranean. The war further tended to the greater consolidation of the Roman power in Italy. It crushed the last reasonable hopes of the Ligurians and Gauls in the north. It riveted their fetters more firmly than ever on the non-Latin races of the centre and the south, the Umbrians, Etruscans, Sabines, Picentians, Apulians, Bruttians. Throughout Italy large tracts of land

were confiscated by the sovereign state; and fresh colonies of Romans and Latins were sent out. In Campania and the southern Picenum, the whole soil was declared forfeit. The repulse of Hannibal involved a second subjugation of Italy, more complete and more harsh than the first. Everywhere, except in Latium, the native races were depressed, and a Latin dominion was established over the length and breadth of the land.

Note the strengthening of old and the foundation of new colonies at this period:—Venusia strengthened in B.C. 200, Narnia in B.C. 199, Cosa in B.C. 197; Sipontum, Thurii (Copia), Croton, Salernum, and Puteoli, established in B.C. 194; Vibo (Valentia) in B.C. 192. In many places, moreover, where no town was built or occupied, the veterans were established on the confiscated lands as *coloni*.

15. Another result of the Hannibalic War, which completed the subjugation of the Western Mediterranean basin, was to hasten the collision between the aggressive Republic and the East, which had long been evidently impending. Already, as early as B.C. 273, Rome had entered into friendly relations with Egypt, and even before this she had made a commercial treaty with Rhodes (see p. 307). About B.C. 245, she had offered to King Ptolemy Euergetes a contingent for his Syrian War (see p. 272); and soon afterwards she interceded with Seleucus Callinicus on behalf of the Ilians, her "kindred." Her wars with the Illyrian pirates, B.C. 229 to 219, had brought her into contact with the states of Greece, more particularly with the Ætolians (see § 7); and finally, the alliance of Philip, king of Macedon, with Hannibal, had forced her to send a fleet and army across the Adriatic, and had closely connected her with Elis, with Sparta, and even with the Asiatic kingdom of Pergamus (see pp. 304, '5). Circumstances had thus drawn her on, without any distinctly ambitious designs on her part, to an interference in the affairs of the East—an interference which, in the existing condition of the Oriental world, could not but have the most momentous consequences. For throughout the East, since the time of Alexander, all things had tended to corruption and decay. In Greece, the spirit of patriotism, feebly kept alive in the hearts of a select few, such as Aratus and Philopœmen, was on the point of expiring. Intestine division made the very name

Collision hastened between Rome and the East.

of Hellas a mockery, and pointed her out as a ready prey to any invader. In Macedonia luxury had made vast strides; military discipline and training had been neglected; loyalty had altogether ceased to exist; little remained but the inheritance of a great name and of a system of tactics which was of small value, except under the animating influence of a good general. The condition of the other Alexandrine monarchies was even worse. In Syria and in Egypt, while the barbarian element had been raised but slightly above its natural level by Hellenic influence, the Hellenic had suffered greatly by its contact with lower types of humanity. The royal races, Seleucids and Ptolemies, were effete and degenerate; the armed force that they could bring into the field might be numerous, but it was contemptible; and a general of even moderate abilities was a rarity. It was only among the purely Asiatic monarchies of the more remote East that any rival, really capable of coping with Rome, was now likely to show itself. The Macedonian system had lived out its day, and was ready to give place to the young, vigorous, and boldly aggressive power which had arisen in the West.

Second Macedonian War, B.C. 200–197.

16. The conclusion of peace with Carthage was followed rapidly by an attack on Macedonia, for which the conduct of Philip had furnished only too many pretexts. Philip had probably lent aid to Carthage in her final struggle: he had certainly without any provocation commenced an aggressive war against Rome's ancient ally, Egypt, and he had plunged also into hostilities with Attalus and the Rhodians, both of whom were among the friends of Rome, the former being protected by a treaty (see p. 306). Rome was bound in honor to aid her allies; and no blame can attach to her for commencing the Second Macedonian War in B.C. 200, and dispatching her troops across the Adriatic. Her conduct of the war was at first altogether mediocre; but from the time that T. Quinctius Flamininus took the command (B.C. 198) it was simply admirable, and deserved the success which attended it. The proclamation of general liberty to the Grecian states, while it could not fail of being popular, and was thus excellently adapted to deprive Philip of his Hellenic allies, and to rally to the Roman cause the whole power of Hellas, involved no

danger to Roman interests, which were perfectly safe under a system that established universal disunion. The gift of liberty to the Greeks by Rome in B.C. 198, is parallel to the similar gift of universal autonomy to the same people by Sparta and Persia in B.C. 387 (see p. 214) at the "Peace of Antalcidas." On both occasions, the idea under which the freedom was conceded was that expressed by the maxim "Divide et impera." The idea was not indeed now carried out to an extreme length. There was no dissolution of the leagues of Achæa, Ætolia, or Bœotia. These leagues were in fact too small to be formidable to such a power as Rome. And as they had embraced the Roman side during the continuance of the war, their dissolution could scarcely be insisted on. Thessaly however was, even at this time, in pursuance of the policy of separation, split up into four governments.

For the details of the Second Macedonian War, and for the terms on which peace was concluded, see pp. 307, '8.

Battle of Cynoscephalæ, its importance.

17. The battle of Cynoscephalæ, by which the Second Macedonian War was terminated, deserves a place among the "Decisive Battles of the World." The relative strength of the "legion" and the "phalanx" was then for the first time tried upon a grand scale; and the superiority of the "legion" was asserted. No doubt, man for man, the Roman soldiers were better than the Macedonian; but it was not this superiority which gained the day. The phalanx, as an organization, was clumsy and unwieldy; the legion was light, elastic, adapted to every variety of circumstances. The strength and weakness of the phalanx were never better shown than at Cynoscephalæ; and its weakness—its inability to form quickly, to maintain its order on uneven ground, or to change front—lost the battle. The loss was complete, and irremediable. Macedonia was vanquished, and Rome became thenceforth the arbitress of the world.

War with the Boii and Insubres, B.C. 201-191.

18. While her arms were thus triumphant in the East, Rome was also gaining additional strength in the West. In the very year of the conclusion of peace with Carthage, B.C. 201, she recommenced hostilities in the plain of the Po, where the Gauls had ever since the invasion of Hannibal defied the Roman authority and

maintained their independence. It was necessary to reconquer this important tract. Accordingly, from B.C. 201 to 191, the Romans were engaged in a prolonged Gallic War in this district, in which, though ultimately successful, they suffered many reverses. Their garrisons at Placentia and Cremona were completely destroyed and swept away. More than one pitched battle was lost. It was only by energetic and repeated efforts, and by skillfully fomenting the divisions among the tribes, that Rome once more established her dominion over this fair and fertile region, forcing the Gauls to become her reluctant subjects.

DETAILS OF THE WAR, B.C. 201 to 191. Hostilities commence in the country of the Boii, who are assisted by the Carthaginian general, Hamilcar. The Romans are defeated, B.C. 201. Sack of Placentia, B.C. 200, and siege of Cremona. Hamilcar defeated near that city. Roman army defeated by the Insubres, B.C. 199. The Cenomani become allies of the Romans and help them to defeat the Insubres on the Mincius, B.C. 197. Fall of Comum, B.C. 196. Peace made with the Insubres. War continues with the Boii, B.C. 195 to 191. Great Roman victory of Mutina, B.C. 193. Submission of the Boii, who cede one-half of their territory, B.C. 191.

Result of the war.

19. The conquest of Gallia Cisalpina was followed by a fresh arrangement of the territory. The line of the Po was taken as that which should bound the strictly Roman possessions, and while "Gallia Transpadana" was relinquished to the native tribes, with the exception of certain strategic points, such as Cremona and Aquileia, "Gallia Cispadana" was incorporated absolutely into Italy. The colonies of Placentia and Cremona were re-established and reorganized. New foundations were made at Bononia (Bologna), Mutina (Modena), and Parma in the Boian country. The Æmilian Way was carried on (B.C. 187) from Ariminum to Placentia. The Boians and Lingones were rapidly and successfully Latinized. Beyond the Po, the Gallic communities, though allowed to retain their existence and their native governments, and even excused from the payment of any tribute to their conquerors, were regarded as dependent upon Rome, and were especially required to check the incursions of the Alpine or Transalpine Celts, and to allow no fresh immigrants to settle on the southern side of the mountain-chain.

20. Meanwhile, in the East, the defeat of Philip, the withdrawal of the Romans, and the restoration of the Greeks to

Unsettled state of Greece and the East.

freedom, had been far from producing tranquillity. The Ætolian robber-community was dissatisfied with the awards of Flamininus, and hoped, in the scramble that might follow a new war, to gain an increase of territory. Antiochus of Syria was encouraged by the weakness of Macedon to extend his dominions in Asia Minor, and even to effect a lodgment in Europe, proceedings which Rome could scarcely look upon with indifference. War broke out in Greece in the very year that Flamininus quitted it, B.C. 194, by the intrigues of the Ætolians, who were bent on creating a disturbance. At the same time, Antiochus showed more and more that he did not fear to provoke the Romans, and was quite willing to measure his strength against theirs, if occasion offered. In B.C. 195 he received Hannibal at his court with special honors; and soon afterwards he entered into negotiations which had it for their object to unite Macedonia, Syria, and Carthage against the common foe. In B.C. 194 or 193 he contracted an alliance with the Ætolians; and finally, in B.C. 192, he proceeded with a force of 10,500 men from Asia into Greece.

War of Rome with Antiochus the Great, B.C. 192–190.

21. This movement of Antiochus had been foreseen by the Romans, who about the same time landed on the coast of Epirus with a force of 25,000 men. War was thus, practically, declared on both sides. The struggle was, directly and immediately, for the protectorate of Greece; indirectly and prospectively, for political ascendency. Antiochus "the Great," as he was called, the master of all Asia from the valley of the Indus to the Ægean, thought himself quite competent to meet and defeat the upstart power which had lately ventured to intermeddle in the affairs of the "Successors of Alexander." Narrow-minded and ignorant, he despised his adversary, and took the field with a force absurdly small, which he could without difficulty have quadrupled. The natural result followed. Rome easily defeated him in a pitched battle, drove him across the sea, and following him rapidly into his own country, shattered his power, and established her own prestige in Asia, by the great victory of Magnesia, which placed the Syrian empire at her mercy. Most fortunate was it for Rome that the sceptre of Syria was at this time wielded by so weak a mon-

Great victory of Magnesia.

arch. Had the occupant of the Seleucid throne possessed moderate capacity; had he made a proper use of his opportunities; had he given the genius of Hannibal, which was placed at his disposal, full scope; had he, by a frank and generous policy, attached Philip of Macedon to his side, the ambitious Republic might have been checked in mid-career, and have suffered a repulse from which there would have been no recovery for centuries.

DETAILS OF THE WAR WITH ANTIOCHUS, B.C. 192 to 190. Antiochus lands at Demetrias, B.C. 192, but with only 10,000 foot, 500 horse, and six elephants. He is made General-in-Chief of the Ætolians. The Athamanians, Chalcis in Eubœa, Elis, and Bœotia join him. Epirus negotiates. Philip, offended at the encouragement given by Antiochus to a pretender to the Macedonian crown, declares for the Romans. The Romans, with 40,000 men, enter Thessaly, B.C. 191, and advance southward. Antiochus occupies Thermopylæ with his small force, and gives the guard of the path over the mountains to the Ætolians, who are easily dislodged, whereupon the whole army of Antiochus breaks up and flies in disorder. He himself returns to Asia and assumes an attitude of defense. His partisans in Greece are forced to submit either to Philip or to the Romans. At sea, his fleet is defeated by the Romans near Cyprus, in Ionia. Struggle for the mastery of the Ægean between the Romans, Pergamenes, and Rhodians on the one hand, and Antiochus, assisted by Hannibal, on the other, B.C. 190. Contest decided by the defeat of Hannibal at Aspendus, and of Polyxenidas, the admiral of Antiochus, at Corycus. The Roman army, under the command of the two Scipios, lands in Asia. Attempt of Antiochus to negotiate fails. Battle of Magnesia decides the war. Antiochus cedes Asia Minor north of the Taurus, and consents to pay the sum of 12,000 talents (nearly £3,000,000 sterling).

Results of the victory.

22. The "moderation" of Rome after the battle of Magnesia has been admired by many historians; and it is certainly true that she did not acquire by her victory a single inch of fresh territory, nor any direct advantage beyond the enrichment of the State treasury. But indirectly the advantages which she gained were considerable. She was able to reward her allies, Eumenes of Pergamus and the Rhodians, in such a way as to make it apparent to the whole East that the Roman alliance was highly profitable. She was able to establish, and she did establish, on the borders of Macedonia, a great and powerful state, a counterpoise to the only enemy which she now feared in Europe. She was able to obtain a cheap renown by proclaiming once more the liberty of Greece, and insisting that the Greek cities of Asia Minor, or at any rate those

which had lent her aid, should be recognized as free—a proclamation which cost her nothing, and whereby she secured herself a body of friends on whose services she might hereafter count in this quarter. That she was content with these gains, that she evacuated Asia Minor, as she had previously evacuated Greece (see § 20), was probably owing to the fact that she was not as yet prepared to occupy, and maintain her dominion over, countries so far distant from Rome. She had found the difficulty of holding even Spain as a part of her empire, and was forced by the perpetual attacks of the unconquered and revolts of the conquered natives to maintain there perpetually an army of 40,000 men. She had not yet made up her mind to annex even Greece; much less, therefore, could she think of holding the remote Asia Minor. It was sufficient for her to have repulsed a foe who had ventured to advance to her doors, to have increased her reputation by two glorious campaigns and a great victory, and to have paved the way for a future occupation of Western Asia, if circumstances should ever render it politic.

The chief benefit which Asia Minor derived from this premature entrance into it of the Roman arms was through the campaign of Cn. Manlius Volso (B.C. 189) against the Gauls or Galatians. The losses inflicted on the two tribes of the Tolistoboii and the Tectosagi secured tranquillity to the neighboring nations for a long term of years. But the motive of Manlius seems to have been plunder.

State of Greece.

23. In Greece, the defeat of Antiochus was followed, necessarily, by the submission of the Ætolians, who were mulcted in large portions of their territory and made to pay a heavy fine. Rome annexed to her own dominions only Cephallenia and Zacynthus, distributing the rest among her allies, who, however, were very far from being satisfied. The Achæan League and Philip were both equally displeased at the limits that were set to their ambition, and were ready, should opportunity offer, to turn their arms against their recent ally.

Wars of Rome in the West.

24. In the West, four wars continued to occupy a good deal of the Roman attention. (*a*) Spain was still far from subdued; and the Roman forces in the country were year after year engaged against the Lusitani or the Celtiberi, with very doubtful success, until about

B.C. 181 to 178, when some decided advantages were gained. (*b*) In the mountainous Liguria the freedom-loving tribes showed the same spirit which has constantly been exhibited by mountaineers, as by the Swiss, the Circassians, and others. War raged in this region from B.C. 193 to 170; and the Roman domination over portions of the Western Apennines and the maritime Alps was only with the utmost difficulty established by the extirpation of the native races or their transplantation to distant regions. No attempt was made really to subjugate the entire territory. It was viewed as a training-school for the Roman soldiers and officers, standing to Rome very much as Circassia long stood to Russia, and as Algeria even now stands to France. (*c*) In Sardinia and (*d*) in Corsica perpetual wars, resembling slave-hunts, were waged with the native races of the interior, especially in the interval from B.C. 181 to 173.

Relations of Rome with Macedon during the last years of Philip, B.C. 190–179.

25. The discontent of Philip (see § 23) did not lead him to any rash or imprudent measures. He defended his interests, so far as was possible, by negotiations. When Rome insisted, he yielded. But all the while, he was nursing the strength of Macedonia, recruiting her finances, increasing the number of her allies, making every possible preparation for a renewal of the struggle, which had gone so much against him at Cynoscephalæ. Rome suspected him, but had not the face to declare actual war against so recent an ally and so complaisant a subordinate. She contented herself with narrowing his dominions, strengthening Eumenes against him, and sowing dissensions in his family. Demetrius, his younger son, who lived at Rome as a hostage, was encouraged to raise his thoughts to the throne, which he was given to understand Rome would gladly see him occupy. Whether Demetrius was willing to become a "cat's-paw" is not apparent; but the Roman intrigues on his behalf certainly brought about his death, and caused the reign of Philip to end in sorrow and remorse, B.C. 179. (See p. 310.)

Position and plans of Perseus, B.C. 179–172.

26. The accession of Perseus to the Macedonian throne was only so far a gain for Rome that he was less competent than Philip to conduct a great enterprise. In many respects the position of Macedonia was bettered by the change of sovereigns. Perseus,

a young and brave prince, was popular, not only among his own subjects, but throughout Greece, where the national party had begun to see that independence was an impossible dream, and that the choice really lay between subjection to the wholly foreign Romans and to the semi-Hellenic and now thoroughly hellenized Macedonians. Perseus, again, had no personal enemies. The kings of Syria and Egypt, who could not forgive his father the wrongs which they had suffered at his hands, had no quarrel with the present monarch; to whom the former (Seleucus IV.) readily gave his daughter in marriage. The design of Philip to re-establish Macedonia in a position of real independence was heartily adopted by his successor; and Rome learnt by every act of the new prince, that she had to expect shortly an outbreak of hostilities in this quarter.

27. Yet, for a while, she procrastinated. Her wars with Liguria, Sardinia, and Corsica still gave her occupation in the West, while a new enemy, the Istri, provoked by the establishment of her colony of Aquileia (B.C. 183), caused her constant trouble and annoyance in the border land between Italy and Macedon, the Upper Illyrian country. But, about B.C. 172, it became clear that further procrastination would be fatal to her interests —would, in fact, be equivalent to the withdrawal of all further interference with the affairs of Greece and the East. Perseus was becoming daily bolder and more powerful. His party among the Greeks was rapidly increasing. The Ætolians called in his aid. The Bœotians made an alliance with him. Byzantium and Lampsacus placed themselves under his protection. Even the Rhodians paid him honor and observance. If the protectorate of Greece was not to slip from the hands of Rome and to be resumed by Macedon, it was high time that Rome should take the field and vindicate her pretensions by force of arms. Accordingly, in the autumn of B.C. 172, an embassy was sent to Perseus, with demands wherewith it was impossible that he should comply; and when the envoys were abruptly dismissed, war was at once declared.

Third Macedonian War commences, B.C. 171.

For the details of the Third Macedonian War, and the causes of the ill success of Perseus, see Book IV., Period III., Part III. (pp. 311, 312).

28. The victory of Pydna, gained by L. Æmilius Paullus

(June 22, B.C. 168), was a repetition of that at Cynoscephalæ, but had even more important consequences. Once more the legion showed itself superior to the phalanx; but now the phalanx was not merely defeated but destroyed, and with it fell the monarchy which had invented it and by its means attained to greatness. Nor was this the whole. Not only did the kingdom of Alexander perish at Pydna, 144 years after his death, but the universal dominion of Rome over the civilized world was thereby finally established. The battle of Pydna was the last occasion upon which a civilized foe contended on something like equal terms with Rome for a separate and independent existence. All the wars in which Rome was engaged after this were either rebellions, aggressive wars upon barbarians with a view to conquest, or defensive wars against the barbarians who from time to time assailed her. The victories of Zama, Magnesia, and Pydna convinced all the world but the "outer barbarians" that it was in vain to struggle against Roman ascendency, that safety was only to be found in submission and obedience. Hence the progress of Rome from this time was, comparatively speaking, peaceful. Her successes had now reduced the whole civilized world to dependence. When it was her pleasure to exchange dependence for actual incorporation into her empire, she had simply to declare her will, and was, generally, unresisted. Occasionally, indeed, the state marked out for absorption would in sheer despair take up arms; e. g., Achæa, Carthage, Judæa. But for the most part there was no struggle, merely submission. Greece (except Achæa), Macedonia, Asia Minor, Syria, Egypt, were annexed peaceably; and the only remaining great war of the Republic was with the barbarian, Mithridates of Pontus.

Important results of the war.

29. But Rome, though her military successes had elevated her to this commanding position, was still loath to undertake the actual government of the countries over which she had established her ascendency. Her experiment in Spain was not encouraging; and she would willingly have obtained the advantages of a widely-extended sway, without its drawbacks of enlarged responsibilities and ever-recurring difficulties and entanglements. Accordingly, her policy was still to leave the conquered re-

Settlement made of the territory.

gions to rule themselves, but at the same time so to weaken them by separation, that they might never more be formidable, and so to watch over and direct their proceedings that these might in no way clash with the notions which she entertained of her own interests. Moreover, as she saw no reason why she should not obtain permanent pecuniary advantage from her victories, she determined to take from both Illyricum and Macedonia a land-tax equal to one-half of the amount which had been previously exacted by the native sovereigns.

SETTLEMENT OF THE HELLENIC PENINSULA. (*a*) Macedonia was disarmed and broken up into four separate states, without rights of intermarriage or of acquiring land within each other's territories. Each of the four states was a federative republic (see p. 312). The Royal demesnes and the right of working the mines (a royal prerogative) were assumed by Rome; and the land-tax was commuted into an annual payment to Rome of 100 talents. (*b*) Illyria was divided into three small states. Certain cities which had favored Rome were exempted from taxation. The rest of the country was taxed at the rate of half of the former land-tax. The entire Illyrian fleet was declared forfeit, and was presented to the Greek towns on the coast. (*c*) In Greece, the treatment of the several states varied considerably. The Ætolians were deprived of Amphipolis, and the Acarnanians of Leucas; Epirus was ravaged, 150,000 of the inhabitants sold into slavery, and the rest of the population delivered over to the government of a tyrant. All the leagues, except that of Achæa, were dissolved; and each city was made independent. The members of the patriotic party in the various states were accused of having favored Perseus, in act or thought, and were either executed or deported to Italy. Even Achæa, which had been the faithful ally of Rome throughout the struggle, was required to deliver up for trial a thousand of her chief men, who were thenceforward detained in Roman prisons as hostages for her good behavior.

Roman system of commissioners.

30. While, however, professedly leaving the countries which she had conquered to govern themselves, Rome could not bring herself really to let them act as they pleased. What she did was to substitute for government a system of surveillance. Everywhere she was continually sending commissioners (*legati*), who not merely kept her acquainted with all that passed in the states which they visited, but actively interfered with the course of government, suggesting certain proceedings and forbidding others, acting as referees in all quarrels between state and state, giving their decisions in the name of Rome, and threatening her vengeance on the recalcitrant.

Treatment of Pergamus and Rhodes.

31. The subjugation of the enemies of Rome was always followed by a tendency on her part to quarrel with her friends. Her friends were maintained and strengthened merely as counterpoises to some foe; and when the foe ceased to exist or to be formidable, the friends were no longer needed. Thus the fall of Macedonia and complete prostration of Greece produced an immediate coolness between Rome and her chief Eastern allies, Pergamus and Rhodes.

The statement that Eumenes had thoughts of joining Perseus against Rome, and even entered into negotiations with him, seems quite unworthy of credit. The coolness certainly began with Rome, and arose from her no longer needing Eumenes. Hence her intrigues with his brother Attalus, B.C. 167; her rejection of his request for Œnus and Maroneia; her refusal to admit him to an audience, B.C. 166; and her grant of independence to Pamphylia, which was disputed between him and Antiochus.

The Rhodians offended Rome by an offer to mediate between her and Perseus, B.C. 168; but there is reason to believe that the Roman consul himself urged them to make the offer. Having fallen into the trap, they were punished by the loss of all their possessions upon the main-land, by serious interferences with their trade, and by the establishment of a free port at Delos, which greatly diminished their commercial gains.

Interference between Syria and Egypt, B.C. 168.

32. The vast prestige which Rome acquired by the victory of Pydna is strikingly shown by the fact that she was able in the same year to deprive Antiochus Epiphanes of the fruits of all his Egyptian successes, by a mere command haughtily issued by her commissioner, Popillius. (See pp. 256, 278.) Antiochus withdrew from Egypt when he was on the point of conquering it; and even relinquished the island of Cyprus to his antagonist. Rome allowed him, however, to retain possession of Cœlé-Syria and Palestine.

Unimportant wars from B.C. 168–150.

33. The pacification of the East was followed by another of those pauses which occur from time to time in the history of the Roman Republic, after a great effort has been made and a great success attained, when the government appears to have been undecided as to its next step. Eighteen years intervene between the close of the Third Macedonian and the commencement of the Third Punic War—eighteen years, during which Rome was engaged in no contest of the least importance, unless it were that which continued to be waged in Spain against the

Lusitanians and a few other native tribes. She did not, indeed, ever cease to push her dominion in some quarter. In the intervals between her great wars, she almost always prosecuted some petty quarrels; and this was the case in the interval between B.C. 168 and 150, when she carried on hostilities with several insignificant peoples, as the Celtic tribes, in the Alpine valleys, the Ligurians of the tract bordering on Nicæa (Nice) and Antipolis (Antibes), the Dalmatians, the Corsicans, and others.

Important successes of C. Sulpicius Gallus against the Eastern Ligurians and of his colleague M. Claudius Marcellus against the Celts in the Alps, B.C. 166. War in Corsica, B.C. 163 to 162. War with the Dalmatians, B.C. 156 to 155. War with the Western Ligurians, B.C. 154. War with the Celtiberians and Lusitanians, B.C. 153 to 150.

34. But the time came when the government was no longer content with these petty and trivial enterprises. After eighteen years of irresolution, it was decided to take important matters in hand—to remove out of the way the city which, however reduced, was still felt to be Rome's sole rival in the Western world, and to assume the actual government of a new dependency in a new continent. The determination to destroy Carthage and to form Africa into a province, was in no way forced upon Rome by circumstances, but was decided upon after abundant deliberation by the predominant party in the state, as the course best calculated to advance Roman interests. The grounds of quarrel with Carthage were miserably insufficient; and the tyranny of the stronger was probably never exerted in a grosser or more revolting form, than when Rome required that Carthage, which had observed, and more than observed, every obligation whereto she was bound in treaty, should nevertheless, for the greater advantage of Rome, cease to exist. It was not to be expected that the idea of a political suicide would approve itself to the Carthaginian government. But less than this would not content Rome, which, having first secured every possible advantage from the inclination of her adversary to make sacrifices for peace, revealed finally a requirement that could not be accepted without war.

Change of policy. Determination to extend the empire.

35. The Third Punic War lasted four years—from B.C. 149 to 146 inclusive. It was a struggle into which Carthage en-

Third Punic War, B.C. 149–146: absorption of "Africa."

tered purely from a feeling of despair, because the terms offered to her—the destruction of the city, and the removal of the people to an inland situation—were such that death seemed preferable to them. The resistance made was gallant and prolonged, though at no time was there any reasonable hope of success. Carthage was without ships, without allies, almost without arms, since she had recently surrendered armor and weapons for 200,000 men. Yet she maintained the unequal fight for four years, exhibiting a valor and an inventiveness worthy of her best days. At length, in B.C. 146, the Romans under Scipio Æmilianus, forced their way into the town, took it almost house by house, fired it in all directions, and ended by levelling it with the ground. The Carthaginian territory was then made into the "province" of "Africa;" a land-tax and poll-tax were imposed; and the seat of government was fixed at Utica.

The utter destruction of Carthage was parallel to that of Veii in B.C. 393, of Corinth in the same year with Carthage, and of Jerusalem, A.D. 70. Rome was unwilling that there should anywhere exist a city which could be viewed as rivalling her in size, wealth, or splendor. It is impossible that she could have really feared any thing from the power of Carthage.

Macedonian and Achæan Wars. Macedonia and Achæa become "provinces."

36. During the continuance of the Carthaginian War, troubles broke out in the Hellenic peninsula, which enabled Rome to pursue in that quarter also the new policy of annexation and absorption. A pretender, who gave out that he was the son of Perseus, raised the standard of revolt in Macedonia, defeated the Romans in a pitched battle, B.C. 149, and invaded Thessaly, but was in the following year himself defeated and made prisoner by Metellus. The opportunity was at once taken of reducing Macedonia into the form of a "province." At the same time, without even any tolerable pretext, a quarrel was picked with the Achæan League, B.C. 148, which was required to dissolve itself. A brief war followed (see p. 314), which was terminated by Mummius, who plundered and destroyed Corinth, B.C. 146. Achæa was then practically added to the empire, though she was still allowed for some years to amuse herself with some of the old forms of freedom, from which all vital force had departed.

37. But while Rome was thus extending herself in the

South and in the East, and adding new provinces to her empire, in her old provinces of the West her authority was fiercely disputed; and it was with the utmost difficulty that she maintained herself in possession. The native tribes of the Spanish Peninsula were brave and freedom-loving; their country was strong and easy of defense; and Rome found it almost impossible to subjugate them. The Roman dominion had indeed never yet been established in the more northern and western portions of the country, which were held by the Lusitani, the Gallæci, the Vaccæi, and the Cantabri; and a perpetual border war was consequently maintained, in which the Roman armies were frequently worsted. The gallantry and high spirit of the natives was especially shown from B.C. 149 to 140 under the leadership of the Lusitanian, Viriathus; and again from B.C. 143 to 133, in the course of the desperate resistance offered to the Roman arms by the Numantians. Rome was unable to overcome either enemy without having recourse to treachery.

War in Spain, B.C. 149–133.

DETAILS OF THE WAR IN SPAIN, from B.C. 149 to 133. The Lusitani invade Turditania, B.C. 149. Viriathus, being made general, extricates them from a perilous position, and defeats the prætor Vetilius. For five years (B.C. 149 to 145) he continues the struggle with uniform success. In B.C. 145, the consul Fabius Maximus Æmilianus, undertakes the war and defeats him; but he gains over most of the Celtiberians and becomes more powerful than ever. In B.C. 142, Viriathus was first defeated by, and then victorious over, Servilianus, the adopted brother of Æmilianus, after which he obtained a peace on fair terms, which was ratified by the Senate, B.C. 141. This peace, however, the Romans broke in the ensuing year, B.C. 140, when the consul Servilius Cæpio first attacked Viriathus with his troops and then procured his assassination. The Lusitani, upon this, submitted; but the Numantians, who had the year before completely defeated the consul Q. Pompeius, continued the struggle with success, gaining victories over the pro-consul Popillius, in B.C. 138, and over the consul Hostilius Mancinus, in B.C. 137. On the second of these occasions a peace was made, which saved a Roman army of 20,000 men. But, as after the Caudine Forks, Rome repudiated her engagements. War was renewed in B.C. 136, but with little success, the pro-consul Lepidus suffering a severe defeat. Calpurnius Piso, in B.C. 135, effected nothing. At last, in B.C. 134, the war was undertaken by Scipio Africanus Æmilianus, who so improved the discipline of the Roman forces, that in the following year, B.C. 133, he succeeded in bringing the war to an end by starving out the Numantians, who fired their city and then slew themselves, rather than fall into the hands of the Romans.

38. While the freedom-loving tribes of the West showed

so much reluctance to surrender their liberties into the hands of Rome, in the East her dominion received a large extension by the voluntary act of one of her allies. Attalus III., king of Pergamus, who held under his sovereignty the greater part of Asia Minor, was found at his death (B.C. 133) to have left his kingdom by will to the Roman people. This strange legacy was, as was natural, disputed by the expectant heir, Aristonicus, bastard son of Attalus, and was afterwards denied by Mithridates V.; but there is no real ground for calling it in question. Rome had no doubt intrigued to obtain the cession, and consequently she did not hesitate to accept it. A short war with Aristonicus (B.C. 133 to 130) gave the Romans full possession of the territory, the greater portion of which was formed into a province; Phrygia Major being, however, detached, and ceded to Mithridates IV., king of Pontus, who had assisted Rome in the brief struggle.

Rome inherits the kingdom of Pergamus, B.C. 133.

The territory of Rome at this time included, besides all Italy up to the Alps, the "provinces" (*provinciæ=providentiæ*, i. e., "cares" or "charges") of Hispania Ulterior and Hispania Citerior, of Africa (the old territory of Carthage), of Sicily, and of Sardinia and Corsica, in the West; and in the East, of Macedonia, Achaia, and Asia, or the absorbed portion of the kingdom of Pergamus. Gallia Cisalpina and Liguria were also "provinces." Each province was administered by a governor, who was either a "pro-consul," a "prætor," or a "proprætor." These governors received no stipend, but were entitled to certain contributions from the provincials for the support of themselves and their court, and might also receive voluntary gifts—two fertile sources of abuse and misgovernment. Their suite or court (*cohors*) consisted of a certain number of quæstors, of secretaries, notaries, lictors, augurs, public criers, etc. They had at once the chief civil authority and the military command in their provinces. They were irremovable during their term of office, which might be prolonged from year to year; nor could any complaint be brought against them till their office was at an end. If serious complaints were then made, they could be brought to trial, either criminally before the people, or by civil action before judges chosen from among the senators. In neither case, however, was there much chance of condemnation; and in the latter, the condemnation could be nothing but a fine, which was easily paid by the extortionate governor, who would often remain after it one of the richest men in Rome. It is evident that this system must have been grievously oppressive to the provincials, and fearfully corruptive of public morals at Rome.

Roman system of "provinces:" its tendency.

39. The internal changes in the Roman government during the period here under consideration were gentle, gradual, and for the most part informal; but they amounted in

Changes in the Roman government at this time gradual.

course of time to a sensible and far from unimportant modification. The long struggle between the Patrician and Plebeian orders was terminated by the Genucian revolution; and, the chief Plebeian families being now placed on a par with the Patricians, a united nobility stood at the head of the nation, confronting and confronted by a proletariate, with only a rather small and not very active middle class intervening between them. The proletariate, however, was in part amenable to the nobility, being composed of persons who were its Clients; and it was not difficult to keep the remaining members in good-humor by bestowing upon them from time to time allotments of land in the conquered territories. On the whole, it may be said that the proletariate was, during this period, at the beck and call of the nobles, while the only opposition which caused them anxiety was that of the middle class—Italian farmers principally—who, supported by some of the less distinguished Plebeian "houses," formed an "opposition," which was sometimes formidable.

40. It was the object of the nobles, (1) to increase the power of the Senate as compared with the "comitia;" and (2) to bring the "comitia" themselves under aristocratic influence. The exaltation of the Senate was effected very gradually. The more important foreign affairs became—and every thing was foreign out of Italy—the greater grew to be the power of the Senate, which settled all such matters without reference to the "comitia." And, with respect to home affairs, the more widely the franchise was extended (and it reached through the *Roman* colonies to very remote parts of Italy), the more numerous and varied the elements that were admitted to it, the less were the "comitia" possessed of any distinct and positive will, and the more easy did it become to manipulate and manage them. As a rule, the people stood and assented to all proposals made by the magistrates. They were too widely scattered over the territory to be instructed beforehand, too numerous to be addressed effectively at the time of voting—besides which, no one but the presiding magistrate had the right of addressing them.

Exaltation of the Senate.

41. To bring the "comitia" more completely under the hands of the government, the vast bodies of freedmen, who

Corruption of the "comitia." constituted at this time the chief portion of the retainers (*clientes*) of each noble house, were continually admitted to the franchise, either by a positive enactment, as in B.C. 240, or by the carelessness or collusion of the censors, who every five years made out anew the roll of the citizens. The lower classes of the independent voters were also systematically corrupted by the practice of largesses, especially distributions of corn, and by the exhibition of games at the private cost of the magistrates, who curried favor with the voters by the splendor and expense of their shows. It was also, perhaps, to increase the influence of the nobles over the centuries that the change was made by which each of the five classes was assigned an equal number of votes; for the wealthier citizens not within the noble class were at this time the most independent and the most likely to thwart the will of the government.

42. Still, no hard-and-fast line was drawn between the nobles and the rest of the community, no barrier which could not be overstepped. A family became noble through its members obtaining any of the high offices of the State, and through its thus having "images of ancestors" to show. And legally the highest office was open to every citizen. Practically, however, the chief offices came to be confined almost to a clique. This was owing, in the first place, to the absolute need of great wealth for certain offices, as especially the ædileship, and to the law (passed in B.C. 180) by which a regular rotation of offices was fixed, and no one could reach the higher till he had first served the lower. But, beyond this, it is evident that after a time a thoroughly exclusive spirit grew up; and all the influence of the nobles over the "comitia" was exerted to keep out of high office every "new man"—every one, that is, who did not belong to the narrow list of some forty or fifty "houses" who considered it their right to rule the commonwealth.

Rome falls practically under the rule of a clique.

See the work of RUPERTI, *Stemmata gentium Romanarum*. Göttingen, 1795; 8vo.

43. The attempts of the "opposition" (see § 39) were limited to two kinds of efforts. First, they vainly wasted their strength in noble but futile efforts to check the spread of luxury and corruption, in-

Weak and narrow policy of the "opposition."

cluding however under those harsh names much that modern society would regard as proper civilization and refinement. Secondly, they now and then succeeded by determined exertions in raising to high office a "new man"—a Porcius Cato, or a C. Flaminius—who was a thorn in the side of the nobles during the remainder of his lifetime, but rarely effected any political change of importance. Altogether, the "opposition" seems fairly taxable with narrow views and an inability to grapple with the difficulties of the situation. The age was one of "political mediocrities." Intent on pursuing their career of conquest abroad, the Roman people cared little and thought little of affairs at home. The State drifted into difficulties, which were unperceived and unsuspected, till they suddenly declared themselves with startling violence at the epoch whereat we have now arrived.

By far the best account of the internal condition of Rome at this period, which has been strangely neglected by most writers of Roman history, will be found in the *Römische Geschichte* of MOMMSEN, book iii., chaps. xi. and xii.

FIFTH PERIOD.

From the Commencement of internal Troubles under the Gracchi to the Establishment of the Empire under Augustus, B.C. 133 *to* A.D. 30.

SOURCES. The continuous histories of this period, composed by ancient writers, whether Greek or Latin, if we except mere sketches and epitomes, are all lost. For the earlier portion of it—B.C. 133 to 70—our materials are especially scanty. PLUTARCH, in his *Lives* of the *Gracchi*, of *Marius*, *Sylla*, *Lucullus*, *Crassus*, and *Sertorius*, and APPIAN, *De Bellis Civilibus*, are the chief authorities; to which may be added SALLUST's *Jugurtha*, a brilliant and valuable monograph, together with a few fragments of his *Histories*. In this comparative scarcity of sources, even the brief compendium of the prejudiced PATERCULUS, and the *Epitomes* of the careless and inaccurate LIVY, come to have an importance. From about B.C. 70, there is an improvement both in the amount and in the character of the extant materials. Appian continues to be of service, as also does Plutarch in his *Lives* of *Cicero*, *Pompey*, *Julius Cæsar*, *Cato the younger*, *Brutus*, and *Antonius;* while we obtain, in addition, abundant information of the most authentic kind, first, from the contemporary *Speeches* and *Letters* of CICERO, and then from the *Commentaries* of CÆSAR and HIRTIUS. The continuous narrative of DIO CASSIUS begins also from the year B.C. 69; the *Catiline* of SALLUST belongs to the years B.C. 66 to 62; and SUETONIUS's *Lives* of *Julius* and *Octavius* fall, the one entirely, the other partially, within the date which terminates the period.

Among modern works wholly or specially devoted to this period of Roman History may be mentioned—

DE BROSSES, *Histoire de la République Romaine dans le cours du 7ième*

Siècle. Dijon, 1777; 3 vols. 4to. (Translated into German, with additions, by SCHLEUTER, in 1790.)

LONG, G., *Decline of the Roman Republic.* London, 1864; 2 vols. 8vo. A careful collection of facts, embracing an unusually small amount of theory. (This work belongs in part to the preceding period; since it commences with the history of B.C. 154, and contains an account of the wars in Spain with Viriathus and the Numantians, and of the contemporary civil history.)

DRUMANN, W., *Geschichte Roms in seinem Uebergange von der Republik zur Monarchie.* Königsberg, 1834–44; 6 vols. 8vo.

LAU, TH., *Die Gracchen und ihre Zeit;* Hamburg, 1854, 8vo; and the same author's *Cornelius Sulla, eine Biographie;* Hamburg, 1855; 8vo.

NITZSCH, K. W., *Die Gracchen und ihre Vorgänger.* Berlin, 1847; 8vo.

General character of the period. Time of civil trouble and disturbance.

1. An epoch is now reached at which the foreign wars of Rome become few and unimportant, while the internal affairs of the State have once more a grave and absorbing interest. Civil troubles and commotions follow one another with great rapidity; and finally we come to a period when the arms of the Romans are turned against themselves, and the conquerors of the world engage in civil wars of extraordinary violence. The origin of these disturbances is to be found in the gulf which had been gradually forming and widening between the poor and the rich, the nobles and the proletariate. For a long series of years, from the termination of the Second Samnite War to the final settlement of Northern Italy (B.C. 303 to 177), the pressure of poverty had been continually kept down and alleviated, partly by the long and bloody struggles which decimated the population and so relieved the labor-market, partly by distributions of plunder, and, above all, by assignations of lands. But the last Italian colony was sent out in B.C. 177; and a new generation had now grown up which had neither received nor expected any such relief. The lands of Italy were all occupied; no nation within its borders remained to be conquered; and settlements beyond the seas possessed for the ordinary Roman citizen few attractions. As the wars came to be less constant and less sanguinary, the population increased rapidly, and no vent was provided for the new-comers. The labor-market was overcrowded; it became difficult for a poor man to obtain a living; and those dangers arose which such a condition of things is sure to bring upon a State.

The number of adult male Roman citizens, which was but 269,015 in B.C. 173, had increased to above 320,000 by B.C. 136, and in B.C. 125 stood at 390,736. In B.C. 114 it was 394,336, and in B.C. 86, after the admission of the Italians, it was 463,000.

Contrast of the rich and poor. Non-employment of free labor on the State lands.

2. The state of affairs would have been very different, had the Licinian law with respect to the employment of free labor been enforced against the occupiers of the public domain. This domain, which had now become extremely large (see p. 426), had, naturally enough, been occupied by the capitalist (which was nearly identical with the governing) class, who had at the time seemed to compensate fairly the non-capitalists by extremely liberal allotments of small plots of ground in absolute property. But, while the poorer classes increased in number, the richer were stationary, or even dwindled. Old "houses" became extinct, while new "houses" only with great difficulty pushed themselves into the ruling order. There were no means of obtaining much wealth at Rome except by the occupation of domain lands on a large scale, by the farming of the revenue, or by the government of the provinces. But these sources of wealth were, all of them, at the disposal of the ruling class, who assigned them, almost without exception, to members of their own families. Thus the wealthy were continually becoming more wealthy, while the poor grew poorer. There was no appreciable introduction of new blood into the ranks of the aristocracy. The domain land was in B.C. 133 engrossed by the members of some forty or fifty Roman "houses" and by a certain number of rich Italians, of whom the former had grown to be enormously wealthy by inheritance, intermarriages, and the monopoly of government employments. The "modus agrorum" established by Licinius had fallen into oblivion, or at least into disuse; and several thousand "jugera" were probably often held by a single man. Still, in all this there would have been no very great hardship, had the domain land been cultivated by the free labor of Roman citizens, either wholly or in any decent proportion. In that case, the noble "possessor" must have conveyed to his estate, in whatever part of Italy it was situated, a body of poor Roman freemen, who would have formed a sort of colony upon his land, and would

have only differed from other colonists in working for wages instead of cultivating on their own account. The Roman labor-market would have been relieved, and no danger would have threatened the State from its lower orders. But it seemed to the "possessor" more economical and more convenient to cultivate his land by means of slaves, which the numerous wars of the times, together with the regular slave-trade, had made cheap. The Licinian enactment was therefore very early set at naught; and it was not enforced. Everywhere over Italy the public domain was cultivated by gangs of slaves.

Apprehension of danger to the State induces Ti. Sempronius Gracchus to bring forward his laws.

3. Among the more wise and patriotic of the Romans it had long been seen that this state of things was fraught with peril. At Rome a proletariate daily becoming poorer and more unwieldy, content hitherto to be at the beck and call of the nobles, but if it once grew to be hungry and hopeless, then most dangerous—in Italy a vast slave population, composed largely of those who had known liberty and were not deficient in intelligence, harshly treated and without any attachment to its masters, which might be expected on any favorable opportunity to rise and fight desperately for freedom—the government, if an outbreak occurred, dependent on the swords of the soldiers, who might largely sympathize with the poorer classes, from which they were in great measure taken—such a combination boded ill for peace, and claimed the serious consideration of all who pretended to the name of statesmen. Unhappily, at Rome, statesmen were "few and far between;" yet, about B.C. 140, Lælius (the friend of Scipio) had recognized the peril of the situation, and had proposed some fresh agrarian enactments as a remedy, but had been frightened from his purpose by the opposition which the nobles threatened. Matters went on in the old groove till B.C. 133, when at length a tribune of the Plebs, Ti. Sempronius Gracchus by name, a member of one of the noblest Plebeian houses, came forward with a set of propositions which had for their object the relief of the existing distress among the Roman citizens, and the improvement of the general condition of Italy by the substitution of free cultivators of the small yeoman class for the gangs of disaffected slaves who were now spread over the country. The exact

measures which he proposed were, (1) The revival of the obsolete law of Licinius, fixing the amount of domain land which a man might legally occupy at 500 jugera, with the modification that he might hold also 250 jugera for each of his unemancipated adult sons; (2) The appointment of a standing commission of three members to enforce the law; (3) The division among the poorer citizens of the State lands which would by the operation of the first provision become vacant; (4) The compensation of the *possessores* on account of their losses from improvements made on the lands which they relinquished by the assignment to them of the portions of land which they legally retained in absolute ownership; and (5) The proviso that the new allotments, when once made, should be inalienable.

There is no reason to believe that Gracchus was actuated by any but pure and patriotic motives. The servile war which was raging in Sicily (B.C. 134 to 132) indicated a danger which might at any moment extend to Italy, and which did in fact show itself in places, as particularly at Minturnæ and Sinuessa. And some poor-law or other, some legal provision for the relief of the distress at Rome, was a State necessity.

4. The propositions of Gracchus were intensely disagreeable to the bulk of the nobility and to a certain number of the richer Italians, who had, legally or illegally, become occupiers of the domain to an extent beyond that which it was proposed to establish as the limit. Naturally therefore his laws were opposed. The opposition was led by one of his own colleagues, the tribune Octavius, who by his *veto* prevented the vote of the tribes from being taken. An unseemly contention followed, which Gracchus, unfortunately for himself and for his cause, terminated by proposing to the tribes, and carrying, the deposition of his adversary. The laws were then passed, a commission was appointed (Gracchus, his brother Caius, and Ap. Claudius, his father-in-law), and the work of resumption and distribution commenced.

His laws opposed but passed, B.C. 133.

5. But it was more easy to initiate than to carry out a measure of such extent and complication, and one that aroused such fierce passions, as that which the bold tribune had taken in hand. As he advanced in his work his popularity waned. His adversaries took heart; and, to secure himself and his cause, he was forced to

His murder.

propose fresh laws of a more and more revolutionary character. The propositions which he made, and his conduct in endeavoring to secure his re-election, for the purpose of carrying them, goaded his enemies to fury; and the Senate itself, with Scipio Nasica at its head, took the lead in a violent attack upon him as he presided in the Tribes, and murdered him in open day together with 300 of his partisans.

The proposals of Gracchus to give the Equestrian Order a distinct political status, by conferring on it the right to furnish one-half of the *judices*, hitherto taken only from the Senate, to grant an appeal to the people in *civil* causes, and to claim for the people the entire right of administering the newly-gained kingdom of Pergamus (besides determining the disposition of the treasure in their own favor), were measures of a far more revolutionary character than his Agrarian Law, which was less severe than that of Licinius.

The Agrarian Commission of Ti. Gracchus sets to work; but after a while its proceedings are suspended, B.C. 129.

6. The open murder of a tribune of the Plebs engaged in the duties of his office was an unprecedented act in Roman history (for the assassination of Genucius, B.C. 471, had been secret), and sufficiently indicated the arrival of a new period, when the old respect for law and order would no longer hold its ground, and the State would become a prey to the violent and the unscrupulous. For the moment, however, the evil deed done recoiled upon its authors. Nasica, denounced as a murderer on all hands, though unprosecuted, was forced to quit Italy and go into banishment. The Agrarian Commission of Gracchus was renewed, and allowed to continue its labors. Moderation on the part of the democratic leaders who had succeeded to the position of Gracchus would have secured important results for the poor from the martyrdom of their champion; but the arbitrary conduct of the new commissioners, Carbo and Flaccus, disgusted the moderate party at Rome and large numbers of the Italians; the Senate found itself strong enough to quash the Commission and assign the execution of the Sempronian Law to the ordinary executive, the consuls; and finally, when, by the assassination of the younger Africanus, the democrats had put themselves decidedly in the wrong, it was able to go a step farther, and suspend proceedings under the law altogether.

7. A lull in the storm now occurred—a period of comparative tranquillity, during which only a few mutterings were

Tranquillity interrupted by the claims of the Italians.

heard, indications to the wise that all was not over. A claim to the franchise began to be urged by the Latins and Italians, and to find advocates among the democratic Romans, who thought that in the accession of these fresh members to the tribes they saw a means of more effectually controlling the Senate. Q. Fabius Flaccus, the consul of B.C. 125, formulated these claims into a law; but the Senate contrived to tide over the difficulty by sending him upon foreign service. The revolt of the disappointed Fregellæ followed; and the bloody vengeance taken on the unhappy town frightened the Italians, for the time at any rate, into silence. Meanwhile, the younger Gracchus, who had gone as quæstor into Sardinia, B.C. 126, was detained there by the Senate's orders till B.C. 124, when he suddenly returned to Rome and announced himself as a candidate for the tribunate.

Revolt of Fregellæ.

PETTY WARS OF THIS PERIOD. Revolt of Aristonicus in Asia, B.C. 131. Revolt put down, B.C. 129. War in Illyria, ibid. Guerrilla War in Sardinia, B.C. 126 to 124. War with the Salluvii (Ligurians) for the protection of Massilia, B.C. 125 to 123. Balearic isles conquered by Metellus, B.C. 123.

8. The measures of C. Gracchus were more varied and more sweeping than those of his elder brother; but they were cast in the same mould. He had the same two objects in view—the relief of the poorer classes, and the depression of the power of the Senate. Like his brother, he fell a victim to his exertions in the popular cause; but he effected more. His elevation of the Equestrian Order, and his system of corn-largesses—the "Roman poor-law," as it has been called—survived him, and became permanent parts of the constitution. To him is also attributable the extension of the Roman colonial system into the provinces. He was a great and good man; but he had a difficult part to play; and he was wanting in the tact and discretion which the circumstances of the times required. The Senate, being far more than his match in finesse and manœuvre, triumphed over him, though not without once more having recourse to violence, and staining the streets and prisons of Rome with the blood of above 3000 of her citizens.

Democratic reforms of the younger Gracchus. He is murdered, B.C. 121.

MEASURES OF THE YOUNGER GRACCHUS. 1. Renewal of his brother's Agrarian Law, with modifications—viz. (*a*) A diminution in the size of the allotments; (*b*) The retention of the allottees in the position of *possessores* by the proviso that they should pay an annual quit-rent to the State; (*c*) The requirement of good character as a condition in all claimants of allotments; (*d*) An arrangement for settling the new allottees, or at any rate a portion of them, in colonies, at Capua, Tarentum, Carthage, and elsewhere. 2. Law requiring the State to sell corn at a loss to all Roman citizens who should apply for it, unsound in principle and injurious to the State in practice, but founded on the old precedent of similar sales in time of famine. 3. Law fixing the *minimum* of age for enlistment at 17, and requiring the State to furnish the soldiers' clothes. 4. Law transferring the duty of furnishing juries (*judices*) from the Senate to the knights (*equites*), and thereby elevating the knights into a distinct "Order." 5. Law requiring the Senate to determine the consular provinces beforehand, and to leave it to the consuls themselves to decide by lot or agreement which province each should administer. 6. Law assigning the taxation of the new province of "Asia" to the Roman censors. 7. Law assigning the management of the public roads in Italy to the tribunes of the Plebs. And 8. Proposal, which did not become law, to extend the Roman franchise, at any rate to all the Latin colonies; perhaps to all free Italians. This last proposition, which was at once just and really advantageous to the State, lost C. Gracchus his popularity with the existing voters; and the Senate then, by encouraging the tribune Livius Drusus to outbid him in popular offers, which were never intended to be carried out, completed his ruin. When, in B.C. 121, he failed to obtain his re-election to the tribunate, the aristocrats knew that they might safely sweep him from their path.

The colony sent, at the instance of C. Gracchus, to Carthage in B.C. 122, was followed by another, which was founded at Aquæ Sextiæ (Aix in Provence) in the same year, and by a third, Narbo Marcius (Narbonne), founded four years later, B.C. 118, on the coast of Gaul where it approaches Spain.

His Agrarian law is repealed.

9. The death of C. Gracchus was followed within a short space by the practical repeal of his Agrarian law. First the proviso that the allotments made under it should be inalienable was abrogated, so that the rich might recover them through mortgage or purchase. Then a law was passed forbidding any further allotments ("Lex Boria"), and imposing a quit-rent on all "possessores," the whole amount of which was to be annually distributed among the poorer classes of the people. Finally, by the "Lex Thoria," the quit-rents were abolished, and the domain land in the hands of the "possessores" was made over to them absolutely.

The other laws of C. Gracchus, except those which were in their nature temporary, seem to have remained in force either permanently or for some considerable time. The "Lex Frumentaria" became the foundation of a regular system. That with respect to the "judices" lasted till the time of Sulla, who restored the right of furnishing them to the Senate, B.C. 80.

The History of the Gracchi and their period has been a favorite subject for historical monographs. Besides the works on this point mentioned above (pp. 460, '61), the reader may consult

HEGEWISCH, D. H., *Geschichte der Gracchischen Unruhen.* Altona, 1801.
HEEREN, A. H. L., *Geschichte der bürgerlichen Unruhen der Gracchen* in his *Vermischte historische Schriften*, vol. iii. Göttingen, 1824.

Tranquil period. Progress of corruption.

10. The twenty years from B.C. 120 to 100 formed a time of comparative internal tranquillity. Rome during this period was under the government of the aristocratical party, which directed her policy and filled up most of the high offices. But the party was during the whole period losing ground. The corruption of the upper classes was gradually increasing, and — what was worse for their interests — was becoming more generally known. The circumstances of the Jugurthine War brought it prominently into notice. At the same time the democratic party was learning its strength. It found itself able by vigorous efforts to carry its candidates and its measures in the Tribes. It learnt to use the weapons which had proved so effectual in the hands of the nobles—violence and armed tumult—against them. And, towards the close of the period, it obtained leaders as bold and ruthless as those who in the time of the Gracchi had secured the victory for the opposite faction.

The severe exercise of the censorship (especially B.C. 115), the sumptuary laws, the trials and inquiries (*quæstiones*) of this period, revealed rather than checked the growing corruption. Almost every man at Rome was found to have his price. Foreign princes bought their crowns of the Roman nobles, who in their turn bought their offices of the people. The judges, whether senators or knights, sold their decisions. Wealth continually flowed in from the gifts of the dependent monarchs and the plunder of the provincials. Enormous fortunes were made by almost every governor, quæstor, and farmer of the revenue.

Wars of the period.

11. While internally Rome remained in tolerable tranquillity, externally she was engaged in several most important and even dangerous wars. The year of the death of C. Gracchus, B.C. 121, saw the conquest of Southern Gaul effected by the victories of Domitius and Fabius, and the formation of that new "Province" whereto the title has ever since adhered as a proper name (Provence). Three years later, B.C. 118, the troubles began in Africa which led to the Jugurthine War. That war was chiefly important

for the revelation which it made of Roman aristocratic corruption, and for the fact that it first brought prominently into notice the two great party-leaders, Marius and Sulla. Scarcely was it ended when a real danger threatened Rome from the barbarians of the North, a danger from which Marius, the best general of the time, with difficulty saved her.

Jugurthine War, B.C. 111-106.

DETAILS OF THE JUGURTHINE WAR. Assassination of Hiempsal by Jugurtha, B.C. 118. Appeal of Adherbal to Rome, and partition of the kingdom between him and Jugurtha, B.C. 117. Aggressions of Jugurtha on Adherbal, B.C. 116 to 113. His siege of Cirta—Adherbal taken prisoner and killed, B.C. 112. The tribune C. Memmius forces the Senate to declare war against Jugurtha; and the consul Calpurnius Bestia is sent against him; but he bribes Calpurnius to make peace, B.C. 111. Jugurtha is summoned to Rome, and obeys the summons. Memmius accuses, but another tribune, Bæbius, protects him, and he is allowed to depart, notwithstanding that he has contrived at Rome the murder of his kinsman, Massiva, on whom the Romans were about to confer his crown. War resumed, B.C. 110, by the consul Albinus, who, however, effects nothing. His brother, Aulus, succeeds to the command as pro-prætor, B.C. 109, and, being defeated, makes a peace which the Senate refuses to confirm; and the war is intrusted to Metellus, who takes Marius with him as his lieutenant. Metellus captures Cirta, B.C. 108, and most of the other cities; Jugurtha takes refuge at the court of the Mauretanian king, Bocchus. Marius, having gone to Rome, obtains the consulship, and is sent out, B.C. 107, to supersede Metellus. L. Cornelius Sulla is appointed his quæstor. Marius twice defeats Bocchus. Long negotiations follow, which Sulla conducts, and at last Bocchus consents to surrender Jugurtha, B.C. 106, who is led in triumph and then starved to death, B.C. 104.

Cimbric ravages.

12. Before the war with Jugurtha was over, that with the Northern barbarians had begun. The Cimbri and Teutones —Celts probably and Germans—issuing, as it would seem, from the tract beyond the Rhine and Danube, appeared suddenly in vast numbers in the region between those streams and the Alps, ravaging it at their will, and from time to time threatening, and even crossing, the Roman frontier, and inflicting losses upon the Roman armies. The natives of the region especially subject to their ravages, in great part, joined them, especially the Ambrones, Tigurini, and Tectosages. As early as B.C. 113 a horde of Cimbri crossed the Alps and defeated the consul Cn. Papirius Carbo, in Istria. In B.C. 109, Cimbri appeared on the borders of Roman Gaul (Provence) and demanded lands. Opposed by the consul M. Junius Silanus, they at-

tacked and defeated him; and from this time till B.C. 101 the war raged almost continuously, Marius finally bringing it to a close by his victory near Vercellæ in that year.

Cimbric War, B.C. 109–101.

DETAILS OF THE CIMBRIC WAR. Defeat of Junius Silanus in Gaul, B.C. 109. Of L. Cassius Longinus, B.C. 107. Great defeat of Q. Servilius Cæpio and Cn. Mallius in the same region, B.C. 105. Marius made consul, B.C. 104. The Cimbri invade Spain, and engage the Celtiberians, who after a while defeat them and compel them to recross the Pyrenees. Marius, meanwhile, with Sulla as his legate, organizes his army. First appearance of the Teutones upon the scene, B.C. 103—they join the Cimbri in Gaul, and arrange a combined attack on Italy, the Teutones undertaking to force their way through Provence and the Western passes, while the Cimbri entered Switzerland and sought the passes already known to them towards the East. Marius, who is re-elected consul year after year, remains in Provence to resist the Teutones, while his colleague of the year B.C. 102, C. Lutatius Catulus, awaits the Cimbri in North Italy. Great victory of Marius over the Teutones and Ambrones near Aquæ Sextiæ (Aix)—150,000 slain and 90,000 made prisoners, B.C. 102. Invasion of Italy by the Cimbri, B.C. 101. Defeat of Lutatius on the Athesis (Adige). The Cimbri ascend the valley of the Po, expecting to form a junction with the Teutones. They are met near Vercellæ by the combined armies of Marius and Lutatius, and suffer a complete defeat—140,000 fall; 60,000 are made prisoners; and the war is thus brought to a close.

Civil troubles at Rome; Marius and Saturninus, B.C. 101–100.

13. The victories of Aquæ Sextiæ and Vercellæ raised Marius to a dangerous eminence. Never, since the first establishment of the Republic, had a single citizen so far outshone all rivals. Had Marius possessed real statesmanship, he might have anticipated the work of Julius, and have imposed himself on the State as its permanent head. But, though sufficiently ambitious, he wanted judgment and firmness. He had no clear and definite views, either of the exact position to which he aspired, or of the means whereby he was to attain to it. His course was marked by hesitation and indecision. Endeavoring to please all parties, he pleased none. At first allying himself with Glaucia and Saturninus, he gave his sanction to the long series of measures by which the latter—the first thorough Roman demagogue—sought to secure the favor of the lower orders. He encouraged the persecution of Metellus, and gladly saw him driven into exile, thus deeply offending the senatorial party. But when the violence and recklessness of his allies had provoked an armed resistance and civil disturbances began, he shrank from boldly casting in

his lot with the innovators, and, while attempting to screen, in fact sacrificed, his friends.

Election of Marius to his sixth consulship, B.C. 101. Saturninus seeks the tribunate, but is defeated by Nonius; whereupon he has Nonius murdered and himself elected by a packed assembly in his place. He then, B.C. 100, brings forward the following measures:—(1) A law to assign extensive tracts of land in Cisalpine Gaul, and in Africa, to all those, whether Romans or Italians, who had served under Marius; the amount which individuals were to receive being as much, in some instances, as 100 jugers. (2) A law to plant large colonies in Sicily, Achæa, and Macedonia. (3) A law to supply the settlers with money from the public treasury to enable them to stock their lands. Degradation of the Senate, which is required to *swear* to the first law. Refusal of Metellus leads to his exile. Fourth law of Saturninus —to reduce the price of the corn annually distributed to Roman citizens (see p. 466) from $6\frac{1}{3}$ asses the modius to $\frac{5}{6}$ of an as. Riots excited by the nobles prevent the passing of this law. Fresh riots at the consular elections. C. Memmius beaten to death by the partisans of Glaucia and Saturninus. The Senate declare Glaucia and Saturninus public enemies, who thereupon seize the Capitol. Hesitation of Marius; he at last consents to act against them. They surrender, trusting to his protection. He endeavors to secure them a formal trial; but the partisans of the Senate attack them in the Curia Hostilia, where Marius has confined them, and put them to death.

Time of tranquillity, B.C. 99–91. Renewed troubles. Laws of M. Livius Drusus.

14. The fall of Saturninus was followed, B.C. 99, by the recall of Metellus from banishment, and the voluntary exile of the haughty and now generally unpopular Marius. That great general but poor statesman retired to Asia and visited the court of Mithridates. The triumph of his rival, though stained by the murder of another tribune, seemed for a time to have given peace to Rome; but the period of tranquillity was not of long duration. In B.C. 91, M. Livius Drusus, the son of the Drusus who had opposed C. Gracchus, brought forward a set of measures which had for their object the reconcilement, at Rome, of the Senatorian with the Equestrian Order, and, in Italy, of the claims of the Italians with those of the old citizens of Rome. There had now been for thirty years a struggle at Rome between the nobles and the *bourgeoisie* on the question of which of the two should furnish the *judices* (see p. 464); expectations had been also for about the same space of time held out to the Italians generally that they would be accepted into full citizenship. It was venturesome in Drusus to address himself at one and the same time to both these great questions. Successfully

to grapple with them a man was required of first-râte powers, one who could bend opposing classes to his will, and compel or induce them to accept, however reluctantly, the compromise which he considered just or expedient. Drusus seems to have possessed mere good intentions, combined with average ability. He carried his "lex de judiciis," but was unable to pass that extending the franchise. Once more the Roman conservatives had recourse to assassination, and delayed a necessary reform by a bold use of the knife. Drusus was murdered before his year of office was out; and the laws which he had passed were declared null and void by the government.

The "Lex Sempronia judiciaria," which made the knights furnish the "judices," B.C. 123 (see p. 464), was repealed, B.C. 106, by a law of Q. Cæpio Servilius, which restored their old right to the Senate. But this Servilian law was set aside by that of the tribune C. Servilius Glaucia, B.C. 104, which recalled into force the Sempronian enactment. The compromise of Drusus placed the knights and the Senate on an equal footing. Three hundred knights elected by the order, were to form the panel together with three hundred senators. The repeal of this law restored to the knights the exclusive possession of the much-coveted privilege.

15. The murder of Drusus drove the Italians to despair. Accustomed for many years to form an important element in the Roman armies, and long buoyed up with hopes of obtaining the advantages of citizenship —the chief of which were lands, cheap corn, and the covert bribery of largesses—the tribes of Central and Southern Italy, finding their champion murdered and their hopes dashed to the ground, flew to arms. Eight nations, chiefly of the Sabine stock, entered into close alliance, chose Corfinium in the Pelignian Apennines for their capital, and formed a federal republic, to which they gave the name of "Italia." At the outset, great success attended the effort; and it seemed as if Rome must have succumbed. Lucius Cæsar, one of the consuls, Perperna, one of his legates, and Postumius, the prætor, were defeated. The allies overran Campania, destroyed a consular army under Cæpio, and entered into negotiations with the northern Italians, whose fidelity now wavered. But the sagacious policy of Rome changed the face of affairs, and secured her a triumph which she could not have accomplished by arms alone. The "Julian Law" conferred full citizenship both on such of the Italians as had taken no

Social War, B.C. 90–88.

part in the war hitherto, the Etruscans, Umbrians, Sabines proper, Hernicans, etc., and also on all such as upon the passage of the law ceased to take part in it. By this proviso the revolt became disorganized; a "peace party" was formed in the ranks of the allies; nation after nation fell away from the league; Rome gained successes in the field; and at last, when only Samnium and Lucania remained in arms, the policy of concession was once more adroitly used, and the "Lex Plotia," which granted all that the allies had ever claimed, put an end to the war.

DETAILS OF THE SOCIAL WAR. Formation of the League between the eight nations—viz., the Marsi, Marrucini, Peligni, Vestini, Picentini, Samnites, Apuli, and Lucani, B.C. 90. Pompædius and Papius made "consuls." Great successes of the allies. Revolt threatens to spread into North Italy. Passage of the "Lex Julia." Resistance of the allies slackens, B.C. 89. Sulla and the elder Pompey gain advantages. Campania recovered. Corfinium taken. Passage of the "Lex Plotia." Submission of the Peligni and Vestini, B.C. 88—then of the Marrucini and Marsi. Rebellion trampled out in Lucania and Samnium.

Exaltation of Sulla. Jealousy of Marius. His triumph, B.C. 88.

16. The part taken by Marius in the Social War had redounded little to his credit. He had served as legate to the consul Rutilius, in the first disastrous year, and had declined battle when Pompædius offered it. Probably his sympathies were with the revolters, and he had no desire to push them to extremities. Sulla, on the other hand, had greatly increased his reputation by his campaigns of B.C. 89 and 88; and it was therefore natural that he should be selected by the Senate as the commander who was to undertake the war against Mithridates, which needed a first-rate general. But this selection deeply offended Marius, who had long regarded the conduct of that struggle as his due. Determined to displace his rival, or perhaps actuated by a less selfish motive, he suddenly undertook the open championship of the Italians, whose forced admission to the franchise the government was attempting to make a mockery by confining them, despite their large numbers, to some eight or ten tribes. At his instigation, the tribune Sulpicius proposed and, by means of tumult, carried a law distributing the new voters through all the tribes, and thus giving them the complete control of the Comitia. At the same time, he enrolled in the tribes a

large number of freedmen. Comitia thus formed passed, as a matter of course, an enactment depriving Sulla of his post, and transferring the command to Marius, B.C. 88.

17. The insulted consul was not prepared to submit to his adversary. Quitting Rome, he made an appeal to his legions, and finding them ready to back his claims, he marched straight upon the capital. The step seems to have been a complete surprise to Marius, who had taken no precautions to meet it. In vain did the Roman people seek to defend their city from the hostile entrance of Roman troops under a Roman general. A threat of applying the torch to their houses quelled them. In vain Marius, collecting such forces as he could find, withstood his rival in the streets and at first repulsed him. The hasty levies which alone he had been able to raise were no match for the legionaries. The victory remained with Sulla; and the defeated Marians were forced to seek safety in flight. Through a wonderful series of adventures, the late director of affairs at Rome, with his son, reached Africa an almost unattended fugitive.

Sulla takes up arms and enters Rome as a conqueror.

18. Meantime, at Rome, the consul, confident in his armed strength, proscribed his adversaries, repealed the Sulpician laws, put Sulpicius himself to death, and passed various measures favorable to the nobility. But he could not remain permanently at the capital. The affairs of the East called him away; and no sooner was he gone than the flames of civil war burst out afresh. Cinna, raised to the consulate by the popular party, endeavored to restore the exiled Marius and to re-enact the laws of Sulpicius. But the aristocrats took arms. Cinna, forced to fly, threw himself, like Sulla, upon the legionaries, and having obtained their support, and also that of the Italians generally, while at the same time he invited Marius over from Africa, marched on Rome with his partisans. Again the city was taken, and this time was treated like one conquered from an enemy. The friends of Sulla were butchered; the houses of the rich plundered; and the honor of noble families put at the mercy of slaves. Prosecutions of those who had escaped the massacre followed. Sulla was proscribed, and a reign of terror was inaugurated which lasted for several months. But the death of Marius,

He departs for the East. Reaction. League of Cinna and Marius, B.C. 87.

early in B.C. 86, put a stop to the worst of these horrors, though Rome remained for two years longer under a species of dictatorship, constitutional forms being suspended.

Capture of Rome, B.C. 87. Marius and Cinna assume the consulship. Death of Marius, Jan. 13, B.C. 86. Cinna sole consul. Law of Valerius Flaccus reduces debts to one-third of their real amount. Cinna continues his consulship, and joins with himself Cn. Papirius Carbo, B.C. 85. Threatening attitude assumed by Sulla in the East. The consuls determine to proceed against him, but the soldiers decline to engage in civil war, and murder Cinna at Ancona. Carbo sole consul till B.C. 84, when Norbanus and L. Scipio are *elected.* Agrarian law proposed, and extension of the franchise to all who had served under Cinna or Marius.

First Mithridatic War, B.C. 88–84.

19. Meanwhile, in the East, Sulla had been victorious over Mithridates, had recovered Greece, Macedonia, and Asia Minor, crushed Fimbria, the Marian partisan, who sought to deprive him of his laurels; collected vast sums of money, and, above all, brought a large Roman army to feel that devotion to his person which is easily inspired in soldiers by a successful general. It is creditable to Sulla that he at no moment allowed his private quarrels to interfere with the public interests, but postponed the rectification of his own wrongs until he had taken ample vengeance for those of his country. The peace of Dardanus was in the highest degree honorable to Rome and humiliating to Mithridates, who not only abandoned all his conquests, but consented to a fine of 2000 talents and surrendered his fleet. Having accomplished in five campaigns, conducted mainly from his private resources, all the objects of the war, Sulla could with propriety address himself to the settlement of his quarrel with the Marians, and having put down Fimbria in Asia, could make his arrangements for fighting out the civil struggle, which had long been inevitable, in Italy and at Rome itself.

DETAILS OF THE FIRST MITHRIDATIC WAR. Mithridates overruns Asia Minor, and defeats the Roman general, Ma. Aquillius. General massacre of the Romans in Asia, B.C. 88. Revolt of Athens, into which Mithridates throws a strong garrison, B.C. 87. Sulla lands in Epirus, with 50,000 men. Siege of Athens and Piræus. Athens taken, March 1, B.C. 86. The Mithridatic generals, Archelaüs and Taxilas, defeated at Chæroneia. Archelaüs and Dorylaüs defeated near Orchomenus. The Marian, Flaccus, sent to supersede Sulla, is murdered by his legate, Fimbria, who leads his army across the Hellespont and engages Mithridates in Asia, B.C. 85. Victory of Fimbria in Bithynia. Sulla detained in Europe by the resistance of Mithridates's allies in Thrace. Victory of Lucullus over the Mithridatic fleet off Tenedos. Mithridates sues for peace. Peace agreed upon in a personal interview between Sulla and Mithridates at Dardanus, B.C. 84.

Return of Sylla to Italy, B.C. 83; and First Civil War.

20. The determination of Sulla to return to Italy at the head of his army, and measure his strength against that of the Marians, had been apparent from the moment when he declined to yield his command to Valerius Flaccus, B.C. 86. The gage of battle had in fact been thrown down to him by his adversaries, when they declared him a public enemy, and he would have been more than human if he had not accepted it. He knew that the party of the nobles, whereof he was the representative, was still strong at Rome, and he felt that he could count on the army which he had now so often led to victory. The death of Marius had made him beyond dispute the first of living generals. There was none among the leaders of the opposite faction for whom he could feel much respect, unless it were the self-restrained and far from popular Sertorius. The strength of his adversaries lay in the Roman mob and in the Italians. For the former he had all a soldier's contempt; but the latter he knew to be formidable. He therefore, with adroit policy, prefaced his return by a declaration that he "intended no interference with the rights of any citizen, new or old." The Italians accepted the pledge, and stood neutral during the opening scenes of the contest.

History of the First Civil War. Sulla landed in Italy with no more than about 40,000 men. He was joined, however, almost immediately by Metellus Pius, by Crassus, and by Pompey. Having defeated the consul Norbanus near Capua, and seduced into his service the army of Scipio, the other consul, he passed the winter of B.C. 83 in Central Italy, where he established the influence of his party. In B.C. 82 the Marians took the field with 200,000 men under Carbo and the young Marius, the new consuls. Carbo fixed his quarters at Clusium, in Etruria, where the Marian cause was popular. Young Marius occupied the strong Latin city of Præneste. Sulla attacked his more youthful antagonist first. Having defeated him in the great battle of Angiportus, he shut him up in Præneste, and passing through Rome, which was undefended, he attacked Carbo in his intrenchments, but failed to effect any thing. Meanwhile young Marius had made an appeal to the Lucanians and the Samnites, and had prevailed on them to espouse his cause. But the gallantry of C. Pontius Telesinus and his brave Italians was exerted in vain. The Northern army was destroyed in detail by Carbo's unskillfulness, and the last hopes of the Marians were ruined by the battle of the Colline Gate, where Sulla and Crassus, after a desperate struggle, succeeded in defeating the remnants of Carbo's army reinforced by the Italians under Telesinus. After the victory Sulla showed the stuff of which he was made by massacring in cold blood 6000 Samnite prisoners.

Cruel severity of Sulla after his victory. He abdicates, B.C. 79.

21. The triumph of Sulla and the nobles was stained by a murderous cruelty such as Rome had never yet witnessed. Not only were the leaders of the late war, and every relation of Marius that could be found, put to death, but at Rome the wealthy *bourgeoisie*, and in the provinces the disaffected Italians, were slaughtered by thousands. The fatal "lists" of the "proscribed" began; and numbers of wholly innocent persons were executed merely on account of their wealth. Nearly 3000 are said to have perished at Rome, 12,000 at Præneste, and numbers not much smaller at other Italian cities which had favored the Marians. The property of every victim was confiscated. Sulla remained lord of Rome, first with no title, then as "dictator," for the space of nearly three years, when he astonished the world by a voluntary abdication of power, a retirement to Puteoli, and a dedication of the remainder of his life to amusement and sensual pleasures. First, however, by his dictatorial power he entirely reformed the Roman Constitution, depriving it of all elements of a popular character, and concentrating all power in the hands of the Senate.

Sulla's new Constitution.

INTERNAL CHANGES EFFECTED BY SULLA. (1) Degradation of the tribunate by the extinction of all its powers except that of protecting the persons of citizens against the other magistrates. (2) Sole right of initiating legislation given to the Senate. (3) The *judicia* placed once more in the hands of the Senate only. (4) Election to the high priestly offices of pontiffs and augurs abolished, and the principle of filling them up by "co-optation" re-established. (5) Restoration in a rigorous form of the "lex annalis," which required all candidates for high office to have passed through all the lower grades in a regular order, with fixed intervals of time between them. (6) Judicious measures against crimes—*lex de sicariis, de veneficiis*, etc. Besides these permanent enactments, Sulla, as dictator, undertook and effected a reconstruction of the Senate, the Tribes, and the Centuries, which he arranged as he thought best. The Senate he filled up to the number of 300 from his own creatures. The Tribes he "purified" by rejecting all, Italians or others, who had taken part with the Marians in the late war, and giving the franchise to 10,000 emancipated slaves. Of the Centuries he made out his own list, on what principles we are not told. He then submitted all his laws to the body which he had thus constituted. Their acceptance was, it is plain, under the circumstances, a matter of course.

On the character and legislation of Sulla, the student may consult with advantage the work of

Lau, Th., *Cornelius Sulla, eine Biographie.* Hamburg, 1855; 8vo.

22. It was not to be expected that the violent changes introduced by Sulla into the Roman constitution could long remain unmodified. The popular party might be paralyzed by terror for a time; but it was sure to revive. The excesses of the nobles, now that their power was wholly unchecked, could not but provoke reaction. The very nobles themselves were scarcely likely to submit long to the restraints which the "lex annalis" placed upon their ambition. Accordingly, we find that immediately after Sulla's death, B.C. 78, an attempt was made by Lepidus, the consul, to rescind his laws and restore the former constitution. This attempt, it is true, failed, as being premature; and so did the effort of the tribune Cn. Sicinius, in B.C. 76, to restore its powers to the tribunate. But, six years later, after the Sertorian and Gladiatorial Wars had been brought to an end and the strength of Mithridates broken, Sulla's constitution was wholly set aside, and the power of the nobles received a check from which it never subsequently recovered.

Symptoms of reaction.

Attempts of Lepidus and Sicinius fail.

23. The individual who had the greatest share in bringing about the reversal of Sulla's reforms rose into notice under Sulla himself, but acquired the influence which enabled him to effect a great constitutional change in the wars which intervened between the years B.C. 77 and 70. Cn. Pompeius, whose father was a "new man" (*novus homo*), and who was thus only just within the pale of the nobility, secured for himself a certain consideration by the zeal with which he worked for Sulla. Having crushed the Marians in Sicily and Africa, and lent effectual aid to the consul Catulus against Lepidus, he was rewarded in B.C. 77 by being sent as proconsul to Spain, where Sertorius, recently one of the Marian leaders, had established an independent kingdom, and defied all the efforts of the aged Metellus to reduce him. Originally the object of Sertorius was to maintain himself in a position of antagonism to Rome by the swords of the Spaniards; but when Perperna and the remnant of the Marian party fled to him, his views became enlarged, and he aspired to reinstate his parti-

Rise of Pompey to power.

War with Sertorius, B.C. 79-72.

sans in authority at Rome itself. He would probably have succeeded in this aim, had not Perperna, thinking that he had found an opportunity of supplanting him in the affections of the Spaniards, removed him by assassination. The war was after this soon brought to a close, Perperna having neither Sertorius's genius for command nor his power of awakening personal attachment.

DETAILS OF THE SERTORIAN WAR. Flight of Sertorius from Italy to Spain, B.C. 83. He is expelled from Spain by C. Annius and crosses to Africa. At the invitation of the Lusitanians, he returns, B.C. 81, and, putting himself at their head, establishes a small independent kingdom. Metellus is sent against him, B.C. 79, but fails to effect any thing. By successive victories almost the whole peninsula is won from the Romans. A government is organized in which Spaniards and Romans share equally. Perperna joins Sertorius with the remnant of the army of Lepidus, B.C. 77. Pompey sent to Spain as proconsul; jealousy between him and Metellus. War continues with alternations of victory and defeat, B.C. 76 to 75. Sertorius negotiates with Mithridates, and aspires to impose his will on Rome. He becomes harsh to the Spaniards and addicts himself to the immoderate use of wine. Siege of Palencia, B.C. 74. Pompey retires with loss. Murder of Sertorius by Perperna, after the former had ordered the execution of the Spanish hostages, B.C. 72. Complete defeat of Perperna by Pompey, and end of the war within a few weeks of Sertorius's death.

War of the Gladiators, B.C. 73–71.

24. Before the Sertorian war was ended, that of the Gladiators had broken out. Spartacus, a Thracian chief, who had been made prisoner and then forced to become a gladiator, persuaded those in the same condition as himself at Capua to rise against their tyrants. Joined by vast numbers of slaves and outlaws, he soon found himself at the head of 100,000 men. Four generals sent against him were defeated signally, and during two entire years he ravaged Italy at his will, and even threatened Rome itself. But intestine division showed itself in his ranks; his lieutenants grew jealous of him; and in B.C. 71, the war was committed to the prætor Crassus, who in six months brought it to a termination. Spartacus fell, fighting bravely, near Brundusium. His followers generally dispersed; but a body of 5000, which kept together, forced its way through Italy and had nearly reached the Alps, when Pompey on his return from Spain fell in with it and destroyed it utterly. About the same time, Crassus crucified all those whom he had made prisoners, amounting to 6000.

25. The successful termination of these two important

struggles exalted in the public esteem two men especially, the rich and shrewd Crassus, and the bland, attractive, and thoroughly respectable Pompey. To them the State had in its dangers committed itself; and they now claimed, not unnaturally, to be rewarded for their services by the consulship. But the Sullæan constitution forbade their election; and to effect it the "lex annalis" had to be broken through. The breach thus made was rapidly enlarged. Though hitherto Sullæans, Pompey and Crassus had now, it would seem, become convinced, either that it was impossible to maintain a strictly oligarchical constitution, or that such a constitution was not for their own personal interest. They had determined to throw themselves upon the support and sympathies of the Roman *bourgeoisie*, or upper middle class, and resting upon this basis to defy the oligarchy. The moving spirit in the matter was, no doubt, Pompey, who easily persuaded his less clever colleague. Three measures were determined upon:—(1) The restoration of the power of the tribunes, and the consequent resuscitation of the tribes; (2) The transference of the *judicia* to a body of which one-third only should be furnished by the Senate, the knights furnishing one-third, and the remaining third being drawn from the Tribuni Ærarii; (3) A purification of the government from its grossest scandals, partly by prosecutions, as that of Verres, partly by a revival of the office of censor, which had been suspended by Sulla. Despite a fierce opposition on the part of the Senate, these measures were carried. The Senate was purged by the expulsion of sixty-four of its members. Verres was driven into exile. The control of the *judicia* was transferred from the nobles to the upper middle class. The paralysis of political life, which Sulla's legislation had produced, was terminated by the restoration of a double initiative, and the consequent rivalry between two parties and two classes for the direction of the affairs of the State.

Consulship of Pompey and Crassus, B.C. 70.

Their legislation.

The accession of Cicero to the party of Pompey was an event of considerable importance. It is doubtful whether any other orator could so thoroughly and effectively have exposed the rottenness of the system upon which the provinces were administered; and without such an exposure the Senatorial party would scarcely have suffered defeat.

26. A pause now occurred in the career of Pompey, who

took no province at the close of his consulship, apparently contented with his achievements, or waiting till some great occasion should recall him to the service of the State. In this interval—B.C. 69 to 67—a new character appeared upon the scene. C. Julius Cæsar, the nephew of Marius and son-in-law of Cinna, whom Sulla had spared in a moment of weariness or weakness, acting probably in concert with Crassus and Pompey, exhibited at the funeral of Julia, his own aunt and the widow of Marius, the bust of that hero. At the same time, he pleaded the cause of his uncle, Cornelius Cinna, and obtained his recall, together with that of other Marian partisans. His wife, Cornelia, dying, he connected himself with Pompey by marriage. At this time the quæstorship, and soon afterwards the ædileship, were conferred upon him. The Pompeians regarded him with favor as a useful, but scarcely dangerous, adherent; the men of more advanced opinions already looked upon him as their leader, the chief who might, and probably would, give effect to their ideas.

Reserve of Pompey. First appearance of Julius Cæsar.

27. After two years of affected retirement, Pompey was once more, in B.C. 67, impatient for action. A danger had long been growing up in the Eastern Mediterranean, which by this time had become an evil of the first magnitude. The creeks and valleys of Western Cilicia and Pamphylia (or Pisidia) had fallen into the hands of pirates, whose numerous fleets had continually increased in boldness, and who now ventured to plunder the coasts of Italy and intercept the corn-ships on which the food of Rome depended. Pompey undertook the war against this foe, and the opportunity was seized by his creatures to invest him with a species of command never before enjoyed, and dangerous as a precedent. He was given by the *lex Gabinia* authority over all the Mediterranean coasts, and over every city and territory within fifty miles of the sea-board, B.C. 67. These extraordinary powers were used quite unexceptionally; Pompey applied them solely to the purposes of the war, which he began and ended in three months.

Pompey undertakes the war against the pirates. Vast powers granted to him, B.C. 67.

First war with the pirates in Isauria (part of Pisidia), B.C. 75. Conducted with some success by the proconsul, Q. Servilius—thence called Isauricus. Encouragement given to them by Mithridates. Appointment of M. Antonius to conduct the war, B.C. 75. He attacks Crete, which has fallen into their power, but fails, and dies there. Q. Metellus is sent against Crete, B.C. 68, and reduces it to the form of a province. Gabinian law authorizes the Senate to appoint a general with extraordinary powers, and is passed, notwithstanding the opposition of the nobles. Pompey appointed, B.C. 67. By the simultaneous movements of a number of squadrons, he obtains a complete success.

He concludes the war with Mithridates, B.C. 65.

28. The precedent set by the Gabinian law was soon followed. In B.C. 66 the tribune C. Manilius moved, and Cicero urged, that the entire command of the whole East should be intrusted to Pompey for an indefinite term, "until he had brought the Mithridatic war to an end;" and he once more set forth to employ his military talents for the advantage of his country. The Mithridatic war, conducted by Lucullus since B.C. 74, dragged on but slowly, partly in consequence of the aid given to Mithridates by Tigranes, partly owing to the economic measures of Lucullus himself, which alienated from him the affections of his soldiers. (See p. 333.) Pompey, by relaxing the strict rules of his predecessor, and by the politic device of an alliance with the Parthian king Phraates, terminated the war gloriously in the space of two years, driving Mithridates into the regions beyond the Caucasus, B.C. 65.

For the details of the Third Mithridatic War, see pp. 333, 334. So long as Mithridates lived, the war was not regarded as wholly over. It might at any time have been rekindled. But the suicide of the aged monarch, in B.C. 63, consequent upon the rebellion of his son, removed the last fear of a fresh outbreak, and left Pompey at liberty to settle the East at his pleasure.

His conquest of Syria and Palestine, B.C. 64–63.

29. After driving Mithridates beyond the Caucasus, Pompey proceeded to overrun and conquer the rest of Asia within the Euphrates. He made himself master of the kingdom of the Seleucidæ without a blow, and reduced it into a Roman province. He proceeded through Cœlé-Syria to Judæa, besieged and took Jerusalem, and entered the Holy of Holies. War with the Idumæan Arabs followed, but was interrupted by the death of Mithridates; after which the Roman general, content with his gains, applied himself to the task of regulating and arranging the conquered territory—a task which occupied him for the rest of the year. He then returned home in a triumphal progress, B.C. 62, and arrived at Rome early in B.C. 61.

Besides Syria, Bithynia and Pontus were made Roman provinces. Pharnaces, the son of Mithridates, was allowed to retain the Crimea. Ariobarzanes once more received Cappadocia. Deiotarus, prince of Galatia, had his dominions extended. Hyrcanus was established as king of Judæa.

Conspiracy of Catiline, B.C. 63–62.

30. Meanwhile at Rome, the State had incurred the danger of subversion at the hands of a daring profligate. L. Sergius Catilina, a patrician of broken fortunes, a man representing no party unless it were that of the ruined spendthrifts and desperadoes with which Rome and Italy now abounded, having failed in an attempt to better his condition, by means of the consulate, with its reversionary province, B.C. 64, combined with others in a similar position to himself, and formed a plot to murder the consuls, seize Rome, and assume the government. Support was expected, not only from the class of needy adventurers, but from the discontented Italians, from the veterans of Sulla, eager for excitement and plunder, from the gladiatorial schools, from slaves and criminals, and from foreigners. The tacit aquiescence of the Marian party was counted on; and Cæsar, and even Crassus, were said to have been privy to the conspirators' designs. But the promptitude and address of Cicero, consul at the time, frustrated the scheme; and, after a short civil war, the danger was removed by the defeat of the rebels in Etruria, B.C. 62, and the death of the arch-conspirator.

First conspiracy of Catiline, B.C. 65, fails through the death of Piso, who was to have supported it with his Spanish levies. Second conspiracy, B.C. 63. Catiline, denounced by Cicero, quits Rome. Execution of Lentulus and Cethegus. Catiline defeated by the proconsul, Antonius, B.C. 62. Falls in the battle.

Influence of Cato, Cicero, and Crassus. Growing power of Cæsar.

31. In the absence of Pompey, the guidance of affairs at Rome had been assumed chiefly by three men. These were Cato, Cicero, and Cæsar. Crassus, who is sometimes mentioned with them as a leader, was in reality too indolent and too weak in character to be of any real account, and could only influence affairs by means of his enormous wealth. Cato, a descendant of the old censor, and a man of similar character, was at the head of the Senatorial party; Cæsar was the acknowledged chief of the Marians; while Cicero held an intermediate position, depending for his power almost wholly on his

unrivalled eloquence, and having the confidence of neither of the two great factions. Of the three, the one whose genius was the greatest, and whose influence manifestly tended to preponderate, was Cæsar. Though bankrupt in fortune, such was the adroitness of his conduct, and such the inherent strength of the principles with which he was identified, that at every turn of affairs he rose higher, and tended to become more and more manifestly the first man in the Republic. Entitled to assist in the administration of justice after his ædileship, he boldly condemned to death agents in the Syllæan assassinations; he defeated the chief of the Senate, Catulus, in a contest for the office of Pontifex Maximus; accused of complicity in the conspiracy of Catiline, he forced Cicero to admit that, on the contrary, he had given the information which led to its detection; elected prætor in B.C. 62, he bearded the Senate by the protection of Masintha, baffled their attempt to entangle him in a quarrel with the profligate Clodius, and finally, having obtained a loan of 830 talents (£200,000) from Crassus, he assumed in B.C. 61 the government of the Farther Spain, where he completed the conquest of Lusitania, and made himself the favorite of an important army. His star was clearly in the ascendant when Pompey, after an unwise delay in the East, at length returned to Rome soon after Cæsar had quitted it.

Return of Pompey to Rome, B.C. 61. FIRST TRIUMVIRATE or league of Pompey, Cæsar, and Crassus, B.C. 60.

32. During his absence Pompey had become more and more an object of suspicion to the Senate; and his own proceedings, as the time of his return approached, were little calculated to inspire confidence. His creature, Metellus Nepos, who arrived in Rome B.C. 62, was in constant communication with the Marian chief, Cæsar, and proposed early in that year the recall of Pompey, with his army, to Italy, and the assignment to him of all the powers of the State, for the purpose of concluding the Catilinarian war. The boldness of Cato baffled this insidious attempt; and, when the proconsul returned in B.C. 61, it was with a studious appearance of moderation and respect for the law. He disbanded his troops as soon as he touched the soil of Italy, came to Rome accompanied by only a few friends, obtained the consent of the Senate to his triumph, claimed no extraordinary honors, and merely demanded allotments for his sol-

diers and the ratification of his Asiatic "acts," which were all certainly within the terms of his commission. But the Senate had passed from undue alarm to undue contempt, and were pleased to thwart one whom they disliked and had so lately feared. Pompey's requests were refused—his "acts" were unconfirmed—and his veterans denied their promised allotments. Hereupon, Pompey accepted the overtures made to him by Cæsar, who effected the private league or cabal known afterwards as the "First Triumvirate," between himself, Pompey, and Crassus, the basis of which was understood to be antagonism to the Senatorial party, and the maintenance against all rivals of the triumvirs' power and influence.

33. The formation of the triumvirate was immediately followed by the election of Cæsar to the consulate, and the passing, by means of tumult and violence, of a number of laws for the advantage of the people. The first of these was an Agrarian Bill on an extensive scale, which provided for the veterans of Pompey, and at the same time gave estates in Campania to a large portion of the Roman populace. A second forced the Senate to swear to the Bill under penalty of death. A third relaxed the terms on which the knights were farming the revenues of Asia. At the close of a consulate which was almost a dictatorship, Cæsar obtained for himself the government of the two Gauls and of Illyricum for a space of five years, thus securing himself a wide field for the exercise of his military talents, and obtaining the opportunity of forming a powerful army devoted wholly to his interests.

Consulship of Cæsar, B.C. 59.

The bonds between the two chief triumvirs were drawn tighter by the marriage of Pompey to Julia, the daughter of Cæsar. Cæsar at the same time married Calpurnia, the daughter of L. Calpurnius Piso.

34. The triumvirs could not count on the firm establishment of their power, so long as the two party-leaders, Cicero and Cato, maintained unimpaired their high and dignified position. Accordingly, they set themselves through their creatures at once to remove from the seat of government these two statesmen, and to cast a permanent slur upon their characters. The tribune Clodius drove Cicero into banishment on the charge of his having acted illegally in putting to death Lentulus and Cethegus. The great orator's property was confiscated, and his houses

Exile of Cicero, B.C. 58.

were demolished. As against Cato no plausible charge could be made, his removal was effected by thrusting upon him an unwelcome commission which was likely to bring odium on those engaged in it. He was sent to deprive Ptolemy of his kingdom of Cyprus on pretexts utterly frivolous, and to convert that island into a Roman province. Though Cato conducted himself with skill and with unimpeachable integrity in this delicate transaction, yet the decline of his influence may be dated from his acceptance of an office unsuited to his character.

Cato sent to Cyprus.

35. On Cicero the blow dealt by the triumvirs fell even more heavily. Though recalled from banishment within eighteen months of his quitting Italy, he never recovered his former position either in the opinion of others or in his own. Constitutionally timid, his exile effectually cowed him. He lost all confidence in the gratitude of his countrymen, in the affection of his friends, in his own firmness and prudence. Henceforth he no longer aspired to direct the counsels of the State: his efforts were limited to moderating the violence of parties and securing his own personal safety by paying court to those in power. Towards the close of his career, indeed, he ventured once more to take a bolder attitude, but it was when the star of Antony was beginning to pale before the rise of a brighter luminary.

In the *Letters* and *Orations* of Cicero we have by far the most important contributions to the history of the period between Sulla and Augustus, which the ravages of time have spared to us. The best works on the life and character of the great orator are—

MIDDLETON'S *Life of Cicero.* London, 1823; 2 vols. 8vo. Not superseded by any later publication.

WIELAND, *Sämmtliche Briefe des Cicero.* Zürich, 1808 et seqq.; 7 vols. 8vo.

MERIVALE, Rev. C., *Life and Letters of Cicero.* London, 1854; 8vo.

36. The tribune Clodius, who had moved and carried the measures by which Cicero and Cato were forced to quit Rome, was not content to be a mere tool in the hands of the triumvirs. His measures for the gratuitous distribution of corn, for the limitation of the censors' powers over the Senate, and for the re-establishment of the guilds, were probably concerted with Pompey; but it was not long before he exhibited an

Recall of Cicero, B.C. 57; and prosecution of Clodius.

independent spirit, outraged his protector, and stood forward as a separate party-leader of the more violent kind. Pompey was thus forced to incline for a while towards the Senatorians, to encourage the recall of Cicero, and to allow the prosecution of Clodius. It was the hope of the triumvir that affairs would fall into such a condition as manifestly to require a dictator, and that he would be selected for the office. But the Senate's vigor was not yet exhausted; it was content to reward Pompey by a new commissionership (the *præfectura annonæ*); to oppose its own "bravo," Milo, to Clodius; and to foment discord between Pompey and Crassus, who naturally tended to become more and more jealous of each other.

Fresh understanding between the triumvirs, B.C. 56.

37. Civil war would probably at this time have broken out, had it not been for the management of Cæsar. At interviews which he held with Crassus and Pompey at Ravenna and Lucca, he succeeded in bringing them to an agreement, and in arranging plans for the further aggrandizement both of himself and them. He urged them to seek the consulate for the ensuing year, and to obtain for themselves such governments as suited them at its close. For himself he required the prolongation of his proconsulship for a second term of five years. Within this period he could hope to have gained such successes as would dazzle the eyes of the Romans at home, and to have acquired unbounded influence over the veteran army, which would have then served ten years under his banner.

Second Consulate of Pompey and Crassus, B.C. 55. Crassus killed by the Parthians.

38. The Second Consulate of Pompey and Crassus, B.C. 55, brought about by violence and tumult, was a further step towards the demoralization of the State, but produced a temporary lull in the strife of parties. The triumvirs severally obtained their immediate objects. Despite the efforts of Cato, Cæsar was assigned the Gauls for an additional term of five years. Pompey received the Spains for an equal period, while the rich East was made over to the avaricious Crassus, who became proconsul of Syria and commander-in-chief of the Roman forces in the Oriental provinces. Pompey, moreover, managed to establish the new principle of combining the administration of a province with residence in the

capital. Under the pretext that his office of "præfectus annonæ" required his presence at Rome, he administered Spain by his legates, and, in the absence of Crassus, acquired the sole direction of affairs at the seat of empire. This position was still further secured to him by the death of Crassus in his rash expedition against the Parthians, B.C. 53.

Departure of Crassus for the East, B.C. 55. He invades Mesopotamia, B.C. 54, and takes some unimportant towns, but returns into Syria for the winter. Second invasion, B.C. 53. Crassus completely defeated in the country between the Belik and the Khabour, and soon afterwards treacherously seized by the Parthian general at a conference, and, in the tumult which ensued, slain.

39. The death of Crassus, by reducing the triumvirate to a duumvirate, precipitated the struggle which had been long impending. The tie of relationship which united Pompey and Cæsar had been dissolved by the death of Julia, B.C. 54. Another check on Pompey's ambition was removed by the murder of Clodius in an affray with Milo, B.C. 53. After this Pompey apparently thought that the time was at length come when, if Cæsar could be disgraced, the State must fall wholly into his hands. He therefore encouraged the proposals that were made by the extreme aristocrats to deprive Cæsar prematurely of his proconsular office, or at any rate to prevent him from suing for the consulship until he had ceased to be the lord of legions. After himself holding the office of sole consul for the space of six months, B.C. 52, and obtaining the prolongation of his own proconsulship for a further term of five years, he sought to reduce his partner and rival to the mere rank of an ordinary citizen. It was not to be supposed that Cæsar would consent to this change, a change which would have placed his very life at his enemies' mercy. War was certain from the moment when, in spite of the veto of two tribunes, the Senate, at Pompey's instigation, appointed Cæsar's successor, and required him, before standing for the consulate, to resign his proconsular command. Cæsar would have lost all at which he had aimed for ten years, had he yielded obedience to this mandate. To expect him to do so was to look for antique self-denial and patriotism in an age when these virtues had been long out of date, and in an individual who had never shown any signs of them.

Ambition of Pompey. He forces Cæsar to a rupture, B.C. 50.

CAMPAIGNS OF CÆSAR between B.C. 58 and B.C. 50. Great migration of the Helvetii from Switzerland to Central Gaul, B.C. 58. They are pursued by Cæsar, defeated in two battles, and forced to return. Campaign against the German chief, Ariovistus; the Suevi are driven across the Rhine. Conquest of Gallia Belgica, and submission of Northern Aquitania, B.C. 57. Galba, sent to occupy the Rhone valley above the Lake of Geneva, is defeated and forced to retire. Great revolt of the Veneti and other tribes in Aquitania, B.C. 56. The Veneti receive help from Britain, but are shortly reduced to subjection. Southern Aquitania reduced by P. Crassus. Fresh invasion of Gaul by German tribes, B.C. 55. Cæsar defeats them, drives them across the Rhine, and carries the war into Germany proper by a raid across the Rhine. Later in the same year he invades Britain, and receives the submission of some chiefs, but loses most of his fleet by a storm. Second invasion of Britain, B.C. 54. Defeat of Cassevelaun, and nominal subjection of his kingdom to a small tribute. Revolt breaks out in Gaul, but is suppressed. Destruction of the Eburones, B.C. 53. Gaul continues unsettled. Great rebellion under Vercingetorix, B.C. 52. Cæsar defeated at Gergovia. Danger of his position. Vercingetorix rashly offers battle, is defeated, blockaded in his fortified camp, and forced to surrender. Last remnants of the rebellion trampled out, B.C. 51.

Second Civil War, B.C. 49–45. Flight of Pompey.

40. On hearing of the Senatorial decrees, the resolve of Cæsar was soon taken. He would appeal to the arbitrament of arms. At the head of a veteran army devoted to his person, with all the resources of Gaul to draw upon, and endeared to the Italians generally as the successor of Marius, he felt himself more than a match for Pompey and the Senate; and was ready to engage any force that they could bring against him. Accordingly he "crossed the Rubicon," and began his march upon Rome. Pompey had probably expected this movement, and had determined upon the line of conduct which he would pursue. He would not attempt to defend Italy, but would retire upon the East. In that scene of his old glories he would draw together a power sufficient, not only to secure him against his rival, but to re-enter and re-conquer Italy. He would drag the Senate with him, and having carried it beyond the seas, would be its master instead of its slave. Having the command of the sea, he would coop up his rival in Italy, until the time came when his land forces were ready to swoop down upon their prey. With these views he retired as Cæsar advanced, making only a show of resistance, and finally crossed from Brundisium to Epirus without fighting a battle.

41. By the retirement of Pompey, all Italy was thrown into Cæsar's arms. He acquired the immense moral advantage of holding the seat of government, and of being thus able to impart to all his acts the color of legitimacy. He secured also important material gains; first, in the acquisition of the State-treasure, which Pompey most unaccountably neglected to carry off; and, further, in the power which he obtained of drawing recruits from the Italian nations, who still furnished their best soldiers to the Roman armies. The submission of Italy drew with it almost of necessity that of Sardinia and Sicily; and thus the power of the proconsul was at once established over the entire middle region of the Empire, reaching from the German Ocean to the Sea of Africa, and from the Pyrenees to Mount Scardus. Pompey possessed the East, Africa, and Spain; and, had his counsels been inspired with energy and decision, he might perhaps have advanced from three sides on his rival, and have crushed him between the masses of three converging armies. But the conqueror of Mithridates was now old, and had lost the vigor and promptitude of his early years. He allowed Cæsar, acting from a central position, to strike separately at the different points of his extended line. First, Spain was attacked, and, for the time, reduced to subjection; then, the war was transferred to the East, and its issue (practically) decided at Pharsalia; after this, the Pompeians were crushed in Africa; and finally, the party having rallied in Spain, was overwhelmed and blotted out at Munda. These four wars occupied the great soldier during the chief portion of five years (B.C. 49 to 45); in the course of which, however, he found time also to reduce Egypt, and to chastise Pharnaces, son of Mithridates, at Zela.

Cæsar master of Italy.

He takes the offensive everywhere, and is everywhere victorious.

DETAILS OF CÆSAR'S WARS between B.C. 49 and B.C. 45. (*a*) FIRST WAR IN SPAIN. March of Cæsar through Gaul to the Pyrenees, B.C. 49. Siege of Massilia, which declares for Pompey. Cæsar encounters the Pompeian forces under Afranius and Petreius at Ilerda (Lerida). After suffering one defeat, he outmanœuvres his opponents, and forces them to surrender themselves. Terentius Varro in Southern Spain, after vacillating between the two causes, declares against Cæsar, but is deserted by his soldiers and capitulates. Soon afterwards Massilia is taken. Defeat of Cæsar's lieutenant, Curio, in Africa, and destruction of his army by the Pompeians and Juba. (*b*) WAR IN THE HELLENIC PENINSULA. Cæsar, through the negligence of the Pompeian admirals, crosses the Adriatic unopposed, January, B.C. 48. Pompey meets him at Dyrrhachium, but declines a battle, intrenching himself, so as to cover the town. Cæsar blockades his position, but Pompey, after watching patiently for his opportunity, breaks up the blockade and gains a victory over the Cæsarean army. This success ruined his cause. It rendered his officers unmanageable, and forced him to give the Cæsareans battle at Pharsalia, in an open plain, where the superiority of Cæsar's troops, and the better generalship of their commander, led to the complete defeat of the grand army on which rested all Pompey's hopes of final triumph. Had he possessed more resolution, he might no doubt have prolonged the contest, as his party did, even after his death; but, however he had acted, it is scarcely possible that he could have retrieved his signal defeat. His choice of Egypt as a refuge was, as the event proved, ill-judged; but the treachery to which he fell a victim could scarcely have been anticipated, and we can understand, even if we can not justify, his reluctance to quit the East. (*c*) WAR IN EGYPT. The necessity of following up his adversary, and striking, if it were necessary, a last blow, drew Cæsar to Egypt, where he found himself in a most critical position. He landed with a force not exceeding 4000 men, and, being ensnared by the charms of Cleopatra, was soon regarded with jealousy by the young king, her brother and rival, while the hatred with which the Egyptians generally viewed foreign interference with their concerns was easily roused against him by the king's ministers. Quarrels and street fights between his soldiers and the Alexandrians gave him a pretext for assuming a hostile attitude. Accordingly he seized and fortified the Pharos, burnt the Egyptian fleet, and sent hastily for reinforcements. The Egyptians on their side blockaded him in the Pharos, cut off his supplies of water, and endeavored to starve him into submission. But the advance of Mithridates of Pergamus (B.C. 47) relieved the Roman general; and the Egyptian army, placed between two fires, was speedily defeated and destroyed. The young king perished; and Cæsar was able to arrange matters to the satisfaction of all parties by investing Cleopatra, under certain conditions (see p. 283), with the actual sole government. (*d*) WAR WITH PHARNACES. The dissensions of the Romans among themselves encouraged the son of Mithridates to attempt the recovery of his father's empire. Immediately after the battle of Pharsalia, he advanced into Lesser Armenia and Cappadocia. Opposed by Calvinus, one of Cæsar's lieutenants, he defeated him in a pitched battle and destroyed his army. He then occupied Pontus. Cæsar, who was at this time blockaded in Egypt, could do nothing; but no sooner was he released, than he marched with all speed to encounter this new enemy. The hosts met at Zela in Pontus, and Cæsar was as usual victorious. The laconic bulletin, "Veni, vidi, vici," expressed the rapidity of his conquest. Pharnaces escaped from the battle, but was soon afterwards killed, and his kingdom served to reward Mithridates of Pergamus. (*e*) WAR IN AFRICA. The Pompeians who escaped from Pharsalia established themselves in the Roman province of Africa, where they had the support of Juba, the king of Numidia. They were commanded by Scipio, the father of Pompey's widow, Cato, and Varus, proconsul of the province. Much jealousy existed among the commanders. Cæsar landed in Africa in December, B.C. 47. In his first engagement near Leptis he was worsted; but early in B.C. 46 he redeemed this mischance by the great victory of Thapsus, which destroyed the republican force in this quarter. Scipio, Cato, and Juba killed themselves; and Africa submitted to the conqueror. (*f*) SECOND WAR IN SPAIN. Revolt first broke out in Spain among the Cæsarean legionaries, who were seduced by the republican spirit which prevailed among the Romanized natives. The revolters received important accessions to their ranks after the battle of Thapsus, being reinforced by the remnants of the African army. Varus, Labienus, and the two sons of Pompey, Cnæus and Sextus, joined them; and Cn. Pompeius was intrusted with the chief command. A vigorous stand was made against the troops which Cæsar led in person across the Pyrenees; and in the final battle, which took place at Munda (March, B.C. 45), the dictator was in greater personal danger than ever before. But the victory when gained was complete. Thirty thousand Pompeians were left on the field; among them Labienus and Varus. Cn. Pompeius fled, but was overtaken and slain. Sextus alone escaped, and found a refuge with some of the hill tribes, who defied the Roman arms. The settlement of Spain after the battle of Munda was a work of difficulty, and occupied the dictator for nearly six months.

Cæsar's civil administration.

42. The claim of Cæsar to be considered one of the world's greatest men rests less upon his military exploits, important as these undoubtedly were, than upon his views and efforts as a statesman and social reformer. It was his great merit that he understood how the time for the Republic had gone by; how nothing but constant anarchy at home and constant oppression abroad could result from the continuance of that governmental form under which Rome had flourished so wonderfully in simpler and ruder ages. He saw distinctly that the hour had arrived for monarchy; that, for the interests of all classes, of the provincials, of the Italians, of the Romans, of the very nobles themselves, a permanent supreme ruler was required; and the only man fit at the time to exercise that office of supreme ruler he knew to be himself. He knew, too, though perhaps he failed to estimate aright, the Roman attachment to old forms, and he therefore assumed, in B.C. 47, the perpetual "dictatorship," whereby he reconciled the actual establishment of an absolute monarchy with the constitutional purism which had weight with so many of his contemporaries. Having thus secured the substance of power, he proceeded, even in the midst of his constant wars, to bring forward a series of measures, which were, in most cases, at once moderate, judicious, and popular. He enlarged the Senate to the number of 900, and filled up its ranks from the pro-

vincials no less than from the class of Roman citizens. He once more confined the *judicia* to the senators and equites. He raised to the rank of citizens the entire population of Transpadane Gaul, and numerous communities in Gaul beyond the Alps, in Spain, and elsewhere. He enfranchised all professors of the liberal sciences. He put down the political clubs. He gave his veterans lands, chiefly beyond the seas, planting them, among other places, at Corinth and Carthage, cities which he did not fear to rebuild. He arranged matters between the two classes of debtors and creditors on a principle which left financial honesty untouched. He re-enacted the old Licinian law, which required the employment of free labor on estates in Italy in a certain fixed proportion to the number of slaves. He encouraged an increase in the free population by granting exemptions to those who had as many as three children. He proposed the codification of the laws, commenced a survey of the empire, and reformed the calendar. When it is remembered that Cæsar only held power for the space of about five years, and that the greater portion of this period was occupied by a series of most important wars, such legislative prolificness, such well-planned, varied, and (in some cases) most comprehensive schemes, can not but provoke our admiration.

43. But the dictator, though endued with political insight far beyond any of his contemporaries, was, after all, only a fallible mortal. He may neither have been wholly corrupted by his passion for Cleopatra, nor so much intoxicated by the possession of supreme power as to have wantonly disregarded the prejudices which stood in the way of his ambition. But at any rate he misjudged the temper of the people among whom his lot was cast, when, because his own logical mind saw that monarchy was inevitable, he encouraged its open proclamation, without making sufficient allowance for the attachment of large classes of the nation to phrases. He thus provoked the conspiracy to which he fell a victim, and can not be exonerated from the charge of having contributed to his own downfall. The conspiracy against the life of J. Cæsar, formed by Brutus and Cassius, found so many abettors, not from the mere blind envy of the nobles towards a superior, but because there was ingrained into the Roman mind a detestation of

His death, March 15, B.C. 44.

royalty. The event proved that this prejudice might be overcome, in course of time, by adroit management; but Cæsar boldly and without disguise affronted the feeling, not aware, as it would seem, of the danger he was incurring. His death, March 15, B.C. 54, introduced another period of bloody struggle and civil war, which lasted until the great victory gained by Octavius at Actium, B.C. 31.

The biography of Julius Cæsar has been a favorite subject with historians; but it can scarcely be said that any "Life" yet published is thoroughly satisfactory. Among those which demand notice are the following:

CELSUS, JUL., *De Vita et Rebus gestis J. Cæsaris.* London, 1697; 8vo.

DE BURY, *Histoire de la Vie de Jules César.* Paris, 1758; 2 vols. 8vo.

MEISSNER, A. G., *Leben Cæsar's*, continued by HAKEN, J. C. L. Berlin, 1811; in four parts.

NAPOLEON, LOUIS, *Histoire de Jules César.* Paris, first volume published in 1865; second volume in 1866. The second volume ends with the passage of the Rubicon and entrance into Italy. A work written with the mere view of justifying a modern usurpation can scarcely be expected to be impartial.

Weakness and vacillation of the conspirators. Chief power seized by Antony.

44. The knot of enthusiasts and malcontents, who had ventured on the revolutionary measure of assassinating the chief of the State, had made no adequate provision for what was to follow. Apparently, they had hoped that both the Senate and the people would unite to applaud their deed, and would joyfully hasten to re-establish the old republican government. But the general feeling which their act aroused was not one of rejoicing, but of consternation. The noble and rich feared the recurrence of a period of lawlessness and anarchy. The poorer classes, who were indifferent as to the form of the government, provided it fed and amused them, looked coldly on the men who, merely on account of a name, had plunged the State into fresh troubles. The numerous class of those who had benefited by Cæsar's legislation trembled lest his murder should be followed by the abrogation of his laws. None knew what to expect next—whether proscription, civil war, or massacre. Had the conspirators possessed among them a commanding mind, had they had a programme prepared, and had they promptly acted on it, the Republic might perhaps have been galvanized into fresh life, and the final establishment of despotism might have been deferred, if it could not be averted. But at the exact time when resolution and

quick action were needed, they hesitated and procrastinated. Their remissness gave the sole consul, Antony, an opportunity of which he was not slow to avail himself. Having secured the co-operation of Lepidus, Cæsar's master of the horse, who alone had an armed force on the spot, he possessed himself of the treasures and papers of the dictator, entered into negotiations with the "Liberators," and while professedly recognizing the legitimate authority of the Senate, contrived in a short time to obtain the substance of supreme power for himself. His colleague, Dolabella, elected consul in the place of Cæsar, became his tool. The "Liberators," fearful for their personal safety, despite the "amnesty" whereto all had agreed, quitted Rome and threw themselves upon the provinces. Antony was on the point of obtaining all that his heart desired, when the claims and proceedings of a youth—almost a boy—who unexpectedly appeared upon the scene, introduced fresh complications, and, checking Antony in mid-career, rendered it doubtful for a while whether he would not fall as suddenly as he had risen.

Arrival of Octavius upon the scene. He joins the Senate against Antony.

45. C. Octavius, the youthful rival of Antony, was the grand-nephew of J. Cæsar, being the grandson of his sister, Julia. He had enjoyed for several years a large portion of the dictator's favor, and in his last testament had been named as his chief heir and son by adoption. Absent from Rome at the date of Cæsar's murder, he lost no time in proceeding to the capital, claiming the rights and accepting the obligations which devolved on him as Cæsar's heir. With consummate adroitness he contrived to gain the good-will of all parties. The soldiers were brought to see in him the true representative of their loved and lost commander; the populace was won by shows, by stirring appeals, by the payment of Cæsar's legacy to them out of his own private resources; the Liberators, and especially Cicero, who had made common cause with them, were cajoled into believing that he had no personal ambition, and only sought to defeat the selfish designs of Antony. Even with Antony there was established, we can not say how early, an understanding, that the quarrel between the two Cæsareans was not to be pushed *à l'outrance*, but was to be prosecuted as between enemies who might one day be friends. Thus guarded on all sides, Octa-

vius ventured, though absolutely without office, to collect an army, which he paid out of his own resources, and to take up a position, from which he might either defend or threaten Rome. Encouraged by his proceedings, Cicero re-entered the political arena, and took up the attitude against Antony which had been successful against Catiline. By the series of speeches and pamphlets known as "the Philippics," he crushed the popularity of the proconsul, drove him from Rome, and freed the Senate from his influence. Antony retired to his province of Cisalpine Gaul, and there commenced the Third Civil War by besieging Decimus Brutus, the previous governor, in Mutina. Hereupon the Senate bade the new consuls, Hirtius and Pansa, to act against him, and, at Cicero's instance, invested the young Octavius with the prætorship, and joined him in the command with the consuls.

Third Civil War commences with the "Bellum Mutinense," B.C. 44-43. Octavius becomes master of Rome.

46. The short war known as the "Bellum Mutinense" followed. In two battles, one at Forum Gallorum, the other under the walls of Mutina, Antony's troops were defeated by the army of the Senate, and he himself, despairing of present success, crossed the Alps to join Lepidus in Gaul. But the two victories were dearly won, at the cost of two most important lives. Hirtius and Pansa, the two honest consuls, both fell; and Octavius, finding himself the sole commander, was encouraged to put aside his reserve and show himself in his true colors. He refused to join Decimus Brutus in the pursuit of Antony, and thus aided the latter's escape. He claimed the whole merit of the war, and boldly demanded a triumph; finally, he sent a detachment of his soldiers to Rome, to demand the consulship for him; when the Senate, alarmed at his attitude, refused these requests, he at once threw off the mask, marched with all his troops on Rome, plundering as he advanced, and at the head of his legions imposed his will on the government. Possessed of supreme power, it pleased him to assume the title of consul, and to give himself, as a nominal colleague in the office, his cousin, Q. Pedius.

The Mutine War began in December, B.C. 44. It terminated with the battle of Mutina, April 14, B.C. 43. Octavius and Pedius were proclaimed consuls, September 22 of the same year.

47. It was the policy of Octavius to secure for all his acts,

so far as he possibly could, legal sanctions. He now, therefore, required and obtained the confirmation of his adoption. Determined to proceed to extremities against the "Liberators," he had them attainted, and, as they had all fled from Rome upon his entrance, condemned in their absence. A similar sentence was, at his instance, passed on Sext. Pompeius. Octavius was made generalissimo of all the forces of the Republic, and was authorized to act against, or, if it pleased him better, treat with, Antony and Lepidus. It was on this latter course that he had long before decided. Only by the aid of Antony could he hope to triumph over Cassius and the Bruti, whose party in the West was in no wise contemptible, and who had all the resources of the East at their disposal. Accordingly, Antony and Lepidus were invited to confer with Octavius on an island in the river Reno, and the result was the formation of the (so-called) "Second Triumvirate"—the first government which really bore the name—a self-constituted Board of Three, who were conjointly to rule the State.

Formation of the SECOND TRIUMVIRATE, B.C. 43.

The triumvirs concluded their agreement, November 27, B.C. 43. Its terms were:—(1) The establishment of the rule of the Three for a space of five years under the title of "Triumviri Reipublicæ constituendæ;" (2) A division of the provinces among the Three—Lepidus was to have Spain and Gallia Narbonensis; Antony the rest of Gaul beyond the Alps and Gallia Cisalpina; Octavius (or Octavian, as he was now called), Sicily, Sardinia, and Africa; (3) A proscription on a large scale, partly to strike terror into the adverse ranks, partly to obtain funds for carrying on the war effectively; (4) The assignment of eighteen Italian cities with their lands as settlements for the legionaries, when the war should be over; and (5) Certain arrangements as to the immediate conduct of affairs.—Lepidus was to receive the consulship, and to remain in Italy with three legions; Octavian and Antony were to conduct the war in the East, each with twenty legions.

48. On the opening of negotiations between Octavian and Antony, Decimus Brutus had been deserted by his soldiers, and, when he attempted to escape from Italy, had been seized and put to death. The West was thus pacified; and the triumvirs could therefore concentrate their whole attention, first upon the destruction of their enemies at home, and then upon the war in the East. The proscription was relentlessly enforced. Among its victims were Cicero, the tribune Salvius, Annalis, one of the prætors, Cicero's brother Quintus, and his nephew,

Death of Decimus Brutus. Enforcement of the proscription.

Quintus's son. The lists, which followed rapidly one upon the other, contained altogether the names of 300 senators and 2000 knights. The property of the proscribed was seized. The soldiers, let loose through Italy under the pretense of hunting out the proscribed, ravaged and wasted at their pleasure. Private malice obtained its gratification with impunity. Numbers were murdered merely because they were rich, and their property was coveted by the triumvirs or their creatures.

War between the Triumvirs and the "Liberators."

49. Early in B.C. 42 military operations were commenced. Octavian, whose province of Sicily had been occupied by Sextus Pompeius, made an attempt to wrest it from his hands; but his admiral, Salvidienus, being defeated in a naval engagement near Messana, the enterprise was given up. Antony had already crossed from Italy to Epirus; Octavian now followed him. Their combined forces, which exceeded 120,000 men, marched unresisted through Epirus and Macedonia, and had reached Thrace before they were confronted by the "Liberators." These now brought up the full strength of the East against the Western legions; their legionary infantry amounted to 80,000; their cavalry to 20,000; and they had Asiatic levies in addition. Still, however, their forces were outnumbered by those of their adversaries; whose legionaries were probably not fewer than 120,000, while their cavalry was reckoned at 13,000.

Brutus and Cassius had departed for the East in the autumn of B.C. 44, when their position in Rome became desperate. They were by decree of the Senate the lawful governors of Macedonia and Syria. Brutus entered quietly on his province; but Cassius had to fight for his with Dolabella, who had obtained it *from the people* after Cassius's departure. Dolabella, having put to death Trebonius, proconsul of Asia, one of Cæsar's murderers, was attacked by Cassius, shut up in Laodiceia, and driven to commit suicide, June 5, B.C. 43. From this time the authority of the "Liberators" was acknowledged generally throughout the East, and they drew freely on the resources of the country.

Battles at Philippi, Nov., B.C. 42.

50. The two armies met at Philippi (the ancient Crenides); and the fate of the Roman world was decided in a twofold battle. In the first fight Brutus defeated Octavian, but Antony gained a decided advantage over Cassius, who, unaware of his colleague's victory, committed suicide. In the second, three weeks later,

the army of Brutus was completely overcome, and he himself, escaping from the field, could only follow the example of Cassius, and kill himself. With Brutus fell the Republic. The usurpation of Cæsar had suspended, but not destroyed it. It had revived after his death. The coarse brutality of Antony, the craft of Octavian, had separately failed to put it down. Conjoined they achieved greater success. The Republic, albeit some of its forms remained, was in reality swept away at Philippi. The absolute ascendency of individuals, which is monarchy, was then established. There might afterwards be several competitors for the supreme power; and struggles, fierce and bitter, might be carried on between them; but no thought was entertained of resuscitating any more the dead form of the Republic; the contest was simply one between different aspirants to the supreme authority.

Arrangements after the second battle.

51. The immediate consequence of the victory at Philippi was a fresh arrangement of the Roman world among the triumvirs. As Antony preferred the East, Octavian consented to relinquish it to him; but it was necessary that he should be compensated for the sacrifice. His colleague therefore yielded to him Italy and Spain, which last Lepidus was required to relinquish, obtaining instead the Roman "Africa." The facile Lepidus submitted readily to the new partition; and while Antony received the homage of the East, and himself succumbed to the charms of Cleopatra at Tarsus, Octavian undertook the direction of affairs at the seat of government.

Civil War in Italy between Octavian and the party of Antony.

52. But there was no real cordiality, no mutual respect, no sense even of a common interest, among the triumvirs. The Roman world was scarcely theirs before they began to quarrel over it. Octavian being in difficulties at Rome from the scarcity of provisions consequent on the attitude of Sextus Pompeius, from the despair of the Italians driven from their cities and lands to make room for the veterans, and from the discontent of many of the veterans themselves, whose rewards fell short of their hopes, Antony began to intrigue against him and to seek his downfall. The embers of discontent were fanned into a flame by the triumvir's brother, Lucius, and his wife Fulvia, who shortly put themselves at the head of

an insurrectionary force, and disputed with Octavian the mastery of Italy. The hopes, however, of the insurgents were smothered in the smoke of Perusia (B.C. 40); and on the return of Antony to Italy, the rivals, at the instance of the soldiery, came to an accommodation. Octavian received the whole West, including both the Gauls and also Illyricum; Antony was obliged to content himself with a diminished East; Lepidus kept Africa. Fulvia having opportunely died, the "Peace of Brundusium" was sealed by a marriage, Octavian giving the hand of his widowed sister, Octavia, to his reconciled colleague.

Peace of Brundusium, B.C. 40.

53. The pact of Brundusium was modified in the ensuing year, B.C. 39, by the admission of Sextus Pompeius into partnership with the triumvirs. It was agreed that he should retain Sicily, Sardinia, and Corsica; and that he should further receive Achæa, on condition of his evacuating certain strongholds which he possessed in Italy. He for his part undertook to provide Rome plentifully with corn. This agreement, however—known as the "Treaty of Misenum"—was never executed. Sextus did not receive Achæa, and therefore kept possession of the strongholds. Octavian, in retaliation, encouraged the defection of his lieutenants, and received from one of them, Menodorus, a fleet and several forts in Sardinia and Corsica. Sextus, upon this, flew to arms; and a naval war began between him and Octavian, which led, after several turns of fortune, to his complete defeat and expulsion from Sicily.

Treaty of Misenum. War of Octavian with Sextus Pompeius, B.C. 38–36.

DETAILS OF THE POMPEIAN WAR. Sextus plunders Campania, and cuts off the Roman supplies of corn, B.C. 38. His admiral, Menecrates, defeats one of Octavian's fleets near Cumæ, while he destroys another, under Octavian himself, in the Straits of Messina. Folly of Sextus, who makes no use of his victories. Octavian builds fresh fleets, receives 130 ships from Antony, and prepares to renew the war, B.C. 37. War renewed in the summer of B.C. 36. Lepidus, summoned from Africa, brings a squadron. Victory gained by Agrippa over a Pompeian squadron off Mylæ, counterbalanced by the complete defeat of Octavian at Tauromenium. War determined by a great sea-fight off Naulochus, where the Cæsarean fleet, commanded by Agrippa, gains a signal victory. Sextus, in despair, flies to Asia.

54. But Octavian had scarcely time to congratulate himself on his success, when he became aware of a new danger.

Downfall of Lepidus, B.C. 36.

The Pompeian land forces, which were considerable, opened communications with Lepidus, and having, conjointly with his troops, plundered Messana, saluted him as their imperator, and ranged themselves under his banner. The weak noble, finding himself at the head of twenty legions, was intoxicated with his good-fortune, and assuming an attitude of complete independence and even of hostility, set Octavian at defiance. A fresh and bloody struggle would have followed but for the prompt boldness of the young Cæsar; who, entering his rival's camp, unarmed and almost unattended, made an eloquent appeal to the soldiers, which was successful. Deserting Lepidus in a body, they declared for Octavian; who degraded his fallen rival from the triumvirship, but spared his life, and allowed him to retain his office of chief pontiff.

Lepidus lived till B.C. 12. He was at first required to reside at Circeii, but was afterwards brought to Rome, not so much out of favor, as for his greater humiliation.

55. With the removal of Lepidus a war between Octavian and Antony became imminent. The bond of affinity by which it had been attempted to unite the interests of the rivals had failed. The wild and rough Antony soon tired of his discreet but somewhat cold spouse; and his roving fancy returned to the voluptuous Egyptian, from whom it had strayed for a while. In B.C. 37, on setting out for the Parthian War, he left Octavia behind him in Italy; and ere the year B.C. 36 was out, he had reunited himself to his old mistress. Henceforth until his death she retained her influence over him unimpaired; and we must ascribe the deterioration in Antony's character to this degrading connection. His great preparations against the Parthians had no commensurate result. After three campaigns, one in Media Atropatênê (B.C. 36), wherein he acquired no honors, the others in Armenia (B.C. 35 to 34), where he was somewhat more successful, Antony abstained from military enterprise and devoted himself to pleasure. The autumn of B.C. 34 was given up to debauchery and dissipation. In the infatuation caused by his passion, Antony not only acknowledged Cæsarion, and assigned crowns to his own children by Cleopatra, but actually ceded to Cleopatra, a foreigner, the Roman provinces

Coolness between Octavian and Antony. Proceedings of Antony in the East, B.C. 37–34.

of Cœlé-Syria and Cyprus. Such conduct was no doubt treasonable, and furnished Octavian with the decent pretext for a declaration of war, for which he had long been waiting.

PARTHIAN AND ARMENIAN WARS OF ANTONY. In B.C. 40, after the fall of Brutus and Cassius, the Parthians, under Pacorus, and assisted by the Roman refugee Q. Labienus, had overrun the East and carried all before them. They lost ground, however, in the following year, being attacked by Ventidius, one of Antony's lieutenants, who defeated and slew Labienus (B.C. 39), and, in B.C. 38, gained a victory over Pacorus. Antony's expedition (B.C. 36) was undertaken against Phraates, the brother of Pacorus, who had become king. Having allied himself with Artavasdes, king of Armenia, he led an expedition into Media Atropatêné, which was under another Artavasdes, a dependent of the Parthian monarch. Antony penetrated as far as Praaspa, the capital, and laid siege to it, but was baffled and forced to retreat. His Armenian allies deserted him, and his retreat was disastrous in the extreme. The next year, he made an attack upon Armenia; and the year following, B.C. 34, having again invaded the country, he seized the person of Artavasdes and conveyed him to Alexandria, to grace his triumph.

Successes and popularity of Octavian.

56. Meanwhile Octavian had been exercising his legions, raising his reputation, and adding important tracts to the Roman Empire in the West. In B.C. 35 he attacked the Salassi and Taurisci, nations of the Western Alps; and in the course of the two following years he reduced to subjection the Liburni and Iapydes in Dalmatia and the Pannonians in the valley of the Save. A new province was here added to the State. Octavian himself received a wound; and his popularity, to which he artfully added by causing Agrippa as ædile to lavish vast sums on the improvement and adornment of the capital, was now at its height. His good-fortune enabled him at the same juncture to add a second province to the Empire in Mauretania, which was annexed peaceably on the death of Bocchus. Feeling himself assured of his position and of the good-will of the Roman people, Octavian now resolved to precipitate the rupture with his rival, for which he had been preparing ever since the formation of the triumvirate.

War between Octavian and Antony decided by the "Battle of Actium," B.C. 31.

57. The year B.C. 32 was passed by the rivals in mutual recriminations, in threats, insults, and preparations for the coming struggle. Antony divorced Octavia with all the harshness allowable by Roman law; made an alliance with the Parthians; collected a vast fleet; levied troops throughout all the East; as-

sembled his armaments on the coast of Epirus, and prepared to cross into Italy. Octavian inveighed against Antony in the Senate; drove his partisans from Rome; caused his will to be opened and published; had Cleopatra declared a public enemy; and, collecting together all the forces of the West, occupied the eastern shore of Italy with his fleets and armies. For a while the two rivals watched each other across the strait. At length, in the spring of B.C. 31, Octavian, though his forces were inferior in number, made the plunge. His fleet took Corcyra. His army was safely conveyed to Epirus. Both were rapidly directed towards the Ambracian Gulf, where lay the fleet and army of his adversary. The work of seduction then began. Octavian found little difficulty in drawing over to his service one Antonian officer after another, Antony's indecision and his infatuation for Cleopatra having greatly disgusted his followers. These repeated defections reduced the triumvir to a state of despondency, and led him most unhappily to accept Cleopatra's fatal counsels. Under pretense of giving battle to his adversary's fleet, Antony, on the morning of September 2, B.C. 31, put to sea with the deliberate intention of deserting his land force and flying with Cleopatra to Egypt. Actium was not a battle in any proper sense of the term. It was an occasion on which a commander voluntarily sacrificed the greater portion of his fleet in order to escape with the remainder. We can with difficulty understand how Antony was induced to yield every thing to his adversary without really striking a blow. But the fact that he did so yield is plain. He left his land army without orders, to fight or make terms, as it pleased; he left his fleet, not when it was defeated, but when it was still struggling manfully, and but for his flight might have been victorious. It was his desertion which decided the engagement, and, with it, the fate of the Roman world. It is with good reason that the Empire is regarded as dating from the day of Actium. Though Antony existed, and resisted, for nearly a year longer in Egypt, it was only as a desperate man, clinging to life till the last moment. From the day of Actium Octavian was sole master of the Roman world.

Conclusion of the Struggle with Antony. When Antony fled, his fleet lost heart, and the remainder of it was annihilated. His land force, after waiting a week for him to return to it, surrendered. Octavian, having founded Nicopolis and spent the winter at Rome, proceeded in B.C. 30 to Egypt, landing at Pelusium, which submitted to him without a blow. Antony attempted to defend Alexandria, and was successful in a cavalry skirmish, but soon afterwards suffered a defeat. His fleet and army then deserted him; and, having no resource left, he committed suicide. Cleopatra followed his example; and Octavian, being now master of Egypt, reduced it into the form of a Roman province. Anthyllus, Antony's son by Fulvia, Cæsarion, Canidius, commander of the land force at Actium, Cassius Parmensis, one of Cæsar's murderers, and several other "Antonians," were ruthlessly put to death.

SIXTH PERIOD.

From the Establishment of the Empire under Augustus to the Destruction of the Roman Power in the West by Odoacer, from B.C. 31 *to* A.D. 476.

Preliminary Remarks on the Geographical Extent and Principal Divisions of the Roman Empire.

Extent and boundaries of the Empire.

1. The boundaries of the Roman Empire, as established by Augustus, may be stated in a general way, as follows:—On the north, the British Channel, the German Ocean, the Rhine, the Danube, and the Euxine; on the east, the Euphrates and the desert of Syria; on the south, the great African desert; and on the west, the Atlantic. It extended from east to west a distance of fifty degrees, or about 2700 miles, between Cape Finisterre and the vicinity of Erzeroum. Its average breadth was about fifteen degrees, or above 1000 miles. It comprised the modern countries of Portugal, Spain, France, Belgium, Western Holland, Rhenish Prussia, parts of Baden and Wurtemberg, most of Bavaria, Switzerland, Italy, the Tyrol, Austria Proper, Western Hungary, Croatia, Slavonia, Servia, Turkey in Europe, Greece, Asia Minor, Syria, Palestine, Idumæa, Egypt, the Cyrenaïca, Tripoli, Tunis, Algeria, and most of Marocco. Its area may be roughly estimated at a million and a half of square miles.

Three groups of provinces.

2. The entire Empire, exclusive of Italy, was divided into "Provinces," which may be conveniently grouped under three heads: viz., the Western, or European; the Eastern, or Asiatic; and the Southern, or African. The Western, or European, provinces were fourteen in number; viz., Spain, Gaul, Germany, Vindelicia, Rhætia, Noricum, Pannonia, Mœsia, Illyricum, Macedonia, Thrace, Achæa,

Sicily, and Sardinia; the Eastern, or Asiatic, were eight, viz., Asia Proper, Bithynia, Galatia, Pamphylia, Cappadocia, Cilicia, Syria, and Palestine; the Southern or African were five, viz., Egypt, the Cyrenaïca (including Crete), Africa Proper, Numidia, and Mauretania. The entire number was thus twenty-seven.

WESTERN OR EUROPEAN: Spain.

3. Spain (Hispania, Iberia), the most western of the European provinces, included the entire peninsula, and was washed on all sides by the sea excepting towards the north-east, where it was separated from Gaul by the Pyrenees. It was subdivided into three distinct portions, generally administered by three different governors: viz. (*a*) Lusitania, or the country of the Lusitani, corresponding nearly to the modern Portugal; (*b*) Bætica, the country about the Bætis (or Guadalquivir), the modern Andalucia; and (*c*) Tarraconensis, comprising all the rest of the peninsula.

Lusitania.

(*a*) Lusitania was inhabited by three principal races, the Gallæci in the north (Gallicia), the Lusitani in the centre, and the Turdetani in the south. It had three great rivers, the Durius (Douro), the Tagus (Tajo), and the Anas (Guadiana). The chief towns were Augusta Emerita on the Anas, now Merida, and Olisipo on the Tagus, now Lisboa (Lisbon).

Bætica.

(*b*) Bætica was inhabited by the Turduli towards the north and the Bastuli towards the south. Its only important river was the Bætis. Its chief towns were Corduba (Cordova) and Hispalis (Sevilla) in the interior, and on the coast Gades, now Cadiz.

Tarraconensis.

(*c*) Tarraconensis, by far the largest of the three subdivisions, comprised the upper courses of the Durius, Tagus, and Anas, and the entire tract watered by the Iberus (Ebro), Turia, Sucro (Jucar), and Tader (Segura) rivers. It was inhabited, towards the north, by the Astures, Cantabri, Vaccæi, Vascones, and others; in the central regions, by the Carpetani, Celtiberi, and Ilergetes; and, along the east coast, by the Indigetes, Ausetani, Cosetani, Ilercavones, Suessetani, Contestani, etc. Its chief cities were Tarraco, the capital, on the east coast, now Tarragona; Carthago Nova (Carthagena); Cæsar-Augusta (Zaragoza or Saragossa), on the Iberus; Toletum (Toledo), on the Upper Tagus; and Ilerda (Lerida). In Tarraconensis were also included the Balearic isles, Major

(Majorca) and Minor (Minorca), and the Pityusæ, Ebusus (Ivica), and Ophiusa (Formentera).

Gaul.

4. Gaul (Gallia), which adjoined Spain to the north-east, corresponded nearly with the modern France, but included also portions of Belgium and Switzerland. It was bounded on the west and north by the ocean; on the east by Roman Germany, Rhætia, and Gallia Cisalpina; on the south by the Pyrenees and the Mediterranean. It had five principal rivers: the Scaldis (Scheldt) and Sequana (Seine) in the north; the Liger (Loire) and Garumna (Garonne) towards the west; and the Rhodanus (Rhone) in the south. Augustus subdivided it into four regions: viz. (*a*) Aquitania, the country of the Aquitani, towards the south-west, from the Pyrenees to the Loire; (*b*) Lugdunensis, to the north-west, reaching from Cape Finisterre to Lyons (Lugdunum), the capital; (*c*) Narbonensis, towards the south-east, between Aquitania and the maritime Alps; and (*d*) Belgica, towards the north-east, reaching from the British Channel to the lake of Geneva. (*a*) Aquitania comprised the basins of the Garumna (Garonne), Duranius (Dordogne), Carantonus (Charente), and half the basin of the Liger (Loire). Its chief tribes were the Aquitani in the south, the Santones and Pictones towards the north-west, the Bituriges towards the north-east, in the tract about Bourges, and the Arverni to the south-east, in Auvergne. The most important cities were Climberris and Burdigala (Bourdeaux).

Aquitania.

(*b*) Lugdunensis consisted of the region between the Loire and the Seine, together with a tongue of land stretching along the Saone to a little below Lyons. Its principal tribes were the Ædui in the south; the Senones, Parisii, Carnutes, and Cadurci in the interior; the Veneti, Osismii, Curiosolitæ, Unelli, and Lexovii upon the coast. The capital, Lugdunum, was inconveniently placed at the extreme south-east of the province. The other important towns were Lutetia Parisiorum (Paris), Genabum (Orleans), and Juliomagus (Angers).

Lugdunensis.

(*c*) Narbonensis extended from the Upper Garonne on the west to the Var upon the east, lying along the Pyrenees and the Mediterranean. Inland it reached as far as the Cevennes, the Middle Rhone, and the lake of Geneva. The chief tribes inhabiting it were the Volcæ in the west,

Narbonensis.

the Allobroges in the tract between the Rhone and the Isere (Isara), the Vocontii between the Isere and the Durance, and the Salluvii on the coast near Marseilles. Its principal cities were Narbo, the capital, now Narbonne, on the Mediterranean; Tolosa (Toulouse), Vienna (Vienne), Nemausus (Nismes), Geneva, and Massilia (Marseilles). (*d*) Belgica lay between the Seine and the Scheldt, and extended southward to the Bernese Alps and the northern shore of the lake of Geneva. It was bounded on the east by the Roman Germany and Rhœtia, on the west by Gallia Lugdunensis, and on the south by Gallia Narbonensis and Gallia Cisalpina. The principal tribes were, in the north, the Caletes, Ambiani, Bellovaci, Atrebates, Morini, and Nervii; in the central region, the Suessiones, the Remi, the Treviri, the Leuci, and the Lingones; towards the south, the Sequani and the Helvetii. The most important towns were Noviodunum (Soissons), Durocortorum (Reims), Augusta Trevirorum (Trêves), Divodurum (Metz), Vesontio (Besançon), and Aventicum (Avenches, in Switzerland).

Belgica.

5. Germany (which is sometimes included in Gaul) comprised two divisions, the Lower (Inferior) and the Upper (Superior). Lower Germany lay upon the sea-coast, between the mouth of the Scheldt and that of the Rhine. It comprised Eastern Belgium, Western Holland, and Rhenish Prussia as far south as the Ahr. Its chief tribes were the Batavi and Menapii in the north; the Ubii on the Rhine near Cologne; the Eburones and Condrusi on the Mosa (Meuse); and the Segni in the Ardennes. The principal towns were Noviomagus (Nimeguen), Colonia Agrippinensis (Cologne), and Bonna (Bonn). Upper Germany was a narrow strip of land along the course of the Rhine from Remagen, at the mouth of the Ahr valley, to the point at which the Rhine receives the waters of the Aar. It was inhabited by the Caracates, the Vangiones, the Nemetes, the Triboci, and the Rauraci. The principal cities were Ad Confluentes (Coblenz), Mogontiacum (Mayence), Borbetomagus (Worms), Argentoratum (Strasburg), and Augusta Rauracorum (Basle).

Germany: Lower.

Upper.

6. Vindelicia, or the country of the Vindelici, lay between the Danube and the Bavarian Alps. It corresponded nearly with Bavaria south of the Danube, including however a cor-

Vindelicia. ner between the Rhine and the Upper Danube, which now belongs to Wurtemberg and Baden. It was inhabited, towards the north, by the Vindelici; towards the south, by the Brigantes. The chief cities were Augusta Vindelicorum (Augsburg) and Brigantia on the Lake of Constance (Bregenz).

7. Rhætia lay south of Vindelicia and east of the country of the Helvetii. It included the modern Tyrol, the Vorarlberg, and the part of Switzerland known as the Grisons. Among its tribes were, besides the Rhæti, the Venostes, Vennones, Brixentes, Tridentini, Medoaci, etc. Its chief cities were Veldidena (Wilten, near Insprück), Curia (Chur or Coire), and Tridentum (Trent).

Rhætia.

8. Noricum, which lay east of Vindelicia and Rhætia, stretched along the Danube from its junction with the Inn to a point a little above Vienna. It comprised Styria, Carinthia, and the greater part of Austria Proper. The chief cities were Juvavia (Salzburg) and Boiodurum (Passau).

Noricum.

9. Pannonia, one of the most important of the Roman provinces, lay east and partly south of Noricum. It was bounded on two sides, the north and east, by the Danube, which in this part of its course makes the remarkable bend to the south by which its lower is thrown three degrees south of its upper course. On the west an artifical line divided Pannonia from Noricum; on the south it was separated from Illyricum by the mountains directly south of the valley of the Save. It thus comprised all Hungary south of the Danube, together with all Slavonia, and parts of Austria Proper, of Styria, Croatia, and Bosnia. It was divided, like Germany, into Upper and Lower. Upper Pannonia adjoined Noricum, extending along the Danube from a little above Vienna to the mouth of the Arrabo (Raab). Its chief tribes were the Boii in the north, the Latovici, Jassii, and Colapini in the south, along the course of the Save. The principal towns were Vindobona (Vienna) and Carnuntum on the Danube, Siscia (Zissek) on the Save, and Æmona (Laybach) between the Save and the Alpes Juliæ. Lower Pannonia lay along the Danube from the mouth of the Arrabo to that of the Save. Its most important cities were Acincum

Pannonia.

Upper.

Lower.

Buda)-Pesth) and Aciminicum (Peterwardin) on the Danube, Mursa (Esseg) on the Drave, and on the Save Sirmium (Zabatz or Alt-Schabaaz) and Taurunum (Semlin).

10. Mœsia was the last of the Danubian provinces. It lay along the river from its junction with the Save to its mouth, extending southward to the line of the Balkan. Its western boundary, which separated it from Illyria, was the course of the Drinus (Drina). It corresponded thus almost exactly to the modern Servia and Bulgaria. The Romans divided it, like Pannonia, into Superior and Inferior. Mœsia Superior reached from the Drinus and the mouth of the Save to the little river Cebrus or Ciabrus (Ischia), whence a line drawn southward separated it from Mœsia Inferior. It comprised thus Servia and a part of Western Bulgaria. The chief towns were Singidunum (Belgrade) and Naissus (Nissa). Mœsia Inferior, a longer but a narrower tract, stretched from the Ciabrus to the mouth of the great river. It comprised about nine-tenths of the modern Bulgaria, together with a small portion of Roumelia. The chief towns were Dorostolum (Silistria) and Axiopolis (Rassova) on the Danube, and Odessus (Varna), Tomi (Tomisvar), and Istrus (Kustendjeh), on the coast of the Euxine.

Mœsia.

Upper.

Lower.

11. Illyricum lay along the western shore of the Adriatic from the peninsula of Istria to Aulon (Avlona) in Epirus. It thus comprised the present Montenegro, the Herzegovina, and the greater part of Albania. The more northern portion of Illyricum was known as Dalmatia, the more southern as Illyria Proper. Among the principal tribes inhabiting it were the Iapydes and Liburni in the north; the Breuci, Mazæi, Dæsitiatæ, and Deimates in the mid-region; and the Autariatæ, Parthini, and Taulantii in the south. Its chief towns were Scardona (which retains its name), Narona on the Naro (Narenta), Epidaurus on the Gulf of Cattaro, Scodra (Scutari, on the Bojana), Lissus (Lesch or Allessio, on the Drin), Dyrrhachium (Durazzo), and Appollonia (Pollina). These were all situated on or near the coast.

Illyricum.

12. Macedonia lay south of Illyricum and Mœsia Superior, and extended across the peninsula from the Adriatic to the

Macedonia. Ægean. On the east it was bounded by Thrace, the line of separation being the river Nestus. On the south an artificial line, carried from the Ambracian to the Maliac Gulf, divided it from Achæa. It comprised, besides the ancient Macedon, most of Epirus and the whole of Thessaly. Its chief towns were Nicopolis, on the Gulf of Ambracia or Actium, built by Augustus to celebrate his victory; Edessa, Pella, Berœa, Thessalonica, and Philippi.

13. South of Mœsia Inferior and east of Macedonia was Thrace, which under the first Cæsars still retained a semi-independent position, being governed by kings of its own, Rhescuporis, and others; but was reduced into the form of a province by Claudius. The principal tribes in Roman times were the Odrysæ, the Bessi, and the Cœletæ. The cities of most importance were Byzantium and Apollonia (Sizeboli) upon the coast, and Philippolis (Filibé), and afterwards Hadrianopolis, in the interior.

Thrace.

14. Achæa lay directly south of Macedonia, corresponding almost exactly with the modern Kingdom of Greece. It included the Ionian islands and the Cyclades, but not Crete, which belonged to the Cyrenaïca. The chief towns were Patræ (Patras), Corinth, and Athens.

Achæa.

15. The Eastern or Asiatic provinces have now to be briefly described. As already stated (p. 504), they were eight in number: viz., Asia Proper, Bithynia, Galatia, Pamphylia, Cappadocia, Cilicia, Syria, and Palestine.

EASTERN OR ASIATIC:

16. Asia Proper, which included the ancient Mysia, Lydia, Caria, and a part of Phrygia, occupied the whole western coast of Asia Minor, extending from the Cianian Gulf in the Propontis to Caunus on the Sea of Rhodes. Inland it reached to about the 32d degree of east longitude, where it adjoined Galatia and Cappadocia. Bithynia bounded it on the north, Pamphylia on the south. The Roman capital of Asia Proper was Ephesus; but the following towns were of almost equal importance: Smyrna, Pergamus, Sardis, Apameia Cibotus, and Synnada.

Asia Proper.

17. Bithynia, which lay north, or rather north-east, of "Asia," had nearly its old dimensions, extending along the coast from the mouth of the Macestus on the west to that of the Parthenius upon the east. Inland it reached a little south of the 40th parallel, being bounded

Bithynia.

towards the south-east by the upper course of the Sangarius (Sakkariyeh), which separated it from both "Asia" and Galatia. Its Roman capital was Nicomedia (now Ismid), in the inner recess of the Gulf of Astacus. Its other important cities were Nicæa (Iznik), Chalcedon (Scutari), and Heracleia (Eregli).

18. Galatia was situated to the east of Bithynia. It included the ancient Paphlagonia, North-eastern Phrygia, and a part of Western Cappadocia. The southern part of the province, which lay on both sides the river Halys, was Galatia Proper, and was inhabited by the three tribes of the Tolistoboii, the Tectosages, and the Trocmi. The chief city of Galatia was Ancyra (Angora) on the Upper Sangarius. Other important towns were Pessinus on the western border, in the country of the Tolistoboii, Tavia east of the Halys, in the country of the Trocmi, and Sinôpê on the Euxine.

Galatia.

19. Pamphylia, situated to the south of "Asia," contained the four subdivisions of Pamphylia Proper, the region originally bearing the name (see p. 29), Lycia, Pisidia, and Isauria. It extended along the southern coast of Asia Minor from Caunus to Coracesium, and reached inland to the Lakes of Bei-Shehr and Egerdir. Its chief city was Perga in Pamphylia Proper; besides which it contained the following towns of note: Xanthus in Lycia, Etenna and Antioch in Pisidia, Oroanda and Isaura in Isauria.

Pamphylia.

20. Cappadocia adjoined Galatia and Pamphylia towards the east. Like Pamphylia, it comprised four regions: viz., Lycaonia, the most western, which adjoined Isauria and "Asia;" Cappadocia Proper, east of Lycaonia, on both sides of the river Halys; Pontus, north of Cappadocia Proper, between it and the Euxine; and Armenia Minor, south-east of Pontus, a rugged mountain tract lying along the Upper Euphrates. The chief city of Cappadocia was Cæsarea Mazaca (Kaisariyeh), between Mount Argæus and the Halys. It contained also the important towns of Iconium (Koniyeh) in Lycaonia; Tyana and Melitênê (Malatiyeh) in Cappadocia Proper; and Amisus, Trapezus (Trebizond), Amasia, Sebastia, and Nicopolis in Pontus.

Cappadocia.

21. Cilicia lay east of Pamphylia and south of Cappadocia. It reached along the south coast of Asia Minor from Corace-

Cilicia.

sium to Alexandria (Iskanderoun). The eastern portion of the province was known as Campestris, the western as Montana or Aspera. Tarsus, on the Cydnus, was its capital. Other important towns were Issus in the pass of the name, Mopsuestia on the Pyramus, and Seleuceia on the Calycadnus, near its mouth.

Syria.

22. Syria, which adjoined Cappadocia and Cilicia, extended from about the 38th parallel upon the north to Mount Carmel towards the south, a distance of nearly 400 miles. It was bounded on the east by the Euphrates as far as Thapsacus and then by the waterless Syrian desert. Southward it adjoined on Palestine. The province was divided into ten principal regions:—(1) Commagênê, towards the north, between Cilicia and Armenia; chief city, Samosata (Sumeïsat) on the Euphrates. (2) Cyrrhestica, south of Commagênê, between Cilicia and Mesopotamia; chief cities, Cirrhus, Zeugma (Rum-kaleh), and Bambycé or Hierapolis (Bambuk). (3) Seleucis, on the coast, south of Cilicia and south-west of Cyrrhestica; chief city, Antioch, with its suburb, Daphné, and its port, Seleuceia. (4) Casiotis, south of Seleucis, so called from the Mons Casius, extending along the shore from the foot of that mountain to the river Eleutherus (Nahr-el-Kebir); chief cities, Laodiceia and Marathus. (5) Phœnicia, a thin slip of coast, due south of Casiotis, reaching from the river Eleutherus to Mount Carmel; chief towns, Antaradus, Berytus (Beyrut), Sidon, Tyre, and Ptolemaïs (Acre). (6) Chalybonitis, south of Cyrrhestica, and east of Seleucis, lying between Seleucis and the Euphrates; chief city, Chalybon (now Aleppo). (7) Chalcis or Chalcidicé, south of Chalybonitis; chief city, Chalcis, on the lake into which the river of Aleppo empties itself. (8) Apamênê, south of Chalcidicé, and east of Casiotis, comprising a large portion of the Orontes valley, together with the country east of it; chief city, Apameia; important towns, Epiphaneia (Hamah) and Emesa (Hems). (9) Cœlé-Syria, south of Apamênê and east of Phœnicia, consisting of the valley between the Lebanon and Anti-Lebanon, together with the Anti-Lebanon itself and the fertile tract at its eastern base towards Damascus; chief cities, Damascus, Abila, and Heliopolis (Balbek). And (10) Palmyrênê, the

desert tract south of Chalybonitis and east of Chalcidicé and Apamêné, comprising some fertile oases, of which the principal contained the famous Tadmor or Palmyra, "the city of Palms." The capital of the entire Syrian province was Antioch, on the Lower Orontes. The most important of the other cities in Roman times were Damascus and Emesa.

Palmyrêné.

23. Palestine, which adjoined Syria on the south, was, like Syria, divided up into a number of districts. The chief of these were Galilee, Samaria, Judæa, Idumæa, and Peræa, which last included Ituræa, Trachonitis, Auranitis, Batanæa, etc. Galilee was entirely an inland region, being shut out from the coast by the strip of territory belonging to Phœnicia. It reached from Hermon on the north to the plain of Esdraelon and valley of Beth-shan upon the south. The most important of its cities were Cæsarea Philippi, near the site of the ancient Dan, Tiberias, on the lake of the name, Capernaum, and Jotapata. Samaria, which lay south of Galilee, extended from the plain of Esdraelon to the hill-country of Benjamin (about lat. 32°). It reached across from the sea to the Jordan, including the rich plain of Sharon as well as the hill-country of Manasseh and Ephraim. The chief cities in Roman times were Cæsarea, upon the coast; Sebasté (Samaria), Neapolis (Shechem), now Nablus, and Shiloh, in the interior. Judæa, which succeeded Samaria towards the south, occupied the coast line from a little to the north of Joppa (Jaffa) to Raphia (Refah). Eastward it was bounded by the Jordan and the Dead Sea, southward by Idumæa or Edom. It comprised the hill-country of Judah and Benjamin, the desert towards the Dead Sea, and the rich Shefêlah or plain of the Philistines. The chief towns were Jerusalem, Hebron, and Joppa (Jaffa). Idumæa, or "Roman Arabia," was the tract between Judæa and Egypt; it included the Sinaitic peninsula, Idumæa Proper, and a narrow tract along the eastern coast of the Red Sea, reaching as far south as lat. 24°. The chief city was Petra. Peræa, or the tract *across* Jordan, comprised the entire habitable country between the great river of Palestine and the Syrian desert. The more northern parts were known as Ituræa and Tracho-

Palestine: Galilee.

Samaria.

Judæa.

Idumæa.

Peræa.

nitis; below these came Auranitis (the Hauran), Galaditis (Gilead), Ammonitis, and Moabitis. The chief cities were Gerasa (Jerash) and Gadara.

SOUTHERN OR AFRICAN:

24. The African or Southern provinces were six in number: viz., Egypt; the Cyrenaïca, including Crete; Africa Proper; Numidia; and Mauretania. Of these Egypt was by far the most important, being the granary of the Empire.

Egypt.

25. Egypt, according to Roman notions, included, besides the Delta and the valley of the Nile, first, the entire tract between the Nile and the Red Sea; secondly, the north coast of Africa from the western mouth of the Nile as far as Paratonium; and thirdly, the oases of the Libyan desert as far west as long. 28°. Southward the limit was Syênê, now Assouan. In Egypt Proper, or the Nile valley and Delta, three regions were recognized—Ægyptus Inferior, or the Delta, which contained thirty-five nomes; Heptanomis, the mid-region, containing seven; and Ægyptus Superior, the Upper valley, containing fifteen. The capital of the province was Alexandria; other important towns were, in Lower Egypt, Pelusium, Sais, and Heliopolis; in the Heptanomis, Arsinoë, Heracleopolis, Antinoë, and Hermopolis Magna; in Ægyptus Superior, Thebes, Panopolis, Abydus, Ombos, and Syênê.

Cyrenaïca.

26. The Cyrenaïca adjoined Egypt upon the west, and extended along the coast from long. 27° to 19°. It was a tolerably broad tract, reaching so far inland as to include the oasis of Ammon, and perhaps that of Aujilah. The chief towns were Berenicé (now Benghazi), Arsinoë (Teuchira), Ptolemaïs, near Barca (now Dolmeta), and Cyrênê (now Grennah). In Crete, which belonged to this province, the most important towns were Gnossus on the north coast, and Gortyna in the interior.

Africa.

27. Africa Proper corresponded nearly to the two modern Beyliks of Tunis and Tripoli. It extended along the shore from Automalax on the Greater Syrtis to the river Tusca (Wady-ez-zain), which divided it from Numidia. The province was made up of two very different regions, viz., a narrow strip of flat coast reaching from Automalax to the Gulf of Khabs or Lesser Syrtis, and a broad, hilly, and extremely fertile region, north of the Syrtis and

the salt lake known as the Shibkah, the former corresponding to the modern Tripoli, the latter to Tunis. The chief towns were, in the western hill-tract, Hadrumetum, Carthage, Utica, and Hippo Zaritus; in the low eastern region, Tacapé and Leptis Magna, or Neapolis.

Numidia.

28. Numidia was, comparatively speaking, a small tract, its sea-board reaching only from the Tusca to the Ampsaga, a distance of about 150 miles. Inland it extended as far as the Atlas mountains. Its chief town was Hippo Regius, the modern Bona.

Mauretania.

29. Mauretania, the country of the Mauri or Moors, extended from the river Ampsaga on the east to about Cape Ghir (lat. 30° 35′) upon the west. It corresponded in a measure to the modern Marocco and Algeria, but did not reach so far either eastward or westward. The province was subdivided into two portions, which were called respectively Tingitana and Cæsariensis. Tingitana reached from Cape Ghir to the mouth of the Mulucha (Mulwia). It took its name from Tingis, the capital, now Tangiers. Cæsariensis lay between the Mulucha and the Ampsaga. The chief cities were Cæsarea and Igilgilis, both on the Mediterranean.

Further extension of the empire.

30. Such was the extent, and such were the divisions and subdivisions of the Roman Empire under Augustus. During the century, however, which followed upon his decease (A.D. 14 to 114) several large additions were made to the Roman territory; these will now require a few words of notice. The most important of them were those of the Agri Decumates, of Britain, Dacia, Armenia, Mesopotamia, and Assyria.

Agri Decumates.

31. The Agri Decumates fell under Roman protection towards the close of the reign of Augustus, but were not incorporated into the Empire till about B.C. 100. They consisted of a tract between the Upper Danube and the Middle Rhine, reaching from about Ingolstadt on the one stream to the mouth of the Lahn upon the other, and thus comprising most of Wurtemberg and Baden, together with a portion of South-western Prussia. The most important city in this region was Sumalocenna on the Upper Main.

32. Britain was conquered as far as the Dee and the Wash

under Claudius, and was probably at once reduced to the form of a Roman province. The chief tribes of this portion of the island were the Cantii in Kent, the Trinobantes in Essex, the Iceni in Norfolk and Suffolk, the Catyeuchlani, Dobuni, and Cornavii, in the midland counties, the Regni in Sussex, Surrey and Hants, the Belgæ in Somerset and Wilts, the Damnonii in Devon and Cornwall, the Silures in South Wales, and the Ordovices in North Wales. The most important cities were Camulodunum (Colchester), Londinium (London), Verulamium (St. Alban's), Isca (Caerleon upon Usk), and Deva (Chester). Under Nero and Vespasian further conquests were made; and under Titus the frontier was advanced as far north as the Friths of Forth and Clyde, which thenceforth formed the real limit of "Britannia Romana." The Highlands of Scotland remained in the possession of the Caledonii, and no attempt was ever made to conquer Ireland (Hibernia or Ierne). The tribes of the North were chiefly the Damnii, Selgovæ, and Otadeni in the Scotch Lowlands; the Brigantes in Yorkshire, Lancashire, Cumberland, Westmoreland, and Durham; and the Coritani in Lincoln and Notts. The most important of the Northern cities was Eboracum (York).

Britannia.

33. Dacia, which was added to the Empire by Trajan, comprised Hungary east of the Theiss, together with the modern principalities of Wallachia and Moldavia. On the west the Theiss separated it from the Jazyges Metanastæ, who held the tongue of land between the Danube and Theiss rivers. The Carpathians formed its boundary upon the north. Eastward it reached to the Hierasus, which is either the Sereth, or more probably the Pruth. Southward it was divided from Mœsia by the Danube. The native capital was Zermizegethusa, which became Ulpia Trajana under the Romans. Other important towns were Tibiscum (Temesvar), Apulum (Carloburg), and Napoca (Neumarkt).

Dacia.

34. Armenia, which, like Dacia, was conquered by Trajan, adjoined upon the east the Roman province of Cappadocia, and extended thence to the Caspian. On the north it was bounded by the river Kur or Cyrus, on the south by the Mons Masius, on the south-east by the high mountain-chain between the lakes of Van and Urumi-

Armenia.

yeh, and by the river Araxes (Aras). Its chief cities were Artaxata on the Araxes, Amida (Diarbekr) in the upper valley of the Tigris, and Tigranocerta on the flanks of Mount Niphates.

35. Mesopotamia, likewise one of Trajan's conquests, lay south of Armenia, extending from the crest of the Mons Masius almost to the shore of the Persian Gulf, and comprising the whole tract between the Euphrates and Tigris rivers. Its chief regions were Osrhoëné and Mygdonia in the north, in the south Babylonia and Mesêné. In Roman times, Seleucia, on the Tigris, was its most important city. Other places of some consequence were Edessa and Carrhæ (Haran) in Osrhoëné, Nisibis in Mygdonia, Circesium near the mouth of the Khabur, and Hatra in the desert between the Khabur and the Tigris.

36. Assyria, conquered by Trajan, and again by Septimius Severus, lay east of the Tigris, between that stream and the mountains. Southward it extended to the Lesser Zab, or perhaps to the Diyaleh. The only town of importance which it contained was Arbela.

HISTORICAL SKETCH OF THE ROMAN EMPIRE.

FIRST SECTION.

From the Battle of Actium, B.C. 31, *to the Death of Commodus*, A.D. 192.

SOURCES. The only continuous history which we possess for this period is that of DIO CASSIUS (books li. to lxii.), the lost portions of whose work may be supplied from the abridgment of XIPHILINUS. For the earlier Emperors the most important authority is TACITUS, whose *Annals* and *Histories* gave a continuous account of Roman affairs from the closing years of Augustus to the death of Domitian. Unfortunately, large portions of both these works are lost, and no abridgment supplies their place. Much interesting information is conveyed by the biographical work of SUETONIUS (*vitæ* xii. *Cæsarum*), in which time has luckily made no gaps; but the scandalous stories told by this anecdote-monger are not always to be received as truth. Some light is thrown upon the reigns of Augustus and Tiberius by the *History* of VELLEIUS PATERCULUS, and on those of Galba and Otho by their *Lives* in PLUTARCH. The Oriental history of the period receives important illustration from the two great works of JOSEPHUS (*Antiquitates Judaicæ* and *De Bello Judaico*).

Among monuments bearing upon the time, may be mentioned as of great interest and importance the—

Marmor Ancyranum, or Great Inscription of Augustus found at Angora (Ancyra), containing his own account of the chief facts of his administration. Best edition, that of MOMMSEN (*Res gestæ D. Augusti.* Berolini, 1865; 8vo), in which the fragments of a Greek translation of the document, found at Apollonia in Pisidia, are collated.

Of modern works treating the history of this period, the following are the most valuable:

HOECK, K., *Römische Geschichte vom Verfall der Republik bis zur Vollendung der Monarchie unter Constantin.* Göttingen, 1841–50; 8vo.

MERIVALE, Rev. C., *History of the Romans under the Empire.* London, 1860–1862; 7 vols. 8vo.

THIERRY, AMÉDÉE, *Tableau de l'Empire Romain jusqu'à la Chute du Gouvernement Impérial en Occident.* Paris, 1862; 12mo.

DE CHAMPAGNY, *Les Césars.* Paris, 1859 (3d edition); 3 vols. 8vo. With its continuation *Les Antonins.* Paris, 1863; 3 vols. 8vo.

Reign of Augustus, B.C. 31 to A.D. 14. His titles and powers.

1. IF we regard the reign of Augustus as commencing with the victory of Actium, we must assign to his sole administration the long term of forty-five years. He was thirty-two years of age when he obtained the undisputed mastery of the Roman world: he lived to be seventy-seven. This long tenure of power, joined to his own prudence and sagacity, enabled him to settle the foundations of the Empire on so firm and solid a basis, that they were never, except for a moment, shaken afterwards. To his prudence and sagacity it was also due that the Empire took the particular shape which in point of fact it at first assumed; that, instead of being, like the kingdoms of the East, an open and undisguised despotism, it was an absolute monarchy concealed uuder republican forms. Warned by the fate of Julius, the inheritor of his position resolved to cloak his assumption of supreme and unlimited authority under all possible constitutional formalities. Carefully eschewing every illegal title, avoiding even the name "Dictator," to which unpleasant recollections attached from its having been borne by Marius and Sulla, he built up a composite power by simply obtaining for himself, in a way generally recognized as legal, all the various offices of the State which had any real political significance. These offices, moreover, were mostly taken not in perpetuity, but for a term of years, and were renewed from time to time at the pressing instance of the Senate.

Some of them were also, to a certain extent, shared with others—a further *apparent* safeguard. State and grandeur were at the same time avoided; no new insignia of office were introduced; the manners and deportment of the ruler were citizen-like. Thus both the great parties in the State were fairly satisfied: it was not difficult for republicans to flatter themselves that the Republic still existed; while monarchists were with better reason convinced that it had passed away forever.

The titles and offices assumed by Augustus were the following:—(1) That of *Imperator*, or commander-in-chief, conferred on him B.C. 30, which implied the *proconsulare imperium*, or command of all the provinces; (2) That of *Princeps Senatus* (B.C. 28), which enabled him to lead the Senate by entitling him to speak first on all questions which came before it; (3) That of perpetual *tribune*, involved in the *tribunicia potestas*, which he obtained B.C. 23; (4) That of perpetual *consul*, involved in the *consularis potestas*, assumed for life in B.C. 19; (5) That of perpetual *censor*, involved in the *potestas censoria*, obtained at the same date; and (6) That of *Pontifex Maximus*, taken at the death of Lepidus, B.C. 12. The *agnomen* of "Augustus," and the honorary title of "Pater Patriæ," were mere distinctions, conferring no rights.

Position of the Senate under Augustus and his successors.

2. The chief apparent check on the authority of Augustus was the Senate. Retaining the prestige of a great name, favorably regarded by large numbers among the people, and possessed of considerable powers in respect of taxation, of administration, and of nomination to high offices, the Senate, had it been animated by a bold and courageous spirit, might have formed not merely an ornamental adjunct to the throne, but a real counterbalancing power in the State, a barrier against oppression and tyranny. The Senate had its own treasury (*ærarium*), which was distinct from the privy purse (*fiscus*) of the Emperor; it divided with the Emperor the government of the Roman world, having its own senatorial provinces (*provinciæ Senatus*), as he had his imperial ones (*provinciæ Cæsaris*); it appointed "presidents" and "proconsuls" to administer the one, as he did his "lieutenants" (*legati*) to administer the other. It was recognized as the ultimate seat of all civil power and authority. It alone conferred the "imperium," or right to exercise rule over the provincials and the citizens. Legally and constitutionally, the Emperor derived his authority from the Senate; and it was always the acknowledgment of the Senate, by whatever means obtained,

which was regarded as imparting legitimacy to the pretensions of any new aspirant. The Senate was, however, prevented from proving any effectual check upon the "prince" by the cupidity and timidity which prevailed among its members. All the bolder spirits had perished in the civil wars; and the senators of Augustus, elevated or confirmed in their seats by him, preferred courting his favor by adulation to imperilling their position by the display of an inconvenient independence. As time went on, and worse Emperors than Augustus filled his place, the conduct which had been at first dictated by selfish hopes continued as the result of fear. Over the head of every one who thwarted the imperial will impended, like the sword of Damocles, the "lex de majestate." By degrees the Senate relinquished all its powers, or suffered them to become merely nominal; and the Roman "prince" became as absolute a despot as ever was Oriental shah or sultan.

The Senate of Augustus was limited to 600 members. It was composed of persons whose continuance in it he had sanctioned on those occasions when, as censor, he "purged the Senate," or whom he had himself appointed. To obtain a seat in it, a property qualification was necessary; and this was gradually raised by Augustus from 400,000 to 1,200,000 sesterces. It was composed, not simply of Romans and Italians, but also to a certain extent of provincials. Provincial members, however, were obliged to reside, and, in later times, to hold landed property, in Italy.

Gradual extinction of popular rights.

3. During the principate of Augustus, the "people" continued to possess some remnants of their ancient privileges. While the Emperor nominated absolutely the consuls and one-half of the other magistrates, the tribes elected, from among candidates whom the Emperor had approved, the remainder. Legislation followed its old course, and the entire series of "Leges Juliæ" enacted under Augustus, received the sanction of both the Senate and the Centuries. The judicial rights alone of the people were at this time absolutely extinguished, the prerogative of pardon which the Emperor assumed taking the place of the "provocatio ad populum." But the tendency of the Empire was, naturally, to infringe more and more on the remaining popular rights; and, though a certain show of election, and a certain title to a share in legislation, were maintained by the great assemblies up to the time when the Empire fell,

yet practically from the reign of Tiberius the people ceased to possess any real political power or privilege.

Institution of a Privy Council.

4. The political power, of which the Senate and people were deprived, could not, in so large an empire as Rome, be all exercised by one man. It was necessary that the Emperor should either devolve upon his favorites great part of the actual work of government, or that he should be assisted in his laborious duties by a regularly constituted Council of State. The temper and circumstances of Augustus inclined him to adopt the more liberal course; and hence the institution in his time (B.C. 27) of a Privy Council (*concilium secretum principis*), in which all important affairs of State were debated and legislative measures were prepared and put into shape. The jealousy of his successors allowed this institution to drop out of the imperial system, and substituted favorites—the mere creatures of the prince—for the legally constituted councillors of Augustus.

The Council of Augustus consisted of the chief annual magistrates, and of fifteen Senators elected by the rest of the Senate for a period of six months. It was thus a sort of Standing Committee of the Senate.

Continuation of old and creation of new offices.

5. As it was the object of Augustus to conceal, so far as possible, the greatness of the change which his measures effected in the government, the magistrates of the Republic were in almost every instance maintained, though with powers greatly diminished. The State had still its consuls, prætors, quæstors, ædiles, and tribunes; but these magistracies conveyed dignity rather than authority, and were coveted chiefly as distinctions. The really important offices were certain new ones, which the changed condition of affairs rendered necessary; as especially, the "præfecture of the city" (*præfectura urbis*), an office restored from the old regal times, and the commandership of the prætorian guard (*præfectura cohortium prætoriarum*), which became shortly the second dignity in the State.

The Prætorian Guard, instituted by Augustus for the security of his person, comprised ten cohorts of a thousand men each. It consisted exclusively of Italian soldiers, and included both horse and foot. Three cohorts only were quartered in Rome—the remainder were dispersed among the neighboring cities. Tiberius collected the whole body in a camp just outside the walls of Rome.

6. It was, indeed, in the military rather than in the civil institutions of the empire, that something like a real check existed upon the caprices of arbitrary power, so that misgovernment beyond a certain point was rendered dangerous. The security of the empire against both external and internal foes required the maintenance of a standing army of great magnitude; and the necessity of conciliating the affections, or at least retaining the respect, of this armed force imposed limits, that few but madmen overstepped, on the imperial liberty of action. Not only had the prætorians and their officers to be kept in good-humor, but the five-and-twenty or thirty legions upon the frontiers—no carpet soldiers, but hardy troops, the real salt of the Roman world—had to be favorably impressed, if an emperor wished to feel himself securely seated upon his throne. This check was the more valuable, as, practically, none other existed. It sufficed, during the period with which we are here more especially concerned—that from Augustus to Commodus—to render good government the rule, and tyranny the comparatively rare exception, only about fifty-seven years out of the 223 having been years of suffering and oppression.

Power of the army.

7. The organization of the army was somewhat complicated. The entire military force may be divided under the two heads of those troops which preserved order at Rome, and those which maintained the terror of the Roman name in the provinces. The troops of the capital were of two kinds: (*a*) the prætorians, of whom an account has already been given (supra, § 5), and (*b*) the "city cohorts" (*cohortes urbanæ*), a sort of armed police, whose number in the time of Augustus was 6000. The troops maintained in the provinces were likewise of two kinds: (*c*) those of the regular army, or the legionaries, and (*d*) the irregulars, who were called "auxilia," i. e., auxiliaries. The legions constituted the main strength of the system. They were "divisions," not "regiments." Each of them comprised the three elements of a Roman army—horse, foot, and artillery—in certain definite proportions, and (in the time of Augustus) numbered probably a little under 7000 men. Augustus maintained twenty-five legions, who formed thus a military force, armed and trained in the best possible

Its organization.

way, which did not fall much short of 175,000. The auxiliaries, or troops supplied by the provincials, were about equal in number. Thus the entire force maintained in the early empire may be reckoned at 350,000 or 360,000 men.

The legion of Augustus was organized as follows: (1) *Infantry*—ten "companies" (*cohortes*), containing 555 men each, except the first, which was of double strength, and therefore contained 1110 men; total, 6105 men. (2) *Cavalry*—ten "troops" (*turmæ*), containing 66 men each, except the first, which had twice the number; total, 726 men. (3) *Artillery*—two large and ten small "machinæ," with a sufficiency of men to work them, number unknown; probably not less than 70. Total (probable) strength of the entire legion, 6901.

Disposition of the legions.

8. The disposition of the legions varied from time to time, but only within somewhat narrow limits, the military strength of the empire being always massed principally upon the northern and eastern frontiers, or on the lines of the Rhine, the Danube, and the Euphrates, where alone had the Romans at this date any formidable foreign enemies. Thirteen or fourteen legions usually guarded the northern, or European, frontier, distributed in nearly equal proportions between the Rhenish and the Danubian provinces. In the East, from four to seven legions sufficed to keep in check the barbarians of Asia. Three legions were commonly required by Spain, which always cherished hopes of independence. The important province of Egypt required the presence of two legions, and the rest of Roman Africa was guarded by an equal number. Two legions were also usually stationed in Britain after its conquest. The older and more peaceful provinces, as Gallia Narbonensis, Sardinia, Sicily, Macedonia, Achæa, Asia, Bithynia, etc., were unoccupied by any regular force, order being maintained in them by some inconsiderable native levies.

Finances of the Empire.

9. The financial system of the Empire differed but little from that of the later Republic, both the sources of revenue and the items of expenditure being, for the most part, identical. Augustus contented himself, in the main, with simplifying the practice which he found established, only in a very few cases adding a new impost. The revenue continued to be derived from the two great sources of (1) the State property, and (2) taxes; and these

last continued to be either (*a*) Direct, or (*b*) Indirect. The chief expenditure was on the military force, land and naval; on the civil service; on public works; and on shows and largesses. It is difficult to form an exact estimate of the probable amount of these several items; but, on the whole, it seems most likely that the entire annual expenditure must have amounted to at least twenty-five millions of pounds sterling.

The principal alterations made by Augustus were:—(1) The substitution of a fixed money payment for the tribute in kind previously levied in the provinces; (2) The imposition of the *vicesima hæreditatium et legatorum*, or five per cent. legacy duty, payable by all Roman citizens on property left them by any other than their next of kin; and (3) The imposition of restrictions on celibacy by the *Lex Papia Poppœa*, which augmented the revenue by the forfeitures incurred under it. Augustus also distributed at his will the different items of revenue between the *ærarium* and the *fiscus* (see § 2), enriching the latter at the expense of the former.

Wars of Augustus in Spain, Rhætia, Arabia, Pannonia, etc.

10. Though it was as a civil administrator that Augustus obtained his chief reputation, yet much of his attention was also given to military affairs, and the wars in which he engaged, either in person or by his lieutenants, were numerous and important. The complete subjugation of Northern and North-western Spain was effected, partly by himself, partly by Agrippa and Carisius, in the space of nine years, from B.C. 27 to 19. In B.C. 24, an attempt was made by Ælius Gallus to extend the dominion of Rome into the spice region of Arabia Felix; but this expedition was unsuccessful. Better fortune attended on the efforts of the Emperor's step-sons, Drusus and Tiberius, in the years B.C. 16 and 15, to reduce the independent tribes of the Eastern Alps, especially the Rhætians and Vindelicians. Two campaigns sufficed for the complete reduction of the entire tract between the Lombardo-Venetian plain and the course of the Upper Danube, the "fortress of modern freedom." More difficulty, however, was experienced in subduing the tribes of the Middle and Lower Danube. In Noricum, Pannonia, and Mœsia, a gallant spirit of independence showed itself; and it was only after frequent revolts that the subjugation of these tracts was effected (between B.C. 12 and A.D. 9).

11. But the most important of all the Roman wars of this period was that with the Germans. The rapid conquest of

Failure of the attempt to subdue Germany.

Gaul and of the tracts south of the Danube encouraged the Romans to hope for similar success against the tribes who dwelt in Central Europe, between the Danube and the Baltic. In a military point of view, it would have been a vast gain, could they have advanced their frontier to the line of the Vistula and the Dniester. Augustus seems to have conceived such a design. Accordingly, from about the year B.C. 12, systematic efforts were made for the subjugation of the German races east of the Rhine and north of the Danube, the Usipetes, Chatti, Sigambri, Suevi, Cherusci, Marcomanni, etc. From the year B.C. 12 to A.D. 5, a continuous series of attacks was directed against these nations, first by Drusus, and then, after his death (B.C. 9), by Tiberius. Vast armies penetrated deep into the interior; fleets coasted the northern shore and ascended the great rivers to co-operate with the land force; forts were erected; the Roman language and laws were introduced; and the entire tract between the Rhine and the Elbe was brought into apparent subjection. But the real spirit of the nation was unsubdued. After a brief period of sullen submission (A.D. 5 to 8), revolt suddenly broke out (A.D. 9). Arminius, a prince of the Cherusci, took the lead. The Romans were attacked, three entire legions under Varus destroyed, and German independence recovered. Henceforth, though Rome sometimes, in ostentation, or as a measure of precaution, marched her armies into the district between the Rhine and the Elbe, yet no attempt was made at conquest or permanent occupation. The Rhine and Danube became the recognized limits of the empire, and, except the Agri Decumates, Rome held no land on the right bank of the former river.

DETAILS OF THE WAR WITH GERMANY. The war began with an attack by Drusus in B.C. 12, which was chiefly from the sea-board, and had no great success. Fresh expeditions were made, however, by land, in B.C. 11 and 9, under the conduct of the same prince, and in these he had better fortune. He reduced the Chatti, caused the Marcomanni to retire eastward, ravaged the country of the Cherusci, and reached (B.C. 11) the banks of the Weser, and (B.C. 9) those of the Elbe. He died, however, in the last-named year, from the effects of an accident, on his return from his expedition. The command was then assigned to Tiberius, who held it for two years (B.C. 8 to 7), when he was succeeded by Domitius Ænobarbus, who was followed by Vinicius. Tiberius then, on his return from Rhodes, once more took the conduct of the war (A.D. 4), and making his attack both by land and sea, gained important successes. Almost all the tribes between the Rhine and Elbe submitted to him. He was proceeding (in A.D. 6) to invade the Marcomanni in their new country of Bohemia, when the revolt in Pannonia (see § 10) called him off to the recovery of that province. Quintilius Varus succeeded him in the command, and, discontinuing warlike operations, applied himself to the organization of the submitted territory; but his measures, which were harsh, disgusted the populations, and drove them to revolt under Arminius (A.D. 9). The destruction of the legions and recovery of independence followed in the same year. In A.D. 10, Tiberius for the third time took the command; but his efforts were now confined to the mere re-establishment of the honor of Rome by incursions across the Rhine, which the Germans did not venture to resist. The same course was pursued by Germanicus during the short remainder of Augustus's reign (A.D. 12 to 14).

Flourishing condition of the Roman world under Augustus.

12. The internal tranquillity of Rome was during the whole of Augustus's long reign never once interrupted. Revolutionary passions had to a great extent exhausted themselves, and the prudence and vigilance of the Emperor never relaxed. The arts of peace flourished. Augustus "found Rome of brick and left it of marble." He gave a warm encouragement to literature, and with such effect that the most brilliant period of each nation's literary history is wont to take name from him. Virgil, Horace, Ovid, Tibullus, Propertius, Varius, Livy, adorned his court, and formed an assemblage of talent never surpassed and rarely equalled. Commerce pursued its course securely under his rule, and, though a little checked by sumptuary laws, became continually more and more profitable. Much attention was given to agriculture; and the productiveness of the land, both in Italy and the provinces, increased. Altogether, the Augustan age must be regarded as one of much material prosperity, elegance, and refinement; and it can create no surprise that the mass of the population were contented with the new *régime*.

Domestic misfortunes of Augustus. He adopts his step-son, Tiberius, and designates him as his successor.

13. The "good-fortune" of Augustus, which the ancients admired, was limited to his public, and did not attach to his private life. He suffered greatly from ill health, more especially in his earlier years. Though thrice married—to Claudia, to Scribonia, and to Livia—he had no son; and his only daughter, Julia, disgraced him by her excesses. His first son-in-law, Marcellus, was cut off by sickness in

the flower of his age; and his second, Agrippa, died when he was but a little more than fifty. Towards his third, Tiberius, he never felt warmly; and it was from necessity rather than choice that he raised him to the second place in the empire. It was no doubt among his most cherished wishes to have been succeeded by one of his own blood; but of the three sons born to his daughter, Julia, the two elder, Caius and Lucius, died just as they reached manhood, the latter in A.D. 2, the former in A.D. 4, while the third, Agrippa Posthumus, was of so dull and stolid a temperament, that not even the partiality of family affection could blind the Emperor to his unfitness. Deprived thus of all support from those of his own race and lineage, Augustus in his old age was forced to lean wholly upon his wife and the male scions of her family. These were Tiberius, the son, and Germanicus, the grandson of Livia, son of the deceased Drusus. When the aged Emperor, feeling the approach of death, resolved to make distinct arrangements for the succession, his choice fell on the former, whom he adopted, and associated with himself in some of the most important of the imperial functions. At the same time, he required Tiberius to adopt his nephew, Germanicus, and gave the latter the hand of his own granddaughter, Agrippina. Augustus lived to see (A.D. 12) the birth of a great-grandson, the issue of this union, and thus left one male descendant, who in course of time inherited his crown.

Special works on the life and times of Augustus were written in the last century by BLACKWELL and LARRY; but these can not be recommended to the reader. Of far greater importance are the following:

LOEBELL, *Ueber das Principat des Augustus*, in RAUMER'S *Historisches Taschenbuch*, for the year 1834.

WEICHERT, A., *Imperatoris Cæsaris Augusti Scriptorum Reliquiæ;* Fasc. i., Grimæ, 1841; 4to.

Reign of Tiberius, A.D. 14–37. Disturbances at his accession.

14. Augustus died A.D. 14, in the seventy-seventh year of his age. There is no reason to believe that his end was hastened by Livia, or by any of those about him. His health had long been giving way, and, but for the tender care of his attached wife, he would probably have died sooner. His place was taken, after some coquetry, by Tiberius, with the entire assent of the Senate and people of Rome, though not without opposi-

tion on the part of the army. It is important to observe that, even at this early date, the legions had an inkling of their strength, and would have proclaimed an emperor, and drawn their swords in his cause, had not the object of their choice, Germanicus, shrunk from the treason. Tiberius was indebted to the generosity of his young kinsman, or to his want of ambition, for his establishment in the imperial dignity without a struggle. It is perhaps not surprising that he felt more jealousy than gratitude towards one who had been proclaimed his rival; but he can not be exonerated from blame for so manifesting his jealousy as to make it generally felt that to vex, thwart, or injure his nephew was the shortest way to his favor.

Triple division of his reign. First Period, A.D. 14-25.

15. The reign of Tiberius may be conveniently divided into three periods:—(1) From his accession to his retirement from the capital (A.D. 14 to 26=12 years); (2) From his retirement to the death of Sejanus (A.D. 26 to 31=5 years); and (3) From the death of Sejanus to his own (A.D. 31 to 37=6 years). The main events of the first period were the exploits and death of Germanicus; the rise of Sejanus to power; and the death of Drusus, Tiberius's only son. During three years Germanicus attempted the re-conquest of Western Germany, and ravaged with his legions the entire country between the Rhine and the Elbe. But no permanent effect was produced by his incursions; and Tiberius, after a while, removed him from the West to the East, fearful perhaps of his becoming too dear to the German legions. In the management of the East he gave him as a coadjutor the ambitious and reckless Piso, who sought to bring his administration into contempt, and was believed to have removed him by poison. It is perhaps uncertain whether Germanicus did not really die a natural death, though his own conviction that he was poisoned is indubitable.

Cappadocia and Commagêné were not formally reduced to the condition of Roman provinces till the arrival of Germanicus in the East, A.D. 17. Previously to this they were Roman dependencies under native kings. Armenia continued in this condition.

Rise of Sejanus to power.

16. The rise of Sejanus to power is to be connected with the general policy of Tiberius as a ruler, which was characterized by a curious mixture of sus-

piciousness with over-confidence. Distrusting his own abilities, doubtful of his right to the throne, he saw on every side of him possible rivals—aspirants who might thrust him from his high place. The noblest and wealthiest of the Patricians, the members and connections of the Julian house, and the princes of his own family, were the especial objects of his jealousy. These, therefore, he sought to depress; he called none of them to his aid; he formed of them no "Privy Council," as Augustus had done, but resolved to administer the entire empire by his own unassisted exertions. Indefatigable as he was in business, this, after a while, he found to be impossible; and he was thus led to look out for a helper, who should be too mean in origin and position to be dangerous, while he possessed the qualities which would render him useful. Such an one he thought to have found in Ælius Sejanus, the mere son of a Roman knight, a provincial of Vulsinii, whom he made "Prætorian Prefect," and who gradually acquired over him the most unbounded influence.

As with his chief assistant at Rome, so with his lesser assistants in the provinces, Tiberius chose them carefully from among those whom he did not fear, and then continued them, without change or recall, in their governments.

Death of Drusus and retirement of Tiberius to Capreæ.

17. The death of Drusus was the result of the criminal ambition of Sejanus, which nothing could content short of the first place in the empire. Having seduced Livilla, the wife of Drusus and niece of Tiberius, Sejanus, with her aid, took him off by poison (A.D. 23). His crime being undiscovered, he soon afterwards (A.D. 25) requested the permission of Tiberius to marry the widow. The request took Tiberius by surprise; it opened his eyes to his favorite's ambition, but it did not at once destroy his influence. Declining the proposal made to him, he allowed his minister to persuade him to quit Rome, retire to Capreæ, and yield into his hands the entire conduct of affairs at the capital.

Second Period, A.D. 26–31. Fall of Sejanus.

18. The influence of Sejanus was now at its height, and was made use of in two ways—to remove the chief remaining members of the imperial family, and to obtain his own admission into it. By lies and intrigues he procured the arrest and imprisonment

of Agrippina and her two elder sons, Nero and Drusus. By pressing his claims, he obtained at last the consent of the Emperor to the marriage whereto he aspired, and was actually betrothed to Livilla. At the same time, he was made joint consul with his master. But at this point his good-fortune stopped. In the very act of raising his favorite so high, the Emperor had become jealous of him. Signs of his changed feelings soon appeared; and Sejanus, anxious to anticipate the blow which he felt to be impending, formed a plot to assassinate his master. Failing, however, to act with due promptness, he was betrayed, degraded from his command, seized, and executed, A.D. 31.

Third Period, A.D. 31–37. Reign of Terror.

19. It might have been hoped that Tiberius, relieved from the influence of his cruel and crafty minister, would have reverted to the (comparatively) mild policy of his earlier years. But the actual result was the reverse of this. The discovery that he had been deceived in the man on whom alone he had reposed confidence, rendered him more suspicious than ever. The knowledge, which he now acquired, that his own son had been murdered, affrighted him. Henceforth Tiberius became a monster of tyranny, because he trusted no one, because he saw in merit of whatever kind at once a reproach and a danger. Hence a "Reign of Terror" followed the execution of Sejanus. In the fall of the favorite all his friends, all who had paid court to him, were implicated; in the guilt of Livilla, the equal guilt of the other relatives of Germanicus was regarded as proved. Nero, therefore, Drusus, and Agrippina, as well as Livilla, were put to death; hundreds of nobles, men, women, and even children, were massacred. The cruel tyrant, skulking in his island abode, issued his bloody decrees, and at the same time gave himself up to strange and unnatural forms of profligacy, seeking in them, perhaps, a refuge from remorse. At length, when he had reached his seventy-eighth year, his strong constitution failed, and he died after a short illness, A.D. 37.

Tiberius dies.

Legal and constitutional changes during his reign.

20. The political and legal changes belonging to the reign of Tiberius were not many in number, but they were of considerable importance. Among his first acts was the extinction of the last vestige of pop-

ular liberty, by the withdrawal from the "comitia tributa" of all share in the appointment of magistrates. Their right of selection from among the Emperor's candidates was transferred to the Senate, and henceforth the tribes met merely *pro forma*, to confirm the choice of that body. A second, and still more vital, change was the usurpation by the Emperor of the right to condemn to death, and execute *without trial*, all those who were obnoxious to him, or at any rate all whom the tribunals had once committed to prison. A third innovation was the extension of the "lex de majestate" to words and even thoughts, and the introduction by these means of "constructive treason" into the list of capital offenses. It is scarcely necessary to observe how these changes tended in the direction of despotism, which was still further promoted by the establishment of the entire body of prætorian guards in a camp immediately outside of Rome, for the sole purpose of overawing, and, if need were, coercing the citizens.

On the character of Tiberius, the reader may consult the work of A. STAHR, *Tiberius*. Berlin, 1863; 8vo.

Caius (or Caligula) succeeds Tiberius.

21. The demise of Tiberius revealed a vital defect in the imperial system, viz., the want of any regular and established law of succession. Tiberius had associated nobody, had designated nobody by his will, had left the State to shift for itself, careless whether or no there followed on his decease a deluge. Under these circumstances, the Senate, the prætorians, and the people might all conceive that the right of appointing an imperator, if not even that of determining whether or no any new imperator should be appointed, rested with them. A collision might easily have occurred, but the circumstances were fortunately such as to produce a complete accord between the three possible disputants. Soldiers, Senate, and people united in putting aside any glowing dream of the Republic, and in calling to the throne Caius, the only surviving son of Germanicus and Agrippina, whose parentage rendered him universally popular, while his age was suitable, and his character, so far as it was known, unobjectionable.

Besides Caius, the only two persons whose connection with previous imperators pointed them out to notice were Claudius, the brother of Germanicus, and Tiberius Gemellus, the son of Drusus and grandson of Tiberius.

But the latter was too young (he was but 17) to be regarded as capable of discharging the duties of an emperor; while the former was a recluse, whose existence was scarcely known outside the palace. Thus Caius had, practically, no rival.

22. The reign of Caius, or Caligula, as he is generally termed, lasted less than four years (from March, A.D. 37, to January, A.D. 41), but was long enough to fully display the disastrous effects of the possession of arbitrary power on a weak and ill-balanced mind. At first mild, generous, and seemingly amiable, he rapidly degenerated into a cruel and fantastic tyrant, savage, merciless, and mocking. Dissipating in a few months the vast hoards of Tiberius, who had left in the treasury a sum exceeding twenty-one millions of our money, he was driven to supply his needs, in part by an oppressive taxation, but mainly from confiscations of large estates, to procure which it was only necessary to make a free use of the law of "majestas." Executions, suicides, exiles followed each other throughout his reign in an unceasing succession, the Emperor becoming more and more careless of bloodshed. The most wanton extravagance exhausted the resources of the State. Not content with the ordinary forms of profligacy, Caius lived in open incest with his sister, Drusilla. After his own severe illness, and her death (A.D. 38), the violence of his feelings, which he had long ceased to control, and the strange contrast, which those events brought home to him, between his weakness and his strength, his unlimited power over the lives of others, and his impotence to avert death, seem to have shattered his reason, and to have rendered him actually insane. His self-deification, his architectural extravagances, his absurd expeditions and still wilder projects, which all belong to the latter half of his reign, have been justly thought to indicate that his mind was actually unhinged. The awful spectacle of a madman absolute master of the civilized world is here presented to us; and the peril inherent in the despotic form of government is shown in the clearest light. The human suffering compressed into Caligula's short reign can scarcely be calculated. What would have been the result, had he been allowed to live out his natural term of life? Fortunately for the world, tyranny, when it reaches a certain point, provokes resistance.

Reign of Caius, A.D. 37–41.

His murder.

Caius was struck down in the fourth year of his reign, and the thirtieth of his life, by the swords of two of his guards, whom he had insulted beyond endurance.

Importance of the crisis.

23. This sudden blow, whereby the State was left wholly without a head, was an event for which the imperial constitution had made no provision; and its occurrence produced a crisis of vast importance for its effect on the imperial constitution itself, which suffered a modification. Two questions presented themselves to be determined by the course of events:—(1) "Was the Empire accidental and temporary, or was it the regular and established form of government?" And (2) "In the latter case, with whom did it rest, in case of a sudden vacancy for which no preparation had been made, to select a successor?" The all but entire abolition of the Comitia put the claim of the people to be heard on either point out of the question: the determination necessarily rested with the Senate or the soldiers. Had the Senate been sufficiently prompt, it might not improbably have determined both points in its own favor; it might have restored the Republic, or it might have nominated an emperor. But it was unprepared; it hesitated; it occupied itself with talk; and the opportunity, which it might have seized, passed away forever. For the prætorians, accidentally finding Claudius in the palace, and aware of the hesitation of the Senate, assumed the right of choice, proclaimed him emperor, and thereby asserted and established both the fixity of the Empire and the right of the army to nominate the imperator. Henceforth for more than half a century the nominees of the army wore the crown, and the Senate was content with the mere ratification of the army's choice.

It was not till the tyranny of Domitian had thrown discredit on the soldiers' emperors that the Senate (A.D. 96) once more took heart, and ventured to nominate a sovereign.

Reign of Claudius, A.D. 41–54. Influence of his wives and freedmen.

24. Claudius, who succeeded Caius, was his uncle, being the younger brother of Germanicus, and thus, though connected with the Julian house, not by birth a member of it. His reign lasted between thirteen and fourteen years, from January, A.D. 41, to October, A.D. 54. Though mild, diligent, and well-intentioned, he was by nature and education unfitted to rule,

more especially in a corrupt commonwealth. Shy, weak, and awkward, he had been considered from his birth "wanting," had been debarred from public life till he was forty-six years of age, and had acquired the temper and habits of a recluse student. Left to himself, he might have reigned respectably; but it was his misfortune to fall under the influence of persons grievously unprincipled, whose characters he was unable to read, and who made him their tool and cat's-paw. His wives, Messalina and Agrippina, and his freedmen, Pallas and Narcissus, had the real direction of affairs during his reign; and it was to them, and not to Claudius himself, that the corruption and cruelties which disgraced his principate were owing. The death of the infamous Messalina, to which he consented, can not be charged against him as a crime, for it was thoroughly merited; and the sway of Agrippina, though in the end it had disastrous effects, was not without counterbalancing advantages. The princess who recalled Seneca from exile and made him her son's tutor, who advanced to power the honest Burrhus, and protected many an accused noble, can not be regarded as wholly a malign influence. Her fear of suffering the punishment due to her infidelity, and her natural desire to see her son upon the throne, led her on at last to crime of the deepest dye. She took advantage of her position to poison the unhappy Claudius in the sixty-fourth year of his age, and the fourteenth of his reign.

Murdered by Agrippina.

In the reign of Claudius several useful and important works were constructed; the empire received further consolidation; and in one direction its bounds were considerably extended. Of the "works," the most remarkable were the "Aqua Claudia" and the "Aqua Aniena Nova," two great aqueducts which brought water to Rome from a distance of forty miles; the "Portus Romanus," or new harbor at Ostia; and the "Emissarium Fucinum," or tunnel to carry off the superfluous waters of Lake Fucinus. The consolidation of the empire was advanced by changing Mauretania (A.D. 42), Lycia (A.D. 43), Judæa (A.D. 44), and Thrace (A.D. 47) from dependencies into actual provinces. The extension of the empire was towards the northwest, where Britain was conquered, mainly by A. Plautius, but partly by Claudius in person, as far north as a line drawn from the Wash to the mouth of the Dee (see pp. 514, 515).

25. Claudius left behind him a son, Britannicus, who was however but thirteen years old at his father's death. The crown, therefore, naturally fell to his adopted son, Nero, who

Reign of Nero, A.D. 54–68. His early promise.

had married his daughter, Octavia, and who was, moreover, a direct descendant of Augustus. Proclaimed by the prætorians as soon as the demise of his father-in-law was known, he was at once accepted by the Senate, whom the circumstances of the elevation of Claudius (see § 23) had made conscious of their weakness. The feelings which greeted his accession were similar to those called forth on a similar occasion by Caligula. Nothing but good could, it was thought, proceed from the grandson of Germanicus, the comrade of Lucan, the pupil of Seneca. Nor were these hopes disappointed for a considerable time. During the first five years of his principate—the famous "quinquennium Neronis"—all went well, at any rate, outside the palace; the "golden age" seemed to have returned; Nero forbade delation, remitted taxes, gave liberal largesses, made assignments of lands, enriched the treasury from his private stores, removed some of the burdens of the provincials. During this period Seneca and Burrhus were his advisers; and their judicious counsels produced a mild but firm government. Within the palace there were, indeed,

His first great crime.

already scandals and crimes: the impatient son and the exacting mother soon quarrelled; and the quarrel led to the first of Nero's domestic tragedies, the poisoning of Britannicus (A.D. 55). This was soon followed by the disgrace of the queen-mother, who was banished from court and made the object of cruel suspicions. The gay prince, passing his time in amusements and debaucheries, fell now (A.D. 58) under the influence of a fierce and ambitious woman, the infamous Poppæa Sabina, wife of Otho, who consented to be his mistress, and aspired to become

His later profligacy and tyranny.

his queen. At her instigation Nero assassinated first his mother Agrippina (A.D. 59), and then his wife Octavia (A.D. 62), whom he had previously repudiated. He now plunged into evil courses of all kinds. He murdered Burrhus, broke with Seneca, and put himself under the direction of a new favorite, Tigellinus, a man of the worst character. Henceforth he was altogether a tyrant. Reckless in his extravagance, he encouraged delation in order to replenish his treasury; he oppressed the provincials by imposing on them forced contributions, over and above the taxes; he shocked public opinion by performing as a singer and a charioteer before his subjects; he displayed complete indifference to the sufferings of the Romans at the time of the great fire; he openly encouraged prostitution and even worse vices; and he began the cruel practice of persecuting Jews and Christians for their opinions, which disgraced the empire from his time to that of Constantine. After this tyranny had endured for five years, something of a spirit of resistance appeared; conspiracy ventured to raise its head, but only to be detected and struck down (A.D. 65). Fear now made the Emperor more cruel than ever. Executions and assassinations followed each other in more and more rapid succession. All the rich and powerful, all the descendants of Augustus, all those who were noted for virtue, lost their lives. At last he grew jealous of his own creatures, the legates who commanded legions upon the frontiers, and determined on sacrificing them. The valiant Corbulo, commander of the forces of the East, was entrapped and executed. Rufus and Proculus Scribonius, who had the chief authority in the two Germanies, were recalled and forced to kill themselves. A similar fate menaced all the chiefs of legions, who, on learning their peril, rose in arms against the tyrant. Galba and Otho in Spain, Vindex in Gaul, Claudius Macer in Africa, Virginius Rufus and Fonteius Capito in Germany, raised the standard of revolt almost at the same time. The multitude of pretenders to empire seemed at first to promise ill for the cause of rebellion, and in one case there was actual war between the troops of two of them, terminating in the death of one (Vindex); but after a while, by general agreement, Galba was chosen to conduct the contest, and, all chance of dividing his adversaries being over, the hopes of Nero fell. Deserted on all hands, even by Tigellinus and the prætorians, he was forced to call on a slave to dispatch him, that he might not fall alive into the hands of his enemies. Nero died on the 9th of June, A.D. 68, at the age of thirty, in the fourteenth year of his principate.

Revolt of his generals. His death.

The chief events in the external history of Rome belonging to the reign of Nero were:—1. The revolt of Britain under Boadicea (A.D. 61), with the destruction of Camulodunum and Londinium, and the recovery of the province by Suetonius Paulinus; 2. The war with the Parthians and Armenians waged by Corbulo (A.D. 56 to 63), which advanced Terminus slightly at the extreme north-east corner of the empire; and 3. The commencement of the Jewish war (A.D. 66), in consequence of the oppressive government of Gessius Florus. The discipline of the legions was still for the most part maintained successfully; and the superiority of the Roman arms was exhibited or confessed on every frontier.

26. Though the law of hereditary succession in the empire had at no time been formally established, or even asserted with any distinctness under the early Cæsars, yet there can be no doubt that the extinction of the Julian family by the death of Nero paved the way for fresh civil commotions, by practically opening the prospect of obtaining supreme power to numerous claimants. Hitherto the Romans had not in fact looked for an imperator beyond the members, actual or adopted, of a single house. Henceforth the first place in the State was a prize at which any one might aim, no family ever subsequently obtaining the same hold on power, or the same prestige in the eyes of the Romans as the Julian.

Results of the extinction of the Julian house.

27. S. Sulpicius Galba, who became emperor in April, A.D. 68, by the will of the Spanish legions, and the acquiescence of his brother-commanders in Gaul and Germany, was a Roman cast in the antique mould—severe, simple, unbending. He was thus ill fitted to bear rule in a state so corrupt as Rome had come to be; and the disasters which followed his appointment might have been anticipated by any one possessed of moderate foresight. His strictness and his parsimony disgusted at once the soldiers and the populace; and when Otho, who had hoped to be nominated his successor, turned against him on account of his adopting Piso Licinianus, he found himself with scarcely a friend, and was almost instantly overpowered and slain (January 15, A.D. 69). His adopted son, Piso, shared his fate; and the obsequious Senate at once acknowledged Otho as Emperor.

Reign of Galba, A.D. 68-69.

28. M. Salvius Otho, the husband of the infamous Poppæa Sabina, was a dissolute noble, who had run through a long course of vice, and who, having exhausted all other excitements, determined in the spirit of a gambler to play for empire. Successful in seizing the throne, he found his right to it disputed by another of Galba's officers, the commander of the German legions,

Reign of Otho, Jan. to April, A.D. 69.

Vitellius. Nothing daunted, he resolved to appeal to the arbitrament of arms, and to bring matters to an issue as soon as possible. When in the great battle of Bedriacum fortune declared against him, he took her at her word, gave up the struggle as carelessly as he had begun it, and by a prompt suicide made the empire over to his rival. Otho died, April 16, A.D. 69, after a reign of barely three months.

29. In exchanging the rule of Otho for that of Vitellius, the Roman world lost rather than gained. Otho was profligate, reckless, sensual; but he was brave. Vitellius had all Otho's vices in excess, and, in addition, was cowardly and vacillating. He gained the empire not by his own exertions, but by those of his generals, Cæcina and Valens. Having gained it, he speedily lost it by weakness, laziness, and incapacity. We search his character in vain for any redeeming trait: he possessed no one of the qualities, moral or mental, which fit a man to be a ruler. What was most peculiar in him was his wonderful gluttony, a feature of his character in which he was unrivalled. It is not surprising that the Roman world declined to acquiesce long in his rule; for while, morally, he was equally detestable with the worst princes of the Julian house, intellectually he was far their inferior. The standard of revolt was raised against him, after he had reigned a few months, by Vespasian, commander in Judæa, who was supported by Mucianus, the president of Syria, and the legions of the East generally. The analogy of the previous civil contests would have led us to expect the defeat of an aspirant who, with troops derived from this quarter, assailed the master of the West. But Vespasian had advantages at no former time possessed by any Oriental pretender. He was infinitely superior, as a general and statesman, to his antagonist. He had all the "respectability" of the empire in his favor, a general disgust being felt at the degrading vices and stupid supineness of Vitellius. Above all, he did not depend upon the East solely, but was supported also by the legions of the central provinces—Mœsia, Pannonia, Illyricum—troops as brave and hardy as any in the whole empire. Hence his attack was successful. Securing in his own person Egypt, the granary of Rome, he sent his generals, Antonius Primus and Muci-

Reign of Vitellius, April to Dec., A.D. 69.

Revolt of Vespasian. Reasons of his success.

anus, into Italy. The (second) battle of Bedriacum, which was gained by Antonius, in fact decided the contest; but it was prolonged for several months, chiefly through the obstinacy of the Vitellian soldiery, who would not permit their leader to abdicate. In a struggle which followed between the two parties inside the city, the Capitol was assaulted and taken, the Capitoline temple burnt, and Flavius Sabinus, the brother of Vespasian, slain. Soon afterwards the Flavian army stormed and took Rome, defeated and destroyed the Vitellians, and, obtaining possession of the Emperor's person, put him to an ignominious death.

30. Though Vitellius did not perish till December 21, A.D. 69, yet the accession of his successor, T. Flavius Vespasianus, was dated from the 1st of July, nearly six months earlier. Vespasian reigned ten years (from A.D. 69 to 79), and did much to recover the empire from the state of depression and exhaustion into which the civil struggles of the two preceding years had brought it. By his general, Cerialis, he suppressed the revolt of Germany and eastern Gaul, which, under Civilis, Sabinus, and Classicus, had threatened to deprive Rome of some of her most important provinces. By the skill and valor of his elder son, Titus, he put down the rebellion of the Jews, and destroyed the magnificent city which alone, of all the cities of the earth, was, by her beauty and her prestige, a rival to the Roman metropolis. The limits of the empire were during his reign advanced in Britain from the line of the Dee and Wash, to that of the Solway Frith and Tyne, by the generalship of Agricola. The finances, which had fallen into complete disorder, were replaced upon a sound footing. The discipline of the army, which Otho and Vitellius had greatly relaxed, was re-established. Employment was given to the people by the construction of great works, as, particularly, the Temple of Peace, and the Flavian Amphitheatre or "Coliseum." Education and literature were encouraged by grants of money to their professors. The exceptional treatment of the Stoics, who were banished from Rome, arose from political motives, and was perhaps a state necessity. Altogether, Vespasian must be regarded as the best ruler that Rome had had since Augustus—a ruler who knew how to combine firmness with leniency, economy with liberality,

Reign of Vespasian, A.D. 69–79.

and a generally pacific policy with military vigor upon proper occasion.

DETAILS OF VESPASIAN'S WARS. (1) WAR WITH CIVILIS, A.D. 69, 70. Civilis aimed at establishing an independent Germany on the left bank of the Rhine. Professing a wish to help Vespasian and injure Vitellius, he gradually overpowered the Roman troops which guarded the province, or induced them to join him. Not satisfied with this success, he urged the Gauls to follow his example, and prevailed on Sabinus and Classicus to proclaim a Gallic empire. But the proclamation awoke no response among the weak and plastic Celts, who were satisfied with their position under the Romans. Gaul was easily pacified, and Civilis, after three defeats, was forced to quit his newly-formed kingdom and retire across the Rhine. (2) WAR WITH THE JEWS. Vespasian was appointed to conduct this war by Nero, A.D. 66. His first campaign was in Galilee, A.D. 67. He took Jotapata, capturing the historian Josephus, made himself master of Tiberias and Tarichea, and reduced all northern Palestine. In the course of the next year, A.D. 68, he advanced southward to Jericho and Cæsarea. Inactive during the earlier part of A.D. 69, on account of the civil contests, he left the prosecution of the war to his son Titus, when he quitted Palestine for Egypt; and Titus, early in A.D. 70, commenced the siege of the capital. Jerusalem was taken, after a desperate resistance, in the autumn of the same year; its inhabitants were massacred or sold as slaves; and the whole city was razed to the ground. (3) WAR IN BRITAIN. Agricola, made governor of Britain by Vespasian in A.D. 78, began his career by the complete reduction of the Ordovices, the chief tribe of North Wales. He then (A.D. 79) attacked the Brigantes and other inhabitants of the tract between the Wash and the Tyne, and subdued the island as far as the Tyne and Solway, establishing a line of forts across the isthmus which unites England with Scotland. (The remainder of the British War belongs to the reigns of Titus and Domitian.)

On the legislation of Vespasian, the student may consult the work of—

CRAMER, A.G., *D. Vespasianus, sive de vita et legislatione T. Flavii Vespasiani commentarius.* Jenæ, 1785.

31. Vespasian had taken care before his decease to associate his elder son, Titus, in the empire; and thus the latter was, at his father's death, acknowledged without any difficulty as sovereign. His character was mild but weak; he cared too much for popularity; and was so prodigal of the resources of the State, that, had his reign been prolonged, he must have had recourse to confiscations or exactions in order to replenish an empty treasury. Fortunate in his early death, he left behind him a character unstained by any worse vice than voluptuousness. Even the public calamities which marked his reign—the great eruption of Vesuvius, which overwhelmed Pompeii and Herculaneum, a terrible fire at Rome, and a destructive pesti-

Reign of Titus, A.D. 79–81.

lence—detracted but little from the general estimation in which he was held, being regarded as judgments, not on the prince, but on the nation. Titus held the throne for the short term of two years and two months, dying Sept. 13, A.D. 81, when he was not quite forty.

Titus continued Agricola in his British command, and the third and fourth campaigns of that general belong to his reign. In these campaigns Agricola reduced the Scotch lowlands, and advanced the Roman frontier from the line of the Tyne and Solway to that of the Friths of Forth and Clyde.

Reign of Domitian, A.D. 81-96.

32. Domitian, the younger brother of Titus, though not associated by him in the empire, had been pointed out by him as his successor; and the incipient right thus conferred met with no opposition from either Senate or army. Of a morose and jealous temper, he had sorely tried the affection of both his father and brother; but they had borne patiently with his faults, and done their best to lessen them. It might have been hoped that on attaining to a position in which he had no longer a rival, he would have become better satisfied, and more genial; but a rooted self-distrust seems to have rendered him morbidly suspicious of merit of any kind, while an inward unhappiness made him intolerant of other men's pleasures and satisfactions. Had he succeeded in gathering real laurels on the banks of the Rhine and Danube, the gratification of his self-love would probably have improved his temper; but, as it was, his inability to gain any brilliant success in either quarter disappointed and still further soured him.

His tyranny and murder.

Morose and severe by nature, as time went on he became cruel; not content with strictly enforcing obsolete laws, he revived the system of accusations, condemnations, and forfeitures, which had been discontinued since the days of Nero; having decimated the ranks of the nobles, and provoked the conspiracy of Saturninus, he became still more barbarous through fear; and, ending by distrusting every one and seeking to strike terror into all, he drew upon himself, just as his sixteenth year had begun, the fate which he deserved. He was murdered by the freedmen of the palace, whom his latest executions threatened, on the 18th of September, A.D. 96.

WARS OF DOMITIAN. (1) WAR IN BRITAIN. Agricola, retained by Domitian in his command for three years, proceeded in A.D. 83 to attack the

Caledonians in the low country north and north-east of the Frith of Forth. Having defeated them in several engagements, and explored the character of the country, he again attacked them in A.D. 84, defeated their leader, Galgacus, in a great battle (probably near Forfar), and threatened to conquer the whole island. His fleet explored the coast as far as Cape Wrath, and ascertained the limits of Britain northward. Further successes were prevented by his sudden recall, towards the close of A. D. 84, by his jealous master. (2) WAR IN GERMANY. In A.D. 84, Domitian crossed the Rhine, and made an expedition in person against the Chatti, which was attended with no important success, but served to strike terror into the tribes in this quarter. In A.D. 87 he attacked the Marcomanni and their neighbors the Quadi and Sarmatæ, but his arms met with reverses. (3) WAR WITH THE DACIANS. This, which was far the most important of Domitian's wars, commenced in his first year, A.D. 81, by an incursion of the Daci into Mœsia, where they defeated a Roman legion, and ravaged the province to the foot of Mount Hæmus. It was not till A.D. 86 that Domitian made an attempt to avenge this disaster. His troops crossed the Danube and invaded Dacia, but were completely defeated by the enemy. This defeat was followed in A.D. 87 by a Roman victory; but three years afterwards (A.D. 90), a peace was made with this formidable enemy on terms disgraceful to the Romans. It was agreed to pay the Dacians an annual tribute on condition of their undertaking to abstain from incursions into Mœsia. This was the first time that imperial Rome had consented to purchase peace of an enemy.

Advantage taken of the crisis by the Senate to increase its powers.

33. The cruelties of Domitian had thrown discredit on the hereditary principle, to which, though it had no legal force, his elevation to the principate was, in point of fact, due. The Senate, which now for the first time since the death of Caligula found itself in a position to claim and exercise authority, proceeded therefore to elect for sovereign an aged and childless man, one whose circumstances rendered it impossible that he should seek to impose upon them a dynasty. It is remarkable that the prætorians, though they felt aggrieved by the murder of Domitian, and demanded the punishment of his assassins, made no opposition to the Senate's selection, but tacitly suffered the Fathers to assume a prerogative which, however it might be viewed as legally inherent in them, they had never previously exercised. Perhaps the lesson taught by Otho's fall was still in their minds, and they feared lest, if they attempted to create an emperor, they might again provoke the hostility of the legions. At any rate, the result was that the Senate at this juncture increased its power, and by its prompt action obtained a position and a consideration of which it had been deprived for more than a century.

34. M. Cocceius Nerva, on whom the choice of the Senate fell, was a man of mild and lenient temperament, of fair abilities, and of the lax morals common in his day. He was sixty-five or seventy years old at his accession, and reigned only one year and four months. For the bloody *régime* of Domitian he substituted a government of extreme gentleness; for his extravagant expenditure, economy and retrenchment; for his attempted enforcement of antique manners, an almost universal tolerance. He relieved poverty by distributions of land, and by a poor-law which threw on the State the maintenance of many destitute children. He continued the best of Domitian's laws, and made some excellent enactments of his own, as especially one against delation. When the public tranquillity was threatened by the violence of the prætorians, who put to death without trial and without his consent the murderers of Domitian, he took the wise step of securing the future of the State by publicly appointing, with the sanction of the Senate, a colleague and successor, selecting for the office the person who of all living Romans appeared to be the fittest, and adopting him with the usual ceremonies. The example thus set passed into a principle of the government. Henceforth it became recognized as the duty of each successive emperor to select from out of the entire population of the empire the person most fit to bear rule, and make him his adopted son and successor.

Reign of Nerva, A.D. 96–98.

Adoption of Trajan.

The adoption practised by the princes of the Julian house was different from this, since they chose only from among their own relatives and close connections. The act of Galba in adopting Piso (see § 27) was similar in intention, but the choice was unhappy.

35. M. Ulpius Trajanus, on whom the choice of Nerva had fallen, was a provincial Roman, a native of the colony of Italica in Spain. His father had been consul and proconsul; but otherwise his family was undistinguished. He himself had been bred up in the camp, and had served with distinction under his father. He had obtained the consulship in A.D. 91, under Domitian, and had been commander of the Lower Germany under both Domitian and Nerva. Readily accepted by the Senate, and thoroughly popular with the legions, he ascended the throne under favorable auspices, which the events of his reign did

Reign of Trajan, A.D. 98–117.

not belie. The Romans regarded him as the best of all their princes; and, though tried by a Christian, or even a philosophic standard, he was far from being a good man, since he was addicted to wine and to low sensual pleasures, yet, taking the circumstances of the times into account, we can understand his surname of "Optimus." He was brave, laborious, magnanimous, simple and unassuming in his habits, affable in his manners, genial; he knew how to combine strictness with leniency, liberality with economy, and devotion to business with sociability and cheerfulness. And if we may thus consider him, in a qualified sense, "good," we may certainly without any reserve pronounce him "great." Both as a general and as an administrator he stands in the front rank of Roman rulers, equalling Augustus in the one respect, and nearly equalling Julius in the other. Though he could not materially improve the imperial form of government, which took its color wholly from the character of the reigning prince, yet he gave to the government while he exercised it the best aspect of which it was capable. He sternly suppressed delation, allowed the Senate perfect freedom of speech, abstained from all interference in its appointments, and in social converse treated its members as equals. Indefatigable in business, he managed almost alone the affairs of his vast empire, carrying on a voluminous correspondence with the governors of provinces, and directing them how to proceed in all cases, hearing carefully all the appeals made to him, and sometimes even judging causes in the first instance. His administration of the finances was extraordinarily good. Without increasing taxation, without having recourse to confiscations, he contrived to have always so full an exchequer, that neither his military expeditions nor his great works (which were numerous both in Rome and the provinces), nor his measures for the relief of the necessitous among his subjects, were ever cramped or stinted for want of means. He extended and systematized the irregular poor-law of Nerva; made loans at a low rate of interest to the proprietors of encumbered estates; repaired the ravages of earthquakes and tempests; founded colonies; constructed various military roads; bridged the Rhine and Danube; adorned with works of utility and ornament both provincial towns and the capi-

His character.

His policy.

tal. He spent little upon himself. His column and his triumphal arch may be regarded as constructed for his own glory; but his chief works, his great Forum at Rome, his mole at Centumcellæ (Civita Vecchia), his harbor at Ancona, his roads, his bridges, his aqueducts, were for the benefit of his subjects, and justly increased the affection wherewith they regarded him. If he had any fault as a ruler, it was an undue ambition to extend Terminus, and to be known to future ages as a conqueror. There were no doubt reasons of policy which led him to make his Dacian and Oriental expeditions, but nevertheless they were mistakes. The time for conquest was gone by; and the truest wisdom would have been to have rested content with the limits which had been fixed by Augustus—the Rhine, the Danube, and the Euphrates. Trajan's conquests had for the most part to be surrendered immediately after his decease; and the prestige of Rome was more injured by their abandonment than it had been advanced by his long series of victories.

His great works.

His conquests no real gain to the empire.

WARS OF TRAJAN. (1) WAR WITH THE DACIANS, A.D. 101–106. The war was aggressive on the part of the Romans, and commenced with an invasion of Dacia in A.D. 101, which was completely successful. Zermizegethusa, the capital, was occupied. The next year a great battle was fought at Tapæ, in which Decebalus was worsted; whereupon he sued for peace. Hard terms were granted him, A.D. 103. In A.D. 104 he rebelled, and Trajan again took the field and carried all before him. Decebalus and his nobles slew themselves. Dacia was made into a province, colonies being planted at Zermizegethusa, Apulum, Napoca, and Cerna. (2) WAR IN THE EAST. The generally unquiet state of the East, and particularly the machinations of the Jews, induced Trajan to strike a blow at Parthia. The conflicting claims of the two empires to direct the affairs of Armenia was the nominal ground of quarrel. The war began by Trajan's invading Armenia, A.D. 115, and taking possession of the country, which he reduced at once to the condition of a province. He then rapidly overran and conquered Mesopotamia and Assyria, which he put upon the same footing. The next year, A.D. 116, he marched southward, took Ctesiphon and Seleucia, and ravaged the Parthian territory as far as Susa. But now revolts broke out in his rear. Seleucia rebelled and was retaken. Hatra (El Hadr) successfully resisted Trajan himself. Retreat from an untenable position became necessary. Trajan therefore relinquished his most southern conquests to a Parthian prince, Parthamaspates, who consented to hold his kingdom as a Roman fief, and retired to Antioch, still retaining, however, as the fruits of the war, the three new provinces of Armenia, Mesopotamia, and Assyria.

A portion of Arabia, the tract about Petra, was also added to the empire under Trajan, by an expedition under the conduct of Cornelius Palma.

36. Trajan, on his return from the East, found his health failing. He was sixty-five years old, and had overtaxed his constitution by the fatigue and exposure which he had undergone in his recent campaigns. He had nominated no successor before quitting Rome, and it was now of the last importance to supply this omission. But regard for the constitutional rights, which it had been his policy to recognize in the Senate, induced him to postpone the formal act as long as possible, and it is uncertain whether he did not delay till too late. The alleged adoption of Hadrian by his predecessor was perhaps a contrivance of the Empress, Plotina, after the death of her husband. It was, at any rate, secret and informal; and the new throne was consequently unstable. But the judicious conduct of Hadrian in the crisis overcame all difficulties; and his authority was acknowledged without hesitation both by the army and the Senate.

Death of Trajan. Difficulties with respect to the succession.

Among special sources for the history of Trajan, the most important are (1) the *Panegyricus* of the younger PLINY; and (2) the correspondence between the same Pliny and Trajan himself, when the former was governor of Bithynia, which forms the Tenth Book of Pliny's *Letters*. This last, a unique remnant of antiquity, gives us an insight which is most valuable, both into the character of the particular emperor and into the general method of Roman administration.

Of modern writers on the reign of Trajan it is only necessary to mention FRANCKE, whose *Geschichte Trajans und seiner Zeitgenossen* (published in 1837) has superseded all former works on the period.

37. Hadrian, who succeeded Trajan in A.D. 117, had a reign of nearly twenty-one years (from August, A.D. 117, to July, A.D. 138). He was forty-two years old at his accession, and had the advantage (as it was now considered) of being childless. Distantly related to Trajan, he had served under him with distinction, and had been admitted to an intimacy both with him and with the Empress. In many features of his character he resembled Trajan. He had the same geniality, the same affable manners, the same power of uniting liberal and even magnificent expenditure with thrift and economy, the same moderation and anxiety to maintain a show of free government. Again, like Trajan, he was indefatigable in his attention to business, and ready to grapple with an infinite multiplicity of details; he was a friend to

Reign of Hadrian, A.D. 117–138.

His character.

literature, and a zealous patron of the fine arts; though lax in his morals, he avoided scandals, and never suffered his love of pleasure to interfere with his duties as prince. He differed from Trajan, partly, in a certain jealousy and irritability of temper, which towards the close of his life betrayed him into some lamentable acts of cruelty towards those about his person; but chiefly, in the absence of any desire for military glory, and a preference for the arts of peace above the triumphs and trophies of successful warfare. Hadrian's reign was marked by two extraordinary novelties: first, the voluntary relinquishment of large portions of Roman territory (Armenia, Mesopotamia, and Assyria), which were evacuated immediately after his accession; and secondly, the continued visitation by the Emperor of the various provinces under his dominion, and his residence for prolonged periods at several provincial capitals. York (Eboracum), Athens, Antioch, Alexandria, were in turns honored by the presence of the Emperor and his court. Fifteen or sixteen years out of the twenty-one years of his reign were occupied by these provincial progresses, which he was the first to institute. Hadrian showed himself manifestly not the chief of a municipality, but the sovereign of an empire. He made no difference between the various races which peopled his dominions. With all he associated in the most friendly way; ascertained their wishes; made himself acquainted with their characters; exerted himself to supply their wants. The great works which he loved to construct were distributed fairly over the different regions of the empire. If Rome could boast his mausoleum, and his grand Temple of Rome and Venus, to Tibur belonged his villa, to Athens his Olympeium, to Britain and the Rhenish provinces his great ramparts, to Tarraco his temple of Augustus, to Nismes (Nemausus) one of his basilicas, to Alexandria a number of his most costly buildings. Hadrian's reign has been pronounced with reason "the best of the imperial series." To have combined for twenty years unbroken peace with the maintenance of a contented and efficient army; liberal expenditure with a full exchequer, replenished by no oppressive or unworthy means; a free-speaking Senate with a firm and strong monarchy, is no mean glory. Hadrian also deserves praise for the choice

He surrenders most of Trajan's conquests.

His choice of a successor.

which he made of a successor. His first selection was indeed far from happy. L. Ceionius Verus may not have deserved all the hard things which have been said of him; but it seems clear that he was a fop and a voluptuary—one, therefore, from whom the laborious discharge of the onerous duties of an emperor could scarcely have been expected. On his death, in A.D. 138, Hadrian at once supplied his place by the formal adoption of T. Aurelius Antoninus, a man of eminent merit, qualified in all respects to bear rule. He would perhaps have done best, had he left to his successor the same power of free selection which he had himself exercised; but the ties of affection induced him to require Antoninus to adopt as sons his own nephew, M. Annius Verus, together with L. Verus, the son of his first choice, L. Ceionius (or, after his adoption, L. Ælius) Verus.

The only wars of any importance during the reign of Hadrian were one with the Roxolani in his second year, A.D. 118, which he terminated by an agreement to pay them an annual subsidy; and one with the revolted Jews, under Barcochebas, which lasted from A.D. 131 to 135. This war ended with the complete defeat of the Jews, their final dispersion, and absolute banishment from Palestine. It was followed by the establishment of Ælia Capitolina as a Roman colony, on the site of Jerusalem.

Our chief sources for the history of Hadrian are his *Life* by SPARTIANUS (contained in the *Historiæ Augustæ Scriptores vi*), and XIPHILINUS's *Epitome* of the Sixty-ninth Book of DIO CASSIUS. Much light is thrown on the period by his coins and inscriptions, which are numerous.

Among special works on the history of this prince, written by moderns, the following are worthy of notice:

WOOG, C. CH., *De eruditione Hadriani Imperatoris et libris ab eo scriptis.* Lipsiæ, 1769; 4to.

FLEMMER, J. M., *De itineribus et rebus gestis Hadriani secundum numorum et scriptorum testimonia.* Havniæ, 1836; 8vo.

GREGOROVIUS, F., *Geschichte des Römischen Kaisars Hadrian.* Königsberg, 1851; 8vo.

38. T. Aurelius Antoninus, the adopted son and successor of Hadrian, ascended the throne in July, A.D. 138. He was fifty-one years old at this time, and reigned twenty-three years, dying A.D. 161, when he had attained the age of seventy-four. It has been said that the people is fortunate which has no history; and this was eminently the condition of the Romans under the first Antonine. Blameless alike in his public and his private life, he maintained the empire in a state of peace and general

Reign of Antoninus Pius, A.D. 138–161.

content, which rendered his reign peculiarly uneventful. A few troubles upon the frontiers, in Egypt, Dacia, Britain, and Mauretania employed the arms of his lieutenants, but gave rise to no war of any magnitude. Internally, Antoninus made no changes. He continued the liberal policy of his predecessors, Nerva, Trajan, and Hadrian, towards the Senate; discouraged delation; was generous in gifts and largesses, yet never exhausted the resources of the treasury; encouraged learning; erected numerous important buildings; watched over the whole of the empire with a father's care, and made the happiness of his subjects his main, if not even his sole, object. Indulgent by temperament and conviction, he extended even to the Christians the leniency which was a principle of his government, and was the first emperor who actively protected them. In his domestic life Antoninus was less happy than his virtues deserved. His wife, Faustina, was noted for her irregularities; his two boys died before his elevation to the throne; and his daughter, Annia Faustina, whom he married to the elder of his adopted sons, M. Aurelius, was far from spotless. He enjoyed, however, in the affection, the respect, and the growing promise of this amiable and excellent prince, some compensation for his other domestic troubles. With just discernment, he drew a sharp line of distinction between the two sons assigned him by Hadrian. Towards the elder, M. Annius (or, after his adoption, M. Aurelius) Verus, he showed the highest favor, marrying him to his daughter, associating him in the government, and formally appointing him his sole successor. In the younger (L. Ælius Verus) he reposed no confidence whatever; he advanced him to no public post; and gave him no prospect, however distant, of the succession.

The troubles, scarcely deserving to be dignified with the name of wars, which ruffled the tranquillity of this reign, were principally (1) A revolt of the Brigantes in Britain, A.D. 140, which was chastised by Lollius Urbicus, who also occupied the tract between the Solway and the Clyde, and erected the barrier drawn from the Clyde to the Forth, which was known as the "Wall of Antonine." (2) A rebellion (probably of the Jews) in Egypt. (3) Troubles in Dacia, complicated perhaps by the simultaneous attacks of a new enemy, the Alani. (4) Disturbances in Mauretania, where the nomads sought to recover lands won by the Romans from the desert. The dates of the Jewish, Dacian, and Mauretanian troubles can not be fixed.

The chief ancient authority for the events of this reign is the *Life of Anto-*

ninus Pius, by JUL. CAPITOLINUS, contained in the *Historiæ Augustæ Scriptores* already quoted (p. 547). This meagre biography is scantily eked out from the *Epitome* of XIPHILINUS, who had before him only a few fragments of Dio, from EUTROPIUS, AURELIUS VICTOR, and FRONTO. The best edition of FRONTO is that of AUG. MAIUS. Mediolani, 1815; 2 vols. 8vo.

Of modern works on the period, the most important is that of the COMTE DE CHAMPAGNY (already mentioned, supra, p. 517), *Les Antonins*, which treats, however, of the entire period from Vespasian to Commodus.

Reign of Marcus Aurelius, A.D. 161–180.

39. M. Aurelius, who took the name of Antoninus after the death of his adoptive father, ascended the throne, A.D. 161, at the age of forty. He reigned nineteen years, from March, A.D. 161, to March, A.D. 180. Although the embodiment of the highest Roman virtue—brave, strict, self-denying, laborious, energetic, patient of injuries, affectionate, kind, and in mental power not much behind the greatest of previous emperors—he had, nevertheless, a sad and unhappy reign, through a concurrence of calamities, for only one of which had he himself to blame. His unworthy colleague, Lucius Verus, was by his own sole act associated with him in the empire; and the anxiety and grief which this prince caused him must be regarded as the consequence of a foolish and undue affection. But his domestic troubles—the loose conduct of his wife Faustina, the deaths of his eldest son and of a daughter, the evil disposition of his second son, Commodus—arose from no fault of his own. Aurelius is taxable with no unfaithfulness to his marriage-bed, with no neglect of the health or moral training of his offspring; still less can the great calamities of his reign, the terrible plague, and the aggressive attitude assumed by the barbarians of the East and North, be ascribed to any negligence or weakness in the reigning monarch. He met the pretensions of the Parthians to exercise sovereignty over Armenia with firmness and vigor; and though here he did not take the field in person, yet the success of his generals and lieutenants reflects credit upon him. When the barbarians of the North began to show themselves formidable, he put himself at the head of the legions, and during the space of fourteen years—from A.D. 167 to his death in A.D. 180—occupied himself almost unceasingly in efforts to check the invaders and secure the frontier against their incursions. Successful in many battles against all his enemies, he nevertheless failed in the great object of the war, which was effect-

ually to repel the Northern nations, and to strike such terror into them as to make them desist from their attacks. From his reign the barbarians of the North became a perpetual danger to Rome—a danger which increased as time went on. But the causes of this change of attitude are to be sought—mainly, at any rate—not within, but beyond the limits of the Roman dominion. A great movement of races had commenced in the lands beyond the Danube. Slavonic and Scythic (or Turanian) hordes were pressing westward, and more and more cramping the Germans in their ancient seats. The Slaves themselves were being forced to yield to the advancing Scyths; and the wave of invasion which broke upon the Roman frontier was impelled by a rising tide of migration far in its rear, which forced it on, and would not allow it to fall back. At the same time, a decline was going on in the vigor of the Roman national life; the race was becoming exhausted; the discipline of the legions tended to relax; long periods of almost unbroken peace, like the reigns of Hadrian and Antoninus Pius, produced a military degeneracy; and by the progress of natural decay the empire was becoming less and less capable of resisting attack. Under these circumstances, it is creditable to Aurelius that he succeeded in maintaining the boundaries of the empire in the north, while he advanced them in the east, where once more Mesopotamia was made a Roman province, and the line of demarkation between Rome and Parthia became the Tigris instead of the Euphrates.

New attitude of the Northern nations.

DETAILS OF THE WARS OF AURELIUS. (1) PARTHIAN WAR, A.D. 162–166. On the accession of Aurelius, the Parthians break the peace by an invasion of Armenia, A.D. 161. Severianus marches against them, but is defeated and slain. Verus, sent to assume the command (A.D. 162), proceeds no farther than Antioch; but Avidius Cassius, prefect of Syria, and Statius Priscus take the offensive. The latter drives the Parthians from Armenia; the former invades Mesopotamia, captures Seleucia, Ctesiphon, and Babylon, burns the royal palace at Ctesiphon (A.D. 165), and forces the Parthians to sue for peace. Peace is granted, A.D. 166, Mesopotamia being ceded to Rome, and Armenia restored to its old condition of a semi-independent monarchy. (2) WAR WITH THE QUADI AND MARCOMANNI, A.D. 167–174. The Quadi and Marcomanni ravage Pannonia, cross the Alps into Italy, and reach Aquileia, A.D. 167. Both emperors proceed against them—they retreat across the Alps. In A.D. 168 the emperors cross the Alps, and, having provided for the defense of the passes, return to Italy. Death of Verus.

The weakness of the Roman efforts in these two years encouraged a general rising of the tribes along the Danube, almost all of whom now took arms, A.D. 169. Aurelius now took post on the Danube, and remained there, summer and winter, for at least three years—probably A.D. 169–172. In A.D. 174 he gains a great victory over the Quadi, ascribed to miraculous rain and lightning. On hearing of the revolt of Cassius, A.D. 175, he makes a peace or truce. (3) WAR WITH THE SARMATIANS, MARCOMANNI, QUADI, etc., A.D. 178–180. The Marcomanni break the peace and gain successes. Aurelius and Commodus proceed against them, A.D. 178. Victory of Paternus, A.D. 179. Death of Aurelius at Vindobona (Vienna), A.D. 180.

The rebellion of Avidius Cassius in Asia was put down without any conflict, Cassius being slain by his own soldiers; but it called Aurelius to the East, where he passed portions of two years, A.D. 175–6.

The special ancient sources for the history of this reign are the *Lives* of M. Aurelius, L. Verus, and Avidius Cassius, in the *Historiæ Augustæ Scriptores*, the two former composed by JUL. CAPITOLINUS, the last by VULCATIUS GALLICANUS. Light is thrown on the character of Aurelius himself, from his correspondence with FRONTO (see p. 549), and his *Meditations* (Τὰ εἰς ἑαῦτον), of which the best edition is probably still that of STANHOPE (London, 1697; 4to). The best edition of the *Historiæ Augustæ Scriptores* is that of JORDAN and EYSSENHARDT (Berolini, 1864; 2 vols. 8vo).

Among modern works on the subject may be mentioned the following:

BACH, N., *De Marco Aurelio Antonino Imperatore philosophante ex ipsius Commentariis scriptio philologica.* Lipsiæ, 1826; 8vo.

WESTENBERG, J. O., *Divus Marcus, seu dissertationes ad Constitutiones M. Aurelii Antonini Imperatoris.* Lugd. Bat., 1736; 4to.

MEINERS, CH., *De M. Aurelii Antonini ingenio, moribus, et scriptis;* in the *Commentationes Societat. Gotting.*, vol. vi.

Return to the principle of hereditary succession. Reign of Commodus, A.D. 180–192.

40. The eighty-four consecutive years of good government which Rome had now enjoyed were due to the practical substitution for the hereditary principle of the power of nominating a successor. This power had been exercised in the most conscientious and patriotic way by four successive rulers, and the result had been most beneficial to the community. But the four rulers had been all childless, or at any rate had had no male offspring; and thus it had not been necessary for any of them to balance a sense of public duty against the feeling of parental affection. With M. Aurelius the case was different. Having a single dearly-loved son, in some respects promising, he allowed the tender partiality of the father to prevail over the cold prudence of the sovereign; and, persuading himself that Commodus would prove a tolerable ruler, associated him in the government (A.D. 177) at the early age of fifteen. Hence Commodus

necessarily succeeded him, having begun to reign three years before his father's death. Few dispositions would have borne this premature removal of restraint and admission to uncontrolled authority. Such a trial was peculiarly unfitted for the weak character of Commodus. Falling under the influence of favorites, this wretched prince degenerated rapidly into a cruel, licentious, and avaricious tyrant. He began his sole reign (March, A.D. 180) by buying a peace of the Marcomanni and Quadi; after which he returned to Rome, and took no further part in any military expeditions. For about three years he reigned decently well, suffering the administration to retain the character which Aurelius had given it. But in A.D. 183, after the discovery of a plot to murder him, in which many senators were implicated, he commenced the career of a tyrant. Delation thinned the ranks of the Senate, while confiscation enriched the treasury. Justice was commonly bought and sold. The ministers, Perennis, prætorian prefect, and after him Cleander, a freedman, were suffered to enrich themselves by every nefarious art, and then successively sacrificed, A.D. 186 and 189. Passing his time in guilty pleasures and in the diversions of the amphitheatre, wherein "the Roman Hercules" exhibited himself as a marksman and a gladiator, Commodus cared not how the empire was governed, so long as he could amuse himself as he pleased, and remove by his warrants all whom he suspected or feared. At length, some of those whom he had proscribed and was about to sacrifice—Marcia, one of his concubines, Eclectus, his chamberlain, and Lætus, prefect of the prætorians—learning his intention, anticipated their fate by strangling him in his bedroom. Commodus was murdered, A.D. 192, after he had reigned twelve years and nine months.

The wars of this reign were unimportant. Clodius Albinus and Pescennius Niger defended Dacia against the attacks of the Sarmatians and Scyths. In Britain, Marcellus Ulpius re-established the Roman authority over the tract between the Solway and the Clyde, which had been again occupied by the barbarians, A.D. 184.

The authorities for the reign of Commodus are (besides the fragments of DIO), his *Life*, by ÆLIUS LAMPRIDIUS, in the *Historiæ Augustæ Scriptores*, and the *History* of HERODIAN, which commences with his accession. (Best edition, that of BEKKER; Berlin, 1826; 8vo.) The regular narrative of GIBBON also here commences.

41. The disorganization of the empire, which commenced as early as Galba, arrested in its natural progress by such wise and firm princes as Vespasian, Trajan, Hadrian, and the two great Antonines, made rapid strides under Commodus, who was too weak and too conscious of his demerits to venture on repressing disorders, or punishing those engaged in them. The numerous desertions, which enabled Maternus to form a band that ravaged Spain and Gaul, and gave him hopes of seizing the empire, the deputation of 1500 legionaries from Britain, which demanded and obtained the downfall of Perennis, and the open conflict between the prætorians and the city cohorts which preceded the death of Cleander, are indications of military insubordination and of the dissolution of the bonds of discipline, such as no former reign discloses to us. It is evident that the army, in which lay the last hope of Roman unity and greatness, was itself becoming disorganized. No common spirit animated its different parts. The city guards, the prætorians, and the legionaries, had different interests. The legionaries themselves had their own quarrels and jealousies. The soldiers were tired of the military life, and, mingling with the provincials, engaged in trade or agriculture, or else turned themselves into banditti and preyed upon the rest of the community. Meanwhile, population was declining, and production consequently diminishing, while luxury and extravagance continued to prevail among the upper classes, and to exhaust the resources of the State. Above all, the general morality was continually becoming worse and worse. Despite a few bright examples in high places, the tone of society grew everywhere more and more corrupt. Purity of life, except among the despised Christians, was almost unknown. Patriotism had ceased to exist, and was not yet replaced by loyalty. Decline and decrepitude showed themselves in almost every portion of the body politic, and a general despondency, the result of a consciousness of debility, pervaded all classes. Nevertheless, under all this apparent weakness was an extraordinary reserve of strength. The empire, which under Commodus seemed to be tottering to its fall, still stood, and resisted the most terrible attacks from without, for the further space of two full centuries.

Increasing disorganization of the Empire.

Some excellent remarks on the general condition of the empire at this period will be found in the concluding chapter of Mr. MERIVALE's *Romans under the Empire.*

SECOND SECTION.

From the Death of Commodus to the Accession of Diocletian, A.D. 193–284.

SOURCES. (1) *Authors:* DIO CASSIUS, as reported in the work of XIPHILINUS (Lib. lxiii.–lxxx), is still our most trustworthy guide for the general history; but this fragmentary production must be supplemented from HERODIAN (see p. 552), and from the *Historiæ Augustæ Scriptores,* as well as from the epitomists, EUTROPIUS, AURELIUS VICTOR, and SEXTUS RUFUS. The works of these last-named writers cover the entire space, whereas DIO's history stops short at his consulate, A.D. 229, and Herodian's terminates at the accession of the third Gordian, A.D. 238. ZOSIMUS (*Historiæ novæ libri sex;* ed. BEKKER, in the *Corpus Hist. Byz.* Bonnæ, 1837); and ZONARAS (*Annales;* ed. PINDER, in the same series. Bonnæ, 1841), are also occasionally serviceable. From A.D. 226 the history of AGATHIAS (ed. NIEBUHR. Bonn, 1828) is of importance. To these various authors may be added the Fragments of DEXIPPUS, whereof there are several collections. The best, probably, is that in the *Fragmenta Historicorum Græcorum* of C. MÜLLER (Paris, 1841–9; vol. iii., pp. 666–687). (2) *Coins and medals,* valuable for the preceding period, are still more useful for this. Works illustrating the History of the Empire from them have been written by

FOY-VAILLANT, J. (*Numismata Augustorum et Cæsarum.* Rome, 1743; 3 vols. folio), and

COOKE, W. (*The Medallic History of Imperial Rome.* London, 1781; 2 vols.).

For representations of the coins, see vol. vii. of the great work of ECKHEL (*Doctrina Nummorum Veterum.* Vindobonæ, 1792; 8 vols. 4to; and compare MIONNET, *Description des Médailles.* Paris, 1806–37; 18 vols. 12mo).

The great modern work on the period is the celebrated *History of the Decline and Fall of the Roman Empire,* by EDWARD GIBBON, of which the best edition is that of Dr. W. SMITH. London, 1854; 8 vols. 8vo. This work, though less accurate and trustworthy than it was formerly thought to be, is still the best on the subject whereof it treats. The sensible reader will make allowance for the unfairness and bias natural in a professed skeptic.

Among other works which, like that of Gibbon, while they embrace the period, go considerably beyond it, may be mentioned:

MONTESQUIEU, *Considérations sur les causes de la grandeur des Romains et de leur décadence,* in his *Œuvres complètes.* Paris, 1718; 5 vols. 8vo. And

SISMONDI, *Histoire de la chute de l'Empire Romain et du déclin de la civilisation.* Paris, 1835; 2 vols. 8vo.

1. The special characteristic of the period on which we now enter is military tyranny—the usurpation of supreme power by the soldiers, who had at last discovered their

General character of the period from Pertinax to Diocletian.

strength, and nominated or removed emperors at their pleasure. Constant disquiet and disturbance was the result of this unhappy discovery—twenty-five emperors wore the purple in the space of ninety-two years, their reigns thus averaging less than four years apiece. Two reigns only during the entire period—those of the two Severi—exceeded ten years. Deducting these, the average for a reign is reduced to two years. It was of course impossible under these circumstances that any renovation of the empire or restoration of pristine vigor should be effected. The internal administration was indeed scarcely a subject of attention. Each emperor was fully occupied by the necessity of maintaining his own power against rival pretenders, generally with as good claims as his own, and resisting the attacks of the barbarians, who were continually increasing in strength and audacity. The few good princes who held the throne exerted themselves mainly to strengthen and invigorate the army by the re-establishment and strict enforcement of discipline. Reform in this quarter was sadly needed; but to accomplish it was most difficult. A strict emperor usually fell a victim to his reforming zeal, which rapidly alienated the affections of the soldiers.

Reign of Pertinax, Jan. 1, to March 28, A.D. 193.

2. The assassins of Commodus, having effected their purpose, acted with decision and promptness. Lætus and Eclectus proceeded to the house of Pertinax, prefect of the city, revealed their deed, and offered him the crown. With a reluctance which may well have been unfeigned, this aged senator, a man of experience in business, and of unblemished character, one of the few remaining friends of M. Aurelius, signified his consent. Influenced by Lætus, the prætorians consented somewhat sullenly to accept him; the Senate, surprised and overjoyed, hailed the new reign with acclamations. But the difficulties of Pertinax began when his authority was acknowledged. An empty treasury required economy and retrenchment, while a greedy soldiery and a demoralized people clamored for shows and for a donative. The donative, which had been promised, was paid; but this necessitated a still stricter curtailment of other expenses. The courtiers and the citizens grumbled at a frugality to which they were unaccustomed;

the soldiers dreaded lest a virtuous prince should enforce on them the restraints of discipline; the "king-maker," Lætus, was disappointed that the ruler whom he had set up would not consent to be a mere puppet. Within three months of his acceptance of power, Pertinax found himself almost without a friend; and when the prætorians, instigated by Lætus, broke out in open mutiny, he unresistingly succumbed, and was dispatched by their swords.

The only special source for the history of Pertinax is his *Life* by JUL. CAPITOLINUS, in the *Hist. August. Scriptores*.

Reign of Didius Julianus, March 28 to June 2, A.D. 193.

3. The prætorians, who had murdered Pertinax, are said to have set up the office of emperor to public auction, and to have sold it to M. Didius Julianus, a rich senator, once governor of Dalmatia, whose elevation cost him more than three millions of our money. Julianus was acknowledged by the Senate, and reigned at Rome for rather more than two months; but his authority was never established over the provinces. In three different quarters—in Britain, in Pannonia, and in Syria—the legions, on learning the death of Pertinax and the scandalous circumstances of Julianus's appointment, invested their leaders, Albinus, Severus, and Niger, with the purple, and declared against the choice of the prætorians. Of the three pretenders, Severus was at once the most energetic and the nearest Rome. Taking advantage of his position, he rapidly led his army across the Alps, advanced through Italy upon the capital, seduced the prætorians by his emissaries, and was accepted by the Senate as emperor. The luckless Julianus was deposed, condemned to death, and executed.

The *Life* of Didius Julianus, by ÆLIUS SPARTIANUS, in the *Hist. August. Scriptores*, is the chief source for his history.

Reign of Septimius Severus, A.D. 193–211.

4. The first act of Severus on obtaining the empire was to disarm and disband the existing prætorians, who were forbidden to reside thenceforth within a hundred miles of the capital. He then addressed himself to the contest with his rivals. First temporizing with Albinus, the commander in Britain, whom he promised to make his successor, he led his whole force against the Eastern emperor, Pescennius Niger, defeated his troops in two great battles, at Cyzicus and Issus, captured him, and

put him to death. He then declared openly against Albinus, who advanced into Gaul and tried the fortune of war in an engagement near Lyons, where he too suffered defeat and was slain. Severus was now master of the whole empire, and might safely have shown mercy to the partisans of his rivals, against whom he had no just grounds of complaint. But he was of a stern and cruel temper. Forty-one senators and great numbers of the rich provincials were executed for the crime of opposing him; and his government was established on a more tyrannical footing than any former emperor had ventured on. The Senate was deprived of even the show of power, and openly oppressed and insulted. The empire became a complete military despotism. In lieu of the old prætorians, a body of 40,000 troops, selected from the legionaries, formed the garrison of Rome, and acted as the Emperor's body-guard. Their chief, the prætorian prefect (*Præfectus prætorio*), became the second person in the kingdom, and a dangerous rival to the sovereign. Not only the command of the guards, but legislative and judicial power, and especially the control of the finances, were intrusted to him. Severus attempted, but without much effect, to improve the general discipline of the legionaries; he also showed himself an active and good commander. His expedition against the Parthians (A.D. 197–8) was, on the whole, remarkably prosperous, the Parthian capital, Ctesiphon, falling into his hands, and Adiabênê being made a dependency. In Britain his arms had no such decisive success; but still he chastised the Caledonians, A.D. 208–9, and extended the limits of the empire in this quarter. His later years were saddened by the unconcealed enmity of his two sons, who were scarcely restrained, by their common dependence upon their father, from an open and deadly quarrel. Determined that neither should be left at the mercy of the other, he associated both in the empire, and recommended both to the army as his successors. He died at York, A.D. 211, at the age of sixty-five, having reigned eighteen years.

Advance of the government towards despotism.

The "Augustan History" contains, besides the *Life* of Severus by SPARTIANUS, *Lives* of Pescennius Niger and Clodius Albinus, the former by SPARTIANUS, the latter by JUL. CAPITOLINUS.

5. The two sons of Severus, Caracallus (wrongly called

Caracalla) and Geta, reigned conjointly for the space of a single year, mutually hating and suspecting one another. At the end of that time, after a fruitless attempt had been made to settle their quarrel by a division of the empire, Caracallus, under pretense of a reconciliation, met his brother Geta in the apartments of the Empress-mother, Julia Domna, and there had him murdered in her arms (Feb. A.D. 212). After this he reigned for five years alone, showing himself a most execrable tyrant. Twenty thousand persons were put to death under the vague title of "friends of Geta;" among them a daughter of M. Aurelius, a son of Pertinax, a nephew of Commodus, and the great jurist Papinian. Caracallus then, made restless by his guilty conscience, quitted Rome never to return, and commenced a series of aimless wanderings through the provinces. He visited Gaul, Rhætia, Dacia, Thrace, Asia Minor, Syria, Egypt, and Mesopotamia, everywhere marking his track with blood, and grievously oppressing the provincials. Knowing himself to be generally hated, he endeavored to secure the affections of the soldiers by combining excessive rewards for service with very remiss discipline, thus doubly injuring the empire. The vigor of the army melted away under his lax rule; and the resources of the State were exhausted by his ruinous profuseness, which led him to devise new and ingenious modes of increasing taxation. It may have been also his desire to gratify his army which induced him to plunge into his great war. In the West he had engaged in no hostilities of importance, having merely when in Gaul made an insignificant expedition against the Alemanni, A.D. 214; but after he had transferred his residence to the East, he determined on an attempt to conquer Parthia. Fixing his head-quarters at Edessa in Mesopotamia, he proceeded to tread in his father's footsteps, crossed the Tigris, took Arbela, and drove the Parthians to seek refuge in the mountains, A.D. 216. Another campaign would have followed; but, before it could begin, Caracallus was murdered by the prætorian prefect Macrinus, who knew his own life to be in danger.

Reign of Caracallus, A.D. 211-217.

In order to extend the incidence of the "succession-tax" (*vicesima hæreditatium*), Caracallus suddenly conferred the rights of citizenship on the whole Roman world. At the same time, he increased the tax from five per cent. to ten.

The *Lives* of Caracallus and Geta, by ÆLIUS SPARTIANUS, contained in the *Hist. August. Scriptores*, form the chief special source for the history of these princes.

6. Macrinus, proclaimed emperor after some hesitation by the soldiers, and acknowledged by the Senate, began his reign by attempts to undo the evil policy of Caracallus, the ruinous effects of which were manifest. He withdrew at once from the Parthian war, which threatened to be tedious and expensive, consenting to purchase peace of the enemy. Not venturing to interfere with the rewards of the existing soldiery, he enlisted recruits upon lower terms. He diminished the burdens of the citizens by restoring the "succession-tax" to its old rate of five per cent. These proceedings were no doubt salutary, and popular with the mass of his subjects; but they were disagreeable to the army, and the army was now the real depository of supreme power. Hence Macrinus, like Pertinax, soon fell a victim to his reforming zeal. The disaffection of the soldiers was artfully fomented by Mæsa, sister of Julia Domna, the late empress, who induced them to raise to the throne her grandson Avitus, or Bassianus, then high-priest of Elagabalus, in the great temple at Emesa (Hems), whom she declared to be a son of Caracallus. Macrinus did not yield without a struggle; but, quitting the field while the battle was still doubtful, he ruined his own cause by his cowardice. Pursued by the soldiers of his rival, he was captured at Chalcedon, brought back to Antioch, and put to death. His son, Diadumenus, on whom he had conferred the title of Cæsar, shared his fate.

Reign of Macrinus, A.D. 217–218.

Two Lives in the *Hist. August. Scriptores* bear upon this reign—that of Macrinus by CAPITOLINUS, and that of Diadumenus by LAMPRIDIUS.

7. Avitus, or Bassianus, on his accession to the throne took the name of M. Aurelius Antoninus, and assumed as an undoubted fact his descent from Severus and Caracallus. The name of "Elagabalus," by which he is generally known, was perhaps also used by himself occasionally, though it is not found upon his coins. His reign, which lasted four years only, is, though not the most bloody, yet beyond a doubt the most disgraceful and disgusting in the Roman annals. Elagabalus was the most effeminate and dissolute of mortals. He openly

Reign of the monster Elagabalus, A.D. 218–222.

paraded his addiction to the lowest form of sensual vice. The contemptible companions of his guilty pleasures were advanced by him to the most important offices of the State. Syrian orgies replaced the grave and decent ceremonies of the Roman religion. A vestal virgin, torn from her sacred seclusion, was forced to be one of his wives. It is astonishing that the Romans, degenerate as they were, could endure for nearly four years the rule of a foreign boy, who possessed no talent of any kind, and whose whole life was passed in feasting, rioting, and the most infamous species of debauchery. Yet we do not find that his gross vices provoked any popular outburst. It was not till he threatened the life of his cousin, Alexander Severus, whom he had been prevailed upon to make "Cæsar," that opposition to his rule appeared, and then it came from the prætorians. These "king-makers" had, it seems, conceived a certain disgust of the effeminate monarch, who painted his face and wore the attire of a woman; and they had become attached to the virtuous Alexander. When, therefore, they found that of the two one must be sacrificed, they mutinied, slew Elagabalus, and placed his cousin upon the throne.

Consult ÆL. LAMPRIDII, *Vit. Antonin. Heliogabali,* in the *Hist. August. Scriptores.*

Reign of Alexander Severus, A.D. 222–235.

8. In Alexander Severus, who succeeded his cousin, A.D. 222, we come upon an emperor of a different type. Carefully educated by his mother, Mammæa, the younger daughter of Mæsa, he presents the remarkable spectacle of a prince of pure and blameless morals cast upon a corrupt age, striving, so far as his powers went, to reform the degenerate State, and falling at length a victim to his praiseworthy but somewhat feeble efforts. It is perhaps doubtful whether at this time any degree of ability could have checked effectually the downward progress of the empire, and arrested the decay that was leading on to absolute ruin. But Alexander, at any rate, did not possess such ability—like his cousin, he was a Syrian, and the taint of weakness was in his blood. However well-intentioned we may consider him to have been, there can be no doubt that he was deficient in vigor of mind, in self-assertion, and in the powers generally which make the firm and good sovereign. He allowed his mother to rule him

throughout his whole reign. He shrank from grappling with the mutinous spirit of the army, and from those stern and bold measures which could alone have quelled insubordination. Hence his reign, though its tendency was towards good, failed permanently to benefit the empire, and can only be regarded as a lull in the storm, a deceitful calm, ushering in a more furious burst of the tempest. It was in vain that Alexander by his simple life set a pattern of frugality; that, by re-establishing the Council of State, he sought to impose limits on his own power; that by deference to the Senate he endeavored to raise it in public esteem, and to infuse into it a feeling of self-respect; that by his intimacy with learned and literary men, he aimed at elevating the gown above the sword. He had not the strength of character to leave his mark upon the world. His attempts at reform failed or died with him. Military license asserted itself the more determinedly for his efforts to repress it, forcing Dio into retirement, and taking the life of Ulpian. Constant mutinies disgraced his reign, and at length, in the German war, the soldiers, despising his military incapacity, drew their swords against the Emperor himself, and murdered him, together with his mother.

WARS OF THIS REIGN. (1) PERSIAN WAR. The great revolution, A.D. 226, by which the Parthian kingdom was brought to an end, and the New Persian Monarchy established in its room (see p. 624), led rapidly to hostilities between Rome and her eastern neighbor. Artaxerxes demanded the restoration to Persia of all her ancient provinces. Alexander Severus met the demand with an invasion, A.D. 231. His troops advanced in three lines, along the Tigris, the Euphrates, and the intermediate region, but were met and checked by the Persians. The war lasted two years. Alexander pretended to have gained a great victory, but appears to have barely held his own. Peace seems to have been made, but on what terms is uncertain, A.D. 233. (2) GERMAN WAR. From the Tigris Alexander passed to the Rhine, A.D. 234, where the German tribes had taken the aggressive, and were plundering Gaul. He stationed himself at Mogontiacum (Mainz), and was killed there early in A.D. 235.

The *Life* of Alex. Severus, in the *Hist. August. Scriptores*, by LAMPRIDIUS, is one of the worst of the series, being almost pure panegyric. HERODIAN is the best authority for his reign. A good estimate of his character will be found in the work of HEYNE, *De Alexandro Severo Judicium;* in vol. vi. of his *Opuscula Academica.*

9. The mutinous soldiers who murdered Severus had acted at the instigation of an officer named Maximin, and this

Reign of Maximin, A.D. 235-238.

man they at once proclaimed emperor. He was by birth a Thracian peasant, and, though he must have shown considerable ability to have obtained the command of a legion, yet he still remained rude and coarse, fierce and brutal, more than half a savage. The cruelties of Maximin, directed against all the noble and wealthy, and still more his constant extortions, soon made him generally detested; and the tyranny of one of his creatures in "Africa" produced a revolt against him in his fourth year—A.D. 238. The people of the province rose up, and made Gordian, their proconsul, together with his son, emperors. With a boldness that nothing but utter despair could have prompted, the Senate ratified their choice. Hearing this, Maximin, who was in winter-quarters at Sirmium on the Danubian frontier, immediately commenced his march towards Italy, hoping to crush his enemies by his promptness. His original rivals, the first and second Gordian, gave him no trouble, being put down by Capellianus, governor of Mauretania, little more than a month after their rebellion. But the Senate, with unwonted energy, supplied their place by two of their own body, Pupienus and Balbinus, and undertook the defense of Italy against Maximin. They garrisoned the towns, laid waste the country, and prepared to weary out the army which they could not venture to meet. The plan succeeded. Maximin, stopped by the resistance of Aquileia, and growing daily more savage on account of his want of success, became hateful to his own soldiers, who rose up against him and slew him, with his son, in his tent. Maximin was killed, probably, in the early part of May, A.D. 238.

Rebellion of the two Gordians, and their death.

Balbinus and Pupienus Emperors.

But little is known of the wars of this reign, which seem, however, to have been important. Maximin, after the death of Severus, remained for nearly two years (A.D. 235–6) on the Rhenish frontier, employed in chastising the Germans. He then removed his head-quarters to Sirmium on the Save, and engaged in a war with the Sarmatians on the borders of Dacia, A.D. 237. From this war he was called off by the news of the Senate's defection.

The "Augustan History" contains *Lives* of Maximin, of the Gordians, and of Pupienus and Balbinus, by JUL. CAPITOLINUS.

10. The triumph of the Senate, which seemed assured by the murder of Maximin, was regarded by the soldiers as fatal to their pretensions; and they soon came to a reso-

Murder of Balbinus and Pupienus.

lution that the Senatorian emperors should not remain at the head of affairs. Already, before the death of Maximin, they had asserted their right to have a voice in the nomination of the supreme authority, and had forced Balbinus and Pupienus to accept at their bidding a third Gordian, grandson and nephew of the former princes of the name, as Cæsar. On the downfall of Maximin, and the full establishment of Pupienus and Balbinus as emperors, they thought it necessary for their interests to advance a step farther. The Senate's nominees were not to be tolerated on any terms; and within six weeks of their triumph over Maximin the prætorians murdered them, and made the third Gordian sole emperor.

Reign of the third Gordian, A.D. 238–244.

11. This unfortunate youth, who at the age of thirteen was elevated to the position of supreme ruler over the entire Roman world, continued to occupy the throne for the space of six years, A.D. 238 to 244, but can not be said to have exercised any real authority over the empire. At first, he was the mere tool of the eunuchs of the palace; after which he fell under the influence of Timesicles, or Timesitheus, whose daughter he married, and who held the office of prætorian prefect. Timesitheus was an able minister; and the reign of Gordian was not unprosperous. He maintained the Roman frontier intact against the attacks of the Persians, A.D. 242, and suppressed an insurrection in Africa, A.D. 240. On his return from the Persian war he was murdered near Circesium by Philip "the Arabian," who had succeeded Timesitheus in the command of the guard.

CAPITOLINUS'S *Life* is the chief authority for this reign (see the *Hist. August. Scriptores*). ZOSIMUS (book i.) is also serviceable.

Reign of Philip, A.D. 244–249.

12. M. Julius Philippus, of Bostra in Arabia (probably a Roman colonist), who was made emperor by the soldiers after they had killed the young Gordian, had a reign of five years only, from A.D. 244 to 249. He concluded a peace with the Persians on tolerable terms, A.D. 244, celebrated the senelar games in commemoration of the thousandth year from the founding of the city, A.D. 248, and defeated the Carpi on the middle Danube, A.D. 245. The notices which we possess of his reign are brief and confused, but sufficiently indicate the growing disorgan-

ization of the Empire. Discontented with their governor, Priscus, Philip's brother, the Syrians revolted, and set up a rival emperor, named Jotapianus. About the same time, the troops in Mœsia and Pannonia, from hatred of their officers, mutinied, and invested with the purple a certain Marinus. These two mock emperors lost their lives shortly; but the Mœsian and Pannonian legions continuing disaffected, Philip sent a senator named Decius to bring them under. The rebels, however, placed Decius at their head, marched on Italy, and defeated and slew Philip at Verona, September, A.D. 249.

The statement of the ecclesiastical historians, that Philip was a Christian, is not altogether unworthy of belief. (See NIEBUHR, *Lectures of Roman History*, vol. iii., Lecture 126.) Origen certainly addressed a letter to him.

13. Decius, made emperor against his will by the Mœsian and Pannonian legions, was gladly accepted by the Senate, which was pleased to see the throne again occupied by one of its own number. His short reign of two years only is chiefly remarkable for the first appearance of a new and formidable enemy—the GOTHS—who invaded the empire in vast force, A.D. 250, traversed Dacia, crossed the Danube, spread devastation over Mœsia, and even passed the Balkan and burst into Thrace. Decius, unsuccessful in A.D. 250, endeavored in the following year to retrieve his ill-fortune, by destroying the Gothic host on its retreat. He was defeated, however, in a great battle near Forum Trebonii, in Mœsia, and, together with his eldest son, whom he had associated in the empire, lost his life.

Reign of Decius, A.D. 249-251.

14. Under these unhappy circumstances, the Senate was allowed to regulate the succession to the empire; which was determined in favor of Gallus, one of the generals of Decius, and of Decius's young son, Hostilianus. Volusianus, the son of Gallus, was also associated in the imperial dignity. The real authority rested, however, with Gallus, whose age and experience placed him far above his colleagues. He commenced his reign by purchasing a peace from the Goths, to whom he consented to pay an annual tribute, on condition of their respecting the Roman frontier, A.D. 252. He then returned to Rome, where he rapidly became unpopular, partly because

Reign of Gallus, A.D. 251-253.

of the disgraceful peace which he had made, partly on account of his inertness amid the fresh calamities which afflicted the unhappy State. Pestilence raged in Rome, and over most of the empire; while fresh hordes of barbarians, incited by the success of the Goths, poured across the Danube. Æmilianus, governor of Pannonia and Mœsia, having met and defeated these marauders, was proclaimed emperor by his army, and, marching upon Rome, easily established his authority. Gallus and his son (Hostilian had died of the plague) led out an army against him, but were slain by their own soldiers at Interamna on the Nar, near Spoletium. Æmilian was then acknowledged by the Senate.

Reign of Æmilian, A.D. 253.

15. The destruction of Gallus and Volusianus was soon avenged. Licinius Valerianus, a Roman of unblemished character, whom Decius had wished to invest with the office of censor, and whom Gallus had sent to bring to his aid the legions of Gaul and Germany, arrived in Italy soon after the accession of Æmilian, and resolved to dispute his title to the crown. The opposing armies once more met near Spoletium, and, by a just retribution, Æmilian suffered the fate of his predecessors, three months after he had ascended the throne.

Reign of Valerian, A.D. 253–260. Calamities of the empire.

16. The calamities of the empire went on continually increasing. On the Lower Rhine there had been formed a confederacy of several German tribes, the Chauci, Cherusci, Chatti, and others, which, under the name of Franks (i. e., Freemen), became one of Rome's most formidable enemies. South of these, the Alemanni, in the tract between the Lahn and Switzerland, had broken through the Roman rampart, absorbed the Agri Decumates, together with a portion of Vindelicia, and assumed from this position an aggressive attitude, threatening not only Gaul but Rhætia, and even Italy. On the Lower Danube and on the shores of the Euxine, the Goths, who had now taken to the sea, menaced with their numerous fleets Thrace, Pontus, Asia Minor, Macedonia, and Greece. Finally, in the remote East, Persia, under its new monarchs, the Sassanidæ, was growing in strength, and extending itself at the expense of Rome towards the north-west. Valerian, already sixty years of age at his accession, felt his inability to grapple with these various dangers, and associated,

in his second year, A.D. 254, his son Gallienus in the empire. But the young prince was no more equal to the occasion than his aged father. The entire joint reign of Valerian and his son (A.D. 254 to 260), as well as the succeeding sole reign of the latter (A.D. 260 to 268), was one uninterrupted series of disorders and disasters. The Franks harried Gaul and Spain at their will, and even passed into Africa. The Alemanni crossed the Rhætian Alps, invaded Italy, and advanced as far on the way to Rome as Ravenna. The Goths occupied Dacia, and, issuing with their fleets from the Cimmerian Bosphorus, ravaged Northern and Western Asia Minor, destroyed Pityus, Trebizond, Chalcedon, Nicomedia, Nicæa, Prusa, Cius, Cyzicus, and Ephesus, overran Greece, took Athens and Corinth, and carried off an immense booty into the regions beyond the Danube. The Persians, under Sapor, conquered Armenia, invaded Mesopotamia, defeated Valerian and took him prisoner near Edessa, advanced into Syria, surprised and burnt Antioch, took Tarsus and Cæsarea Mazaca, and returned triumphant into their own country. At the same time, and in consequence of the general disorganization which these various invasions produced, numerous independent sovereigns started up in different parts of the Roman empire, as Odenathus in the East, who reigned at Palmyra over Syria and the adjacent countries, Posthumus and Victorinus in Gaul, Celsus in Africa, Ingenuus and Aureolus in Illyria, Macrianus in Asia Minor, Piso in Thessaly, Æmilianus in Egypt, etc. These sovereigns—known as the "Thirty Tyrants"—had for the most part brief and inglorious reigns; and their kingdoms were generally as short-lived as themselves. In two quarters, however, a tendency to a permanent splitting-up of the empire was exhibited. The kingdom of Odenathus passed from that prince to his widow Zenobia, and lasted for ten years—from A.D. 264 to 273. The Gallic monarchy of Posthumus showed still greater vitality, continuing for seventeen years, under four successive princes, Posthumus, Victorinus, Marius, and Tetricus. Gallienus, quite incapable of grappling with the terrible difficulties of the time, aimed at little more than maintaining his authority in Italy. Even there, however, he was attacked by Aureolus; and in the war which followed, his own sol

Reign of Gallienus, A.D. 260-268.

Time of the "Thirty Tyrants."

diers slew him as he lay before Milan, into which Aureolus had thrown himself, A.D. 268.

The chief authority for this troublous period is TREBELLIUS POLLIO, whose *Lives* of Valerian, Gallienus, and the "Thirty Tyrants" are contained in the "Augustan History." AURELIUS VICTOR, ZOSIMUS, and ZONARAS must also be consulted. For the Gothic wars the best authority is JORNANDES, *De Getarum sive Gothorum origine et rebus gestis.* Hamburg, 1611; 4to. For the history of the "Thirty Tyrants," the student may consult with advantage MANSO's Dissertation at the end of his *Leben Constantins des Grossen.* Breslau, 1817; 8vo.

Partial recovery of the Roman Empire.

17. From the state of extreme weakness and disorganization which Rome had now reached, a state which seemed to portend her almost immediate dissolution, she was raised by a succession of able emperors, who, although their reigns were unhappily short, contrived at once to reunite the fragments into which the empire had begun to split, and to maintain for the most part the integrity of the frontiers against the barbarians. Claudius, Aurelian, Tacitus, Probus, and Carus — five warlike princes—reigned from A.D. 268 to 283, and in this space of fifteen years, the progress that was made towards a recovery of the power and prestige of Rome is most remarkable.

Reign of Claudius, A.D. 268–270.

M. Aurelius Claudius, the successor of Gallienus, who reigned from A.D. 268 to 270, gained a great victory over the Alemanni in Northern Italy in A.D. 268, and another over the Goths at Nissa in Mœsia, A.D. 269. His successor, L. Domitius Aurelianus, routed an army of Goths in Pannonia, A.D. 270, and effectually checked the Alemanni in North Italy. Bent on reuniting the fragments of the empire, he undertook a war against Zenobia, A.D. 272, and brought it to a happy conclusion the year after. He then turned his arms against the great Western kingdom of Gaul, Spain, and Britain, which was held by Tetricus, and succeeded in re-establishing the authority of Rome over those regions, A.D. 274. He was about to proceed against the Persians, A.D. 275, when he fell a victim to the malice of his private secretary, Eros (or Mnestheus), whose misconduct he had threatened to punish.

Reign of Aurelian, A.D. 270–275.

The "Augustan History" contains a *Life* of Claudius by TREBELLIUS POLLIO, and one of Aurelian by FLAVIUS VOPISCUS.

The splendor of its ruins and the romantic story of its queen, Zenobia, have attached a special interest to Palmyra and its brief life as an independent kingdom. Odenathus, the founder, first distinguished himself by raising an army against Sapor, when that prince had defeated Valerian, and inflicting losses upon him during his retreat. He was acknowledged as a sort of colleague to Gallienus, A.D. 264. Murdered by his nephew, Mæonius, A.D. 267, he was succeeded by his widow, Zenobia, who avenged him by putting Mæonius to death, and ruled from A.D. 267 to 273, as regent for her son Vabalathus. In the reign of Claudius she made an attempt to conquer Egypt, which was unsuccessful, A.D. 269. Aurelian attacked her, A.D. 272, defeated her in two great battles, near Antioch and Emesa (Hems), pursued her to Palmyra, and (A.D. 273) forced her to surrender. The city was mildly treated at first, but, revolting as soon as Aurelian had returned to Europe, was destroyed. Zenobia, transferred to Italy, became a Roman matron.

On the architectural glories of Palmyra the student may consult the following works:

WOOD, R., *The Ruins of Palmyra.* London, 1753; folio. A magnificent work for the time at which it was published. Not superseded by any later one.

ADDISON, C. G., *Damascus and Palmyra.* London, 1838; 2 vols. 8vo.

He abandons Dacia and fortifies Rome.

18. The military glories of Aurelian's reign have thrown into some obscurity his prudential measures; yet to these Rome probably owed as much. He finally relinquished to the Goths and Vandals the outlying province of Dacia, which had proved from the time of its occupation by Trajan nothing but an incumbrance to the empire. The Roman inhabitants were removed across the Danube into Mœsia, a part of which was henceforth known as "Dacia Aureliani." Aurelian also fortified the capital anew, thus securing it from a *coup de main*, which the incursions of the Alemanni had shown to be a real danger. His walls, which were restored by Honorius, continue, with some small exceptions, to be those of the modern city.

On the walls of Aurelian, see BECKER, *De Romæ veteris muris atque portis.* Lipsiæ, 1842; 8vo; and BUNSEN, *Beschreibung der Stadt Rom.* (See p. 388.)

Reign of Tacitus, A.D. 275–276.

19. The assassination of Aurelian was displeasing to the army which he commanded; and the soldiers, instead of allowing any of their officers to assume the purple, applied to the Senate to appoint a new emperor. The Senate hesitated; but, after an interval of six months, complied with the request, and elected M. Claudius Tacitus, one of their body. A pleasing dream was entertained for a few weeks of restoring something like the old

Republic; but the illusion soon vanished. Tacitus was called away from Rome by an irruption of the Alani into Asia Minor, and there perished, six or seven months after his accession, either from weakness or through military violence.

The *Life* of Tacitus, by VOPISCUS, in the *Hist. August. Scriptores*, is the special authority for this reign.

20. On learning the death of Tacitus, Florian, his brother, assumed the imperial dignity at Rome, while the army of the East raised to the purple their general, M. Aurelius Probus. A bloody contest for the empire seemed impending; but it was prevented by the lukewarmness of Florian's soldiers in his cause. Sacrificing their leader, who survived his brother little more than three months, they passed over to his rival, who thus became undisputed emperor. Probus was a warlike, and at the same time a careful and prudent prince, anxious to benefit his subjects, not merely by military expeditions, but by the arts of peace. He delivered Gaul from the German hordes which infested it, and carried the Roman arms once more beyond the Rhine to the banks of the Neckar and the Elbe. The "Agri Decumates" became again a portion of the empire, and the rampart of Hadrian was restored and strengthened. On the Danube Probus chastised the Sarmatians, and by the mere terror of his arms induced the Goths to sue for peace. In Asia Minor he recovered Isauria, which had fallen into the hands of robbers. In Africa he pacified Egypt. The court of Persia sought his alliance. The troubles raised by the pretenders, Saturninus in the East, and Proculus and Bonosus in the West, he suppressed without any difficulty. Among his plans for recruiting the strength of the empire two are specially noticeable—(1) the settlement in most of the frontier provinces of large bodies of captured or fugitive barbarians, Franks, Vandals, Bastarnæ, Gepidæ, etc., and (2) the improvement of agriculture by the drainage of marshy tracts and the planting of suitable localities with the grape. The first of these plans was attended with a good deal of success; the second unfortunately provoked an outbreak which cost Probus his life. He had ventured to employ his soldiers in agricultural labors, which were distasteful to them, and perhaps injurious to their health. On this account they mutinied, seized their arms, and, in a moment of

Reigns of Florian, A.D. 276, and Probus, A.D. 276–282.

passion, stained their hands with his blood. Probus died, A.D. 282, after a reign of six years and six months.

The "Augustan History" contains *Lives* of Florian, Probus, Saturninus, Proculus, and Bonosus, all written by FLAVIUS VOPISCUS, who flourished under Diocletian and Constantine.

21. After murdering Probus, the soldiers conferred the purple on M. Aurelius Carus, prefect of the prætorians, who proclaimed his two sons, Carinus and Numerianus, "Cæsars," and associated the elder, Carinus, in the cares of empire. Leaving this prince to conduct affairs in the West, Carus proceeded at the head of a large army to Illyricum, where he inflicted a severe defeat on the Sarmatians, killing 16,000, and taking 20,000 prisoners; after which he proceeded to Persia, where he carried all before him, overrunning Mesopotamia, and taking Seleucia and Ctesiphon. The complete conquest of Persia was anticipated; but the sudden death of the Emperor—whom different authors report to have been murdered, to have died of disease, and to have been killed by lightning—put a stop to the expedition, and saved the kingdom of the Sassanidæ. Carus died, A.D. 283, after he had reigned a little more than a year. On his death, his son Numerian was acknowledged as emperor.

Joint reign of Carus and Carinus, A.D. 282-283.

22. The year following, A.D. 284, saw the death of Numerian, who was murdered at Perinthus by his father-in-law, the prætorian prefect, Arrius Aper. Carinus still ruled in the West; but the army of the East, discovering the death of Numerian, which was concealed, set up a rival emperor in the person of Diocletian, who slew Aper with his own hand, and, marching westward, defeated Carinus, who was then assassinated by one of his officers, A.D. 285.

Reign of Numerian, A.D. 283-284.

The "Augustan History" concludes at this point with *Lives* of Carus, Carinus, and Numerian, the work of their contemporary, FL. VOPISCUS.

23. The period of extreme military license here terminates. For ninety-two years, from A.D. 193 to 284, the soldiers had enjoyed almost continuously the privilege of appointing whomsoever they pleased to the office of supreme ruler. In a few instances they had allowed a favorite prince—a Severus, a Valerian, a Claudius, a Carus—to nominate an associate or a successor; and on one occasion they had put the nomination unreservedly into

General review of the period.

the hands of the Senate; but generally they had asserted and maintained their right, at each vacancy of the throne, to choose and proclaim the imperator. They had likewise taken upon themselves to remove by assassination even the rulers of their own choice, when they became oppressive or in any way unpopular. Ten emperors had thus perished by military violence in the space of sixty-six years (A.D. 217 to 283), among them the virtuous Alexander, the mild Gordianus, the excellent Probus—and thus every emperor knew that he held office simply during the good pleasure of the troops, and that if he offended them his life would be the forfeit. Such a system was tolerable in only one respect—it tended naturally to place power in the hands of able generals. But its evils far more than counterbalanced this advantage. Besides the general sense of insecurity which it produced, and the absence of any thing like plan or steady system in the administration, consequent upon the rapid change of rulers, it necessarily led to the utter demoralization of the army, which involved as a necessary result the absolute ruin of the empire. The army was, under the imperial system, the "salt" of the Roman world; to corrupt it was to sap the very life of the State. Yet how could discipline be maintained, when every general was bent on ingratiating himself with his troops, in the hope of gaining what had come to be regarded as the great prize of his profession, and every emperor was aware that to institute a searching reform would be to sign his own death-warrant? It was fortunate for Rome that she had powerful enemies upon her frontiers. But for the pressure thus put both upon the men and the officers, her armies would have degenerated much more rapidly than they actually did, and her ruin would have been precipitated.

THIRD SECTION.

From the Accession of Diocletian, A.D. 284, *to the final Division of the Empire,* A.D. 395.

SOURCES. Besides the Epitomists, EUTROPIUS, AURELIUS VICTOR, RUFUS, ZONARAS, and OROSIUS, the most important authorities for this period are, (1) ZOSIMUS, whose *Historia Nova* covers the space between the accession of Macrinus, A.D. 217, and the sixteenth year of Honorius, A.D. 410; (2) AMMIANUS MARCELLINUS, whose eighteen books of *Histories* contain a prolix account of the events which happened between A.D. 353 and 378; and

(3) the obscure authors of the *Panegyrics*, MAMERTINUS, EUMENIUS, NAZARIUS, etc., who must be consulted for the entire period between Diocletian and Theodosius (A.D. 284 to 395). Of inferior importance, yet still of considerable value, are the Christian writers, EUSEBIUS (*Historia Ecclesiastica;* ed. BURTON. Oxoniis, 1856; 8vo, and *Vita Constantini Magni;* ed. HEINICHEN. Lipsiæ, 1830), LACTANTIUS (*Opera.* Biponti, 1786; 2 vols. 8vo), JOHN OF MALALA (in C. MÜLLER'S *Fragm. Hist. Græc.*, vol. iv.), JOHN OF ANTIOCH (in the same collection), SOCRATES, SOZOMEN, THEODORET, EVAGRIUS, etc. The *Armenian History* of MOSES OF CHOREN is occasionally serviceable (see p. 341). Another important source is the *Codex Theodosianus* (ed. SISMONDI. Lipsiæ, 1736-45; 6 vols. folio), which gives the laws passed between A.D. 313 and 438, and the *Codex Justinianus* (ed. KRIEGEL. Lipsiæ, 1844; 3 vols. 8vo), which contains numerous laws of emperors between Hadrian and Constantine. *Coins, medals,* and *inscriptions* are also valuable for the period.

Among modern works treating especially, or inclusively, of the period, are the following:

LE BEAU, *Histoire du Bas-Empire commençant à Constantin le Grand* (continued by AMEILHON). Paris, 1824; 20 vols. 8vo.

GIBBON, *Decline and Fall of the Roman Empire* (see p. 554). Chapters xiii. to xxviii. treat of this period.

NIEBUHR, *Lectures on the History of Rome;* edited by Dr. L. Schmitz. London, 1849; 3 vols. 8vo. Lectures cxxix. to cxxxviii.

Fresh revival of the empire. Second and stronger phase of Imperialism.

1. With the accession of Diocletian the declining empire experienced another remarkable revival, a revival, moreover, of a new character, involving many changes, and constituting a fresh phase of imperialism, which contrasts strongly with the previous one. Power passed away from the hands of the soldiers, and tended to become dynastic; the principle of association, adopted on a wide scale, gave stability to the government; the helm of the State was grasped by firm hands, and various new arrangements were made, all favorable to absolutism. Such restraint as the Senate had up to this time exercised on the despotic authority of the emperors—a restraint slightest no doubt in the cases where it was most needed, yet still in the worst case not wholly nugatory—was completely removed by the departure of the Court from Rome, and the erection of other cities—Nicomedia, Milan, Constantinople—into seats of government. When Rome was no longer the capital, the Roman Senate became a mere municipal body, directing the affairs of a single provincial town; and as its lost privileges were not transferred to another assembly, the Emperor remained the sole source of

law, the sole fountain of honor, the one and only principle of authority. Again, the influence of the prætorians, who, in their fortified camp, at once guarding and commanding Rome, had constituted another check on the absolute power of the princes, ceased with the reforms of Diocletian and Constantine, who respectively diminished their numbers and suppressed them. The Orientalization of the Court, the comparative seclusion of the monarch, and the multiplication of officers and ceremonies, weakened, if it did not even destroy, such little control as public opinion had hitherto exercised over the caprices of the monarch. Above all, the multiplication of emperors and the care taken to secure the throne against such an occurrence as a vacancy, took from the legionaries the power, which they had so long exercised and so much abused, of making and destroying monarchs at their will, and placed the imperial authority almost beyond the risk of danger from military violence.

Establishment of Christianity as the State religion, an infusion of fresh life.

2. While the principle of authority was thus gaining in strength, and the anarchy which had prevailed for more than half a century was giving place to the firm, if somewhat over-despotic, rule of princes who felt themselves secure in their possession of the throne, another quite separate and most important change was taking place, whereby new life was infused into the community. Christianity, hitherto treated as inimical to the State, contemned and ignored, or else down-trodden and oppressed, found itself at length taken into favor by the civil power, being first tolerated by Galerius, after he had vainly endeavored to root it out, and then established by Constantine. As there can be no doubt that by this time the great mass of the intellect and virtue of the nation had passed over to the Christian side, the State can not but have gained considerably by a change which enabled it to employ freely these persons.

Advantages of the Establishment weakened by certain ill results.

3. But scarcely any political change is without its drawbacks. The establishment of Christianity as the State religion, while it alienated those who still adhered to heathenism, tended to corrupt Christianity itself, which persecution had kept pure, turned the attention of the rulers from the defense and safety of the empire to minute questions of heterodoxy and ortho-

doxy, and engaged the civil power in new struggles with its own subjects, whom it was called upon to coerce as heretics or schismatics. Moreover, the adoption of Christianity by a state, all whose antecedents were bound up with heathenism, was like the putting of a "new patch on an old garment," which could not bear the alteration. All the old associations, all the old motives to self-sacrifice and patriotism, all the old watch-words and rallying cries were discredited; and new ones, in harmony with the new religion, could not at once be extemporized. A change of religion, even though from false to true, can not but shake a nation to its very core; and the Roman body-politic was too old and too infirm not to suffer severely from such a disturbance. The change came too late thoroughly to revive and renovate; it may therefore, not improbably, have weakened and helped towards dissolution.

Evils attending the other changes of the period.

4. Nor were the other political changes of the period wholly and altogether beneficial. The partition of the supreme power among numerous co-ordinate emperors was a fertile source of quarrel and misunderstanding, and gave rise to frequent civil wars. The *local* principle on which the partition was made increased the tendency towards a disruption of the empire into fragments, which had already manifested itself (see p. 566). The degradation of Rome and the exaltation of rival capitals worked in the same direction, and was likewise a breaking with the past which could not but be trying and hazardous. The completer despotism gave, no doubt, new vigor to the administration; but it was irksome and revolting to the feelings of many, more especially in the provinces of the West; it alienated their affections, and prepared them to submit readily to a change of governors.

Balance of advantage in favor of the changes.

5. But, if the remedies devised by the statesmen of the Diocletianic period were insufficient to restore the Empire to its pristine strength and vigor, at any rate they acted as stimulants, and revived the moribund State very wonderfully for a space of time not inconsiderable. From the accession of Diocletian to the death of Theodosius the Great (A.D. 284 to 395), is a period exceeding a century. During the whole of it, Rome maintained her frontiers and her unity, rolled back each wave of invasion as it broke upon her, and showed herself superior to

all the surrounding peoples. For the gleam of glory which thus gilds her closing day, must we not regard her as in a great measure indebted to the reforms of Diocletian and Constantine?

Reign of Diocletian and Maximian, A.D. 284–305. Galerius and Constantius "Cæsars."

6. Diocletian was proclaimed emperor by the soldiers, in September, A.D. 284. He defeated Carinus, and entered on his full sovereignty, in the following year. His first public measure (A.D. 286) was to associate in the Empire, under the title of "Augustus," his comrade in arms, Maximian, a man who had risen from the ranks, and who had few merits besides that of being a good general. A few years later (A.D. 292), he completed his scheme of government by the further creation of two "Cæsars," who were to stand to the two "Augusti" as sons and successors. Galerius and Constantius, selected respectively for this important office by Diocletian and Maximian, were both of them active and able generals, younger than their patrons, and well suited to fill the position which was assigned to them. They readily accepted the offers of the two emperors, and, after repudiating their own wives, married respectively the daughter and the step-daughter of their patrons. The Imperial College being thus complete, Diocletian proceeded to a division of the empire analogous to that which had formerly taken place under the triumvirs (see p. 496). Reserving to the elder "Augusti" the more settled provinces, he assigned to the "Cæsars" those which required the care of younger and more active men. Gaul, Spain, and Britain, with the defense of the Rhine against the Germans, were intrusted to Constantius; the Danubian provinces, Noricum, Pannonia, and Mœsia, to Galerius; Italy and Africa to Maximian; while Diocletian himself retained Thrace, Macedon, Egypt, and the East. It was understood, however, that the unity of the empire was to be preserved; the "Cæsars" were to be subordinate to the "Augusti;" and the younger "Augustus" was to respect the superior dignity of the elder. The four princes were to form an imperial "Board" or "College," and were to govern the whole State by their united wisdom.

On the relative position of the "Augusti" and the "Cæsars," the reader may consult a Dissertation by MANSO at the end of his *Leben Constantins des Grossen* (see p. 567).

7. The complex governmental system thus established by Diocletian worked thoroughly well while he himself retained the superintendence of the machine which he had invented. No quarrels arose; the "Cæsars" restrained themselves within the limits set them; and Maximian was always ready to submit his judgment to that of his benefactor. Many dangers from without, and some from within, threatened the State; but they were met with energy and combated with success by the imperial rulers. In Britain, for a while (A.D. 287 to 293), a rebel chief, Carausius, a German probably, defied the Roman arms, and maintained an independent sovereignty; but the authority of Rome was re-established in this quarter (A.D. 296) by the victories of Constantius. Maximian put down the troubles which, as early as A.D. 287, had broken out in Gaul; while at a later date (A.D. 297), Constantius delivered the same province from a furious invasion of the Alemanni. Galerius, after maintaining for many years the honor of the Roman arms upon the Danube, engaged the Persians in the far East, and although at first signally defeated (A.D. 297), made up for his defeat by a great victory in the year following, which led to a peace very advantageous to the Romans. Finally, Diocletian and Maximian subdued revolt in Africa, chastised the Moors and the Egyptians, and put to death the pretenders who had raised the standard of revolt in those regions.

Success of the new system of government. Wars of the period prosperous.

DETAILS OF THE BRITISH AND PERSIAN WARS. (1) BRITISH WAR. Revolt of Carausius, A.D. 287. He is attacked by Maximian and repulses him, A.D. 289. Peace made; Carausius allowed the title of Augustus, A.D. 290. Death of Carausius, who is murdered by his first minister, Allectus, A.D. 293. Allectus becomes king. Landing of Constantius in Britain, A.D. 296. Defeat and death of Allectus, and recovery of the island. (2) PERSIAN WAR. War provoked by the Romans, who seize Armenia and make it over to their vassal, Tiridates, A.D. 286. Armenia recovered by the Persians, A.D. 296. Galerius enters Mesopotamia, A.D. 297, and, after one or two indecisive engagements, is met and defeated by the Persians near Carrhæ (Harran). Having collected a new army, he advances through Armenia upon Assyria, and defeats the Persian king, Narses, in the mountains, A.D. 298. Peace is made the same year, by the cession to the Romans of several small provinces beyond the Tigris, and the enlargement of the dominions of Tiridates.

8. But while success attended the arms of Diocletian and his colleagues against whatever enemy they were turned,

Defects in the internal administration. Persecution of the Christians.

whether foreign or domestic, the results achieved by the internal administration of the empire were less satisfactory. After long consideration, Diocletian determined, towards the close of A.D. 302, to compel uniformity of religion, and for this purpose issued an edict against the Christians (A.D. 303), which led to terrible excesses. Throughout the entire empire, except in the extreme West, where Constantius protected those of the "new religion," one half of the community found itself proscribed; the most relentless persecution followed; thousands were put to death in almost every province; the churches were demolished, endowments confiscated, the sacred books burnt, meetings for worship prohibited, the clergy declared enemies of the State. A war of extermination commenced, to which there seemed to be no end; for, as usual, the "blood of the martyrs" proved the "seed of the Church," and the ranks of the Christians were replenished as fast as they were thinned. A state of things worse than civil war prevailed, authority being engaged in a conflict in which it could not succeed, and being thus brought into disrepute, while the most cruel sufferings were day by day inflicted on the citizens who were least deserving of them.

9. Nor was suffering at this period confined to the Christians. The establishment of four Courts instead of one, and

General suffering from oppressive taxation.

the multiplication of officials and of armies, vastly augmented the expenditure; and a heavy increase of taxation was the necessary consequence. The provinces groaned under the burden of oppressive imposts; which were wrung from the reluctant tax-payer by violence and even by torture. Industry sank beneath a system which left it without reward; production diminished; and the price of all commodities rose. To meet this evil, a futile attempt was made to fix by law a maximum of prices for all the necessaries, and most of the commodities, of life, for corn, wine, and oil, salt, honey, butchers'-meat, vegetables, clothes, fish, fruit, laborers' wages, schoolmasters' and advocates' fees, boots and shoes, harness, timber, and beer. Such an interference with the natural course of trade could only aggravate the evils which it was intended to allay.

The celebrated "Edict of Diocletian," discovered by Col. Leake at Eski-Hissar in Asia Minor, appears to have been issued in A.D. 301. It runs in the name of the four emperors, and fixes the price of all the articles above named, and of many others, in denarii. An excellent edition of the Edict has been published by MOMMSEN, under the title, *Das Edict Diocletians de pretiis rerum venalium.* Leipzig, 1851; 8vo.

Diocletian and Maximian abdicate, A.D. 305: Severus and Maximin are made "Cæsars."

10. The severe illness which afflicted Diocletian in A.D. 304, was probably the chief cause determining him on the most celebrated act of his life—his abdication. His health made rest necessary for him; and he may naturally have desired to preside over the steps which required to be taken in order to secure the continuance of his system after he himself should have quitted life. Accordingly, he formally abdicated his power in A.D. 305, after a reign of twenty-one years, and compelled Maximian to do the same. The two "Cæsars," Galerius and Constantius, became hereupon "Augusti," and should, according to the original design of Diocletian, have respectively succeeded to the provinces of the East and of the West, and have each appointed a "Cæsar" to rule a portion of his dominions. But the partiality of Diocletian for his own "Cæsar" and son-in-law, Galerius, or his conviction that the empire required a *chief* ruler to prevent it from breaking up, produced a modification of the original plan. Galerius, with Diocletian's sanction, appointed both the new "Cæsars," and assigned them their governments, giving to his nephew Maximin, Syria and Egypt; to his friend Severus, Italy and Africa. Constantius simply retained what he already had. Galerius reserved for his own share the entire tract between Gaul and Syria, and was thus master, in his own person or by his deputies, of three-fourths of the empire.

Constantius dies, A.D. 306. Severus is made "Augustus."

11. The new partition of the empire was followed shortly by the death of Constantius, who expired at York, July 24, A.D. 306. On his decease, the legions immediately proclaimed his son, Constantine, his successor. This was an infringement of the new order of things; but Galerius felt himself obliged to condone it, to recognize a legitimate "Cæsar" in the new prince, while he raised Severus to the rank of "Augustus." The harmony of the empire was thus still preserved, in spite of the irregularity which had threatened to disturb it, and the Roman world continued to be still amicably governed by four princes, two of whom were "Augusti" and two "Cæsars."

12. But it was not long before the tranquillity was interrupted. Maxentius, son of Maximian, took advantage of the discontent prevalent in Rome and Italy owing to the loss of privilege and dignity, to raise the standard of revolt, assume the imperial ornaments, and boldly proclaim himself emperor. His father, Maximian, joined him, and resumed the rank of "Augustus." In vain Severus hurried to Rome, and endeavored to crush the insurrection. Abandoned by his troops, he fell into his enemy's hands, and was compelled to end his life by suicide, A.D. 307. In vain Galerius, at the head of all the forces of the central and eastern provinces, sought to impose his will on the rebellious Romans and Italians; after a short campaign he was obliged to retreat without effecting any thing. Maximian and Maxentius, who had allied themselves with Constantine, held their ground successfully against the efforts of their antagonists; and for a brief space the empire was administered peacefully by six emperors, Constantine, Maximian, and Maxentius in the West; in the East, Galerius, Maximin, and Licinius, who had received the imperial dignity from Galerius after the death of Severus.

Revolt of Maxentius; joint rule of six emperors, A.D. 307–309.

13. The inherent evil of the new system of government now began to show itself. First, Maximian and Maxentius quarrelled, and the former was forced to take refuge with Constantine. Then Constantine himself had to defend his position against the intrigues of his father-in-law, and having defeated him, put him to death, A.D. 310. In the next year Galerius perished by the miserable death which has often befallen persecutors; and the rulers of the Roman world were thus reduced to four, Constantine in the West, Maxentius in Italy and Africa, Licinius in Illyricum and Thrace, Maximin in Egypt and Asia. But no friendly feeling now united the members of the Imperial College. War broke out between Constantine and Maxentius in A.D. 312, and between Licinius and Maximin in the year following. In each case the struggle was soon decided. Constantine vanquished his adversary in two battles—one near Verona, the other at the Colline gate—and became master of Rome and Italy. Maxentius perished in the Tiber. Maximin was defeated by Licinius in a single great fight, near Heracleia; but the victory was de-

Wars between the emperors; reunion of the empire under Constantine, A.D. 324.

cisive, being followed shortly by the defeated emperor's suicide. It remained that the two victors, lords respectively of the East and of the West, should measure their strength against each other. This they did in A.D. 314; and after a long and bloody struggle, interrupted by an interval of peace (A.D. 315 to 322), victory declared itself in favor of the Western legions, and Constantine, who is not without reason given the epithet of "the Great," became sole master of the reunited Roman Empire. The defeated Licinius was, as a matter of course, put to death, A.D. 324.

DETAILS OF THE WAR BETWEEN CONSTANTINE AND LICINIUS, A.D. 314 to 324. War provoked by the intrigues of Licinius. First battle at Cibalis on the Save. Licinius, defeated with great loss, escapes with difficulty, A.D. 314. Second battle at Mardia, in Thrace. Constantine again successful. Peace made. Pannonia, Illyricum, Mœsia (or Dacia), Macedonia, and Greece ceded to Constantine. Peace broken by the ambition of Constantine, who is bent on obtaining the whole empire, A.D. 323. Licinius, defeated near Hadrianople, throws himself into Byzantium. Siege of Byzantium and flight of Licinius to Asia. Last battle at Chrysopolis in Bithynia. Licinius, once more defeated, submits, and is put to death, A.D. 324.

Reign of Constantine, A.D. 306–337. He carries out the system of Diocletian.

14. The reign of Constantine the Great is the turning-point of this period of the history. He completed the revolution which Diocletian had begun. By his entire abolition of the prætorians, and conversion of their prefects into purely civil officers, he secured the State as far as was possible from the tyranny of the sword. By the erection of his new capital, and the formal transfer of the seat of government from Rome to Byzantium, he put the finishing stroke to the degradation of the old metropolis, destroyed forever the power of the Senate, and freed the emperors from all those galling restrictions which old constitutional forms and usages imposed upon them. By his organization of the Court on a thoroughly Eastern model, he stamped finally on the later empire the character of Orientalism which attaches to it. Finally, by his new division of the empire into *Prefectures*, and his assignment of different portions of his dominions to his sons and nephews, on whom he conferred the titles of "Cæsar," or "King," he maintained in a modified form the principles of a federated as distinct from a centralized government, and of joint as distinct from sole rule, which was the most original, and at the same time the most doubtful, of Diocletian's conceptions.

An excellent account of the new organization of the empire under Constantine has been written by MARQUARDT, and will be found in BECKER'S *Handbuch der Römischen Alterthümer*, vol. iii., part i. (Leipzig, 1843–64; 5 vols. 8vo). The chief points of the organization were the following:

New arrangement of the provinces.

The whole empire was divided into four prefectures (*præfecturæ*), each under its prætorian prefect (*præfectus prætorio*). These were, I. THE PREFECTURE OF THE GAULS (*præfectura Galliarum*), comprising three *dioceses*, each under a vicar (*vicarius*), those, namely, of (1) Spain, (2) Gaul, or the Seven Provinces, and (3) Britain; which were further subdivided into governments, under consulars (*consulares*) or presidents (*præsides*), seven in Spain, seventeen in Gaul, and five in Britain—Total, 29. II. THE PREFECTURE OF ITALY, comprising likewise three *dioceses*, those of (1) the city of Rome, (2) Italy, and (3) Africa, and subdivided into thirty governments, under consulars, presidents, correctors (*correctores*) or dukes (*duces*), five in Africa, ten in the diocese of the city of Rome, which corresponded to Southern and Central Italy, and fourteen in the Italian diocese, which comprised North Italy, Rhætia, Pannonia, Noricum, and Dalmatia—Total, 30. III. THE PREFECTURE OF ILLYRICUM, divided into two *dioceses*, (1) Dacia, and (2) Macedonia, the former comprising five, and the latter six governments; to which must be further added Achæa, which had its own proconsul. Total number of governments, 12. IV. THE PREFECTURE OF THE EAST (*præfectura Orientis*), which contained five *dioceses*, those of (1) the East (*Orientis*), (2) Egypt, (3) Asia, (4) Pontus, and (5) Thrace; forming altogether forty-six governments, under consulars, presidents, correctors, dukes, and counts (*comites*), fifteen of which were in "the East," or Syria and Mesopotamia, six in the diocese of Egypt, eight in that of "Asia" (Asia Minor), eleven in Pontus, and six in Thrace; while two others were extra-diocesan, those of the Hellespont and the Greek islands. Total, in this prefecture, 48. Grand total of governments in the four prefectures, 119.

Organization of the Court and its officers.

The organization of the Court was as follows: At its head were seven chief officers—(1) the grand chamberlain (*præpositus sancti cubiculi*); under whom was, first, his deputy (*vicarius*), and secondly, the counts of the palace and the bedchamber (*comites palatii* and *cubicularii*), who had the superintendence respectively of the royal table and wardrobe, and were marshalled in four divisions. (2) The chancellor, or "master of the offices" (*magister officiorum*), who was at once a judge and a minister, it being his duty to determine all causes in which persons connected with the Court were concerned, to receive and answer memorials, to direct the ports and arsenals, and to receive the envoys of foreign powers. The business of this important functionary was transacted in four distinct offices (*scrinia*), and employed 148 clerks. (3) The quæstor, an officer who has no correspondent in modern times. He was the organ of the Emperor in legislation, composed and usually suggested his edicts, and resolved the doubts of inferior judges. (4) The treasurer-general, or "count of the sacred largesses" (*comes sacrarum largitionum*), who superintended the collection and disbursement of the revenue, a business conducted in eleven different offices, and employing several hundreds of people. (5) The master of the privy purse (*comes rei principis*), who managed the Emperor's private estate. (6) and (7) The two commanders of the household troops (*comites domesticorum*), the heads respectively of the two bands of cavalry and infantry, which had taken the place of the old prætorians, and watched over the safety of the Emperor. This service was now intrusted almost exclusively to Armenians!

The chief authority for these details is the *Notitia dignitatum utriusque imperii*, of which a good edition has been published by Böcking. (Bonnæ, 1839–53; 2 vols. 8vo.)

Further reforms of Constantine: creation of a nobility.

15. But the reforms of Constantine were not limited by the range of his predecessor's conceptions. He established, not merely at the Court, but throughout the empire, a graduated nobility, the archetype of the modern systems, mainly but not wholly official, composed of three ranks: (1) the "illustrious" (*illustres*); (2) the "respectable" (*spectabiles*); and (3) the "right honorable" (*clarissimi*). To the "illustrious" class belonged (*a*) the consuls during their term of office; (*b*) the patricians, life peers, who received the title of "patricius" at the will of the Emperor; (*c*) the prætorian prefects, six in number, four provincial and two metropolitan—the prefects respectively of Rome and Constantinople; (*d*) the masters-general of the cavalry and infantry; and (*e*) the seven chief officers of the Court, mentioned in the preceding section. Under the head of "respectable" were included (*a*) the proconsuls of Asia, Africa, and Achæa; (*b*) the heads of the thirteen dioceses, whatever their special title, whether vicar, count, or augustal prefect; and (*c*) the second rank of officers in the army, thirty-five in number, of whom ten were "counts" and the remainder "dukes." The subordinate governors of provinces, consulars, presidents, and correctors, together with the other members of the Roman and Constantinopolitan Senates, constituted the class of "right honorables" or "clarissimi."

Reorganization of the army.

Constantine likewise reorganized the Roman army. He multiplied the number and reduced the strength of the legions, which were raised from thirty or thirty-one to a hundred and thirty-two, while the strength of each sank from 6000 to 1000 or 1500. He divided the soldiers into the two classes of "palatines" and "borderers," the former quartered in the chief towns of the empire, the latter stationed upon the frontiers. The whole army he placed under two (later, under four) commanders, called respectively, "master of the horse" (*magister equitum*) and "master of the foot" (*magister peditum*), but each practically commanding mixed armies in the field. Next in rank to them were the various "counts" and "dukes," who acted as lieutenant or divisional generals, and were stationed in the more exposed provinces.

Commencement of the "Indictions."

16. It is not certain that Constantine made any change in the nature or amount of the taxes which the imperial government exacted from its subjects. But the fact that the "era of indictions" dates from a year within his reign (Sept. 1, A.D. 312) would seem to imply that the practice of making a new survey of the empire for financial purposes every fifteen years was commenced by him. The land-tax (*capitatio* or *indictio*), with its supplement, the poll-tax (*capitatio humana* or *plebeia*), the tax on trades (*aurum lustrale*), the indirect taxes, customs, etc., the forced contributions (*aurum coronarium*) were, all of them, imposts of old standing at this time; and it is not easy to see that Constantine added any others. He was probably rigid in his exaction of taxes, and may have been the first to require that all payments to the treasury should be made in gold; but the charge of oppressing his subjects by the imposition of new and unheard-of burdens, which rests upon the sole testimony of the prejudiced Zosimus, is certainly "not proven."

The "era of indictions" did not come into use till the twelfth century, and thus belongs to modern, rather than to ancient, history. But the financial employment of a cycle of fifteen years probably dates from the seventh year of Constantine.

On the general subject of the later Roman taxation the student should consult the great work of SAVIGNY, *Geschichte des Römischen Rechts im Mittelalter*. Heidelberg, 1834–1851; 7 vols. 8vo. Second edition.

Change of the State religion. Heathenism discarded. A partial alliance made with Christianity.

17. But the great change, the crowning reform, introduced and carried through by Constantine was his reformation of religion. Here he did not so much go beyond as directly contradict the ideal of Diocletian. Diocletian, and after him Galerius, had endeavored to destroy Christianity, root and branch, by the fire of persecution. But they had failed; and Galerius had acknowledged the failure by an edict issued from his death-bed, which permitted to the Christians the free exercise of their religion, and invited them to aid the

suffering emperor by their prayers. Galerius, however, and the emperors of his appointment, though they tolerated Christianity, had remained heathens, and had continued to maintain heathenism as the State religion. It remained for Constantine not merely to tolerate, but in a certain sense to establish, the new religion; to recognize its bishops and clergy as privileged persons, to contribute largely towards its endowment, to allow the meetings and give effect to the decrees of its councils, to conform the jurisprudence of the State to its precepts and its practices. Hence the laws against infanticide, against adultery, against pederasty, against rape and seduction passed at this period; hence the edict for the general observance of Sunday, and the new and strong restrictions upon the facility of divorce. Constantine did not indeed, as has sometimes been supposed, proscribe heathenism; he did not shut up the temples, neither did he forbid the offering of sacrifice. But he completely dissociated the State from heathenism, and to a certain extent allied it with Christianity; he stopped all *magisterial* offering of sacrifice; he shut up the temples where the ritual was immoral. Though not a *baptized* Christian till shortly before his death, he threw the whole weight of his encouragement on the Christian side; and the rapid increase in the number of professing Christians, which now set in, must be regarded as in great part the effect of his patronage.

Consequent changes in the jurisprudence.

18. The character of Constantine has been variously estimated, according as his patronage of Christianity has been liked or disliked. The most impartial writers view him as a man in whom vice and virtue, weakness and strength of mind were curiously blended. His military talents and his power of organization are incontestable. His activity, courage, prudence, and affectionateness can not be questioned. But he was less clement and humane than it was to have been expected that the first Christian emperor would have shown himself; he was strangely superstitious; and his religion, so far as it can be gathered from his public acts, his coins, his medals, and his recorded speeches, was a curious medley of Christianity and paganism, which it is not pleasant to contemplate. His character deteriorated as time went on. His best period is

Character of Constantine.

that of his administration of Gaul, A.D. 306 to 312. As he grew older, he became more suspicious, more irritable, more harsh and severe in his punishments. The darkest shadow which rests upon his reign is connected with the execution of his son, Crispus, and his nephew, Licinius, events of the year A.D. 326; but it is impossible to say whether these acts were, or were not, a State necessity—whether they punished a contemplated crime, or were cruelties which had their origin in a wicked and unworthy jealousy. The harmony which subsisted between Constantine and his other sons, and the kindness which he showed towards his half-brothers and their offspring, may reasonably incline us to the belief that in the great tragedy of his domestic life Constantine was rather unfortunate than guilty.

The story that Constantine put to death his second wife, Fausta, on the charge of intriguing with a groom, discredited even by Gibbon, is more than doubtful.

His wars and designs with respect to the succession.

19. The later years of Constantine were troubled by the barbarians of the North and East, who once more assumed the aggressive, and invaded, or threatened to invade, the Roman territory. In the vigor of his youth and middle age he had repelled such attacks in person, defeating the Franks and Alemanni in Gaul, A.D. 309, and the Goths and Sarmatians upon the Danube, A.D. 322. Less active as he approached old age, he employed the arms of his eldest son, Constantine, to chastise the Goths in A.D. 332, and allowed the hostile proceedings of the Persians (A.D. 336) to pass unrebuked. At the same time he made preparations for the succession, in anticipation of his own demise, creating his third son, Constans, and his nephew, Dalmatius, "Cæsars," making another nephew, Hannibalianus, REX, and assigning to these two nephews and his three surviving sons the administration of different portions of his dominions. Constantine died, May 22, A.D. 337, having reigned nearly thirty-one years.

His death, A.D. 337.

The young Constantine was assigned the *præfectura Galliarum;* Constantius the *præfectura Orientis*, excepting Pontus, Cappadocia, and Armenia Minor; Constans the *præfectura Italiæ;* Dalmatius the *præfectura Illyrici.* Hannibalianus received Pontus, Cappadocia, and Armenia Minor for his "kingdom."

Several *Lives* of Constantine the Great have been written. The best is that of

MANSO, J. C. F., *Leben Constantins des Grossen.* Breslau, 1817; 8vo.

The student may also consult with advantage

BURKHARDT, J., *Die Zeit Constantins des Grossen.* Basel, 1853; royal 8vo.

The dealings of Constantine with the Christians and the ecclesiastical aspect of his reign are best given in Dean MILMAN'S *History of Christianity* (3 vols. 8vo, London, 1840), vol. ii.

Joint reign of the three sons of Constantine.

20. The designs of Constantine with respect to the succession were not allowed to take full effect. Troubles followed close upon his decease, which led to the removal of Dalmatius and Hannibalianus, and the murder of most of their near relations and partisans. The three sons of Constantine divided his dominions between them, Constantine retaining the portion assigned him by his father, viz., the Gauls, Constans receiving the share of Dalmatius besides his own, and Constantius absorbing the "kingdom" of Hannibalianus. But the brothers could not long remain at peace among themselves. Constantine, the eldest, discontented with his share, required Constans to relinquish to him the diocese of Africa, and when the latter demurred, invaded his territories and sought to compel the surrender. He had, however, miscalculated his strength, and was easily defeated and slain (A.D. 340). Constans took possession of his government, but, ruling tyrannically, was, ten years later (A.D. 350), conspired against by his generals and ministers, one of whom, Magnentius, assumed the purple, captured and slew Constans, and reigned in his stead. Meanwhile, Constantius was engaged in an unsuccessful war against the Persians under their king, Sapor, who aimed at recovering the provinces ceded to Galerius by his grandfather. Recalled by the dangerous condition of the West, where, besides Magnentius, another officer, Vetranio, general in Illyricum, had been proclaimed emperor, Constantius in the space of three years (A.D. 350 to 353) put down all opposition, forcing Vetranio to abdicate his dignity and retire into private life (A.D. 350), and driving Magnentius, after twice defeating him—at Mursa in Pannonia, A.D. 351, and at Mount Seleucus in Gaul, A.D. 353—to take refuge in suicide. Constantius thus, in the sixteenth year after the death of his father Constantine, reunited under his sole rule the scattered fragments of the Roman world.

Rise and fall of Magnentius, A.D. 350-353.

21. The sole reign of Constantius, which lasted from A.D. 353 to 361, was a period of mixed disaster and success, exhausting to the empire, but not inglorious. His bloody contest with Magnentius had greatly weakened the Roman military force, and exposed the empire almost without defense to the attacks of the barbarians. German tribes had been actually encouraged by Constantius to cross the Rhine, and had planted themselves firmly on its left bank. The Quadi and Sarmatians ceased to respect the frontier of the Danube. In the East Sapor resumed his aggressive operations, and poured his hosts into the Roman province of Mesopotamia. But though the Roman arms sustained many reverses, especially in the East, and though the provinces suffered grievously from hostile inroads, yet on every side the honor of the empire was upheld or vindicated, and no permanent conquest of Roman territory was effected. Constantius repulsed the Quadi and attacked them in their own abodes, A.D. 357; set a king devoted to his interests over the Sarmatæ, A.D. 359; and prevented Sapor from occupying the regions which he overran with his army, A.D. 360. In the West, the efforts of Julian were crowned with still more decided success. The Franks and Alemanni, defeated in a number of battles (A.D. 356 to 358), evacuated their new conquests and retired to the right bank of the Rhine; but even here the vengeance of the Romans followed them. Julian led three expeditions across the great river, ravaged Germany far and wide, and returned into Gaul with a rich booty.

Sole reign of Constantius, B.C. 353–361. His wars.

22. In his relations with the princes of his family Constantius was peculiarly unhappy. At his accession, A.D. 337, he had sanctioned, if he had not even commanded, the massacre of his two surviving uncles and seven of his cousins. Two cousins only, Gallus and Julian, boys of six and twelve respectively, he had spared. Having no male offspring, and having lost his two brothers, who died childless, it was only to these two princes that he could look, if he desired heirs of his own blood and lineage. Accordingly, when the troubles caused by Magnentius summoned him to the West, A.D. 350, he drew forth Gallus from the retirement in which he bred him up, conferred upon him the title of "Cæsar," and intrusted to him the administration

His treatment of his cousins, Gallus and Julian.

of the East. But the ill-trained prince having grievously abused his trust, was in A.D. 354 summoned to appear before Constantius at Milan, and, when he obeyed, was seized while upon his journey, imprisoned and put to death. Shortly afterwards (A.D. 355) Julian was, by the influence of the Empress, Eusebia, advanced to the dignity made vacant by his half-brother's decease and invested with the government of the Gauls; but the Emperor was from first to last jealous of his young kinsman and harsh in his treatment of him. At length, when he found himself about to be deprived of the troops who constituted his sole defense, Julian allowed his soldiers to proclaim him emperor (A.D. 360), and marched eastward to maintain his cause in arms. Another civil war would have followed had not Constantius opportunely died (A.D. 361) and left the throne open to his rival.

His death.

The persecution of the orthodox Christians by Constantius, and his encouragement of Arianism, belong to ecclesiastical rather than to civil history. His reign is the time of "Athanasius contra mundum."

23. Julian, the last prince of the house of Constantine, who succeeded to the undivided empire on the death of Constantius, was a man of unquestionable ability and of nearly blameless moral character; but his reign was a misfortune for the empire. A pagan from conviction, he not only restored Paganism to its old position as the established religion of the State, but endeavored to destroy Christianity by depriving its professors of the advantages of wealth, knowledge, and power, and pertinaciously directing against them every weapon of petty persecution. The success of his enterprise, had it been possible, would have deeply injured the State, since it would have substituted a degraded morality and an effete religion for an ethical system in which even skeptics can find no fault, and a faith whose vitality is evidenced by its continuing to exist and to flourish at the present day. But success was wholly impossible; even a partial success could only have been gained at the expense of a prolonged civil war; and thus the sole result of the emperor's futile attempt was to cause a large amount of actual suffering, to exasperate the two parties against each other, and to prolong a struggle which could only end in one way. The religious counter-

Reign of Julian, A.D. 360-363.

revolution which he designed was altogether a mistake and an anachronism; and it was well for the empire that the brevity of his reign confined the time of suffering and of struggle within narrow limits.

His expedition against the Persians, A.D. 363.

24. Nor was the great military expedition which Julian undertook against the Persians more fortunate in its results than his crusade against the faith of half his subjects. The end at which he aimed—the actual destruction of the Persian empire—was grand, and the plans which he formed for the accomplishment of his object were not ill-devised; but he had underrated the difficulty of his undertaking, and had counted too much on all his plans being carried out successfully. The allies on whose assistance he reckoned—Armenia and Liberia—failed him; his second army, which had been directed to take the line of the Tigris and join him before Ctesiphon, never made its appearance; he himself accomplished without disaster his march along the Euphrates and the Nahr-Malcha to the Persian capital, but he found his forces insufficient to undertake its siege, and after an imprudent delay he was compelled, just as the heats of summer were coming on, to commence his retreat. But the multitudinous enemy hung about his rear, cut off his stragglers, deprived him of supplies, and even ventured, where the ground was favorable, to occupy and interrupt his line of march. Like the Ten Thousand Greeks (see p. 120) in their retreat through the same regions, the Roman army had day after day to fight its way. At length in one of these numerous combats Julian fell. The soldiers, forced to supply his place, created the Christian, Jovian, emperor; and Jovian procured himself a safe retreat from Persia with the remnant of Julian's army by relinquishing the provinces ceded to Galerius in A.D. 248 (see § 7), together with a portion of Mesopotamia.

His death.

The best account of the Emperor Julian and his times is in the work of NEANDER, A., *Ueber den Kaiser Julian und sein Zeitalter.* Leipzig, 1812; 8vo.

Reign of Jovian, A.D. 363–364.

25. The reign of Jovian lasted only a few months—from June, A.D. 363, to February, A.D. 364—but it was long enough to enable him to reverse his predecessor's religious changes, and restore Christian-

ity to its former position. He conducted the army of Julian from the eastern bank of the Tigris to Ancyra in Phrygia, religiously performed the stipulations of his treaty with Sapor, replaced Athanasius on his episcopal throne, and issued an edict of universal toleration. His death, February 17, A.D. 364, was sudden and mysterious, but is most probably to be ascribed to natural causes.

Joint reign of Valentinian and Valens. Valentinian, A.D. 364–375.

26. An interregnum of ten days followed the death of Jovian. At its close the great officials of the empire took upon themselves to nominate a monarch, and selected Valentinian, a Christian and a brave officer, who had served with distinction both on the Rhine and in Persia. The army ratified the choice, but required the new emperor to associate a colleague, being anxious (apparently) to prevent the recurrence of such a time of uncertainty and suspense as they had just experienced. Valentinian conferred the purple on his younger brother, Valens, and committed to his hands the administration of the "præfectura Orientis," reserving the rest of the empire for himself. He fixed his court at Milan, and from this centre, or sometimes from Trèves, he governed with vigor and success, though not without occasional cruelty, the various provinces of the West. In person, or by his generals, he defeated the Picts and Scots in Britain, the Saxons in Northern Gaul, the Franks and Alemanni upon the Rhine, and the Quadi upon the Danube, everywhere maintaining the frontier and defending it by castles and ramparts. He suppressed the revolt of Firmus in Africa, and re-established the Roman authority over Numidia and Mauretania. As early as A.D. 367, he associated his son, Gratian, in the honors of the imperial dignity, but gave him no share in the government. He died at Bregetio, on the Danube, November 17, A.D. 375, when he had reigned between eleven and twelve years.

Valens, A.D. 364–378.

27. Meanwhile, the weaker Valens in the East, cruel, timid, and governed by favorites, with difficulty maintained himself upon the throne which he owed, not to his own merit, but to the affection or the jealousy of his brother. The insurrection of Procopius had nearly brought his reign to an end in the year after his accession, A.D. 365, but was suppressed by the courage and devotion of

the brave and unselfish Sallust. War with the Visigoths, who had embraced the cause of Procopius, followed, A.D. 367, and was concluded by a peace, A.D. 369, of which the barbarians dictated the terms. A campaign against Sapor, A.D. 371, had no result of importance. In the following year there was a conspiracy at Antioch which threatened the life of the Emperor. But the great event of the reign of Valens was the irruption of the HUNS into Europe, and the consequent precipitation on the Roman Empire of the dispossessed Goths, who, received as suppliants and fugitives, were in a little while driven by ill-treatment to declare themselves enemies, and in the two battles of Marcianople and Adrianople proved their superiority over the Roman armies, defeating first the generals of Valens, and then Valens himself, who was slain at Adrianople, with two-thirds of his soldiers, A.D. 378.

That the Huns were Turanians from the steppes of Northern or Central Asia seems to be certain, but their exact race is a point which can never be settled. They were probably either Mongols, Turks, or Oigurs. Their identity with the Hiong-nu, assumed by Gibbon, is disputable. Nothing is known of the causes which led to their migration; but we have sufficient evidence of their appearance as a new nation, about A.D. 370, on the northern shores of the Black Sea, of their conquest of the Alani in the tract between the Wolga and the Don, and of their repeated victories over the Goths under Hermanric and his successor, Withimer. The Gothic kingdom of Hermanric had extended from the Baltic to the Black Sea, comprising South-western Russia, Poland, and Eastern Prussia, and extending over various cognate tribes, of which the two most important were the Ostrogoths (Eastern Goths) and the Visigoths (Western Goths) in the tract between the Theiss and the Dnieper. Driven from their lands by the Huns, the Visigoths first, and the Ostrogoths after them, requested and obtained leave from the Romans to cross the Danube into Mœsia. The numbers of the Visigoths alone have been estimated at a million. The difficulty of feeding such a multitude, and perhaps acts of oppression and extortion on the part of the Roman officials, led to the armed outbreak in which Valens lost his life. The result might have been different if he had waited for the forces of the West, which were marching to his aid at the time when he provoked an engagement.

28. On the death of Valentinian, A.D. 375, he had been succeeded by his son Gratian, a youth of seventeen, who immediately associated in the government his brother, Valentinian II., a boy of five. Gratian, the pupil of the Christian poet, Ausonius, was amiable but weak. So long as the instructors of his youth

Reign of Gratian, A.D. 375–383. Valentinian II. and Theodosius I. associated.

maintained their authority over him, he conducted himself with credit and seemed to be an excellent ruler. Gaul was delivered from the Alemanni under his auspices by the victory of Argentaria (A.D. 378); and the East, which the precipitation of his uncle had prevented him from saving, was wisely placed under the superintendence of Theodosius, whom Gratian raised from a private station to be his colleague, A.D. 379. The prefecture of Illyricum was voluntarily ceded by the Western to the Eastern Emperor. But as advancing manhood emancipated Gratian from control, the natural softness and weakness of his character displayed itself. Unworthy favorites obtained from him the direction of public affairs, and cruelly abused his confidence. Hunting became his passion; and the hours which should have been given to business were devoted to the pleasures and excitement of the chase. The army was neglected and resented its treatment; the indolent emperor was despised; in a short time revolt broke out. Maximus, a Roman settled in Britain, was invested with the purple by the British legions, and passed over into Gaul, with the intention of engaging Gratian. But the Gallic legions refused to fight; and Gratian, quitting Paris, where he held his court, fled to Lyons, and was there overtaken and slain, A.D. 383.

Reign of Maximus, A.D. 383–388.

29. Maximus, successful thus far, obtained an acknowledgment of his dignity from Theodosius, on condition of his acknowledging in his turn the title of Valentinian II., and leaving him in undisturbed possession of the Italian prefecture, which had been made over to him by his brother. But the ambition of the usurper induced him after a few years to break his engagement. In August, A.D. 387, he crossed the Alps, invaded Italy, and drove Valentinian to take refuge in the East. There the great Theodosius, after some hesitation, embraced the cause of his nephew, married his sister Galla, and, defeating Maximus in Pannonia, A.D. 388, replaced the young Valentinian upon the throne.

Second reign of Valentinian II., A.D. 388–392.

30. Valentinian II., who now at the age of eighteen became for the second time emperor, was amiable and weak, like his brother. He allowed a subject, Argobastes, a Frank by race, to obtain a position in the kingdom similar to that occupied by the

"mayors of the palace" under the Merovingian kings of France; and then, becoming aware of his own want of authority, attempted to remove him, but in vain. Argobastes asserted his power, refused to lay down his office, and after a few days murdered his master, A.D. 392, and placed a creature of his own, one Eugenius, upon the throne.

Reign of Eugenius, A.D. 392–394.

31. The new emperor was not acknowledged by Theodosius, whose natural indignation at the contempt shown for his arrangements was stimulated by the prayers and tears of his wife, Galla, the sister of the murdered monarch. After temporizing for some months, while he collected a formidable force, the Eastern emperor invaded the provinces of the West, defeating his rival by the help of his own troops near Aquileia, and caused his head to be struck from his shoulders, A.D. 394. The Frank, Argobastes, became a fugitive, and soon afterwards terminated his life by suicide.

Reign of Theodosius I. (the Great), A.D. 379–395. He subjects the Goths.

32. The reign of Theodosius in the East runs parallel with those of Gratian, Maximus, Valentinian II., and Eugenius in the West, commencing A.D. 379, in the fourth year of Gratian, and terminating A.D. 395, the year after the death of Eugenius. It is a reign which surprises us by its wonderful vigor. Theodosius truly deserved the name of "Great." By a combination of patience and caution with vast military skill, he in the course of five years (A.D. 379 to 384) effectually reduced the hordes of the Visigoths to subjection, converted them from enemies into subjects, and was able to use their swords against his other adversaries. It was no doubt an evil that these barbarians, and the Ostrogoths also, after their defeat in A.D. 386, were settled within the limits of the empire, in Mœsia, Thrace, Illyricum, and Asia Minor; since they were not sufficiently civilized to amalgamate with the other subjects of the State. But Theodosius had only a choice of evils. If he had not given the barbarians settlements, he would have driven them to despair; and more was to be feared from their despair than even from their fickleness and turbulence. Theodosius himself kept the Goths quiet while he lived. He employed them with good effect against Maximus and Eugenius. If his successors had had his talents, the new subjects of the empire might, very possibly, have

been kept under control, and have become its strength instead of proving its weakness.

His persecution of pagans and heretics.

33. The vigor of Theodosius, which was employed with such good effect against the Goths, and against the usurpers who troubled the repose of the West, found another and more questionable vent in the regulation of the faith of his subjects and in earnest and prolonged efforts to establish uniformity of religion. A qualified persecution of heathenism had been sanctioned by some previous emperors. Theodosius broadly forbade all exercise of the chief rites of the old pagan religion under the extreme penalty of death; shut up or destroyed the temples; confiscated the old endowments; and made every act of the worship penal. Towards heretics he acted with equal decision, but with somewhat less harshness. The Arians and other sects condemned by the Councils of Nice (A.D. 325) and Constantinople (A.D. 381) were compelled to relinquish their churches, vacate their sees, and make over their endowments to the orthodox; they were forbidden to preach, to ordain ministers, and even to meet for public worship; but the penalty in case of disobedience rarely went beyond a fine or exile, and practically the penalties were very seldom enforced. The administration of Theodosius was very much less severe than his laws; and to judge him from his code alone would give a false idea of his character.

His clemency and severity.

34. Still Theodosius can not be wholly absolved from the charge of violence and cruelty. His temper was capricious; and, while upon some occasions he exhibited an extraordinary degree of clemency and gentleness under extreme provocation, as when (in A.D. 387) he pardoned the insolence of Antiochenes, yet on others he allowed the fury which opposition awoke in him to have free course, and involved the innocent and the guilty in one sweeping sentence of punishment. The most notable example of this culpable severity is to be found in the famous massacre of the Thessalonians, for which he was compelled to do penance by St. Ambrose (A.D. 390).

Final division of the empire.

35. The victory of Theodosius over the usurper, Eugenius, A.D. 394, had made him master of the West, and reunited for the last time the whole of the Roman world under the sceptre of a single monarch. But the

union did not last longer than a few months. It had come to be an accepted principle of the imperial policy that the weight of the internal administration, and the defense of the frontiers against the barbarians, was a burden beyond the powers of any single man. From the accession of Diocletian the Roman world had been governed, excepting on rare occasions, by a plurality of princes; and it had been the usual practice to partition out the provinces among them. Theodosius, therefore, had no sooner defeated Eugenius, than he sent for his younger son, Honorius, a boy of eleven, and prepared to make over to him the Western Empire. Soon afterwards, finding his end approaching, he formally divided his dominions between his two sons, leaving the East to Arcadius, the elder, and the West to Honorius, whom he placed under the guardianship of the general Stilicho.

Theodosius's death.

Theodosius expired at Milan in the fiftieth year of his age and the sixteenth of his reign, January 17, A.D. 395.

A *Life* of Theodosius was written in the seventeenth century by FLÉCHIER, bishop of Nismes (Paris, 1679; 4to); but it can not be recommended to the student. A better idea of the time will be derived from the work of

MUELLER, P. E., *De genio sæculi Theodosiani.* Havniæ, 1798; 2 vols. 8vo.

FOURTH SECTION.

History of the Western Empire from the Accession of Honorius, A.D. 395, *to the Deposition of Romulus Augustus,* A.D. 476.

SOURCES. For the reign of Honorius ZOSIMUS is our chief authority; but his prejudiced history must be supplemented and often corrected from the works of the poet CLAUDIAN (ed. KÖNIG, Gottingæ, 1808; 8vo), who is however too eulogistic. Both for this and for the subsequent period, the *Epitome* of OROSIUS, and the *Chronicles* of PROSPER and MARCELLINUS are of service. JORNANDES, the Gothic historian (see p. 567), rises in importance, as the history of the Goths becomes more and more closely intermixed with that of the Romans. The ecclesiastical historians, SOCRATES, SOZOMEN, THEODORET, etc., and the chronologers, IDATIUS, ISODORUS, etc., have an occasional value. Other authors will be mentioned under particular heads.

No modern writers of repute have specially treated this last and saddest period of the history of Rome. The student must consult GIBBON, chaps. xxix. to xxxviii., and NIEBUHR, *Lectures on the History of Rome*, lectures cxxxv. to cxxxviii. He may also with advantage compare MILMAN, *History of Latin Christianity* (London, 1854; 5 vols. 8vo); books ii. and iii.

1. Hitherto the East and West, if politically separate governments, had been united by sympathy, by the mutual

Last period of the Western Empire, A.D. 395–476.

lending and receiving of assistance, and by the *idea*, at any rate, that in some sense they formed one empire. With Arcadius and Honorius this idea begins to fade and disappear; relations of friendship between the governments are replaced by feelings of jealousy, of mutual repulsion, of suspicion, distrust, and dislike. Hence the disruption of the empire is ordinarily dated from this time, though the separation was really so gradual that the historian acts somewhat arbitrarily in fixing on any definite point. There is, however, none better than the date commonly taken; and, as the Eastern or Byzantine Empire belongs confessedly to Modern and not to Ancient History, the fortunes of the Western Empire will alone be followed in this concluding section of the history of Ancient Rome.

Estrangement between the East and West.

2. The origin of the estrangement between the East and West appears to have been the mutual jealousy and conflicting pretensions of Rufinus, the minister of the Eastern, and Stilicho, the general and guardian of the Western emperor. This jealousy cost Rufinus his life, and rendered the relations between the two states unsatisfactory. The ill-will was brought to a head, when the Goths of Mœsia and Thrace, having revolted under Alaric, instead of being sternly repressed by the Eastern emperor, were treated with and induced to remove to a region from which they threatened Italy. When ALARIC was made by Arcadius master-general of the Eastern Illyricum, A.D. 398, it was felt at once that the West was menaced; and the dreadful invasions which followed were ascribed, not without some show of reason, to the connivance of the Emperor of the East, who, to save his own territories, had let the Goths loose upon his brother's. The first invasion, in A.D. 402, carried devastation over the rich plains of Northern Italy, but was effectually checked by Stilicho, who completely defeated Alaric in the battle of Pollentia (March 29, A.D. 403) and forced him to retire into Illyricum. The second invasion, A.D. 408, was more disastrous. The empire had lost the services of Stilicho, who had been sacrificed to the jealousy of an ungrateful master. Alaric marched upon Rome, and formed the siege of the city, but after some months consented to spare it on the receipt of an enormous ransom, A.D. 409.

Invasions of the Goths under ALARIC.

He then sought to come to terms with Honorius, who had fixed his court at Ravenna; but, being insulted during the negotiations, he broke them off, once more marched on Rome, starved the city into submission, and entered it as its master, A.D. 410. A puppet emperor was set up in the person of a certain Attalus, who was however, after a few months, again degraded by Alaric to a private condition. The court of Ravenna still refusing the terms of peace which Alaric offered, he finally, in August, A.D. 410, resolved to push hostility to the utmost. Advancing a third time upon Rome, he took and sacked the city, overran Southern Italy, and made himself master of the whole peninsula from the walls of Ravenna to the Sicilian sea. The Roman Empire of the West would probably have now come to an end, had not death overtaken the bold Goth in the midst of his conquests. His brother-in-law, Adolphus, who succeeded him, had neither his talents nor his ambition. After exhausting Southern Italy by plunder and ravage for the space of two years, he made peace with Honorius, accepted his sister, Placidia, in marriage, and withdrew his army from Italy into Gaul, A.D. 412.

Sack of Rome, A.D. 410.

3. Nor were the sack of Rome and the devastation of Italy by the Goths the only calamities which afflicted the empire during this miserable period. The invasion of the combined Vandals, Suevi, Burgundians, and Alani, under Rhadagaisus (A.D. 405), which carried fire and sword over the regions between the Alps and the Arno, would have been regarded as a misfortune of the first magnitude, if it had not been thrown into the shade by the more terrible visitation of the Goths. Stilicho, indeed, with consummate generalship, defeated this formidable host, slew Rhadagaisus, and forced the remainder of his army to retire. Italy, after suffering ravage through its whole extent from the wild and savage hordes of Sarmatia and Germany, was by the year A.D. 412 cleared of all its invaders, and was once more ruled in peace by the son of Theodosius. But, if no worse calamity than utter exhaustion was inflicted on the centre of the empire, a sadder fate began to overtake the extremities, from which Rome withdrew her protection, or which were torn from her by the barbarians. The remnant of the host of Rhadagaisus, Van-

Other troubles. Invasion of Rhadagaisus. Loss of provinces.

dals, Burgundians, and others, after quitting Italy, passed into Gaul (A.D. 406), overran the region between the Rhine and the Pyrenees, and took possession of a broad tract which became known as "Burgundy." Passing thence into Spain, they carried all before them, spreading themselves over the entire peninsula from the Pyrenees to the straits of Gibraltar. In Southern Gaul and Spain they were shortly followed by the Goths, who, under Adolphus, crossed the mountains, drove the Vandals into Gallicia and Bætica (thence called *Vandal*usia or Andalusia), and established in Spain and Aquitaine the "Kingdom of the Visigoths," which, although for a time (A.D. 414 to 418) nominally subject to Rome, became under Theodoric I. (A.D. 418) completely independent. About the same time Britain was finally cut adrift from the empire. In Gaul the Franks followed the example of the Burgundians, and, crossing the Lower Rhine, established themselves in the region about Cologne and Trèves. Thus almost the whole of the *prefectura Galliarum* passed out of the hands of the Romans, who retained nothing west of the Alps but the province of Gallia Lugdunensis.

Revolts and usurpations.

4. It is not surprising that during this troublous period Honorius found his right to the throne disputed by pretenders. Besides Attalus (see § 2), there arose in Africa a Moorish usurper, named Gildo, who assumed the government of the "Five Provinces," A.D. 398, but was defeated by the Romans under Mascezel, Gildo's brother. In Britain a Constantine was proclaimed emperor, A.D. 407, who associated on the throne his son, Constans, and extended his dominion at one time (A.D. 408 to 409) over the greater portion of Gaul and Spain; but after the revolt of his general, Gerontius, in the last-named province, he was defeated and put to death by Constantius, one of Honorius's commanders, A.D. 411. A second revolt occurred in Africa under Count Heraclian, A.D. 413. Assuming the purple, he ventured to invade Italy, but was defeated in the neighborhood of Rome, and, on returning to his province, was put to death by his indignant subjects. After the death of Constantine, the sovereignty of Roman Gaul was assumed by Jovinus, A.D. 412, who associated on the throne his brother, Sebastian; but these usurpers were easily put down by the Gothic leader, Adolphus, A.D. 413. The latter years of Ho-

norius (A.D. 413 to 423) were free from troubles of this kind. The weak prince strengthened himself by marrying his sister, Placidia, the widow of the Gothic chief, Adolphus, to Constantius, his successful general, and associating the latter in the government, A.D. 421. Constantius, however, reigned only seven months, and he was soon followed to the tomb by his unhappy colleague, who died of a dropsy, August 27, A.D. 423, without making any arrangements for the succession.

Reign of John the "Secretary," A.D. 423-425.

5. The vacant throne was seized by John, principal secretary of the late emperor; but Theodosius II., who had succeeded his father, Arcadius, in the Empire of the East, refused to acknowledge the usurper; and claimed the throne for his infant nephew, Valentinian, the son of Constantius and Placidia. A naval and military expedition, which he sent to Italy, was at first unsuccessful; but, after a while, signs of disaffection appeared among the Italian soldiers, who preferred a monarch descended from the great Theodosius to an unknown upstart. Treachery opened the gates of Ravenna to the Eastern army, and John, delivered into the hands of his enemies, was beheaded at Aquileia, A.D. 425.

Reign of Valentinian III., A.D. 425-455.

6. The nephew of Honorius, who was now raised to the throne, was a child of no more than six years of age. He was therefore placed under the guardianship of his mother, Placidia, who administered the empire from A.D. 425 to 450. The government of an infant and a woman was ill suited for a kingdom placed in desperate circumstances, and precipitated the ruin which had long been visibly impending. The jealousy felt by the general Aëtius towards Boniface, Count of Africa, and the unworthy treatment of the latter, drove him into rebellion, induced him to invite over the Vandals from Spain, A.D. 428, and led to the loss of the African diocese, and the establishment of a Vandal kingdom in that region by the renowned GENSERIC, A.D. 429 to 439. Family arrangements connected with the betrothment of Valentinian to Eudoxia, daughter of Theodosius II., had even before this (A.D. 425) detached from the West and made over to the East the provinces of Pannonia, Noricum, and Dalmatia. Excepting for some precarious possessions in Gaul and Spain, the Western Empire

was now confined to the three countries of Vindelicia, Rhætia, and Italy. The sword of Aëtius maintained with tolerable success the dimensions of Roman Gaul against the attacks, from opposite sides, of the Visigoths and the Franks, A.D. 435 to 450; but his contest with the latter brought into the field a new foe, the terrible ATTILA, king of the Huns, who, professing to embrace the cause of a fugitive Frankish king, crossed the Rhine into Gaul at the head of a vast army, and spread devastation far and wide over the country. The Romans and Visigoths were forced into a temporary alliance, and united their arms against the Scyth. On the field of Châlons the question was tried and determined (A.D. 451), whether the predominance of power in Western Europe was to fall to the Tatars or to the Teutons, to a savage race, heathen, anarchical, and destructive, or to one which had embraced Christianity, which had aptitudes for organization and law, and could construct as well as destroy. The decision was, fortunately, in favor of the Teutons. Attila retreated beyond the Rhine; and although in A.D. 452 he endeavored to retrieve his failure, invading Italy, and spreading desolation over the whole plain of the Po, yet it was only to retreat once more to his palace in the wilds of Hungary. The year following, A.D. 453, he burst a blood-vessel, and died suddenly; and the West was delivered from all peril of becoming the prey of Tatar hordes. Two years later, Valentinian also lost his life, being murdered, A.D. 455, by Maximus, whose wife he had dishonored, and the retainers of Aëtius, whom, on grounds of suspicion, he had executed.

The history of Attila has engaged the pens of several able writers. Among them may be noticed

MUELLER, J., *Attila, der Held des fünften Jahrhunderts.* Leipzig, 1806; 8vo.

KLEMM, G. F., *Attila nach der Geschichte, Sage, und Legende dargestellt.* Berlin, 1827; 8vo.

HERBERT, DEAN, *Attila, King of the Huns: a Poem.* London, 1838; 8vo. The Notes to this work are elaborate and highly valuable.

Reign of Maximus, March 16 to June 12, A.D. 455.

7. Maximus, the murderer of Valentinian III., succeeded him as emperor, but reigned less than three months (March 16 to June 12, A.D. 455). Anxious to strengthen his hold upon the throne by connect-

ing himself with the royal house of Theodosius, he married his son, Palladius, to the daughter of Valentinian, and forced Eudoxia, Valentinian's widow, and daughter of Theodosius II., to become his wife. The outraged matron implored the aid of Genseric, whose fleet commanded the Mediterranean; and the bold Vandal, greedy after the spoil of Italy, readily responded to her call. His landing at Ostia was the signal for the Romans to rise against their sovereign, in whom they saw the author of their calamities; but the murder of the Roman emperor failed to propitiate the Vandalic king, whose mind was intent upon plunder. Despite the intercession of Pope Leo, Genseric entered Rome with his troops, and gave it up to them to pillage for fourteen days. Whatever Attila had left was now carried off. Eudoxia and her two daughters were made prisoners and borne away to Carthage. Even the churches were not spared. All that yet remained in Rome of public or private wealth, of sacred or profane treasure, was transported to the vessels of Genseric, and removed to Africa.

Rome plundered by Genseric.

8. This terrible calamity so paralyzed the Romans, that they appointed no emperor in the place of Maximus. When, however, the news that the throne was vacant reached Gaul, Avitus, the commander of the legions there, induced his soldiers to proclaim him; and, as he was supported by the Visigoths of Western Gaul and Spain, Rome and Italy for a brief space acknowledged him as their sovereign. But Italian pride chafed against the imposition of a monarch from without; and Count Ricimer, a Goth, who commanded the foreign troops in the pay of Rome, disliked the rule of an emperor in whose appointment he had had no hand. Avitus was therefore required to abdicate, after he had held the throne a little more than a year; he consented, and, laying aside the imperial office, became Bishop of Placentia, but died within a few months of his abdication, whether by disease or violence is uncertain.

Reign of Avitus, A.D. 455-456.

9. It was evidently the wish of Count Ricimer to assume the crown which he had forced Avitus to resign; but he saw that Rome was not yet prepared to submit herself to the rule of a barbarian, and he therefore, after an interval of six months, placed an

Interregnum. Reign of Majorian, A.D. 457-461.

emperor on the throne in the person of Majorian, who ruled well for four years, from A.D. 457 to 461. Majorian, who was a man of talent and character, addressed himself especially to the struggle with the Vandals of Africa, whose constant depredations deprived Italy of repose. Not content with chastising the disorderly bands which ravaged his coasts, he prepared to invade the territory of Genseric with a fleet and army. These were collected at the Spanish port of Carthagena; but the emissaries of Genseric secretly destroyed the fleet; and Majorian, having returned to Italy, was, like Avitus, forced to abdicate, Count Ricimer being jealous of his *protégé*, and desirous of appointing an emperor of inferior ability.

Rule of Ricimer, A.D. 461–467. Severus nominally Emperor from A.D. 461–465.

10. The imperial title and ensigns were now conferred on a puppet named Severus, who served as a convenient screen, behind which Count Ricimer concealed the authority which he himself really wielded. But Severus dying at the end of four years, A.D. 465, Ricimer at length felt himself sufficiently strong to take openly the sole and entire direction of the affairs of Italy. He respected Roman prejudices, however, so far as to abstain from the assumption of the imperial name. His position was a difficult one, for the Emperor of the East looked coldly on him, while he was exposed to constant attack from the powerful fleets of Genseric and Marcellinus, the sovereigns of Africa and Dalmatia, and had further to fear the hostility of Ægidius, Roman commander in Gaul, who refused to acknowledge his authority. The peril of his situation compelled him, two years after the death of Severus, A.D. 467, to apply for aid to the Eastern emperor, Leo, and to accept the terms on which that prince was willing to succor him. The terms were galling to his pride. Italy was required by Leo to submit to a sovereign of his choice, which fell on Anthemius, a Byzantine nobleman of distinction.

Reign of Anthemius, A.D. 467–472.

11. The establishment of Anthemius as "Emperor of the West" was followed by a serious effort against the terrible Vandals, who were now the enemy from whom Italy suffered the most. Alliance was made between Leo, Anthemius, and Marcellinus; and while the Dalmatian fleet protected Italy and retook Sar-

dinia, two great expeditions were directed by the Eastern emperor upon Carthage, A.D. 468. One of these, starting from Egypt, attacked Tripoli, surprised the cities of that province, and proceeded along the coast westward. The other, which consisted of 1113 ships, having on board 100,000 men, was directed upon Cape Bona, about forty miles from Carthage, and should at once have laid siege to the town. But Basiliscus, the commander, allowed himself to be amused by negotiations while the cunning Genseric made preparations for the destruction of the fleet, which he accomplished by means of fire-ships, thus entirely frustrating the attack. The remnant of the expedition withdrew; Genseric recovered Sardinia, and shortly afterwards established his power over Sicily, thus obtaining a position from which he menaced Italy more than ever before. But the "Empire," as it was still called, was to be subverted, not by its external, but its internal foes. Though Ricimer had consented to the nomination of Anthemius as emperor, and had bound himself to his cause by accepting his daughter in marriage, yet it was not long before discord and jealousy separated the professed friends. As Anthemius had fixed his court at Rome, Ricimer retired to Milan, whence he could readily correspond with the barbarians of Spain, Gaul, and Pannonia. Having collected a considerable army, he marched to the gates of Rome, proclaimed Olybrius, the husband of Placidia (youngest daughter of Valentinian III.), emperor, and, forcing his way into the city, slew Anthemius, and established Olybrius upon the throne (July 11, A.D. 472).

Reigns of Olybrius, Glycerius, Nepos, and Romulus Augustus, A.D. 472–476.

12. The Western Empire had now, in the space of sixteen years, experienced the rule of six different sovereigns. In the four years of continued existence which still remained to it, four other "emperors" were about to hold the sceptre. The first of these, Olybrius, retained his authority for little more than three months, ascending the throne, July 11, and dying by a natural death, October 23. The chief event of his reign was the death of Count Ricimer, who expired forty days after his capture of Rome, August 20, leaving the command of his army to his nephew, Gundobald, a Burgundián. Gundobald gave the purple, in A.D. 473, to Glycerius, an obscure soldier; but the Eastern emperor, Leo, interposed for the second time,

and assigned the throne to Julius Nepos, the nephew of Marcellinus, and his successor in the sovereignty of Dalmatia. Nepos easily prevailed over Glycerius, who exchanged his imperial dignity, A.D. 474, for the bishopric of Salona; but the new emperor was scarcely settled upon the throne, when the barbarian mercenaries, who were now all-powerful in Italy, revolted under the patrician Orestes, A.D. 475, and invested with the purple his son, Romulus Augustus, called, by way of contempt, "Augustulus." Augustulus, the last of the Western emperors, reigned less than a year (October 31, A.D. 475 to August 23, A.D. 476). The mercenaries, shortly after his accession, demanded one-third of the lands of Italy, and, when their demand was refused, took arms under the command of their German chief, Odoacer, slew Orestes, the Emperor's father, and deprived Augustulus of his sovereignty. The dignity of Emperor of the West was then formally abolished; and Odoacer ascended the throne as the first barbarian "King of Italy."

Duration of the Empire. Causes of its decline and fall.

13. The history of the Western Roman Empire here terminates. The Empire had endured 507 years (B.C. 31 to A.D. 476), under seventy-seven princes. Attaining its greatest magnitude in the reign of Trajan, when it extended from the Pillars of Hercules and the Friths of Forth and Clyde to the Caspian and the Persian Gulf, it had gradually broken up and contracted its limits, until it had come to be almost confined to Italy. Its ruin had been caused partly by internal decay, but mainly through the repeated invasions of vast hordes of barbarians. Goths, Vandals, Huns, Burgundians, Suevi, Alani, Alemanni, Franks, Heruli had precipitated themselves in a ceaseless succession on the regions which Roman civilization had turned into gardens, and poured in a resistless torrent over province after province. The force of the attack fell mainly upon the West. After the first rush of the Goths across the Lower Danube, in the time of Valens, the tide of migration took wholly a westerly course. Pannonia, Spain, Africa, most of Gaul, were occupied by the invaders. Italy attracted each more powerful spoiler, and host after host desolated its fertile plains. Rome herself was taken repeatedly, and was sacked twice, by Alaric and by Genseric. She felt that she needed all her resources for her own defense, and was

therefore obliged to relinquish such outlying provinces as no foe had captured. Hence, Britain, parts of Gaul, Vindelicia, and probably Rhætia, were abandoned: Pannonia, Noricum, and Dalmatia were parted with; at last, nothing remained but Italy; and Italy could not undertake to defend herself. Her rulers had long ceased to put any trust in Italian soldiers, and had drawn their recruits from the outlying provinces rather than from the heart of the empire. Finally, they had thought it excellent strategy to take the barbarians themselves into pay, and to fight Huns with Goths, and Goths with Burgundians or Vandals. But this policy at last proved fatal. The barbarians, perceiving their strength, determined to exert it, and to have Italy for themselves. It was more pleasant to be masters than servants. The imperial power had in fact been long existing upon sufferance; the edifice was without due support, and it only needed the touch of a finger to make it fall. What Odoacer did, Ricimer might have done with as much ease; but the facility of an enterprise is not always apparent beforehand.

PART II. HISTORY OF PARTHIA.

Geographical Outline of the Parthian Empire.

Extent of the empire.

1. THE Parthian Empire at its greatest extent comprised the countries between the Euphrates and the Indus, reaching northward as far as the Araxes, the Caspian, and the Lower Oxus, and southward to the Persian Gulf and the Indian Ocean. It thus covered, in the main, the same ground with the Persian empire of Cyrus and with the original kingdom of the Seleucidæ; but it was less extensive than either of those great monarchies. It did not include Syria, or Phœnicia, or Palestine, or Armenia, or any portion of Asia Minor, nor does it seem to have comprised the valley of the Upper Oxus, much less that of the Jaxartes. Its greatest length, between the Euphrates and the Indus, may be estimated at about one thousand nine hundred miles, while its greatest width, between the Lower Oxus and the Indian Ocean, may have equalled, or a little

exceeded, a thousand miles. Its area can not have fallen much short of a million square miles.

2. But of this vast space a very large proportion was scarcely habitable. The Mesopotamian, Persian, Kharesmian, Gedrosian, and Carmanian deserts occupy at least one-half of the region between the Euphrates and the Indus; and, though not absolutely incapable of supporting human life, these tracts can at the best sustain a very sparse and scanty population. Such possessions add but little to the strength of the empire which comprises them, and thus may be omitted from consideration when we seek to form an estimate of its power and resources. About half a million square miles remain when we have deducted the deserts; an area only one-third of that of Rome (see p. 503), but still very much larger than that of any modern European state excepting Russia.

Large area occupied by deserts.

3. The Parthian Empire was, like most others, divided into provinces. Of these the most important were, in the west, Mesopotamia and Babylonia; in the mid-region, Atropatênê, Media, Assyria, Susiana, and Persia; towards the east, Parthyênê or Parthia Proper, Hyrcania, Margiana, Aria, Zarangia, Carmania, Sacastanê, Arachosia, and Gedrosia. Other minor divisions were Chalonitis, Cambadênê, Mesênê, Rhagiana, Choarênê, Comisênê, Artacênê, Apavarcticênê, etc. It will be observed that the main provinces were for the most part identical, in name at any rate, with provinces of the old Persian Empire, already described in this work (see pp. 30–35). As, however, even in provinces of this class certain changes have often to be noted in respect of boundaries, or principal towns, it seems best to run briefly through the entire list.

Division into provinces.

i. *Mesopotamia.* The name of Mesopotamia was applied by the Parthians, not to the whole region between the Tigris and Euphrates rivers, but only to the upper portion of it—the tract bounded on the north by the Mons Masius, and on the south by a canal uniting the two streams a little above the 33d parallel. Its chief cities were Anthemusia, Nicephorium, Carrhæ, Europus, Nisibis, and Hatra.

Mesopotamia.

ii. *Babylonia* lay below Mesopotamia, extending to the confluence of the Euphrates and Tigris, and including a tract

Babylonia. of considerable size and importance on the right bank of the former river. Its chief towns were Seleuceia on the Tigris, Babylon, Borsippa, and Vologesia.

iii. *Mesênê*, called also Characênê, was the tract below Babylonia, reaching to the shores of the Persian Gulf. Its capital was Charax Spasini, at the confluence, probably, of the Kuran with the Euphrates. The only other city of any importance was Teredon or Diridotis, on the Gulf, at the mouth of the Euphrates. Mesênê was famous for its thick groves of palm-trees.

Mesênê.

iv. *Susiana* had nearly its old boundaries and dimensions (see p. 34). Its chief cities were Susa and Badaca.

v. *Assyria*, according to the nomenclature of the Parthian period, designated a tract which lay wholly to the east of the Tigris, extending from Armenia on the north to Susiana on the south, and interposed between Mesopotamia and Media Magna. It was divided into numerous districts, among which the most important were Cordyênê (the country of the Kurds) in the north, Adiabênê, the tract about the two Zab rivers, Arbelitis, the region about Arbela, Chalonitis, the country about Holwan, and Apolloniatis or Sittacênê, the tract upon the lower course of the Diyaleh river. In this district was situated Ctesiphon, the capital of the whole empire. Other important towns were Arbela, the capital of Arbelitis, Apollonia, the old capital of Apolloniatis, and Artemita, in the same region, which became under the Parthians, Chalasar.

Assyria.

vi. *Atropatênê* lay between the northern part of Assyria (Cordyênê) and the western shore of the Caspian, thus corresponding nearly to the modern Azerbijan. Its chief city was Gaza or Gazaca (afterwards Canzaca), now *Tahkt-i-Suleïman*. Atropatênê was not so absolutely a part of the Parthian Empire as most of the other provinces. It was a fief over which the Parthian monarch claimed a sort of feudal supremacy; but was governed by its own princes, who were sometimes not even appointed by the Parthian king.

Atropatênê.

vii. *Media* lay south and south-east of Atropatênê, extending from the Kizil Uzen and the Caspian on the north, to about the 32d parallel towards the south, where it adjoined on Susiana and Persia. It contained

Media.

several districts, of which the chief were Media Inferior, Media Superior, Cambadênê, and Rhagiana. The chief towns were Ecbatana (now Hamadan), Bagistana (Behistun), Concobar (Kungawur), Aspadana (Isfahan), Rhages or Europus (Kaleh Erij), and Charax.

Persia.

viii. *Persia*, like Susiana, retained its old dimensions and boundaries, except that it had ceased to be regarded as comprising Carmania, which was reckoned a distinct country. After the destruction of Persepolis by Alexander, Pasargadæ seems to have been the chief city.

Carmania.

ix. *Carmania* adjoined Persia upon the east. It extended from the Persian Gulf to about the 33d parallel, thus including a large portion of the desert of Iran. The chief town was Carmana (now Kerman).

Parthia.

x. *Parthyênê*, or Parthia Proper, lay north of Carmania and west of Media Magna. It comprised the old country of the name, together with most of the desert which in early times was known as Sagartia. (See p. 31.) Among its subdivisions were Choarênê, Comisênê, Artacênê, Tabiênê, etc. The capital city was Hecatompylus. Other important towns were Apameia in Choarênê, near the Caspian Gates, and Parthaunisa, or Nisæa (Nishapur).

Hyrcania.

xi. *Hyrcania* was north of Parthia, being the tract at the south-eastern corner of the Caspian, along the course of the river Gurgan. Its chief cities were Syrinx, Tapé, on the shore of the Caspian, Carta (perhaps the earlier Zadracarta), Talabrocé, and Samariané.

Margiana.

xii. *Margiana* was situated east and north-east of Parthia and Hyrcania, in the low plain between the Elburz range and the Sea of Aral. It lay along the course of the river Margus (now the Murg-ab). The only city in Parthian times was Antiocheia (Merv ?).

Aria.

xiii. *Aria* included the district which bore the same name under the Persians (see p. 32), but comprised also the tract between Herat and the Hamoon or Sea of Seistan. Its chief city was Artacoana (Herat). Other towns of some consequence were Phra (Furrah), Gari (Girisk), and Bis (Bist).

Zarangia.

xiv. *Zarangia*, or Drangiana, had come to be used in a narrower acceptation than the ancient one. (See p. 32.) It was now only a small tract close upon the Hamoon, the district upon the Haroot-rud and Furrah-rud being reckoned to Aria, and that on the Lower Helmend being separated off, and forming the new province of Sacastané. The chief town of Zarangia was Prophthasia.

Sacastané.

xv. *Sacastané* lay south of Zarangia, corresponding to the Segestan of the Arabian geographers, which is now known as Seistan. Its chief cities were Sigal and Alexandropolis. Sacastané (i. e., the land of Sacæ) had probably been occupied by a colony of Scyths in the interval between Alexander's conquests and the formation of the Parthian Empire.

Arachosia.

xvi. *Arachosia* (or "White India," as the Parthians called it) seems to have been identical with the country known by the same name to the Persians. (See p. 32.) It lay east of Sacastané, and corresponded nearly with the modern Kandahar. The capital was Alexandropolis, on the Arachotus (Arghand-ab). Its other chief cities were Demetrias, Pharsana, and Parabesté.

Gedrosia.

xvii. *Gedrosia* retained in the main its ancient limits, which were nearly those of the modern Beluchistan (see p. 32). It was, however, perhaps somewhat encroached upon towards the north by Sacastané. The province lay south of this tract and of Arachosia and east of Carmania.

HISTORICAL SKETCH OF THE PARTHIAN EMPIRE.

FIRST PERIOD.

From the Foundation of the Kingdom, about B.C. 255, *to the Creation of the Empire by Mithridates or Arsaces VI., about* B.C. 174.

SOURCES. The sources for the history of Parthia are scanty and scattered. Of native sources, we possess only a very incomplete series of coins, generally without dates and without the special name of the king; and a few mutilated inscriptions. No classical author, so far as we know, ever treated of the history of Parthia as a whole; and few ever made Parthian history, in any of its portions, even a special subject of attention. ARRIAN'S *Parthica* was a mere account of the Parthian War of Trajan, written from a Roman point of view; and of this work there only remain about twenty short fragments. (See the fragments collected in C. MÜLLER'S *Fragmenta Hist. Græcorum*, vol. iii., pp. 586–591.) STRABO'S account of the Parthian manners and customs in the sixth book of his *Historical Memoirs*, and the second book of his

Continuation of Polybius, would have been most interesting; but these works have wholly perished. The extant writer who tells us most about the Parthians is JUSTIN; but this careless historian has most imperfectly reported his authority, TROGUS POMPEIUS, and needs perpetual correction. For the earlier history we are reduced to scattered notices in STRABO, ARRIAN, JUSTIN, POLYBIUS, LUCIAN, and PHLEGON of Tralles; for the middle portion, from the time of Phraates III. to Vonones I., we have APPIAN in his *Mithridatica* and *Syriaca*, JUSTIN, PLUTARCH in his *Lives* of Lucullus, Pompey, Crassus, and Antony, JOSEPHUS in his *Antiquitates Judaicæ*, and DIO CASSIUS (bks. xxxv., lv.); for the later history, from Vonones to the destruction of the monarchy, our authorities are TACITUS in his *Annals*, JOSEPHUS, SUETONIUS, HERODIAN, the *Historiæ Augustæ Scriptores*, and, above all, DIO (bks. lvi.–lxxviii.).

Modern works treating specially on the subject of Parthian history are not very numerous. The best are the following:

FOY-VAILLANT, J., *Arsacidarum Imperium, sive Regum Parthorum Historia ad fidem numismatum accommodata.* Parisiis, 1725; 4to.

DU FOUR DE LONGUERUE, *Annales Arsacidarum.* Argentorat., 1732; 4to.

RICHTER, C. F., *Historisch-kritischer Versuch über die Arsaciden und Sassaniden-Dynastien.* Göttingen, 1804; 8vo.

TYCHSEN, T. C., *Commentationes de nummis Persarum et Arsacidarum*, published in the *Commentationes novæ Societat. Scient. Gotting.*, vols. i. and iii.

Abstracts of the history are given in Dr. SMITH'S *Dictionary of Greek and Roman Biography*, sub voc. ARSACIDÆ, and by Mr. CLINTON in his *Fasti Romani.* Oxford, 1845–50; 2 vols. 4to. (See vol. ii. pp. 243–250.)

Foundation of the kingdom about B.C. 255.

1. Parthia, which, in the earlier times of the Persian monarchy, formed a portion only of a large satrapy extending from the Iranic desert to the Jaxartes, and from the Caspian to Samarcand, appears towards the close of the Persian period to have constituted a satrapy by itself (or with the mere addition of Hyrcania), in which condition it was continued by the successors of Alexander. Tranquillity was preserved till about B.C. 255, when the weakness of Antiochus Theus, and the success of the Bactrian rebellion (see p. 342), encouraged the Parthians to rise against their Greek masters, and to declare themselves an independent people. Their leader in the revolt was a certain Arsaces. This person was the commander of a body of Scythian Dahæ from the banks of the Ochus, who migrated into Parthia, and obtaining the ascendency in the country, raised their general to the position of king. There was, probably, sufficient affinity between the immigrant Dahæ and the previous inhabitants of the region for the two

races readily to coalesce; both appear to have been Turanian; and the Dahæ were so completely absorbed that we hear nothing of them in the subsequent history. The names of "Parthia" and "Parthian" prevailed; and the whole nation presents to us one uniform type.

Character of the people.

2. This type is one of a low and coarse character. The manners of the Parthians, even at the height of their power, had a tinge of Tatar barbarism. Their mimetic art was rude, compared, not only with that of the Greeks, but even of the Persians. In their architecture they imitated the heavy and massive constructions of the Babylonians. Their appearance was repulsive. They were treacherous in war, indolent and unrefined in peace. Still they possessed qualities which fitted them to become a ruling nation. They were brave, enterprising, and fond of war; while they had also a certain talent for organization and administration. They are not ill-represented by the modern Turks, who are allied to them in race, and rule over some of the same countries.

Reign of Arsaces I., about B.C. 255–253.

3. Arsaces, the first king, reigned, we are told, only two years, probably from B.C. 255 to 253. He occupied himself chiefly in consolidating his dominion over the Parthians themselves, many of whom resisted his authority. Antiochus Theus, whose rule he had subverted, seems to have made no effort to recover his hold on Parthia, being too much engaged in his war with Ptolemy Philadelphus. (See p. 251.) Arsaces, however, appears to have fallen in battle.

Reign of Arsaces II. (Teridates I.), about B.C. 253–216.

4. The first Arsaces was succeeded by his brother, Teridates, who had assisted him in his original revolt. He took the title of Arsaces after his brother's death; and the practice thus begun passed into a custom, which continued to the very close of the empire. Teridates, or Arsaces II., reigned thirty-seven years, from B.C. 253 to 216. He made himself master of Hyrcania, probably about B.C. 240, thereby drawing upon himself the hostility both of Seleucus Callinicus, whom he deprived of a province, and of Diodotus I. of Bactria, who became alarmed at the increasing power of his neighbor. Callinicus and Diodotus, accordingly, made common cause; and the former led an expedition against Teridates, B.C. 237, which alarmed

him so that at first he fled from Parthia into Scythia. Diodotus I., however, dying and being succeeded by his son, Diodotus II., Teridates found a means of breaking up the alliance, and drew over the Bactrian prince to his side. A great battle followed; and, Callinicus being signally defeated, Parthian independence was regarded as at length fully established.

In JUSTIN'S *Epitome* of the History of Trogus Pompeius the acts of the first and second Arsaces are assigned to a single monarch. He is to be corrected from SYNCELLUS, who followed ARRIAN.

Reign of Arsaces III., about B.C. 216–196.

5. Teridates was succeeded by a son, whose real name is unknown, but who reigned as Arsaces III. Pursuing the aggressive policy of his father, he overran Eastern Media, and threatened to conquer the entire province, about B.C. 214. Antiochus the Great, upon this, marched against him (B.C. 213), drove his troops from Media, took his capital, Hecatompylus, and pursuing him into Hyrcania, there brought him to an engagement, the issue of which was doubtful. Arsaces greatly distinguished himself; and the Syrian monarch, finding the conquest of the new kingdom impossible, came to terms with his foe, confirming him in the possession of both Parthia and Hyrcania, but probably requiring him to furnish a contingent to his projected Eastern expedition, B.C. 206. It is uncertain how long Arsaces III. lived after this; but the best authorities assign him a reign of about twenty years—from B.C. 216 to 196.

Reign of Priapatius (Arsaces IV.), about B.C. 196–181.

6. Priapatius (Arsaces IV.) now became king, and reigned for fifteen years—from about B.C. 196 to 181. He appears to have been an unwarlike prince, and to have been content with maintaining, without any attempt to extend, his dominions. The Bactrian monarchs of this period were aggressive and powerful (see pp. 343, 344), which may in part account for this pause in the Parthian conquests. Priapatius left two sons, Phraates and Mithridates, the former of whom succeeded him.

Reign of Phraates I. (Arsaces V.), about B.C. 181–174.

7. Phraates I. (Arsaces V.) had a short reign, probably from about B.C. 181 to 174. Nothing is known of him excepting that he extended his dominions by the conquest of the Mardi, one of the most powerful tribes of the Elburz, and, though he had many

children, left his crown to his brother, Mithridates, whom he regarded as peculiarly fitted for the kingly office. Mithridates justified this opinion by the extensive conquests of which an account will be given in the next section. He transformed the small kingdom which he received from Phraates into a vast and flourishing empire, and established the governmental system on which that empire was thenceforth administered.

SECOND PERIOD.

From the Foundation of the Empire by Mithridates I., about B.C. 174, *to the Commencement of the Wars with the Romans,* B.C. 54.

Reign of Mithridates I. (Arsaces VI.), about B.C. 174–136.

1. The Parthian dominion had hitherto been confined to a comparatively narrow territory between the Caspian Gates on the one hand and the districts of Aria (Herat) and Margiana (Merv) upon the other. The neighboring Bactria, with its Greek princes (see pp. 342–344) and its semi-Greek civilization, had been a far more powerful state, and had probably acted as a constant check upon the aspirations of its weaker sister. Conscious of their weakness, the Parthian monarchs had cultivated good relations with the Bactrians; and, so far as appears, no war had hitherto broken out between the conterminous powers. But with the accession of Mithridates I. (Arsaces VI.) this state of things came to an end. The Bactrian princes were about this time directing their arms towards the East, bent on establishing their authority in Affghanistan and North-western India. It would seem that while their main strength was employed in this quarter, the provinces nearer home were left without adequate defense, and tempted the cupidity of the Parthians. Mithridates I., who was contemporary with Eucratides of Bactria, began aggressions on the Bactrian kingdom, probably soon after his accession. Success attended his efforts, and he deprived Eucratides of at least two provinces. A few years later, on the death of Antiochus Epiphanes, B.C. 164, he turned his arms against the West. After a protracted struggle, he succeeded in reducing Media to obedience. He then conquered Susiana, Persia, and Babylonia, extending his dominion on this side as far as the lower course of the Euphrates. Nor did these gains content him. After the death of Eucratides

(about B.C. 160), he resumed his war with the Bactrians, and completely destroyed their kingdom. In vain did these unfortunately isolated Greeks implore the help of their Syrian brethren. Demetrius Nicator, who in B.C. 140 endeavored to relieve them, was defeated and made prisoner by Mithridates, who retained him in captivity till his own death, about B.C. 136.

The Indian conquests of Mithridates I., which rest on the authority of Diodorus and Orosius, are extremely doubtful. Trogus appears to have known nothing of them.

2. The satrapial system, which had been introduced by the Persians, and continued by Alexander and his successors, was not that adopted by Mithridates in the organization of his empire. On the contrary, he reverted to the older and simpler plan, which prevailed in the East before the rise of the Persians to power. This was to allow each nation to have its own native king, its own laws and usages, and simply to require the subjection of all these monarchs to the chief of the ruling nation as lord paramount, or feudal head. Hence the title "King of Kings," so common on the Parthian coins from the time of Mithridates. Each "king" was bound to furnish a contingent of troops when required, and likewise an annual tribute; but otherwise they were independent.

Organization of the empire.

3. The constitution under which the Parthians themselves were ruled was a kind of limited monarchy. The king was permanently advised by two councils, one consisting of the members of his own royal house, the other of the great men (μεγιστᾶνες), comprising both the temporal and spiritual chiefs of the nation (the σοφοὶ and the μάγοι). The monarchy was elective, the kings, however, being necessarily taken from the family of the Arsacidæ. When the *megistanes* had nominated a monarch, the right of placing the diadem on his head belonged to the surena, or field-marshal. The *megistanes* claimed a right to depose a monarch who displeased them; but any attempt to exercise this privilege was sure to lead to a civil war, and it was force, not law, which determined whether the prince should retain or forfeit his crown.

Constitution of Parthia.

4. The Parthians affected, in the main, Persian customs. The same state and dignity were maintained by the Arsaci-

Manners and customs, art, etc.

dæ as by the Achæmenidæ. The Court migrated at different seasons of the year to Ctesiphon, Ecbatana, and Hyrcania. Polygamy was practised on a large scale, not only by the monarch, but by the nobles. Luxury, however, was at no time carried to the same extent by the Parthians as it had been by the Persians; the former continued to the last a rude, coarse, vigorous people. In some few respects they adopted Greek manners, as in the character of their coins and the legends upon them, which are Greek from first to last, and evidently imitated from the coins of the Seleucidæ. Their mimetic art shows also Grecian influences; but it never attained to any high degree of excellence.

5. The founder of the Empire, Mithridates I., was succeeded upon the throne by his son, Phraates II., who is known as Arsaces VII., and reigned about nine or ten years, from about B.C. 136 to 127. The earlier part of his reign seems to have been quiet and peaceful; but about B.C. 129, Antiochus Sidetes, who reigned over Syria, undertook an expedition to the East for the purpose of releasing his brother Demetrius, and humbling the pride of the Parthians. Success at first attended his efforts. Phraates was defeated in three battles, and Babylonia was recovered by the Syrians. A general disposition to revolt showed itself among the Parthian feudatories. Phraates, reduced to straits, released Demetrius and sent him into Syria (see p. 258), while at the same time he invoked the aid of the Turanian hordes who bordered his northern frontier. Before these allies, however, could arrive, he had brought the Syrian monarch into difficulties, attacked and overpowered his army in its winter-quarters, and slain Sidetes himself in a battle. He now determined to invade Syria; but the Turanians, whose aid he had invoked, discontented with their treatment, attacked him. A war with these nomads followed, in which Phraates was unsuccessful. His army, composed in part of captured Greeks, played him false; and he himself fell in the fight, about B.C. 127.

Reign of Phraates II. (Arsaces VII.), B.C. 136–127.

6. On the death of Phraates II., his uncle, Artabanus, was placed upon the throne. The Syrian wars now entirely ceased, no effort being made by the Seleucidæ, after the death of Sidetes, to recover their Eastern provinces. But

Reign of Artabanus (Arsaces VIII.), about B.C. 127–124.

the place of this enemy was taken by one more formidable. The Turanian races of the tract beyond the Oxus had been long increasing in power. Their incursions across the river, in some of which they reached Hyrcania and Parthia Proper, were constant. We have seen that Phraates II., alarmed at the attack of Sidetes, called them in to his aid, and afterwards lost his life in a war with them. The same fate befell his successor. In an engagement with a Turanian tribe called Tochari, he received a wound in his arm, from the effects of which he died, about B.C. 124.

7. Artabanus was succeeded by his son, Mithridates II., who is known as Arsaces IX. He was a warlike and powerful prince, whose achievements procured him the epithet of "the Great." He effectually quelled the spirit of the northern nomads, whom he defeated in several engagements; and, in a long series of wars, he extended the Parthian power in many directions. At length he engaged in a contest with the Armenian king, Ortoadistes (Artavasdes?), who was compelled to a disadvantageous peace, for his observance of which he gave hostages, among them Tigranes, a prince of the blood royal. Tigranes induced the Parthian monarch to aid him in gaining the Armenian throne, by undertaking to cede to him a part of Armenia; and this cession took place about B.C. 96. But here the successes of Mithridates came to an end. Tigranes, having become king of Armenia, declared war against his benefactor, recovered the ceded territory, invaded Parthia itself, conquered Adiabênê, and forced the kings of Atropatênê and Gordyênê to become his tributaries, about B.C. 90 to 87. (See p. 339.) Soon after this Mithridates seems to have died, after a reign which must have exceeded thirty-five years.

Reign of Mithridates II. (Arsaces IX.), about B.C. 124–87.

The first contact of the Parthians with the Romans occurred in this reign, Mithridates's envoy, Orobazus, having had an interview with Sulla, the Senatorian commissioner in Asia, B.C. 92.

8. It is uncertain who was the immediate successor of Mithridates II. The list of Trogus, as reported by Justin, is here faulty; and from the incidental notices of other writers, the succession of the kings can only be determined conjecturally. It is usual to place after Mithridates II. a

Uncertain succession. Supposed reign of Mnasciras (Arsaces X.), about B.C. 87-76.

certain Mnasciras, who is mentioned by Lucian as a Parthian monarch. But there is no evidence that Mnasciras followed *immediately* after Mithridates II., or even that he reigned at this period. The next king whom we can positively place after Mithridates II. is Sanatrœces, who mounted the throne about B.C. 76.

Reign of Sanatrœces, B.C. 76-69.

9. Sanatrœces (Arsaces XI.), at the age of eighty, became king of Parthia by the assistance of the Sacaraucæ, one of the Turanian tribes of the north. He reigned seven years only, from about B.C. 76 to 69. He was contemporary with Tigranes of Armenia and Mithridates of Pontus, and seems to have been engaged in war with the former; but the particulars of this contest are unknown.

The name of this king appears in the classical writers under various forms, as Sintruces, Sintricus, and Sinatruces. But the native form, as appears by a coin, is Sanatrœces (Σανατροίκης).

Reign of Phraates III. (Arsaces XII.), B.C. 69-60.

10. Phraates, son of Sanatrœces, succeeded him, and took the title of Θεός ("God"). Ascending the throne at the moment when the Mithridatic War entered on a new phase, the losses of the Pontic monarch having forced him to seek a refuge in Armenia (see p. 333), and Rome being about to transfer the struggle into this quarter, he was naturally drawn into the contest. Both sides sought his alliance; but it was not till Pompey took the direction of the war, B.C. 66, that the Parthian monarch desisted from an attitude of neutrality. He then made an alliance with the Romans, and while Pompey pressed Mithridates with all his forces, Phraates made an attack upon Tigranes. The diversion determined the Mithridatic War in favor of Rome; but, as usual, when her object was gained, the great republic repaid assistance with ingratitude. Tigranes was, in B.C. 65, aided by the Romans against Phraates. The province of Gordyênê, which Phraates had recovered, was retaken by the Romans and assigned to Armenia. It was in vain that the Parthian king remonstrated. Pompey was inexorable; and Phraates, about B.C. 63, came to terms with Tigranes. Shortly afterwards (B.C. 60) he died, poisoned, as was reputed, by his two sons, Mithridates and Orodes.

By the results of the Mithridatic War, the Roman and Parthian Empires became conterminous. Rome absorbed Syria (see p. 261), which bordered on the Parthian province of Mesopotamia, the Euphrates flowing between them. Hence collision between the two great powers became imminent.

Reign of Mithridates III. (Arsaces XIII.), B.C. 60-55.

11. Mithridates, the elder of the two sons of Phraates III., succeeded him. Tigranes I. having died in Armenia, and Artavasdes, his second son, having seized the throne, Mithridates became engaged in a war with Armenia on behalf of his brother-in-law, Tigranes, the eldest son of the late king. His efforts, however, were unsuccessful, and had no effect but to alienate Artavasdes. After a reign of a few years, Mithridates was deposed by the Parthian nobles (see § 3); and, though he maintained himself for some considerable time in Babylon, he was at last captured and put to death. Orodes, his brother, whom the Parthians had made king in his room, succeeded him, about B.C. 55.

THIRD PERIOD.

From the Commencement of the Wars with Rome, B.C. 54, *to the Destruction of the Parthian Empire by the Persians,* A.D. 226.

Reign of Orodes I. (Arsaces XIV.). Expedition of Crassus, B.C. 54-53.

1. The aggressive policy systematically pursued by the Roman Republic rendered a war with Parthia the natural sequel to the victories over Mithridates and Tigranes. The struggle with these princes had revealed to Rome the existence of an Oriental power greater and richer than either Pontus or Armenia; and the jealousy, as well as the cupidity, of the republic was stirred by the revelation. No special grounds of complaint or quarrel were regarded as necessary before the war could be commenced. It was enough that the time had arrived when it seemed to be for the interest of Rome to increase her empire at the expense of Parthia. War was declared without even a pretext, B.C. 55, and in the following year Crassus attacked Orodes.

The failure of the expedition of Crassus (see p. 487) was owing, in part to his age and incapacity, in part to an undue contempt of the Parthian prowess. It was only by bitter experience that the Romans learnt to respect the Parthians as soldiers, and to regard them as greatly superior to most other Orientals.

2. The immediate result of the disastrous expedition of Crassus was the advance of the Parthians across the Euphrates. In B.C. 52, and again in the year after, Pacorus, the son of Orodes, at the head of a large and well-appointed army, crossed from Mesopotamia into Syria, and ravaged the Roman territory far and wide. Upper Syria was overrun, Cilicia invaded, Antioch and Antigoneia threatened, the Roman general, Bibulus, defeated. Cassius, however, gained certain successes; and suspicion having been thrown upon the loyalty of Pacorus, Orodes recalled him, and withdrew his troops within the Euphrates. But eleven years later he made a second advance. Once more Pacorus, this time assisted by the Roman refugee, Labienus, crossed the Euphrates, B.C. 40, and invaded the Syrian presidency. A Roman army, under Decidius Saxa, was destroyed; Antioch, Apameia, Sidon, Ptolemaïs, were occupied; Jerusalem was entered and plundered, and Antigonus set, as Parthian viceroy, upon the throne (see p. 354). The Parthians were complete masters of Syria, Phœnicia, and Palestine; and proceeded to invade Asia Minor, occupying the whole south coast, as far as Caria, and sending their plundering bands into Ionia and the Roman "Asia." At this point, however, their progress was stayed, and reverses began to befall them. Ventidius defeated and slew Labienus in B.C. 39, and gained a similar success over Pacorus in the next year. The Parthians retired from Syria, never to reoccupy it, and henceforth were content to resist the attacks and aggressions of the Romans.

Parthian expeditions into Syria, B.C. 52–51, and 40–38.

3. The death of Orodes followed closely upon this defeat, B.C. 37. He either died of grief for the loss of Pacorus, or was murdered by Phraates, the son whom he had put forward as his successor when he heard of Pacorus's decease. Phraates IV. succeeded him, and reigned as Arsaces XV. Against him Antony, in B.C. 36, led his great expedition. (For this, see p. 501.) Once more on Parthian soil the Romans were completely baffled; and the retreat of Antony was almost as disastrous as that of the army of Crassus. The Parthian power issued from these early contests with Rome intact; each side held its own; and it seemed as if the Euphrates was to be a permanent barrier which the Terminus of neither nation could cross.

Death of Orodes and accession of Phraates IV., B.C. 37. Expedition of Antony, B.C. 36.

4. An uninteresting period of the Parthian history now sets in. Rome and Parthia abstain equally from direct attacks upon each other, while each endeavors to obtain a predominant influence in Armenia, which alternately leans on one or other of the two powers. Troubles are excited by the Romans within the Parthian royal family; and almost every reign exhibits one or more pretenders to the throne, who disturb and sometimes expel the legitimate monarch. This period lasted 150 years —from the retreat of Antony, B.C. 36, to the sixteenth year of Trajan, A.D. 114. It is unnecessary to do more than briefly indicate the succession of the kings during this space.

Dull period of Parthian history, from B.C. 36 to A.D. 114.

LINE OF KINGS FROM PHRAATES IV. TO CHOSROËS, B.C. 37 to A.D. 107. Phraates IV. (Arsaces XV.) reigned from B.C. 37 to A.D. 4. He was annoyed by a pretender named Tiridates, whom Augustus encouraged, and was finally murdered by his female slave, Thermusa, whom he had married. Phraataces, the son of Phraates IV. and this Thermusa, succeeded as Arsaces XVI. He reigned only a few months, being put to death by the Parthians, who gave the crown to a certain Orodes, a member of the royal family, whose exact relationship to the preceding monarchs is unknown. Orodes II. (Arsaces XVII.) reigned, like Phraataces, for a few months only, being put to death about A.D. 5, on account of his cruelty. The Parthians then sent to Rome for Vonones, the eldest of the sons of Phraates IV., who was sent to them by Augustus, and ruled from about A.D. 6 to 14, as Arsaces XVIII., when he was compelled to yield his crown to another member of the royal family, Artabanus. Artabanus II. (Arsaces XIX.) held the throne from about A.D. 14 to 44. His reign was stormy, troubled by a revolt of the Babylonian Jews, by pretenders whom Tiberius supported, and by rebellions of the tributary monarchs. At his death, war broke out between two of his sons, Gotarzes and Vardanes, who both claimed the kingdom. Vardanes, the younger, was successful after a sharp struggle, and reigned as Arsaces XX., from about A.D. 44 to 48, when Gotarzes renewed the fight, and the Parthians, deserting Vardanes, slew him and made Gotarzes king. Gotarzes (Arsaces XXI.) held the throne from A.D. 48 to 50. The chief event of his reign was a war with the pretender Meherdates, son of Vonones I., who was supported by the Romans, but fell after a short contest. Gotarzes himself died soon afterwards, probably by a natural death. The next king was Vonones II. (Arsaces XXII.). He was a member of the royal family, and had governed Media Atropatênê under Gotarzes, but seems not to have been a near relation. His reign, which lasted only a few months, was unmarked by any unimportant event. Vologeses I. (Arsaces XXIII.), the eldest of his sons, succeeded him. He reigned for the space of forty years, from about A.D. 50 to 90, and was contemporary with eight Roman emperors—Claudius, Nero, Galba, Otho, Vitellius, Vespasian, Titus, and Domitian. The contention between Rome and Parthia, with respect to supremacy over Armenia, came to a head during his reign, when his brother, Tiridates, to whom he had given the Armenian crown, was so harassed by the Romans—more especially by Nero's general, Corbulo, A.D. 56 to 64—that he consented at last to renounce his allegiance to Parthia, and to accept the Armenian kingdom from Nero, which he held thenceforth as a Roman fief, A.D. 65. After this, Parthia remained at peace with Rome for nearly half a century, and very little is known of its condition. Vologeses seems to have died about A.D. 90. He left two sons, Pacorus and Chosroës, the elder of whom, Pacorus, succeeded him. Pacorus (Arsaces XXIV.), who succeeded Vologeses, reigned from about A.D. 90 to 107. Nothing is known of him except that he beautified Ctesiphon. He was succeeded, about A.D. 107, by his brother Chosroës, in whose reign the Parthian history again becomes important and interesting.

Reign of Chosroës (Arsaces XXV.), A.D. 107–121. Expedition of Trajan.

5. Chosroës (Arsaces XXV.), on obtaining the crown, proceeded almost immediately to assert the authority of Parthia over Armenia by deposing the reigning monarch, Exedares, and placing his nephew, Parthamasiris, the son of Pacorus, upon the Armenian throne. This act furnished an excuse to Trajan for his Eastern expedition, a part of his great scheme of conquest. (See p. 544.) The earlier operations of the Roman emperor were altogether successful; he deprived Parthamasiris of his kingdom, and made Armenia a Roman province without a struggle; he rapidly overran Mesopotamia and Assyria, taking the cities one after another, and added those countries to the empire; he pressed southward, took Seleuceia, Ctesiphon, and Babylon, descended the Tigris to the sea, and received the submission of Mesênê, the tract upon the Persian Gulf. In another direction his arms penetrated as far as Susa. But it was easier to conquer than to hold. Revolts broke out in the countries already occupied, at Seleuceia, at Edessa, at Nisibis, at Hatra, and elsewhere. Trajan felt that he must retire. To cover the ignominy of his retreat, he held an assembly at Ctesiphon, and placed his more southern conquests under the sovereignty of a mock king, a native named Parthamaspates. His other conquests, Armenia, Mesopotamia, and Assyria, he maintained and strongly garrisoned. But they continued Roman for only about two years (A.D. 115 to 117). The first act of Hadrian was to relinquish the whole results of the Parthian war of Trajan, and to withdraw the legions within the line of the Euphrates (see p. 546). Chosroës returned to his capital, Parthamaspates quitting it and falling back on his Roman friends, who made him king

His conquests abandoned by Hadrian.

of Armenia. The Parthian empire was restored to its old limits; and friendly relations subsisted between Chosroës and Hadrian until the death of the former, probably about A.D. 121.

6. The successor of Chosroës was his son, Vologeses II. (Arsaces XXVI.), who reigned from about A.D. 121 to 149. He kept the peace with Rome throughout the whole of his reign, though sorely tempted to interfere with the affairs of Armenia, which had reverted to the position of a Roman fief. He was contemporary with Antoninus Pius. The only important event of his reign was an invasion of Media Atropatênê by the Alani, who were becoming formidable in the tract between the Black Sea and the Caspian. Vologeses bribed these enemies to retire.

Reign of Vologeses the IId (Arsaces the XXVIth), A.D. 121–149.

7. His successor was another Vologeses, the third of the name, who was probably his son. He reigned from about A.D. 149 to 192. During the lifetime of Antoninus Pius, he remained at peace with the Romans; but soon after the accession of M. Aurelius (B.C. 161) he provoked a war by invading Armenia for the purpose of severing its connection with Rome. At the outset he was successful; Armenia was occupied; Severianus, Roman prefect of Cappadocia, was defeated, his army destroyed, and he himself slain; the Parthian hordes once more crossed the Euphrates, and carried devastation into Syria; but their triumph was short-lived. Verus was sent to the East; and though individually he did nothing, yet his generals gained great advantages. The Parthians were driven from Syria and Armenia; Mesopotamia was occupied; Seleuceia, Ctesiphon, and Babylon taken; and the royal palace at Ctesiphon burnt (A.D. 165). Parthia then sued for peace, and obtained it by ceding Mesopotamia, and allowing Armenia to return to the position of a Roman dependency (see p. 551). Vologeses, thus humbled, remained quiet during his later years, living on friendly terms with M. Aurelius and with Commodus.

Reign of Vologeses the IIId (Arsaces the XXVIIth), about A.D. 149–192.

8. Vologeses III. left two sons, Vologeses and Tiridates, of whom the elder, Vologeses, succeeded him. This prince, having unfortunately attached himself to the cause of Pescennius Niger, A.D. 193, was attacked by the Roman em-

Reign of Vologeses the IVth (Arsaces the XXVIIIth), about A.D. 192–213.

peror, Septimius Severus, after he had defeated Niger, and suffered important reverses. The Roman army advanced through Mesopotamia to the Tigris, crossed into Assyria, and occupied Adiabênê, descended the river in ships to Ctesiphon, which it took and plundered, captured also Seleuceia and Babylon, and returned without suffering any worse defeat than a double repulse from the walls of Hatra. The only permanent fruit of the campaign was, however, the addition of Adiabênê, or Northern Assyria, to the empire, which the Parthian monarch was forced to cede to his adversary, A.D. 199. Nothing more is known of Vologeses IV., excepting that he left several sons, and that he reigned till about A.D. 212 or 213.

Some writers (as Clinton) interpose between Vologeses III. and IV. a certain Pacorus, whose name exists upon a coin, with a date equivalent to A.D. 198. But as it seems certain from DIO that a Vologeses, and not a Pacorus, was the opponent of Severus in that year, and almost certain that this same Vologeses lived on into the reign of Caracallus, we must regard Pacorus as a pretender, who, when Vologeses IV. was driven from his capital, claimed the throne.

9. Upon the death of Vologeses IV., a contention arose between his sons with respect to the succession, which seems to have fallen, after a short struggle, to another Vologeses, who was king when Caracallus, wishing to pick a quarrel with Parthia, sent to demand the surrender of two refugees, Tiridates and Antiochus. Vologeses at first refused; but, when he was threatened with invasion, yielded, A.D. 215. Soon after this he must have ceased to reign, for we find Caracallus, in A.D. 216, negotiating with Artabanus.

Reign of Vologeses the Vth (Arsaces the XXIXth), about A.D. 213–216.

10. Artabanus (Arsaces XXX.), the last king of Parthia, is thought to have been a son of Vologeses IV. and a brother of Vologeses V. He reigned from A.D. 215 or 216 to 226. Caracallus, bent on a Parthian campaign, in which he was to rival Alexander, sent, in A.D. 216, to demand the daughter of Artabanus in marriage. Artabanus refused, and Caracallus immediately crossed the Euphrates, took possession of Osrhoënê, proceeded through Mesopotamia to the Tigris, invaded Adiabênê, took Arbela, and drove the Parthians into the mountains. He then returned to Edessa in

Reign of Artabanus the IIId (Arsaces the XXXth), about A.D. 215–226. Destruction of the empire.

Osrhoëné, and was proceeding in the year following to renew his attack, when he was murdered by order of Macrinus, his prætorian prefect. Macrinus then carried on the war for a short time, but, being twice defeated by Artabanus near Nisibis, he was content to purchase peace by the expenditure of a large sum of money and the surrender of all the Roman possessions beyond the Euphrates. The dominions of the Parthians were thus once more extended to their ancient limits, and Artabanus had even reclaimed and exercised the old Parthian suzerainty over Armenia, by appointing his own brother to be king, when suddenly an insurrection broke out in the south. The Persians, under Artaxerxes, the son of Sassan, rebelled, after four centuries of subjection, against their Parthian lords, defeated the forces of Artabanus in three great battles, and in the third slew that king himself. The Parthian empire came thus suddenly to an end, A.D. 226, when it had given few signs of internal decay or weakness. It was succeeded by the New Persian Monarchy, or Kingdom of the Sassanidæ, which lasted from A.D. 226 to 652.

This revolution was a recovery by the old Arian race of the supremacy so long wielded by the Tatars. It was accompanied by a complete change in the government and the religion. The new Persian kingdom had important relations with Rome during almost the whole period of its continuance; but, as these relations were chiefly with the Eastern empire, whose history the design of this work does not include, no account will be here given of the Sassanian dynasty. Those who wish for information on the subject will find it in the following works:

RICHTER, C. F., *Historisch-Kritischer Versuch*, etc. (see p. 654).

MALCOLM, Sir J., *History of Persia.* London, 1815; 2 vols. 4to.

DE SACY, S., *Mémoires sur diverses Antiquités de la Perse, et sur les Médailles des Sassanides, avec l'histoire des Sassanides par Mirkhond.* Paris, 1793; 4to.

D'HERBELOT, *Bibliothèque Orientale ou Dictionnaire universel, contenant tout ce qui fait connaitre les peuples de l'Orient.* Paris, 1781–83; 6 vols. 8vo.

A brief outline of the history is given by Mr. CLINTON in his *Fasti Romani*, vol. ii. pp. 259–263; and a somewhat fuller account will be found in Dr. SMITH'S *Dict. of Greek and Roman Biography*, sub voc. SASSANIDÆ.

GENEALOGICAL TABLES.

I. MACEDONIAN ROYAL HOUSES.

A. HOUSE OF ALEXANDER THE GREAT.

- (1) AMYNTAS II.
  - (4) PHILIP, m. 1. Olympias; 2. Cleopatra; 3. Concubines.
    - (5) ALEXANDER THE GREAT, m. 1. Roxana; 2. Concubines.
      - (7) ALEXANDER.
      - Hercules.
    - Cleopatra, m. Alexander of Epirus.
    - (6) PHILIP ARRHIDÆUS, m. Eurydicé.
  - (2) ALEXANDER II.
  - Thessalonica, m. Cassander.
  - Cynané, m. Amyntas.
  - (3) PERDICCAS III.
    - Amyntas, m. Cynane.
      - Eurydicé, m. Philip Arrhidæus.

B. HOUSE OF ANTIPATER.

- ANTIPATER.
  - (8) CASSANDER, m. Thessalonica.
    - (9) PHILIP II.
    - (10) ANTIPATER II.
    - (11) ALEXANDER.
  - Philip.
  - Eurydicé, m. Ptolemy Lagi.
  - Phila, m. 1. Craterus; 2. Demetrius Poliorcetes.
  - Nicæa. m. Perdiccas.

C. HOUSE OF ANTIGONUS.

- ANTIGONUS I.
  - (12) DEMETRIUS I. (Poliorcetes), m. Phila, daughter of Antipater.
    - (13) ANTIGONUS II. (Gonatas), m. Phila, daughter of Seleucus Nicator.
      - (14) DEMETRIUS II., m. 1. Stratonice; 2. Phthia.
        - (16) PHILIP III.
          - (17) PERSEUS, m. Laodicé, daughter of Seleucus Philopator.
          - Demetrius.
        - Apama.
      - Halcyoneus.
    - Craterus.
      - Alexander.
    - Demetrius the Handsome.
      - (15) ANTIGONUS III. (Doson), m. Phthia, widow of Demetrius II.
    - Stratonice, m. 1. Seleucus Nicator; 2. Antiochus Theus.
    - Echecrates.
      - Antigonus.
  - Philip.
  - Phila.

II. ROYAL HOUSE OF THE SELEUCIDÆ.

(1) SELEUCUS I. (Nicator).
m. 1. Apama; 2. Stratonicé, daughter of Demetrius Poliorcetes.

(2) ANTIOCHUS I. (Soter), *m.* 1. Stratonicé (his father's wife); 2. Another. — Phila, *m.* Antigonus Gonatas.

(3) ANTIOCHUS II. (Theus), *m.* 1. Laodicé, daughter of Achæus; 2. Berenicé, daughter of Ptolemy Philadelphus. — Apama, *m.* Magas of Cyrêné. — Stratonicé, *m.* Demetrius II. of Macedon.

(4) SELEUCUS II. (Callinicus), *m.* Laodicé, daughter of Andromachus. — Antiochus Hierax. — Stratonicé, *m.* Ariarathes III. of Cappadocia. — A daughter, *m.* Mithridates III. of Pontus.

(5) SELEUCUS III. (Ceraunus). — (6) ANTIOCHUS III. (the Great), *m.* Laodicé, daughter of Mithridates IV. of Pontus. — Stratonicé, *m.* Mithridates IV. of Pontus.

Antiochus, *m.* his sister, Laodicé. — Ardys. — Mithridates. — (7) SELEUCUS IV. (Philopator). — (8) ANTIOCHUS IV. (Epiphanes). — Laodicé, *m.* her brother, Antiochus. — Cleopatra, *m.* Ptolemy V. (Epiphanes). — Antiochis, *m.* Ariarathes IV. of Cappadocia. — Another, *m.* Eumenes II. of Pergamus.

(10) DEMETRIUS I. (Soter). — Laodicé, *m.* Perseus of Macedon. — (9) ANTIOCHUS V. (Eupator). — (11) ALEXANDER BALAS (?) — Laodicé.

(13) ANTIOCHUS VI.

(12) DEMETRIUS II. (Nicator), *m.* 1. Cleopatra, d. of Ptolemy Philometor. 2. Rhodogyné, a Parthian. — Antigonus. — (14) ANTIOCHUS VII. (Sidetes), *m.* Cleopatra, his sister-in-law.

Seleucus. — (15) ANTIOCHUS VIII. (Grypus), *m.* Tryphæna. — (16) ANTIOCHUS IX. (Cyzicenus), *m.* Cleopatra, daughter of Ptolemy Physcon. — Antiochus. — Seleucus.

(17) SELEUCUS V. (Epiphanes). — (19) PHILIP. — Antiochus Epiphanes. — Demetrius Eucærus. — Antiochus Dionysus.

(18) ANTIOCHUS X. (Eusebes), *m.* Cleopatra Selene, daughter of Ptolemy Physcon.

(20) ANTIOCHUS XI. (Asiaticus).

III. ROYAL HOUSE OF THE PTOLEMIES.

PTOLEMY I. (son of Lagus), *m.* 1. Eurydice, daughter of Antipater; 2. Berenicé.

Magas, king of Cyrêné. — Berenicé.

Arsinoë, *m.* 1. Lysimachus; 2. Ptolemy Ceraunus; 3. Ptolemy Philadelphus.

Lysandra, *m.* Agathocles, son of Lysimachus. — Ptolemy Ceraunus, king of Macedon, *m.* his half-sister, Arsinoë. — PTOLEMY II. (Philadelphus), *m.* 1. Arsinoë, d. of Lysimachus; 2. his sister, Arsinoë.

PTOLEMY III. (Euergetes), *m.* Berenicé, d. of Magas. — Lysimachus. — Berenicé, *m.* Antiochus Theus.

PTOLEMY IV. (Philopator), *m.* 1. his sister, Arsinoë; 2. the courtesan Agathoclea. — Magas. — Arsinoë, *m.* her brother, Ptolemy IV.

PTOLEMY V. (Epiphanes), *m.* Cleopatra, daughter of Antiochus the Great.

PTOLEMY VI. (Philometor), *m.* his sister, Cleopatra. — Cleopatra, *m.* 1. Ptolemy VI.; 2. Ptolemy VII. — PTOLEMY VIII. (Physcon), *m.* 1. his sister, Cleopatra; 2. his niece, Cleopatra.

PTOLEMY VII. (Eupator). — Cleopatra, *m.* Ptolemy VIII. — Cleopatra, *m.* 1. Alexander Balas; 2. Demetrius Nicator; 3. Antiochus Sidetes.

PTOLEMY IX. (Lathyrus), *m.* 1. his sister, Cleopatra; 2. his sister, Selêné. — PTOLEMY X. (Alexander). — Apion, king of Cyrêné. — Selêné, *m.* 1. Ptolemy IX.; 2. Antiochus Epiph.; 3. Antiochus Eusebes. — Cleopatra, *m.* 1. Ptolemy IX.; 2. Antiochus Cyzicenus. — Tryphæna, *m.* Antiochus Grypus.

Ptolemy, king of Cyprus. — Cleopatra (?) — PTOLEMY XI. (Alex. II.), *m.* Berenicé. — A daughter.

BERENICÉ, *m.* Ptolemy (Alex. II.). — PTOLEMY XII. (Auletes). — Arsinoë.

PTOLEMY XIII. (the elder), *m.* his sister, Cleopatra. — PTOLEMY XIV. (the younger), *m.* his sister, Cleopatra.

TRYPHÆNA. — BERENICÉ, *m.* Archelaüs. — CLEOPATRA, *m.* her two brothers; 3. Antonius. — Ptolemy. — Cleopatra.

Cæsarion. — Alexander.

IV. ROYAL HOUSE OF PERGAMUS.

Unknown.

Eumenes. — Attalus, *m.* Antiochis, d. of Achæus.

(1) PHILETÆRUS. — (2) EUMENES I. — (3) ATTALUS I., *m.* Apollonias.

Philetærus. — Athenæus.

(4) EUMENES II., *m.* 1. Stratonicé, d. of Ariarathes IV. of Cappadocia; 2. a dau. of Antiochus the Great. — (5) ATTALUS II. (Philadelphus).

(6) ATTALUS III. (Philometor). — (7) ARISTONICUS.

V. ROYAL HOUSE OF BITHYNIA.

(1) BOTEIRAS.
(2) BAS.
(3) ZIPŒTES.

Children of Zipœtes: (4) NICOMEDES I., *m.* 1. Ditizèlé; 2. Etazeta. — Zipœtes. — Two other sons.

Children of Nicomedes I.: (5) ZEÏLAS. — Prusias. — Tibœtes. — Lysandra.

(6) PRUSIAS I. (the Lame).
(7) PRUSIAS II. (the Hunter).

Children of Prusias II.: (8) NICOMEDES II. (Epiphanes), *m.* Laodicé, widow of Ariarathes VI. of Cappadocia. — Another.

Children of Nicomedes II.: (9) NICOMEDES III. (Philopator), — Socrates.

VI. ROYAL HOUSE OF PONTUS.

(1) ARIOBARZANES I.
(2) MITHRIDATES I.
(3) MITHRIDATES II.
(4) ARIOBARZANES II.
(5) MITHRIDATES III., *m.* a daughter of Antiochus II.

Children of Mithridates III.: (6) PHARNACES I. — Laodicé, *m.* Antiochus III. — Laodicé, *m.* Achæus, son of Andromachus.

(7) MITHRIDATES IV. (Euergetes).

Children of Mithridates IV.: (8) MITHRIDATES V., the Great (Eupator), *m.* his sister Laodicé, and several others. — A son, name unknown. — Laodicé, *m.* her brother, Mithridates. — Laodicé, *m.* 1. Ariarathes VI. of Cappadocia; 2. Nicomedes of Bythinia. — Roxana and two others.

Children of Mithridates V.: Arcathias. — PHARNACES. — Ariarathes. — Mithridates. — Five other sons. — Cleopatra, *m.* Tigranes I. of Armenia. — Six other daughters.

VII. ROYAL HOUSE OF CAPPADOCIA.

Ariamnes.

(1) ARIARATHES I. — Holophernes.

(2) ARIARATHES II. — Aryses.

(3) ARIAMNES. — Two other sons.

(4) ARIARATHES III.,
m. Stratonicé, daughter of Antiochus Theus.

ARIARATHES IV.,
m. 1. Unknown; 2. Antiochis, daughter of Antiochus the Great.

A daughter by first wife, Stratonicé, *m.* Eumenes II. of Pergamus. — Mithridates or ARIARATHES V., *m.* 1. Unknown; 2. Laodicé. — Two daughters by second wife.

By first wife, Demetrius. — By Laodicé, ARIARATHES VI., *m.* Laodicé, sister of Mithridates the Great. — By Laodicé, five other sons.

ARIARATHES VII. — ARIARATHES VIII.

VIII. JEWISH ROYAL HOUSES.

A. HOUSE OF THE MACCABEES.

(1) MATTATHIAS.

(2) JUDAS MACCABÆUS. — (3) JONATHAN. — (4) SIMON.

(5) JOHN HYRCANUS.

(6) ARISTOBULUS I. — ALEXANDER JANNÆUS, *m.* (8) ALEXANDRA (who reigns after his death).

(9) HYRCANUS. — (10) ARISTOBULUS II.

Alexander, *m.* Alexandra. — (11) ANTIGONUS.

Aristobulus. — Mariamné, *m.* Herod the Great.

JEWISH ROYAL HOUSES—*Continued.*

B. HOUSE OF THE HERODS.

Antipater.

(1) HEROD I. (the Great), *m.* 1. Doris; 2. Mariamné; 3. Several others. — Salomé, *m.* Costobarus.

Berenicé, *m.* Aristobulus.

Antipater. — Alexander. — Aristobulus, *m.* Berenicé. — (2) ARCHELAUS. — (3) ANTIPAS, *m.* Herodias. — (4) PHILIP, *m.* Herodias.

Aristobulus, *m.* Jotapa. — (5) AGRIPPA I., *m.* Cypros. — HEROD of Chalcis. — ARISTOBULUS of Armenia Minor. — Herodias, *m.* 1. her uncle Philip; 2. her uncle, Antipas.

Jotapa.

(6) AGRIPPA II. — Berenicé, *m.* 1. Herod of Chalcis; 2. Polemo of Cilicia. — Mariamné. — Drusilla, *m.* Felix.

IX. ROMAN IMPERIAL HOUSES.

A. THE JULIAN HOUSE.

C. Julius Cæsar, *m.* Aurelia.

C. JULIUS CÆSAR, *m.* Cornelia. — Julia, *m.* M. Atius Balbus.

Julia, *m.* Cn. Pompeius Magnus. — Atia, *m.* C. Octavius.

A son. — A daughter.

C. Octavius (adopted as son by the will of Julius) became C. JULIUS CÆSAR OCTAVIANUS AUGUSTUS, *m.* 1. Clodia; 2. Scribonia; 3. Livia. — Octavia, *m.* 1. C. Claudius Marcellus; 2. M. Antonius (Triumvir).

Julia, *m.* 1. M. Marcellus; 2. M. Vipsanius Agrippa; 3. Tiberius.

TIBERIUS (adopted as son by Augustus). (See *Claudian House.*) *m.* 1. Vipsania; 2. Julia.

Drusus, *m.* Livilla, sister of Germanicus.

C. Cæsar. — L. Cæsar. — M. Agrippa (Posthumus). — Agrippina, *m.* Germanicus. — Julia, *m.* Æmilius Paullus.

Nero, *m.* Julia, daughter of Drusus. — Drusus, *m.* Æmilia Lepida. — CAIUS (Caligula), *m.* Cæsonia. — Three other sons. — Agrippina, *m.* Cn. Domitius. — Drusilla, *m.* 1. Cassius Longinus; 2. Æmil. Lepidus. — Two other daughters.

Julia Drusilla.

L. DOMITIUS NERO, *m.* Poppæa Sabina.

Claudia Augusta.

M. Æmilius Lepidus, *m.* Drusilla. — Æmilia Lepida, *m.* 1. CLAUDIUS; 2. Junius Silanus.

Tiberius Gemellus. — Julia, *m.* 1. Nero, son of Germanicus; 2. Rubellius Blandus.

Rubellius Plautus.

M. Junius. Silanus. — L. Junius Silanus. — D. Torquatus Silanus. — Junia Calvina, *m.* VITELLIUS. — Junia Lepida, *m.* C. Cassius.

L. Silanus Torquatus.

ROMAN IMPERIAL HOUSES—*Continued.*

B. THE CLAUDIAN HOUSE.

Tiberius Claudius Nero,
m. Livia Drusilla (afterwards wife of AUGUSTUS).

TIBERIUS Claudius Nero,
m. 1. Vipsania Agrippina; 2. Julia.

Drusus (by first wife),
m. Livilla, his first cousin.

Son, who died an infant
(by second wife).

Tiberius
Gemellus.

Son (twin to
Gemellus),
died an infant.

Julia,
m. 1. Nero, son of Germanicus;
2. L. Rubellius Blandus.

Rubellius Plautus,
m. Antistia Pollutia.

Drusus Claudius Nero,
m. Antonia, daughter of the Triumvir.

Germanicus,
m. Agrippina.
(For issue, see
Julian House.)

Livilla,
m. her first
cousin, Drusus.

Ti. CLAUDIUS Drusus,
m. 1. Æmilia Lepida;
2. Livia Medullina;
3. Plautia Urgulanilla;
4. Ælia Petina;
5. Valeria Messalina;
6. Agrippina, d. of Germanicus.

By third wife.

Drusus,
died an infant.

Claudia,
died an infant.

By fourth wife.

Antonia,
m. 1. Cn. Pompeius;
2. Corn. Sulla.

By fifth wife.

Octavia,
m. NERO.

Britannicus.

By adoption.

NERO.

C. THE HOUSE OF CONSTANTINE.

CONSTANTIUS Chlorus, *m.* 1. Helena; 2. Theodora.

By his first wife.

CONSTANTINE I. (the Great),
m. 1. Minervina; 2. Fausta.

By first wife.

Crispus,
m. Helena.

By second wife.

CONSTANTINE II.

CONSTANTIUS II.

Constantia,
m. GRATIAN.

CONSTANS.

Constantia,
m. 1. Hannibalianus;
2. GALLUS.

Constantia,
a nun.

Hellena,
m. JULIAN.

By his second wife.

Constantine.

Hannibalianus.

Dalmatius.

Hannibalianus,
m. Constantia,
d. of Constantine I.

Constantius,
m. 1. Galla;
2. Basilina.

GALLUS, *m.* Constantia, widow of
Hannibalianus.

JULIAN,
m. Helena, d. of
Constantine I.

A son.

A daughter.

Constantia,
m. LICINIUS.

Fl. Licinianus
Licinius.

Anastasia,
m. Bassianus.

Eutropia,
m. Popilius
Nepotianus.

Fl. Popilius
Nepotianus.

ROMAN IMPERIAL HOUSES—*Continued.*

D. THE THEODOSIAN HOUSE.

Theodosius.
- THEODOSIUS I. (the Great), *m.* 1. Flaccilla; 2. Galla, sister of Valentinian II.
  - Gratianus.
  - Pulcheria.
  - ARCADIUS, *m.* Eudoxia.
    - THEODOSIUS II., *m.* Eudocia.
      - Eudoxia, *m.* VALENTINIAN III.
      - Flaccilla.
    - Pulcheria, *m.* MARCIAN.
    - Three other daughters.
  - HONORIUS, *m.* Maria, d. of Stilicho.
  - Placidia, *m.* 1. Adolphus; 2. CONSTANTIUS.
    - VALENTINIAN III., *m.* Eudoxia.
      - Eudoxia, *m.* 1. Palladius, son of MAXIMUS; 2. Hunneric, son of Genseric.
        - Ilderic.
      - Placidia, *m.* OLYBRIUS.
    - Honoria.
- Honorius.
  - Serena, *m.* Stilicho.
    - Maria.
  - Thermantia.

X. ROYAL HOUSES OF PARTHIA.

A. HOUSE OF ARSACES I.

Unknown.
- ARSACES I.
- TIRIDATES (Arsaces II.).
  - ARSACES III.
    - PRIAPATIUS (Arsaces IV.).
      - PHRAATES I. (Arsaces V.).
      - MITHRIDATES I. (Arsaces VI.).
        - PHRAATES II. (Arsaces VII.).
      - ARTABANUS I. (Arsaces VIII.).
        - MITHRIDATES II. (Arsaces IX.).

B. HOUSE OF SANATRŒCES.

SANATRŒCES (Arsaces XI.).
- PHRAATES III. (Arsaces XII.).
  - MITHRIDATES III. (Arsaces XIII.).
  - ORODES I. (Arsaces XIV.).
    - Pacorus.
    - PHRAATES IV. (Arsaces XV.), *m.* Thermusa.
      - VONONES I. (Arsaces XVIII.).
        - Tiridates (?).
        - Meherdates.
      - Phraates.
      - Seraspadanes.
      - Rhodaspes.
      - PHRAATACES (Arsaces XVI.).
    - Twenty-nine sons, murdered by Phraates IV.
  - A daughter, *m.* Tigranes II. of Armenia.

ROYAL HOUSES OF PARTHIA—*Continued.*

C. HOUSE OF ARTABANUS II.

- ARTABANUS II. (Arsaces XIX.).
  - Arsaces (made king of Armenia by his father).
  - Orodes.
  - VARDANES (Arsaces XX.).
  - GOTARZES (Arsaces XXI.).
  - Artabanus.
    - A son, put to death by Gotarzes.

D. HOUSE OF VONONES II.

- VONONES II. (Arsaces XXII.).
  - VOLOGESES I. (Arsaces XXIII.).
    - Vardanes.
    - PACORUS (Arsaces XXIV.).
      - Parthamasiris (made king of Armenia by Chosroës).
    - CHOSROËS (Arsaces XXV.).
      - VOLOGESES II. (Arsaces XXVI.).
        - ⋮ VOLOGESES III.* (Arsaces XXVII.).
          - VOLOGESES IV. (Arsaces XXVIII.).
            - VOLOGESES V. (Arsaces XXIX.).
            - ARTABANUS III. (Arsaces XXX.).
              - A daughter, sought in marriage by Caracallus.
            - Another son (made king of Armenia by Artabanus III.).
          - Tiridates.
  - Tiridates (king of Armenia).
    - Exedares (king of Armenia).
  - Pacorus (king of Media).

[* The relationship of this king to his predecessor is uncertain.]

VALUABLE STANDARD WORKS

FOR PUBLIC AND PRIVATE LIBRARIES,

PUBLISHED BY HARPER & BROTHERS, NEW YORK.

☞ *For a full List of Books suitable for Libraries, see* HARPER & BROTHERS' TRADE-LIST *and* CATALOGUE, *which may be had gratuitously on application to the Publishers personally, or by letter enclosing Five Cents.*

☞ HARPER & BROTHERS *will send any of the following works by mail, postage prepaid, to any part of the United States, on receipt of the price.*

MOTLEY'S DUTCH REPUBLIC. The Rise of the Dutch Republic. By JOHN LOTHROP MOTLEY, LL.D., D.C.L. With a Portrait of William of Orange. 3 vols., 8vo, Cloth, $10 50.

MOTLEY'S UNITED NETHERLANDS. History of the United Netherlands: from the Death of William the Silent to the Twelve Years' Truce—1609. With a full View of the English-Dutch Struggle against Spain, and of the Origin and Destruction of the Spanish Armada. By JOHN LOTHROP MOTLEY, LL.D., D.C.L. Portraits. 4 vols., 8vo, Cloth, $14 00.

NAPOLEON'S LIFE OF CÆSAR. The History of Julius Cæsar. By His Imperial Majesty NAPOLEON III. Two Volumes ready. Library Edition, 8vo, Cloth, $3 50 per vol.

Maps to Vols. I. and II. sold separately. Price $1 50 *each,* NET.

HAYDN'S DICTIONARY OF DATES, relating to all Ages and Nations. For Universal Reference. Edited by BENJAMIN VINCENT, Assistant Secretary and Keeper of the Library of the Royal Institution of Great Britain; and Revised for the Use of American Readers. 8vo, Cloth, $5 00; Sheep, $6 00.

MACGREGOR'S ROB ROY ON THE JORDAN. The Rob Roy on the Jordan, Nile, Red Sea, and Gennesareth, &c. A Canoe Cruise in Palestine and Egypt, and the Waters of Damascus. By J. MACGREGOR, M.A. With Maps and Illustrations. Crown 8vo, Cloth, $2 50.

WALLACE'S MALAY ARCHIPELAGO. The Malay Archipelago: the Land of the Orang-Utan and the Bird of Paradise. A Narrative of Travel, 1854–1862. With Studies of Man and Nature. By ALFRED RUSSEL WALLACE. With Ten Maps and Fifty-one Elegant Illustrations. Crown 8vo, Cloth, $3 50.

WHYMPER'S ALASKA. Travel and Adventure in the Territory of Alaska, formerly Russian America—now Ceded to the United States—and in various other parts of the North Pacific. By FREDERICK WHYMPER. With Map and Illustrations. Crown 8vo, Cloth, $2 50.

ORTON'S ANDES AND THE AMAZON. The Andes and the Amazon; or, Across the Continent of South America. By JAMES ORTON, M.A., Professor of Natural History in Vassar College, Poughkeepsie, N. Y., and Corresponding Member of the Academy of Natural Sciences, Philadelphia. With a New Map of Equatorial America and numerous Illustrations. Crown 8vo, Cloth, $2 00.

WINCHELL'S SKETCHES OF CREATION. Sketches of Creation: a Popular View of some of the Grand Conclusions of the Sciences in reference to the History of Matter and of Life. Together with a Statement of the Intimations of Science respecting the Primordial Condition and the Ultimate Destiny of the Earth and the Solar System. By ALEXANDER WINCHELL, LL.D., Professor of Geology, Zoology, and Botany in the University of Michigan, and Director of the State Geological Survey. With Illustrations. 12mo, Cloth, $2 00.

WHITE'S MASSACRE OF ST. BARTHOLOMEW. The Massacre of St. Bartholomew: Preceded by a History of the Religious Wars in the Reign of Charles IX. By HENRY WHITE, M.A. With Illustrations. 8vo, Cloth, $1 75.

LOSSING'S FIELD-BOOK OF THE REVOLUTION. Pictorial Field-Book of the Revolution; or, Illustrations, by Pen and Pencil, of the History, Biography, Scenery, Relics, and Traditions of the War for Independence. By BENSON J. LOSSING. 2 vols., 8vo, Cloth, $14 00; Sheep, $15 00; Half Calf, $18 00; Full Turkey Morocco, $22 00.

LOSSING'S FIELD-BOOK OF THE WAR OF 1812. Pictorial Field-Book of the War of 1812; or, Illustrations, by Pen and Pencil, of the History, Biography, Scenery, Relics, and Traditions of the Last War for American Independence. By BENSON J. LOSSING. With several hundred Engravings on Wood, by Lossing and Barritt, chiefly from Original Sketches by the Author. 1088 pages, 8vo, Cloth, $7 00; Sheep, $8 50; Half Calf, $10 00.

ALFORD'S GREEK TESTAMENT. The Greek Testament: with a critically-revised Text; a Digest of Various Readings; Marginal References to Verbal and Idiomatic Usage; Prolegomena; and a Critical and Exegetical Commentary. For the Use of Theological Students and Ministers. By HENRY ALFORD, D.D., Dean of Canterbury. Vol. I., containing the Four Gospels. 944 pages, 8vo, Cloth, $6 00; Sheep, $6 50.

ABBOTT'S HISTORY OF THE FRENCH REVOLUTION. The French Revolution of 1789, as viewed in the Light of Republican Institutions. By JOHN S. C. ABBOTT. With 100 Engravings. 8vo, Cloth, $5 00.

ABBOTT'S NAPOLEON BONAPARTE. The History of Napoleon Bonaparte. By JOHN S. C. ABBOTT. With Maps, Woodcuts, and Portraits on Steel. 2 vols., 8vo, Cloth, $10 00.

ABBOTT'S NAPOLEON AT ST. HELENA; or, Interesting Anecdotes and Remarkable Conversations of the Emperor during the Five and a Half Years of his Captivity. Collected from the Memorials of Las Casas, O'Meara, Montholon, Antommarchi, and others. By JOHN S. C. ABBOTT. With Illustrations. 8vo, Cloth, $5 00.

ADDISON'S COMPLETE WORKS. The Works of Joseph Addison, embracing the whole of the "Spectator." Complete in 3 vols., 8vo, Cloth, $6 00.

ALCOCK'S JAPAN. The Capital of the Tycoon: a Narrative of a Three Years' Residence in Japan. By Sir RUTHERFORD ALCOCK, K.C.B., Her Majesty's Envoy Extraordinary and Minister Plenipotentiary in Japan. With Maps and Engravings. 2 vols., 12mo, Cloth, $3 50.

ALISON'S HISTORY OF EUROPE. FIRST SERIES: From the Commencement of the French Revolution, in 1789, to the Restoration of the Bourbons, in 1815. [In addition to the Notes on Chapter LXXVI., which correct the errors of the original work concerning the United States, a copious Analytical Index has been appended to this American edition.] SECOND SERIES: From the Fall of Napoleon, in 1815, to the Accession of Louis Napoleon, in 1852. 8 vols., 8vo, Cloth, $16 00.

BANCROFT'S MISCELLANIES. Literary and Historical Miscellanies. By GEORGE BANCROFT. 8vo, Cloth, $3 00.

BALDWIN'S PRE-HISTORIC NATIONS. Pre-Historic Nations; or, Inquiries concerning some of the Great Peoples and Civilizations of Antiquity, and their Probable Relation to a still Older Civilization of the Ethiopians or Cushites of Arabia. By JOHN D. BALDWIN, Member of the American Oriental Society. 12mo, Cloth, $1 75.

BARTH'S NORTH AND CENTRAL AFRICA. Travels and Discoveries in North and Central Africa: being a Journal of an Expedition undertaken under the Auspices of H. B. M.'s Government, in the Years 1849-1855. By HENRY BARTH, Ph.D., D.C.L. Illustrated. 3 vols., 8vo, Cloth, $12 00.

HENRY WARD BEECHER'S SERMONS. Sermons by HENRY WARD BEECHER, Plymouth Church, Brooklyn. Selected from Published and Unpublished Discourses, and Revised by their Author. With Steel Portrait. Complete in 2 vols., 8vo, Cloth, $5 00.

LYMAN BEECHER'S AUTOBIOGRAPHY, &c. Autobiography, Correspondence, &c., of Lyman Beecher, D.D. Edited by his Son, CHARLES BEECHER. With Three Steel Portraits, and Engravings on Wood. In 2 vols., 12mo, Cloth, $5 00.

BOSWELL'S JOHNSON. The Life of Samuel Johnson, LL.D. Including a Journey to the Hebrides. By JAMES BOSWELL, Esq. A New Edition, with numerous Additions and Notes. By JOHN WILSON CROKER, LL.D., F.R.S. Portrait of Boswell. 2 vols., 8vo, Cloth, $4 00.

www.ingramcontent.com/pod-product-compliance
Lightning Source LLC
LaVergne TN
LVHW021059110826
845150LV00001B/120
* 9 7 8 1 4 2 5 5 6 6 2 8 9 *